CITYGUIDE

SEATTLE

1ST EDITION

FODOR'S TRAVEL PUBLICATIONS

NEW YORK • TORONTO • LONDON • SYDNEY • AUCKLAND

WWW.FODORS.COM

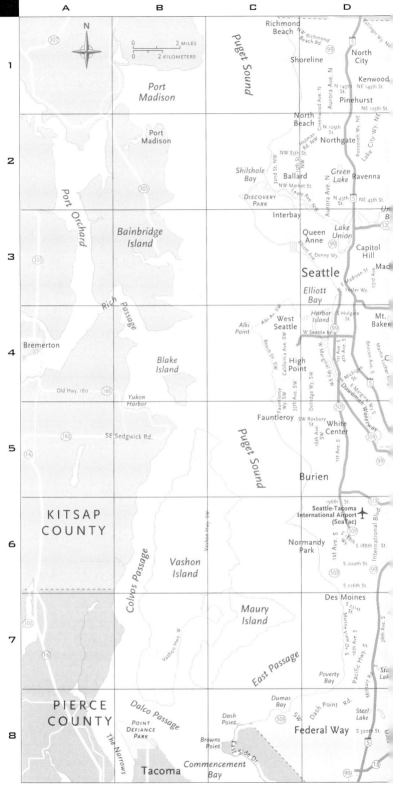

1

	A	B	C	D

1

N

0 — 2 MILES
0 — 2 KILOMETERS

Puget Sound

Richmond Beach
Richmond Beach Rd.

Shoreline

North City

Kenwood
NE 145th St.

N 145th St.

Pinehurst

Port Madison

Aurora Ave. N

Greenwood Ave. N

NE 125th St.

2

Port Madison

North Beach

N 105th St.

Holman Rd. NW

Northgate

Roosevelt Wy. NE

Lake City Wy. NE

NW 85th St.

32nd St. NW

15th Ave. NW

Shilshole Bay

Ballard

NW Market St.

NW Leary Ave. NW

Aurora Ave. N

Green Lake

Ravenna

DISCOVERY PARK

N 45th St.

NE 45th St.

Un
B

3

Bainbridge Island

Interbay

Queen Anne

Lake Union

5

520

Port Orchard

103

Elliott Ave.

Denny Wy.

Capitol Hill

Rich Passage

Seattle

E Madison St.

23rd Ave.

Mad

Elliott Bay

Yesler Wy.

4

Bremerton

Alki Point

Alki Av SW

West Seattle

Harbor Island

S Holgate St.

Mt. Baker

W Seattle Br.

99

Old Hwy. 160

166

Blake Island

Beach Dr. SW

California Ave. SW

High Point

Delridge Wy. SW

35th Ave. SW

Marginal Wy. S

1st Ave. S

4th Ave. S

E Marginal Wy. S

S Michigan St.

Beacon Ave. S

Martin Luther

C

Duwamish Waterway

Yukon Harbor

5

160

SE Sedgwick Rd.

Fauntleroy Wy. SW

Fauntleroy

SW Roxbury St.

16th Ave. SW

White Center

509

16

Puget Sound

1st Ave. S

Burien

99

6

KITSAP COUNTY

Colvos Passage

Vashon Hwy. SW

Vashon Island

156th St.

Seattle-Tacoma International Airport (SeaTac) ✈

518

Normandy Park

1st Ave. S

S 160th St.

S 188th St.

International Blvd.

509

S 200th St.

99

503

S 216th St.

7

102

16

Vashon Hwy. W

Maury Island

Des Moines

S 211st

Marine View Dr. S

16th Ave. S

Pacific Hwy. S

36th Ave. S

East Passage

Poverty Bay

Military Rd. S

Sta
Lak

8

PIERCE COUNTY

Dalco Passage

POINT DEFIANCE PARK

Dash Point

Dumas Bay

509

SW Dash Point Rd.

Steel Lake

The Narrows

Browns Point

East Side Dr.

Federal Way

S 320th St.

5

Tacoma

Commencement Bay

99

18

STREETFINDER

2

	A	B	C	D

1

Shoreline
Lake Forest Park

NW 137th St.
N 145th St.
NE 145th St.
HALLER LAKE
Roosevelt Wy. N
NW 120th St.
N 130th St.
NE 125th St.
LAKE CITY
Greenwood Ave. N
Aurora Ave. N
Meridian Ave. N
Lake City Wy. NE
Sand Point Wy. NE
Riviera Pt. NE
N 110th St.
NE Northgate Wy.

Puget Sound

2

BLUE RIDGE
N 105th St.
NE 105th St.
Meadow Point
NORTH BEACH
N 100th St.
NORTHGATE
522
NE 95th St.
28th St. NW
Holman Rd. NW
Roosevelt Wy. NE
15th Ave. NE
NE 85th St.
35th Ave. NE
45th Ave. NE
NW 85th St.
INVERNESS
LOYAL HEIGHTS
15th Ave. NW
24th Ave. NW
15th Ave. N
8th Ave. N
NW 80th St.
Phinney Ave. N
N Green Lk. Dr. N
99
Green Lake
Lake City Wy. NE
NE 75th St.
NE 70th St.
32nd Ave. NW

Shilshole Bay

3

West Point
BALLARD
NW Market St.
Woodland Park
E Green Lk. Wy. N
NE Ravenna Blvd
RAVENNA
VIEW RIDGE
513
Salmon Bay
NW Leary Ave.
WALLINGFORD
Aurora Ave. N
NE 55th St.
UNIVERSITY
Sand Point Wy. NE
DISCOVERY PARK
Gilman Ave. W
W Nickerson St.
N 50th St.
N 45th St.
5
NE 45th St.
NE 41st St.
LAURELHURST
W Emerson St.
FREMONT
Meridian Ave. N
University Wy. NE
Montlake Blvd
W Dravus St.
INTERBAY
W Bertona St.
N 40th St.
NE Pacific St.
W 34th St.
Stone Wy. N
N Pacific St.
Portage Bay
Union Bay

4

34th Ave. W
3rd Ave. W
W McGraw St.
99
MONTLAKE
520
Gov. Albert D. (Evergreen Pt.)
Magnolia Blvd. W
Thorndike Ave. W
15th Ave. W
QUEEN ANNE
Queen Anne Ave. N
Aurora Ave. N
Westlake Ave.
10th Ave. E
Boyer Ave. E
MADISON PARK
MAGNOLIA BLUFF
W Galer St.
Magnolia Br.
Elliott Ave. W
Olympic Pl.
Aloha St.
Lake Union
Fairview Ave. E
Eastlake Ave. E
E Madison St.
Lake
Mercer St.
CAPITOL HILL
Broad St.
Queen Anne Ave.
E Roy St.
E Aloha St.
Denny Wy.
E Denny Wy.
MADRONA PARK

5

Seattle
Olive Wy.
Broadway
12th Ave. E
15th Ave. E
23rd Ave. E
E Union St.
E Cherry St.
Madison St.
Yesler Wy.
Lake Washington Blvd
Elliott Bay
S Dearborn St.
90
Homer M. Hadley Mem.
Lacey V. Murrow Mem.

N

6

Alki Ave. SW
Admiral Wy.
S Holgate St.
MT. BAKER
Alki Point
63rd Ave. SW
WEST SEATTLE
Harbor Ave. SW
Harbor Island
Alaskan Fwy.
Airport Wy. S
1st Ave. S
4th Ave. S
15th Ave. S
BEACON HILL
Mt. Baker Park
Lake Washington Blvd S
SW Charlestown St.
W Seattle Br.
99
S Spokane St.
38th Ave. S
Beach Dr. SW
39th Ave. SW
SW Genesee St.
Beacon Ave. S
Martin Luther King Jr. Wy.
S Genesee St.
COLUMBIA
Wilson Ave. S

7

48th Ave. SW
California Ave. SW
Delridge Wy. SW
W Marginal Wy. SW
S Lucile St.
PIONEER VALLEY
S Orcas St.
Rainier Ave. S
Fauntleroy Wy. SW
Sylvan Wy. SW
S Michigan St.
5
VAN ASSELT
S Graham St.
LINCOLN PARK
35th Ave. SW
Holden St.
9th Ave. SW
WESTWOOD
E Marginal Wy. S
Duwamish Waterway
S Othello St.
Beacon Ave. S
SW Barton St.
SW Henderson St.
509
S Henderson St.

8

FAUNTLEROY
WHITE CENTER
SW Roxbury St.
S 96th St.
RAINIER BEACH
Marine View Dr.
SW 106th St.
16th Ave. SW
TOP HAT
8th Ave. S
99
Martin Luther King Jr. Wy. S
S Bangor St.
Des Moines Mem. Dr. S
Military Rd. S
Beacon Ave. S
BOULEVARD PARK
SW 116th St.
1st Ave. S
Tukwila
Burien

0 ___ 1 MILE
0 ___ 1 KILOMETER

Puget Sound

STREETFINDER

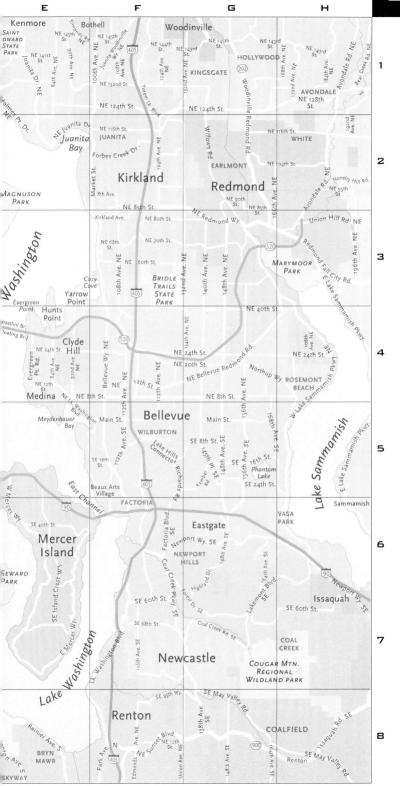

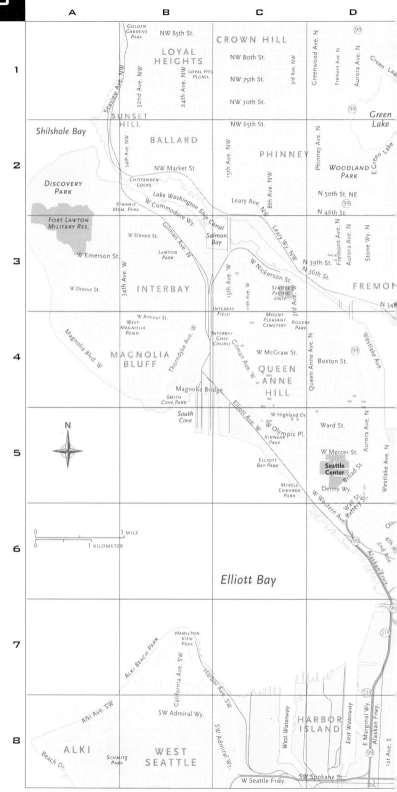

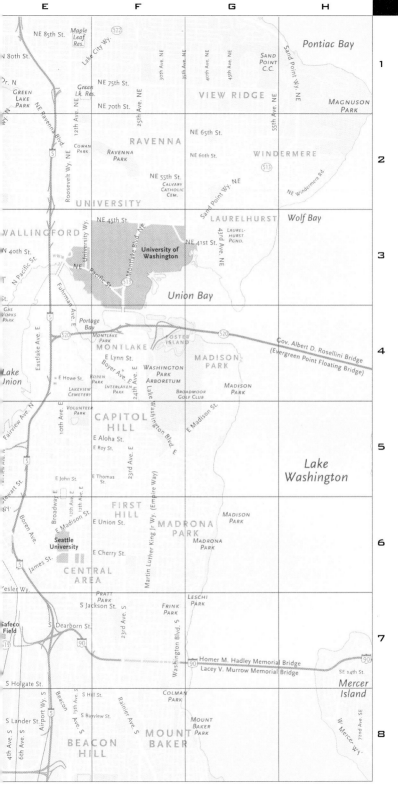

E F G H

1

NE 85th St.
Maple
Leaf
Res.
522
Lake City Wy.
Pontiac Bay

N 80th St.
Dr. N
GREEN
LAKE
PARK
NE Ravenna Blvd.
Green
Lk. Res.
NE 75th St.
NE 70th St.
30th Ave. NE
35th Ave. NE
4th Ave. NE
45th Ave. NE
SAND
POINT
C.C.
Sand Point Wy. NE
VIEW RIDGE
55th Ave. NE
MAGNUSON
PARK

2

Roosevelt Wy. NE
12th Ave. NE
5
COWAN
PARK
RAVENNA
RAVENNA
PARK
NE 65th St.
NE 60th St.
Sand Point Wy. NE
513
WINDERMERE
NE Windermere Rd.

NE 55th St.
CALVARY
CATHOLIC
CEM.

UNIVERSITY

3

WALLINGFORD
N 40th St.
University Wy. NE
NE 45th St.
Montlake Blvd. NE
University of
Washington
NE Pacific St.
513
NE 41st St. NE
Sand Point Wy. NE
43rd Ave. NE
LAURELHURST
LAUREL-
HURST
PGND.
Wolf Bay

N Pacific St.
Fuhrman Ave. E
GAS
WORKS
PARK
Union Bay

4

Eastlake Ave. E
520
Portage
Bay
MONTLAKE
PARK
MONTLAKE
E Lynn St.
Boyer Ave. E
FOSTER
ISLAND
520
MADISON
PARK
Gov. Albert D. Rosellini Bridge
(Evergreen Point Floating Bridge)

Lake
Union
= E Howe St.
BOREN
PARK
INTERLAKEN
PARK
LAKEVIEW
CEMETERY
24th Ave. E
WASHINGTON
PARK
ARBORETUM
Lake Washington Blvd. E
BROADMOOR
GOLF CLUB
MADISON
PARK

5

Fairview Ave. N
5
10th Ave. E
VOLUNTEER
PARK
CAPITOL
HILL
E Aloha St.
E Roy St.
23rd Ave. E
E Madison St.
Lake
Washington

E John St.
E Thomas
St.
Broadway E
12th Ave. E

6

Boren Ave.
E Madison St.
12th Ave.
FIRST
HILL
E Union St.
E Cherry St.
Martin Luther King Jr Wy. (Empire Way)
MADRONA
PARK
MADISON
PARK
MADRONA
PARK

Seattle
University
James St.
CENTRAL
AREA
Yesler Wy.

7

Safeco
Field
99
5
S Dearborn St.
90
PRATT
PARK
S Jackson St.
23rd Ave. S
FRINK
PARK
Washington Blvd. S
LESCHI
PARK
90
Homer M. Hadley Memorial Bridge
Lacey V. Murrow Memorial Bridge
90
SE 24th St.
Mercer
Island

S Holgate St.

8

S Lander St. S
4th Ave. S
6th Ave. S
Airport Wy. S
Beacon Ave. S
15th Ave. S
S Hill St.
S Bayview St.
Rainier Ave. S
COLMAN
PARK
MOUNT
BAKER
PARK
BEACON
HILL
MOUNT
BAKER
W Mercer Wy.
72nd Ave. SE

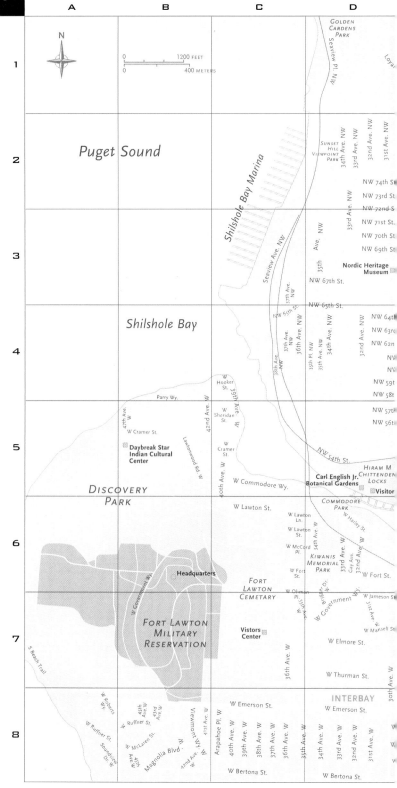

4

A   B   C   D

N

0 ——— 1200 FEET
0 ——— 400 METERS

1

GOLDEN GARDENS PARK

Seaview Pl. NW

Loyal

2

Puget Sound

Shilshole Bay Marina

SUNSET HILL VIEWPOINT PARK

34th Ave. NW
33rd Ave. NW
32nd Ave. NW
31st Ave. NW

NW 74th S
NW 73rd St
NW 72nd S
NW 71st St.
NW 70th St
NW 69th St

Seaview Ave. NW

33rd Ave. NW

Ave. NW

35th

Nordic Heritage Museum

NW 67th St.

3

Shilshole Bay

37th Ave. NW

NW 65th St.

NW 65th St.

38th Pl. NW

37th Ave. NW

36th Ave. NW

34th Ave. NW

35th Pl. NW
35th Ave. NW

32nd Ave. NW

NW 64t
NW 63r
NW 62n
NV
NV
NW 59t
NW 58t

4

38th Ave. NW

W Hooker St.

39th Ave. W

Parry Wy.

42nd Ave. W

NW 57t
NW 56t

47th Ave. W

W Cramer St.

W Sheridan St.

NW 54th St.

Lakewood Rd. W

Daybreak Star Indian Cultural Center

W Cramer St.

40th Ave. W

W Commodore Wy.

Carl English Jr. Botanical Gardens

HIRAM M CHITTENDEN LOCKS

Visitor

5

DISCOVERY PARK

W Lawton St.

COMMODORE PARK

W Lawton Ln.

W Lawton St.

34th Ave. W

W Harley St.

6

S Beach Trail

W Government Wy.

Headquarters

FORT LAWTON CEMETERY

W McCord Pl.

W Fort St.

KIWANIS MEMORIAL PARK

33rd Ave. W

Gay Ave.

32nd Ave. W

W Fort St.

W Olmin Pl.

W Bright Dr.

35th Ave.

W Government Wy.

31st Ave. W

W Jameson St

W Mansell St.

7

FORT LAWTON MILITARY RESERVATION

Vistors Center

36th Ave. W

W Elmore St.

W Thurman St.

30th Ave. W

8

W Roberts Wy.

45th Ave. W

43rd Ave. W

W Ruffner St.

W McLaren St.

Viewmont Wy. W

Magnolia Blvd.

41st Ave. W

Arapahoe Pl. W

40th Ave. W

39th Ave. W

38th Ave. W

37th Ave. W

36th Ave. W

35th Ave. W

34th Ave. W

33rd Ave. W

32nd Ave. W

31st Ave. W

W Emerson St.

INTERBAY

W Emerson St.

W Soundview Dr. W

47th Ave. W

W Bertona St.

W Bertona St.

STREETFINDER

E   F   G   H

NW 86th St.

CROWN HILL

NW 85th St.

1

NW 83rd St.

24th Ave. NW
Jones Ave. NW
23rd Ave. NW
22nd Ave. NW
21st Ave. NW
20th Ave. NW
19th Ave. NW
18th Ave. NW
17th Ave. NW
16th Ave. NW
15th Ave. NW

NW 83rd St.

NW 80th St.

NW 80th St.

LOYAL HEIGHTS

29th Ave. NW
28th Ave. NW

NW 77th St.

LOYAL
HEIGHTS
PLAYGROUND

NW 75th St.

NW 73rd St.

Mary Ave. NW
14th Ave. NW

2

Mary Ave. NW
Alonzo Ave. NW
14th Ave. NW
13th Ave. NW
12th Ave. NW
11th Ave. NW
10th Ave. NW
9th Ave. NW
Dibble Ave. NW
8th Ave. NW

Earl Ave. NW
27th Ave. NW
26th Ave. NW
25th Ave. NW

NW 70th St.   SALMON
BAY PARK

NW 68th St.
NW 67th St.
NW 66th St.

NW 67th St.

Division Ave. NW
Cleoparra Pl. NW

3

NW 65th St.

NW 65th St.

28th Ave. NW
26th Ave. NW
24th Ave. NW
22nd Ave. NW
20th Ave. NW
17th Ave. NW

NW 64th St.
NW 63rd St.
NW 62nd St.

1st St.
0th St.

NW Brygger Pl.

PHINNEY   NW 61st St.
NW 60th St.

BALLARD

NW 59th St.

4

NW Market St.

NW 58th St.

15th Ave. NW
14th Ave. NW
11th Ave. NW
9th Ave. NW
8th Ave. NW

NW 57th St.
NW 56th St.

enter

Shilshole Ave. NW
Ballard Ave. NW
Leary Ave.
Russell Ave. NW
NW Vernon Pl.
Tallman Ave. NW
Barnes Ave.

NW Market St.
NW 54th St.
NW 53rd St.   GILMAN
PLAYGROUND
NW 52nd St.

5

Salmon Bay

NW Central Pl.
NW Ione Pl.
NW Dock Pl.

NW 51st St.

NW 50th St.

NW 49th St.   NW 49th St.

NW Leary Ave.   NW 48th St.

NW Ballard Wy.   NW 47th St.

NW 46th St.
NW 45th St.

6

W Commodore Wy.

Boat
Launch

Leary Wy. NW

7

28th Pl. W
28th Ave. W
Williams Ave. W
27th Ave. W
26th Ave. W
Gilman Pl. W
Gilman Ave. W
24th Ave. W
23rd Ave. W
22nd Ave. W
21st Ave. W

W Jameson St.

W Elmore St.

9th Ave. NW   NW 43rd St.

NW Fern Pl.

11th Ave. NW   NW 42nd St.

W Elmore
Pl.
28th View Pl.

Barton Pl.

29th Ave. W

W Emerson Pl.

W Ewing St.

LAWTON
PARK

W Jameson Pl.
W Manor Pl.
25th Ave. W
25th Pl. W
24th Pl. W
26th Ave. W
W Emerson St.
Fishermans
Terminal

W Emerson St.

Ewing
Pl.

W Nickerson St.

W Emerson St.

W Ewing
St.

8

ilden St.
uffner St.
rover St.

W Ruffner St.

23rd Ave. W
22nd Ave. W
21st Ave. W

Thorndyke Ave. W
16th Ave. W
14th Ave. W
13th Ave. W

W   Ruffner St.

12th Ave. W
11th Ave. NW
10th Ave. NW
9th Ave. W
8th Ave. W

BALLARD, PHINNEY RIDGE, AND THE SHIP CANAL

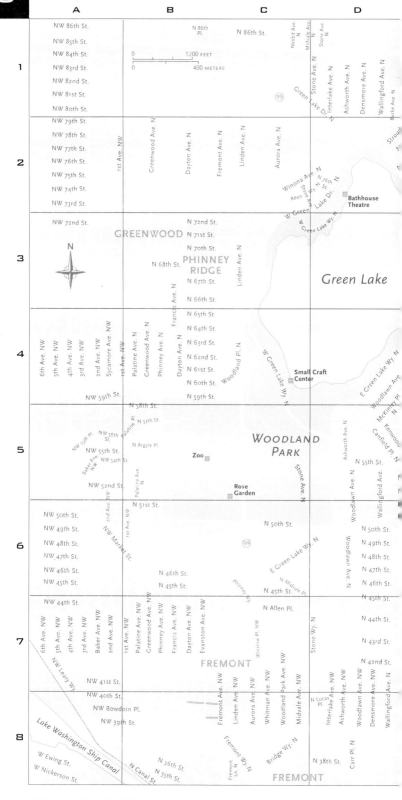

5

	A	B	C	D

NW 86th St. · N 86th Pl. · N 86th St. · Nesbit Ave N · Midvale Ave N · Stone Ave N

NW 85th St.

NW 84th St.

NW 83rd St.

NW 82nd St.

NW 81st St.

NW 80th St.

0 — 1200 FEET
0 — 400 METERS

Green Lake Dr N · Stone Ave N · Interlake Ave N · Ashworth Ave N · Densmore Ave N · Wallingford Ave N · Burke Ave N

NW 79th St.

NW 78th St.

NW 77th St.

NW 76th St.

NW 75th St.

NW 74th St.

NW 73rd St.

1st Ave NW · Greenwood Ave N · Dayton Ave N · Fremont Ave N · Linden Ave N · Aurora Ave N · Stroud N

Winona Ave N · N 76th St · Keen · Stone · N · W Green · W Green Lake Dr N · **Bathhouse Theatre**

NW 72nd St. · N 72nd St.

GREENWOOD · N 71st St.

N 70th St.

N 68th St. · **PHINNEY RIDGE** · N 67th St.

N 66th St.

W Green Lake Wy N · *Green Lake*

N ↑

Francis Ave N · Linden Ave N

N 65th St.

6 Ave NW · 5 Ave NW · 4 Ave NW · 3 Ave NW · 2 Ave NW · Sycamore Ave NW · 1st Ave NW · Palatine Ave N · Greenwood Ave N · Phinney Ave N · Dayton Ave N · N 64th St. · N 63rd St. · N 62nd St. · N 61st St. · N 60th St. · N 59th St.

Woodland Pl N · W Green Lake Wy N · **Small Craft Center** · E Green Lake Wy N · Woodlawn Pl · McKinley Pl

NW 59th St.

N 58th St. · N 57th St. · Palatine Pl

NW 56th St.

NW 55th Pl · N Argyle Pl · Palatine Ave N · Baker Ave NW · NW 55th St · NW 54th St · **Zoo** · **WOODLAND PARK** · Ashworth Ave N · N 55th St. · Woodlawn Ave N · Wallingford Ave N · Kenwood · Canfield Pl N

NW 52nd St. · N 51st St. · **Rose Garden** · Stone Ave N

2nd Ave NW · 1st Ave NW

NW 50th St. · N 50th St. · N 50th St.

NW 49th St. · N 49th St.

NW 48th St. · N 48th St.

NW 47th St. · N 47th St.

NW 46th St. · N 46th St. · N 46th St.

NW 45th St. · N 45th St. · N 45th St. · N 45th St.

NW Market St. · E Green Lake Wy N · (99) · Phinney Wy · N Midvale Pl · Woodlawn Ave N

NW 44th St. · N 44th St. · N 44th St.

6 Ave NW · 5 Ave NW · 4 Ave NW · 3 Ave NW · Baker Ave NW · 2 Ave NW · 1st Ave NW · Palatine Ave NW · Greenwood Ave NW · Phinney Ave NW · Francis Ave NW · Dayton Ave NW · Evanston Ave NW · N Allen Pl. · N 43rd St.

Winslow Pl NW · Fremont Ave NW · Linden Ave NW · Woodland Park Ave NW · Stone Wy N · N 42nd St.

NW Leary Wy · **FREMONT** · NW 41st St. · Interlake Ave NW · Ashworth Ave NW · Woodlawn Ave NW · Densmore Ave NW · Wallingford Ave N

NW 40th St.

NW Bowdoin Pl.

NW 39th St. · N Lucas Pl.

Lake Washington Ship Canal

Aurora Ave NW · Whitman Ave NW · Midvale Ave NW · Fremont Ave NW · Linden Ave NW · Woodland Park Ave NW

Fremont Wy N · Bridge Wy N · Carr Pl. N · N 38th St.

W Ewing St. · N Canal St. · N 36th St. · N 35th St. · Fremont Ln N · **FREMONT**

W Nickerson St.

STREETFINDER

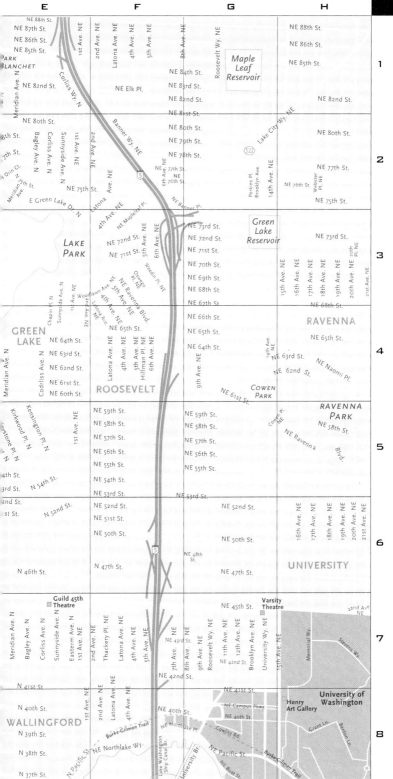

5

GREEN LAKE, FREMONT, AND WALLINGFORD

	A	B	C	D

1

23rd Ave.
Ravenna Ave.
26th Ave.
27th Ave.
Ave. NE
30th Ave.
32nd Ave.

NE 89th St.
NE 88th St.
NE 87th St.
NE 86th St.
NE 85th St.

42nd Ave. NE
NE 89th St.
NE 89th St
NE 88th Pl.

Inverness

22nd Ave. NE
22nd Pl. NE
23rd Ave. NE
26th Ave. NE
28th Ave. NE

NE 83rd St.
NE 82nd St.

NE 84th St.
NE 83rd St.
NE 82nd St.
NE 81st St.
NE 80th St.

41st Ave. NE
42nd Ave. NE

NE Forest Vista
Fairway Dr. NE
Forest Cr. Dr. NE

NE 81st Pl.
NE 81st St.

University Prep Academy

2

DAHL WALDO PLAYGROUND

NE 77th St.

36th Ave. NE
37th Ave. NE
38th Ave. NE
39th Ave. NE
40th Ave. NE

43rd Ave. NE
44th Ave. NE
45th Ave. NE

Forest Cr.

NE Urban Vista
Par

NE 75th St.

3

Ravenna Ave. NE
23rd Ave. NE
24th Ave. NE
25th Ave. NE
26th Ave. NE
27th Ave. NE
28th Ave. NE
29th Ave. NE
30th Ave. NE
33rd Ave. NE
34th Ave. NE
35th Ave.

73rd St.

NE 74th St.
NE 73rd St.
NE 72nd St.

NE 70th St.

46th Ave. NE
47th Ave. NE
47th Ave. NE
3N

VIEW RIDGE PLAYGROUND

NE 71st St.

VIEW R

4

RAVENNA

NE 68th St.

NE 65th St.

BRYANT PARK

NE 62nd St.

46th Ave. NE
47th Ave. NE
48th Ave. NE
49th Ave. NE

NE 62nd St.
NE 61st St.
24th Ave. N
25th Ave. NE
26th Ave. NE
27th Ave. NE
28th Ave. NE
29th Ave. NE
30th Ave. NE
31st Ave. NE
32nd Ave. N

41st Ave. NE
43rd Ave. NE
44th Ave. NE
45th Ave. NE

Ann Arbor Ave. NE
Vassar Ave. NE
Washington
Oberlin Ave. NE

5

NE 60th St.

33rd Ave. N
34th Ave. N
35th Ave.

36th Ave. NE
37th Ave. NE
38th Ave. NE
39th Ave. NE
40th Ave. NE

NE 58th St.
NE 57th St.
NE 56th St.

Stanford Ave.
Purdue Ave.
Princeton Ave.
NE Tulane Pl.
NE

RAVENNA PARK

NE 57th St.

NE 55th St.

6

22nd Ave. NE
Ravenna Ave. NE
Ravenna Pl.
Burke-Gilman Trail

NE 54th St.
NE 53rd St.
NE Blakely St.
30th Ave. NE

CALVARY CATHOLIC CEMETERY

NE 52nd St.

NE 50th St.

NE 48th St.

NE 61st Pl.
NE 52nd Pl.

BURKE GILMAN PARK

Sand Point Pl. NE
Terrace Dr. NE
513

NE 54th St.
46th Ave. NE
47th Ave. NE
48th Ave. NE

NE 50th St.
44th Ave. NE
45th Ave. NE

NE 49th St.

University Village

University View Pl. NE
34th Ave. NE

Union Bay Pl.

NE 47th Pl.
39th Ave. NE
43rd Ave. NE

NE 47th St.

7

Pend Oreille Rd.
Montlake Blvd. NE
Walla Walla Rd.
Walla Walla Pl.
24th Ave. NE
25th Ave. NE

NE 45th St.
Clark Rd.
Union Bay Pl.
NE 45th Pl.
Union Cross Mason Rd.
34th Ave. NE

NE 43rd St.
NE 42nd St.
NE 41st St.

42nd Ave. NE
43rd Ave. NE

NE 45th St.
NE 44t
LAURELHURST PLAYGROUND NE 43r
NE 42n
NE 41st St.

8

Mason Rd.
513
Wahkiatum Ln.
Canal Rd.

Canal Rd.
Douglas Rd.

University of Washington

Union Bay

Sunber Dr. NE
41st Ave. NE
NE Belvoir Pl.
NE 38th St.
NE 38th St.
42nd Ave. NE

LAURELHURST
NE 40th St
44th Ave. NE
45th Ave. NE
44th Pl. NE
47th Ave. NE
48th Ave. NE
46th Ave. NE
W. Laurelhurst Dr. NE
NE 39t

E   F   G   H

1

Lake Washington

Pontiac Bay

r. NE
NE 87th St.
NE 86th St.
NE 85th St.

54th Ave. NE
86th Ave. NE
Burke-Gilman Trail

2

Lakemont Dr. NE
Lakemont Vista
Club House Dr.
Crest Dr. NE
Pl.
Sand Point
Country Club
NE Sunrise Dr.
57th Ave. NE
449S Pl.
NE 77th St.

3

NE 74th St.
NE 73rd St.
GE
53rd Ave. NE
54th Ave. NE
55th Ave. NE
56th Ave. NE
57th Ave. NE
58th Ave. NE
NE 75th St.
Sand Point Wy. NE

MAGNUSON
PARK

4

51st Ave. NE
52nd Ave. NE
NE 49th St.
57th Ave. NE
58th Ave. NE
(513)
53rd Ave. NE
54th Ave. NE
NE 63rd St.
NE 65th St.
Park Entrance Rd.
NE 64th St.
NE 63rd St.
NE Radford Dr.

5

NE 60th St.
Burke-Gilman Trail
ullman Ave. NE
Coniston Rd. NE
NE 60th St.
NE 58th St.
NE 57th St.
NE 56th St.
NE 61st St.
NE 62nd St.
59th Ave. NE
60th Ave. NE
61st Ave. NE
63rd Ave. NE
64th Ave. NE
65th Ave. NE
NE 60th St.

6

Ivanhoe
NE 52nd St. Pl. NE
Harold Pl. NE
Nickias Pl. NE
54th Ave. NE
55th Ave. NE
Kenilworth Pl. NE
NE Penrith Rd.
Ellray Ln. NE
NE 55th St.
NE Ambleside Rd.
NE Kelden Pl.
NE Keswick Dr.
Windermere Rd.
WINDERMERE
PARK

WINDERMERE

Wolf Bay

7

51st Ave. NE
52nd Ave. NE
53rd Ave. NE
54th Ave. NE
55th Ave. NE
Laurel Dr. W.
NE Laurelcrest Ln.
NE 44th St.
NE 42nd St.

Lake Washington

8

51st Ave. NE
NE Laurelcrest Ln.

N

0   1200 FEET
0   400 METERS

RAVENNA, UNIVERSITY DISTRICT, AND LAKE WASHINGTON

A | B | C | D

1

W Bertona St.

W Dravus St.
29th Ave. W
28th Ave. W
27th Ave. W
26th Ave. W
25th Ave. W
24th Ave. W

23rd Ave. W
22nd Ave. W
21st Ave. W
20th Ave. W

17th Ave. W
16th Ave. W
15th Ave. W

W Dravus St.
14th Ave. W
13th Ave. W
12th Ave. W
11th Ave. W

10th Ave. W
9th Ave. W
Conkling Pl. W
Cremon
7th Ave.
Dravu
W Etruria St.
W Florenti Pl.

W Barrett St.

Patten Pl. W

W Fulton St.

W Barrett St.

W Fulton St.

INTERBAY
ATHLETIC
FIELD

2

W Armour St.

BAYVIEW
PLAYGROUND

W Raye St.

W Halladay St.

W Smith St.

29th Ave. W

Thorndyke Ave. W

21st Ave. W

W Raye St.

INTERBAY
GOLF
COURSE

Prosch Ave. W

W Armour St.

W Newell
St.
MT
PLEASAN
CEMETER

W Raye St.
W Bothwell
St.

W Raye St.

13th Ave. W
12th Ave. W
11th Ave. W

Westview Dr. W

10th Ave. W

W Halladay St.

W Wheeler St.

3

W McGraw St.
W Lynn St.
Lynn Pl.
W Boston St.
W Crockett St.
W Newton St.
W Plymouth St.
W Howe St.

23rd Ave. W

Thorndyke Ave. W

W Armory Wy.

National
Guard
Armory

W Armory Wy.

14th Ave. W

W Boston St.

15th Ave. W

W Newton St.

Gilman Ave. W

McGraw St.

W Crockett St.

W Howe St.

UP

W Blaine St.

4

W Hayes St.

Magnolia Wy. W

23rd Ave. W

Magnolia

Bridge

W Garfield St.

11th Ave. W
10th Ave. W
9th Ave. W
8th Ave. W

W Galer St.

SMITH COVE
PARK

W Marina Pl.

W Galer St.

Van Buren Ave. W

Elliott Ave. W

Olympic Wy. W

9th Pl. W

PARSON
GARDEN

5

Marina

Smith Cove

16th Ave. W

Alaskan Wy. W

KINNEA
PARK

W Mer

6

Elliott Bay
Fishing Pier

ELLIOT
BAY PAR

7

Elliott Bay

8

N

0 — 1200 FEET
0 — 400 METERS

STREETFINDER

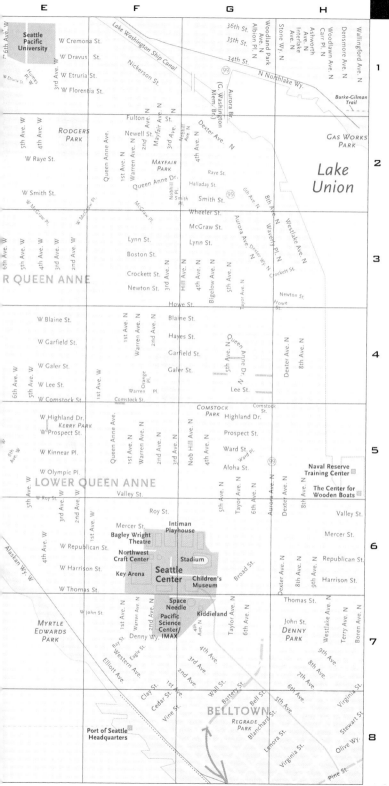

QUEEN ANNE AND SEATTLE CENTER

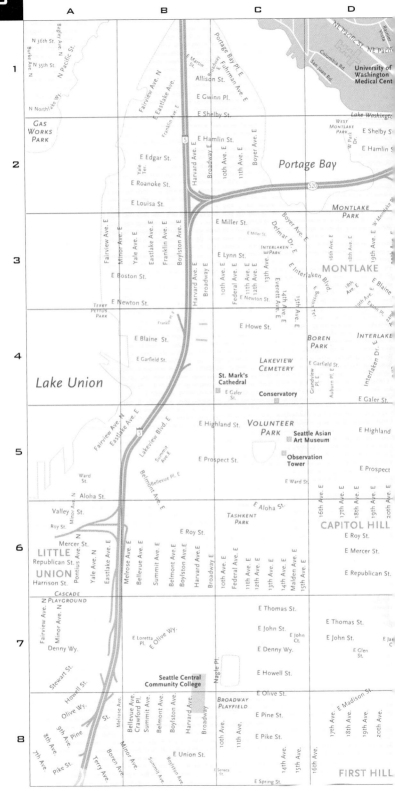

8

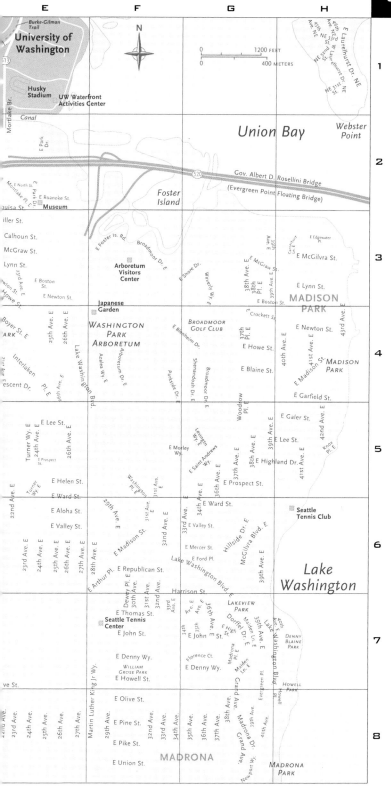

E   **F**   **G**   **H**

Burke-Gilman Trail

University of Washington

513

Husky Stadium

UW Waterfront Activities Center

Mortlake Br.

Canal

E Park Dr.

Union Bay

Webster Point

520

Gov. Albert D. Rosellini Bridge
(Evergreen Point Floating Bridge)

E North St.

Montlake Pl. E

Park Dr. E

E Roanoke St.

Louisa St.

Museum

Foster Island

1200 FEET
400 METERS

N

iller St.

Calhoun St.

McGraw St.

Lynn St.

23rd Ave. E

E Boston St.

Newton St.

E Newton St.

Howe St.

E Foster Is. Rd.

Broadmoor Dr. E

Arboretum Visitors Center

E Shore Dr.

Waverly Wy. E

39th Ave. E

E McGraw St.

38th Ave. E

38th Pl. E

39th Ave. E

Canterbury Ln. E

E Edgewater

E McGilvra St.

E Lynn St.

E Boston St.

MADISON PARK

Japanese Garden

WASHINGTON PARK ARBORETUM

Boyer St. E

ARK

25th Ave. E

26th Ave. E

Lake Washington Blvd.

Arboretum Dr. E

Azalea Wy. E

E Blenheim Dr.

BROADMOOR GOLF CLUB

Broadmoor Dr. E

Shenandoah Dr. E

Parkside Dr. E

37th Pl. E

Crockett St.

E Howe St.

E Blaine St.

40th Ave. E

E Newton St.

E Madison St.

41st Ave. E

43rd Ave. E

MADISON PARK

E Garfield St.

Interlaken

escent Dr.

26th Ave. E

Turner Wy. E

24th Ave. E

E Lee St.

26th Ave. E

E Prospect St.

Turner Wy. E

Woodow Pl. E

Lenawee Wy.

Leschi Wy.

E Morley Wy.

E Saint Andrews Wy.

36th Ave. E

37th Ave. E

38th Ave. E

39th Ave. E

E Galer St.

42nd Ave. E

E Lee St.

41st Ave. E

Knox Pl. E

E Highland Dr.

E Prospect St.

22nd Ave. E

E Helen St.

E Ward St.

E Aloha St.

E Valley St.

23rd Ave. E

24th Ave. E

25th Ave. E

26th Ave. E

27th Ave. E

28th Ave. E

29th Ave. E

Washington Pl. E

31st Ave. E

32nd Ave. E

33rd Ave. E

34th Ave. E

E Ward St.

E Valley St.

E Mercer St.

E Ford Pl.

Lake Washington Blvd.

Hillside Dr. E

McGilvra Blvd. E

39th Ave. E

Seattle Tennis Club

Lake Washington

E Arthur Pl.

E Republican St.

E Dewey Pl. E

30th Ave. E

31st Ave.

32nd Ave. E

33rd Ave. E

Harrison St.

LAKEVIEW PARK

34th Ave. E

35th Ave. E

36th Ave. E

Dorffel Dr. E

E High Dr.

Maiden Ln. E

39th Ave. E

40th Ave.

Lake Washington Blvd.

DENNY BLAINE PARK

Seattle Tennis Center

E Thomas St.

E John St.

34th Ave. E

35th Ave. E

E John St.

E Denny Wy.

WILLIAM GROSE PARK

E Howell St.

Florence Ct.

E Denny Wy.

Madrona Pl. E

Maiden Ln. E

Grand Ave. E

Evergreen Pl.

Howell Rd.

HOWELL PARK

ve St.

22nd Ave.

23rd Ave.

24th Ave.

25th Ave.

26th Ave.

27th Ave.

Martin Luther King Jr Wy.

29th Ave.

E Olive St.

32nd Ave.

33rd Ave.

34th Ave.

E Pine St.

E Pike St.

E Union St.

MADRONA

35th Ave.

36th Ave.

37th Ave.

38th Ave.

Madrona Dr.

Grand Ave.

Newport Way

39th Ave.

40th Ave.

MADRONA PARK

CAPITOL HILL, MONTLAKE, AND MADISON PARK

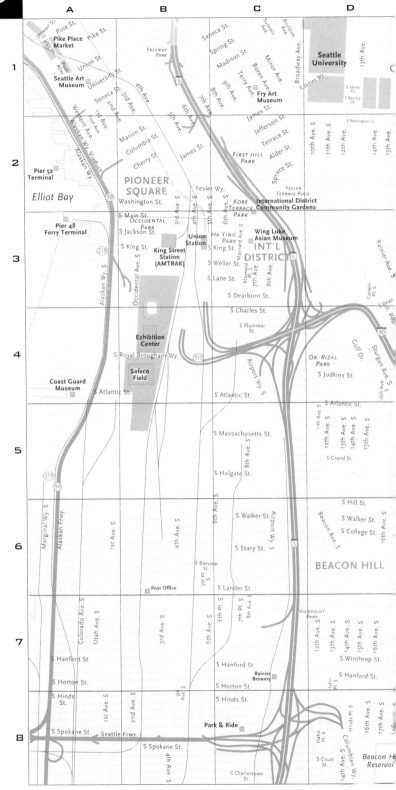

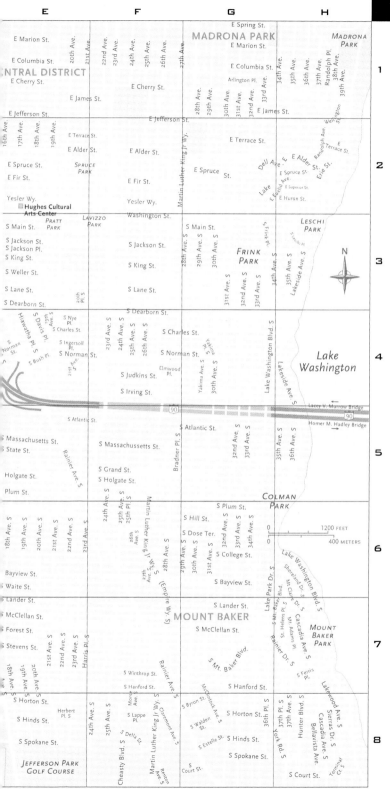

	E	F	G	H	
	6th Ave. N / Aurora Ave. N	8th Ave. N / Broad St.	Valley St.	Valley St. / Minor Ave. N / Roy St. / Mercer St.	1
	Broad St. / Dexter Ave. N / Aurora Ave. N	8th Ave. N / 9th Ave. N	Republican St. / Harrison St.	Fairview Ave. N / Minor Ave. N / Pontius Ave. N / CASCADE PLAYGROUND	2
	6th Ave. N / Aurora Ave. N	John St. / DENNY PARK / Denny Wy. / Westlake Ave. N	Terry Ave. N / Boren Ave. N	Thomas St. / Denny Wy.	3
	Monorail / 5th Ave.	8th Ave. / 7th Ave. / 6th Ave.	Terry Ave. / 9th Ave.	Minor Ave. / Yale Ave. / Boren Ave. / Stewart St. / Howell St.	4
	4th Ave. / REGRADE PARK / Blanchard St.		Virginia St. / Olive Wy. / 7th Ave.	Olive Wy. / Terry Ave. / 9th Ave. / 8th Ave. / Pine St.	5
	BELLTOWN / Lenora St. / Virginia St.	4th Ave. / Stewart St.	6th Ave. / 5th Ave. / Bus Tunnel	Pike St. / Washington State Convention & Trade Center	6
	Post Alley / Stewart St. / Pike Place Market / Pike Pl.	Pine St. / Bus Tunnel / Pike St. / Post Alley	3rd Ave.	Union St. / FREEWAY PARK / 8th Ave. / 6th Ave. / 7th Ave.	7
	WATERFRONT PARK / Alaskan Wy. Viaduct / Alaskan Wy.	Union St. / Western Ave. / Post Ave. / 1st Ave. / Spring St.	Benaroya Hall / Seattle Art Museum / University St. / 2nd Ave. / Seneca St. / FINANCIAL DISTRICT / Federal Reserve / 4th Ave.	5th Ave. / Public Library / Madison St. / Marion St.	8

SEATTLE CENTER, BELLTOWN, AND DOWNTOWN

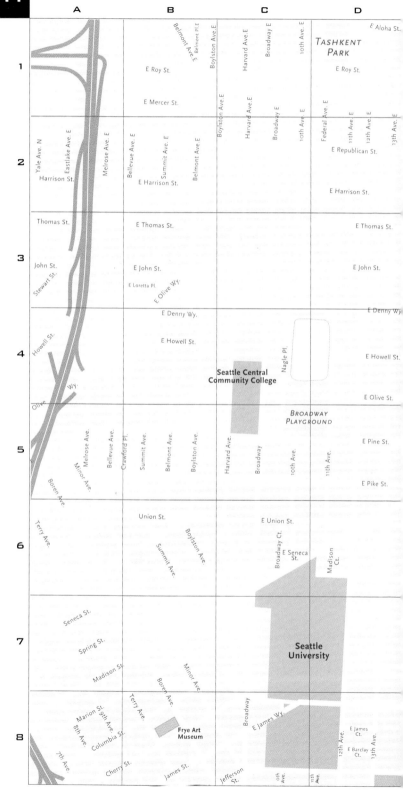

STREETFINDER

CENTRAL DISTRICT, FIRST HILL, AND CAPITOL HILL

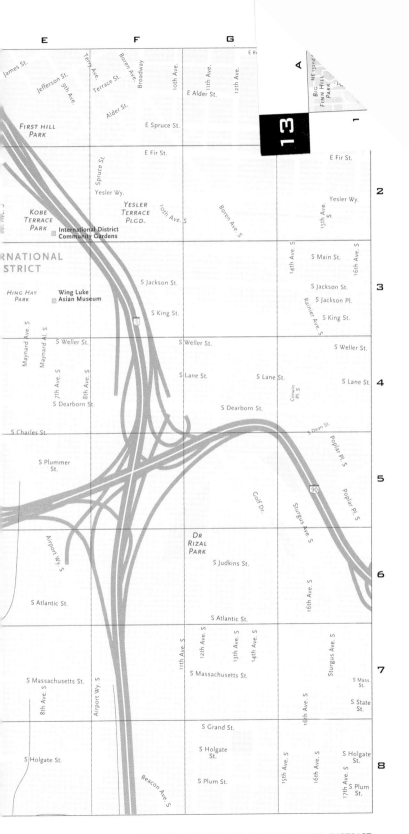

James St.

Jefferson St.
9th Ave.

Terry Ave.

Terrace St.

Boren Ave.

Broadway

10th Ave.

11th Ave.

12th Ave.

E Alder St.

FIRST HILL
PARK

Alder St.

E Spruce St.

E Fir St.

E Fir St.

Spruce St.

Yesler Wy.

Yesler Wy.

KOBE
TERRACE
PARK

YESLER
TERRACE
PLGD.

10th Ave. S

Boren Ave. S

15th Ave. S

International District
Community Gardens

INTERNATIONAL
DISTRICT

14th Ave. S

16th Ave. S

S Main St.

HING HAY
PARK

Wing Luke
Asian Museum

S Jackson St.

S Jackson St.

S Jackson Pl.

Rainier Ave. S

S King St.

Maynard Ave. S

Maynard Al. S

S Weller St.

S King St.

S Weller St.

S Weller St.

7th Ave. S

8th Ave. S

S Lane St.

S Lane St.

Corwin
Pl. S

S Lane St.

S Dearborn St.

S Dearborn St.

S Charles St.

S Dean St.

Poplar Pl. S

S Plummer
St.

Golf Dr.

I-90

Poplar Pl. S

Airport Wy. S

Sturgus Ave. S

DR
RIZAL
PARK

S Judkins St.

16th Ave. S

S Atlantic St.

S Atlantic St.

11th Ave. S

12th Ave. S

13th Ave. S

14th Ave. S

Sturgus Ave. S

S Massachusetts St.

S Massachusetts St.

8th Ave. S

Airport Wy. S

16th Ave. S

S Mass.
St.

S State
St.

S Grand St.

S Holgate
St.

S Holgate
St.

S Holgate St.

15th Ave. S

16th Ave. S

Beacon Ave. S

S Plum St.

17th Ave. S

S Plum
St.

PIONEER SQUARE AND INTERNATIONAL DISTRICT

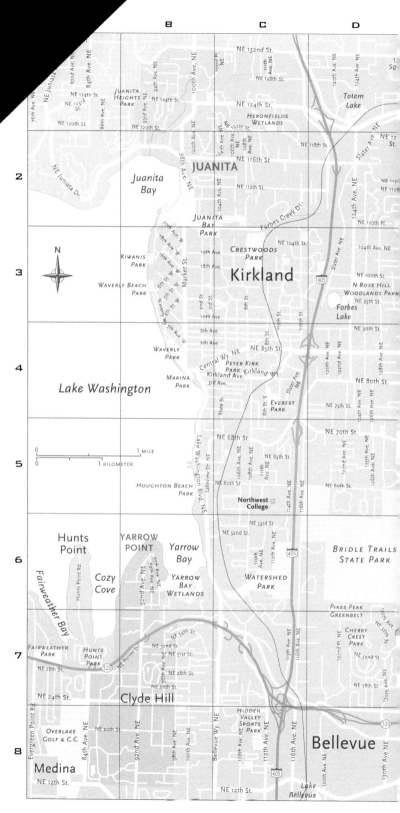

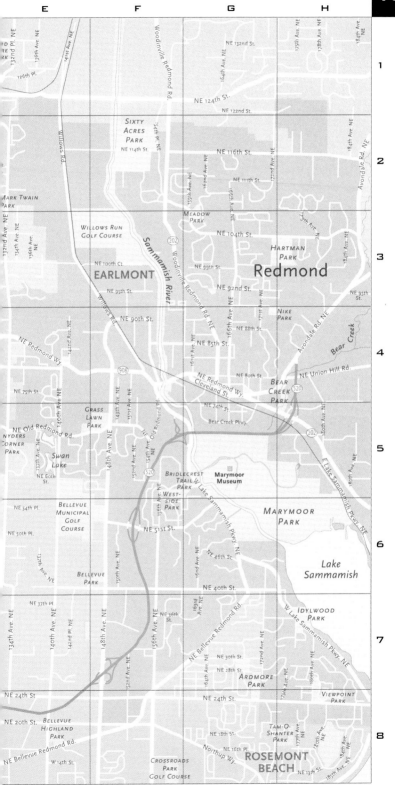

KIRKLAND AND REDMOND (EASTSIDE)

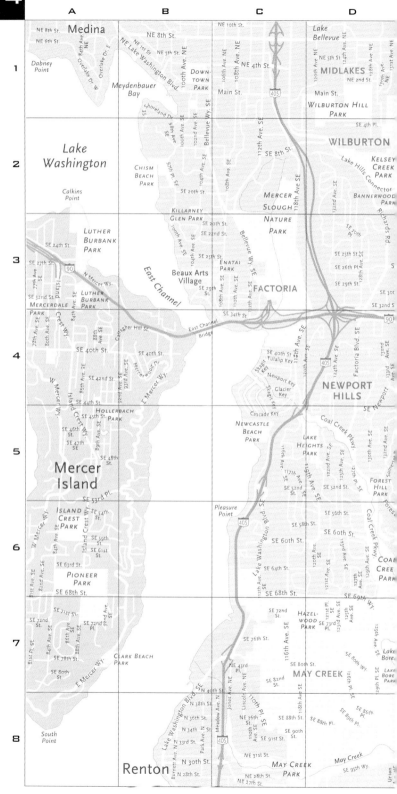

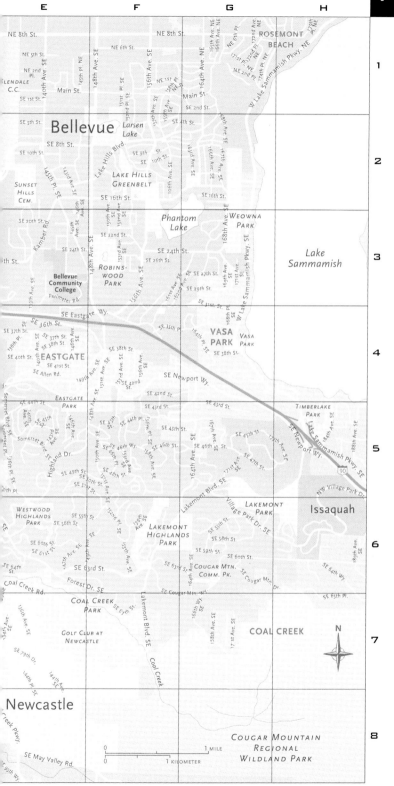

MERCER ISLAND AND BELLEVUE (EASTSIDE)

A   B   C   D

1

2

3

4

5

6

7

8

Carkeek Park

Jackson Park Golf Course

NE Northgate St

North Seattle Park

Thornton Creek Park

Licton Springs Park

Sacajewe Playground

Maple Leaf Playfield

NE 100th St

NE 96th St

Soundview Playfield

Crown Hill Glen

Golden Gardens Park

North Beach Park

Eddie Vine Boat Ramp

Loyal Heights Playground

Salmon Bay Park

Ballard Pool

Webster Playground

Ballard Playfield

Gilman Playground

Chittenden Locks

Lake Washington Ship Canal

14th Ave Boat Ramp

Ross Playfield

Shilshole Bay

Discovery Park

Lawton Park

Mounger Pool

Bayview Playfield

Interbay Athletic Complex

West Magnolia Playfield

Magnolia Park

Smith Cove Park

Elliott Bay Park

Myrtle Edwards Park

Sandel Playground

Greenwood Park

North Seattle Park

Green Lake Park

Green Lake

Evans Pool

Froula Playground

Cowan Park

Woodland Park

Meridian Playground

Wallingford Playfield

Burke-Gilman Trail

Sunnyside Boat Ramp

West Montlake Park

Montl Park

Gas Works Park

Roanoke Park

Interl Park

Boren Park

Volunteer Park

David Rogers Park

Queen Anne Pool

NEQueen Anne Greenbelt

Bhy Kracke Park

Seattle Center

South Lake Union Park

Waterfront Park

Harborview Park

Safeco Field

Dr Rizal Park

Pre Pa

Judi

Taejor Park

West Duwamish Greenbelt

Jeffers Park Golf Co

Elliott Bay

Don Armeni Boat Ramp

Hamilton View Park

Seacrest Park

Alki Beach Park

Duwamish Head Greenbelt

Alki Playfield

Schmitz Preserve Park

Bar-S Playground

Duwamish Head Greenbelt

West Seattle Frwy

SW Spokane St.

Mee-Kwa-Mooks Park

Deiridge Playfield

West Seattle Golf Course and Recreational Center

Puget Park

Fairmount Playground

Puget Creek Natural Area

Langfellow Creek Greenspace

West Duwamish Greenbelt

Maple Wood Playground

Georgetown Playfield

Cleveland Playfield

PARKS AND RECREATION

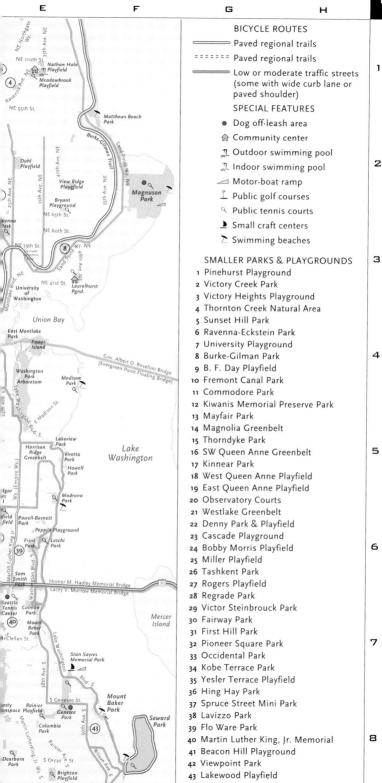

E   F   G   H

BICYCLE ROUTES

═══ Paved regional trails

======= Paved regional trails

━━━ Low or moderate traffic streets
(some with wide curb lane or
paved shoulder)

SPECIAL FEATURES

● Dog off-leash area

🏠 Community center

⚲ Outdoor swimming pool

⚲ Indoor swimming pool

◁ Motor-boat ramp

⌇ Public golf courses

⚲ Public tennis courts

⤙ Small craft centers

⋝ Swimming beaches

SMALLER PARKS & PLAYGROUNDS

1 Pinehurst Playground
2 Victory Creek Park
3 Victory Heights Playground
4 Thornton Creek Natural Area
5 Sunset Hill Park
6 Ravenna-Eckstein Park
7 University Playground
8 Burke-Gilman Park
9 B. F. Day Playfield
10 Fremont Canal Park
11 Commodore Park
12 Kiwanis Memorial Preserve Park
13 Mayfair Park
14 Magnolia Greenbelt
15 Thorndyke Park
16 SW Queen Anne Greenbelt
17 Kinnear Park
18 West Queen Anne Playfield
19 East Queen Anne Playfield
20 Observatory Courts
21 Westlake Greenbelt
22 Denny Park & Playfield
23 Cascade Playground
24 Bobby Morris Playfield
25 Miller Playfield
26 Tashkent Park
27 Rogers Playfield
28 Regrade Park
29 Victor Steinbrouck Park
30 Fairway Park
31 First Hill Park
32 Pioneer Square Park
33 Occidental Park
34 Kobe Terrace Park
35 Yesler Terrace Playfield
36 Hing Hay Park
37 Spruce Street Mini Park
38 Lavizzo Park
39 Flo Ware Park
40 Martin Luther King, Jr. Memorial
41 Beacon Hill Playground
42 Viewpoint Park
43 Lakewood Playfield

The Sourcebook for Your Hometown

MANY MAPS • WHERE & HOW

FIND IT ALL • NIGHT & DAY

ANTIQUES TO ZIPPERS

BARGAINS & BAUBLES

ELEGANT EDIBLES • ETHNIC EATS

STEAK HOUSES • BISTROS

DELIS • TRATTORIAS

CLASSICAL • JAZZ • COMEDY

THEATER • DANCE • CLUBS

COCKTAIL LOUNGES

COUNTRY & WESTERN • ROCK

COOL TOURS & TRIPS

HOUSECLEANING • CATERING

GET A LAWYER • GET A DENTIST

GET A NEW PET • GET A VET

MUSEUMS • GALLERIES

PARKS • GARDENS • POOLS

BASEBALL TO ROCK CLIMBING

FESTIVALS • EVENTS

DAY SPAS • DAY TRIPS

HOTELS • HOT LINES

PASSPORT PIX • TRAVEL INFO

HELICOPTER TOURS

DINERS • DELIS • PIZZERIAS

BRASSERIES • TAQUERÍAS

BOOTS • BOOKS • BUTTONS

BICYCLES • SKATES

SUITS • SHOES • HATS

RENT A TUX • RENT A COSTUME

BAKERIES • SPICE SHOPS

SOUP TO NUTS

Fodor's

CITYGUIDE
SEATTLE

FODOR'S TRAVEL PUBLICATIONS
NEW YORK • TORONTO • LONDON • SYDNEY • AUCKLAND
WWW.FODORS.COM

FODOR'S CITYGUIDE SEATTLE

EDITOR
Melisse J. Gelula

EDITORIAL CONTRIBUTORS
Shelley Arenas, Sharon Pian Chan, Julie Fay, Vanessa Lazo Greaves, Sara-Jean Green, Laura Kidder, Katrina Larsen, Stacey Levine, Eric Lucas, Lois Maffeo, Melanie McFarland, Holly S. Smith, Margaret Spain

EDITORIAL PRODUCTION
Linda K. Schmidt

MAPS
David Lindroth Inc., *cartographer;* Bob Blake and Rebecca Baer, *map editors*

DESIGN
Fabrizio La Rocca, *creative director;* Allison Saltzman, *text design;* Tigist Getachew, *cover design;* Melanie Marin, *photo editor*

PRODUCTION/MANUFACTURING
Yexenia (Jessie) Markland

COVER PHOTOGRAPH
Richard Cummins (sculpture outside Wells Fargo Tower)

COPYRIGHT

SPECIAL SALES

PRINTED IN THE UNITED STATES OF AMERICA

10 9 8 7 6 5 4 3 2 1

CONTENTS

METROPOLITAN LIFE

On a bad day in a big city, the little things that go with living shoulder-to-shoulder with a few million people wear us all down. But the special pleasures of urban life have a way of keeping us out of the suburbs—and thankful, even, for every second of stress. The field of daffodils in the park on a fine spring day. The perfect little black dress that you find for half price. The markets—so fabulously well stocked that you can cook any recipe without resorting to mail-order catalogs. The way you can sometimes turn a corner and discover a whole new world, so foreign you can hardly believe you're less than a mile from home. The never-ending wealth of possibilities and opportunities.

If you know where to find it all, the city cannot defeat you. With knowledge comes power. That's why Fodor's has prepared this book. It will put phone numbers at your fingertips. It'll take you to new places and remind you of those you've forgotten. It's the ultimate urban companion—and, we hope, your **new best friend in the city.**

It's the **citywise shopaholic,** who always knows where to find something, no matter how obscure. We've made a concerted effort to bring hundreds of great shops to your attention, so that you'll never be at a loss, whether you need a special birthday present for a great friend or some obscure craft items to make Halloween costumes for your kids.

It's the **restaurant know-it-all,** who's full of ideas for every occasion—you know, the one who would never send you to Café de la Snub, because he knows it's always overbooked, the food is boring, and the staff is rude. We'll steer you around the corner, to a perfect little place with five tables, a fireplace, and a chef on her way up.

It's a **hip barfly buddy,** who can give you advice when you need a charming nook, not too noisy, to take a friend after work. Among the dozens of bars and nightspots in this book, you're bound to find something that fits your mood.

It's the **sagest arts maven you know,** the one who always has the scoop on what's on that's worthwhile on any given night. In these pages, you'll find dozens of concert venues and arts organizations.

It's also the **city whiz,** who knows how to get you where you're going, wherever you are.

It's the **best map guide** on the shelves, and it puts **all the city in your briefcase** or on your bookshelf.

Stick with us. We'll lay out all the options for your leisure time—and gently nudge you away from the duds—so that you can truly enjoy metropolitan living.

YOUR GUIDES

No one person can know it all. To help get you on track around the city, we've hand-picked a stellar group of local experts to share their wisdom.

Shelley Arenas is co-author of *Lobster Kids Guide to Exploring Seattle* and has contributed to six Northwest travel and family resource books. She is regional site manager and editor of Parentcafe.com and former online director of *Seattle's Child* magazine. Shelley was born to contribute to the Shopping chapter, having come into this world at Northgate Hospital, adjacent to the nation's first shopping mall, also called Northgate. Her parks research began shortly thereafter, as a toddler at Green Lake.

Seattle-based journalists **Sara Jean Green** and **Sharon Chan** tag-teamed the outdoor activities and sports section. Sara Jean reports on lifestyles, travel, and arts and entertainment for the *Seattle Times*. Sharon has written outdoor-adventure features for the *Seattle Times* and travel features for the *Times'* Northwest Weekend supplement. A point of pride for Sharon: she has biked the Burke-Gilman Trail in the pouring rain, run circles around Green Lake, and plowed into snow banks at all the surrounding ski resorts.

An enthusiastic champion of good food, great service, and comfortable beds, the admittedly hedonistic **Julie Fay** is a freelance writer who has contributed to Fodor's guidebooks since 1997. Most recently she revised and expanded the dining, lodging, and side trips chapters of *Fodor's Seattle*, and wrote the Lodging chapter for this book. A native of Seattle, she is now raising her two children in Seattle's Columbia City neighborhood with her husband, and serves on the Board of Directors for Cinema Seattle.

Katrina Larsen is a Seattle-based writer and editor, who contributed to the Dining chapter. As the former editor of a trade publication for the fine dining and specialty coffee industries, *Coffee & Cuisine*, she's gotten to interview such culinary luminaries as Julia Child and Charlie Trotter. She's currently the associate editor at *WHERE Seattle*, a magazine for visitors to the Emerald City. She's also been a restaurant reviewer for *Metropolitan Living* and covered Seattle spas for *Spa* magazine. "I specialize in the good life," she says.

Stacey Levine is a Seattle-based writer who writes about food, restaurants, and culture for the *Seattle Weekly* and Seattle's alternative newspaper *The Stranger*. She is a novelist and the author of *My Horse and Other Stories*, which won the 1994 PEN/West Fiction Award. She is currently working on a new novel, and thereafter plans to expand her search for perfection in both osso bucco and macaroni and cheese.

Dining chapter contributor **Eric Lucas** is a Seattle-area travel and natural history writer. He has been a newspaper columnist and magazine editor and is the author or coauthor of several guidebooks focusing on the West. He lives on a small farm on Vashon Island, Washington.

Nightlife writer **Lois Maffeo** is a freelance music journalist from Olympia, Washington. Since 1995, she has been a contributing writer at *The Stranger*, covering music and culture. She also writes for the *College Music Journal Monthly*, *The Boston Phoenix*, *The Portland Mercury*, and *Time Out New York*.

As an arts and pop-culture writer for the *Seattle Union Record* and the *The Seattle Times*, **Melanie McFarland** has gotten to know some of Seattle's best-known places and best-kept secrets by stumbling around its bor- oughs and back streets. Melanie reviewed spas for this book and wrote the CitySources and Places to Explore chapters with **Winda Benedetti,** an avid traveler and a *Seattle Post-Intelligencer* reporter, who has written about everything from rock bands to criminal justice.

Margaret Spain, Nightlife contributor, is an artist currently living in Seat- tle. She keeps a keen eye on the Northwest scene, and knows a thing or two about getting in on the guest list.

You've probably spotted Shopping writer **Holly S. Smith** browsing stores with her camera, tape recorder, and notebook in hand—plus her two-year- old son in tow in the backpack and her three-year-old daughter in the stroller. As a writer living and working in Seattle for years, she knows where to find the latest high-quality fashions and deepest discounts for working parents and kids. As an editor for numerous Fodor's titles and a writer for *Fodor's Bali, Indonesia,* and *Southeast Asia* guides, Holly and fam- ily currently split their time between their Fox Island home and their bases in Singapore and Indonesia.

It goes without saying that our contributors have chosen all establish- ments strictly on their own merits—no establishment has paid to be included in this book.

HOW TO USE THIS BOOK

The first thing you need to know is that everything in this book is **arranged by category and in alphabetical order within category.**

Now, before you go any further, check out the **city maps** at the front of the book. Each map has a number, in a black box at the top of the page, and grid coordinates along the top and side margins. On the text pages, every listing in the book is keyed to one of these maps. Look for the map number in a small black box preceding each establishment name. The grid code follows in italics. For establishments with more than one location, additional map numbers and grid codes appear at the end of the listing. To locate a museum that's identified in the text as as **7** *e-6*, turn to Map 7 and locate the address within the e-6 grid square. To locate restaurants that are nearby, simply skim the text in the restaurant chapter for listings identified as being on Map 7.

Where appropriate throughout the guide, we name the neighborhood in which each sight, restaurant, shop, or other destination is located. We also give you complete opening hours and admission fees for sights; closing information for shops; credit-card, price, reservations, and closing information for restaurants; and cover prices for nightspots.

At the end of the book, in addition to an **alphabetical index,** you'll find a directory of restaurants by neighborhood.

Chapter 7, CitySources, provides resources and essential information for residents and visitors alike—everything from vet and lawyer-referral services to entertainment hot lines.

We've worked hard to make sure that all of the information we give you is accurate at press time. Still, time brings changes, so always confirm information when it matters—especially if you're making a detour.

Feel free to drop us a line. Were the restaurants we recommended as described? Did you find a wonderful shop you'd like to share? If you have complaints, we'll look into them and revise our entries in the next edition when the facts warrant. So send us your feedback. Either e-mail us at editor@fodors.com (specifying Fodor's CITYGUIDE Seattle on the subject line), or write to the Fodor's CITYGUIDE Seattle editor at 280 Park Avenue, New York, New York 10017. We look forward to hearing from you.

Karen Cure
Editorial Director

chapter 1

RESTAURANTS

general information

Unless otherwise noted, the restaurants listed in this guide are open daily for lunch and dinner. Downtown Seattle restaurants generally serve food until 10 PM on weekdays and later on Friday and Saturday. Outside the city, many restaurants stop serving around 9 PM. Some restaurants take checks from local banks.

NO SMOKING

There is no smoking at Seattle area restaurants, a fact established by ordinance and by custom. Even in those rare situations where smoking might be theoretically possible—say, a private dinner—it is almost always considered unacceptable. This is especially true in business situations, where it's also important to note that hard liquor is generally frowned upon at lunch.

RESERVATIONS

We only list reservations when they're essential or not accepted. If you've got a big party, by all means, call ahead.

TIPPING

Most Seattleites tip around 15% to 20%. You might consider leaving 25% if the service was outstanding, or the server or kitchen fulfilled special requests.

PRICE CATEGORIES

CATEGORY	COST*
Very Expensive ($$$$)	over $30
Expensive ($$$)	$20–$30
Moderate ($$)	$10–$20
Inexpensive ($)	under $10

*per person, for a main course at dinner

restaurants by cuisine

AFGHAN

5 e-6
KABUL
In the busy Wallingford district, this long-standing ethnic favorite with its mint-and-cardamom-scented dining room is a serious spot to relax. The lightly smoky, charbroiled kebab of lamb, Kabul's signature dish, gives new meaning to the word succulent. For vegetarians, the *ashak* (small purses of pasta stuffed with leek and scallion) are a delicate delight. Live sitar music on Tuesdays and Thursdays can keep you entranced well after your meal's end. *2301 N. 45th St. (at Corliss Ave.), Wallingford, 206/545–9000. AE, MC, V. No lunch. $$*

AFRICAN

10 c-4
AFRIKANDO
A great mix of folks file into this Senegalese storefront eatery on a regular basis, ex-peace corps workers and cab drivers among them. Many novices have come to love it, too. Such fresh-squeezed juices as tamarind, ginger, and hibiscus sparkle with flavor, and the excellent *thiebu djen* (stuffed halibut steak in red sauce with jolof rice) is richly satisfying but not heavy. Entrées come with generous sides of vegetables like eggplant, cabbage, and cassava. *2904 1st Ave. (near Broad St.), Belltown, 206/374–9714. MC, V. No lunch weekends. $–$$*

AMERICAN

14 c-2
CHACE'S PANCAKE CORRAL
Like a little vacation lodge, Chace's has been nestled along this woodsy Bellevue road since 1957—and it feels like the place hasn't changed much. Pancakes are the name of the game here, and they're comforting, scrumptious, and served with warm syrup. Try the Swedish plate with lingonberry sauce, or the oniony-brown potato pancakes with

sour cream. Evoking a bygone era, the Teenagers' Plate serves up hearty amounts of cakes, sausage, and eggs, while the Ladies' Plate has more demure portions. *1606 Bellevue Way SE (at 16th Ave. SE), Bellevue, 425/454–8888. MC, V. No dinner.* $

9 *b-6*

LEMIEUX'S

Here's a dependable diner just south of just south of Safeco Field, with a charming air of faded elegance imparted by the decades-old wallpaper, soda fountain, and tan vinyl booths. Employees of the nearby Starbucks headquarters fill the place at lunch, and the cocktail lounge is often bustling with old-timers even at midday. Omelets are the most popular item, though sandwiches with thick steak fries are fresh and good, too. *97 S. Lander St. (at 1st Ave. S), Downtown, 206/624–9851. AE, MC, V. Closed Sun.* $

10 *e-7*

LOWELL'S

Aside from the tasty breakfasts, the big draw here is the picture-window view of Puget Sound, and the ferries trailing across the water slowly as a dream. Tourists and the long-standing gang of Market workers who make up its clientele value the friendly service, clean tables, and those thick white ceramic coffee mugs. Try the corned beef hash, or for lunch, a bowl of clam steamers in garlic broth along with a cold brew. *1519 Pike Pl. (Main Arcade, next to the Athenian), Pike Place Market, 206/622–2036. AE, MC, V.* $

3 *c-8*

LUNA PARK CAFE

Time-travel to the 1950s at this retro-garbed diner with its stockpiles of memorabilia, tasty meat loaf, and thick malts. Straight-up turkey dinners, mashed potatoes, and burgers are served to the tunes on a relic jukebox; breakfast is hearty diner-American, too. With a slight nod to contemporary food trends, you can also get veggie burgers and healthful tossed salads. *2918 SW Avalon Way (at the West Seattle Bridge), West Seattle, 206/935–7250. MC, V.* $

5 *b-4*

MAE'S PHINNEY RIDGE CAFE

Several dining rooms, each outfitted with an incredible avalanche of objets de kitsch, can keep you amused for hours. Folks have flocked here weekend mornings for years to savor the huge, soft cinnamon rolls (also in French toast form), cheddar-topped piles of homemade hash browns, or the (Milk) Shake n' Eggs and a seat on the back porch. Kindly faced owner Jeannie Mae is proud of the house-smoked fish in the popular kippered salmon scramble and the Trout n' Eggs. Lunch is served at Mae's, but that isn't really the point. Things shut down daily at 3. *6412 Phinney Ave. N (at N. 65th St.), Phinney Ridge, 206/782–1222. AE, MC, V. No dinner.* $

10 *f-5*

PALACE KITCHEN

The most recent of Tom Douglas's ventures, which include Dahlia Lounge and Etta's Seafood, does upscale versions of American diner food: applewood-rotisserie free-range chicken, pan-roasted quail, and "farmers" salads sit well next to the fantastic cheese selection. Although the kitchen serves as the commissary for his other two restaurants, drinks in the massive bar, under the Chihuly-esque chandelier, are indeed the order of the day. *2030 5th Ave., at Lenora St., Belltown, 206/448–2001. AE, D, DC, MC, V. No lunch weekends.* $$$

5 *b-2*

PETE'S EGGNEST

Big breakfasts and warm service have made loyalists out of neighbors to this all-day breakfast hangout. It's packed on weekend mornings, when joggers in Lycra-and-fleece jackets order eggs Benedict, the gyros omelet, and rich, cups o' regular Joe. Even software designers have been known to order the kids' pancakes, arranged on the plate to look like a teddy bear face. The Greek salad, with its snappy blue cheese and grilled chicken, isn't on the menu, but ask for it. *7717 Greenwood Ave. N (near 77th St.), Greenwood, 206/784–5348.* $

7 *e-6*

THE SHANTY

As the name implies, it's little more than a rough-hewn, boxy shack in what once was a blue-collar neighborhood of fish merchants and longshoremen. Although condos, design shops, and office buildings have sprung up along the waterfront, gentrification hasn't affected the decidedly nontrendy lunch counter. The clientele—old and new—

stop in here for basics: hearty BLTs and a good-looking tuna melts on sourdough. Breakfast comes in the form of malted waffles, chicken-fried steak and eggs, and the like, and is served daily 'til closing at 3 PM. *350 Elliott Ave. W (at Harrison St.), Waterfront, 206/282–1400. AE, D, MC, V. No dinner. $*

10 *e-7*

THREE GIRLS BAKERY

Famous for its huge sandwiches soft breads or rolls, Three Girls—one of the oldest businesses in the Market—is most comfortable off-season after the tourists have cleared out. Even so, you'll sit elbow-to-elbow at the lunch counter year-round, where friendly banter is unavoidable. Try the meat loaf, egg salad, or baked eggplant; sandwiches are so big you can save half for later. The bakery also sells its goods around the corner at a take-out window, so you pick up some sweet-potato-pecan bread on your way home. *1514 Pike Pl. (around the corner from Frank's Produce), Pike Place Market, 206/622–1045. MC, V. No dinner. Breakfast. $*

AMERICAN CASUAL

10 *e-7*

ALIBI ROOM

Rockers, models, and wanna-bes often inhabit this half-lit bar-restaurant that pulses until the wee hours. (The kitchen's open until 11 PM on weekdays, and until midnight on weekends.) Tucked inside a bend in a cobblestone alley beneath the Market, Alibi is owned by a group of Hollywood types, including actor Tom Skerritt, who live in town. A loud downstairs dance floor is fairly out of earshot, so you can dig into entrées of flank steak, roast chicken, or the risotto or ravioli of the day in relative peace. Brunch is also served daily. A selection of import beers and port wines fills out the drink menu. *85 Pike St. (Lower Post Alley), Pike Place Market, 206/623–3180. AE, MC, V. Brunch. $–$$*

4 *c-5*

THE BAIT HOUSE

It's no joke: In the summer fishermen stop here at 4 AM to pick up their bait (but the kitchen's closed then). You can come during a more reasonable hour for a deli sandwich, crab cocktail, the

famous open-faced crab-cheese melt, and definitely for the view. The patio and small, crooked, rough-hewn dining room overlook boats gliding by on their way to the Ballard Locks. Take a peek behind the counter, too: All hot food is baked or warmed in little toaster ovens. Expect local nautical charm. *5517 Seaview Ave. NW (between Ballard Locks and train bridge overpass), Ballard, 206/297–9109. MC, V. Closed Mon. No dinner Sun. or Tues. $$*

5 *e-6*

JITTERBUG CAFE

A diner-cum-bistro, the tiny Jitterbug with its cozy booths and white tablecloths has a rotating menu of international ethnic cuisine—just like its companion café, the Coastal Kitchen. On the basic menu you'll find pork chops and juicy rib-eye steak, with specials like halibut with pasta in white wine sauce or pan-seared marlin. For breakfast, try the cheery gingerbread waffles. As at the Coastal, you'll hear voices in the bathrooms here: hilarious, wooden-sounding foreign-language lessons on tape. *2114 N. 45th St. (between Meridian and Bagley Sts.), Wallingford, 206/547–6313. MC, V. No dinner Sun. $*

10 *e-7*

THE MARKET GRILL

It's easy to miss this earnest, no-nonsense little counter in the center of cacophonous Pike Place Market. But its low-fat, clean-tasting grilled fish sandwiches on Market sourdough bread are marvelously textured and delicious. The fish comes fresh from the seafood merchant stall; plates of grilled salmon, halibut, or cod are served with rice and sweet, crisp coleslaw. The clam chowder is surprisingly good, too, full-flavored and not as heavy as the usual breeds. *1509 Pike Pl. (Main Arcade, across from fish market), Pike Place Market, 206/682–2654. AE, MC, V. $*

5 *b-3*

RED MILL

Seattleites have been seduced by the Red Mill. Burgers here are assembled superbly by a crack assembly-line staff. You can order your burgers dressed simply, with lettuce and smoky-mayo "Mill Sauce," or more elaborately, with menu combinations of luscious roasted Anaheim peppers, blue cheese, barbecue sauce, or Tillamook cheddar. Vegetarians note: Order the meatless patties as substitutions on the regular burger menu, rather than from the veggie menu—the regular burger buns and dressings are much better. *312 N. 67th (at Greenwood Ave. N), Phinney Ridge, 206/783–6362. No credit cards. $*

2 *b-3*

1613 W. Dravus (at 16th Ave. W), Magnolia, 206/284–6363. $

5 *f-4*

SCARLETT TREE

Here's a reputable jazz/R&B bar by night, and a find for breakfast seekers by day. Established in the 1940s, the Tree is as well-known for its chipper career waitresses as it is for its huge breakfasts and grilled crab sandwich with cheddar. Try the strawberry-stuffed French toast with yogurt and cream cheese. Long-time customers know each other here, so friendly chitchat shoots across the busy room. It's easy to hear the music and see the stage if you're eating dinner on the restaurant side. *6521 Roosevelt Way NE (at NE 66th St.), Roosevelt, 206/523–7153. AE, MC, V. No dinner Sun. and Mon. $*

10 *e-7*

SISTERS
EUROPEAN SNACKS

A melange of international-style sandwiches and fresh grains-and-greens salads have given this colorful, casual, open-air market stall a solid reputation. Go for the *croque monsieur* (a grilled ham-and-cheese sandwich dipped in egg and sautéed in butter) or the baked eggplant with olive paste on focaccia, with a side of gazpacho or Hungarian mushroom soup. Breakfast egg sandwiches are popular, too. Sisters closes daily at about 5:30. *1530 Post Alley (Sanitary Market Building), Pike Place Market, 206/623–6723. No credit cards. No dinner. $*

10 *e-5*

SIT N' SPIN

Part Laundromat, part retro-industrial hangout, and part healthful café, Sit N' Spin offers you vinyl booths in which to play board games and swill "live" juices while you wash your whites. Favorite fare includes the five-bean vegetarian chili, pastas tossed with chicken, and a famous Snickers pie. Counter service is laconic at best. *2219 4th Ave. (between Bell and Blanchard Sts.), Downtown, 206/441–9484. MC, V. Sun.–Wed. café*

closes at midnight; Thurs.–Sat. closes at 2 AM. Last load 10:30 PM Sun.–Wed. and 12:30 AM Thurs.–Sat. $

2 *f-3*

THE SLIP

The name describes it aptly: alongside the Kirkland Marina, this spot is just about large enough to hold a sailboat. But in warm weather the open patio creates more space, which is necessary since there's no lack of takers for the popular shrimp burger, dressed with wasabi mayonnaise. Other tasty offerings include the salmon burger and a vegetarian burger made from bulgur and mushrooms. The smoky-tasting homemade ketchup tastes great on the roasted fries. *80 Kirkland Ave. (at Lake Washington Blvd.), Kirkland, 425/739–0033. AE, D, DC, MC, V. $*

10 *e-5*

TWO BELLS TAVERN

This funky tavern with a low-key dining room was once a hangout for artists and writers, and to some degree still is. The humble joint hasn't suffered much from the upscaling of Belltown the way some long-standing businesses have; one reason is that Downtown workers and residents have discovered the large and marvelous burgers. They come on sourdough buns, smothered with onions and cheese, with a choice of a side dishes or salad. Accompanied by a cold beer, all sandwiches here are satisfying. *2313 4th Ave. (between Bell and Battery Sts.), Belltown, 206/441–3050. AE, D, MC, V. $*

BARBECUE

1 *c-4*

BACKDOOR BBQ

Located outdoors and at the rear of a neighborhood tavern, it's not more than a little porch kitchen with three adjacent picnic tables, but the sweet, tender brisket and boneless pork practically fall apart at the touch of a fork. Fruitwood-smoked meats slow-cook here for 10 to 12 hours, says the owner. You have four choices of sauce intensity: mild, spicy, turbo, and nitro. The chicken sandwich, topped with smoked Tillamook cheddar, is succulent. Sides are done well, too, including home-baked corn bread and corn on the cob. Get ribs elsewhere, but stay here for the brisket, boneless pork, and other meats, which you can also buy by the pound. *6459 California Ave. SW (between Fauntleroy Way and Beveridge Pl.), West Seattle, 206/932–RIBS. MC, V. $$*

2 *f-4*

DIXIE'S BBQ

Originally an auto repair shop where the owner dished out family recipes cooked on a portable meat smoker, this family-owned gem sees hordes of appreciative followers line up for weekday lunch. The hot sauce is strong and sweet, and the thick, heartily smoked ribs with sides like red beans and rice, corn bread, and baked beans make for a very filling meal. After the homemade lemon cake, you might need a nap, or coffee. Closes at 4:30 daily. *11522 Northup Way (at 116th Ave. NE), Bellevue, 425/828–2460. No credit cards. Closed Sun. No dinner. $*

2 *d-6*

JONES BARBEQUE

When one of the local weeklies recently declared Jones' the best in town, the secret was out. It boasts complex layers of flavor, and the pork ribs are consistently large and generously meaty. The small, cheery kitchen with counter service and bright red tablecloths also serves astoundingly velvety macaroni and cheese, as well as candied yams, greens, and sweet-potato pie. *3216 S. Hudson St. (at Martin Luther King Way, one blk. south of Ferdinand), Rainier Valley, 206/725–2728. MC, V. Closed Mon. $–$$*

9 *b-6*

PECOS PIT BBQ

Across from Starbucks corporate headquarters and a short distance from Safeco Field, this window-service hut serves up quick, decent meat sandwiches: brisket, pork, Pecos beef, ham, or links. Business suits and construction workers alike wait in the lunch line on weekdays for the sauced goods. Ask the counterman to "spike" your sandwich and it'll arrive with an extra sliced link. *2260 1st Ave. S (across from Sodo Center–Starbucks HQ), Downtown, 206/623–0629. No credit cards. Closed weekends. $*

5 *b-1*

PIG N' WHISTLE

It looks like an English pub from the outside, but the fare calls Louisiana to mind. The grand piano and brightly colored paintings create a comfortable atmosphere where you can dig into applewood-smoked pork ribs and baby back ribs glazed with a secret sauce. For a less gooey meal, try the po'boy sandwich or the house specialty, Appaloosa chili made with chicken sausage. The bar serves local microbrews. Live music makes the place noisier at night. *8412 Greenwood Ave. N (at 85th St.), Greenwood, 206/782–6044. AE, MC, V. $*

2 *c-6*

WILLIE'S TASTE OF SOUL BAR-B-QUE & CUSTOM SMOKE HOUSE

Reviewers have raved over the sauce at Willie's, with its sweetness that seems to ebb and flow against the heat and spice of the recipe. You'll find alder- and cherry-smoked meats here, including ribs, ultratender beef with blackened edges, lusciously tender chicken, and fine brisket. The homemade hot links aren't to everyone's liking, but there's plenty else to choose from. Sides are fresh, especially the potato salad, which is surprisingly good and mustardy. The dining room is immaculate, with a TV always on. Try the 7-Up cake for dessert. *605 Beacon Ave. S (at Graham St.), Beacon Hill, 206/722–3229. MC, V. Closed Sun. $–$$*

BRAZILIAN

5 *g-5*

CAFFE BRAZIL

Next to a Brazilian grocery and travel agency, this casual café has small cheese rolls and meat-stuffed pastries, as well as homemade national dishes like *feijoada* (pork and black-bean stew) and *moxiqua* (whitefish in red sauce). The vegetarian plate is a huge, comforting combination of smooth-as-butter red beans, moist rice, and garlic-sautéed okra. Cashew-fruit juice is a treat, as is the flan. *5259 University Way NE (between 52nd and 55th Sts.), University District, 206/525–1993. MC, V. $*

5 *g-5*

TEMPERO DO BRASIL

Folks come from far afield to this festive place for a taste of Brazil. The popular cod, prawn, and halibut dishes simmered in golden-coconut-based sauces are complex and satisfying; entrées arrive with moist, chewy long-grain rice and delectable black beans. For a larger meal, try the charbroiled Argentine steak, *bife grelhado*. Finish with cold passionfruit mousse or tangy guava paste served with farmer's cheese, and strong, dark coffee. The outstanding food, attention to detail, and earnest staff make dining here a pleasure. The airy patio is perfect for icy Brazilian cocktails in the summer. *5628 University Way NE (between 56th and Ravenna Sts.), University District, 206/523–6229. AE, MC, DC, V. $$*

CAFÉS

3 a-8
ALKI BAKERY

You can't help but notice the pies bursting with fruit and pillowy cakes filling the café's attractive display case. But before you indulge yourself, order a colorful salad or fettuccine with roasted vegetables, and take in the wide, calming view of the Olympics and Bainbridge Island. This bakery does a brisk business and also owns a retail outlet in Georgetown, south Seattle. *2738 Alki Ave. SW (at 61st St.), West Seattle, 206/935–1352. AE, D, MC, V. $*

2 d-6
BOTH WAYS CAFE

Pastries reign here: sour-cream coffee cake, lemon bars, and delectable pecan sticky buns. Patrons are often runners, bicyclists, or moms with strollers out for a walk in nearby Seward Park, so the atmosphere here, even for dinner, is classic Seattle-casual. Large, comfortable wooden tables promote community dining and conversation. Dinner takes cues from Italian, French, or Middle Eastern recipes, like the scallop bisteeya, a flaky crust encasing scallops, spinach, pasta, lemon, and Middle Eastern spices. The Both Ways' split-pea soup is a creamy wonder. *4922 S. Genesee Ave. (at 49th Ave.), Columbia City, 206/722–5799. AE, D, DC, MC, V. No dinner Sun.–Tues. $–$$*

5 f-7
BUNGALOW WINE BAR & CAFE

The snugly and warm upper-story den and living room of a house forms the dining room. A fireplace is the centerpiece in cooler months, and with warmer weather, an airy patio opens up. Clientele is often solo and reading: one of the main attractions here is the West Coast's only exclusively poetry bookstore, located downstairs. Servers' wine knowledge is strong, and entrées are wide ranging, including a number of game dishes (quail over polenta, venison medallions). *2412 N. 45th St. (between Eastern and Sunnyside Aves.), Wallingford, 206/632–0254. AE, D, MC, V. Closed Sun.–Mon. $–$$*

12 b-2
CAFE PALOMA

You might swoon over the lovely atmosphere in this tiny café close to art galleries, with its decorative bronze trays and big basketfuls of glossy eggplants and tomatoes. Along with coffee service, there's light lunch and dinner fare with a Mediterranean/Turkish accent: handmade dolmas, hummus, and *baba ghanoush* (a puree of eggplant), made with yogurt in this case, not tahini. The owner's daily lunch specials can veer toward down-home American, though: a juicy pork tenderloin is frequently the lunch centerpiece. First Thursday of the month dinners, which correspond with Pioneer Square's Art Gallery Walk, are more elaborate. Try the rice pudding topped with golden raisins. *93 Yesler Way (between 1st and Elliott Aves.), Pioneer Square, 206/405–1920. No credit cards. $*

10 g-6
FIFTH AVENUE CAFE

Behind floor-to-ceiling windows reminiscent of a New York deli, owners Andy and Shelby Tran make one of the better chicken-salad sandwiches in town, sprinkled with walnuts, and served on soft, house-baked nine-grain bread. Some folks swear by the homemade chicken soup—full of doughy, tender dumplings—served daily. Homemade desserts, like the pecan chocolate chunks, may widen your eyes. *1522 5th Ave. (between Pike and Pine Sts.), Downtown, 206/621–7137. MC, V. $*

4 f-5
GRAPES WINE SHOP & BISTRO

Amid a number of tables and a comfy sofa, the wine-and-cheese merchant's counter area is usually jumbled looking with paperwork and magazines. Piaf's voice might be resonating through the rafters, though; a sea breeze from Shilshole Bay might be drifting in, and the grilled cheese sandwich of the day on rustic bread might be scrumptious raclette, a nutty, semifirm cheese similar to Gruyère. The large by-the-glass and bottled-wine selection is a veritable tour of Italy's wine regions. *5424 Ballard Ave. NW (between 20th and 22nd Aves.), Ballard, 206/297–1460. D, MC, V. $*

9 *d-6*

JAVA LOVE ESPRESSO

Neighborhood residents and Amazon.com employees from a nearby branch office stop at this storefront for strong coffee and lunch in the form of Mexican-style *tortas* (sandwiches) on large, chewy French-style rolls. The turkey, ham, and vegetarian varieties are layered with avocado, spinach leaves, red onion, and crumbly white ranchero cheese. Demonstrating the "eat locally" motto, chicken, pork, and cheese tamales are hand-made by a nearby Beacon Hill resident, and Mexican popsicles, Paletas Frescos, are also sold here. It closes daily at 3 PM. *2414 Beacon Ave. S (at 15th Ave.), Beacon Hill, 206/323–1157. No credit cards. No dinner. $*

4 *h-1*

LIBRARY CAFE

The building was once a fireplace shop, so the walls are exposed brick and lined with built-in hearths, marble mantles, brick arches, and niches that bespeak cozy warmth and ports in storms. Books line the mantles and fill glass cabinets, making the homey Library a good place for a solitary spot of breakfast, tea, and browsing. After 2 PM, you can order afternoon tea for two or more—reservations are essential; service includes scones, finger sandwiches, and fruit. Mimosas and champagne are extra but promise to make the afternoon melt away. *850 NW 85th St. (at Dibble Ave.), Crown Hill, 206/789–5682. AE, MC, V. Closed Mon. No dinner. $*

10 *d-5*

MACRINA BAKERY

If you see an empty table here, make a dash for it. Long-famous for the fresh, take-away bread by head baker Leslie Mackie, the café can get packed. Don't let the limited seating deter you: the Mediterranean-influenced soups, salads, sandwiches, and mezes are above-par. *2408 1st Ave. (between Blanchard and Wall Sts.), Downtown, 206/448–4032. AE, DC, MC, V. $*

4 *f-5*

MR. SPOTS CHAI HOUSE

In-the-know locals won't put up with syrupy-sweet competitors once they've partaken of Mr. Spots' peppery, subtle drink, dubbed Morning Glory Chai. In fact, what started as a chai-brewing operation in owner Jessica Vidican-Neisius's basement quickly became a successful wholesale business with a storefront café (and computers with Internet access). Tea is worshiped here, so you'll find high-quality leaf as well as unusual blends like rose congou, plum, and hairpoint green, along with jars of more mysterious herbs. The thumbnail-size menu offers an especially gooey and satisfying grilled cheese. *2213 NW Market St. (between 20th and 22nd Aves.), Ballard, 206/297–CHAI. MC, V. $*

5 *g-7*

UGLY MUG

Pleasantly worn couches, lamps on the tables, and jazz standards on the stereo recall the funky Seattle that once was. A sign at the cash register admonishes, "Friends don't let friends go to Starbucks!" Indeed, the Ugly Mug doesn't aspire to be anything more than itself, with warming, inventive soups like garbanzo-cabbage or black bean cooked with wine and orange zest. The meatloaf sandwich, with its wonderfully smoky flavor, makes you want seconds. For breakfast, try the Belgian waffles with yogurt and fruit, or the exceptional raspberry scone. *1309 NE 43rd St. (between University and Brooklyn Aves.), University District, 206/547–3219. No credit cards. $*

11 *e-2*

VICTROLA

When this hip-'n'-homey café appeared in the summer of 2000, it added a dose of community and life to Capitol Hill's east neighborhood. There are plenty of café lizards here—they don't move for hours—enjoying the Berardo coffee, wood-roasted in Rome. A recently added, to-the-point menu of decidedly healthful sandwiches are stuffed with free-range turkey, basil, tomato, and goat cheese. Homemade soups appeal as well to the health-conscious, often bobbing with tofu. Sandwiches sell out, so get there early. *411 15th Ave. E (between Republican and Harrison Sts.), Capitol Hill, 206/325–6520. MC, V. $*

CAJUN/CREOLE

4 g-6

BURK'S CAFE

With homey wooden floors, a tiny but comfortable bar, and plenty of light, immaculate Burk's is well versed in gumbos, jambalayas, and ribs, making it a godsend in a city with relatively few Creole restaurants. Big crocks of hot pickled okra sit on each table; servers are competent and even witty. Blackened rockfish is exceedingly tender inside, and alder-wood-smoked sausages are made and smoked on the premises. Try the fetching sandwiches, which come on chewy rolls. Be warned: most dishes are extra-spicy and can't be made milder. *52411 Ballard Ave. NW (at 22nd Ave.), Ballard, 206/782–0091. MC, V. Closed Sun.–Mon. $–$$*

10 f-7

DELCAMBRE'S RAGIN' CAJUN

Chef-owner Danny Delcambre studied under cookbook-magnate and Louisiana chef Paul Prudhomme before moving to Seattle and developing his own style of creamy catfish étouffée, spicy gumbo crowded with Louisiana-smoked sausage (flown in fresh from the bayou), and a mean muffuletta. Delcambre is deaf and legally blind, and he runs a tight ship, communicating across the dining room with his mostly deaf staff in ASL. Even former president Clinton has sampled his fine Cajun fare. *1525 1st Ave. (between Pike and Pine Sts.), Pike Place Market, 206/624–2598. AE, MC, V. No lunch Sun. No dinner Mon.–Wed. $–$$*

9 b-2

NEW ORLEANS

Aspirations to authenticity demand more than a name, and better versions of Creole and Cajun cuisine can be had elsewhere in Seattle. But at least they put filé powder (a woodsy-flavored spice) and okra in the gumbo, and crayfish shows up on the menu. And the setting—unpretentious tables in a high-ceiling, 19th-century brick building—comes as close to the French Quarter as you can get on the West Coast. After dinner, it transmogrifies into one of the Pioneer Square bars, with blues the predominant genre. *114 1st Ave. S (at Yesler Way), Pioneer Square, 206/622–2563. AE, MC, V. $*

10 g-8

SAZERAC

The bright colors and festive Mardi Gras feel of Sazerac are as sumptuous as the enormous cocktails (including the whiskey cocktail that inspired the restaurant's name) and heady entrées. For starters you'll find chicory salad with basted pears and Brie or butternut-squash crab bisque. Dishes might be as elegant as grilled salmon atop a sweet corn–and–chile pepper ragout, crab–and–rock shrimp cake drizzled with cayenne mayonnaise, or more straightforward, like the smoky Zinfandel pork chops with grits (from scratch), or "beans that make you crazy" (served at breakfast). Delightful presentations and strong flavor combinations make meals here worthwhile any time of day. *Hotel Monaco, 1101 4th Ave. (at Spring St.) Downtown, 206/624–7755. Reservations essential. AE, D, DC, MC, V. $$–$$$*

CAMBODIAN

12 e-3

PHNOM PENH NOODLE HOUSE

This room accented with bamboo, a tank of gaping koi, and a steaming fountain, seems to draw Seattleites from all walks of life, and the menu is written in Cambodian, Vietnamese, English, and Chinese. Dishes are seasoned with lemongrass, lime, and pickled garnishes; servers aren't overly friendly but are helpful enough with describing dishes. You can't go wrong with the noodle soup bowls—try the *batambang* with ground peanuts, pickled radish, cucumber, and slices of hard-boiled egg. *Chow-geutaol*, stir-fried rice noodles, is a good bet, too. *660 S. King St. (between 7th and Maynard Aves.), International District, 206/748–9825. MC, V. Closed Wed. $*

CARIBBEAN

10 c-5

WESTERN VINE CARIBBEAN GRILL

Caribbean eateries seem to come and go in Seattle, but this one has a good foothold in Belltown, close to the water. In the relaxed tropics-inspired atmosphere, the specialty is jerk half-chicken served with yam puree. Complex spices ranging from delicate to strong meld in the dish, with allspice, chile, ginger, cinnamon, and cloves all pitching in to make your mouth water. In fact, flavors may draw from West Africa, Portugal, and India. If you're faint of heart when it comes to heat and spice, though, tell your server, or try something milder like fried tilapia, dressed in a banana leaf with tamarind sauce. *81 Vine St. (at Western Ave.), Belltown, 206/728–1959. AE, MC, V. Closed Mon. No lunch. $$*

CHINESE

Many Chinese restaurants have branches around town, but these are mostly the spin-offs of successes born in the International District. If you'd prefer a multisensory or a late-night dining experience, the International District restaurants are for you.

7 *g-6*
BAMBOO GARDEN

Look no further: You've found one of the few vegetarian (and kosher!) Chinese restaurants in town. All dishes are made with mock meat: textured vegetable protein that's in most cases fairly convincing. The Buddhist Basket, literally woven from dried taro and filled with emerald-green vegetables, is a gorgeous dish. *364 N. Roy St. (between 3rd and 4th Aves.), Queen Anne, 206/282–6616. AE, D, MC, V. $$*

6 *c-3*
BLACK PEARL

There are only six booths and a few counter seats here—a drawback at night when the place is packed. Luckily, a fleet of white delivery vans is at the ready, speeding across Wedgewood with the goods. People love the chewy homemade noodles, and the Lover's Eggplant—batter-crisp on the outside, tender within. Try the shrimp-stuffed tofu or sea bass steamed in oolong tea. Prices are good in general, but the lunch special is a serious bargain. *7347 35th Ave. NE (at 75th St.), Wedgewood, 206/526–5115. AE, DC, MC, V. $*

1 *d-1*
14602 15th Ave. NE, at 145th, Shoreline, 206/365–8989. $

2 *b-2*
DOONG KONG LAU HAKKA CUISINE

Your schlep to its unlikely location, amidst tire shops and cheap pancake diners, is rewarded by a wild ride of a menu that satisfies with at least 250 tasty items. The Hakka are a nomadic Chinese ethnic group with their own cuisine style—although it negotiates the mildness of Cantonese and the spiciness of Mandarin—and flavor comes from strong soup stocks and spice combinations; no MSG is used. Seafood hot pots are terrific, as is the salt-bake chicken, Hakka crispy half duck, and the regular or vegetarian-style Mah Poh Tofu with bell peppers. Chinese breakfast is always available in the form of congees, sweet soy milk and crullers, or unusual forms of dim sum. *9710 Aurora Ave. N (at 97th St.), North Aurora, 206/526–8828. DC, MC, V. $–$$*

12 *e-3*
FORTUNA CAFE

If you love an odd, irregular gem, you might like this Cantonese/Szechwan spot, with a timeworn interior and rickety upstairs balcony that dates back to the International District of yore, when the area was called Chinatown. Emphasis is given to barbecued pork and duck—in the daily "lunchbox," they're served plainly, on a bed of rice—but barbecue is also sold by the pound. Other interesting dishes include something called swamp cabbage (served with tofu), and an assortment of light noodle stir-frys, congees, and soups. *711 S. King St. (between 8th and 7th Aves.), International District, 206/223–5343. MC, V. $*

12 *d-4*
HING LOON SEAFOOD RESTAURANT

A low-key underdog in a neighborhood of stylish competitors, Hing Loon's atmosphere isn't subtle (fluorescent lights loom overhead; metallic clangs from the kitchen are frequent), but the staff is extra friendly, and the menu's broad and interesting. Daily Cantonese and Szechwan specials, written on colorful paper and hung on the wall, list dishes like chicken with cake noodle or quail in salt. Noodle soups have a deep chicken-broth flavor, and the dumplings are good, as are flash-cooked greens and panfried noodle dishes like *chow foon*, and the very popular steamed whole crab with black bean sauce. Some of Hing Loon's plates are on the oily side, though. Stick with these dishes, soups, hot pots, or fresh seafood. *628 S. Weller St. (at Maynard Ave.), International District, 206/682–2828. MC, V. $–$$*

2 *d-6*

JUMBO

The enormous dining room with bright chandeliers spreads around you, as does the din in this hopping spot that's especially busy during weekend lunches, when dim sum—possibly the best in town—is served. Details aren't lost here: A tiny dash of roe and coriander leaves top the translucent *har gow* (shrimp dumplings), and lobster comes prepared five different ways. Though the extensive Cantonese menu includes a separate listing of Vietnamese dishes including *pho* (noodle soup), the Chinese preparations here seem to shine much more. *4208 Rainier Ave. S (at Genessee St.), Rainier Valley, 206/760–9200. MC, V. $–$$*

12 *e-3*

KAU KAU

It seems that Kau Kau has been eclipsed of late by more fashionable joints moving into the ever-expanding International District. But the barbecued pork, duck, and spareribs here, always reliably tasty, haven't changed. Or mix-and-match seasonal vegetables (Chinese okra, young greens, bitter melon) with various meats to design your own stir-fry. Hot pots and good crispy- or soft-noodle dishes round out the Cantonese menu at this very serviceable restaurant. *656 S. King St. (between 7th and Maynard Aves.), International District, 206/682–4006. AE, MC, V. $–$$*

12 *e-3*

L.A. SEAFOOD

Come here if you want something unusual in your Cantonese/Mandarin fare. The chef hearkens back, through his menu, to the youth he spent in a small rural village: steamed frog, duck tongue in spicy sauce, dried scallops with Chinese melon, fried prawns with walnuts, and a number of egg-and-vegetable dishes are prominent on the menu. There are less exotic items, too, like noodle soups, but they can be bland; steer toward the other menu items, if you dare. There's another plus: L.A. Seafood stays open until 2:30 AM on weeknights, even later on weekends. *424 7th Ave. S (at King St.), International District, 206/622–8181. AE, MC, V. $$–$$$*

4 *g-6*

LOUIE'S

The decor at Louie's looks straight out of a 1960s James Bond flick. Cavernous booths, mirror-paneled walls, and a huge (reservable) banquet room can make for a fun excursion. Besides the Cantonese/Szechwan fare, the menu includes dim sum and American chow like burgers and roast beef au jus sandwiches. Like many Chinese restaurants in town, Louie's is open past midnight on weekends. *5100 15th Ave. NW (just north of the Ballard Bridge), Ballard, 206/782–8855. AE, D, MC, V. $–$$*

12 *e-3*

MIKE'S NOODLE HOUSE

On chill, rainy days, the steamy front windows of this clean soup-only café look inviting. So do the lovely, savory soups and congees. Homemade *sui-kau* (shrimp and pork) dumplings, also stuffed with wood-ear mushrooms, rise easily above most competition, even in this neighborhood. Order a Chinese "donut" to dunk in your broth. The affable chef Mike Huang uses no MSG in his kitchen. *418 Maynard Ave. S (between King and Jackson Sts.), International District, 206/389–7099. No credit cards. $*

12 *e-3*

OCEAN CITY

On one side of the building, it's a full restaurant with an enormous dining room, banquet rooms, the whole nine yards; on the other, it's a bare-bones "noodle café" where you'll find quick soups, barbecued pork, and duck dishes. Each side has approximately the same Cantonese menu, but the café, with its view to the street, holds the rough charm and more interesting clientele. On winter days, peer through your teacup's steam to the rain-slicked street below. *609 S. Weller St. (at 6th Ave.), International District, 206/623–2333. MC, V. $–$$*

9 *d-6*

PERRY KO'S SOUTH CHINA RESTAURANT

They don't necessarily come here for the food, which consists of old-fashioned Cantonese American chow mein, sub gums, burgers, and the like. No, it's the Dragon Room lounge that's been drawing some hip nightcrawlers here of late. Clad in cocktail outfits or black leather, these young hipsters sit side by side with the rather impacted old-timers, drinking Manhattans and martinis till 2 AM in divey, retro splendor. Take a peek at the dining room, too, outfitted with kitsch decor. *2714 Beacon Ave. S (at*

McLellan St.), Beacon Hill, 206/329–
5085. MC, V. $

12 *e-3*
SEA GARDEN

As the name implies, the specialty here is
seafood, and it's fetched from the restaurant's own tanks. Chefs turn out impeccable Cantonese and Mandarin dishes,
and the menu has a good deal of variety.
Try the expertly made dumpling noodle
soup. The dining room with its Formica
tables is always crowded; an upstairs
room for large parties is often in use, but
its ambience seems rather disconnected.
Expect service to be anywhere from adequate to maddeningly slow. Or come for
a midnight meal: The very late hours
(until 2 AM weekdays and until 3 AM weekends) make this an ideal place to go during bouts of insomnia. 509 7th Ave. S
(between Weller and King Sts.), International District, 206/623–2100. $

14 *c-2*
200 106th Ave. NE (at NE 2nd St.), Bellevue, 425/450–8833. Closes weekdays and
Sun. at 10; Fri.–Sat. at 11. $

12 *e-3*
SHANGHAI GARDEN

The decor is pink on pink, the clientele
is mostly Asian, and the menu is vast,
full of adventurous twists and turns. But
the big draw at Shanghai are the hand-shaved noodles—thick, irregular, and
fresh-cut from blocks of handmade
dough—which are available in a "high
nutrition barleygreen" form, made from
barley grass plants. The popular owner-chef Hau Te Su prepares dishes from
every Chinese province, and regional
accents change seasonally. 524 6th Ave.
S (at Weller St.), International District,
206/625–1689. MC, V. $$

14 *c-2*
Shanghai Cafe, 12708 SE 38th St. (Factoria Square Mall), Bellevue, 425/603–1689.
$$

2 *c-2*
SNAPPY DRAGON

Your dumpling radar will immediately
locate the small round gems on the
menu: doughy and filling, they come
only in orders of 15 or 25, meat-filled or
vegetarian, and are rolled, stuffed, and
boiled at a special station where you can
watch. This usually crowded restaurant
is headed up by chef Judy Fu, formerly of
Panda, and specializes in northern Chi-

nese dishes. If you steer away from stir-fries and hover near the dumplings,
homemade noodles, and mu shu, you'll
do best. 8917 Roosevelt Way NE (at 89th
St.), Maple Leaf, 206/528–5575. AE, DC,
MC, V. No lunch Sun. $

CONTEMPORARY

There are many wonderful aspects to
finer Seattle cuisine, but one of the
nicest is the price. Only a short eight to
ten years ago, the options for creative
cuisine were sorely limited here, and
much of the culinary landscape was
plain, cheap, causal, and not always up
to par. With the development of Belltown and other areas, well-designed,
well-executed menus have upped the
ante, and contemporary Northwest cuisine has gained cachet, too. In terms of
creativity (and the lengths chefs go to
use local food sources), it's safe to call
Seattle one of the nation's top contemporary dining meccas. And yet, in spite
the high quality, Seattle prices have
remained comparable with other urban
centers. Aren't you glad you live here?
Bon appetit!

7 *f-6*
1 0 MERCER

This relatively new hot spot is well-appointed, trendy, and crowded nightly.
Lots of exciting ingredient combinations
and zippy sauces abound, for instance,
the smoked sturgeon with avocado
cream cheese and roasted-pepper vinai-grette appetizer. Some dishes' flavors,
like the highly seasoned smoked duck,
can be too intense. 10 W. Mercer St.
(between Queen Anne and 1st Aves.),
Queen Anne, 206/691–3723. AE, MC, V.
No lunch. $$

9 *b-2*
THE BOOKSTORE

Though a little pretentious, this swank
niche on the first floor of the Alexis
Hotel has a big plus: you can order from
the hotel's acclaimed Painted Table
restaurant menu (during regular restaurant hours). Plus, the café's own sandwiches, served on grilled bread, are
fresh and tasty. You'll find books, magazines, and newspapers aplenty for
browsing if you're not mingling with the
well-coiffed clientele. 1007 1st Ave. (at
Madison St.), Downtown, 206/382–1506.
AE, D, DC, MC, V. $

8 *a-5*

BLUWATER BISTRO

In the hands of chef Peter Levine the carefully assembled, but fun menu here takes a concertedly not-boring approach to its bistro fare. Grilled salmon is brushed with ancho chile and honey; Jamaican jerk chicken is served with pineapple and jicama relish. Try the light, pretty salads or fried calamari. Servers are amazingly quick. The youngish after-work bar crowd lingers marina-side on the patio in spring and summer; and no matter what the weather, serious singles action kicks in after 10 PM. *1001 Fairview Ave. N (on the lake, north of Chandler's Cove), Lake Union, 206/447–0769. AE, D, DC, MC, V. $$*

10 *e-5*

BRASA

Though the decor is rather somber and heavy, this large operation with an open kitchen (and applewood-fired stove) turns out consistently great food and gets rave reviews. Well-known local chef Tamara Murphy, formerly of Campagne, oversees this daily-changing menu that she terms "sun-drenched Seattle," for its Mediterranean overtones. You might find suckling pig with chorizo and clams, or Oregon king salmon with tapenade vinaigrette. Watch for early evening bar-gains on the bar menu, which has some-what lighter, less expensive items such as a cheese plate or tapenades. *2107 3rd Ave. (at Leonora St.), Downtown, 206/728–4220. Reservations essential. AE, DC, MC, V. No lunch. $$–$$$*

11 *c-3*

CAFE SEPTIEME

This large, casual room with dusky red walls hung with local artists' works is a meeting place for Capitol Hill scen-esters, artsy types, and students and employees of the nearby community col-lege. Septieme and its dependably strong café au lait—served in ribbed, white ceramic bowls—is definitely a place to see and be seen. The dinner hour bustles, and in a district full of veg-etarian and Asian eateries, its flank steak and free-range roasted chicken with garlic-mashed potatoes are dependable standbys. Euro fare such as the *Schweinsschnitzel* (a pounded and breaded pork cutlet) is popular, too, but before you leap, make sure to ask about nightly specials. Expect a bit of attitude from servers and you won't be annoyed.

214 Broadway Ave. E (between John and Thomas Sts.), Capitol Hill, 260/860–8858. AE, DC, MC, V. $–$$

11 *c-5*

CENTURY BALLROOM CAFE

Upstairs in Capitol Hill's huge, creaking Oddfellows Hall, this café does a brisk business alongside an adjacent ball-room with a 2,000-square-ft maple floor. With live swing on most evenings, the joint jumps. Watch dancers from a balcony table, or find a seat in the jewel-box sized café. A hand-ful of menu items—warm chicken salad with caramelized onions, baked Alaskan salmon with steamed asparagus, and daily pasta specials are the stars of this concise menu. By day, the café serves neighborhood folk and actors and dancers who rehearse in the building. Reservations are essential for ballroom tables. *915 E. Pine St. (half-block east of Broadway), Capitol Hill, 206/324–7263. MC, V. No dinner Mon.–Tues. $$*

11 *e-2*

COASTAL KITCHEN

Here's a chic yet casual place with a three-tiered menu. Local restaurant ubermensches Jeremy Hardy and Peter Levy (of Queen Anne's Five Spot and Wallingford's Jitterbug fame) hit on a surefire formula with their hearty diner-style dishes served alongside Southern-accented meals; the cooks also concoct a rotating menu featuring cuisines of far-flung coastal places like Vietnam, Thailand, and northern Spain, to name a few. The experiments don't always work, but you can't knock their willingness to be adventurous. Besides, you can always fall back on the roast chicken with creamy mashed potatoes or the mildly marinated pork chop, served all day. *429 15th Ave. E (between Republican and Har-rison Sts.), Capitol Hill, 206/322–1145. MC, V. $–$$*

10 *d-5*

CYCLOPS

A decade ago it was a small, funky café where band members of Nirvana and REM were known to dine. With its change of location, Cyclops has adapted and grown with an ever-growing Bell-town. Still patronized by the hip, it's swankier these days, and the bar is friendly, if clamorous, on weekend nights. The kitchen serves an always-good pastiche of flavors inspired from widely different international cuisines such as gnocchi tossed with dried tomatoes, basil, and shallots, or venison *carne asada*. The starter menu is detailed: order a chicken quesadilla and the baby green and mango salad for a fine small meal. *2421 1st Ave. (at Wall St.), Downtown, 206/441–1677. MC, V. $–$$*

10 f-5
DAHLIA LOUNGE

Tom Douglas's first restaurant serves distinctive, finely honed Northwest cuisine in a red-accented, new setting close to its original location. Eclecticism is half the fun on this constantly shifting menu: you might find little tea sandwiches with Old Chatham Camembert or seared foie gras with Bing cherries as starters; and lemon-and-scallion Dungeness crab cakes with local bamboo shoots as an entrée. Fresh local oysters are available every night, and you can't do better than the made-to-order vanilla mascarpone doughnuts. *2001 4th Ave. (at Virginia St.), Downtown, 206/682–4142. AE, D, DC, MC, V. No lunch weekends. $$$*

9 b-1
EARTH & OCEAN

A spare elegance pervades the setting, and also, in some ways, the orchestration of the menu. The fixed-price Growers' Menu (in which all ingredients are harvested from a local organic farm) and Menu Sauvage (incorporating only foraged or wild ingredients like mountain greens or squab) draw the curious and keep them. Heartier plates include the shellfish paella and a grilled black-pepper pork loin with fava beans. The varying daily Dessert of the Moment gets consistently enthusiastic reviews. *W Hotel, 1112 4th Ave. (at Seneca), Downtown, 206/264–6060. AE, D, DC, MC, V. $$–$$$*

5 e-5
EVA

In the quiet residential district near the now-defunct, much-missed Honey Bear Bakery, you'll find this relatively new spot turning out beautifully inventive meals that have reviewers cawing. With a bright palette of Northwest ingredients and seasonal menus, Amy McCray, former lead chef at Chez Shea, dazzles you with such dishes as grilled organic rib eye with roasted potatoes and Gorgonzola butter; and gnocchi connoisseurs will pine for McCray's light, potato-ricotta version. For dessert, sample the Taleggio cheesecake with sautéed pears and lavender honey. By all indications, Eva's popularity will soon skyrocket, so check to see if reservations are needed. *2227 N. 56th St. (at Kirkland St.), Green Lake, 206/633–3538. AE, D, MC, V. Closed Mon. No lunch. $$*

10 f-6
FARE START

It's an inspired idea: train the homeless to work in the hospitality industry, and fund the program by operating a restaurant. Lunch is served weekdays, and once a week, a four-course dinner is designed by a celebrity guest chef from, say, Metropolitan Grill or Ray's Boathouse. For this purpose, the former Hotel Josephinum dining room has been gussied up, and now more than ever resembles the set of a 1940s musical, glittering chandeliers and all. At $16.95 flat, the dinner's quite a steal. *1902 2nd Ave. (between Stewart and Virginia Sts.), Downtown, 206/443–1233 Ext 28. Reservations essential. AE, MC, V. No lunch weekends. $–$$*

10 a-2
KASPAR'S

Kaspar Donier's restaurant is something to experience at least once. The food and attentive servers are no less than excellent. The ever-changing menu consistently offers the signature roast Muscovy duck breast with crispy duck confit, elegant seafood, and meats, like the tenderloin beef tower. Near Seattle Center, the restaurant is full of theater- and ballet-goers on weekend nights. An affordable sampler menu is available in the wine bar. *19 W. Harrison St. (between Queen Anne and 1st Aves.), Queen Anne, 206/298–0123. AE, MC, V. Closed Sun.–Mon. No lunch. $$$*

10 d-5
MARCO'S SUPPER CLUB

A warm, hip, colorful atmosphere; savvy servers; and a sexy, eclectic menu make repeat customers out of both in-the-know Belltowners and those who come in on weekends from the suburbs. They're also nice to "singles," people dining alone. The fried sage-leaves appetizer is irresistible, the Jamaican jerk chicken is subtler than you'd expect, but lovely, and yet the best bite may just be the bistro steak, wrapped in bacon and dripping with juice. Pair it with a glass of Rioja, and you'll swear you've never had better. A cherry clafoutis with almond custard waits in the wings for dessert. A cute back patio full of good vibes opens up in warmer weather. Marco's new sibling, the Italian Lush Life, is around the corner on 2nd Avenue, but to many, Marco's feels like home. *2510 1st Ave., (between Wall and Vine Sts.), Belltown, 206/441–7801. AE, MC, V. No lunch. $$*

4 *g-5*
MARKET STREET GRILL
In a space that mixes restrained, cool decor with the warmth of candlelit tables, chef Frank Springmann, formerly of Flying Fish, oversees the seafood and Northwestern menu. A number of particularly attractive starters can be paired to make whole meals: warm lobster and artichoke salad, shrimp cakes with watercress mayonnaise, and foie gras with sweetbreads. The entrée selections, seasonally focused and equally appetizing, range from sea scallop potpie to grilled pork tenderloin with shaved Reggiano chesse and porcini risotto cake. This relatively new spot is one of the few upscale eateries in this still–fairly Scandinavian neighborhood, begging the question as to whether more urbane dining is on the way. *1744 NW Market St. (between 17th and 20th Aves.), Ballard, 206/789–6766. D, MC, V. $$*

11 *c-4*
ONE WORLD DINING
Inside the first-floor atrium of Seattle's Central Community College, culinary arts students prepare sit-down daily luncheons at more-than-reasonable prices, focusing on international cuisines. A sprawling, cheap, all-you-can-eat Friday buffet also showcases the students' efforts: Extremely incongruent dishes such as paella marinara, Swedish meatballs, and potatoes O'Brien sit side by side, with a free-for-all atmosphere. But that's half the fun. Allow for the minor excesses and gaffes of the student chefs and you'll be fine. It's closed during holiday sessions; call for schedules and menus. *600 Broadway (at Pine St.), Capitol Hill, 206/587–5424. No credit cards. No dinner. Closes at 1 PM. $*

9 *b-2*
THE PAINTED TABLE
Chef Tim Kelly's famous establishment lives up to its sterling reputation. Market-inspired specialties include good meats and fish, but vegetables, combined so unusually here, always surprise. Quirky pairings, like parsnips with Granny Smith apples, or eggplant melded to poblanos, are happily satisfying. *Alexis Hotel, 92 Madison St. (at 1st Ave.), Downtown, 206/624–3646. AE, D, DC, MC, V. No lunch weekends. $$$*

5 *g-7*
RAIN DANCER
Unusually upscale for the University District, you'll find this spot among the cadres of youthful and pierced "Avenue Rats" who routinely hang out along this block. Exposed ceiling beams and dark-painted walls make the place pleasantly cavernous. Sandwiches from the open kitchen include roasted duck, blackened salmon, and a sautéed vegetable bruschetta. Dinner entrées are more ambitious, though during the summer and school holidays, the evening menu is scaled back. *4217 University Way NE (between 42nd and 43rd Sts.), University District, 206/634–2433. AE, D, MC, V. $*

10 *e-5*
RESTAURANT ZOË
One of the city's freshest new restaurants, one of the more shining stars in cuisine-crowded Belltown, has quickly established itself as a chic place to eat and be seen. Its light-industrial look is accented by high windows that make the outdoor street life part of the scene, and the menu focuses on seasonal and regional ingredients with a Mediterranean tang. A young, hip clientele seeks starter plates such as albacore sashimi with cucumber coulis, and entrées like roast chicken with a garlic-spice crust. Desserts aren't as consistently stellar, but the fruit tarts and crème brûlée with brioche french toast often sparkle. *2137 2nd Ave. (at Blanchard), Downtown, 206/256–2060. AE, D, MC, V. No lunch. $$–$$$*

10 *f-5*
ROY'S
Honolulu-based celebrity chef Roy Yamaguchi heads up this Pacific Rim chain that fuses Japanese, French, Thai, and other cuisines—and the results can be rather complicated. Stick with elegant and straightforward dishes like grilled meats or seafood. For dessert, it's best to go with the merely semi-ostentatious: try the house signature melting hot chocolate soufflé, or Kilauea, a gorgeous

baked Alaska. Weekend brunches are impressive. *Westin Hotel, 1900 5th Ave. (at Stewart St.), Downtown, 206/256–7697. AE, D, DC, MC, V. Weekend brunch. $$–$$$*

5 *e-2*

SIX DEGREES

Natural light, bright colors, and a spirited atmosphere imbue this tavern, recapitulating it Seattle style. The menu has some original strokes, and the result is fun, easy-to-eat food served with panache. You'll find a smoky pork-loin sandwich with caramelized onion and melted fontina, and a spinach-pecan salad with orange-sesame-ginger dressing and goat cheese, and thick onion rings (served on a peg). The bar is seriously packed at night, where drinking both microbrews and international wines is the thing. *7900 E. Green Lake Dr. N (at Wallingford Ave.), Green Lake, 206/523–1600. AE, D, DC, MC, V. $$*

2 *e-2*

121 Park La. (at Lake St.), Kirkland, 425/803–1766. $$

5 *b-3*

STALK EXCHANGE

Most of the ingredients here are organic—meat, produce, flour, coffee—which is no small feat at these reasonable prices. Doubling as a catering business, Stalk Exchange occupies a cute cottage with an upright piano. Wonderfully smoked organic meats, free-range chicken, roasted vegetables, breads, and pastry treats issue from the applewood-burning brick oven. *6711 Greenwood Ave. N (between 67th and 68th Sts.), Greenwood, 206/782–3911. MC, V. Closed Mon. No dinner Sun. No lunch weekends. Weekend brunch. $$*

5 *b-3*

STUMBLING GOAT

Deep red velvet curtains lend a touch of drama and style to this relatively new bistro, whose name is an irreverent spin-off of the owners' first choice, the Drunken Boat, vetoed by the Liquor Board. The short, to-the-point, seasonally changing menu includes juicy pan-roasted chicken, pan-seared seafood with inventive vegetable sides, and colorful salads. The wine list is priced right. *6722 Greenwood Ave. N (between 67th and 68th Sts.), Greenwood, 206/784–3535. MC, V. Closed Mon. No lunch. $$*

8 *f-8*

SUPREME

Clean and spare with green highlights and ceiling skylights that drench you in light, Supreme feels a bit otherworldly. Evenings the bar is busy with the after-work crowd and a brisk dinner business. Chef Chris Hunter, formerly of Etta's Seafood, breaks out here with exciting brunch and dinner items: there's ricotta or carrot gnocchi, or grilled pork tenderloin wrapped in pancetta with cherry-and-onion relish. Finish with a chocolate silk tart with a walnut base. Attractively presented plates echo the room's crisp, contemporary look, and word about this new restaurant is spreading quickly. *1404 34th Ave. (at Union St.), Madrona, 206/322–1974. AE, MC, V. Weekend brunch. $$–$$$*

6 *c-7*

UNION BAY CAFE

At Union Bay, you'll see crisp white tablecloths, pretty glassware, and a creative, careful Northwest menu at prices that will really make you grin. Try a starter like spinach and blue cheese ravioli with lemon-chive butter, and an entrée of free-range chicken breast in coconut milk with mango salsa and creamy polenta. Chef-owner Mark Manley has kept his menu's quality consistently strong for years. *3515 NE 45th St. (one blk. east of Mary Gates Way), Laurelhurst, 206/527–8364. AE, D, DC, MC, V. Closed Mon. No lunch. $$*

2 *f-3*

YARROW BAY CAFE

The downstairs bar-café of the upscale Yarrow Bay Grill is a destination in its own right, with a boisterous crowd, weekly live music, and a rotating international menu, including seafood entrées and sandwiches that are a little less dear. *1270 Carillon Point (at Lakeview Dr.), Kirkland, 425/889–0303. AE, D, DC, MC, V. No lunch Sat. $–$$*

CONTINENTAL

2 *g-4*

TOSONI'S RESTAURANT

This Eastside favorite manages to make its space, essentially a storefront in a strip mall, both inviting and sophisticated. On any given night, chef and owner Walter Walcher's menu might include classic schnitzel, prawns in red curry, or a recipe of his mother's: pheasant in a raspberry-herb sauce. Service is friendly and competent. In fact, Walcher remembers regulars' names and stops by every table to check on the meal, sometimes pulling up a chair and sitting a spell. *14320 NE 20th St. (between 140th Ave. NE and 148th Ave. NE), Bellevue, 425/644–1668. Reservations essential. AE, DC, MC, V. No lunch. $$–$$$*

2 *f-3*

VIDAL'S EUROPEAN BISTRO

Chef Vidal Bitton focuses on Northwest fare prepared in the French tradition, but he doesn't stop there. You'll also find dishes like citrus-marinated Moroccan chicken on hummus with a lemon-thyme sauce, and an elegant American surf-and-turf appetizer: a mini steak and lobster tail with sesame dressing. Vidal's wine selection has won accolades from *Wine Spectator* magazine and the restaurant often offers wine-tasting evenings and live jazz. Call to see what's happening and consider making a reservation. *107 Lake St. (at Central Way), Kirkland, 425/822–0977. AE, D, DC, MC, V. No lunch. $$$*

CUBAN

1 *b-3*

CAFE NOLA

With dishes like sugar-cane shrimp on the menu, it's easy to see why Bainbridge Island's Cafe Nola has been described as serving Cuban cuisine. But there's more than a Latin influence here: Pork chops provide home-style comfort, grits cakes a taste of the American South. The small size and cozy atmosphere is great for romance—especially since you start with a ferry ride—but a children's menu means kids are welcome, too. The service, while usually friendly, can occasionally be a bit chilly. Outdoor dining is available in summer. *101 Winslow Way (at Madison Ave.), Bainbridge Island, 206/842–3822. MC, V. No dinner Mon.–Tues. Brunch weekends. Beer and wine only. $$*

7 *f-4*

EL DIABLO COFFEE COMPANY

Hot red, yellow, and pink-painted devils decorate the walls of this lively shop, where classic coffee *Cubano* (two shots with caramelized sugar) is served. So is

Mexican hot chocolate, *batidos* (Cuban fruit shakes), and tropical-tasting pastries like coconut cake or key lime tart. A brief, savory menu offers tapas-like snacks including house-marinated kalamata olives and a cheese plate topped off with Spanish blue Cabrales and manchego varieties; thick slices of bread are included. A sweet back patio and Lucy and Ricky Ricardo–themed rest rooms make this cheery place one that can brighten your day. *1811 Queen Anne Ave. N (between Blaine and Howe Sts.), Queen Anne, 206/285–0693. AE, D, MC, V. No dinner Mon.–Tues. $*

5 *b-7*

PASEO

The centerpiece of Lorenzo Lorenzo's slim Cuban-influenced menu is a highly secret sauce that was years in the making; word has it that Lorenzo even hides the recipe from his employees. The marinated pork sandwich, topped with sautéed onions, is doused with this sauce and keeps folks coming back for more. The entrées are also a bargain, from scallops with cilantro to prawns in red sauce. *4225 Fremont Ave. N (between 42nd St. and Motor Pl.), Fremont, 206/545–7440. No credit cards. No lunch Sun. $*

DELICATESSENS

12 *c-1*

BAKEMAN'S RESTAURANT

Long before *Seinfeld*'s "soup Nazi," there was Bakeman's, a very funky, very popular lunch spot in Pioneer Square. Hungry office workers line up for homemade bread and lunch specials like meat loaf and chicken-fried steak—and woe to the poor patron who doesn't give his order quickly enough, or asks for bread other than white or wheat. The sandwiches are good-sized, but save room for homemade desserts such as slabs o'chocolate cake and oatmeal cookies. Once you've got your lunch tray (think grade-school cafeteria), you can sit in the fluorescent-lit dining area, or venture into what was once a bar (no alcohol is served now)—a dark room with black plastic booths. *122 Cherry St. (at 2nd Ave.), Downtown, 206/622–3375. No credit cards. Closed weekends. No dinner. $*

10 *g-5*

PAMELA'S FINE FOODS

With NPR on the radio and comforting delicacies like oatmeal, four-cheese macaroni casserole, and homemade brownies, Pamela's is a rarity in the feed 'em fast world of lunch-hour dining. (It's been run by the same family for more than a dozen years.) Hang out while your sandwich is made and look at the community posters or read the latest *Vanity Fair*. If it's hot out, get an ice-cream cone on your afternoon coffee break. In short, make yourself at home. *607 Stewart St. (at 6th Ave.), Downtown, 206/623–2347. No credit cards. Closed weekends. No dinner. $*

10 *f-8*

ROXY'S DINER

Roxy's Diner, while not strictly kosher, is definitely a traditional New York–style delicatessen. Pastrami rules here, whether you want it in a sandwich or in a "pastrambow," Roxy's take on the Chinese *hombow* (a meat-filled steamed bun). There's also corned beef, chopped liver, and, of course, brisket. Chicken matzoh ball soup, knishes, cheese blintzes, and Dr. Brown's sodas round out the experience. *1329 1st Ave. (at Union St.), Downtown, 206/381–8800. AE, D, MC, V. No dinner. $*

4 *f-1*

2364 NW 80th St. (between 24th and Jones Aves.), Loyal Heights, 206/784–6121. $

ECLECTIC

10 *d-5*

AXIS

Though the food is good, Axis is definitely a see-and-be-seen kind of place. You don't have to be in black Armani, but it helps. Located in trendy Belltown, it's a great spot for after-work apps and martinis, or for late-night schmoozing. In addition to providing these social opportunities, Axis (also associated with Ponti's Seafood Grill in Fremont) serves up some mean dishes: Must-bites include the cabernet-marinated flank steak, grilled squid steaks with curried roasted oysters, and parchment-wrapped salmon. The wine list is excellent; the service a bit less so. *2212 1st Ave. (between Bell and Blanchard Sts.), Belltown, 206/ 441–9600. AE, DC, MC, V. No lunch. $$$*

5 *e-5*

EVA RESTAURANT & WINE BAR

Chef Amy McCray's new restaurant, in the much-mourned former Brie & Bordeaux digs, lives up to the former inhabitant's standards with tasty, European-inspired fare. Try the Cabrales flan with sweet pear relish appetizer, the decadent braised lamb with mascarpone polenta, or any seasonal vegetable. Co-owner James Hondros is an oenophile extraordinaire, without the pretension. He'll fix you up with just the right glass to go with your food. *2227 N. 56th St. (at Keystone Pl.), Wallingford, 206/633–3358. Reservations essential. MC, V. Closed Mon. No lunch. $$*

10 *f-5*

ICON GRILL

Foodies, trendies, and tourists swarm this very pink, very decorated room clotted (even on its dining tables) with Chihuly-style glass sculptures and other voluminous bric-a-brac. Though the menu is peppered with trite quotations from socialites and writers, the "aroused Americana" fare is enticing. Chef Nick Musser riffs creatively on basics like the turkey club (with Gruyère and avocado salsa), and the macaroni & cheese (with four cheeses and tomato "snow"). Also on the menu are Asian-inspired fish dishes and pasta any Italian restaurant would be proud of. The desserts are as mountainous as the ambience here, especially the Superbowl Sundae. Quixotic service and cranky crowds may be the joint's only pitfalls. *1933 5th Ave. (between Stewart and Virginia Sts.), Belltown, 206/441–6330. AE, MC, V. No lunch weekends. $$$*

10 *e-7*

MATT'S IN THE MARKET

Shhh . . . once you find Matt's you won't want to tell anyone else about it. Upstairs at Pike Place Market (next to chichi Chez Shea), Matt's is a casual, teensy-tiny space with big-flavored food and a terrific view of the Market. The menu changes quite often, though there's usually an emphasis on seafood, and almost always Penn Cove mussels in some kind of fantastic broth like lemon-ouzo is available. Though the folks who seat you often have to be curt (there's just no room for the undecided), Matt himself is often there, greeting and pouring the wine. Still unsure? It's where the restaurant folk go to eat once they're off work. *94 Pike Pl. (Corner Market Building), Pike Place Market, 206/467–7909. MC, V. Closed Sun.– Mon. No breakfast. $$*

9 *C-1*

THE HUNT CLUB

If it's dark paneling, a men's club atmosphere, and ultra-traditional meat-and-potatoes fare you have in mind, it'll be a surprise to see the eclectic menu here—lots of Mediterranean touches like olive oil and spices other than salt are added to that ultra-traditional beef. And if it's on the menu, try the mussel bisque. If you don't feel like the full-meal deal, try dessert and drinks in the romantic Fireside Room. *Sorrento Hotel, 900 Madison St. (between 9th Ave. and Terry Ave.), First Hill, 206/343–6156. AE, D, DC, MC, V. $$$–$$$$*

2 *f-3*

YARROW BAY GRILL

Surrender your culinary categories at the door: The Northwest cuisine here has Japanese accents, like sake-marinated salmon, but also veers toward Italian with such dishes as the roast chicken breast with spinach, ricotta, and a red pepper sauce. And then there's the upscale take on the roast pork loin chop, with bourbon and currant sauce. If the menu sounds a bit schizophrenic, rest assured there's a method to Chef Felix Acosta's madness. After all, he's prepared dinner at the prestigious James Beard House in New York. Sit back and enjoy the lake view and the savvy service. *1270 Carillon Point (off Lake View Dr.), Kirkland, 425/889–9052. AE, D, DC, MC, V. No lunch Sat. $$$*

ENGLISH

10 *f-7*

THE CRUMPET SHOP

Served straight off the griddle, these English muffin–like pastries have been delighting Pike Place Market visitors for more than 25 years. The simple rounds lend themselves to a variety of culinary interpretations, from a slathering of jam to a ham sandwich. Order a pot of tea with your crumpet and let the rest of the world hurry past. *1503 1st Ave. (between Pike and Pine Sts.), Pike Place Market, 206/682–1598. AE, MC, V. Closed Sun. No dinner. $*

10 *g-7*

THE ELEPHANT & CASTLE

Okay, so it's part of a chain. And maybe it's not fair to call a pub that serves nachos English. But the fish-and-chips are first rate, and it's not easy to find steak-and-kidney pie or *cock-a-leekie* (a traditional Scottish soup made with chicken and leeks) this side of the Atlantic. But it *is* a pub, so enjoy the billiards room and the highly quaffable tap beers. Not only is there Guinness and Bass, there's Caffrey's Cream Ale, too. *West Coast Grand Hotel, 1415 5th Ave. (between Union and Pike Sts.), Downtown, 206/624–9977. AE, DC, MC, V. $*

7 *f-6*

ROY ST. BISTRO

Despite the joke that English cuisine is an oxymoron, London chefs have been making names for themselves for a long time now; and though not every dish here is English per se, Roy St. Bistro serves up some swellegant British chow. They do it under a time constraint, too. Near Seattle Center, the bistro is often a pre-func spot for theater-goers. Check out the British meat pie, covered in puff pastry, stuffed with ostrich breast, and served in a Walla Walla onion–and–rhubarb sauce. We *told* you it was upscale. *174 Roy St. (between 2nd Ave. N and Warren Ave.), Queen Anne, 206/284–9093. AE, MC, V. Closed Sun. Closed Mon. in summer. No lunch. $$*

ETHIOPIAN

9 *g-1*

ASSIMBA

Eat with your hands here using *dabo*, bread made with semolina, spiced with cumin, and basted with butter and oil. Chef Messelu Feide Messeret has attracted quite a following by offering both traditional fare and twists on tradition: The Assimba combo is a house favorite—Messert takes a typically vegetarian dish and covers it with an Ethiopian beef sauce. *2722 E. Cherry St. (between 27th Ave. and Martin Luther King Way), Downtown, 206/322–1019. No credit cards. Closed Sun. $*

8 *f-8*

CAFE SOLEIL

Residents of the Madrona neighborhood love having a place like this within easy walking, driving, or busing distance. On a street filled with quality cafés, Soleil stands out for its interesting fare and delicate service: Every diner receives a hot towel to clean up with, and the cheerful staff explains unfamiliar dishes without making you feel silly for asking. The tall windows make this a perfect sunny breakfast and lunch spot, which serves filling vegetarian frittatas and hearty sandwiches. At dinner, more flavors of proprietor Kuri Teshome's native Ethiopia emerge in dishes like the spicy lentils. *1400 34th Ave. (between E. Union and E. Pike Sts.), Madrona, 206/325–1126. MC, V. Weekend brunch. $*

FRENCH

1 *f-1*

BARKING FROG

Chef Stephane Desgaches (formerly of Brasserie Margaux) tackles haute cuisine in a lodge setting. As always, his sea bass (crisp outside, moist and tender inside) is a winner, especially served with the pea-mashed potatoes. Once you get past the fact that your mashed potatoes are green, you may enjoy 'em. The wine list is intriguing: It's organized by taste rather than grape, which helps novices who know their likes but not their vintages. Service at dinner is excellent, but you may want to skip breakfast. Since it's a lodge, they've got to serve it. But it's not their favorite meal of the day and it shows. *Willows Lodge, 14580 NE 145th St. (at Sammamish River Park), Woodinville, 425/424–2999. AE, V. Weekend brunch. $$$*

5 *g-8*

BOAT STREET CAFE

Boat Street is one of those hidden places only those-in-the-know go. The casual, found-object decor and such Provençal-style dishes as the sardine plate, replete with red potatoes, haricot vertes, and capers, are just two reasons this place has earned a loyal following. Its location on Portage Bay is doubtless another. The bite that can't be beat here is the *strata*: layer after layer of roasted pepper, herbs, and paper-thin potatoes melt in your mouth. Pair it with a glass of crisp white wine at lunch and take the rest of the day off. *909 NE Boat St. (off Pacific St.), University District, 206/632–4602. No credit cards. Closed Mon. No dinner Sun. Weekend brunch. $$*

10 *f-7*

CAFE CAMPAGNE

Sure, this is the more casual version of the mothership Campagne, but the charming Paris bistro atmosphere and delicious country French food insure Cafe Campagne stands on its own. Dinner is terrific: Try the lamb burger, steak frites, or go for the night's rotisserie special, and go back for brunch. Whether you opt for the French toast made with brioche, the baked eggs with white beans and cream, or the upscale croque monsieur, start with a *kir du soleil*, champagne, and Mandarin Napoleon brandy. *1600 Post Alley (between Pine and Stewart Sts.), Pike Place Market, 206/728–2233. AE, MC, V. $$*

10 *f-7*

CAMPAGNE

Campagne is the tonier parent of Cafe Campagne, but it's not only the prices that make it so. Just upstairs from the bistro in Pike Place Market's Post Alley, this Seattle classic is the perfect place to honor a special occasion or share a romantic dinner. Try the foie gras, nearly perfect here, or the baked goat cheese salad with pancetta, beets, and hazelnuts. Lately there's been talk that Campagne is resting on its laurels, and that the service can be a bit condescending. But if you're in the mood for an elegant evening, Campagne is still difficult to beat. *86 Pine St. (between Pike Pl. and 1st Ave.), Pike Place Market, 206/728–2800. AE, MC, V. No lunch. $$$*

8 *b-3*

CASSIS

It feels like a 1930s Paris bistro, but Cassis serves Provençal dishes. This is of no concern, of course: Art deco elegance combines with friendly service to create a neighborhood restaurant that's become a destination spot. If they've got 'em, the seasonal almond-crusted sweetbreads in a Marsala sauce over pearled potatoes is a gem of a dish. And if the orange semolina pudding topped with black walnuts and Concord grape conserve is on the dessert menu, save room for it. It tastes like nothing so much as French comfort food. *2359 10th Ave. E (at E. Miller St.), Capitol Hill, 206/329–0580. AE, DC, MC, V. No lunch. $$*

10 *g-7*

CREPE DE PARIS

Featuring the "Cabaret de Paris" Thursday through Saturday, Crepe de Paris is a one-of-a-kind Seattle institution. Though the crepes (ratatouille, ham and cheese) are primarily served at lunch (at dinner, crepes are a dessert), there's no shortage of other French dishes: salmon in lobster sauce and game hens are often on the menu. The shows stand on their own, but if you want to go, you might plan on dinner there first (there are dinner and show packages), as owner Annie Agostini and company naturally offer preferred seating to those who purchase both. *1333 5th Ave. (between Union and University Sts.), Rainier Square, Downtown, 206/623–4111. AE, DC, MC, V. Closed Sun. $$*

7 *f-6*
FIGARO BISTRO
That heartiest of French dishes, the cassoulet—duck, sausage, and white beans—is what this Queen Anne restaurant may be known for, but it's the veal that really shines. The *coq au vin* is also a good choice, but you may want to steer clear of the crab ravioli, which can taste as though it were previously frozen. The service is friendly and the atmosphere charming, with French scenes painted on the walls. The full bar is usually full: Figaro is close to Seattle Center and gets plenty of pre- and posttheater patronage. *11 Roy St. (at Queen Anne Ave. N), Queen Anne, 206/284–6465. Reservations essential. AE, MC, V. Closed Mon. $$*

5 *a-5*
LE GOURMAND
The Northwest is a bountiful place, from produce and seafood to game meat and lamb, and few cuisines show this off better than French. Chef Bruce Naftaly knows it. It's his craft that's behind Le Gourmand and its excellent reputation. Known for its unassuming ambience, the restaurant presents fabulous sauces and innovative touches on classic cuisine—like peach sauce on rabbit loin, or Merlot butter sauce on steak—have wowed Seattleites more than 15 years. *425 NW Market St. (at 6th Ave. NW), Phinney Ridge, 206/784–3463. Reservations essential. MC, V. Closed Sun.–Tues. No lunch. $$$–$$$$*

10 *e-7*
LE PICHET
This winning little restaurant feels like it just dropped out of the Paris sky. Though dishes like the hearty country pâté and ham-and-cheese baguettes make a great lunch, dinners here will leave you trying not to lick your plate.

Particularly stunning are the baked eggs with mushrooms and shallots in a Madeira sauce and the roasted chicken (allow an hour; it's cooked to order) seasoned with salt and a delicate Cantal (cheese) sauce. The wine list is terrific, with something to make you happy by the glass, demi-pitcher, *le pichet* (pitcher), or bottle. *1933 1st Ave. (between Virginia and Stewart Sts.), Belltown, 206/256–1499. MC, V. Closed Tues.–Wed. $$*

10 *f-7*
MAXIMILIEN
While southern French cooking garners all the attention these days, Maximilien quietly offers the "other" French fare. Feast on onion soup smothered in Gruyère, harden those arteries with steak topped with seared foie gras and an armagnac-and-butter glaze, nibble on the duck confit . . . all while gazing out at Elliott Bay. Like its neighbor, Place Pigalle, Maximilien's is somewhat hidden in Pike Place Market, and it too features a tiny, friendly bar populated with regulars who seem to know something the rest of us don't, like why French bars make a great hangout. *81 Pike St. (behind the Fish Market), Pike Place Market, 206/682–7270. AE, D, DC, MC, V. Closed Mon. $$$*

10 *e-6*
MISTRAL
If it's casual service, ambience, and food you want, don't go to Mistral. But if you want a fine dining experience where the waitstaff are professionals, the decor (and sound level) so restrained you focus only on the dishes in front of you, and food that's, well, to die for, call for reservations today. Chef and owner William Belickis, who's been working in kitchens since he was a teen, is devoted to his craft and Mistral is his temple; he stops at each table to describe in somewhat hushed tones that evening's prix fixe menu. Ingredients are utterly fresh and usually seasonal: earthy truffles, meltingly rich foie gras, and bright greens come carefully and artfully prepared. Oh, and let Belickis help you with the wine, in fact, let him help you with everything. *113 Blanchard St. (between 1st and 2nd Aves.), Belltown, 206/770–7799. AE, D, MC, V. Closed Sun.–Mon. No lunch. $$$$*

10 *f-7*

PLACE PIGALLE

Want to impress? Make reservations at this wee restaurant hidden behind a Pike Place Market seafood stall. The food is always remarkable, but the romance factor is especially high. With fabulous sound views and discreet tables, the black-and-white-tiled restaurant seems straight from the 1930s. With its Market location it's no accident that seafood's a specialty: Everyone raves about the mussels in a balsamic-and-bacon broth. Desserts are also good; pick a simple one like fresh fruit with cream and brown sugar. Service is friendly, especially in the bar, where a pre-meal cocktail is a must. *81 Pike St. (behind the Fish Market), Pike Place Market, 206/624–1756. AE, DC, MC, V. Closed Sun. $$*

8 *f-6*

ROVER'S

Creating a tasting menu is an art form here. For 13 years or so, Thierry Rautureau has been serving upscale prix fixe menus of polished Provençal cuisine. Each has at least five courses—the Grand Degustation is a whopping eight. So if you're not thrilled with the scrambled eggs with crème fraîche and caviar (though you should be), you can choose, say, the foie gras in a Sauterne sauce. Do it up right and ask Rautureau to prepare a selection of wines to taste with each course of your meal; it's an evening you'll be recounting to friends for weeks. *2808 E. Madison St. (at 28th Ave.), Madison Park, 206/325–7442. Reservations essential. AE, DC, MC, V. Closed Sun.–Mon. No lunch. $$$$*

GERMAN

9 *b-1*

GENEVA

There's a lot more to German cuisine than sauerkraut and bratwurst: And Seattle is fortunate enough to have Geneva to prove this true. Though the schnitzel, spaetzle, and potato pancakes are first rate, the Continental-style veal chop in a chanterelle sauce (seasonal) is something to come back for. Chef Hanspeter Aebersold and his wife, Margret, run the place graciously. The atmosphere may be a bit old-fashioned. The food, however, is anything but. *1106 8th Ave. (between Seneca and Spring Sts.),*

Downtown, 206/624–2222. AE, MC, V. Closed Mon. No lunch. $$$

3 *b-4*

SZMANIA'S RESTAURANT

Lovely seafood, game, and meats with intense sauces stream from the open kitchen at what has become an extremely popular dinner destination. Chef Ludger Szmania tips a hat to his German roots with dishes like *Jaegerschnitzel* (a breaded pork cutlet topped with chanterelle gravy) with spaetzle, and the goat cheese potato pancake, but Northwest-Continental is prominent on the menu: salmon in cream-corn sauce, Oregon lamb, horseradish-brushed mahimahi in lobster-and-shiitake sauce. Plates are garnished with brilliantly colored vegetables and portions are very generous; many entrées are available in half-orders. For dessert, you might find something as soothing and ambitious as a saffron-banana *semifreddo gateau* (literally a "half cold" cake). Reservations are essential on weekends. *3321 W. McGraw St. (between 33rd and 34th Aves.), Magnolia, 206/284–7305. AE, MC, V. Closed Mon. No lunch. $$*

2 *e-2*

148 Lake St. S (at 2nd Ave. S), Kirkland, 425/803–3310. Closed Mon. No lunch Sat. $$

GREEK

2 *b-6*

EPHESUS RESTAURANT

Neighborhood joints like this one are well-worth the trip west. With a garden that provides a good amount of the restaurant's produce—Ephesus is in an old house—you can expect the emphasis to be on fresh, seasonal fare. If it's summer, get a salad; in winter try one of the *topraks* (oven-baked stews made with chunks of meat, potatoes, onions, and other veggies). They're rich and comforting on a cold and rainy day. *5245 California Ave. SW (between SW Findlay and SW Dawson Sts.), West Seattle, 206/937–3302. Reservations essential. MC, V. No lunch. $$*

13 *g-4*

EPIROS GREEK RESTAURANT

Despite the name change from the cutesy Delicious World Bistro, Epiros serves consistently good food. A favorite is the flashy *saganaki*, a flaming cheese dish. Once the fire's out, however, the cheese can be a bit salty. Service is sometimes slow on weekends, but if there's belly dancing the wait is worth it. *16564 Cleveland St. (between 164th and 165th Aves.), Redmond, 425/883–4443. Reservations essential. AE, D, MC, V. No lunch Sun. $$*

7 g-5

PANOS GREEK TAVERNA KLEFTIKO

Loud, friendly, and full of feta, Panos is the kind of traditional place Greeks go for Greek food. You can order an entrée—the lamb in garlic aïoli is excellent—but the four pages of appetizers suggest that you build a meal this way. Start with the classic, creamy *tzatziki* (yogurt sauce) and pita; move on to a fresh green salad with tomatoes, kalamata olives, and lots of feta; finish with the *spanakopita*, a phyllo-dough pie made with fresh spinach. *815 5th Ave. N (between Valley and Aloha Sts.), Queen Anne, 206/301–0393. MC, V. Closed Sun. No lunch. $$*

HAWAIIAN

5 e-5

LUAU POLYNESIAN LOUNGE

Anything that claims to be a polynesian lounge had better deliver the atmosphere. Teeny tiny Luau does it up right, and for better or worse without the grass-skirted servers. In the thatched-roof bar you can order a cocktail served in a ceramic coconut mug and the *pupu* platter (an assortment of spicy appetizers, like the fabulous hot-and-sour, five-spice beef short ribs). Or grab a table to order entrées that include Kahlua pork sandwiches and coconut-crusted Hawaiian game fish in a curry broth. *2253 N. 56th St. (at Kirkwood Pl. N), Wallingford, 206/633–5828. AF, MC, V. No lunch. $$*

10 e-5

'OHANA

'Ohana's a strange hybrid of umbrella drinks and surf murals and the black-clad cool crowd. Suffer through the sceney clientele because the food, with Japanese influences and dishes like sashimi, is worth it. Go for the 28-day aged beef tenderloin topped with crispy Maui onions, the prawn dumplings, or Spam (Hawaii's national dish) fried and

wrapped in nori. *2207 1st Ave. (between Blanchard and Bell Sts.), Belltown, 206/956–9329. AE, MC, V. No lunch Sun. $$*

7 g-7

PALISADE

A 50-ft bridge suspended over an enormous indoor saltwater waterfall and tidepool lends a decidedly island feel to Palisade, whose killer views of Elliott Bay Marina, the city skyline, and Puget Sound place a distractedly second. Lots of grilling and roasting attends the fish, poultry, and pork on the menu; sweet-sour rubs flavor many preparations. Other dishes, like the Dungeness crab cakes with a sweet-and-sour plum beurre blanc, are pretty good, too. The cedar-plank-roasted salmon (advertised as "seen on 'Martha Stewart Living'") and the Mother's Day brunch and get lots of attention. *2601 W. Marina Pl. (at Seattle Marina, at Magnolia Bridge), Magnolia, 206/285–1000. AE, MC, V. $$$–$$$$*

INDIAN

7 f-3

BANJARA

Know what you like, but not what it's called? The mango *lassi*, a yogurt fruit drink, helps cut the garlicky *masala* (spices). The *paneer*, literally defined as an Indian farmer cheese, is used in two dishes, one with *saag* (spinach) and another with *mattar* (peas). Scoop one up with *naan* (soft bread served fresh from the oven). *2 Boston St. (between 1st St. and Queen Anne Ave. N), Queen Anne, 206/282–7752. AE, MC, V. $$*

7 f-6

CHUTNEY'S

With three Seattle locations (Queen Anne, Wallingford, and Capitol Hill), Chutney's is clearly popular. Even among a row of fast-food joints, it's the flagship restaurant in Queen Anne that remains the best. The subdued lighting and Indian artwork and sculptures—oh, and the higher prices—create an upscale feeling. Skip the lunch buffet and go to dinner. Both chicken and lamb masalas are creamy and rich, as is the mattar paneer; and the mango cheesecake makes a refreshing dessert. Though it's near Seattle Center, rethink your plans if you're in a hurry to get to a game or a show; service can be leisurely.

519 1st Ave. N (between Queen Anne Ave. N and Warren Ave. N), Queen Anne, 206/284–6799. Reservations essential. AE, D, MC, V. No lunch Sun. $$

| 12 | b-2 |

FLAVOR OF INDIA

On weekdays it will seem that you and everyone else in Pioneer Square are here for the traditional lunch buffet—partly because it's a great deal and partly because the servers give the impression they don't want you ordering off the menu. For dinner, however, get the chicken *korma*, decadent, creamy, and chock-full of delicate flavors, spooned over some aromatic basmati rice. 625 1st Ave. (between James and Cherry Sts.), Downtown, 206/628–0200. MC, V. $$

| 13 | c-5 |

SHAMIANA RESTAURANT

Interested in less-than-traditional Indian fare? The brother-and-sister team behind this Eastside eatery grew up abroad and the cuisine reflects Pakistani and even African influences. Not every dish is fabulous, but the saag paneer and the *hash-met* (eggplant with yogurt, tomato, and coriander) are standouts. With good food at a good value, the lunch buffet may be the best way to check out this fusion favorite. 10724 NE 68th St. (at 108th Ave. NE), Kirkland, 425/827–4902. Reservations not accepted. AE, D, MC, V. Closed Mon. No lunch weekends. $$

| 5 | g-6 |

TANDOOR

In a neighborhood largely populated by starving students, the restaurants here usually have the bonus of being cheap. Tandoor is no exception. The northern Indian menu focuses on tandoor-prepared dishes, though it's the special naan (in this case stuffed with chicken and nuts), lamb vindaloo, and mulligatawny soup that really sing. An additional bonus: the beer and wine, like the food, are bargain-priced. 5024 University Way NE (between 50th and 52nd Sts.), University District, 206/523–7477. AE, D, DC, MC, V. $$

IRISH

| 12 | b-1 |

FADO IRISH PUB

Fado is part of a chain, so if the decor looks familiar, it's not déjà vu. Lots of Celtic wisdom is stenciled on the walls, and lots of Irish whiskey and beers are poured at the bar. You can get traditional Irish fare here, from shepherd's pie to *boxty* (thin, rolled potato pancakes with a choice of fillings—skip the salmon and get the Guinness-braised beef). Fado fills up fast after work, in both the dining room and the large bar. Sometimes there's an Irish band playing; call for schedules. 801 1st Ave. (at Columbia), Downtown, 206/264–2700. AE, D, MC, V. $$

| 5 | g-5 |

IRISH EMIGRANT

If authenticity means something to you, this is a true Irish bar, owned by Irish folks (they may be the ones playing that fiddle you hear) with lots of Irish regulars. (Although lots of the patrons are U.W. students who do get loud and rowdy on occasion.) In addition to the ubiquitous (and properly poured) pint of Guinness, provisions include bangers-and-mash (Angus sausages and mashed potatoes), fish-and-chips, and chicken potpie. Shoot some pool, or just shoot the breeze with your friends. For those with minds like a lint trap, Monday is trivia night. 5260 University Way NE (between NE 52nd and NE 55th Sts.), University District, 206/525–2955. AE, MC, V. No lunch weekdays. $

| 10 | e-7 |

KELLS IRISH PUB & RESTAURANT

It doesn't seem to matter that the pub entrance is somewhat hidden; this truly Irish pub (run by Irish and frequented by Irish) gets crowded nonetheless. There's often music, sometimes football (soccer) on the telly, and always Guinness and Harp on tap. Eats include sausage rolls, Irish whiskey cake, and at lunch a Half Limerick sandwich, thinly sliced ham served on homemade Irish soda bread. 1916 Post Alley (between Stewart and Virginia Sts.), Pike Place Market, 206/728–1916. AE, MC, V. $$

ITALIAN

| 10 | f-5 |

ASSAGGIO RISTORANTE

La dolce vita is the motto here, so look elsewhere for some place quiet. Owner Mauro Golmarvi greets everyone who comes in like a friend, and many are.

Scores of regulars come for the fabulous sturgeon with red grapes in a champagne sauce and the fusilli with house-made sausage. The wine list and servers are top-notch, too. Though the high prices are no joke, truly the only thing taken seriously here is the food. *Claremont Hotel, 2010 4th Ave. (between Virginia and Lenora Sts.), Belltown, 206/441–1399. AE, D, DC, MC, V. Closed Sun. No lunch weekends. $$$*

5 *d-6*
ASTEROID CAFE
Three rock 'n' rollers who didn't like the sound of "starving musician" created this tiny Wallingford eatery where pasta rules. Nearly three dozen kinds are offered: from savory Portobello ravioli in a sage-and-butter sauce to ultra-spicy chicken diablo. Servings are huge, so be smart and share your entrée. And, especially if you ordered the diablo, cool off with the homemade sorbet, served in frozen lemon or orange peels. *1605 N. 45th St. (between Densmore Ave. N and Interlake Ave. N), Wallingford, 206/547–2514. AE, D, DC, MC, V. No lunch. $$*

5 *d-6*
BIZZARO ITALIAN CAFE
Kitsch may be king at this small, popular restaurant, but die-hard fans love the elegant and inventive dishes. "Loosely Italian" may be the best classification for such creations as Forest Floor Frenzy, lots of Portobello and shiitake mushrooms in a sherry-cream sauce with roasted walnuts and garlic. Less over-the-top is lamb shanks with a fig demiglace served with polenta triangles. The service is equally glamorous: your server might offer an operatic rendition of the night's specials. *1307 N. 46th St. (at Stone Way N), Wallingford, 206/545–7327. AE, D, MC, V. No lunch. $$*

5 *b-7*
BRAD'S SWINGSIDE CAFE
You've probably dreamed of finding a place like this—funky, cramped, and dear to the heart of the owner. Lots of people share this dream, so you can expect to wait a while on weekends. Chef-owner Brad Inserra, who likes to come out and chat—so long as you don't dis the Pittsburgh Pirates—bills Swingside as Seattle's "best little Italian restaurant," but don't come expecting spaghetti and meatballs. You will find an imaginative lamb-and-venison stew with

coconut milk, orange, and mango. Be sure to ask the server what wine Inserra recommends. He's always right. *4212 Fremont Ave. N (between 42nd and 43rd Sts.), Fremont, 206/633–4057. D, MC, V. Closed Sun. No lunch. $$*

12 *c-2*
CAFE BENGODI
A passage from Boccaccio's *Decameron* painted on the bright red walls explains the café's name as a mythical land for foodies. In this teensy-tiny magical land, owner and chef Luigi DeNunzio wheels a cart with a burner to cook at your table, guiding you toward the special dishes. Though the sauce sometimes overwhelms the pasta, you may not mind when it's as savory as the rigatoni *massimo* (charbroiled chicken in sun-dried-tomato-and-tarragon cream sauce) or the lasagna *bengodi* (pasta layered with meat and bechamel sauces). *700 1st Ave. (at Cherry St.), Pioneer Square, Downtown, 206/381–0705. AE, D, DC, MC, V. $$*

2 *e-1*
CAFE JUANITA
Chef Holly Smith's (formerly of Brasa) swanky restaurant operates on the purity principle: everything is worth serving pure and simple or it ain't making it to the table. If necessary, you may be told that the soup didn't pass muster. (No fancy excuses like "our truffle pig got sick" are given.) This means you can trust Smith and her impeccable, if sometimes glib, staff. The shelled lobster with pumpkin gnocchi and chanterelles in a light cream sauce will nearly make you weep; the foie gras with nectarines, grilled onion, and candied ginger will have you begging for more. Pair anything on the menu with champagne, and you have a *very* special meal. *9702 NE 120th Pl. (at 97th Ave. NE), Kirkland, 425/823–1505. Reservations essential. AE, MC, V. Closed Mon. No lunch. $$$*

1 *e-4*
LA MEDUSA
Sherri Serino and Lisa Becklund decided that Seattle needed "Sicilian soul food." And they were right. The duo have two Columbia City restaurants (Salumeria's the other), with La Medusa being the more "sit-down" of the two. Check out Grandma's Greens, slow-cooked endive and escarole with garlic, olives, raisins, and pine nuts, or the spaghetti with sar-

dines, fennel, and more pine nuts, olives, and raisins. Try to save room for the cannoli drizzled with chocolate, though. You never know the next time your soul will get fed. *4857 Rainier Ave. S (near Hudson St.), Columbia City, 206/723–2192. MC, V. Closed Sun.–Mon. No lunch. $$*

10 d-5
LUSH LIFE

Three's definitely a crowd in this candlelit "date" spot, so dine *à deux*, if possible. Owned by the Marco's Supper Club folks, this intimate dinner spot is cared for by Chef Matthew Burian, who fashions unique Italian-inspired dishes like risotto *spinaci arancia* (orange spinach) and thin-crust pizza with red onions and asparagus. The bar in back is a great place to sip a Moretti's before your table's ready, or enjoy an Armagnac later in the evening. *2331 2nd Ave. (at Battery), Belltown, 206/285–0693. AE, MC, V. No lunch. $$*

7 f-6
PERCHE NO

The friendly owners of this small Queen Anne restaurant readily admit that, yes, they're not Italian (they're Malaysian). Thus the name, Perche No, Italian for "Why not?" But chef and co-owner David Kong studied Italian cuisine in North Beach, that famous Italian neighborhood in San Francisco, and knows whereof he cooks. Try the sautéed sweetbreads, porcini risotto, or osso buco, and finish with the chocolate and mascarpone "lasagna." *621½ Queen Anne Ave. N (between 1st Ave. N and 1st Ave. W), Queen Anne, 206/298–0230. Reservations essential. AE, D, DC, MC, V. Closed Sun.–Mon. $$$*

10 e-6
PINK DOOR

Maneuver yourself through the Market to Post Alley and you'll find some solid Italian fare dressed up in shabby-chic (read: oilcloth-covered tables, old mirrors, and lots of pink). First, go for the *bagna cauda* (a warm dip of garlic, olive oil, and anchovies), move on to the vermicelli with pan-seared scallops in a roasted-beet sauce, and, for dessert, have drinks on the deck (weather permitting) and take in the sweet view of Elliott Bay. Tuesday nights are musical cabaret night. *1919 Post Alley (between Stewart and Virginia Sts.), Pike Place Market, 206/443–3241. AE, MC, V. Closed Sun.–Mon. $$*

5 d-1
RIALTO

Taciturn chef-owner Rudy LaValle shows he cares the same way an Italian mama might—through the sauce. Rudy's Red, indeed his mother's recipe, is born of long-simmering tomatoes, garlic, herbs, and meat: sausage, bone marrow, ribs, whatever. The finely pureed sauce tossed with spaghetti is truly one of life's finer things. Other can't-go-wrong dishes are the spaghetti Bolognese (a classic meat sauce with a touch of cream and lemon) and the manicotti, filled with ricotta, mozzarella, and fontina and smothered in *pomodoro* (red tomato) sauce. *1400 N. 80th St. (at Interlake Ave. N), Green Lake, 206/522–6635. D, MC, V. No lunch. $*

2 d-6
SALUMERIA

Salumeria, owned by chefs Sherri Serino and Lisa Becklund (also of La Medusa), is an Italian deli of the highest sort. Look upon the chewy, thin-crust pizzas, upscale lamb or prosciutto sandwiches, and antipasti with spicy meats for yourself at lunch and see if you can say no. Though you can take the food to go (it's a deli after all), the small café tables are perfect for sipping a glass of wine and celebrating the revival of an old neighborhood with new friends. *4918 Rainier Ave. S (at Hudson St.), Columbia City, 206/760–7741. MC, V. Closed weekends. $–$$*

12 d-3
SALUMI

The kind Armandino Batali (father of famed New York chef Mario Batali) doles out samples of his fabulous house-cured meats while you wait for a table (that you simply must be willing to share) at this postage-stamp of a place. Order a meatball, oxtail, sausage, or lamb sandwich—and get a sample of your runners-up. Mainly this is a lunch spot, though once a week Batali serves dinner to a lucky few (reservations are made as much as 12 months ahead). Wine served at lunch is strong, inexpensive, and good. *309 3rd Ave. S (between Jackson and Main Sts.), Pioneer Square, 206/621–8772. AE, D, DC, MC, V. Weekly dinner by reservation only. $$*

8 b-3
SERAFINA

For many long-time Seattle residents, Serafina is *the* Italian restaurant. It's endured local debate being described as cramped by the irked and intimate by the enamored. Still, the generous pasta portions (the puttanesca is a popular dish) and the *polpettini con vitello* house-made veal meatballs in a green olive–tomato sauce, served over *strangozzi* pasta are sure to impress, and some people have been known to go to Serafina just for an after-dinner drink and an order of the mystical hazelnut chocolate torte. *2043 Eastlake Ave. E (at E. Boston St.), Eastlake, 206/285–0693. Reservations essential. MC, V. No lunch weekends. $$*

12 *b-2*

TRATTORIA MITCHELLI

Although the food is good, Trattoria Mitchelli is important for another reason: It's open until 4 AM most nights, and opens at 7 AM. Its Pioneer Square location may account for this, as many pub crawlers find "the Trat" a hospitable establishment for winding up an evening (and for getting some much-needed late-night/early-morning sustenance). The food is traditional—thin crust, applewood-fired pizzas; sizable pasta dishes; Caesar salads with anchovies (if you want). *84 Yesler Way (at 1st Ave.), Pioneer Square, 206/623–3883. D, MC, V. $$*

10 *h-8*

TULIO RISTORANTE

Tulio is a hotel restaurant that manages to be a neighborhood one as well. The tony atmosphere and pricey meals make it a "special occasion" restaurant, but it still draws regulars, even from other cities: Legend has it Paul Newman eats here when in town. Quietly efficient servers will start you off with a glass of wine from the better-than-average list. From there, expect upscale Tuscan fare, like salmon ravioli in a lemon sauce, or gnocchi with sage butter and mascarpone. *Hotel Vintage Park, 1100 5th Ave. (at Spring St.), Downtown, 206/624–5500. Reservations essential. AE, D, DC, MC, V. No lunch weekends. $$$*

JAPANESE

8 *a-5*

I LOVE SUSHI

Places like this are a genre of their own: kind-of-cheesy name, '80s decor, fast and friendly service, good sushi. The sushi novice should try the California roll (crab, avocado, cucumber, flying fish roe, and mayonnaise); the die-hard should go for *sashimi* (uncooked, fresh seafood). A must-have for anyone is the spider roll (soft-shell crab, avocado, mayonnaise, cucumber, and flying fish roe): It's served while the crab is still warm from the frying, and the cooling cucumber, creamy rice, mayo, and avocado blend seamlessly. *1001 Fairview Ave. N (at Ward St.), Lake Union, 206/625–9604. AE, D, MC, V. No lunch weekends. $–$$*

2 *f-5*

11818 NE 8th St. (at 118th Ave. NE), Bellevue, 425/454–5706. No lunch Sun. $–$$

10 *e-6*

NARA GRILL

Nara can appeal to your many moods: Will you sit in the lounge, outside, at the sushi bar, or the Pan-Asian grill (think Benihana, only less chainlike)? The indecisive should at least be firm about ordering the following spectacular dinner dishes: a lobster tail cooked in butter and served in the shell, or the tuna-steak salad, seared and accompanied by organic vegetables. You won't go wrong with the sushi, if that's why you're here, but the grill is where the fun is: A chef tosses utensils into the air as you sit around the grill table. *2027 5th Ave. (between Virginia and Lenora Sts.), Belltown, 206/727–2225. Reservations essential. AE, D, MC, V. No lunch weekends. $$$*

10 *f-5*

NIKKO JAPANESE RESTAURANT

Arguably Seattle's most elegant Japanese restaurant, Nikko's individual tatami rooms (traditional Japanese rooms perfect for special occasions) create privacy in a public space. Social creatures should venture to the sushi bar or lounge. Specialty sushi includes the paradise roll, made with yellowtail, tuna, salmon, avocado, flying fish roe, and a spicy sauce. For something exotic, try the ostrich from the *robata* (grill). As expected in a restaurant of this caliber, the servers excel and the prices soar. *Westin Hotel, 1900 5th Ave. (between Virginia and Stewart Sts.), Belltown, 206/322–4641. Reservations essential. AE, DC, MC, V. Closed Sun. No lunch Sat. $$$–$$$$*

8 *f-6*

NISHINO

Regulars argue whether it's Nishino's spicy tuna rolls, adventurous geoduck, or bright red *maguro* (tunu) sashimi that's the best. Whichever you choose, you're in good hands: executive chef and owner Tatsu Nishino often watches the sushi chefs from the kitchen to ensure things are getting done right. For dessert, cross your fingers that the banana tempura (served with vanilla ice cream and caramel sauce) is on the menu. *3130 E. Madison St. (at Lake Washington Blvd.), Madison Park, 206/322–5800. Reservations essential. AE, MC, V. No lunch. $$$*

10 *e-6*

SAITO'S JAPANESE CAFE & BAR

So where does Seattle Mariner Kazu Sasaki go to eat sushi when he's not busy pitching a winning game? Rumor has it it's Saito's, whose forte is unique fish selections. The spotted mackerel, butterfly fish, or New Zealand snapper are hard to come by, so if you want a really good California roll, go elsewhere. Lots of great sakes make deciding your beverage more difficult than your meal. Service is unfortunately hit and miss. *2122 2nd Ave. (between Blanchard and Lenora Sts.), Belltown, 206/728–1333. AE, MC, V. Closed Sun.–Mon. No lunch Sat. $$*

7 *f-6*

SAM'S SUSHI

Queen Anne-ers breathed a sigh of relief when Sam's opened. Sure QA isn't that far from Belltown sushi mainstay, Shiro's, but hey, Shiro's can get pricey, and this one's between Uptown Espresso (home of some terrific pies) and Uptown Cinema. And Sam's is good. It may not get the raves Nishino does, or have the swank of Nikko, but it's clean, friendly, and the fish is fresh. The rolls (California, spider, and the eponymous Sam's roll—shrimp tempura, crab, salmon, cucumber, and flying fish roe) are first-rate. *521 Queen Anne Ave. N (between W. Mercer and W. Harrison Sts.), Queen Anne, 206/282–4612. MC, V. Closed Sun. $$*

7 *a-4*

SANMI SUSHI

If you tell people that your favorite sushi restaurant is Magnolia's Sanmi Sushi, you'll either get a blank look, or a suspicious one, like "How'd you know about Sanmi?" Whether it's the best sushi restaurant in Seattle may be debatable, but devotees will argue—and be right—that there's none better. Unpretentious, the restaurant's owner is also the head sushi chef and his wife, the hostess. Not only will you be treated graciously and eat some fabulous fresh fish, but you've got a gorgeous view of the Magnolia marina. If you order nothing else, try the scallop roll. You won't find more buttery scallops anywhere else. *2601 W. Marina Pl. (off the Magnolia Bridge), Magnolia, 206/283–9978. AE, MC, V. Closed Mon. No lunch weekends. $$*

10 *d-5*

SHIRO'S SUSHI

Shiro's is famous for its sushi, and well it should be. Owner and head chef Shiro Kashiba has been crafting sushi in Seattle for a couple of decades now. But in addition to the amazing *hamachi* (yellowtail) sushi, the kasuzuke black cod, which is broiled with sake and miso paste, will make you a fan of his hot food as well. Though service at the tables is swell, to get maximum Shiro exposure, eat at the bar and watch Kashiba work his magic. *2401 2nd Ave. (between Battery and Wall Sts.), Belltown, 206/443–9844. AE, MC, V. No lunch. $$*

KOREAN

7 *h-7*

SHILLA RESTAURANT

Though Shilla serves Japanese cuisine, including sushi, it's much better known for its Korean fare. And if you're looking for the real deal, this venerable Downtown establishment has it. Those in the know ignore the less than exciting ambience and order not only *kimchi* and *kalbi* (barbecued short ribs), but specialties such as *yook hwae bi bim bap*, marinated vegetables and raw beef strips served with an egg fried sunny-side up and seasoned with sesame and honey pears. Shilla also has an Eastside location, in Redmond, and a new "express" café in the International District grocery store nonpareil Uwajimaya. *2300 8th Ave. (at Denny Way), Belltown, 206/623–9996. AE, DC, MC, V. $$*

KOSHER

7 g-5

BAMBOO GARDEN VEGETARIAN CUISINE

Though Roxy's Deli is real New Yawk, not every dish is pareve. The same can't be said of Bamboo Garden. Whatever your stance on tofu and wheat gluten that tastes like chicken, it's kosher and it's popular. Chinese veggie standards such as mushrooms, bok choy, asparagus, and snow peas are all fresh and, thankfully, not overcooked. The hot peanut pudding sells like hot cakes. Go more than once and you're likely to be greeted by name. *364 Roy St. (at 3rd Ave.), Queen Anne, 206/282–6616. Reservations essential. AE, D, MC, V. $$*

LATIN

8 b-3

BANDOLEONE

Though small, the storefront dining room is staffed by friendly waiters and the owner herself, Danielle Phillippa. Because there've been a number of chefs over the years, dishes can be hit or miss, though mostly hits. Ingenious ingredients supplement already creative dishes: The sherry-and-garlic soup with ancho chiles and mushrooms is sweetened by almond paste, which deepens the flavor, and a blackened fish is seasoned with a tomato-and-tequila sauce. Cigars are allowed in the full bar, and there's live Latin music on occasion. Despite the insufficient neighborhood parking, Bandoleone has a far-away following. *2241 Eastlake Ave. E (between Boston and Lynn Sts.), Eastlake, 206/329–7559. Reservations essential. MC, V. No lunch. $$*

8 f-8

DULCES LATIN BISTRO

Flattering candlelight makes this a great "date" place on the weekend, but postwork business-casual rules during the week. All audience are here for Julie Ann Guerrero's to-die-for Latin cuisine. Creations like chicken enchiladas baked in a green tomatillo cream sauce draw upon classic recipes. Inventive burst-in-your-mouth dishes, like the homemade red-pepper ravioli (filled with chorizo, mozzarella, and ricotta) in a cilantro-tomatillo cream sauce, make use of Mediterranean ingredients. After dinner,

head to the cigar room for a cognac. *1430 34th Ave. (between E. Union and E. Pike Sts.), Madrona, 206/322–5453. Reservations essential. AE, D, MC, V. Closed Sun.–Mon. No lunch. $$$*

10 d-5

FANDANGO

With a James Beard Award in her possession Christine Keff created this high-design Latin restaurant kitty-corner to her first restaurant, Flying Fish, in Belltown. Though the suckling pig entrée has garnered great reviews, the drinks and appetizers make a more consistently good meal. The meltingly thin slices of beef in the carpaccio come with tart marinated mushrooms; the Brazilian crab soup is drink-the-last-drop good; the *queso asado* (grilled cheese in a tomatillo sauce) is salty enough to make you call for another mojito, Fandango's signature rum drink with lime, crushed mint, and sugar. If it's Belltown, it's crowded, so call for reservations. *2313 1st Ave. (between Battery and Bell Sts.), Belltown, 206/441–1188. Reservations essential. AE, D, DC, MC, V. No lunch. $$*

10 g-5

YAKIMA GRILL

Yakima twists standard Latin menu items into inspired delicacies: the Yakima ranch burger is made with chorizo *and* ground beef; the roast chicken comes with balsamic creamed onions. If you're in the mood for something light, order a margarita and some tapas. Or come during the happy hour from 4 to 6 PM, and again from midnight to 2 AM. *Vance Hotel, 612 Stewart Ave. (between 6th and 7th Aves.), Downtown, 206/956–0639. AE, DC, MC, V. $$*

MALAYSIAN

12 g-2

MALAY SATAY HUT

This inexpensive, inauspicious-looking spot is where transplanted Malaysians go for home cooking. Casually, they signal the number of *roti canai* (a thin, grilled tortilla-like bread served with a curried potato-chicken broth), they want as they enter. Get some for yourself and something from the menu of 80 other rather un-Americanized items. Not into the spicy curried fish-head stew? Start with the accessible Malay pork ribs, small deep-fried pork chops that are then stir-fried in a sweet-and-spicy sauce. *200 12th Ave. S (at Boren Ave. S), International District, 206/324–4091. MC, V. $*

MEDITERRANEAN

7 *g-5*
ADRIATICA

About as classically Mediterranean as you can get, Adriatica has become less popular than in former years, though who knows why. The thinner crowds are a blessing to those in-the-know, though, because the food's still good and so is the location, a multi-story hillside house overlooking Lake Union. Start with the signature deep-fried calamari with the Greek garlic dipping sauce, then, if it's on the menu, order the pork tenderloin in a fruit sauce. Wines by the glass are reasonably priced and pretty good, too. *1107 Dexter Ave. N (between Aloha and Comstock Sts.), Lake Union, 206/285–5000. AE, DC, MC, V. Closed Sun.–Mon. No lunch. $$*

10 *f-6*
ANDALUCA

Andaluca is the more adventurous and atmospheric of the two Mayflower boutique hotel restaurants (the other is Oliver's—famous for martinis), with lots of dark wood, flattering lighting, and warm colors. The tapas craze has hit here, but there's also more to the menu than the bite-size plates. Try the lamb chops, seasoned with garlic, ginger, and cardamom, or the beef tenderloin with a Cabrales crust. The service is fine, but sitting at the bar in the middle of the restaurant may prove a friendlier experience. *Mayflower Park Hotel, 407 Olive Way (between 4th and 5th Aves.), Downtown, 206/382–6999. AE, D, DC, MC, V. $$*

10 *f-7*
96 UNION

If 96 Union doesn't have the best patio in Seattle, at the edge of Pike Place Market with stunning views of Elliott Bay, who does? In a city where it rains a lot, however, even the nicest deck isn't going to keep a restaurant afloat, so Chef Bryan Weener (formerly of Sazerac) has wisely invested in his menu. Most recited dishes include the braised rabbit pasta, crispy polenta with pears, and the gnocchi in a Bolognese sauce. The waitstaff's friendliness is undisputed, but

sometimes the unorganized presentation is, too. *96 Union St. (at 1st Ave.), Downtown, 206/623–3783. Reservations essential. AE, D, MC, V. $$*

2 *a-7*
SAFFRON COW

This espresso shop/gourmet grocery/antiques gallery/restaurant near the Fauntleroy ferry really does seem to have it all. Whether you want to kick back with a Sunday morning latte on one of the big sofas, find an elusive imported ale, or eat a Mediterranean-inspired sit-down meal, you can do it here. Take-away food, particularly sandwiches and baked goods from the ever-popular Alki Bakery, win kudos; dinners can be a tad spottier. The daily curry is usually good and not too spicy; the pork tenderloin (not always on the menu) can be a bit dry. *9261 45th Ave. SW (at Wildwood), West Seattle, 206/923–1729. MC, V. No lunch Sat. $$*

14 *c-1*
SPAZZO
MEDITERRANEAN GRILL

With a variation on the old motto, Spazzo tries to please all the people all the time—and generally succeeds. Got a family? Bring 'em! On a date? Cool! The sweeping views provide romance while the vast menu at this popular Bellevue restaurant pleases nearly every palate. So whether you want pizza, pasta, or one of 30 tapas items, including the classic tortilla Espanola (a potato frittata) or the Greek phyllo pastry stuffed with shrimp, whitefish, cayenne, and cumin, Spazzo will probably have something you'll like. One caveat: Try not to be in a hurry: service can be unpredictably slow. *10655 NE 4th Ave. (between 106th NE and 108th NE), Bellevue, 425/454–8255. Reservations essential. AE, MC, V. No lunch weekends. $$*

MEXICAN

5 *g-8*
AGUA VERDE

You can rent kayaks at Agua Verde—which is hidden in the oddest of places, on a street bordering Portage Bay, and surrounded by boat repair shops and a bike shop—though most people come for the food. Agua Verde has been described as Baja California Mexican, which may refer as much to the bright, beachy colors and order-here window as it does to the cuisine. Tacos are not dripping with grease, cheese, or sour cream, and choices include fish and chile-chicken. With a nod to the U-District diet, there are lots of vegetarian items, too. Join the group of regulars who swear by the black-bean cakes and *mangodillas,* quesadillas with mango and poblano chiles. Warning: The fresh-lime margaritas may hike your otherwise small bill. *1303 NE Boat St. (between Brooklyn Ave. and 15th Ave. NE), University District, 206/545–8570. MC, V. Sun. lunch take-out only. $*

7 *f-1*

EL CAMINO

El Camino's big, strong, and fruity margaritas often take top honors in local publications' reader polls. (The sangria trails not too far behind.) Their popularity packs the lounge and, in warmer weather, the outdoor patio with views of Fremont, the ship canal, and Queen Anne. The dining room is often just as packed on weekends, but the food worth the wait. Look for pan-roasted Penn Cove mussels with ancho chiles and cream, and tacos de carne asada, with four types of cheese, cilantro, and onion. Though often quite spicy, the food is authentically flavored, thanks to the Mexican chefs invited periodically to teach the staff their secrets. *607 N. 35th St. (between Evanston and Fremont), Fremont, 206/632–7303. Reservations essential. AE, MC, V. No lunch. $$*

10 *e-7*

EL PUERCO LLORON

Older than most Seattle residents, El Puerco Lloron—and its furniture (reputedly derived from a Tijuana bullring café)—has been around for years. With age comes culinary wisdom: The corn tortillas are hand-made on the premises, the chile rellenos are about the flavor not an overabundance of cheese, and the tamales are a screaming deal at about $5 a plate. Lunch is the busiest, so come early and hope the tourists take one look at the beat-up tables and jukebox and go elsewhere. *1501 Western Ave. (on the Hillclimb, between Western and Alaskan Way), Pike Place Market, 206/624–0541. AE, MC, V. $*

10 *d-5*

MAMA'S MEXICAN KITCHEN

Before Belltown became the 'hood *du jour,* fun and funky restaurants like

Mama's Mexican Kitchen were the norm, places where the kitsch factor was high and the prices low. Judging from the hoards, Mama's is in no danger of losing her Elvis Room any time soon. The food is good, if what you'd expect. The nachos drown in cheese; you can hear the lard in the refried beans stopping up your arteries. Service can be slow but is endearingly friendly. The diminutive Mamacita's has a smaller menu. *2234 2nd Ave. (between Bell and Blanchard Sts.), Belltown, 206/728–6262. AE, D, DC, MC, V. $*

10 *f-6*

Mamacita's, 216 Stewart St. (between 2nd and 3rd Aves.), Downtown, 206/374–8876. No dinner. $

2 *b-8*

TAQUERIA GUAYMAS

Taqueria Guaymas is a perfect example of how restaurants with multiple locations can serve vastly different food—even if the menu is the same. The Guaymas in Green Lake is a bit Anglicized, the one on Capitol Hill serviceable, the one on California Avenue in West Seattle somewhat more authentic, and the one on Roxbury Street (also in West Seattle) the most authentic of all. If location isn't an issue head to the Roxbury Guaymas as often as decently possible, where the *menudo* (a tripe and posole stew) may not cure your hangover, but it will help. The ceviche is tart with lime juice. The carne asada comes sizzling and spicy. *1622 SW Roxbury St. (between 16th and 17th Aves. SW), White Center, 206/767–4026. No credit cards. $*

MIDDLE EASTERN

9 *b-5*

KOLBEH PERSIAN RESTAURANT

Kolbeh has good food and belly dancing: And it charges big bucks for both. (In addition to your meal, expect to pay $10 to $15 a head if you want to stay past 10 PM to watch the dancing.) If you've got the cash in hand, though, do it: The dancing's fairly unusual in Seattle. During the show, munch on a kebab that's got a pound of perfectly tender lamb on it. Or try the slightly spicy beef tenderloin marinated in lemon and onion, or roasted eggplant and tomatoes mixed with mint, garlic, and homemade yogurt. Drink the cardamom tea;

the wine selection isn't all that great. *1956 1st Ave. S (between Lander and Holgate Sts.), Sodo Center, Downtown, 206/224–9999. Reservations essential. MC, V. No dinner Mon. $$*

7 *g-6*

MEDITERRANEAN KITCHENS

Mediterranean Kitchen serves food just the way owner Kamal Aboul-Hosn's grandfather made it in Lebanon. The vinegar-marinated chicken covered in roasted garlic wins an argument over the value of such authenticity. The unfamiliar should start with the baba ghanoush or hummus and move on to the chicken or beef shawarma, seasoned with grilled onions, green peppers, and tomatoes, and served with tahini. If you're on the Eastside, go to the Mediterranean Kitchen (run by Aboul-Hosn's son, Bassam). *366 Roy St. (4th and Roy Aves.), Queen Anne, 206/285–6713. Reservations essential. AE, DC, MC, V. No lunch weekends. $$*

2 *f-5*

103 Bellevue Way NE (at NE 2nd St.), Bellevue, 425/462–9422. No lunch Sun. $$

MOROCCAN

7 *e-4*

SAPPHIRE KITCHEN & BAR

"Little plates," tapas-size servings of food meant for sharing, may have originated in Spain, but where is it written that the food served upon them can't derive from, say, Morocco or Greece? Insist upon the extra-crispy potato pancake topped with smoked cod and drizzled with truffle oil and the seasonal (and extremely large) antipasti platter, with mussels in a tomato sauce, toasted almonds, fresh mozzarella, and pesto. Note that the space isn't large and the bar, which allows smoking, is within a few inches of the dining section. *1625 Queen Anne N (between W. Garfield and W. Blaine Sts.), Queen Anne, 206/281–1931. Reservations essential. MC, V. Weekend brunch. $$*

PAN-ASIAN

7 *f-3*

CHINOISE CAFE

Few restaurants are as truly Pan-Asian as this crowded, popular neighborhood café. There's Japanese: yaki soba and an extensive sushi menu. Chinese: stir-fried chicken, such as General Tso's. Thai: curries and pad thai. And yet execution of this dizzying range of cuisines is reliable, if not inspired. *12 Boston St. (at Queen Anne Ave.), Queen Anne, 206/284–6671. AE, D, DC, MC, V. $$*

12 *d-4*

610 5th Ave. S (at Lane St.), International District, 206/254–0413. $$

9 *b-3*

2801 E. Madison St. (at 28th Ave.), Capitol Hill, 206/323–0171. $$

10 *h-5*

DRAGONFISH

Glitz and shine, and lots of bright origami mobiles and celebrity posters adorn Dragonfish, owned by a well-known Japanese restaurant family. The menu wanders from salmon kebab to stir-fried seafood to good old fried rice. Breakfasts (it is a hotel restaurant) offer relatively mainstream American fare such as omelets, pancakes, and waffles. *Paramount Hotel, 722 Pine St. (at 8th Ave.), Downtown, 206/467–7777. AE, D, DC, MC, V. $$*

10 *d-5*

NOODLE RANCH

You might need mountaineering equipment to scale some of the heaping plates that issue forth from the Noodle Ranch kitchen. This hugely popular eatery is nothing fancy—the tables are diner-esque Formica. The menu has several dozen versions of noodles and sauce, usually Thai in character (such as red and green curries), and rice bowls laden with fish or chicken and vegetables. The line forms early at lunch, and if you're not there by noon, you wait. *2229 2nd Ave. (at Bell St.), Belltown, 206/728–0463. Reservations not accepted. AE, DC, MC, V. Closed Sun. $*

7 *c-1*

PANDASIA

Essentially a neighborhood Asian bistro, this Interbay (foot of Queen Anne) eatery is locally popular for its noodle dishes, such as homemade spinach noodles larded with chicken and a curry-like sauce. As a neighborhood joint, its take-out business booms. *1645 W. Dravus St. (at 17th Ave.), Queen Anne, 206/283–9030. AE, DC, MC, V. $*

`10` *d-4*

SHALLOTS

Tucked inconspicuously in one of Bell-town's older high-rises, this compact Asian bistro maintains a low profile that belies the remarkable food within. The spare interior—light wood, high ceilings, a few carefully placed pieces of glass art—contrasts with the rich flavors, textures, and aromas of Shallots' soups, stir-fries, and entrées. Wok-seared Pacific stir-fry, for instance, combines calamari, fish, shrimp, and clams in a rich garlicky sauce. The formal tea service is exquisite. Lunch is the main meal here; tables are all spoken for by noon. *2525 4th Ave. (at Vine St.), Downtown, 206/728–1888. AE, D, DC, MC, V. Closed Sun. $$*

`10` *g-7*

WILD GINGER

In a refurbished Art Deco building across from Benaroya Hall, Seattle's Pan-Asian pioneer now has a glistening, airy modern interior marked by brushed metal and black accents—a marked change from its original Market setting. A small army of attendants waits at the formal check-in desk, and the floor-to-ceiling windows in the two dining halls allow you to watch the passing 3rd Avenue scene—and to be seen in turn. The menu remains as always, though: an extensive array of satays to start, Southeast Asian red and green curries, and rarities such as *laksa*, a Malaysian bouillabaisse transfigured with crab, salmon, and other Northwest ingredients. *1401 3rd Ave. (at Union St.), Downtown, 206/623–4450. Reservations essential. AE, D, DC, MC, V No lunch Sun. $$–$$$*

PERUVIAN

`10` *f-7*

COPACABANA

By Seattle standards the Andean cuisine served up here is somewhat dull—meat-and-potato stews, peanuty shrimp soup, a mildly spiced corn pie. It's the jaw-dropping view that draws crowds, especially on sunny days, when you can grab a table on the long second-floor balcony over the Market, and gaze out at Elliott Bay, Puget Sound, and the Olympics in the distance. Want to be sure you get a good table? Best be in line when the wrought-iron gate opens at 11:30.

Crowds diminish at dinner. *1520 Pike Pl. (at Post Alley), Downtown, 206/622–6359. AE, MC, V. Dinner Sat. only in winter. $$*

PHILIPPINE

`10` *f-7*

ORIENTAL FOOD MART

With just a dozen or so stools at two short lunch counters, this hidden Market gem is almost invisible to the throngs that pass nearby (hundreds of whom support the enterprising Filipino family that owns the place by buying the famed "Seattle Slug" paper toys from the novelty store out front). The menu is simple: redolent stews and a daily fried fish. Pork *adobo* (braised in coconut milk and spices) is the mainstay here; alternatives such as beef *buselo* also rely on chiles, tamarind, and tomato. *1506 Pike Pl. (at Pike St.), Pike Place Market, 206/622–8488. MC, V. Closes at 6 PM. $*

PIZZA

`8` *h-4*

MAD PIZZA

The "mad" is for Madison Park, where this small pizza chain originated, but it might just as well describe the wacky combos you can get here, with Asian, Southwestern, and Mexican toppings. The crust is the chewy kind. *4021 E. Madison St. (at 40th Ave.), Madison Park, 206/329–7037. DC, MC, V. $$*

`3` *d-3*

3601 Fremont Ave. N (at 36th St.), Fremont, 206/632–5453. $$

`8` *b-6*

PAGLIACCI PIZZA

These days, down-and-dirty pizza is hard to find. Pagliacci ascetically adheres to a thin-crust, no-nonsense ethic which includes, yes, amazing, a cheese-and-tomato sauce pie. That's all. It's almost zen. *426 Broadway Ave. E (at Harrison St.), Capitol Hill, 206/324–0730 for branch; 206/726–1717 for general delivery. MC, V. $$*

`5` *g-7*

4529 University Way NE (at 45th St.), University District, 206/632–0421. $$

`3` *a-8*

PEGASUS PIZZA & PASTA

Mediterranean touches, all the rage in Seattle in the mid-'90s, still hold sway here with ingredients like artichoke hearts, thick pesto, and pine nuts. The salads are sea-sized, too. Just up the street is where Seattle's settlers landed; bet they wish they'd had a Pegasus pie that first night. *2758 Alki Ave. (at 61st Ave.), West Seattle, 206/932–4849. MC, V. $$*

13 *d-4*

12669 NE 85th St. (at 126th Ave. NE), Kirkland, 425/822–7400. $$

7 *f-1*

ZEEK'S

Zeek's array of weird and wonderful pizzas suits the Northwest character, especially in its original location across from unconventional Fremont. You can get pizza with pad thai; pesto, tomatoes, and mozzarella; and enchilada fixins. These pizzas are not for the weak. *71 Dravus St. (at Nickerson St.), Queen Anne, 206/285–6046. MC, V. $$*

7 *f-8*

6000 Phinney Ave. N (at 60th St.), Green Lake, 206/789–0089. $$

RUSSIAN

8 *b-7*

PIROSHKI ON BROADWAY

Piroshki are peasant food, and the versions served here don't stray far from the originals—small dumpling-like turnovers stuffed with potatoes, meat, cabbage, yogurt. What distinguishes this little stand is its location, in the heart of the Capitol Hill stroll-and-be-seen district, and its hours. It opens early (7 AM) and stays open late (11 PM). *124 Broadway E (at Union St.), Capitol Hill, 206/322–2820. AE, MC, V. $*

SEAFOOD

Thirty years ago when singer and entrepreneur Ivar Haglund was promoting what seemed an inexhaustible resource, North Pacific seafood, he sang about his "happy condition" in acres and acres of clams, which depicted both the wealth of seafood and the dearth of imagination in its presentation.

Today the cuisine is limitless, and the resource less so. Now most of Seattle's salmon comes from Alaska, as does much of the crab. Oysters, clams and

mussels are still plucked from Puget Sound; tuna (albacore) often comes from Oregon, as does the sturgeon that periodically turns up on menus.

The key to good seafood is that it be new and near—that is, caught within days (preferably less than two), and not shipped far. Ask where the ingredients in menu items are from, and whether they ever have been frozen. Note that flash-frozen seafood (common with shrimp) is actually comparable to fresh.

10 *b-4*

ANTHONY'S HOME PORT

Anthony's is a home-grown institution turned mini-conglomerate, with outlets around Puget Sound. The Kirkland original has a splendid view across Lake Washington, casually elegant surroundings, and reliably excellent seafood. Nothing too exotic—cioppino, first-class fish-and-chips, simple grilled salmon or halibut. The Sunday night family crab feeds are legendary. *135 Lake St. S (at Moss Bay Marina), Kirkland, 425/822–0225. AE, DC, MC, V. No lunch. $$–$$$*

4 *c-4*

6135 Seaview Ave. NW (Shilshole Bay Marina), Ballard, 206/783–0780. $$–$$$

10 *c-6*

ANTHONY'S PIER 66

A glistening exemplar of shiny industrial chic design, this sprawling complex can be oh so crowded when there's a docked cruise ship, a concert at Pier 62/63, or a conference in the Bell Harbor Center. It pursues excellence as the other Anthony's branches, with a slightly more experimental menu that drops in Asian and Mediterranean touches, such as cilantro cream and Hawaiian-style ahi. The casual, reliable downstairs fish bar is Anthony's answer to the Ivar's fish stand at the other end of the waterfront. *2201 Alaskan Way (at Pier 66), Waterfront, 206/448–6688. AE, D, DC, MC, V. Reservations essential. $$–$$$*

10 *g-7*

THE BROOKLYN

The clubby, booth and brick ambience, and simple, satisfying food make it seem ever so much like a Baltimore or D.C. chophouse. This emporium spreads its menu wide, with steaks, chops, fish, and shellfish, and has enjoyed a resurgence since Benaroya Hall opened across the street. Oysters come in more than a dozen incarnations, including an admirable selection of raw varieties for comparison, and the grilled beef, lamb, and chicken are splendid. Reservations are essential on concert nights. *1212 2nd Ave. (at University St.), Downtown, 206/ 224–7000. AE, D, DC, MC, V. No lunch weekends. $$–$$$*

8 a-6
CHANDLER'S CRABHOUSE

Not many Seattle restaurants assert a crab specialty. The crab cakes, appropriately, are among the best in town, the flavor of the crabmeat not overly subsumed by other ingredients; the same holds for the whiskey-laced crab soup. You can get snow and king crab, but Dungeness, which is the most local, is best. The Lake Union view is a bonus. *901 Fairview Ave. N (at Mercer St.), Lake Union, 206/223– 2722. AE, D, DC, MC, V. $$$*

10 g-7
CUTTER'S BAYHOUSE

Cutter's has something many of its Pike Place rivals do not—a full-on view across Elliott Bay to the Olympics. The decor is heavy-handed (lots of red), and tourists crowd in; withal, Cutter's has managed to upgrade its cuisine from its mid-'90s doldrums, finessing its traditional seafood repertoire with international touches that liven things up. It's not quite as bracing as its cross-street competitor, Etta's, but flashy items such as wok-seared crab and applewood-grilled salmon heighten the culinary interest sufficient for residents as well as visitors. *2001 Western Ave. (at Virginia St.), Downtown, 206/448–4884. AE, MC, V. Reservations essential. $$*

10 f-7
ELLIOTT'S OYSTER HOUSE

You can sample up to 30 different oyster varieties at this popular waterfront spot, which is basically a lunch café. Go for the dependable oyster, clam, and salmon preparations. The oyster stew is thick and filling, and the daily pasta specials are usually full of fish and shellfish. The outside deck is dandy on sunny days. *1201 Alaskan Way (at Pier 56), Waterfront, 206/623–4340. AE, MC, V. $$*

10 g-7
EMMETT WATSON'S OYSTER BAR

Just as Emmett Watson was a character on par with Ivar Haglund, his Market oyster bar is in a class by itself, aspiring more to the Formica ambience of Gulf Coast oyster bars than the refinements of any labeled cuisine. What you get here are quiet tables tucked in a small courtyard; oysters fried, sautéed, or stewed; chips and bread and no-nonsense service. It's an essential part of the Seattle experience—and Emmett, who spent a lifetime promoting what he called "Lesser Seattle," would never have wanted to contribute to anyone's desire to move here. *1916 Pike Pl., (at Stewart St.), Pike Place Market, 206/448– 7721. No credit cards. Reservations not accepted. $*

10 e-6
ETTA'S

Celebrity chef Tom Douglas first made his mark in this very space at the long-gone Cafe Sport, the birthplace of Northwest contemporary cuisine. His hip, sporty seafood emporium pursues the same fey melding of culinary influences, using seafood as the base and a touch of whimsy: One appetizer pairs two bites of foie gras with one single seared scallop. The spice-rubbed, pit-roast salmon is incomparable in Seattle, and the comfort-food side dishes like mashed potatoes and chard solidify the meal. The view of the passing Market panoply encompasses the social, if not geographic, scenery of Seattle. *2020 Western Ave. (at Virginia St.), Pike Place Market, 206/443–6000. AE, MC, V. $$$*

10 d-5
FLYING FISH

When celebrity chef Chris Keff opened Flying Fish in 1995 it was a revelation: Yes, there is something new to be done with seafood. Now a culinary landmark, it has lost none of its amazing verve. Dozens of fresh items, ranging from the usual salmon to exotics such as opah and escolar are flown in fresh. Flavors and adornments might be Asian (hoisin and ginger), Mediterranean (ricotta and truffle oil), or eclectic (porcini, potatoes, and morels). The most popular items are the by-the-pound platters: mussels, whole rockfish, crab, fish tacos. The wine list is longer than a gill net, and there's not a single ho-hum, mainstream vintage on it. *2234 1st Ave. (at Bell St.), Belltown, 206/728–8595. AE, MC, V. Reservations essential. No lunch. $$*

4 *d-5*

HIRAM'S

Location is the key to Hiram's long-standing popularity, as the Ballard Locks are one of the most popular Seattle attractions. The seafood is uninspired—salmon and halibut, grilled and roasted—but the chance to watch boats move through the locks diverts almost everyone's attention from the meal. *5300 34th Ave. NW (at Hiram Chittenden Locks), Ballard, 206/784–1733. AE, MC, V. $$$*

12 *a-1*

IVAR'S ACRES OF CLAMS

Yes, Ivar's is full of tourists—it's no novelty to hear one announce that he's going to try sautéed geoduck. And, yes, it's old-fashioned mainstream seafood: clam chowder, alder-grilled salmon, baked halibut. Ivar's periodic attempts to freshen the menu languish amid the weight of tradition. But that tradition is eminently worthwhile: the food is done right, the dining room view of the fireboat dock and Elliott Bay is great, and the heritage is unmatched. Ivar Haglund was unabashedly promoting seafood, and Seattle, back in the days that spaghetti was considered racy. *1001 Alaskan Way (at Pier 54), Waterfront, 206/624–6852. AE, MC, V. $$*

12 *a-1*

IVAR'S SEAFOOD BAR

Next to Ivar's Acres of Clams, this simple stand hawks the most dependable fish-and-chips on the waterfront, made with true cod or, for a bit more, halibut. The clam chowder's good, if over-thick with cream, and the fried oysters are fine. If you want to be a real Seattle expert, have a look beneath the statue of Ivar out front—what's there is an unsurpassed Seattle trivia quiz question. *1001 Alaskan Way (at Pier 54), Waterfront, 206/467–8063. MC, V. $*

8 *a-1*

IVAR'S SALMON HOUSE

This replica of a Coast Salish cedar longhouse makes up in earnestness what it lacks in authenticity. Here you get cedar-plank salmon, grilled over alder-wood chips, just as Ivar first served it to an audience that, a half-century ago, had no interest in Native traditions. Today that seems humdrum, and the most exotic dish here is black cod—one of the best of all North Pacific fishes, yet not always found at more upscale restaurants. *401 Northlake Way (at Gasworks Park), Lake Union, 206/632–0767. AE, MC, V. $$*

10 *f-7*

JACK'S FISH SPOT

Jack's is the best place for fish-and-chips at the Market, a seafood stall in the classic (and best) sense. Your choices include fish-and-chips made with cod, halibut, or salmon, best in variety and quality because Jack's is the best fresh fish purveyor at Pike Place. He'll tell you the truth about when the fish came in, and his prices beat everyone else's by about 50 cents. The boiled crabs and smoked salmon are excellent as well. *1514 Pike Pl. (at Pike St.), Pike Place Market, 206/467–0514. MC, V. $*

9 *h-2*

LESCHI LAKE CAFE

It's basic: fish-and-chips, burgers and fries, chowders, and stew. What distinguishes this popular neighborhood joint is the unadorned quality of the food, and the drop-dead view across the water of Mount Rainier and the Cascades. *102 Lakeside Ave. (at Alder and Lake Washington Blvd.), Madrona, 206/328–2233. AE, MC, V. $–$$*

9 *a-2*

MCCORMICK & SCHMICK'S

When Schmick joined McCormick to create this downhill sibling of the original fish house, the nascent corporation was born that now has a dozen nationwide branches. Perched above the steep decline below First Avenue, the restaurant's chophouse atmosphere (dark wood booths, waiters in bow ties) gives it an exclusive air that the meals live up to. Don't try anything too fancy: stick to fresh fish, grilled or sautéed, and it will be as good as anywhere in town. Chops and steaks are thick and redolent, and the single-malt Scotch list matches anyone's. *1103 1st Ave. (at Spring St.), Downtown, 206/623–5500. AE, MC, V. No lunch weekends. $$–$$$*

10 *g-7*

MCCORMICK'S FISH HOUSE

The granddaddy of what has become a far-reaching chain, McCormick's offers something unique in the way of reliability: a partnership with fishing boats, so it ensures the availability of the freshest fish. That's one reason they claim a larger daily fresh sheet than anybody else, a reasonable assertions with 36 fresh-fish entries. The bustling, multi-level financial district location is hugely popular for business lunches, and is one of the few places in town where you might see a martini or two on the table at noon. *722 4th Ave. (at Columbia St.), Downtown, 206/682–3900. AE, MC, V. No lunch weekends. $$*

7 *f-1*

PONTI SEAFOOD GRILL

It's hard to stand out in Seattle's crowded seafood genre. Ponti's distinc-tion is a Mediterranean ambience (the tile-roof stucco building faces the Lake Washington Ship Canal) and a sensa-tional fusion cuisine that mixes pasta, seafood, Asian spices, and Mediter-ranean bases like risotto. That's no longer as exotic as it once was, but Ponti helped invent it. *3014 3rd Ave. N (at Etruria St.), Queen Anne, 206/284–3000. AE, MC, V. No lunch Sat. $$*

10 *d-6*

QUEEN CITY GRILL

This saloon-style seafood café has been here since long before anybody past Tacoma knew the term "Belltown." Like most places of this ilk, it does best what's simplest—grilled and sautéed fish, oysters, salads, and soups. *2201 1st Ave. (at Blanchard St.), Belltown, 206/443–0975. AE, MC, V. $$*

4 *c-4*

RAY'S BOATHOUSE

Seattle's most formal and elegant seafood dining room is known for the magnificence of its view, the excellence of its service, and the refined cuisine. The view across Shilshole Bay takes in Puget Sound, Bainbridge Island, and the Olympic Mountains; if you're going to propose marriage—we only mention it because of its frequency—schedule it at a window table at sunset. The cuisine mixes light exotic touches (curry broth with steamed mussels) into a main-stream seafood palate. Like a half-dozen other Seattle restaurants, this is no place for T-shirt and jeans. The upstairs café has less formal food and atmo-sphere. *6049 Seaview Ave. NW (at 60th St.), Shilshole, Ballard, 206/789–3770. Reservations essential. AE, MC, V. No lunch. $$$–$$$$*

3 *c-7*

SALTY'S ON ALKI

Famed for its Sunday and holiday brunches, and its view across the harbor of Seattle's skyline, Salty's menu (and brunch table) offers more in the way of quantity than quality—and a bit too much of its namesake ingredient. But it's a couple steps up from the main-stream seafood chains. And, oh, that view. *1936 Harbor Ave. W (just past the Port complex), West Seattle, 206/937–1600. AE, MC, V. $$–$$$*

10 *g-7*

SHUCKER'S

Undeservedly overlooked, this small seafood bistro in the Four Seasons Olympic has a simple but expert slate of fish, shellfish, and sandwiches. The raw oyster sampler plates are exceptional; the fish fillet preparations lightly doc-tored (no heavy sauces) to bring out the natural flavors. The dark wood paneling and heavy furniture remind you that you're in Seattle's only five-star hotel, even if this is a pretty casual corner of it. *Four Seasons Olympic, 411 University St. (at 4th Ave.; entrance on 4th Ave.), Down-town, 206/621–1984. AE, MC, V. No lunch Sun. $$*

3 *a-8*

SUNFISH CAFE

Alki's neighbors love Sunfish, and it does a thriving business despite its lack of variety. Unfancy grilled "fishkebabs," stews, and chowders are the fare, and it's cheap, quick, and good. Take a beach stroll before or after dinner—the sun set-ting over the Olympics washes the entire landscape in gold. *2800 Alki Ave. SW (at SW 62nd St.), West Seattle, 206/938–4112. No credit cards. Closed Mon. $*

13 *b-4*

THIRD FLOOR FISH CAFE

Greg Campbell (sous chef to Scott Sta-ples who left to open Restaurant Zoë) has taken the helm at this Eastside favorite. He has a sure Mediterranean-style touch with fish, and he handles meats equally well. The menu focuses on local seafood (such as wild Pacific salmon or pan-seared scallops), but also includes chicken, lamb (as in caber-net-braised lamb shanks), and beef ten-derloin. The extensive wine list, piano bar, and small but select menu of roast meats broaden the appeal—so much so that it's often packed. *205 Lake St. S (at*

2nd St.), Kirkland, 425/822–3553. Reservations essential. AE, MC, V. No lunch. $$$

10 b-5

WATERFRONT

While it's not the only restaurant on Elliott Bay, Waterfront's perch at the very end of Pier 70 affords unmatched 270-degree views of Puget Sound and the Olympics. Star chef Vicky MacCaffree, who made her mark at Kirkland's Yarrow Bay Grill, infuses her dishes with Asian cooking touches using such ingredients as sesame, ginger, lemongrass, and whole fried fish. Thai crab cakes, pepper-seared tuna, and lobster risotto typify the entrées. Waterfront's sister restaurant, El Gaucho, is just up the hill in Belltown; complimentary shuttle service is offered between the two. 2801 AlaskanWay (Pier 70), Waterfront, 206/956–9171. AE, DC, MC, V. No lunch. $$$–$$$$

SOUTHERN

9 g-1

CATFISH CORNER

Towns in the south have diners like Catfish with quick-and-friendly service, farm-raised catfish cornmeal-battered and deep-fried, and the usual sides: chips or onion rings, collard greens, black-eyed peas. What goes best with catfish? Cole slaw. 2726 E. Cherry St. (at Martin Luther King, Jr. Way), Capitol Hill, 206/323–4330. No credit cards. $

9 f-2

EZELL'S FAMOUS CHICKEN

Your basic needs for fried chicken and fixins (cole slaw, mashed potatoes, and sweet potato pie) can be met here. Chicken comes crispy or spicy; some believe it's the best in Seattle. 501 23rd Ave. (at Yesler Way), Downtown, 206/324–4141. No credit cards. Take-out only. $

2 d-8

11805 Renton Ave. S (at S. 118th St.), Skyway (South Seattle), 206/772–1925. $

8 d-6

KINGFISH CAFE

Good Southern cooking is such a novelty in Seattle that the three sisters who own and operate Kingfish are local celebrities. Here you can get a good po'boy (served on a proper po'boy roll) with green tomatoes; buttermilk fried chicken; pulled pork; scrumptious crab cakes; and, of course, sweet potato pie. The atmosphere is spare but made elegant with monotone photographs culled from family albums. 602 19th Ave. E (at Mercer St.), Capitol Hill, 206/320–8757. No credit cards. Closed Tues. $–$$

SOUTHWESTERN

8 h-4

CACTUS

You could call this popular neighborhood café Pan-Southwestern for the breadth of its menu, which includes margaritas, tapas, fajitas, Indian fry bread, and enchiladas. Northwestern touches, such as calamari, mingle with chicken mole and plain old tacos. The wait can be considerable on weekends. 4220 E. Madison St. (at 42nd Ave. E), Madison Park, 206/324–4140. AE, MC, V. No lunch Sun. $–$$

10 g-6

DESERT FIRE

The sandstone-and-tile decor is pure Texas Hill Country; the corn husk–wrapped salmon is definitely not. In fact, numerous Northwest touches infuse the cuisine of this Texas-based chain. Lots of chile-based rubs flavor the meats, but there's relatively little fire, despite the moniker. 600 Pine St. (at 6th Ave. in Pacific Place), Downtown, 206/405–3400. AE, MC, V. $$

13 g-4

7211 166th Ave. NE (at 72nd St., Redmond Town Center), Redmond, 425/895–1500. $$

5 b-4

SANTA FE

This Woodland Park institution pioneered genuine Southwestern cuisine in Seattle and has earned undying loyalty ever since from those who know that posole is a grand side dish for enchiladas, and tamales are not supposed to be mush. Nontraditional innovations such as garlic custard please the adventurous Seattle palate. The stucco-walled building is authentic-looking, too (but no, it's not real adobe). 5410 Phinney Ave. N (at 59th St.), Green Lake, 206/783–9755. AE, MC, V, DC. $–$$

5 f-4

2255 NE 65th St. (at Ravenna Blvd.), Green Lake, 206/524–7736. $–$$

10 g-7
TIA LOU'S

You wonder where all this faux South-western furniture, the enamel-caked tables and chairs, comes from (not New Mexico). Nonetheless, the cuisine, based on traditional New Mexico recipes, is relatively genuine—red and green chile; occasional menudo; red-corn tortillas and chips. Yes, you can get poblano rellenos. Need a little fire? Ask for *Tapatío* hot sauce. The free parking is a big plus. *2218 1st Ave. (at Blanchard St.), Belltown, 206/733–8226. Reservations not accepted. AE, MC, V. Closed Sun. $$–$$$*

STEAK

Though Seattle is far from a steak-and-potatoes town, the financial district—bounded by 2nd and 6th avenues, Columbia and Union streets—is a sort of steak-house district. These corn fed–beef palaces draw dependable crowds—relying on business travelers perhaps more than residents. Steak houses are met with a lighter culinary touch: seafood, salads, and vegetables are more common here than, say, Peter Luger in New York City.

10 g-7
BLACK ANGUS

Black angus is a leaner, meaner cow than the Herefords most prime beef is drawn from—and the steers are typically grain-fed, rather than stuffed with corn to make the maximum fat. The result is a heartier, more robust cut of meat, exactly what Stuart Anderson was selling when he started this home-grown Northwest chain three decades ago. Most of the beef now comes from the Midwest, but the menu still lists certified Black Angus beef, if you want to try something a little less gummous. The ambience is sheer mid-range steak-house: think banquettes and landscape paintings. *1411 156th Ave. NE (at 141st St.), Bellevue, 425/746–1663. AE, MC, V. $$*

2 g-7
CALCUTTA GRILL

The Calcutta's innovation is wood-fired grilling, a technique that makes more difference than you'd expect. (It's why alder wood–grilled salmon was the Northwest's most savory dinner two centuries ago. Calcutta uses alder and apple woods.) The informal, publike atmosphere reflects its Newcastle golf club location, catering to the Eastside's high-tech gentry; the panoramic views of the Seattle basin to the west are match-less. Here, too, you can count on the seafood to be cooked right. *15500 Six Penny La. (at Coal Creek Rd.), Newcastle, 425/793–4646. Reservations essential. AE, MC, V. $$$*

7 g-2
CANLIS

Chef Greg Atkinson's San Juan Islands–bred culinary ethic has melded nicely with the prime-rib and salmon-steak tra-dition at Canlis. On any given night half the diners carve into steaks. But you can also get a Kobe-style cut of Washington beef, and expertly prepared scallops, prawns, and crab. The stone, glass, and light-wood decor of the early '60s looks surprisingly hip these days, and the sen-sational view over Lake Union remains as peerless as ever. *2576 Aurora Ave. N (at Halladay, east side of Hwy. 99), Queen Anne, 206/283–3313. Reservations essential. AE, MC, V. No lunch. $$$*

14 c-1
DANIEL'S BROILER

Daniel's is the Eastside's Metropolitan Grill with a glass-and-steel twist, since it's on the 21st floor of Bellevue's tallest building. This is the one place in town where celebrities and athletes are repeatedly spotted. Like you, they come for the prime, corn-fed steaks, and the absolutely excellent potatoes prepared mashed, shoestring, or baked. The Ellensburg lamb chop is an often-ordered item, too. The westward sunset view of Lake Washington, the Seattle skyline, and the Olympic mountains is unsurpassed. Call far, far ahead to be sure of a window table. The Seattle sib-ling has the opposite view, across Lake Washington toward the Bellevue skyline and the Cascades. *10500 NE 8th Ave. (at 105th St.), Bellevue, 425/462–4662. AE, MC, V. No lunch weekends. $$$–$$$$*

9 h-2
200 Lake Washington Blvd. (at Leschi Park), Madison Park, 206/329–4191. $$$

10 d-5
EL GAUCHO

Stylish El Gaucho's a resembles '60s Seattle supper club. The windowless, spotlighted space melds cabaret ambi-ence with supper-club drama—there are two cigar lounges and a lower-floor dance hall. Waiters light vodka-doused kebabs at tableside, and Sinatra croons from the sound system, while martinis pour at the bar. Over-the-top menu items like bananas Foster and cherries jubilee seal the deal. Coat and tie aren't exactly necessary, but don't show up in jeans and T-shirt. And what did all this used to be? A seamen's hall. So it goes in Belltown. *2505 1st Ave. (at Wall St.), Belltown, 206/728–1337. Reservations essential. No lunch. AE, MC, V. $$$–$$$$*

9 b-1
FLEMING'S

Fleming's, a Northern outpost of a small California chain, has the usual dry-aged Midwest beef: lots of marbling, buttery flavor. It sets itself off in its genre a bit with its setting: lots of cherry wood, big windows, and airy, high-ceilinged rooms. The side dishes, like the excellent mesclun salad, are a bit brighter, too. The California-focused wine list innovatively offers wines by the glass from more than 100 vintages. *1001 3rd Ave. (at Madison St.), Downtown, 206/587–5300. AE, MC, V. No lunch. $$$*

9 b-2
METROPOLITAN GRILL

There's a reason Seattleites have favored the Metropolitan Grill. It's a home-grown, high-end steak house with everything you'd expect in the genre: a clubby, refined, dark-wood bonhomie; superlative dry-aged steaks done expertly; splendid salads, fine wines, and ales to round out the meal. The Met tacks on a Northwest sensibility; you can expect fish to be handled as well as at a first-class seafood house, for instance. The wine list focuses on Northwest vintages, especially the Columbia merlots and cabernets that best suit beef. The service is under-stated and expert. Other steak houses in town now offer similar advantages, but the Met was first. At lunch, this is one of the few places in town where more than half the patrons will be wearing suits. *820 2nd Ave. (at Marion St.), Downtown, 206/624–3287. AE, MC, V. No lunch weekends. $$$–$$$$*

10 g-7
MORTON'S OF CHICAGO

Like Ruth's Chris, Morton's is an upscale chain outlet that draws big crowds and gets high marks for its prime beef and tony atmosphere—mostly from business travelers. The menu's high points are prime Midwest-ern steaks, and lamb and veal chops, but the seafood dishes are also very popular. Hardly anyone seems to mind that the prices are a bit steep, or that the dining room is two flights of steps below street level. The place always seems packed to capacity. Which means that you really should have a confirmed reservation before stepping out. *1511 6th Ave. (at Pike St.), Downtown, 206/223–0550. AE, DC, MC, V. No lunch. $$$*

9 b-2
RUTH'S CHRIS

Although it's consistently packed, a good portion of the diners here are out-of-town visitors who want the same meal they had in Indianapolis last week. Ruth's Chris simply doesn't fit the Seat-tle culinary style, what with fat-laden steaks swimming in butter-drenched platters and wine lists that proffer French vintages pricier than mountain bikes. The steaks are richly flavored and exquisitely tender, of course; soups and salads need a bit of help, and this is not the place to order fish. If you want national-class feedlot beef and Maine lobster, they've got your dinner. The atmosphere and decor are strictly coun-try club, with paneled walls and plush chairs. *800 5th Ave. (at Columbia St.), Downtown, 206/624–8524. AE, D, DC, MC, V. $$$*

10 g-7
UNION SQUARE GRILL

Operated by the same folks as the Met, Union Square is a slightly subdued ver-sion of the grilled-meat, dark-wood ambience of its higher-profile sibling. The atmosphere is a little more con-vivial; the patrons' suits are a few-hun-dred dollars more sensible; the menu items a few dollars less across the board. The bar's long list of martinis includes almost every variation you can think of. *621 Union St. (at 7th Ave.), Downtown, 206/224–4321. AE, MC, V. No lunch weekends. $$$*

TEA

Let's face it: Seattle is a coffee town. With the exception of a few Asian restaurants that have extensive tea menus, there's an absolute paucity of teahouses; Vancouver and Victoria, B.C., where there are dozens, are the places to go for real tea culture. However, there are a couple practitioners of classic British tea, one Mandarin high-tea palace, and a couple teahouses that blend in New Age culture.

11 g-7

BLUE WILLOW

Blue Willow is a hybridized teahouse and store with almost as many herbal and flavored blends as classic black and green teas. Afternoons sherry, port, and sake join the agenda; limited snacks and desserts are available in the scone–and–tea cake genre. *1024 E. Pike St. (at 10th Ave.), Capitol Hill, 206/325–5140. AE, MC, V. $*

10 f-7

THE CRUMPET SHOP

Ah, here's a dandy little British tea-room—friendly, intimate, and with everything hand-made by the propri-etress. This means fresh crumpets every morning, and not the stony version most American bakeries manage. You can pick up a sack of crumpets for a mid-morning snack in the park. Tuesday through Friday turkey and chicken are popped in the oven to make lunch sand-wiches. Kids should investigate the green eggs and ham. Teas are the British standards: English breakfast, Earl Grey, oolongs, and pekoes, plus a few herbal blends. *1503 1st Ave. (at Pike St.), Downtown, 206/682–1598. AE, DC, MC, V. Closed Sun. $*

10 g-7

GEORGIAN ROOM

Seattle's most formal dining room is the new home for the Four Seasons Olympic Hotel's afternoon British tea. High, high ceilings festooned with huge crystal chandeliers set the tone; the tablecloths are not just white linen, they're starched and pressed, and wait-ers are seriously garbed in black. The teas range from oolong to rare jas-mines, and the accompanying snacks, sandwiches, and desserts have a North-west touch (as much salmon as cucum-ber). *411 University St. (at 4th Ave.), Downtown, 206/621–1700. Reservations essential. AE, D, DC, MC, V. $$$*

1 e-7

IMPERIAL TEA COURT

High Mandarin decorum and serenity simultaneously prevail here, along with oolong, jasmine, and green teas. Make the pilgrimage to Kent and reward your-self with hombows (meat-and-vegetable-filled pastries) and pot stickers. *18230 E. Valley Highway (at SE 182nd St., in the Great Wall Shopping Center), Kent, 425/251–8191. DC, MC, V. Closed Tues. $*

5 e-7

TEAHOUSE KUAN YIN

There's almost as much ginger, ginseng, and philosophy in evidence here as clas-sic black or green tea; the New Age healthful ethic is in full swing. Rich scones, berry pies, and green-tea ice cream leaven the mix. The adjoining bookstore focuses on travel and world understanding. Kuan Yin, the shop's namesake, is the goddess of mercy. *1911 N. 45th St. (at Meridian Ave.), Walling-ford, 206/632–2055. MC, V. $*

6 a-5

QUEEN MARY TEAROOM

With tea and crumpets, scones and clot-ted cream, and cucumber sandwiches, the Queen Mary holds the traditional line for afternoon tea. The ambience is plush, too: chintz, bric-a-brac, even doves cooing in their cote. If you've just got to have lemon curd, this is the place. *2912 NE 55th St. (at 30th Ave.), Ravenna, 206/527–2770. MC, V. No din-ner Sun.–Wed. $$*

TEX-MEX

8 b-8

BIMBO'S BITCHIN' BURRITO KITCHEN

No-nonsense burritos and the like are filled with meat, fish, beans, and hot sauce. The food is quick, hot, and right on the money. Eat among the velvet paintings or take it to go. Who's the bimbo? Go ahead, we dare you to ask. *506 E. Pine St. (at Union St.), Downtown, 206/623–4450. DC, MC, V. $*

2 b-2

BURRITO LOCO

The gas station next door reminds you of the unfailing principle that the best Tex-Mex food is found in the least snazzy circumstances. Living up to the credo, burritos are stuffed with top-notch ingredients (such as beans refried in vegetable oil), and the lemonade is a dandy hot-weather cooler. The menu also extends to enchiladas and ceviche.

9211 Holman Rd. NW (at 92nd St.), Greenwood, 206/783–0719. D, MC, V. $

10 *a-1*

TACO DEL MAR

Although it has morphed into a many-outlet chain, Taco del Mar helped inaugurate the fish taco craze in Seattle back in the early '90s. All branches are diner-like stop-and-pop shops where you won't want to linger, but the recipe remains the same. Watch as the amazing tortilla (it's actually more like a burrito than a taco) is lavished with fish or chicken, beans and rice, and hot sauce to your liking. You just can't beat it for a genuine Seattle fast-food fix. A dozen or so shops are scattered throughout Seattle and the Eastside. *1336 1st Ave. (at Union St.), Downtown, 206/623–8741. MC, V. $*

7 *f-8*

90 Yesler Way (at 1st Ave.), Pioneer Square, 206/467–5940. $

7 *f-8*

677 120th St. NE (at 67th Ave.), Bellevue, 425/646–9041. $

7 *f-8*

5431 Ballard Ave. (at Market St.), Ballard, 206/706–9933. $

7 *f-8*

1520 Broadway Ave. (at Pike St.) Downtown, 206/328–4868. $

7 *f-8*

3526 Fremont Pl. NE (at N. 35th St.), Fremont, 206/545–8001. $

7 *f-8*

104 Central Way (at Lake Washington Blvd.), Kirkland, 425/828–3002. $

THAI

With more than 100 restaurants in the metropolitan area—including neighborhood cafés and a few higher-profile restaurants—Thai has long been Seattle's favorite Asian cuisine. If there's a concentration it's in lower Queen Anne, north of Seattle Center (not the International District). Marked by lemongrass, tamarind, cilantro, and basil, and fired by chiles, the soups, curries, noodles, and stir-fries of Thailand have assumed a place in the Seattle diner's repertoire.

Because it depends on readily available ingredients and relatively simple techniques, it's hard to find bad Thai food. It's also rare to find very adventurous

menus. If you're lucky, you'll happen on a night when more exotic items appear, such as a salmon hot pot or black rice pudding, one of the world's most exquisite desserts when done right.

A word about heat: Most dishes get 1 to 5 stars. A 1 is generally not much spicier than catsup; 5 is a euphemism for burst-into-flames. If you want more heat, ask the waitstaff to bring a pepper tray and boost the octane yourself.

10 *g-7*

AYUTTHAYA

Capitol Hill's best sit-down Thai restaurant has a small pastel-theme dining room noted for its seafood, such as whole fried fish in chile paste. Lunch is busy, busy. *727 E. Pike St. (at Harvard Ave.), Capitol Hill, 206/324–8833. AE, DC, MC, V. $*

10 *g-7*

BAHN THAI

A Seattle institution, Bahn Thai was one of the first restaurants to bring Southeast Asian food to the Northwest, and has long been a favorite before Seattle Center events, as the service is prompt. The Craftsman-style house has a softly lit dining room that's more elegant than usual for Thai restaurants. The cuisine is steady but unremarkable, with good curries, peanut sauces, and soups, served with a wide array of meats and vegetables. *409 Roy St. (at 5th Ave. N), Queen Anne, 206/283–0444. AE, D, DC, MC, V. $$–$$$*

1 *d-5*

BAI TONG

Worthwhile dining options near the airport are painfully rare. Years agone Bai Tong was legendary as the place Thai Airways crews came, but Thai Air no longer flies here, and Bai Tong seems to have lost a little steam. The cuisine is as much perfunctory as sensational, and the clientele seems less savvy about the imbalance. But the *tom kai gong* (seafood stew) and hot-pot salmon are dependable. *15859 Pacific Hwy. S (at S. 160th St.), Sea-Tac, 206/431–0893. AE, DC, MC, V. $*

13 *c-4*

CITY THAI

This is no food court: With white linen and antique furniture ambience you'll forget you're in an Eastside shopping center. The food is considered the best on this side of Lake Washington; the rich seafood stew and sweet-and-spicy stir-fries standout among the merely dependable dishes elsewhere. *134 Park Place Center (at 6th St.), Kirkland, 425/827–2875. AE, DC, MC, V. $*

`10` *a-2*

CILANTRO

A quick-and-fast Downtown diner known as much for its take-out meals as for sit-down dining means you can be lazy about cooking in a variety of ways. Stir-fries are a bit better here than the curries, which tend to rely overmuch on coconut milk. *93 Marion St. (at Western Ave.), Downtown, 206/652–9300. D, MC, V. $*

`10` *g-7*

LOTUS

The U-District's local Thai eatery has quick service and simple, tasty curries and noodles. Try the spicy eggplant stir-fry for a welcome change from the usual chicken-shrimp Thai hegemony. *2101 N. 45th St. (at 21st St.), University District, 206/632–2300. MC, V. $*

`5` *f-4*

KRITTIKA NOODLES & THAI

Burnished in purple and gold (yes, the University of Washington colors), this neighborhood Thai café has most of the genre standards (including the tropical fish aquarium). Vegetables, chicken, beef, and shrimp are arrayed in peanut or bean sauces; the orange beef stir-fry is a favorite. *6411 Latona Ave. (at 64th St.), Green Lake, 206/985–1182. MC, V. $$*

`10` *b-2*

MAE PHIM

In the basement of a massive stone building near Pioneer Square, Mae Phim has scant room, no atmosphere, a compact menu—and long lines snaking out the door and down the sidewalk. What draw hordes of lunchtime office workers are the stir-fried chicken, beef, and vegetables with garlicky sauces; basic curries are rock-solid as the surrounding stone walls; and a tasty, token noodle dish or two. Quick service means tables turn quickly, but on nice days you can grab some take-out and head down to the Waterfront. *94 Columbia St. (at 1st Ave.), Downtown, 206/624–2979. No credit cards. Closed Sun. $*

`10` *b-1*

RACHA

Real experts—such as Thai government officials—give their seal of authenticity to high-profile Racha. It's not so much the ingredients or dishes, but the skillful preparation, that distinguishes its soups, curries, and noodle platters. Favorites include the duck noodle soup; shrimp soup, which is light, lemony, and rich; and yellow curry, fragrant and yet not overwhelmed by coconut milk. With more than two dozen noodle dishes, you're bound to find something to meet your exact tastes. *23 Mercer St. (at 1st Ave.), Queen Anne, 206/281–8883. AE, MC, V. $–$$*

`10` *g-7*

SIAM

Little more than a lunch counter, this neighborhood institution is a maelstrom of quick cooking on weekend nights when passersby cruising the Broadway scene are snared by the sounds and smells emanating from the kitchen. What's best is what's simplest: peanut-laden stir-fries, red curry chicken, and *tom kah gai* (a coconut-based chicken soup). *616 Broadway Ave. E (at Mercer St.), Capitol Hill, 206/324–0892. AE, DC, MC, V. $*

`7` *f-8*

1880 Fairview Ave. E (at Blaine St.), Lake Union, 206/323–8101. $

`10` *a-1*

TUP TIM

Tup Tim is a blessedly inconspicuous neighborhood Thai café that excels at delivering reliable food. There's not much need to stray from the basics: Go for the red curry that gently stings your nose and tongue; the pad thai with the freshest bean sprouts; and then the coconut and mango ice cream. The diner-esque atmosphere keeps the out-of-town foodies away. *118 W. Mercer St. (at 1st Ave. W), Queen Anne, 206/281–8833. MC, V. Closed Sun. $$–$$$*

`10` *f-8*

TYPHOON

Portland-born Typhoon inherited Wild Ginger's subterranean spot when the latter moved uphill and upscale. In some ways, the trade was beneficial to all—the no-nonsense menu suits the clubby space, which retains the dark wood and banquettes of old, but a bamboo "wall" eases the atmosphere. Cut-and-paste noodle combos derive from Bangkok noodle shops; soups are mild and rich; and a few curries are quite distinctive (king's curry is a dry-paste, beans, and chicken combo that warms all the way down). Occasionally you'll find black rice pudding. The voluminous tea list, with almost 150 varieties, is truly mind-boggling. *1400 Western Ave. (at Union St.), Downtown, 206/262–9797. AE, DC, MC, V. No lunch Sun. $$*

13 *g-4*

8936 161st Ave. NE (at NE 90th St.), Redmond, 425/558–7666. $$

TURKISH

10 *g-7*

BISTRO ANTALYA

The proprietor of this small sandwich shop makes all his fixins by hand, including the pitas he bakes every morning. Thus, you can hardly get a better sandwich, stuffed with lamb, potatoes, vegetables, eggplant. Take one strolling with you along Broadway, as you peruse the night-time scene. The kebabs are scrumptious, too. *327 Broadway Ave. E (at Harrison St.), Capitol Hill, 206/860–1911. No credit cards. $*

2 *b-7*

EPHESUS

Situated somewhat oddly in a Craftsman-style house on a busy arterial street, Ephesus is essentially a neighborhood restaurant whose atmosphere is quiet and whose food is reliable but never veers from the expected lamb, chicken, and potato plates. The payoff comes at the end of the meal, in the form of Seattle's best baklava—it's not cloyingly sweet, just rich and wondrous. *5245 California Ave. (at SW Dawson St.), West Seattle, 206/937–3302. DC, MC, V. $$*

10 *g-7*

TURKISH DELIGHT

Strollers flock to this street-front lunch cafeteria at the Market for one reason—the simple lentil soup, pitas, and lamb dishes make a heck of a good, filling midday meal. The strong coffee and sweet candy have nothing to do with it. *1930 Pike Pl. (at Western Ave.), Downtown, 206/443–1387. No credit cards. $*

VEGETARIAN & MACROBIOTIC

10 *f-6*

CAFE FLORA

Cafe Flora ventured into serious vegetarian cuisine long before the idea made a ripple on the mainstream cultural scale. Purists accuse the place of tainting the vegetarian ethic with yuppie sensibilities, to which the best answer is: Get a life. No-meat cooking reaches its pinnacle here, with inventive dishes, soothing decor, and a splendid sunroom that keeps winter at bay. The no-alcohol policy was abandoned years ago—so much the better when you can sip pinot noir with Portobello Wellington, one of Flora's best-known (and most delectable) dinner dishes. The one-world friendliness that pervades the atmosphere is absolutely genuine; there's no Seattle chic sourpuss service here. *2901 E. Madison St. (at 29th Ave. E), Madrona, 206/325–9100. AE, DC, MC, V. Closed Mon. $$*

5 *a-2*

CARMELITA

Carmelita fans appreciate the bright café's stylish interior (the founders are designers) as much as the food, which roams the global map—Portobello roulade and risotto with rhubarb and fava beans. Try the vivid tamarind-ginger lemonade. *7314 Greenwood Ave. N (at 73rd St.), Green Lake, 206/706–7703. DC, MC, V. Closed Mon. $$*

10 *b-7*

GREEN CAT CAFE

A little of everything's on the menu here, starting with what seems ever so much like a hearty country breakfast till you notice the bacon is missing. The green-bean potato salad is a hugely popular dinner. *1514 E. Olive Way (at Denny Way), Capitol Hill, 206/726–8756. AE, DC, MC, V. $$*

8 *b-6*

GRAVITY BAR

They take the healthful veggie ethic very seriously here—with great gravity, you could say. Need spirulina? Haven't had enough wheatgrass juice? The more accessible entrées have lots of brown rice, soy, lentils, hummus, and other artfully presented stuff rich in flavor. The decor brings to mind a '50s science fiction TV show set. *415 Broadway Ave. E* *(at Harrison St.), Capitol Hill, 206/325–7186. MC, V. $*

5 *g-4*

SUNLIGHT

"World famous waffles" and surprising hale-nut burgers leave no one hungry. Some feel the service is, well, meditative; others enjoy the serene pace here in the always frantic U-District. *6403 Roosevelt Way NE (at 64th St.), University District, 206/522–0099. Reservations not accepted. DC, MC, V. Weekend brunch. $$*

VIETNAMESE

9 *b-3*

CAFE HUE

Cafe Hue seems a bit like its namesake old colonial capital—its glories past now, quiet and reflective. Once this café helped introduce Seattle to Vietnamese food; now its dishes seem a bit wan compared with the explosion of Thai and Pan-Asian menus, all tangier and saucier. The setting, a late-19th-century beauty of a stone-and-brick building, is still grand as ever. But the food— chicken and fish, lightly sauced, with rice and Asian vegetables—leaves you wondering if something hasn't been left out. *312 2nd Ave. S (at Jackson St.), Pioneer Square, 206/625–9833. MC, V. No dinner Sun. $$*

6 *d-6*

MONSOON

Monsoon is what Cafe Hue once was, an upscale Vietnamese restaurant that elevates the fish, meats, noodles, and rice of the country's cuisine to their fragrant, succulent best. Dishes like salmon steamed in green tea, lemongrass chicken, and stir-fried tofu are artful and zesty. *615 19th Ave. E (at Mercer St.), Capitol Hill, 206/325–2111. AE, DC, MC, V. $$*

5 *g-7*

MY'S

This is the Vietnamese entry in the U-District's United Nations of food. Dishes are standard—*pho* (noodle soups) with beef or chicken, spring rolls, a few curries—but are quick, cheap, and tasty. Thus the crowds of grad students at lunch. *4220 University Way NE (at 42nd St.), University District, 206/623–4450. AE, D, DC, MC, V. $$–$$$*

9 *d-3*

NHA TRANG

It looks like a humdrum noodle café, but Nha Trang goes beyond the usual with innovations like catfish hot pot. Yes, those are artificial plants. *1207 S. Jackson St. (at 12th Ave.), International District, 206/860–0057. AE, DC, MC, V. $*

9 *d-3*

SAIGON BISTRO

Crowds gather at this slightly upscale café in Little Saigon to slurp up fragrant bowls of soup and noodles tossed with fish and poultry. Food here is southern Vietnamese style, which means it's somewhat richer and spicier than the pho so common these days. *132 S. Jackson St. (at 12th Ave.), International District, 206/329–4939. D, MC, V. $*

chapter 2

SHOPPING

Savvy Seattle, with its glitter-ing new Downtown mega-stores and shining waterside shops, makes browsing and buying fun for even the most perfunctory shopper. Home-grown national chains include Nordstrom and Eddie Bauer—and it's an affluent enough region to name-drop such impressive anchors as Barneys New York, Nieman Marcus, Eileen Fisher, and Tiffany's. Here, you dress up to shop Downtown, for going to the sleek stores in the core is usually an event, an experience of wandering through multi-story, glass-and-chrome buildings that house such well-known names as Banana Republic, Gap, Old Navy, and Nike.

But the city center is the exception; the rest of Seattle is a casual market town where most people stroll through week-end festivals and bargain stores in jeans, pullover jackets, and cross-trainers. (Seattleites love to explore their own neighborhoods, each one with its own character, and they'll spend their hard-earned weekends nosing into new little restaurants and shops.) Residents are also deal-hunters at heart, and the abundance of thrift and discount stores proves it—they'll even go across town before dawn to find the best bargains. Their only beef is with parking; from Ballard to Belltown, Madison Park to Magnolia, the University District to the International District, they use every trick to find a space. But you won't find a more polite crowd scanning the spaces or grabbing from the sales racks, for Seattle has the friendly sort of small-town ambience where strangers will exchange haircut tips over the last pair of size-six Jimmy Choos.

Hint: To find all the free parking spots, as well as the cheapest lots, and for a rundown of the meter rules, pick up a copy of the brochure "How to Park in Downtown Seattle," available at most Seattle information displays in major stores.

major destinations

DEPARTMENT STORES

Seattle's two major department stores are the Bon Marché and Nordstrom, both highly regarded for their classic—and classy—clothing, housewares, and services. Prices are comparable with other biggie department stores in town, though, which makes these two local notables worth a look for their North-west flavor. Several upscale, New York–based department stores are found in Downtown Seattle and Bellevue, while less-expensive bargain chains and brand-name outlets are found in the city's many outer malls.

10 g-7

BARNEYS NEW YORK

Barneys injects a breath of haute-cou-ture attitude into casual Seattle. Step through tall glass doors into a cool envi-ronment defined by crisp, basic hues, where your needs are calculated in a glance. The store is long and slim, fronted by a cozy cosmetics room where pros paint glamour onto those heading out to big events. If it's fitted designer duds you're after, strut into the main store to scan the sleek suits and dresses. You'll find every label in these racks, and the efficient staff will help you refine your style. While you're at it, you might as well pair the outfit with that perfect pair of Manolos. *City Centre, 1420 5th Ave. (at Pike St.), Downtown, 206/622–6300.*

10 f-7

BON MARCHÉ

"The Bon," Seattle's oldest and largest department store, has been providing shoppers with classic, yet affordable attire and home accents for more than a century. Attentive service and a range of high-quality merchandise—Gucci, Jones New York, Nine West—account for the store's appeal, and it's always packed with a mix of locals and tourists brows-ing to see what's new. Pop in at 4 PM on a weekday, and you'll become one with the ever-present throng of power-buyers raiding the Clinique and Chanel coun-ters, or threading their way through the jackets for the ultimate ensemble piece.

Weekends are equally crowded but less frenzied; this is the time to visit the popular salon, search for that house-warming gift, or linger in the coffee shop with the friend you bumped into. Look for the latest high-design kitchen items and gourmet foods, and pick up a pretty box of thick Frango truffles. Even if your wallet is close to empty, the fancy bathrooms-cum-lounges, with their ultra-private suite-like stalls and endless mirrors lit by mega-watt bulbs, make you feel like one of upper classes. Watch for the store's incredible one-day sales, when everything is marked down—some pieces up to 75% off. The Bon also sponsors such major city events as the annual Christmas parade and has an informative city and shopping guide desk near the salon entrance on the lower level. *1601 3rd Ave. (at Pine St.), Downtown, 206/506–6000.*

2 *f-4*
Bellevue Square, Bellevue Way (between NE 4th and 8th Sts.), Bellevue, 425/688–6000.

2 *c-1*
Northgate Mall, Northgate Way (at 4th Ave. NE), Northgate, 206/440–6000.

2 *h-4*
GOTTSCHALKS
You'd think it's a local landmark, but it's really from California. Clothing and accessories departments are mostly modern and youthful, with a mix of designer-label items; classic items are more colorful than dull. Most stores include a housewares section—and a bridal registry, cosmetics, and linens. Shop at the end of summer and mid-January, when prices for last-season's lines can drop as much as 75%. *Crossroads Shopping Center, 15600 NE 8th St. (at 156th Ave. NE), Bellevue, 425/644–1111.*

2 *c-1*
Northgate Mall, Northgate Way (at 4th Ave. NE), Northgate, 206/367–7690.

1 *d-8*
SeaTac Mall, 1928 SeaTac Mall Blvd. (between 19th and 20th Aves. SW), Federal Way, 206/872–9895.

2 *f-5*
MERVYN'S
The hook for this California-based store is big-name brands at discount prices—indeed, they're company cousins with Target (and Marshall Fields). Their "trend experts" scan the boutique shops and runways to spot what's hot, and you'll find similar styles here for a lot less. There are clothes for every age, plus cosmetics, handbags, accessories, and housewares. *4216 124th Ave. SE (at NE 4th St.), Bellevue, 425/643–6554.*

2 *h-3*
17601 NE Union Hill Rd. (at 176th Ave. NE), Redmond, 425/558–9500.

9 *e-2*
NORDSTROM
The store that was a small Seattle shoe shop in 1901 (and relocated to new, double-size digs in the Frederick and Nelson Building in 1997) is now a full-service department store found in malls coast to coast. (Who knew that a century later luxury cars parked along Seattle's most notable streets would have license-plate frames declaring, "I'd rather be shopping at Nordstrom?") This high-class, high-quality spot is *the* shopping stop for those who want to project an image that's classic yet cutting-edge. (The little sailboat logo conveys it all.) Expert sales assistants quickly assess your size, best colors, and style, and cull an ensemble—or entire wardrobe—from the racks without missing a breath. Dress smart, sporty, or for business: you'll find shoes, jewelry, handbags, scarves, and accessories to match. The extensive cosmetics department has products and fragrances for both men and women. Hint: For bargains, scan *The Seattle Times* for Nordstrom's deep-discount sales—and don't miss the marked-down merchandise at the Nordstrom Rack (*see Clothing for Women/General, below*). *500 Pine St. (at 5th Ave.), Downtown, 206/628–2111.*

2 *f-4*
Bellevue Square, Bellevue Way (between NE 4th and 8th Sts.), Bellevue, 425/455–5800.

2 *c-1*
Northgate Mall, Northgate Way (at 4th Ave. NE), Northgate, 206/364–0400.

MALLS & MARKETS

The Puget Sound region has more than two dozen large malls that dot the distances between Federal Way to the south, Issaquah to the east, and Shoreline to the extreme north. Each has a different mood; some are indoor spaces, some are outside and span city blocks, with large green parks, fountains, and play areas between stores. There are several "super malls" that include a variety of discount stores, including supermarkets and members-only bulk warehouse stores like Costco and Sam's. It's easy to while away an entire day at one of the big complexes, given the range of restaurants, movie screens, game rooms, and shops in their midst.

But don't discount the small malls, which take on the neighborhood's character and often include shops selling locally handmade items. And you can't live in Seattle without going to one of the open markets at least once a season—in addition to all the delicious and fresh local produce, there's always a vast selection of handmade crafts and clothing, antiques, toys, and natural products for bath and body.

2 f-4
BELLEVUE GALLERIA
Although relatively small as malls go, this indoor shopping area is a convenient satellite to the bigger Bellevue Square mall. Stores include Habits for the Home, Men's Warehouse, Sahara Fine Arts, and Tower Records, but it's best to come for a day of spa pampering at Gene Juarez rather than for a whole day of shopping. There's plenty of evening entertainment to choose from afterward at four restaurants, the Rock Bottom Brewery, and Regal Cinemas. *550 106th Ave. NE (between NE 5th and 6th Sts.), Bellevue, 425/452–1934.*

2 f-4
BELLEVUE SQUARE
More than 200 stores are neatly organized into a stacked square of shops at Seattle's favorite outskirts' mall; notables include Nordstrom, the Bon Marché, Pottery Barn, and Crate and Barrel, and lots of smaller standbys, like Aveda, Banana Republic, Coach, Esprit, and Swatch. The wide walkways and benches make it a great place to take kids; in addition to many children's clothing stores, there's also a first-floor play area and a third-floor children's museum. The attached garage has free parking. *Bellevue Way (between NE 4th and 8th Sts.), Bellevue, 425/454–8096, www.bellevuesquare.com.*

11 c-2
BROADWAY MARKET
Small, locally based entrepreneurs fill many of the 40-some trendy shops at

this indoor three-floor mini-mall, but there are a few national names like the Gap and Urban Outfitters. Fred Meyer supermarket is the anchor store on the corner. The mini-mall has a strong following among Capitol Hill's major gay/lesbian community. There's a movie theater on the top floor and free parking in the underground lot. *401 Broadway St. E (between Thomas and Republican Sts.), Capitol Hill, 206/322–1610.*

2 f-3
CARILLON POINT
In the scoop of Yarrow Bay, Seattle's most attractive mall is fronted by a western view of Lake Washington and the forested hills of the opposite shores. Wander along the waterfront, where white sailboats skim the waves and ducks and muskrats paddle right up into the lily pads. It's a hot spot for sunset dining at the Yarrow Bay Grill or Cucina! Cucina!, but you can stop in at other times for a spa treatment at the Woodmark Hotel or a cut at Michael David Salon. The parking lot is free after 7 PM. *2000 Carillon Point (at Bellevue Way NE), Kirkland, 425/822–1700.*

10 g-6
CITY CENTRE
Representing the refined atmosphere of this high-gloss, high-glamour indoor mall are more than 20 exclusive shops, some with gold-gilded doorways and marble floors. Shops range from Barneys New York to the glittering Galleries of Nieman Marcus and Georgiou to Europa for Men and Facere Jewelry. If you're headed for the vogue shops, take the kids to the two-story FAO Schwarz on the northeast corner first. There's an attached parking garage, but it's pay by the half-hour. *1420 5th Ave. (at Pike St.), Downtown, 206/624–8800, www. shopcitycentre.com.*

2 g-4
CROSSROADS SHOPPING CENTER
Sometimes it's worth the trek to the Eastside. Sixty shops—including Bed, Bath, & Beyond, Gottschalks, and Old Navy—surround the open Public Market Stage where there's free live music 7:30–10 PM Friday and Saturday, and an open mike on Thursday 6–9 PM. A giant chessboard and playground are nearby, and the Crossroads Cinema anchors the southeast corner. If you're hungry, there are 23 restaurants to choose from. *Cross-*

roads Shopping Center, 15600 NE 8th St. (at 156th Ave. NE), Bellevue, 425/644–1111, www.crossroadsbellevue.com.

1 g-4

GILMAN VILLAGE

When you're bored with shopping the typical in-town malls, head up north for a refreshing change of stores. The look of this outdoor mall is up-style country, and, unlike generic stores found everywhere, the garden stores and art galleries add a sense of place and a Northwest feel; many of the clothing separates and gift items you'll find here are locally made. There are several small restaurants and three free parking lots. 317 Gilman Blvd. (at I–90), Issaquah, 425/392–6802.

1 e-2

KIRKLAND PARKPLACE

This big outdoor mall has a bit of everything, from supermarkets to drugstores to restaurants. With several salons, a 24-hour fitness center, a yoga facility, and a movie theater, it's more of an event site than a shopping spot—hence it's popularity with local youth on weekend evenings. There's free valet parking on weekdays near the Parkplace Office Supply (no gratuities accepted). 600 Central Way (at 6th Ave. NE), Kirkland, 425/827–7789.

2 c-1

NORTHGATE MALL

Big department stores anchoring this major northern mall include The Bon Marché, Nordstrom, Gottschalks, and JCPenney. There's a gathering of medium-price-range stores between them—Ann Taylor Loft, BabyGap and GapKids, Garden Botanika, The Limited—as well as a few Northwest favorites like Eddie Bauer. The usual dining court with fast-food fare is in the center. 350 Northgate Mall Blvd. (at 4th Ave. NF), Northgate, 206/362–4777.

10 g-6

PACIFIC PLACE

Cartier, Tiffany & Co., and Nicole Miller: The names read like an *In Style* listing of what the stars wore to the Oscars. Of course, there's informal wear, too—

Tommy Hilfiger, MaxMara, Club Monaco, Nicole Miller, BCBG, and bebe, among others. And there are housewares aplenty at Williams-Sonoma, Pottery Barn, and Restoration Hardware. Take a break at one of the five restaurants, or head to the top-floor cinema. There's a 24-hour parking garage (hint: after 5 PM, it's just $2 for four hours). 600 Pine St. (at 6th Ave.), Downtown, 206/405–2655, www.pacificplace seattle.com.

10 f-78

PIKE PLACE MARKET

So it's the city's quintessential tourist spot—but there are plenty of high-quality goods (and cheap stuff!) here for locals, too. And it's fun to wander between the colorful produce stands, ducking the occasional flying salmon, and sampling local pears or a handful of cinnamon cashews. Head below to the rabbit-warren of little antiques and used-book shops; you'll always find something kooky or kitschy to buy for under $5. Use the lot at 1531 Western Avenue (under the skybridge) and parking is free if you're in and out in an hour; it's also free after 5 PM if you eat in one of the Market restaurants. Don't miss the organic farmers' days (Wed.–Sun., mid-June–Oct. 31) and the Market Festival every Memorial Day weekend when the Parade of Pigs heads through the city streets. The fish stalls, bakeries, and farmers open early, as do restaurants that serve breakfast. Other restaurants stay open late. Otherwise the Market observes pretty regular business hours 10–6 Monday through Saturday and 11–5 on Sunday. 93 Pike St. (at 1st Ave.), Pike Place Market, 206/587–0351, www.pike-placemarket.com.

10 g-7

RAINIER SQUARE

The 5th Avenue Theater and the Rock Bottom Restaurant & Brewery establish this big indoor mall, with small and upscale stores—Barcelino, Brooks Brothers, Escada, Nancy Meyer—but the building is also home to several airline offices and a hotel. There's a big Eddie Bauer store and a branch of the University Bookstore, plus several small coffee-shops and delis. 1333 5th Ave. (at Union St.), Downtown, 206/628–5050.

2 f-2

REDMOND TOWN CENTER

There's an REI with a climbing rock here, as well as a Borders Books, Pier 1 Imports, and Victoria's Secret. The outdoor complex is laid out like an open village and interspersed with fountains

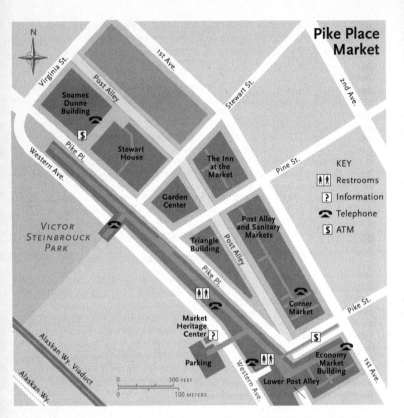

Pike Place Market

KEY

🚻 Restrooms
❓ Information
☎ Telephone
$ ATM

and play areas, so it's a nice place to bring children—note the big Zany Brainy store. Well-known clothing stores like the Gap and the Limited plus numerous bath and body stores like Garden Botanika join the roster of shops. There's also a Loews Cineplex, several large ethnic chain restaurants (Amigos, Cucina! Cucina!, Thai Ginger), and lots of free parking. *16495 NE 74th St. (between 164th and 165th Aves. NE), Redmond, 425/867–0808, www.shopredmondtowncenter.com.*

1 *d-8*

SEATAC MALL

An imposing giant several miles south of the city and right in the traffic crush between Highway 99 and I–5, the "super mall" is a can't-miss attraction on the west side of the highway. Both the vehicle and shopping crowds are divided between residents of Seattle and Tacoma flocking to this half-way point. Most of stores and restaurants are of generic national chains, and the Bon Marché, Gottschalks, Mervyn's, Nord-strom, and Sears are all here. There's a cinema and a big, free parking lot. *1928 S. SeaTac Mall Blvd. (between 19th and 20th Aves. SW), Federal Way, 253/839–6150, www.seatacmall.com.*

1 *e-6*

SOUTHCENTER MALL

Every child dreams of seeing The Rainforest Café, the restaurant with a cavernous tangle of thick tree trunks and leafy vines interspersed with huge fish tanks, live parrots, and animal figures that move within the sounds of a tropical storm. If you acquiesce, know there are several children's stores in the mall, too, each with a play area, and lots of places to sit in between them. There's plenty for adults, too, with 170-plus shops, a Mariner's team store, and all the major department stores. A string of strip malls outside the central building has some alluring shopping stops, so drive around first to plan your spending trip. *Southcenter Mall, 633 Southcenter Mall Blvd. (at I–5), Southcenter, 206/246–7400.*

1 *e-8*

SUPERMALL

The commercial motif here is on discounted brand-name labels. Some of the 130-plus major stores include Mikasa, the Gap, Donna Karan, Nordstrom Rack, Eddie Bauer, DKNY, Ann Taylor Loft, and others. The mall is arranged in a circle and you should bring the kids—there's a calliope, an inflated jumping house, and lots of room to run. Pick up a brochure at any Seattle information center and trade it in here at the guest services desk for a free coupon booklet and souvenir. *1101 Supermall Way (at 15th Ave. SW), Auburn, 253/833–9500, www.supermall.com.*

12 *d-4*

UWAJIMAYA

The International District's Japanese market is a colorful, block-size superstore for all-things Asian. A 30-ft-long red Chinese dragon hangs above the enormous grocery, where piles of produce front rows of packaged goods from Indonesia, the Philippines, India, Thailand, and more. Glass tanks containing fish, crabs, lobster, prawns, and geoducks comprise the incredible seafood section—and the frozen cases contain even more choices. For immediate gratification the food counters in back serve typical Japanese bento-box meals and Chinese stir-fry combos, plus Thai and Vietnamese noodles, Chinese pastries, and an assortment of jellied milk drinks and teas. The extensive housewares section has dishes, appliances, and decorations. There's also a card shop, a Hello Kitty corner, a bank, and Yuriko's cosmetics (*see* Fragrances & Skin Products in Beauty, *below*). Plan an extra hour to browse the attached Kinokuniya bookstore (*see* Special Interest in Books, *below*). The large parking lot is free for three hours on weekdays and two hours on weekends with a minimum $5 purchase (don't forget to have your ticket validated). *600 5th Ave. S (at Weller St.), International District, 206/624–6248, www.uwajimaya.com.*

2 *g-4*

15555 NE 24th (at Bel-Red Rd.), Bellevue, 425/747–9012.

6 *a-6*

UNIVERSITY VILLAGE

Many big names recently moved into this pretty, open-air mall including Anthropologie, Banana Republic, Baby-Gap, Butch Blum, Pottery Barn, and Williams-Sonoma. Casual yet somewhat upscale stores focus on self-pampering and gift items, like those found at Sephora and Restoration Hardware, respectively. Several discount and consignment clothing are in the area, too. If you love gardening, don't miss Molbak's. (On the other hand, if you love ice cream, don't miss Ben & Jerry's.) *NE 45th St. at 25th Ave. NE, University District, 206/523–0622, www.uvillage.com.*

10 *f-6*

WESTLAKE CENTER

Once the star of Seattle's posh shopping set, this flashy, glass-and-gold mall has had heavy competition in recent years from nearby upstarts like City Centre and Pacific Place. But with 70-plus shops, including Aveda, Godiva, the Galleries of Nieman Marcus, Fireworks, and Ann Taylor, Westlake still reigns as queen of the city shopping spree sites. It helps that, with the Monorail station on the third floor, it's directly on the tourist path between Downtown and the Seattle Center; plus the rocking food court, which carries more Northwest-known ethnic cuisine than fast food, is a key lunching spot. You can even park free across town and take a free in-city bus to the Westlake tunnel shop right under the mall. *400 Pine St. (at 4th Ave.), Downtown, 206/467–3044.*

SHOPPING NEIGHBORHOODS

Greater Seattle is a gathering of more than a dozen neighborhoods, each of which has its own look and personality. Seattleites love local goods and thus each area has a thriving core section of innovative shops that showcase the crafts and wares of the city's neighbors around the Sound. Yes, you might gravitate toward the malls for a mindless escape on gray weekends, but when the weather is good, it's the small shops that get a visit. And note how easily spent hours are wandering through the markets and stores. Chat with the owners to get the story behind what's on the shelves—and buy something to support the independent economy.

Neighborhoods are arranged from the Seattle core out in geographical order.

DOWNTOWN

Seattle's Downtown retail core might feel business-crisp by day, but it's casual and arts-centered by evening, and the shopping scene reflects both these moods. Executives bounce between the twin sets of posh malls—Westlake and Pacific Place, and Rainier Square and City Centre—while students, tourists, and weekend shoppers mill about the name-brand stores tucked in between them. Glitzy glass-and-chrome buildings house elite East Coast boutiques and upmarket California chain stores, reflecting the city's growing prominence among the country's major metropolitan areas. The Waterfront, with its kitschy small shops and open-air restaurants, is all tourists, but it's a fun place to dawdle on a day off. *Best shopping: 4th and 6th Aves. between Pine and Spring Sts.*

PIONEER SQUARE

This quaint, cobblestoned neighborhood of small craft shops and art galleries was centered around Pioneer Square, extends several blocks east to Occidental Park and south down to the water. Refurbished, late 19th-century buildings house rows of charming stores with high ceilings, wood floors, and exposed-brick walls. Inside is an amazing variety of handmade local and international crafts: clothing, household items, decorative art pieces, and all manner of *objets*. Small antiques shops are crowded in between the craft stores all the way down to Western Avenue, where the large furniture and home-accessories stores stretch down to Bell Street. *Best shopping: 1st Ave. S, between Cherry and Jackson Sts.*

INTERNATIONAL DISTRICT

Uwajimaya—the mega-market, bookstore, and eatery—is the major shopping attraction of the International District (I.D.). However, the rest of the neighborhood warrants browsing, too, since it's filled with small tea shops, groceries, and five-and-dime stores that show the city's strong Asian character. Here you can pick up authentic (and rare) Chinese teas and pastries, jade and gold jewelry, fresh Asian fruits and vegetables, and every Eastern herb and tincture you could possibly imagine. Look for the little souvenir shops, dusty and deep, where you can pick up Japanese kites, Vietnamese bowls, Chinese slippers, Korean art, and beautiful tea and dish sets. *Best shopping: S. King St., between 5th and 8th Aves. S.*

PIKE PLACE MARKET

The thriving Market captures all the flavors of the Northwest, with great bargains (and excellent views) to top off the experience. Though the main building is full of tourists, the excellent produce sold here comes at negotiable prices and the maze of underground shops houses fun trinkets and cheap treasures. The 9-acre historic district now not only includes the Market, but stretches north down Pike Place and Post Alley all the way to Virginia Street. Also *see* Malls & Markets, *above. Best shopping: In the market.*

BELLTOWN

Over the past decade, this former "fringe" neighborhood has turned into the city's fastest-growing retail corridor. If you haven't been here in awhile, you'll hardly recognize its polished new look, complete with eclectic clothing and housewares shops, humble art galleries, and trendy restaurants. The atmosphere is edgy and international, attracting a base crowd of single professionals who want to enjoy being close to Seattle without paying its price. Many places are closed on Sunday and Monday. *Best shopping: Along Bell St. and 1st Ave.*

CAPITOL HILL

Styling its shopping attractions for the hip and the rich, this hilltop neighborhood is a haunt of Seattle University students and Downtown professionals. The former shop for cheap, funky clothes in the consignment stores; the latter come trend-setting styles in the name-brand outlets. And everyone makes a run to the excellent used bookstores each season, both to stave off the winter blues and to stock up for the summer holidays. Broadway Market is the big style-conscious shopping center, but a gathering of small stores runs for about a mile along Broadway Avenue, and also along 15th Avenue East. The chic area is also the epicenter of Seattle's gay community, who flock to the ever-so-hip restaurants, shops, and clubs. A gathering of small shops runs for about a mile along Broadway, and also along the 15th Avenue East. *Best shopping: Broadway Ave., between E. Olive Way and E. Roy St., and 15th Ave. E, between E. John and Mercer Sts.*

WEST SEATTLE

In the summer, the beachside Alki neighborhood is all California: surfboards, roller skates, and bikinis. The waterside shopping strip has a line of casual restaurants and shops that cater to this easygoing culture, stocking basic necessities like beachwear, quick snacks, reading materials, and souvenirs. The real shopping area is actually a couple miles southwest along the Fauntleroy hill leading out of the ferry docks. This gathering of trendy clothing and tattoo shops, mixed in with antiques, furniture, and art stores, trickles north through the hills into the larger strip malls along California Avenue Southwest before ending at the Duwamish Head and Alki. *Best shopping: Fauntleroy Way SW between the ferry terminal and California Ave. SW.*

QUEEN ANNE

There are actually two shopping areas in this hillside neighborhood—around the Seattle Center at the bottom of the slopes and along Queen Anne Avenue North at the top. Across from the northeast entrance to the Seattle Center is the constantly bustling Larry's Market and a 24-hour Rite Aid, plus east along Queen Anne and Mercer avenues from here are tiny cafés and coffee shops, bookstores, antiques and consignment shops, and bike stores. The cluster of businesses at the top of the hill includes craft shops and coffeehouses. *Best shopping: Along Queen Ave. N between W. Harrison and Roy Sts. and between W. Galer and McGraw Sts.*

FREMONT

Home to all things inspiring and outrageous—including the wacky, impromptu annual Summer Solstice Parade—this openly creative community has built up a gathering of fun, colorful shops across from the Fremont Bridge. The two main roads, Fremont Place North and the busier Fremont Avenue North, merge at this conglomeration of quirky clothing, bed-and-bath, and housewares shops, but there's plenty of parking along the side streets. If you want originals by Seattle designers and artists, the finds here are top-quality and reasonably priced. To get a taste of what's available, don't miss the weekly summer Sunday Market along the waterfront (with free parking nearby). *Best shopping: The blocks bound by Fremont Pl. N and Evanston Ave. N to N. 34th St. and Aurora Ave. N.*

WALLINGFORD

It's just steps between the stores on the one-street business corridor of what's Seattle's Gen-X neighborhood. In the middle is the Wallingford Center—with several women's and children's clothing boutiques, a kids' hair salon, a big toy shop, and couple of furniture stores. Clothing shops, home-decorating boutiques, and bookstores also spread out from here in either direction. Despite the high-quality merchandise, prices are much less than in central Seattle, and there are several excellent used bookstores and clothing consignment shops. One of the city's best bookstores, Wide World Books and Maps, is around the corner from the Center on Wallingford Avenue North. *Best shopping: N. 45th St., between Woodlawn Ave. N and 1st Ave. NE.*

UNIVERSITY DISTRICT

The student clientele has kept the prices here low—and the merchandise unique and attractive. The parallel shopping corridors are along Roosevelt Way Northeast and University Way Northeast, each of which has a line of worn-looking but well-stocked book, clothing, and accessories stores. University Way NE has more shops and small, cheap ethnic restaurants, as well as the venerable main branch of the University Bookstore. (Check out the best of the neighborhood crafts and produce at the Saturday farmers market, which runs May through September). University Village shopping center, at 25th Avenue Northeast and Northeast 45th Street, is a gathering of large, classy brand-name stores like Pottery Barn and Williams-Sonoma, although there are several consignment and children's stores on the premises. *Best shopping: University Way NE between NE 42nd and 47th Sts.*

GREEN LAKE

Most of the shops and restaurants around the lake are concentrated along the north to northeast corners, but with just a few jewelry and clothing stores this is more a place to eat and chat than to browse. You'll find more stores along the west side of Phinney Avenue, which turns into Greenwood Avenue, but it's not a walk-and-shop road. The furniture, housewares, and small chain stores here are interspersed with fast-food restaurants, but to it's credit the neighborhood does have several good antique stores—notably Pelayo's. *Best shopping: Green Lake Dr. N.*

BALLARD

Ballard's two blocks are chock-full of wonderful shops: kitchen and home stores, a children's bookstore, antiques and import shops, and small cafés. Stores are small and attractive, with a friendly yet upscale ambience. Lingering is just fine. The hassles, though, are traffic and parking. Beat the crowds headed for the nearby Ballard Locks by coming early. Or plan to walk a few blocks from the closest parking spot to the shops. *Best shopping: NW Market St. between 20th and 24th Aves. NW.*

BELLEVUE

The shopping scene here rivals—and probably outshines—that of the city center, both in the number of elite, brand-name shops and in customer spending. High-rise buildings with sleek glass exteriors show that this is a powerful sister metropolis in the making, the core of which is Bellevue Square mall (on Bellevue Way, between Northeast 4th and 8th streets). Browsing here is like strolling through a modern king's mansion, but there's an equally attractive gathering of upscale shops and restaurants surrounding the mall's southwest corner. Bellevue Galleria and Bellevue Place are two smaller malls with similar attractions: upscale shops, restaurants, movies, and parking. Bellevue's retail strip is huge, stretching all the way from Bellevue Square between Northeast 4th and 8th streets to the enormous, department store–anchored Crossroads Shopping Center several miles to the east. *Best shopping: Bellevue Square.*

KIRKLAND

Kirkland now has a stretch of boutique shops, elegant restaurants, and patio bars along Lake Street South, which are where the city's rich and famous take their business when they want to get back to a small-town environment. It's not hard to see why—you can't beat the beauty of the waterfront Waverly and Marina parks, where geese and otters frolic in full view of picnickers. The relaxed coastal feel and scenic backdrops make Kirkland a worthwhile trip; if you want a mall-type experience, there are several within five minutes' drive. *Best shopping: Lake St. S between Central Way NE and 3rd Ave. S.*

REDMOND

Northern residents seeking space and solitude from Bellevue's ever-expanding city limits have brought the best of the shopping scene with them. Redmond Town Center is the main mall where the big names reside, many of them Northwest giants: Eddie Bauer, REI, and Gene Juarez, among others. There are also many little strip malls, filled with typical small clothing outlets, fast-food restaurants, and chain stores, along the main roads that link Redmond with Bellevue, Issaquah, and Woodinville. *Best shopping: Redmond Town Center.*

specialty shops

ANTIQUES

Although you'll find quality antiques stores throughout the Greater Seattle area, the largest cluster is Downtown near the water, particularly running from Pioneer Square north to between Westlake and Second avenues, and on through Pike Place Market, Belltown, and lower Capitol Hill. Outside of this wide strip, each neighborhood has at least a few small antiques and collectibles shops; notable among these areas are Fremont, Ballard, and Madison Park. Kirkland, Renton, Centralia, and Snohomish also have antique malls, regular markets, or streets of shops where you can spend a day browsing for rare and unusual items.

antiques centers & flea markets

12 *C-2*

PIONEER SQUARE ANTIQUE MALL

Descend into this 6,000-square-ft rabbit warren where every nook is filled with collectibles sold by 60-plus dealers. Searching for something old, odd, or even obscure? You'll find dishes, shoes, records, cameras, figurines, and all classics and kitsch in between—maybe that piece to complement your hard-to-match pattern. Beware: The items here span space and time, and you're likely to lose an hour or so yourself just wandering among them. Thankfully, there's a bathroom in back. *602 1st Ave. (at James St.), Pioneer Square, 206/624–1164.*

american & european

7 g-1

ANTIQUE ALLEY
Follow the hand-printed signs along the street to find the store with the casual attitude—"Visitors may be accompanied by children, dogs, coffee, and ice cream cones"—and the stash of candy and dog biscuits next to the counter. The merchandise is a mix of old and new items: a solid oak ship's wheel, walnut desks, golf clubs, pendulum clocks, and brightly colored carpets. If the price looks too high, just barter, haggle, or make an offer. Bring in your own attic's contents for appraisal or trade. *3519 Fremont Pl. N (at Evanston Ave. N), Fremont, 206/675–8835.*

1 e-8

ANTIQUE IMPORTERS
There's plenty of room under the highway overpass for cumbersome pieces and furniture sets. The cavernous space full of mostly European-derived wares is stocked with mostly large pieces: dark, heavy armoires, dining sets, bed frames, desks, and more. knickknacks are stuffed between shelves and into every corner—you might find an old glass lamp, a 1920s magazine, or a set of unusual brass keys. There are a couple of free parking spaces out front. *620 Alaskan Way (between Yesler and Columbia Sts.), Waterfront, 206/628–8905.*

10 e-7

ANTIQUE WAREHOUSE INC.
Squeeze through the aisles of American and English furniture to view quality tables, desks, and bedframes carved from mahogany, oak, walnut, and other hardwoods. Look for other antiques tucked into corners: telephones, books, toys, lamps, and knickknacks. With more than 400 old signs, the owner claims to have the Northwest's best selection. There's free parking while you shop. *1400 Alaskan Way (below Pine St.), Waterfront, 206/624–4683.*

4 g-9

ANTIQUES & HEIRLOOMS
Big, open showrooms (in an old, refurbished two-story home) allow for all-angle examination of the tall dressers, stately dish cabinets, slender side tables, and other merchandise, each with its own descriptive tag. A background of classical music creates an appropriate mood for perusing such fine European antiques. Park in one of the three spaces out front, or around the corner. *6019 15th Ave. NW (at 61st St.), Ballard, 206/706–5650. Closed Tues.–Wed.*

10 f-6

GREAT JONES HOME
Popular for its rustic, country-market style store and its 19th- and 20th-century French and American furnishings, Great Jones has iron bed frames, knobby wood tables, leather club chairs, and period accessories. Is the piece you like worn or scratched? Just throw one of the handmade shabby chic quilts, cushions, or slipcovers over the rough spots. *1921 2nd Ave. (between Virginia and Stewart Sts.), Downtown, 206/448–9405. Closed Sun.*

12 b-3

JEAN WILLIAMS ANTIQUES
The entrance is just a slim little shop door, but peek inside and you'll find deep rooms full of 18th- to 19th-century furnishings from England, France, and the United States. Note the upscale props: a gilded vanity with matching bench, elaborate mirrors, and thick, 5-ft-tall matching candlesticks. Although it's not a place to bring young ones, the store has such childhood delights as a Swiss chalet–style dollhouse and a painted gliding horse (with real horsehair for its mane and tail). You can also order handmade reproductions. *115 S. Jackson St. (between Occidental and 1st Aves. S), Pioneer Square, 206/622–1110. Closed Sun.*

5 b-2

PELAYO ANTIQUES
Fine 18th-, 19th-, and 20th-century European furnishings are the brilliance of Pedro Pelayo's shops, the original of which has been open since 1973. Danish country pine gets the attention here, but you'll also find pieces from England, Scandinavia, and Russia. Ceramics and porcelain, small antiques, and religious artifacts are sold, too. *7601 Greenwood Ave. N (at 76th Ave. NW), Green Lake, 206/789–1999.*

10 d-7

8421 Greenwood Ave. N (between 84th and 85th Aves. NW), Green Lake, 206/789–1333.

5 e-7
TIN HORSE
Specializing in children's furniture, the Tin Horse (just opened in summer 2001) carries some antiques and refinishes reproductions with an aged patina. Especially notable is the selection of whitewashed children's dressers, cribs, rocking horses, and chairs. Antique toys are set along a shelf near the ceiling. *Wallingford Center, 1815 N. 45th St. (between Wallingford and Burke Aves. N), Wallingford, 206/547–9966, www.thetinhorse.com.*

12 c-2
WINDOW ON THE PAST
You can bet on finding the perfect accent to fill that empty space on your mantel or baker's rack. Classic European and American restored home furnishings—at up to a 25% discount—including tall china cabinets, wide wooden tables, chunky dining chairs, and a range of country-style furniture, are arranged throughout the showroom. But it's the antique decorations that stand out, including enormous aqua and olive-green French wine bottles, wire egg baskets, and thin metal irons with wooden handles. *322 Occidental Ave. S (between S. Main and Jackson Aves.), Pioneer Square, 206/622–1846.*

asian

12 b-2
ASIAN STYLE
This big, bright shop is the place to go if you're looking for an elaborate, Korean multi-drawer dresser or armoire, or an Asian-style table that's a bit different from the ubiquitous Chinese and Indonesian pieces. Antiques here tend to be slightly more expensive than those in other Western Avenue shops, but the look is unique and the craftsmanship is high-quality. Just browsing for home accents? Grab a little ceramic teapot or a pagoda lamp. *915 Western Ave. (between Marion and Columbia Sts.), Pioneer Square, 206/628–3099.*

12 c-3
AZUMA GALLERY
Seattle has a rapidly growing market for all things Japanese, and this gallery is the core of the city's old Japanese arts. Wares include such antiques and folk art pieces as basketry, ceramics, and paintings. Even if you're not a buyer, it's

worth a look to see the diversity in the simple designs. *530 1st Ave. S (between S. King and Railroad Way S), Pioneer Square, 206/622–5599.*

12 b-1
BIG PEOPLE TOYS
It's a dark little shop, but it's full of large, elaborate Asian dressers, cupboards, and tables—almost all at $1,000 or less. And this is just a peek at the selection; the rest is in the warehouse (visits by appointment). The owners, who are chatty about the history and usefulness of each item, can modify a piece to best suit your space or decor. A brighter side room has exotic butterflies encased in glass, a tiny teapot collection, and a huge display of miniature glass bottles. *2203 1st Ave. S (at Marion St.), Belltown, 206/447–5654.*

12 c-3
CHIDORI ANTIQUES
Well-preserved, hand-painted Javanese leather *wayang kulit* shadow puppets and wooden *wayang golek* puppets top the front shelves at this Asian crafts shop. But look further and you'll find small ceramic pots, dishes, and wood carvings. Cloth panels, some painted with mountain scenes of China, decorate the walls. Note the selection of Asian musical instruments displayed beneath the counter. *108 S. Jackson St. (at 2nd St.), Pioneer Square, 206/343–7736.*

7 f-6
CRANE GALLERY
You can review exquisite, expensive pieces with important histories and browse the array of Chinese, Japanese, and Korean arts and antiques. The owners can also help locate unique Asian items for special collections. Recent exhibits included Vietnamese pieces from a Hoi An shipwreck, including a glass bottle dated 1480. *104 Roy St. (between 1st and 2nd Aves. W), Queen Anne, 206/298–9425. Closed Sun. and Mon.*

12 e-4
EILEEN OF CHINA
Although the banner hanging from this large, corner brick building has long announced a blow-out moving sale, the store doesn't appear to be going anywhere soon. Really it's the neighborhood's best-known antiques shop, and the selection ranges from rosewood din-

ing and living room sets, armoires, and cabinets to stone carvings and fine art. If you're interested in Chinese statues, take a peek into the gated area beneath the building to see replicas of the famous terra-cotta figures. *624 S. Dearborn St. (at Maynard Ave. S), International District, 206/624–0816.*

12 *c-3*

ELLIOTT BAY ANTIQUES
Simple, elegant, understated antiques behind tinted glass windows contribute to the store's professional, classy mise-en-scene. Each item—Chinese wardrobes, Bali daybeds, benches carved into ornate blossoms and swirls, rustic temple doors—is exquisite, and lovingly preserved. Come here for high-quality, high-price pieces, as well as such accents as stone jars, painted wooden statues, wall panels with Chinese lettering, and unique *objets. 165 S. Jackson St. (between Occidental and 2nd Aves. S), Pioneer Square, 206/340–0770. Closed Sun.*

10 *f-3*

GLENN RICHARDS
Depending on the day, you could stumble over items from China, India, Indonesia, Japan, the Philippines, and other points in Southeast Asia in this huge 15,000-square-ft Pan-Asian warehouse. Multi-compartment dressers, tea tables, privacy screens, and wooden chests are just a few items you might find to add panache to a room. Smaller pieces are also available, including lamps and garden accents. *Price–Asher Building, 964 Denny Way (between Fairview and Westlake Aves.), Belltown, 206/287–1877. Closed Mon.*

11 *b-8*

HONEYCHURCH ANTIQUES
This antiques shop and gallery, which has a sister shop in Hong Kong, bills itself as having the Northwest's largest selection of 19th-century Chinese and Japanese furniture. They might be telling the truth: The selection of armoires, credenzas, dressers, bedframes, and tables is vast, plus you'll also find fine-art and folk-art items. Check with the store for the dates of its bimonthly shows of Chinese ceramics and Japanese wood-block prints. *1008 James St. (between Terry and Boren Sts.), First Hill, 206/622–1225. Closed Sun. and Mon.*

collectibles

12 *c-2*

FLURY & COMPANY
With a focus on Native American art and antiques, Flury carries an admirable range of totem poles, woven blankets, baskets, jewelry, and tools. The shop also specializes in vintage photography, and has a comprehensive selection of photogravures, platinum and silver print photos, and goldtones in the original studio frames, some of which are displayed along the walls. *322 1st Ave. S (between S. Main and Jackson Sts.), Pioneer Square, 206/587–0260. Closed Sun. and Mon.*

auction houses

10 *e-5*

PACIFIC GALLERIES
At the southern edge of Belltown, a wide warehouse claims to be the Northwest's largest antique and auction site. Whether or not this is true, you'll find bargains on big furniture pieces: carved Asian teak cabinets, walnut dining sets, and carpets. Decorate your walls with oil paintings, porcelains, and other fine art. A schedule of auctions and events is posted on the front window. *2121 3rd Ave. (between Blanchard and Lenora Sts.), Belltown, 206/441–9990, www.pacgal.com.*

accessories

12 *b-1*

GREG DAVIDSON ANTIQUES
If it's ever been made, you can probably find or order that style of lighting here. The choices are staggering: gas, kerosene, and electric lamps are displayed among fine furnishings to show off their power and shine. Note the selection of Victorian, Tiffany, and Arts and Crafts pieces. *1020 1st Ave. (between Spring and Madison Sts.), Downtown, 206/625–0406.*

10 *e-7*

N.B. NICHOLS & SON
Among the "antiques, import objects, and extraordinary junk" here, some pieces date to 11th-century BC Egyptian finds. Repeat visits might unearth pieces from Asia, Africa, or European countries, much of it attractive and some of it quite valuable. *1924 Post Alley (between Virginia and Stewart Sts.), Pike*

Place Market, 206/448–8906. Closed Sun. and Mon.

10 *f-8*

PORTER DAVIS ANTIQUES
Basically it's a frilly showroom for 18th- and 19th-century European and American furniture and accessories to fill odd spaces. If the polished mahogany pieces or elaborate divans don't catch your eye, the shine of crystal chandeliers, old silver, and dainty glassware surely will. *103 University St. (at 1st Ave.), Downtown, 206/622–5310. Closed Sun.*

10 *f-2*

SEATTLE BUILDING SALVAGE
You'll literally find everything *and* the kitchen sink here, including pre-1940 building fixtures, doorknobs, chandeliers, and claw-foot tubs. Art Deco pieces sit side-by-side Victorian ones. *330 Westlake Ave. (at Harrison St.), Downtown, 206/381–3453. Closed Sun. and Mon.*

10 *e-7*

TWO ANGELS ANTIQUES
High ceilings and creative window displays show off key 17th- to 19th-century pieces and knickknacks, some of which are museum quality. If you can't find what you want here, make an appointment to see the 4,000-square-ft warehouse. *1527 Western Ave. (across from the Pike Place Hill Climb), Pike Place Market, 206/340–6005. Closed Sun.*

11 *e-3*

WEATHERFORD ANTIQUES & INTERIORS
With mostly 18th-century English and French furniture—and scads of Asian carpets, porcelains, and screens—this 1894 mansion could very well be a museum. An on-site design team can advise you on starting a collection of pieces, or on how to display antiques in a modern home setting. The Downtown gallery specializes in commercial collections. *133 14th Ave. E (at E. John St.), Capitol Hill, 206/329–6533, www.gallery.net.*

10 *g-8*

Washington Mutual Tower, 1200 2nd Ave. (at Seneca St.), Downtown, 206/624–3514.

10 *f-3*

WESTLAKE ANTIQUE MALL
More than 65 dealers gather here to sell (and buy) antiques and collectibles, including furniture, paintings, glass, silver, and jewelry. There's a bit of everything, some of it worthy and some of it worthless. Don't miss the antiquarian children's and illustrated bookstore. There's free parking and a deli, too. *222 Westlake Ave. N (between Thomas and John Sts.), Downtown, 206/628–3117.*

ART SUPPLIES

10 *e-6*

SEATTLE ART SUPPLY
Paints, paper, portfolios, and arts-and-crafts materials are available in various price ranges—but look in the weekly papers for frequent sales. It's a great place to browse, too, with more than 1,000 items to give you a million ideas. Bookbinding supplies, custom framing, and free delivery are available. *2108 Western Ave. (at Lenora St.), Belltown, 206/625–0711, www.seattleartsupply.com.*

3 *d-8*

DANIEL SMITH STORE FOR ARTISTS
From professional portfolio materials to children's items, this highly regarded store is a one-stop shop for all things artsy. Free demonstrations, workshops, and custom framing take place on site. To get here, drive 2 mi south of Safeco Field. *4150 1st Ave. S (at S. Dakota St.), South Seattle, 206/223–9599, www.danielsmith.com.*

13 *f-8*

15112 NE 24th St. (at 152nd Ave. NE), Bellevue, 425/643–1781.

BEADS

Handmade jewelry is all the rage in Seattle, among students, professionals, moms, and senior citizens alike. These are the best of the do-it-yourself bead craft shops, where you can often not only learn to make necklaces and such, but also to stitch and weave.

5 *g-4*

ALEXANDER'S BEAD BAZAAR
One-of-a-kind beads here include Czech crystal, gemstones, vintage seeds, and

bone beads. Create your own necklaces and bracelets, or look to the ethnic jewelry displays for ideas. Ask about after-inventory sales, when many beads are marked $6 and under. *6307 Roosevelt Way NE (between 63rd and 64th Sts.), University District, 206/526–8909, www.alexandersbeads.com.*

CRAFT EMPORIUM
See Crafts & Hobby Supplies, *below.*

4 *h-6*
FUSION BEADS
A generalist bead shop with a range of shapes and sizes has classes and a newsletter to help you make your own creations. *1111 NW Leary Way (between 11th and 14th Aves. NW), Ballard, 206/782–4595.*

11 *c-3*
WORLDBEADS
Pick up a tray and designing tools—or ask for professional guidance at the desk and peruse the mosaic of shining colors and shimmering metals. Workshops cost $10 and are held regularly; you can also take private classes. *233 Broadway St. E (between John and Thomas Sts. E), Capitol Hill, 206/323–4998.*

10 *e-6*
98 Virginia St. (between 1st and 2nd Aves.), Belltown, 206/441–7022.

BEAUTY

Grunge may have grown up here and Seattleites may love the easygoing out-doors look, but they're actually suckers for pampering; thus, they've managed to cultivate quite a sophisticated range of shops specializing in personal care. Trendy hair salons and day spas are hot spots for gift certificates, girls'-nights-out, and getaways. And who hasn't spent an hour in a bath shop sniffing and testing all the delicious natural products created by innovative Northwest entrepreneurs?

From barbers to big-name salons, there's a style and price for everyone—and many salons also have inexpensive manicures, pedicures, and facials. If you're going for a new look, set up a consultation first (usually free), and ask about group discounts if you're planning a major event like a wedding. This may not be New York or L.A., but you can still get a high-fashion haircut before a big night out, or spend a low-stress weekend indulging in mud baths and massages. But if you'd rather stay in, you can put together a collection of sensuous international skin products that will add sparkle to a weekend escape.

fragrances & skin products

10 *f-6*
AVEDA
You'll almost feel the toxins easing out of your skin as you enter the cool, clinical store that first brought aromatherapy and beauty products together in the West. Try at least a few of the 700-plus lotions, oils, and hair treatments. All products are plant-based. Housecleaning agents, healthful-lifestyle work-shops, and other services are also available. *Westlake Center, 400 Pine St., Shop 20 (at 4th Ave.), Downtown, 206/623–0766, www.aveda.com.*

2 *f-4*
Bellevue Square, Bellevue Way (between NE 4th and 8th Sts.), Bellevue, 425/454–1375.

10 *g-6*
BODY SHOP
The England-based soap company, known for its environmentally conscious, animal-empathetic testing practices, is also a top stop for self-indulgence and gifts. Grab a fruit-scented soap, test a fragrant floral body lotion, or sample a juicy new lipstick. Prices are competitive with typical drugstore merchandise. *Pacific Place, 600 Pine St. (at 6th Ave.), Downtown, 206/624–4925.*

2 *f-4*
Bellevue Square, Bellevue Way (between NE 4th and 8th Sts.), Bellevue, 425/637–9535.

2 *c-1*
Northgate Mall, Northgate Way (at 4th Ave. NE), Northgate, 206/440–9378.

10 *f-6*
CRABTREE & EVELYN
Known for its upscale British Victorian–inspired products, the shadowed lighting, delicate bottles and jars, and thick washcloths sold here make you wish you could have a bath right in the store—and a downy bed to sleep in afterward. *Westlake Center, 400 Pine St. (at 4th Ave.), Downtown, 206/682–6776, www.crabtree-evelyn.com.*

2 *f-4*

Bellevue Square, Bellevue Way (between NE 4th and 8th Sts.), Bellevue, 425/451–8457.

7 *f-1*

DANDELION

Dark-brown glass jars labeled with names of herbs and little bottles of oils and scents line the walls at this tidy apothecary and perfumery. Look for thick, chunky soaps, like honey oat scented with vanilla. Or just mix up a unique fragrance to fit your mood for the day. *708 N. 34th St. (at Fremont Ave. N), Fremont, 206/545–8892 or 877/778–4869, www.dandelionbotanical.com.*

7 *f-1*

ESSENZA

You can mix and match scents on strips of paper amid the flowing white curtains, whitewashed walls, and soft Spanish music—or rifle through the perfume sachets and makeup. A side room has gift items like robes, pajamas, and children's clothes. *615 N. 35th St. (at Fremont Pl. N), Fremont, 206/547–4895, www.essenzainc.com.*

10 *f-6*

GARDEN BOTANIKA

What began as an environmentally conscious skin, hair, and body products shop by three Northwest natives has taken just a decade to grow into a thriving business with 100-plus stores. And it's all natural—no petroleum products or animal products, no animal testing, and minimal packaging—for minimum environmental impact. For the extra effort, the lotions, shampoos, and cosmetics are competitively priced and quite attractive. *Westlake Center, 400 Pine St. (at 4th Ave.), Downtown, 206/624–8292, www.gardenbotanika.com.*

6 *a-4*

THE HERBALIST

In one stop, you could fill your bathroom for a year with the comprehensive assortment of products here—cosmetics, oils, soaps, shampoos, and fragrances, plus a full range of vitamins and herbs, and books to tell you how to use them. *2106 NE 65th St. (at 21st Ave. NE), Ravenna, 206/523–2600.*

10 *g-6*

L'OCCITANE

The exclusive fragrances and upscale body products here come from all corners of the earth. Look for soothing Vetyver fragrance—the Indian oil of tranquillity—and revitalizing leg gels. Discounts are given for large purchases. *Pacific Place, 600 Pine St., (at 6th Ave.), Downtown, 206/903–6693.*

10 *g-7*

PARFUMERIE ELIZABETH GEORGE

Specializing in custom-made perfumes, this shop's professional consultants will test your skin's pH content, match a scent, and then help you learn to wear it. Have them put it in one of the pretty atomizers or suggest a matching lotion. They can also make less-expensive copies of rare perfumes and designer fragrances. *1424 4th Ave. (at Pike St.), Downtown, 206/622–7212. Closed Sun.*

12 *b-1*

PARFUMERIE NASREEN

Even against its many fragrance-and-bath competitors, this small perfumery still holds strong, with more than 400 perfumes in stock, many of which are international. *Alexis Hotel, 1005 1st Ave. (at Madison St.), Downtown, 206/682–3549. Closed Sun.*

2 *f-4*

SEPHORA

Makeup now has its own department store, with a signature fire-red carpet, and shelves meticulously organized by brand—from Blisslabs to Philosophy. Oversize photos of made-up eyes on the walls aim to inspire. Or let one of the crisply trained staff make you up. *Bellevue Square, Bellevue Way, (between NE 4th and 8th Sts.), Bellevue, 425/467–1337, www.sephora.com.*

6 *a-6*

2566 NE University Village (at 25th Ave. NE), University District, 206/526–9110.

5 *g-7*

SOAP BOX

The city's oldest specialty soap shop now has a range of products from around the world. Check out the bath products, lotions, sponges, brushes, and other toiletries, both for getting clean and for having fun. The staff can also mix any scent you like to personalize a lotion, oil, or bubble bath. *4340 University Way NE (between 43rd and 45th Sts.), University District, 206/634–2379. www.soapboxltd.com.*

10 *f-7*
1916 Pike Pl. (at 1st Ave.), Pike Place Market, 206/441–5680.

3 *b-8*
4531 California Ave. SW (at Alaska Ave.), West Seattle, 206/932–3747.

10 *f-7*
TENZING MOMO & CO.
Duck into the Pike Place Market annex to the left of Rachel the pig and you'll soon catch a whiff of the incense floating above the scent of fresh-baked bread and iced fish. Follow your nose to the jumbled multi-faceted perfumery, herbal apothecary, library, and souvenir stop. Look for the varieties of rosebuds in glass jars and T. Momo aromatherapy products at the counter, where the friendly staff whip up tinctures for every ailment. *93 Pike St. (at 1st Ave.), Pike Place Market, 206/623–9837. Closed Sun.*

12 *d-4*
YURIKO'S
You can buy top-quality makeup and skin products, notably from the Shiseido line, with the help of a cosmetologist who considers the right shades for your skin. Facials, manicures, and pedicures are also available at the small clinic in back. *Uwajimaya, 600 5th Ave. S (at Weller St.), International District, 206/624–6248.*

hair care & salons

10 *g-8*
321 HAIR DESIGN
From high styles to basic trims, this basement shop with the black-and-white decor can meet your hair needs—and fast. Just jog down the stairs; walk-ins are welcome. Note the blackboard specials, like American crew cuts for under $10. *321 Seneca St. (between 2nd and 3rd Aves.), Downtown, 206/587–0130.*

10 *f-8*
BELLA VITA SALON
Trendy cuts, elegant styling, and "natural" makeovers are hallmark services, or you can shop from the full line of body products, including Aveda. If you're really tense, book a massage. *1334 1st Ave. (between Union and University Sts.), Downtown, 206/621–9936.*

5 *d-6*
THE EDGE
Targeting teens and in-betweens with current cuts, this small and busy shop pretty much requires an appointment. It's $21 for those under 12, $24 for teens, and $27 for men and $33 for women 20 and up. Plus, they have stacks of delicious bumblebumble products. *Wallingford Center, 1815 N. 45th St. (between Wallingford and Burke Aves. N), Wallingford, 206/633–2158.*

12 *a-1*
FEROCIOUS ANGELS
The innovative stylists at this little shop, named after a song lyric, will work with you to hone your present look or help you develop a new one. Cuts and colors run about $40. *55 Spring St. (between Western Ave. and Alaskan Way), Waterfront, 206/749–9840.*

10 *g-6*
GENE JUAREZ SALON & SPA
The trendy "stand-up haircut," in which you stand while the stylist insures an even cut, started here. Basic cuts start at $30, or at $40 for an experienced stylist. Consultations, make-up sessions, and follow-up bang trims are free (appointments necessary). At the Pine Street spa, have a cup of tea and luxurious foot soak in water infused with detoxifying algae. From here you can indulge in wraps, massages, facials or a hydromassage with 75 underwater jets that bubble stiffness away. Try the affordable Spa Glo treatment—an all-over salt rub followed by a soothing shower that feels like you're laying under a warm waterfall. (Note: Don't shave your legs the day of the treatment or you will know the meaning of having salt rubbed in your wounds.) Arrive early to take advantage of the eucalyptus steam chamber. Treatments start at $45; a Day of Beauty costs $260. *607 Pine St. (at 6th Ave.), Downtown, 206/326–6000, www.genejuarez.com.*

2 *f-4*
Bellevue Galleria, 550 106th Ave. NE (at NE 8th St.), Bellevue, 425/455–5511.

13 g-4

Redmond Town Center, 16495 NE 74th St. (between 164th and 165th Aves. NE), Redmond, 425/882–9000.

1 e-6

Southcenter Mall, 633 Southcenter Mall Blvd. (at I–5), Southcenter, 425/431–8888.

10 f-6

LEWIS FOX SALON

The humble salon in the back of the Bon Marché's Downtown store has been a Northwest icon for 20 years, achieving its fame by melding classic cuts and current looks. The savvy cuts (and color services) run $30–$70. *1601 4th Ave. (at Pine St.), Downtown, 206/332–0755.*

2 f-4

217 Bellevue Way NE (at NE 2nd Ave.), Bellevue, 425/451–4810.

5 d-6

L'IL CLIPPERS

A playhouse and toy bucket make haircuts less traumatic at this kids-only salon. Wee ones ride wooden figures—a train, a boat, a horse—while stylists work hard to charm their small charges. The prices (hovering around $20) mean that parents leave smiling, too. Be sure to make an appointment. *1815 N. 45th St. (between Wallingford and Burke Aves.), Wallingford, 206/633–2158.*

5 b-8

RUDY'S BARBERSHOP

"It's Cheap! It's Sexy!" say the ads. Cuts are cheap but appealing in a minimalist sort of way. Come when you need a basic buzz or trim—or a straight blade shave. It's really popular: Call to get your name on the list. *475 N. 36th (between Phinney Ave. and Francis St.), Fremont, 206/547–0818.*

10 g-6

614 Pine St. (at 6th Ave.), Downtown, 206/329–3008.

5 b-4

6415 Phinney Ave. N (between N. 64th and 65th Sts.), Phinney Ridge, 206/782–9861.

5 g-7

4738 University Way NE (between NE 45th and 47th Sts.), University District, 206/527–5267.

10 c-4

SALON COLUMBIA

A posh prettifying pit stop gives mostly Downtown professional the works on their lunch hour or before big evening events. Walk in for a cut or a service from the full menu of nail treatments, facials, and waxings. *Columbia Tower, 701 5th Ave., 2nd floor (at Columbia St.), Downtown, 206/386–7740. Closed Sun.*

12 b-3

STUDIO 904

Endure the parking hassles of Pioneer Square for a cut or color at this trend-setting, no-tipping, light and bright salon. A $12 fee is added for styling services (not included in color and treatments), but there's a self-stocked styling bar for self-serve primping. Studio is active in local fund-raising projects and causes. *401 1st Ave. S (at S. Jackson St.), Pioneer Square, 206/626–0904, www.studio904.com.*

2 e-6

3045 78th Ave. SE (between 77th Ave. SE and SE 29th St.), Mercer Island, 206/232–3393.

spas

Given that they live in one of the nation's fittest cities, it's no surprise that Seattleites enjoy feeling as good as they look with lots of heavenly pampering. The city's spas are surprisingly affordable and provide services and treatments that range from the aesthetic to the spiritually based treatment. Some, like Spa Bellissima, which has a psychotherapist on staff, have a more holistic focus, and are concerned with your ongoing well-being.

10 d-1

BRENDA BRYAN

Sometimes you don't want to leave the house. Bryan, a traveling massage therapist, knows this, and keeps all her equipment, including a portable massage table, in her car and is constantly on call. Give her a ring and she'll be there to work out those knots and kinks with reiki, Swedish, and deep-tissue techniques, along with a dose of aromatherapy—all in the comfort of your space. *206/427–3624.*

GENE JUAREZ SALON & SPA

See Hair Care and Salons.

9 e-4
JAROSLAVA SPA
Skin is "in" at this clinical salon, focusing on the care and hydration of what your aesthetician will remind you is your biggest organ. The spa's $470 "Grand Sampler" gives you the works or just get those cavernous pores clean as a whistle in treatments that can cost as much as $115. *1413 4th Ave. (at Union St.), Downtown, 206/623–3336.*

9 e-3
NAPOLITANO DAY SPA SALON
Partaking of spa services in a 1911 Queen Anne Victorian has a comfortable homey appeal. The spa, upstairs from the hair salon, specializes in electrolysis, microdermabrasion, salt polish, waxing, and facials. Crown yourself "Queen Anne For a Day," for six hours of treatments for $275. Or simply try the Tea Bath, a long soak in Napolitano's claw-foot tub steeping in herbs the spa grows in its garden. *614 W. McGraw St. (at 6th Ave. W), Queen Anne, 206/282–4343.*

9 e-4
ROBERT LEONARD DAY SPA
A spacial mute button relegates the honking and braying to the city streets below. Here, in quiet repose, you can treat yourself to a candlelit thalassotherapy massaging bath or get a facial, which rivals those given at Woodmark's. Or, for the truly indulgent, relax into eight hours of treatments in the $485 "Ultimate Day" package. It's worth the late charge on your rent. *2033 6th Ave. (at Virginia St.), Downtown, 206/441–9900.*

9 e-3
SALISH LODGE
Cedar scent and essential oils permeate Salish, a Northwest-flavored escape only minutes from Seattle. In the skylight-illuminated wooden rooms you can be wrapped in detoxifying mud harvested from the dead sea, soak in a hot bath while gazing at the black Cascade foothills, or surrender to a facial. *6501 Railroad Ave. SE (at SE 1st St.), Snoqualmie, 425/888–2556. www.salishlodge.com.*

10 d-1
SPA BELLISIMA
Treating the body as well as the mind, the staff includes aestheticians, massage therapists, and a psychological counselor. Come for the custom-blended facials made from natural ingredients, so raw honey, ground sesame seeds, and citrus show up in products given in rooms with diaphanous gauze "clouds" overhead. Visit the steam room and breathe deeply—essential oils and herbs infuse the mist. Or come for a massage. There's even one for expectant mothers. *2620 2nd Ave. (at Cedar St.), Belltown, 206/956–4156.*

9 e-3
SPA NORDSTROM
Give yourself over to the experts for unreal treatments taken from all over the world. Try the Shirodhara, a relaxing scalp massage using herbal-infused oil that is first dripped on the forehead, followed by a hand and foot massage—all for $90. Or try a stone massage: hot stones placed on your chakras and along your spine provide incomparable penetrating heat. Even the skeptical have to admit it works. The creative treatments here are typically expensive but are worth it. *5th floor; 500 Pine St. (between 5th and 6th Aves.), Downtown, 206/628–1670, www.nordstrom.com/spanordstrom.*

9 e-4
SPA AT THE WOODMARK
The 75-minute European facial gets you relaxed and your face clean. Sink into a heated bed as your face is cleansed, and your face, neck, shoulders, hand and arms receive a soothing massage. By the end you'll be floating on a warm cloud of bliss, with clean skin to boot, and a bag of samples at your side. Not bad for $80–$125. *Woodmark Hotel, 1200 Carillon Point (at Lake Washington Blvd), Kirkland, 425/822–3700 or 800/323–7500.*

9 e-4
SPA AT WILLOWS LODGE
The centerpiece is the spa's outdoor hot tub, a calm pool surrounded by rock sculptures and a miniature bubbling waterfall where you can recline and stare up at the sky. Inside you experience massages and skin treatments. Go for the pedicure, a truly royal treat where you lie back on a chaise while your feet receive the ultimate pampering. *Willows Lodge, 14580 NE 145th St. (by Sammamish River Regional Park), Woodinville, 425/424–2900, www.willowslodge.com/spa.htm.*

9 *e-3*

UMMELINA INTERNATIONAL DAY SPA

International touches include the hand-carved Javanese doors and silks, to a global selection of teas, to various "rituals" (a.k.a. treatments). Couples might try the three-hour Equator package, which includes relaxing under a waterfall before taking a scented steam sauna. This is followed by a salt rub with water massage, then a relaxing mud wrap in dry heat before returning to the waterfall—all for $280. *1525 4th Ave. (between Pike and Pine Sts.), Downtown, 206/624–1370. www.ummelina.com.*

BOOKS

If there's one thing that ties all Seattle residents together, it's a deep love of books. And, judging from the number of stores about town, they're voracious readers, gobbling up everything from highbrow literature to down-and-out bios and tell-all travel tales. As always, we love to save money, and there is a prevalence of used bookstores in many neighborhoods. Our community has always been supportive of the independent bookselling and publishing industry, which flourishes in our region and has given us wonderful small stores that are full of color and character. Besides, there's no better place to spend a gray winter afternoon than sipping a hot drink while browsing through cherished old tomes.

antiquarian, collector's, & out-of-print editions

10 *f-8*

ARUNDEL BOOKS

Choose from more than 80,000 antiquarian, collectible, used, and new books at this well-known store. Bowles, Bukowski, Fante, and other Black Sparrow Press titles are advertised specialties. Want to send a book to a friend? Worldwide shipping is available. *1113 1st Ave. (between Seneca and Spring Sts.), Downtown, 206/624–4442.*

5 *d-8*

BOWIE & COMPANY BOOKSELLERS

Here you can find antiquarian and rare books from as early as the 15th century, as well old maps and book accessories.

Be prepared to pay dearly for the high-quality goods—costs run $5 to upwards of $70,000. Bowie will appraise and buy your books as well. Call for a mail-order catalogue. *3831 Stone Way N (between N. 38th and N. 39th Sts.), Fremont, 206/624–4100.*

12 *c-2*

DAVID ISHII, BOOKSELLER

The store looks like your grandfather's home office, a mish-mash of books stacked to the high ceiling and scattered about the tables. But plan extra time, and bring a few extra dollars, for the search through the titles almost always yields rare finds. Specialties are books on baseball and fly-fishing, and there are lots of oversize coffee-table volumes as well. *212 1st Ave. S (between Main and S. Washington Sts.), Pioneer Square, 206/622–4719.*

12 *c-2*

WESSEL & LIEBERMAN BOOKSELLERS

The store's philosophy imparted in Thoreau's words hangs on a banner out front: "Books are the wealth of the world and the first inheritance of generations and nations." Readers come here for first-edition fiction titles and books of unusual shapes—miniature books, take-apart books, books with cigar-box covers—and to browse interminably. Don't be intimidated by the clipped, upper-class accents of the knowledgeable staff—they love books just as much as you do. *208 1st Ave. S (at S. Washington), Pioneer Square, 206/682–3545. Closed Sun.*

binding

12 *c-2*

ARS OBSCURA

With minimal effort, you can restore or rebind rare and cherished books here. You can also create journals, boxes, and make other projects; the beautiful papers in the window display inspire lots of ideas. *214 1st Ave. S, Studio B11 (between Main and S. Washington Sts.), Pioneer Square, 206/340–8810.*

children's books

2 *d-3*

ALL FOR KIDS BOOKS & MUSIC

When you bring kids to the U-District, keep them busy here with top children's titles, games, and activities. Story time, crafts, music, and other events are scheduled almost daily except in August. *2900 NE Blakely St. (at 29th Ave. NE), University District, 206/526–2768.*

general interest

11 *c-2*

BAILEY/COY BOOKS

Through the red door you'll find books and magazines on all subjects. The open, well-illuminated rooms make for browsing without bumping—and it can get crowded on weekends. "Perfectly lovely books at ridiculously low prices" (a.k.a. remainders) are on a table in front. *414 Broadway E (between Harrison and Republican Sts.), Capitol Hill, 206/323–8842.*

10 *g-6*

BARNES & NOBLE, INC.

Everyone knows this capacious bookselling giant, which now has 12 branches around Puget Sound. If you can't find a book, magazine, newspaper, or CD anywhere else, you can be sure they'll order it for you (and gift wrap it free). *Pacific Place, 600 Pine St. (at 6th Ave.), Downtown, 206/264–1056, www.bn.com.*

2 *f-4*

626 106th Ave. NE (at NE 6th St.), Bellevue, 425/451–8463.

2 *f-4*

15600 NE 8th St. (at 156th Ave. NE), Bellevue, 425/644–1650.

6 *a-6*

2700 NE University Village (at 25th Ave. NE), University District, 206/517–4107.

10 *f-6*

BORDERS BOOKS & MUSIC

The other godfather of all things printed also has nearly all the media you could ask for—or they can get it for you. There's also a café where you can pore over your paper. Regular events include author talks and signings, workshops, and weekend music. *1501 4th Ave. (at Pine St.), Downtown, 206/622–4599, www.borders.com.*

2 *f-4*

505 Bellevue Square, Bellevue Way (between NE 4th and 8th Sts.), Bellevue, 425/990–8171.

13 *g-4*

Redmond Town Center (off Hwy. 520), Redmond, 425/869–1907.

1 *b-3*

EAGLE HARBOR BOOKS

Come to Bainbridge Island's liveliest bookstore to enjoy readings by nationally known authors, a great selection of books, and a good cup of Joe. *157 Winslow Way E (at Madison Ave.), Bainbridge Island, 206/842–5332, www. eagleharborbooks.com.*

12 *c-2*

ELLIOTT BAY BOOK COMPANY

The bookstore with the candy-cane-striped lettering that orders passersby to "READ" is as famous a local landmark as the Space Needle. It's easy to love the creaky wood floors, exposed-brick walls, lots of quiet corners, and wood shelves lined with delicious titles. Head downstairs to the café and browse the well-worn used books that line the walls. *101 S. Main St. (at 1st Ave. S), Pioneer Square, 206/624–6600, www.elliottbaybook.com.*

7 *f-1*

FREMONT PLACE BOOK COMPANY

It's a little shop, with a range of contemporary fiction including women's studies, gay and lesbian titles, and kids' books. A video- and book-rental library lends anything for $3.75 a week. Ask about book groups and conference services. *621 N. 35th St. (at Fremont Pl. N), Fremont, 206/ 547–5970.*

2 *e-6*

ISLAND BOOKS

Mercer Island's main bookstore stocks a selection of current titles, as well as some used books. The sizeable children's section has a playhouse and posts a monthly story-time calendar. If you want to send a book, gift wrapping and domestic shipping are free. *3014 78th Ave. SE (at SE 30th St.), Mercer Island, 206/232–6920.*

10 *f-7*

M COY BOOKS

It's not just the scent wafting from the espresso bar in back that draws you into this bookstore; the Downtown location and the extensive choice of popular and used titles means you invariably walk out with something you want. Come for book-related and author events, too. *117 Pine St. (between 1st and 2nd Aves.), Downtown, 206/623–5354.*

8 *h-4*

MADISON PARK BOOKS

Hum along with the classical music as you browse the shelves, taking note of those stocked with staff recommendations (and lengthy notes as to why). The store covers just about every topic, including lots of pretty coffee-table books and a children's area in back. On cold, rainy days, a circular in-store wood-stove crackles merrily, adding a cozy, home-library feel. *4105 E. Madison St. (between 41st and 42nd Sts. E), Madison Park, 206/328–7273. madisonparkbooks. com.*

10 *f-8*

MUSEUM STORE

One of the city's finest collections of art books is here. From West African stamping to Aboriginal art, nearly art form throughout the world is covered. A cleverly organized section on international artists has bios and books on their works. *100 University St. (at 1st Ave.), Downtown, 206/654–3231. Closed Mon.*

7 *f-4*

QUEEN ANNE AVENUE BOOKS

Don't know what you want to read? Come and browse the well-stocked shelves of this eclectic, independent bookstore—or pick something off the Queen Anne bestseller list. You're bound to find something to satisfy your reading urges here. *1629 Queen Anne Ave. N (at Blaine St.), Queen Anne, 206/283–5624, www.queenanneavebooks.com.*

5 *d-6*

SECOND STORY BOOKS

It's not a big shop, but it's a relaxing one, especially if you grab one of the comfy chairs in back; a separate children's section also quarantines the chaos. Genre highlights include a good selection of regional fiction (buy or check out via the rental library), magazines, and postcards. *Wallingford Center, 1815 N. 45th St. (between Wallingford and Burke Aves.), Wallingford, 206/547–4605.*

4 *f-5*

SECRET GARDEN BOOKSHOP

Formerly a children's bookstore, this shop is now a full-service, general book-store, featuring books for all ages; it still has a great selection of children's books. *2214 NW Market St. (between 22nd and 24th Aves. NW), Ballard, 206/789–5006, www.secretgardenbooks.com.*

1 *e-1*

THIRD PLACE BOOKS

It's not just a bookstore, although it stocks more than 200,000 new, used, and collectible books—it's a book *event* venue, with frequent author readings, book clubs, and free live music on weekend nights. Save your shekels for the annual sale at the end of June, when the store knocks 40% off all used books. *Lake Forest Towne Centre, 17171 Bothell Way NE (at Ballinger Way), Lake Forest Park, 206/366–3333, www. thirdplacebooks.com.*

7 *g-6*

TOWER BOOKS

Although it's best-known for music, this national chain store with the blinding neon sign has a broad books section with titles on every topic. It's open until midnight (365 days). *500 Mercer St. (at 5th Ave. N), Queen Anne, 206/283–4456, www.towerrecords.com.*

2 *f-4*

Bellevue Galleria, 550 106th Ave. NE (at NE 8th St.), Bellevue, 425/451–2557.

5 *g-7*

UNIVERSITY BOOKSTORE

Hailed as the country's largest college bookstore, this crowded, two-story building on the U-District's main shopping avenue can effortlessly steal hours from your day. Dig through the used-book tables in front before hitting your target section. En route you may hear an author reading or encounter book accessories, the children's toys, or the 15%–25% off popular titles. And, after all this time, don't forget to have your parking stub validated! This is also the city's best academic bookstore, so it's best to avoid shopping the first week of each quarter—particularly in fall—unless you enjoy standing in hour-long lines. *4326 University Way NE (at NE 43rd St.), University District, 206/634–3400.*

2 *f-4*

990 102nd Ave. NE (at NE 10th St.), Bellevue, 425/462–4500.

10 g-7

1225 4th Ave. (at University St.), Downtown, 206/545–9230.

special interest

11 b-5

BEYOND THE CLOSET BOOKSTORE

Gay and lesbian authors and topics and
titles get center stage here, but the store
also has lots of general-interest fiction,
including best-sellers, and titles by small
presses. 518 E. Pike St. (at Belmont
Ave.), Capitol Hill, 206/322–4609, 800/
238–8518, www.beyondthecloset.com.

5 f-6

CINEMA BOOKS

Movie magazines, posters, photos, and
books about movies are available at this
store beneath a cinema. 4753 Roosevelt
Way NE (between NE 47th and 50th
Sts.), University District, 206/547–7667.
Closed Sun.

5 f-4

EAST WEST BOOK SHOP

Ethereal titles focus on such New Age
topics as spirituality, self-help, feng shui,
and astrology. Friday night speakers'
forums and workshops cover similar
subjects—check the free newsletter for
the guest list. Tapes, videos, gifts, and
other items are also stocked. 6500 Roosevelt Way NE (at NE 65th St.), University
District, 206/523–3726 or 800/587–6002.
www.eastwestbookshop.com.

12 c-2

FLORA & FAUNA BOOKS

Like a garden gone feral, this store with
more than 25,000 new, used, and rare
titles is brimming over with volumes on
all things plant and animal—biology,
gardening, rare species, the environment, and history, among other topics.
You can sell your books here, too. 121 1st
Ave. S (at S. Washington), Pioneer
Square, 206/623–4727. Closed Sun.

12 d-4

KINOKUNIYA BOOKSTORE

Mostly Japanese-language titles and topics from a broader Asian perspective fill
the two-floor store. (English-language
books are few.) The cooking section is
top-notch, and there's an eclectic range
of children's books—with a long reading

bench in the middle, plus Hello Kitty
merchandise. Uwajimaya, 600 5th Ave. S
(at Weller St.), International District, 206/
624–6248, www.uwajimaya.com.

10 f-7

LEFT BANK BOOKS

New and used titles all with Leftist leanings comprise this co-op Market store.
Poetry, philosophy, political, and gay and
lesbian books are mostly what you'll
find. Pick up a button or bumper sticker
to go with your purchase. Corner Market
Building, 92 Pike St. (at 1st Ave.), Pike
Place Market, 206/622–0195.

10 f-7

MISTER E BOOKS

Although the name's a clever take on
the store's favored genre, you'll also find
popular fiction, travel guides, children's
books, and even LPs. Lots of shelf space
is also given to science fiction, fantasy,
and horror books. Take a look at the
signed editions by such famous authors
as Ray Bradbury and Maurice Sendak.
1501 Pike Place Market, Suite 432, 206/
622–5182.

5 e-7

OPEN BOOKS— A POEM EMPORIUM

Like wine with your poetry? This bar and
bookstore with frequent author readings
encourages a good dose of both. With
nary another bookstore exclusively
devoted to poetry, Open Books carries
new, used, and out-of-print titles. 2414
N. 45th St. (between Eastern and Sunnyside Aves.), Wallingford, 206/633–0811.
Closed Sun.–Mon.

12 b-1

PETER MILLER ARCHITECTURAL AND DESIGN BOOKS & SUPPLIES

The extensive selection of architecture
and design books and supplies makes
the sparse surroundings seem ironic.
Don't miss the section of Japanese and
European drafting implements. 1930 1st
Ave. (between Stewart and Virginia Sts.),
Pioneer Square, 206/441–4114.

11 b-7

PISTIL BOOKS & NEWS

Step into this shop for an alternative
look at world politics and other issues.
Shelves are also stocked with gay and

lesbian material, and there's a strong poetry section. *1013 E. Pike St. (between Nagel Pl. and 11th Ave.), Capitol Hill, 206/325–5401.*

5 *e-7*

SEATTLE MYSTERY BOOKSHOP

Thrillers, spy tales, true crime, and who-dunits line the shelves at this quaint shop—and the bargain prices make it easy to stock up for rainy weekends. *117 Cherry St. (between 1st and 2nd Aves. S), Pioneer Square, 206/587–5737.*

6 *a-4*

TREE OF LIFE JUDAICA

See Ethnic Items, *below.*

5 *e-7*

WIDE WORLD BOOKS & MAPS

With a comprehensive collection of travel guides and books on travel topics, it's one of the best Pacific Northwest stores in the genre. You can grab up all the accessories to go with your books, too, from maps, magazines, and language tapes to luggage, passport photos, and European rail passes. Each staff member is a long-time traveler, and many are authors themselves, so feel free to ask for advice. *4411A Wallingford Ave. N (between N. 45th and 44th Sts.), Wallingford, 206/634–3453, www. travelbooksandmaps.com.*

used books

1 *f-5*

BALLARD BOOKS

Browse the selection of popular used titles in peace and quiet while waiting for others to shop elsewhere. *2232 NW Market St. (between 22nd and 24th Aves. NW), Ballard, 206/782–0820.*

10 *f-6*

BEATTY BOOKSTORE

You never know what you'll find here: a rare fiction title, a worn traveler's diary, a kitschy craftsy coffee-table book, a how-to volume on field hockey, a cat nuzzling at your pant leg. With a large selection of titles (some dating back more than a century), Beatty is inarguably one of the city's best used bookstores—prices are reasonable, and the staff pays well for titles they buy. *1925 3rd Ave. (between*

Stewart and Virginia Sts.), Downtown, 206/728–2665. Closed Sun.

11 *e-2*

CHAMELEON

This simple, one-room shop with a world-weary feel is full of possibilities with lots of oversize and international titles (on art, science, medicine, history) overflowing the plywood shelves. Sorting through the mess produces bargains. Some rare and antiquarian titles are in stock. Call in advance, as hours are by chance except Saturdays from 12 to 4. *514 15th Ave. E (between Republican and Mercer Sts.), Capitol Hill, 206/323–0154.*

5 *g-6*

HALF PRICE BOOKS RECORDS MAGAZINES

We've all been here, and we love the deals, even if we always walk out with twice as much as we planned. The children's and history sections are particularly notable. You can sell your own books, too (though you'll probably get a better deal elsewhere). *4709 Roosevelt Way NE (between NE 47th and 50th Sts.), University District, 206/547–7859.*

2 *g-4*

Crossroads Shopping Center, 15600 NE 8th St. (at 156th Ave. NE), Suite F2, Bellevue, 425/747–6616.

11 *e-2*

HORIZON BOOKS

The 30-year-old store in a blue house is a maze of closet-size rooms lined with tall bookshelves, with every free space patchworked in posters, fliers, cards, and cartoons. The books here are in great condition, with lots of current fiction, nonfiction, magazines, and paperbacks. If it's a sunny day, sit on the blue porch bench by the cat and read your new book. *425 15th Ave. E (between Harrison and Republican Sts.), Capitol Hill, 206/329–3586.*

5 *g-4*

6512 Roosevelt Way NE (between NE 65th and 66th Sts.), University District, 206/523–4217.

5 *c-1*

8570 Greenwood Ave. N (between N. 87th and 88th Sts.), Green Lake, 206/781–4680.

10 b-1

TITLE WAVE BOOKS

This is Queen Anne's sweetest book-store, a neat, one-room shop full of fine used books. The high ceiling, clean-swept wood floor, and fresh air wafting through the screen door make it a refreshing place to browse. *7 Mercer St. (between Queen Anne Ave. N and 1st Ave. W), Queen Anne, 206/282–7687.*

11 c-3

TWICE SOLD TALES

Just surrender to the store's adage, "You can always catch the next bus," if linger-ing makes you late—although you may find yourself here all night on Fridays when the store is open 24 hours. It's not a neat or quiet place, but it has every-thing a beloved bookstore should: worn carpet, cats prowling, jumbled sections, and a deeply knowledgeable (and often opinionated) staff who can answer just about any book question. Popular authors (Kerouac, Foucalt, Marquez, and others) are always in stock, and used books fetch good prices. *905 John St. (at Broadway St.), Capitol Hill, 206/324–2421.*

5 g-7

1311 45th St. NE (between Brooklyn Ave. and University Way), University District, 206/545–4266.

7 g-1

3504 Fremont Ave. N (at N. 35th St.), Fre-mont, 206/632–3759.

5 d-6

VANDEWATER BOOKS

The paperbacks are downstairs, the nonfiction upstairs, and the free books are on the table while you wait to pay for your purchase (50¢ otherwise). If you enjoy spine-tingling subjects, head for the glass-walled "detectives, spies, and vampire room," complete with a big, soft chair where you can dive into a new story. *1716 N. 45th St. (between Dens-more and Wallingford Aves.), Wallingford, 206/633–3040.*

10 f-7

WOMEN'S HALL OF FAME

"Change how you see, not how you look," advises a Barbara Kruger–sound-ing sign at this women's bookstore. The selection of paperbacks, oversize books, and popular titles is small but signifi-cant, and includes an international cast of prize-winning writers. *93 Pike St., Level 3 (at 1st Ave.), Pike Place Market, 206/622–8427.*

CLOTHING & SHOES FOR CHILDREN

Seattle is a kid-friendly town. The parks have playgrounds, the city streets are interspersed with green spaces—and almost all stores have sections devoted to wee ones—plus designated areas for play. Kids' clothing stores often have toy sections. Whether you're shopping for gifts or you have kids in tow, and whether you're browsing with a blank check or a budget, you'll find plenty to buy. Don't miss the numerous consign-ment shops around town, many of which sell barely used clothing at a frac-tion of a cost, or cheaply new-clothes shops like Old Navy and GapKids.

2 f-4

BABY GUESS/GUESS KIDS

Buy this store's bright, high-quality, mix-and-match items for your firstborn and they'll last for all your kids—and per-haps even the grandkids. Tiny babies can snuggle into the soft onesies and blankets, or try on their first pair of miniature jeans. Toddler girls squeal at the pretty floral and patterned dresses, while older girls love the trendy hand-bags, wallets, jewelry, and shoes. Boys' billfolds, athletic shoes, and logo T-shirts are equally cool. *Bellevue Square, Bellevue Way (between NE 4th and 8th Sts.), Bellevue, 425/646–5078.*

1 e-6

Southcenter Mall, 633 Southcenter Mall Blvd. (at I–5), Southcenter, 206/241–7374.

5 d-6

BOSTON ST.

Here you'll find high-quality, low-price kids' clothes and their many props. Sale items, $5–$15, are right up front and along the back shelves. In between are rows of beautiful clothes and gifts, like the soft, handmade comforters or the mugs that read, "Having a bad day? Didn't get your way? Call 1-800-GRANDMA." *Wallingford Center, 1815 N. 45th St. (between Wallingford and Burke Aves.), Wallingford, 206/634–0580.*

13 g-4

Redmond Town Center, 16495 NE 74th St. (between 164th and 165th Aves. NE), Redmond, 425/895–0848.

6 a-6

A CHILD'S CLOSET

Since this consignment shop opened in 2001 it's been a hot spot among parents of young ones. Clothing sizes range from premies to size 7, and all the usual baby equipment is available. Bring in your kids' old clothing for cash. *University Plaza, 5025 25th Ave. NE (between NE 45th St. and Blakely Aves.), University District, 206/985–4402.*

10 g-8

FLORA & HENRI

Since 1998, owner Jane Hedreen has been designing children's clothes in classic fabrics: cotton, linen, silk, and wool. Inspired by vintage garments, the colors are soft and natural, the styles simple and sophisticated. Granted, you'll pay for such quality and finely detailed designs, but isn't your little one worth a splurge? *1215 1st Ave. (at Seneca St.), Downtown, 206/749–9698, www.floraandhenri.com.*

6 a-6

KID'S CLUB

Everything you need for your growing kids is here, including clothing for newborns up to size 10. Many items are 100% cotton. If your kids need a trim, the Hair Chair, a Paul Mitchell salon, is on site. *2676 NE University Village (at 25th Ave. NE), University District, 206/524–2553.*

2 g-4

Crossroads Shopping Center, 15600 NE 8th St. (at 156th Ave. NE), Bellevue, 425/643–5437.

5 d-6

KIDS ON 45TH

Check out the mix of pricey but cool-looking new clothes and hip shoes—and don't miss the dirt-cheap used items in mint condition. The consignments in back are a bargain: $2–$5 outfit separates, and $1 books and toys. *1720 N. 45th St. (between Densmore and Wallingford Aves.), Wallingford, 206/633–KIDS, www.kidson45th.com. Closed Sun.*

14 c-1

MERRY GO ROUND BABY NEWS

Serving Eastside families since 1947 with a full selection of furniture, equipment, clothes, accessories and baby supplies, the staff also knows a little something about nursery design, car seats, and more. Ask for large items to be delivered. *11111 NE 8th St. (at 112th Ave. NE), Bellevue, 425/454–1610.*

2 c-2

MIMI ROSE OUTLET STORE

Look for the pink balloon to find this wonderful children's store. The brand-name clothes are first-class quality—but 30% to 75% off retail-store prices. Sizes for babies through teens are available. *12027 Greenwood Ave. N (at 120th Ave. N), Greenwood, 206/361–1834.*

2 f-4

OILILY

This chain with the colorful clothes was started in 1963 by a Dutch couple who were frustrated with the lack of high-quality clothing they could find for their twin daughters. The lively print knits or bright solids for babies, children, and women are folded into decorative boxes when purchased. *Bellevue Square, Bellevue Way (between NE 4th and 8th Sts.), Bellevue, 425/688–0663.*

8 h-4

ORIGINAL CHILDREN'S SHOP

With exquisite, if expensive, clothing for babies and toddlers, the sticker prices may be shocking at first—$60 and up for top-quality dresses and hand-knit sweaters. Browse the sale rack outside to find last season's stuff discounted. *4114 E. Madison St. (between 41st and 42nd Aves. E), Madison Park, 206/328–7121.*

2 f-6

OSHKOSH B'GOSH

The store that became famous for its colorful overalls also carries high-quality dresses and separates for children. Matching accessories, like hats and toys go with any outfit. For discounts, try Great Northwest Factory Outlet just past Issaquah. *4092 Factoria Square Mall (at 128th Ave. SE), Bellevue, 425/957–7217.*

5 b-2

RISING STARS

If you're looking for unique children's items, try this shop specializing in locally made kids' clothing, toys, and gifts, the most popular of which is the Teddy Toes blanket. Kids stay busy in the store's treehouse while parents shop. *7404 Greenwood Ave. N (at NW 74th St.), Greenwood, 206/782–0238.*

6 a-6

SHOE ZOO

A shoe store where everyone knows your name? Well, sort of. They'll at least know your child's shoe size, if you've visited before. Building relationships with customers is important here, and they've been doing it for more than 20 years. Expect a great selection of high-quality items and attentive service. *2675 NE University Village (at 25th Ave. NE), University District, 206/525–2770.*

13 g-4

Redmond Town Center, 16495 NE 74th St. (between 164th and 165th Aves. NE), Redmond, 425/558–4743.

1 g-4

STARS CHILDREN'S WEAR

This is one big store—a superstore in fact—filled with aisles of moderately priced children's wear, toys, stuffed animals, gifts, books, music, and accessories. It's well worth the trip to Issaquah, especially on the weekends when free entertainment for families is often presented. *Gilman Village, 55 NE Gilman Blvd. (near Front St. N), Issaquah, 425/392–2941.*

8 h-4

SUN PRECAUTIONS

With head-to-toe outfits designed for sun protection, this shop buzzes year-round with those getting ready for summer somewhere in the world. The Solumbra clothing line, made of 30+ SPF fabric in light, pastel hues, provides all-day UVA and UVB protection even in tropical climates. There are grown-up sizes, too—ask for a catalogue. *4105 E. Madison St. (at 43rd Ave. E), Madison Park, 206/322–7057, www.sunprecautions. com. Closed Sun.–Mon.*

2 f-4

TALBOTS KIDS

At this upscale children's branch of the lauded women's fashion store you'll find bright, long-lasting clothes in durable fabrics. Styles follow the latest adult trends in a playful way: knitted cotton cardigans for newborns, two-piece silk and velour outfits for babies, and flowing dresses, striped turtlenecks, and corduroy jumpers for toddlers. *Bellevue Square, Bellevue Way (between NE 4th and 8th Sts.), Bellevue, 425/450–3375.*

CLOTHING FOR MEN/GENERAL

Guys hold their own when it comes to being in fashion. You're smart and style-conscious enough to let that tux or designer suit sneak into your closet, but laid-back enough to spend the weekend in jeans and plaid flannels. After all, this is not only where comfortable outdoor clothes became chic (in "Northwest colors," no less), but it's where the dot-com craze made casual mismatches in vogue.

Plenty of designer-label names have moved into the Downtown and Bellevue shopping centers, so you can put on a New York, California, or international professional look when you need it. But don't fret about expense—just go to the outlet malls and browse for off-season discounts if you're not ready to invest in the full-price goods. Judging from the throngs of men that fill the stores after work hours and on weekends, you'll be in good company.

classic & conservative

10 g-7

BARCELINO

If you're among Seattle's elite—or you'd like to mix with them—try this international clothing store. The business, formal, and sportswear is first-class, mostly in deep, basic colors with little flash. That you can add with the polished shoes, sleek attachés, one-of-a-kind ties, and semiprecious accessories. *Rainier Square, 411 Union (at 4th St.), Downtown, 206/262–9111, www.barcelino.com.*

2 f-4

Bellevue Square, Bellevue Way (between NE 4th and 8th Sts.), Bellevue, 425/462–2000.

10 g-7

BROOKS BROTHERS

This store began selling its fine, tailored clothing in 1818, and the selection is still classic—albeit supplemented by some career-casual pieces. Put together a business suit or formal outfit from a 5-trillion thread-count dress shirt down to the shiniest leather shoes. Watch for the annual sales, which knock 20%–50% off the merchandise. *1335 5th Ave. (between Union and University Sts.), Downtown, 206/624–4400, www.brooksbrothers-clothing.com.*

`2` *f-4*

Bellevue Square, Bellevue Way (between NE 4th and 8th Sts.), Bellevue, 425/646–9688.

`10` *g-7*

DAVID LAWRENCE

Want a cutting-edge look? You probably already shop here for the classic yet clever pieces. Labeled suits fill the racks—Hugo Boss, Donna Karan, Versace, and others—but there's plenty of casualwear, too. Jet-black outfits mix with bright prints and silks, plus hip additions by Dolce & Gabbana, John Varvatos, and Versace Jeans Couture. *1318 4th Ave. (between Union and University Sts.), Downtown, 206/622–2544, www.david-lawrence.com.*

`2` *f-4*

Bellevue Square, Bellevue Way (between NE 4th and 8th Sts.), Bellevue, 425/688–1669.

`10` *g-7*

EUROPA FOR MEN

Add a dose of international attitude to your look the fitted blazers, Remy leathers, St. Croix knits, and Coogie sweaters, which are just a taste of the wares. If you're not feeling brave, dip in first with a pick from the amazing tie selection. *City Centre, 1420 5th Ave. (at Pike St.), Downtown, 206/621–0350.*

`10` *g-7*

MARIO'S

Dare we call it the Barneys of Seattle? Since the Seattle branch opened in 1982, Mario's has defined Northwest high fashion and has been the destination on any stylish shopper's fashion pilgrimage. Racks teem with Armani, Calvin Klein, Helmut Lang, Prada, and pals—and there's a Hugo Boss Shop attached. You can also pick up shoes to match that finely tailored suit or tux. Service is sometimes slow, but the quality makes everything worth the wait. *1513 6th Ave. (at Pike St.), Downtown, 206/447–2677.*

contemporary & casual

`10` *g-6*

BANANA REPUBLIC

The sophisticated sibling of the Gap aims its de rigeur office-chic styles at grown-ups with desk jobs. Technofibers come and go, and the color palate can get a little excessive (who likes that shade of matte turquoise?), but you can always count on mid-priced professional staples, a good shoe selection, and some decidedly casual (but never sloppy) pieces. Some branches also carry housewares. The Downtown store is worth a visit just to see the restored 1916 Coliseum Theater Building in which it resides. *1506 5th Ave. (between Pike and Pine Sts.), Downtown, 206/622–2303, www.bananarepublic.com.*

`2` *f-4*

Bellevue Square, Bellevue Way (between NE 4th and 8th Sts.), Bellevue, 425/454–2431.

`6` *a-6*

5625 NE University Village (at 25th Ave. NE), University District, 206/525–5560.

`10` *g-7*

BUTCH BLUM

A good selection of chichi brands like Brioni, Donna Karan, and Vestimenta, among others, makes this elite store for men and women an efficient stop for designer attire. You'll find Neil Barret jackets and Zipper shoes, leather jackets, and swanky accessories. The store's famous for its first-class customer service and is one of six U.S. locations where you can find the exclusive Armani Black Label. The University District store has more casual wear. *1408 5th Ave. (at between Pike and Union Sts.), Downtown, 206/622–5760, www.butchblumworld.com.*

`6` *a-6*

4512 NE University Village (at 25th Ave. NE), University District, 206/524–5680.

`12` *d-6*

C.C. FILSON

One thing can be said for sure: more than a century of creating outdoor clothing perfected this Northwest icon's top-quality selections. You'll find every component of activewear here: sweaters, jackets, hats, footwear, and luggage. And you can try it all out with the right fishing and hunting gear: vests, chaps, game bags, bibs. The huge, log-stacked store makes you feel like you're already in a mountain cabin—albeit one with an attached clothing factory, an oversize 19th-century bird-hunting diorama, seven outdoor murals of local places, and an 11-ft company timeline. *1555 4th Ave. S (between S. Royal Brougham Way and S. Holgate St.), Downtown, 206/622–3147 or 800/297–1897, www.filson.com.*

10 *g-7*

EDDIE BAUER

The store that first defined Seattle's rumpled, sporty style is as popular as ever today. The men's clothing is still superb, with businesswear, outdoor attire, leisure clothing, and accessories made of thick, soft fabrics and autumnal Northwest colors. Women's and children's clothing are available at all stores, and you can find home furnishings at the University District branch. *1330 5th Ave. (at Union St.), Downtown, 206/622–2766, www.eddiebauer.com.*

6 *a-6*

2720 NE University Village (at 25th Ave. NE), University District, 206/527–2646.

2 *c-1*

Northgate Mall, Northgate Way (at 4th Ave. NE), Northgate, 206/367–7767.

10 *f-6*

FAST FORWARD

Paul Smith, Vivienne Westwood, Tocca, and others outfit big-spenders and splurgers. Whichever you are, you'll be glad to know your outfit won't have one-season wearability. Pieces are cool, but not so trendy that you'll wonder what you were thinking when you laid out a week's pay for an outfit. *1918 1st Ave. (at Olive Way), Downtown, 206/728–8050.*

KENNETH COLE

See Shoes & Boots, *below.*

10 *g-7*

NORTHWEST PENDLETON

The store that opened in 1863 with flannel shirts and sweaters to combat the winter chill has grown into a thriving business. The outdoor clothes and wool blankets are high-priced, but the quality is exceptional. Conservatively cut year-round wool blazers and skirts are also available for women. *1313 4th Ave. (between Union and University Sts.), Downtown, 206/682–4430, www.pendletonblankets.com.*

2 *f-4*

Bellevue Square, Bellevue Way (between NE 4th and 8th Sts.), Bellevue, 425/453–9040.

PANACHE

See Contemporary *in* Clothing for Women, *above.*

2 *f-4*

STRUCTURE

Not for the suit-and-tie crowd, the "Limited for men" hits the mark with college-age budget-minded shoppers. Styles are on the trendy side: The slim pants, thin dress shirts, turtlenecks, and sleek fabrics are perfect for a night out—though you can find casual work clothes and weekend wear here, too. *Bellevue Square, Bellevue Way (between NE 4th and 8th Sts.), Bellevue, 425/455–4160.*

2 *c-1*

Northgate Mall, Northgate Way (at 4th Ave. NE), Northgate, 206/367–5513.

10 *g-6*

TOMMY HILFIGER

Catering to a young, urban, and fresh-faced customer, this New York–based yet all-American sportswear company is big with the hip-hop and high school demographic. (Price tags confirm that the kids are borrowing from the folks.) If the looks are too youthful or fad-conscious, you can always pick up perfume, shoes, or something for the home. *Pacific Place, 600 Pine St. (at 6th Ave.), Downtown, 206/903–8448.*

11 *c-2*

URBAN OUTFITTERS

Mix store-bought punk and post-flannel grunge with some roll-on glitter and you get an idea of the cheap, casual pieces at this hip national chain. Bulldog tanks, trendy jeans, multi-holed belts, and Pumas are cleverly displayed from repurposed surfaces. The low-key design-conscious furniture and housewares at good prices can fill that first college apartment. *Broadway Market, 401 Broadway Ave. E (between Harrison and Republican Sts.), Capitol Hill, 206/322–1800, www.urbanoutfitters.com.*

11 *c-2*

ZEBRACLUB

Enter through the green tunnel past the shoes displayed in small, lighted caves. Once inside, wind your way through the casual, going-out-tonight trendy and kitschy clothes—boys and girls can pick out a Diesel jean jackets and a retro T-shirt, and, *voila!*, a new you! *Broadway Market, 401 Broadway St. E (between Harrison and Republican Sts.), Capitol Hill, 206/623–5572.*

discount & off-price

11 *c-2*

LOEHMANN'S

This large national chain sells clothes for men, women, and kids at deeply discounted prices. Shop carefully and you'll find designer skirts, jackets, suits, shoes, and accessories by DKNY, Emanuel, Fendi, Helmut Lang, and others. (Hint: Don't miss the Back Room, where the clothes are marked down another 30% to 65%.) *3620 128th Ave. SE (between SE 4th and 7th Sts.), Bellevue, 425/641–7596, www.loehmanns. com.*

10 *g-7*

MEN'S WAREHOUSE

Known for its discounts up to as much as 40% on designer outfits, suits, and accessories, men of all sizes (35 short to 54 extra-long are available) find formal wear less of a strain on the wallet and the psyche. In fact, if you're a guy who hates to shop, this is the place for you: everything is organized in an easy-to-browse arrangement and the sales staff lets you be. And you can pick up casual pieces, shoes, hats, and watches, too. *1404 4th Ave. (at Union St.), Downtown, 206/622–0570 or 800/776–7848.*

2 *f-4*

550 106th Ave. NE (between NE 5th and 6th Sts.), Bellevue, 425/453–6014.

10 *d-7*

500 NE Northgate Way (at 25th Ave. NE), Northgate, 206/366–8344.

1 *e-8*

1424 Supermall Way (at Hwy. 18), Auburn, 206/939–4942.

larger sizes

2 *f-4*

KAUFMAN'S

Tall, big, and athletically built men will find stylish work clothes, many with brand names, for every professional occupation and event. There's a nice selection of casual shirts and pants up to size 60. The store has been in business more than 40 years, and the salespeople are knowledgable about the intricacies of fitting all body types. *30 Bellevue Way (at NE 1st St.), Bellevue, 425/453–8255, www.kaufmans.com.*

CLOTHING FOR MEN/SPECIALTY

formal wear

10 *g-6*

BROCKLIND'S

Suits and separates by Christian Dior, Ralph Lauren, Claiborne, and Perry Ellis, among others, stock this century-old men's formal shop. Prices are very reasonable, and same-day tailoring service is available. Students get special rental rates, and the groom's tuxedo is free if the wedding party rents here. *500 Pike St. E (at 5th Ave.), Downtown, 206/325–8700 or 800/878–7900, www.brocklinds. com.*

2 *b-7*

4546 California Ave. SW (between SW 45th and 46th Sts.), West Seattle, 206/937–6720.

2 *b-7*

SHAFRAN'S APPAREL

You'll get expert attention and advice at this cozy shop, which has been in the men's fine apparel business since 1960. Sizes 3 to 60 are available, with discounts for children and groups. The groom gets a free tuxedo if the wedding party rents here. *4546 California Ave. SW (between SW 45th and 46th Sts.), West Seattle, 206/937–6720.*

10 *g-8*

TUX SHOP

With more than 75 styles in sizes 4–70, this chain store is the popular place to rent and buy formalwear. Pierre Cardin, Perry Ellis, and Oscar de la Renta are just a few of the available labels—and once you've nailed down the suit, you can choose from more than 125 vests. If you're renting with a group, ask for a discount. Work uniforms are also sold. *Four Seasons Olympic Hotel, 1212 4th Ave. (between Seneca and University Sts.), Downtown, 206/622–3900, www. thetuxshop.com.*

4 *f-5*

2232 NW Market St. (between 22nd and 24th Aves. NW), Ballard, 206/789–6047.

2 *f-2*

1 Lake St. (at Market St.), Kirkland, 425/822–8866.

2 *c-1*

Northgate Mall, Northgate Way (at 4th Ave. NE), Northgate, 206/365–4422.

ties & accessories

Brooks Brothers, Barneys, Nordstrom, and Mario's have large tie sections and consultants acquainted with how to knot them or purchase them for others. J. Crew and Banana Republic have a smaller selection at your-average-Joe prices.

10 *g-6*

TIFFANY & CO.

Yes, the famous jewelry and silver company, established in 1837, is the ultimate brand name in fine wares and prices are typically commensurate. But even if your dot-com business went bust, you can still score some affordable items from the hallmarked T&CO line, including a silver money clip ($65), cufflinks ($135), or business card case ($175). It's worth a trip to the store just to see the museum-quality displays of gift items, fragrances, and jeweled finery. *Pacific Place, 600 Pine St. (at 6th Ave.), Downtown, 206/264–1400, www.tiffany.com.*

CLOTHING FOR WOMEN/GENERAL

Flannel, polar fleece, Gortex. Seattle women know these fabrics well, but they hardly reflect what's really going on fashionwise. The city has attracted a slew of first-rate designer-label stores, where you can put together an outfit like those you've seen in the magazines. If that's not your thing, there's also a great choice of smaller boutiques featuring New York styles with a Seattle spin, and others with fine, handmade clothing by local artists. Of course, chain stores have joined the mix (who said we weren't interested in a few brand names!) and a new breed of upscale shops has appeared in the newer City Centre and Pacific Place Downtown malls. The Bellevue shopping centers have also brought in numerous power stores for women, but the prices, like those of the Downtown shops, can be heart-stopping. Never fear, though—there are always the outlet malls.

classic

10 *g-7*

ANN TAYLOR

If your style is best described as boardroom chic, you'll love this tailored line. Work suits run about $400, crisp pants about $120, and fitted blouses ($40 and up) come in bold and basic colors that mix and match. Accessories and shoes are available, too, and there's a selection of weekend wear. *City Centre, 1420 5th Ave. (at Pike St.), Downtown, 206/623–4818.*

10 *g-6*

600 Pine St. (at 6th Ave.), Downtown, 206/652–0663.

2 *f-4*

Bellevue Square, Bellevue Way (between NE 4th and 8th Sts.), Bellevue, 425/455–3470.

6 *a-6*

2550 NE University Village (at 25th Ave. NE), University District, 206/729–1132.

10 *g-7*

BARNEYS NEW YORK

See Department Stores, *above.*

10 *g-7*

BROOKS BROTHERS

See Classic & Conservative *in* Clothing for Men, *above.*

10 *g-7*

MARIO'S

See Classic & Conservative *in* Clothing for Men, *above.*

10 *f-7*

PASSPORT

Traveling to tropical climates? Linens and cottons mostly make up the casual below-the-knee dresses, mix-and-match pantsuits, nature-patterned summer outfits, and soft winter sweaters. You can also find jewelry, handbags, hosiery, and other accessories. *123 Pine St. (at 2nd Ave.), Downtown, 206/628–9799.*

12 *c-2*

RAGAZZI'S FLYING SHUTTLE

Since 1982, this shop has held its place as one of Seattle's best upscale boutiques, and it carries the city's largest collection of handmade jewelry and accessories by more than 100 local and nationally renowned artists. Professional consultants can help find you the most flattering styles from the hundreds of fancy dresses, suits, and separates. Top off the outfit with a handmade scarf or a one-of-a-kind piece of jewelry. *607 1st Ave. S (at Yesler St.), Pioneer Square, 206/343–9762.*

10 *f-6*
TALBOTS
Working women with big budgets appreciate the lure of Talbots' classic suits and simple dresses. The extensive selection of accessories and gracious sales clerks make it easy to put together an outfit for fun or business. *Westlake Center, 400 Pine St. (at 4th Ave. St.), Downtown, 206/903–1132.*

2 *f-4*
Bellevue Square, Bellevue Way (between NE 4th and 8th Sts.), Bellevue, 425/455–5058.

1 *e-6*
Southcenter Mall, 633 Southcenter Mall Blvd. (at I–5), Southcenter, 206/246–7400.

contemporary & casual

10 *g-6*
ANTHROPOLOGIE
Stylish shoppers wear this chain store's colorful, trend-setting styles. The fashions are funky with a classic twist—think big sister to Urban Outfitters—meaning you can still wear them off-season. The store also stocks vintage-esque and modern home accessories, furniture, and gifts. *1509 5th Ave. (at Pike St.), Downtown, 206/381–5900, www.anthropologie.com.*

6 *a-6*
University Village, 2673 NE University Village (at NE 45th St.), University District, 206/523–0622.

12 *b-1*
BABY & CO.
Though the name suggests clothes for wee ones, this is actually a women's store that focuses on a variety of popular styles—vintage, retro, casual, and country, to name a few. Stop by the whimsical window display for a hint at what's inside. *1936 1st Ave. (between*

Madison and Spring Sts.), Pioneer Square, 206/448–4077.

10 *g-6*
BCBG
This French acronym for "bon chic bon genre" is almost the equivalent of WASP—but there's nary an oxford shirt in sight. BCBG was one of the first "casual" designers to crash the couture-show circuit with catwalks of its own. Sleek lines, soft fabrics, and subtle hues with just a splash of color are the foundations. Expect light pantsuits, flowing dresses, mix-and-match skirts and blouses, and a selection of casuals. *Pacific Place, 600 Pine St. (at 6th Ave.), Downtown, 206/447–3400, www.bcbg.com.*

2 *f-4*
Bellevue Square, Bellevue Way (between NE 4th and 8th Sts.), Bellevue, 425/454–7691.

7 *f-1*
BLISS
It's The Gap with an edge—a bright white, wood-floor boutique with pulsating music and a range of inexpensive styles. Betsey Johnson dresses of all colors line one wall, while another rack holds a line of simple summer dresses, all $29. Check the discount bin in the back, where you might come across finds like White Rice separates for just $9. *3501 Fremont Ave. (at 35th Ave. N), Fremont, 206/623–6695.*

11 *c-3*
BROADWAY BOUTIQUE
If you want something funky and cheap, shop here for tropical-pattern halter tops, wide-leg pants, and platform shoes. Dress it all up with a zebra backpack or a feather boa for $5. *113 Broadway St. E (between Denny Way and E. John Sts.), Capitol Hill, 206/325–0430.*

10 *g-6*
COLDWATER CREEK
It's hard to believe it's a chain store: the gently rugged apparel has a down-to-earth edge (linen skirts, Tencel pants, drapey boat-neck chemises, turquoise and silver jewelry) so appreciated in the Northwest. *1511 5th Ave. (between Pike and Pine Sts.), Downtown, 206/903–0830, www.coldwatercreek.com.*

7 *f-1*

DREAM

Mix-and-match contemporary fashions are what you'll find here. Be sure to look in the *Seattle Weekly* for sales ads, which feature discount coupons and tickets for free nail polish. Large sizes are available at the First Hill store. *3427 Fremont Pl. N. (between 34th and 35th Aves. N), Fremont, 206/547–1211.*

11 *a-6*

1028 Madison Ave. (at Boren St.), First Hill, 206/839–0362.

10 *d-6*

ENDLESS KNOT

The racks inside this corner shop surround a beautiful teak Javanese day bed, which sets the mood for the Asian atmosphere. Chinese silk pajamas, batik skirts, silk separates, and simple cotton items are available in sizes small through 3X. Jewelry, scarves, and small gift items are also sold. *2300 1st Ave. (at Bell St.), Belltown, 206/448–0355.*

7 *f-1*

ENEXILE

The clothes at this offbeat shop are modern with an edge: classic jeans with an iridescent sheen, simple blouses decorated with long fringe, Hawaiian-print handbags. BCBG, DKNY, Anna Sui are some of the underwriters. Unique home items are used in displays. Shop here before that killer party and you'll walk out looking great—and with the perfect gift, too. *611 N. 35th St. (at Fremont Ave. N), Fremont, 206/633–5771.*

7 *f-1*

FRITZI RITZ

If you're into retro, shop here for that orange-and-melon checkered skirt, that bright pink-and-puke paisley jacket, or that psychedelic handbag. Going casual? Try one of the funky T-shirts, or a pair of lavender or mustard-yellow Converse gym shoes. *3425 Fremont Pl. N (between N. 34th and 35th Sts.), Fremont, 206/633–0929.*

10 *g-6*

GAP

Delivering the young, urban, and nouveau preppy looks that still rule the Northwest, and pretty much every other U.S. region, the casual-wear giant has stores all over town, plus its offsprings, BabyGap and GapKids. The prices are right and predictable—jeans and pants start around $30; sale items are $9.99, $19.99, and $29.99. BodyGap departments corner the cotton lingerie market with underwear, bras, and sleepwear for the ladies. *1530 5th Ave. (at Pine St.), Downtown, 206/625–1470, www.gap.com.*

2 *f-4*

Bellevue Square, Bellevue Way (between NE 4th and 8th Sts.), Bellevue, 425/454–9132.

11 *c-2*

Broadway Market, 401 Broadway St. E (between Harrison and Republican Sts.), Capitol Hill, 206/325–3852.

6 *a-6*

University Village, 2673 NE University Village (at 25th Ave. NE), University District, 206/525–2146.

2 *f-4*

GUESS

Rough-and-tumble, trend-setting styles define this edgy denim-heavy store that stocks such teen staples as jean jackets, zebra-striped skirts, leather coats, and chunky platform shoes. This is a top back-to-school shopping spot, too, where kids can buy the latest A-line skirts, flared pants, and cashmere sweaters. Don't think it's all casual and fad stuff, though—there are some sharp little black dresses and coy handbags that will endure every party season. Get mini sizes of similar stuff at Baby Guess/Guess Kids (*see* Clothing for Children, *above*). *Bellevue Square, Bellevue Way (between NE 4th and 8th Sts.), Bellevue, 425/646–5078, www.guess.com.*

1 *e-6*

Southcenter Mall, 633 Southcenter Mall Blvd. (at I–5), Southcenter, 206/241–7374.

10 *g-6*

J CREW

Preppy and stylish are the hallmark traits of this chain's high-quality collections of career and casual clothing. Business outfits include wool crepe, gabardine, and stretch herringbone suits. Put together a Northwest-style weekend outfit with a silk or cashmere sweater and a pair of cordouroys, chinos, or jeans—petites and tall sizes are available. The shoe and handbags and intimates come in classic styles at mid-range prices. Newer lines are the store's bath and body products and workout wear. *Pacific Place, 600 Pine St., Suite 115 (at 6th Ave.), Downtown, 206/652–9788, www.jcrew.com.*

2 *f-4*

Bellevue Square, Bellevue Way (between NE 4th and 8th Sts.), Bellevue, 425/451–2739.

7 *f-1*

LES AMIS

Tap into your romantic side with this shop's soft, lacy styles. The youthful fashions are fun to wear—and the stock changes with the seasons and trends. *3420 Evanston Ave. N (at N. 34th St.), Fremont, 206/632–2877.*

10 *f-6*

THE LIMITED

Those in search of an affordable knock-off shop here for the contemporary styles. Colors are dark and muted—charcoals, camels, olives, berries—and best fit tall, slender model types. The collections swipe characteristics from the latest designer trends, but the prices are far less—so you can fit looking good into your budget. *Westlake Center, 400 Pine St. (at 4th Ave.), Downtown, 206/624–3930, www.limited.com.*

2 *c-1*

Northgate Mall, 350 Northgate Mall Blvd. (at 4th Ave. NE), Northgate, 206/367–2607.

13 *g-4*

Redmond Town Center, 16409 NE 74th St. (between 164th and 165th Aves.), Redmond, 425/558–7565.

1 *e-6*

Southcenter Mall, 633 Southcenter Mall Blvd. (at I–5), Southcenter, 206/246–4148.

10 *g-6*

OLD NAVY

The big, warehouse-type stores have commercials you've seen, movie-marquee signs on the street, and piles of merchandise in-store—all this to say, you can't miss 'em and you can usually find what you want even amid the constant throng of shoppers. The casual, au courant styles for men, women, and wee ones are colorful and garage-sale cheap. Fabrics and quality are not always top-notch, but then replacement tees and jeans come cheaply. *601 Pine St. (at 6th Ave.), Downtown, 206/264–9341.*

2 *g-4*

Crossroads Shopping Center, 15600 NE 8th St. (at 156th Ave. NE), Bellevue, 425/562–4215.

4 *g-6*

OLIVINE ATELIER

This posh boutique, whose wares are often spotted in fashion magazines, carries such high-style items as Tocca dresses, Earl jeans, and pieces from Diane von Furstenberg, Jill Anderson, and Nuala. Look to the apothecary for nail polishes, soaps and candles, cosmetics, beauty cocktails, and hair products. Stash some extra cash to splurge on the delicate handmade bags, jewelry, scarves, and lingerie. *5344 Ballard Ave. NW (between 20th and 22nd Aves. NW), Ballard, 206/706–4188.*

9 *d-8*

PANACHE

The name is perfect for this light-filled store that carries pretty floral slip dresses with slanted, ruffled edges; batik sarong skirts; and chic silk separates. It stocks the requisite accessories, too: straw hats, woven handbags, platform sandals, and sunglasses. The extensive men's section also has dress clothes and shoes. *225 Broadway St. E (between Thomas and John Sts.), Capitol Hill, 206/726–3300.*

5 *d-7*

ROOM SERVICE

Going out? Amid vintage home furnishings and huge old suitcases pasted with the stickers of international cities, you'll find cute, girlish clothes, like dresses in bright fruit patterns (for a mere $30 and up), petite tops and tanks, sassy skirts, and accessories with flowers and rhinestones. *1717 N. 45th St. (between Densmore and Wallingford Aves.), Wallingford, 206/675–8602.*

5 *d-6*

YADZI FINE CLOTHING

Among the chic international outfits, Asian designs predominate, including a line by the Iranian owner and fashions from Indonesia and India. Faux silk, batik, and shimmering, sheer fabrics fill the racks, and there's jewelry behind the counter. Step across the hall for another room filled with glistening, vividly colored blouses, skirts, and dresses. *Wallingford Center, 1815 N. 45th St.*

(between Wallingford and Burke Aves.), Wallingford, 206/547–6008.

11 *c-2*

Broadway Market, 401 Broadway St. E (between Harrison and Republican Sts.), Capitol Hill, 206/860–7109.

10 *f-7*

93 Pike St. (at 1st Ave.), Pike Place Market, 206/682–0657.

designer

10 *g-7*

BETSEY JOHNSON

Splashy colors and wild prints define the fun, youthful look of this edgy designer. You can find bits of her line at other stores, but you can shop here and see all the dresses (around $200), poufy skirts, and corset tops—and get accessories, too. Check out the fun, vibrant Web site for future trends and hot gossip. *1429 5th Ave. (at Pike St.), Downtown, 206/624–2887, www.betseyjohnson.com.*

10 *g-6*

EILEEN FISHER

The entrepreneur who opened her New York store in 1986 with just five racks of her minimalist, drapey, solid-color garments has brought her expanded selection to Seattle. Petite sizes are in stock at other stores, but you can special-order them here. *525 Pine St. (at 5th and 6th Aves.), Downtown, 206/748–0770, www.eileenfisher.com.*

11 *c-1*

Redmond Town Center, 16495 NE 74th St. (between 164th and 165th Aves. NE), Redmond, 425/885–4560.

10 *g-7*

ESCADA

The tailored silk suits, simple yet stylish EscadaSport casual wear, Rock Chic leather wear, stretchy knit dresses, and even beaded gowns impart serious confidence when worn. Such composure comes at cost, though. Belts, shoes, and purses complete your big bucks outfit. *1302 5th Ave. (at University St.), Downtown, 206/223–9433. www.escada.com.*

5 *g-7*

HELEN'S OF COURSE/ JERI RICE

When you need that key ensemble piece, stop by this sophisticated boutique filled with European fashions and exclusive designer lines. Finds might include Jimmy Choo shoes, items by Rebecca Moses or Zoran, and accessories by a range of Italian designers. *421 University St. (between 4th and 5th Aves.), Downtown, 206/624–4000.*

2 *f-4*

800 Bellevue Way NE (at NE 8th St.), Bellevue, 425/462–1400.

10 *g-6*

MAXMARA

This chic European-style boutique, one of hundreds worldwide, has finally debuted in Seattle. What's here is smoking hot: skin-tight leather, pencil-thin pants, military gear in coffee and khaki, as well as a range of luxurious evening dresses. Best of all, you don't have to be tall and svelte to look good in most of what's available. *Pacific Place, 600 Pine St. (at 6th Ave.), Downtown, 206/264–2400.*

discount & off-price

10 *f-6*

ALEXANDRA'S

The thousands of designer-label pieces here on consignment look like they've hardly been worn. You'll find women's work, casual, and formal outfits by Armani, Calvin Klein, Donna Karan, and Richard Tyler, among many others. *412 Olive Way (between 4th and 5th Aves.), Capitol Hill, 206/623–1214.*

11 *c-2*

BUFFALO EXCHANGE

This big, bright shop of new and recycled fashions is always crowded—even on Saturday night—with UW girls looking for bargains. It will take time to browse the stuffed racks, but the trendy rewards are great: sequinned jeans, leather jackets, vintage-style dresses. Frequent sales slash prices 25%. Tip: This is a great place to find a Halloween costume. *4530 University Way NE (between NE 45th and 47th Sts.), University District, 206/545–0175, www. buffaloexchange.com.*

10 *f-7*

NORDSTROM RACK

Vigilant Seattle executives on the lookout for bargain clothing and shoes shop here. With prices 30%–75% off retail, and things for men, women, and kids, there's something for anyone who takes the time to dig through the racks. *1601*

2nd Ave. (between Pike and Pine Sts.), Downtown, 206/448–8522.

11 c-3

TAKE 2 CONSIGNMENT

The neatly arranged racks are full of smart, casual, new and used women's clothes, like floral skirts, slip dresses, and funky T-shirts. Top them off with a hat or beaded jewelry. 430 15th Ave. E (at Republican St.), Capitol Hill, 206/324–2569.

larger sizes

2 c-2

KATHLEEN'S

The assortment of casual pieces in soft pastels and bright prints come in sizes 16 through 60; business-wear styles, jewelry, and hosiery are also available. A full-size bridal salon has dresses for the entire wedding party (and lingerie, too). 12000 15th Ave. NE (at NE 120th St.), Northgate, 206/367–4564.

2 f-4

LANE BRYANT

One of the spearheading mass-marketers for larger sizes (going back to 1916!), this chain store carries both casual and moderately dressy lines in sizes 14–28. Check the back racks for deep discounts. Bellevue Square, Bellevue Way (between NE 4th and 8th Sts.), Bellevue, 425/453–2811.

1 e-5

TALL FASHIONS NORTHWEST

Women over 5' 6" will find a wealth of contemporary outfits and accessories at this casual clothing shop. Look for the half-off-everything sales in January and June. 216 Wells Ave. S (between S. 2nd and 3rd Sts.), Renton, 425/235–4900.

10 g-6

TALL GIRL

Long-legged, long-waisted women and girls will love the selection of casual, contemporary clothing—including jeans, jackets, swimsuits, lingerie, and accessories—in sizes 6–22. 1529 6th Ave. (at Pine St.), Downtown, 206/262–1985.

vintage

10 e-6

ISADORA'S

The early to mid-1900s attire here includes velvet gowns, wide-brimmed hats, cocktail dresses, and accessories. Exquisite handmade bridal gowns are a shop specialty, and you can find designer and antique bridal dresses in smaller sizes. 1915 1st Ave. (between Stewart and Virginia Sts.), Belltown, 206/441–7711.

11 d-5

LE FROCK

Hip top-label clothing and vintage wear is the rage at this "recycled" clothing store. Displays range from 1940s outfits to last-year's leftovers, including designer samples and shoes. 317 E. Pine St. (between Bellevue and Melrose Aves.), Capitol Hill, 206/623–5339.

11 c-2

RED LIGHT

Mix and match among the decades with miniskirts, feather boas, fab handbags, old-school designer jeans, men's camp shirts, and darling tops—items that were top of their line in their time . . . and campy in ours. Time-warp toys, lunch boxes, underwear sets, and other kitsch are also available. The store accepts consignments daily. 312 Broadway Ave. E (between Thomas and Harrison Sts.), Capitol Hill, 206/329–2200.

5 g-7

4560 University Way NE (between NE 45th and 47th Sts.), University District, 206/545–4044.

10 f-7

RUDY'S

It's the place to pick up mid-century styles (circa 1950s) in clothing (coats to casual outfits) and accessories, including watches. 109 Pine St. (between Pike and Union Sts.), Downtown, 206/682–6586.

CLOTHING FOR WOMEN/SPECIALTY

bridal

10 g-7

CICADA

If you'd rather design your own dress than rack shop—and you have the budget to do it right—Cicada will help you create the ultimate bridal gown. Browse through the books or racks for a look you like, then alter it to your own dreams. Top the dress off with a tiara, or choose from the gorgeous jewelry by local artists. *Rainier Square, 1333 5th Ave. (at Union St.), Downtown, 206/652–2434, www.cicadadesigns.com.*

5 *d-6*

I DO BRIDAL

The light, sunny atmosphere of this elegant one-room store sets the tone for a happy wedding-planning process. Browse the racks of dresses, or bring your own pattern to give the expert sales staff a few ideas. *Wallingford Center, 1815 N. 45th St. (between Wallingford and Burke Aves.), Wallingford, 206/633–7926, www.idobridal.com.*

2 *c-2*

MONIR'S

The professional seamstresses and fashion designers here whip up one-of-a-kind couture dresses for weddings and formal events. The styles lean toward European looks and are created from fine international fabrics special-ordered for the store. A quick look at the dresses shows that they're not only fabulous but functional, and can be easily altered for more casual use. *9226 Roosevelt Way (between NE 92nd and 93rd Sts.), Northgate, 206/547–1711, www.monircouture.com.*

furs

10 *g-7*

BOB MANDERS FURS

Since 1976 Bob Manders has cared for the finery of visiting glitterati. Complete fur service is offered, including cleaning, repairing, and storage. *1424 4th Ave. (at Pike St.), Downtown, 206/622–3076.*

5 *b-1*

EILERS FURS

The city's premier full-service furrier carries a wide selection of high-quality items. It's a one-stop shop, where you'll get fashion advice, cleaning tips, repair service, and attentive, knowledgeable assistance. The store also sells used furs and takes consignment items. *8213 Greenwood Ave. N (between 82nd and 83rd Sts.), Green Lake, 206/782–8563.*

2 *f-4*

FOERESTER FURS

The wealthy of Bellevue and Mercer Island have brought success to this local north Seattle furrier. Glazing, restyling, storage, and appraisals are the main services. *10500 NE 8th St., (at 105th Ave. NE), Bellevue, 425/637–6747.*

handbags

10 *g-6*

COACH

The dependable brand has dozens of classic leather handbags in deep, basic colors and patterns. Choose from signature styles, more whimsical limited editions (like the Girlie Suede Hobo bag, $180), or unique lines like Mercer, Hamptons, and Legacy. Business gifts might include briefcases, desk accessories, and cases for everything: business cards, cell phones, computers, and cosmetics. Belts, shoes, watches, wallets, hats, and gloves are also available. The Pacific Place branch has home furnishings and sassy pet collars. *Pacific Place, 600 Pine St. (at 6th Ave.), Downtown, 206/264–0372, www.coach.com.*

2 *f-4*

Bellevue Square, Bellevue Way (between NE 4th and 8th Sts.), Bellevue, 425/453–0141.

5 *g-7*

427 University St. (between 4th and 5th Aves.), University District, 206/382–1772.

10 *g-7*

FURLA

These high-fashion Italian handbags come in bold colors and frosty pastels. Grab a pair of orange-tinted sunglasses or some silver bangles to match 'em. *City Centre, 1420 5th Ave. (at Pike St.), Downtown, 206/749–5555.*

hats & gloves

Looking for a pair of leather driving gloves or some sleek suede beauties? Don't forget Nordstrom, Barneys New York, Coach, J. Crew, and Mario's.

10 *g-7*

BYRNIE UTZ HATS

The city's premier hat shop—in business since 1934 when it was still called millinery—has the best range of head gear in the Downtown area. From Borsalino to Stetson to Kangol, this is where you'll find the hip and high-quality brands. *310 Union St. (between 3rd and 4th Aves.), Downtown, 206/623–0233.*

10 *e-7*

FINI

This little accessories shop indeed carries the perfect items to polish an outfit. Look for quirky hats, colorful gloves, and a range of belts, handbags, jewelry, and hair accessories. *86 Pine St. (between Western and 1st Aves.), Downtown, 206/443–0563.*

lingerie & nightwear

9 *c-1*

BRA SHOW

This organization often holds fashion shows and events to promote its unique "wearable art" bras designed and donated by local artists. All proceeds go to cancer awareness programs. Check the Web site or *Seattle Weekly* to find out what's next on their schedule. *117 Summit Ave. E (at Broadway St.), Capitol Hill, 206/329–5387, www.thebrashow.org.*

10 *g-7*

NANCY MEYER

Exquisite silks, natural fibers, and imported lingerie for every season are highlighted at this elegant shop. In particular, look for La Perla and Fernando Sanchez loungewear. *1318 5th Ave. (between University and Union Sts.), Downtown, 206/625–9200. Closed Sun.*

7 *f-5*

NELLY STALLION

This little shop has a bright, well-maintained collection of new and used items. Seattle women stop by weekly to browse the incoming merchandise, which often includes designer-label work suits, snappy weekend wear, and shoes. You'll also find all the appropriate scarves, handbags, and even some jewelry to match. *1622 Queen Anne Ave. N (at W. Garfield St.), Queen Anne, 206/285–2150.*

13 *g-4*

PAJAMAMANIA

Design your own pajamas from the many styles and patterns offered by this innovative local company—or do what everyone else does and match your pj's with your kids'. Cotton and silk blends are used to create lounge sets, casual nightwear, and washable silks. Kids choose from Flapdoodles two-piece outfits, PJ Salvage flannels, and Rebel Kids thermal underwear. *6507 214th Ave. NE (between Avondale Ave. and Bel-Red Rd.), Redmond, 425/898–0881, www.pajamamania.com.*

10 *g-6*

VICTORIA'S SECRET

The famous lingerie store has plenty of Seattle outlets, and they all stock many styles of pretty cotton and silk pajamas and underthings. Perfumes, bath items, and hosiery are available, too. Look for seasonal sales on featured bra and underwear styles. *Pacific Place, 600 Pine St. (at 6th Ave.), Downtown, 206/749–9518, www.victoriassecret.com.*

2 *f-4*

Bellevue Square, Bellevue Way (between NE 4th and 8th Sts.), Bellevue, 425/454–6415.

2 *c-1*

Northgate Mall, Northgate Way (at 4th Ave. NE), Northgate, 206/368–7798.

maternity

2 *f-4*

DESIGNER MATERNITY FACTORÉ

Casual wear and dresses come in most sizes, and there's a selection of such handy mom-to-be items as hosiery, bras, books, and pillows. The shop's Baby Daze children's clothing outlet is right next door, so you can browse for the newborn (or older siblings) while you're here. *10676 NE 8th St. (between 106th and 107th Aves. NE), Bellevue, 425/451–1945.*

10 *g-6*

A PEA IN THE POD

Though the name is lighthearted, the clothing is in all seriousness: items are expensive, but the quality is unbeatable. Invest in a couple of really nice work or evening outfits—especially if you think you'll be using them again. *Westlake Center, 400 Pine St. (at 4th Ave.), Downtown, 206/292–9200.*

2 *f-4*

MIMI MATERNITY

The chic, Mimi-brand mother-to-be clothes are top of the line, and they'll make even the most sleep-deprived woman look good. Although the emphasis is on careerwear, there's a wide selection of casual clothes, too, all in basic and bright colors and patterns. If you're going to splurge, do it here. The pros on staff will find something just right—and the hosiery, nursing bras, pajamas, swimsuits, and diaper bags to match. *Bellevue Square, Bellevue Way (between NE 4th and 8th Sts.), Bellevue, 425/637–8785.*

2 *f-4*

MOTHERHOOD MATERNITY

All the kind sales assistants are moms themselves, and they will help you put pillows under the shirts (and in the nursing bras) to see how you'll look as you grow. Prices are moderate and there's always something on sale; if you've really jumped sizes and need a major shopping spree, try the outlet store at the Supermall in Auburn. *Bellevue Square, Bellevue Way (between NE 4th and 8th Sts.), Bellevue, 425/454–1355, www.maternitymall.com.*

1 *e-6*

Supermall, 1601 15th Ave. SW (at I–5), Auburn, 253/833–9500 or 800/729–8258.

6 *a-6*

VILLAGE MATERNITY

This big store won top scores by readers of *Seattle Child* magazine for its maternity line and accessories (including pumps for you and toys for the wee one). You can sign up for the baby gift registry, too. *University Village, NE 45th St. at 25th Ave. NE, University District, 206/523–5167.*

swimsuits

2 *f-2*

BIKINI BEACH

Headed for the Riviera? Looking for something summery to wear? You'll find the suit here. There are enough tropical hues to match any exotic setting, though, oddly enough, the tiniest suits command the highest prices. *30 Lakeshore Plaza (at NE 116th St.), Kirkland, 425/893–9542.*

2 *f-4*

SWIM IN

Swimwear practically flies out of this place in the weeks before spring break, but the stock is usually back to bursting in the months before summer. Suits are neatly arranged by color and size, so it's easy to find what you want. If you want a different size or something unusual, check with the staff about special-ordering. *Bellevue Square, Bellevue Way (between NE 4th and 8th Sts.), Bellevue, 425/454–2668.*

2 *c-1*

Northgate Mall, Northgate Way (at 4th Ave. NE), Northgate, 206/364–8844.

2 *b-1*

TROPICAL TAN

Anyone toned and tan can look good in a swimsuit, but this store has a range of cover-up options for those who went a bit doughy over the winter months. If you're not Gen Next, just ignore the youth shoppers and go in anyway— there are plenty that look good on 'Boomers, too. *9911 Aurora Ave. N (between NW 99th and 100th Sts.), Northgate, 206/523–7561.*

COMPUTERS & SOFTWARE

14 *g-1*

COMPUSA

Since it took over its big box competitor, CompUSA rules the region when it comes to computer superstores. Sales are frequent and the selection is immense. Demos are always available to try before you buy. *100 108th Ave. NE (at NE 2nd St.), Bellevue, 425/452–1264.*

13 *d-1*

Totem Lake Shopping Center, 12526 Totem Lake Blvd. NE (near 124th Ave. NE), Kirkland, 425/825–5500.

3 *b-8*

QUID'NUNC

Owner Bill Hibler has been serving the computer needs of West Seattle residents and businesses since the mid 1990s. You can buy computers and software here; get your computer fixed; and take classes. Quid'nunc is also an Internet Service Provider, with dial-up and DSL service. *4306 SW Oregon St. (at California Ave. SW), West Seattle, 206/932–8795.*

9 *b-7*

RE-PC RECYCLED COMPUTERS & PERIPHERALS

If you find yourself upgrading your equipment every couple of years, recycle your old computer here. RE-PC buys used computers and accessories, which they recycle, refurbish, and sometimes re-use. Check out the vintage computers or look for inexpensive spare parts. *1565 6th Ave. S (near S. Massachusetts St.), Sodo, 206/623–9151.*

COSTUME RENTAL

10 *b-3*

CHAMPION PARTY SUPPLY

It's the place in Seattle to find those ultrapopular life-size cardboard stand-ups of your favorite celebrities and characters. They line the windows, beckoning. Inside, Champion Costume Supply has all the party trimmings and some incredible costume choices for purchase or rent. *124 Denny Way (at 1st Ave. N), Queen Anne, 206/284–1980.*

2 *c-1*

DISPLAY & COSTUME

A costume party and nothing to wear? No problem. A stroll down the costume aisles (that's plural) will give you plenty of ideas. Check out the colorful feather boa aisle—Eva Gabor would drool. *11201 Roosevelt Way NE (near Northgate Way), Northgate, 206/362–4810.*

5 *g-4*

VINTAGE COSTUMERS

Ah, the elegance of lace and long skirt; the gasp-evoking beauty of the early 19th-century tux. For dress-up or costume creation, these folks have the real vintage garments. The rental prices are reasonable, and you'll be the best dressed at the ball. *7011 Roosevelt Way NE (at NE 70th St.), University District, 206/522–5234.*

CRAFT & HOBBY SUPPLIES

10 *e-6*

CRAFT EMPORIUM

Trays of beads and charms and supplies for painting, embroidery, mosaic projects, and other crafts fulfill your creative urges. Novices may consult the good selection of instruction books. *1501 Pike Pl. (in the Main Arcade), Pike Place Market, 206/622–2219.*

14 *g-1*

MICHAEL'S ARTS & CRAFTS

Well-known for its vast selection and discount prices, this national chain has rows and rows of arts-and-crafts supplies, plus framing services. Seasonal crafts and crafts materials are especially well-represented and go on deep discount (up to 90% off!) after the holidays. Classes are offered most weekends, both for kids and adults, and free project instruction sheets are available, too. *Crossroads Shopping Center, 15600 NE 8th, Bellevue, 425/747–1221.*

2 *f-2*

9755 Juanita Dr. NE (near Market St.), Kirkland, 425/821–4444.

model-making

2 *d-1*

AMERICAN EAGLES INC.

From its humble beginnings in the basement of owner Michael Edwards' home in 1969, American Eagles has grown to become the largest hobby shop in the United States. You'll find an incomparable selection of models, from traditional ships to sci-fi aircrafts, plus games, miniatures, railroad products, die-cast cars, wooden ships, and modeling supplies and tools. *12537 Lake City Way NE (at NE 125th St.), Lake City, 206/440–8448.*

other categories

6 *a-6*

PAINT THE TOWN

Create your own original pottery without creating a mess of your home in the process. Choose an unpainted cup, picture frame, bowl, etc., then do your painting magic. When you finish, turn your creation over to the shop to glaze and fire it. They'll have it ready for you to pick up in about a week. *4527 NE University Village (at 25th Ave. NE), University District, 206/527–8554.*

13 *g-4*

Redmond Town Center, 7329 164th Ave. NE (near NE 74th St.), Redmond, 425/861–8388.

4 *g-5*

POURETTE CANDLE MAKING SUPPLY

Even the most un-crafty will find pleasure and accomplishment in the simple act of rolling sheets of beeswax around a wick. Using molds to make candles and soap isn't much more complicated. For this reason, the Pourette mold technique and store were profiled in *Martha Stewart Living* magazine. *1418 NW 53rd St. (at 14th Ave. NW), Ballard, 206/789-3188.*

ELECTRONICS & AUDIO

5 *g-4*

DEFINITIVE AUDIO

High-performance audio and home-theater equipment is the name of the game. Both branches have dedicated home-theater environments where you can "audition" the equipment before you buy it. Each year, special two-day events bring industry experts demonstrating the latest and greatest products. The price? Well, if you have to ask . . . . *6017 Roosevelt Way NE (at NE Ravenna Blvd.), University District, 206/524-6633.*

13 *e-8*

14405 NE 20th St. (near 148th Ave. NE), Bellevue, 425/746-3188.

5 *g-4*

MAGNOLIA HI-FI

Len Tweten started this home-grown electronics store in 1954 as a stationery and camera shop, transitioning to audio specialties in the mid-1960s. The business has grown to include 13 stores in three states and has won repeated industry awards. Though the products have changed over the years, the emphasis on great customer service and technical support has been consistent. It now carries a full line of home audio and video products, plus car stereos, cellular phones, and accessories. *6308 Roosevelt Way NE (at NE 63rd St.), University District, 206/525-0080.*

13 *e-8*

14404 NE 20th St. (near 148th Ave. NE), Bellevue, 425/747-0850.

10 *g-6*

SHARPER IMAGE

You're likely to find a gadget previously unknown to you here that you'll suddenly need. Sure, you could shop from the catalog or on-line, but it's not the same as playing with all these electronic doodads in person (especially the massaging recliner). Once in awhile you'll find a bargain (the techno "has-beens"). And maybe come fall that around-the-neck personal air-conditioner will go on sale. *1501 4th Ave., (at Pike St.), Downtown, 206/343-9125.*

ETHNIC ITEMS

10 *e-6*

COST PLUS WORLD MARKET

See Home Accessories, *below.*

6 *a-4*

GAELSONG

Celtic culture is the theme of Colleen Carroll's store. Imports from Ireland, Scotland, and Wales include jewelry (including the Celtic cross), books, music, and home furnishings. *2207 NE 65th St. (at 22nd Ave. NE), University District, 206/526-8350.*

5 *f-7*

HAWAI'I GENERAL STORE & GALLERY

Take home some aloha spirit in the form of jewelry, music, books, quilts, handmade crafts, artwork, koa-wood bowls, and authentic Hawaiian clothes. Planning a Hawaiian party? Get your supplies here, along with island foods and fresh flower leis. *258 NE 45th St. (at Thackeray Pl. NE), Wallingford, 206/633-5233.*

6 *a-4*

TREE OF LIFE JUDAICA

Jewish life and culture is highlighted here in books, music, jewelry, art, toys, and ceremonial items. The store aims to serve the local Jewish community while also introducing the culture and heritage to people from all backgrounds. In-store events include classes and author readings. *2201 NE 65th St. (at 22nd Ave. NE), University District, 206/527-1130.*

12 *d-4*

UWAJIMAYA

See Malls, *above.*

EROTICA

2 *c-1*

LOVE PANTRY

Lacy lingerie decorating the windows invites even the most coy to come hither. Inside are sex toys, games, body-painting supplies, massage oils, DVDs, and plenty of gag gifts, too. *10333 Aurora Ave. N (at N. 103rd St.), Northgate, 206/ 523–5683.*

13 *e-8*

14220 NE 20th St. (near 140th Ave. NE), Bellevue, 425/643–5683.

13 *e-8*

LOVE SEASON GIFTS FOR LOVERS

Love Season has been supplying fun and fulfilling sex products in their myriad forms for more than 20 years with the belief that they improve and enrich relationships. You'll find toys, lingerie, and books here—and a lot of satisfied couples. *12001 NE 12th St. (at 120th Ave. NE), Bellevue, 425/455–0533.*

11 *c-5*

TOYS IN BABELAND

Women who know their bodies own and run this woman-oriented shop. And they want to help you get to know yours, too, with dildos ($28–$70) and vibrators ($5–$70) in all the colors of the rainbow flag. Familiarize yourself with the gadgets (are there some you've never seen?) or peruse the books and videos. Sign up for one of the improvement courses, including Sex Toys 101 and Lesbian's Tell All: Sex Tips For Straight Guys. *707 E. Pike St. (between Boylston and Harvard Sts.), Capitol Hill, 206/328– 2914, www.babeland.com.*

EYEWEAR

For discount and moderately priced eyewear, you have several chains to choose from, including the Group Health See Centers (at most Group Health medical centers), Vista Optical (in shopping malls and many Fred Meyer stores), Pearle Vision, and LensCrafters.

5 *c-7*

EYES ON FREMONT

Owner Lorali Downes offers the personal touch, advising you to take a chance on a hip new look in eyewear. Contemporary frames from Asia and Europe are privately designed and affordable (at least in comparison with big-name U.S. designers). *4254 Fremont Ave. N (at N. Motor Pl.), Fremont, 206/ 634–3375.*

10 *e-6*

MARKET OPTICAL EYE WEAR

Voted the best eyewear store by readers of *Seattle Weekly*, Market is well-known for its cutting-edge designs and large selection of frames. Of course cutting-edge is costly, but this isn't just a simple matter of vision correction; it's about making a fashion statement. *1906 Pike Pl. (at Stewart St.), Pike Place Market, 206/448–7739.*

14 *b-1*

Bellevue Square, Bellevue Way (between NE 4th and 8th Sts.), Bellevue, 425/451– 1184.

14 *b-1*

OPTHALARIUM ART EYEWEAR

In his gallery-style boutique with unusual and custom-made eyewear, Dr. Mark Hamilton has developed a passion for the precise visual needs of airline pilots, microsurgeons, and anyone feeling slighted by their eye doctor. Jerry Grecian, Opthalarium's master optician, is the man to make you look good. A master woodworker and optical artist, he considers your whole face and finds the pair that accentuates what you've got. *Bellevue Galleria, 550 106th Ave. NE (at NE 6th St.), Bellevue, 425/454–6573.*

FABRICS & NOTIONS

Two major fabric store chains dominate the Seattle scene: JoAnn Fabrics & Crafts and Pacific Fabrics & Crafts. With nearly 20 area stores between them, you're never far from the fabrics needed to whip up a Halloween costume or make home-decorating projects. Quilting is enjoying a resurgence, too, and both stores carry the popular calico-type fabrics for quilts and the other supplies you'll need to get started.

5 *h-1*

IN THE BEGINNING FABRICS

Quilters come here for designs and fabrics—or you can look for these original fabrics at many other local fabric shops. *8201 Lake City Way NE (at NE 82nd St.), Lake City, 206/523–8862.*

4 *h-4*

LIJEPO

When you need unusual buttons, this is your place. All shapes and colors are here, from antique and vintage to modern novelty styles. The store also accepts consignments and will appraise your wares; call first. *503 NW 65th St. (between 7th and 8th Aves. NW), Madison Park, 206/789–4355.*

7 *f-3*

NANCY'S SEWING BASKET

Modern fabrics and supplies and plenty of vintage and antique items appeal to designers of all ilks (and abilities). Look for designer fabrics, bridal ideas, imported cottons and silks, and quilting and craft notions. Behold the ribbon room—and tons of unusual buttons. It's open late on Tuesday and Thursday. *2221 Queen Anne Ave. N (between Boston and Meridian Sts.), Queen Anne, 206/282–9112 or 800/443–2964.*

8 *h-4*

TINA'S ON MADISON

You know you've found a good thing when bolts of fabulous fabric are piled 10-deep around the walls. And this shop, open for more than 20 years, is the real thing, with skeins of shining ribbons, clusters of gold tassels, myriad buttons and sewing items, and nothing over $50. *4232 E. Madison St. (between 41st and 42nd Sts. E), Madison Park, 206/328–0803.*

FLOWERS & PLANTS

florists

4 *g-5*

BALLARD BLOSSOM

The Northwest's largest florist opened in 1927 and prides itself on having the largest delivery area. Fresh flowers arrive several times a day, ensuring that your arrangement will be created to the highest standards. It also carries indoor and outdoor plants, gift items, and silk flowers. *1766 NW Market St. (at 17th Ave. NW), Ballard, 206/782–4213.*

14 *g-1*

BELLEVUE CROSSROADS FLORIST

For generations Eastside residents have marked special occasions with flowers from here. Eastside and Seattle delivery is available and is always free to Overlake Hospital and the Microsoft main campus. *15920 NE 8th St. (at 160th Ave. NE), Bellevue, 425/747–5654.*

8 *f-8*

FLEURISH

Nisha Kelen specializes in floral design by appointment only. Services are geared to corporate accounts, private residences, and weddings. The European-style arrangements (an imported and domestic assortment, arranged in looser style) artfully highlight texture and colors. *1411 34th Ave. (at E. Union St.), Madrona, 206/322–1602.*

12 *c-3*

MEGAN MARY OLANDER FLORIST

Call or stop by to order European-style arrangements, select flowers by the stem, or purchase wildflowers and perennials for your garden. *222 1st Ave. S (at S. Main St.), Pioneer Square, 206/623–6660.*

nurseries & garden supplies

14 *b-2*

BELLEVUE NURSERY

Bellevue's oldest nursery (opened in 1954) has a good selection of stock, a nice gift shop, and an indoor plant area. *842 104th Ave. SE (at SE 10th St.), Bellevue, 425/454–5531.*

11 *e-1*

CITY PEOPLE'S MERCANTILE

See Home Accessories, *below.*

1 *f-1*

MOLBAK'S

Molbak's greenhouse and nursery is a year-round destination. In spring and summer, fill your cart with plants and trees. Bargain hunters should mark their calendars for the two-for-one sale on plants, held in late June and early July. In fall and winter, come for holiday displays or a photo op in the poinsettia-filled greenhouse. The gift shops, espresso café, and the conservatory filled with singing birds amuse even non-gardeners. The University Village shop is smaller, carrying indoor and outdoor plants, supplies, and gifts. The

Pike Place Market shop has seeds, plants, and gardening supplies. *13625 NE 175th St. (near 135th Ave. NE), Woodinville, 425/483–5000.*

6 *a-6*
4601 NE University Village (at 25th Ave. NE), University District, 206/754–6500.

10 *e-6*
1600 Pike Pl. (at Pine St.), Pike Place Market, 206/448–0431.

2 *b-2*
SWANSON'S NURSERY
Nicely organized with helpful signs, Swanson's has 5 acres of gardens to explore, which serve as the nursery. Paved walkways make it accessible. Plant varieties range from the common to the rare, and the selection of perennials and herbs is superb. The knowledgeable staff lends advice on the best plant choices for your needs. There's also a café. *9701 15th Ave. NW (near NW 97th St.), Crown Hill, 206/782–2543.*

2 *e-5*
WELLS-MEDINA NURSERY
Despite the upscale neighborhood, this nursery isn't a fancy sort of place with a gift shop or café. The emphasis is on practical gardening supplies, high-quality stock, and excellent customer service. It's especially noted for the rich variety of perennials, shrubs, and conifer trees. *8300 NE 24th St. (near 84th Ave. NE), Medina, 425/454–1853.*

FOLK ART & HANDICRAFTS

9 *b-3*
FIREWORKS
The work of more than 300 artisans fill these home-accessories shops with colorful, fun handcrafts. Whether made locally or from afar, the emphasis is on the offbeat and unusual, like star-shape metal lanterns, painted dining room sets, and stained-glass night-lights. Items include ceramics, glass, jewelry, books, furniture, home accessories, and a selection of Judaica. *210 1st Ave. S (between S. Washington and S. Main Sts.), Pioneer Square, 206/682–8707, www.fireworksgallery.net.*

10 *f-6*
Westlake Center, 400 Pine St. (at 4th Ave.), Downtown, 206/682–6462.

14 *b-1*
Bellevue Square, Bellevue Way (between NE 4th and 8th Sts.), Bellevue, 425/688–0933.

6 *a-6*
2629 NE University Village (at 25th Ave. NE), University District, 206/527–2858.

10 *e-6*
HANDS OF THE WORLD
Owner Cynthia Hope selects handcrafted items for her Pike Place store from artisans around the world. She searches for folk art that has been created by traditional means, using techniques that have been handed down through the ages. Like other such stores, many items are one of a kind (especially furniture). *1501 Pike Pl. (at 1st Ave.), Pike Place Market, 206/622–1696.*

5 *g-8*
LA TIENDA FOLK ART GALLERY
The U-District La Tienda has been selling unique folk art since 1962; The Ballard store opened more recently. Both carry handblown glass, pottery, jewelry, clothing, masks, toys, musical instruments, and CDs, book, and games from various countries and cultures. *4138 University Way NE (at NE 41st St.), University District, 206/632–1796.*

4 *f-5*
2050 NW Market St. (at Leary Ave. NW), Ballard, 206/297–3605.

10 *e-6*
MILAGROS MEXICAN FOLK ART
With the goal to sell affordable pieces that reflect the whimsy, color, and humor of Mexico, this gallery carries an impressive selection of collectible artworks by some of that country's most noted artisans. Check out the clay figures, detailed yarn paintings, masks, papier-mâché, pottery, tinworks, wood carvings, religious folk art, and more. *1530 Post Alley (between Pike and Pine Sts.), Pike Place Market, 206/464–0490.*

10 *e-6*
PHOENIX RISING
See Decorative Glass, below.

FOOD & DRINK

breads & pastries

6 *a-6*

A LA FRANCAISE

Experience delicate pastries and fine desserts, aromatic soups, great sandwiches, and that lovely cramped French bakery feel all in one place. Baguettes and breads are the real McCoy. *2609 NE University Village (at 25th Ave. NE), University District, 206/524–9300.*

2 *a-6*

ALKI BAKERY

The place is always packed, sits right off the beach, and has lush pastries, including giant cinnamon rolls. *2738 Alki Ave. SW (at 61st Ave. SW), West Seattle, 206/935–1352.*

5 *b-8*

BAGEL OASIS

While a number of the area's bagel shops and chains have closed in recent years, Bagel Oasis has stood the test of time. Swing by in the morning and get a dozen to share with your office mates, or grab a bagel sandwich for lunch with salad, soup, or pasta. The University District shop is certified kosher. *462 N. 36th St. (between Dayton and Francis Aves. N), Fremont, 206/633–2676.*

2 *f-6*

2112 NE 65th St. (near 22nd Ave. NE), University District, 206/526–0525.

5 *e-7*

EROTIC BAKERY

Popping out of cakes is passé. Instead have any body part rendered in marzipan or consider the booby cupcakes for your next tasteless party. *2323 N. 45th St. (at Corliss Ave. N), Wallingford, 206/545–6969.*

6 *d-5*

GREAT HARVEST BREAD CO.

Before you buy, you get a big slab of bread and butter to whet your appetite. The whole grain breads are delectable and the cookies, brownies, and pastries vie for your sweet tooth; holiday specialties include green bread on St. Patrick's Day, orange bread for Halloween, and hot cross buns at Easter. *5408 Sand Point Way NE (at 47th Ave. NE), University District, 206/524–4873.*

2 *f-6*

Loehmann's Plaza, 3610 128th Ave. SE (near SE 36th St.), Bellevue, 425/643–8420.

13 *g-4*

Bear Creek Village, 17192 Redmond Way (near 170th Ave. NE), Redmond, 425/883–6909.

8 *c-8*

LA PANZANELLA

The rustic bread here is made by Ciro, an Italian baker who speaks of bread as if it's his life, his lover, his soul. He's somewhat of a Seattle icon, having brought to many a restaurant and family table the old-fashioned, hard-skinned, oddly shaped loaves that have made Italy a food-lover's destination for centuries. The café also sells soups, salads, pizzas, sandwiches, and box lunches. *1314 E. Union St. (at 14th Ave.), Capitol Hill, 206/325–5217.*

7 *g-8*

MACRINA BAKERY

By combining artistry with baking, Macrina's makes some of the best baked goods in town, including luscious pastries and breads served in the city's finest restaurants. It serves breakfast and lunch, and the baristas are hip, friendly, and know their coffee. It's pricey but worth it. *2408 1st Ave. (at Wall St.), Belltown, 206/448–4032.*

8 *b-7*

NOAH'S BAGELS

Since opening its first shop in Berkeley in 1989, Noah's has expanded up and down the West Coast, offering consistently tasty bagels in traditional and creative flavors. Noah's has some interesting bagel variations, too, including low-fat cinnamon sticks and buns, bialies, and bagel pizzas. Salads, knishes, soups, challah bread, and other assorted treats round out the menu. The Mercer Island and University District store's are kosher. *220 Broadway Ave. E (at E. John St.), Capitol Hill, 206/720–2925.*

13 *c-4*

320 Park Place Center (at Central Way), Kirkland, 425/827–7382.

14 *a-3*

7831 SE 27th St. (at 78th Ave. SE), Mercer Island, 206/232–4729.

7 *f-3*

2133 Queen Anne Ave. N (at W. Crockett St.), Queen Anne, 206/282–6744.

6 *a-6*

University Village, 2746 NE 45th St. (in the QFC store), University District, 206/526–0525.

10 *f-7*

THREE DOG BAKERY

Inspire your canine pals to sit up and beg for the fresh-baked treats such as Beagle Bagles and Scottie Biscotti. 1408 1st Ave. (at Union St.), Pike Place Market, 206/364–9999 or 206/343–8892.

cheese

10 *e-6*

DELAURENTI SPECIALTY FOOD MARKET

See Ethnic Foods, below.

10 *d-5*

JAMES COOK CHEESE CO. LTD.

James Cook knows cheese and he carries the finest varieties from Europe, like Camembert from France, mountain-aged Gorgonzola from Italy, as well as premium American cheeses. Want to expand your knowledge? He'll be glad to answer your questions and provide samples, too. 2421 2nd Ave. (at Battery St.), Belltown, 206/256–0510.

7 *f-6*

LARRY'S MARKET

See Gourmet Foods, below.

9 *c-6*

PACIFIC FOOD IMPORTERS (PFI)

See Gourmet Foods, below.

5 *g-4*

WHOLE FOODS MARKET

See Gourmet Foods, below.

chocolate & other candy

1 *g-4*

BOEHM'S CANDY KITCHEN

The late Julius Boehm, who climbed Mt. Everest at the age of 80, built his candy factory in the style of a Swiss chalet. Since the 1950s, it's sold chocolates and other candies made on the premises. Call ahead during the summer and you can

join one of the free tours, which end with a sampling session. 255 NE Gilman Blvd. (near Front St.), Issaquah, 425/392–6652.

8 *b-6*

DILETTANTE CHOCOLATES

Chocolates fit for royalty are created by third-generation chocolatier, Dana Taylor Davenport. His grandfather was the chocolate-maker to a Russian czar and Viennese emperor, and since 1976 Davenport has been carrying on the family legacy, serving delicious treats to the common folk of Seattle. Well at least those willing to pay the price! A pound of truffles can be had for $32, a bag of chocolate chips for about $3. The Broadway location serves desserts in a café setting. Visit the Cherry Street shop for seconds—the less than perfect chocolates that taste just as good, but cost much less (less than half price for truffles). 416 Broadway Ave. E (at E. Harrison St.), Capitol Hill, 206/329–6463.

10 *e-7*

1603 1st Ave. (at Pine St.), Downtown, 206/728–9144.

9 *f-1*

2300 E. Cherry St. (at 23rd Ave.), Capitol Hill, 206/728–9144.

6 *a-6*

FRAN'S CHOCOLATES

Fran Bigelow is the esteemed queen of Seattle chocolate, tempting the local sweet tooth since 1982. Her Gold Bars—a marriage of soft caramel, crunchy nuts, and bittersweet chocolate—are justifiably famous, as are her many other delectable chocolate confections. Every piece is handmade and hand-wrapped; prices reflect the high standards. Fran's ice cream is available at the University Village shop. University Village, 2594 NE University Village (at 25th Ave. NE), University District, 206/528–9969.

14 *b-1*

10305 NE 10th St. (at 103rd Ave. NE), Bellevue, 425/453–1698.

coffee & tea

Seattle is, of course, known for its love of coffee. Yes, it's the birthplace of Starbucks, and you'll find dozens of their establishments throughout the area— on street corners, in shopping malls, in supermarkets, in bookstores, and even as drive-thrus. If you want to brew your own, Starbucks coffee can be purchased by the bag at your neighborhood grocery store. Seattle's Best Coffee and Tully's Coffee also play a prominent role in the city's coffee craze.

8 *b-7*

ESPRESSO VIVACE ROASTERIA

The motto here is "una bella tazza di caffe" which means "a beautiful cup of coffee." The owners have done extensive research to perfect their espresso preparation and roasting methods, and the company is known world-wide for their expertise. They sell two blends of espresso (plus decaf) available by the half-pound (minimum 2-lb order by mail) or in espresso drinks. Both locations are open almost around the clock (6:30 AM to 11 PM). The Denny Way shop has an 85-seat café; the Broadway location is a sidewalk bar only. *901 E. Denny Way (at Broadway Ave. E), Capitol Hill, 206/860–5869.*

8 *b-7*

321 Broadway Ave. E (at E. Harrison St.), Capitol Hill, 206/860–5869.

5 *b-7*

LIGHTHOUSE ROASTERS FINE COFFEE

Using a 1937 Danish roaster, owner Ed Leebrick roasts small batches, ensuring a finer, fresher blend. The store sells six varietal coffees, six blends, dark roasts, and decaf. Grab a pastry with your java at the cozy Fremont café. *400 N. 43rd St. (at Phinney Ave. N), Fremont, 206/633–4444.*

10 *e-6*

PERENNIAL TEA ROOM

Fathom this: Some people actually prefer tea. You can choose from more than 60 varieties from around the world, and stock up on all things tea—tea cozies, kettles, infusers, books, and a huge selection of teapots. *1910 Post Alley (at Stewart St.), Pike Place Market, 206/448–4054.*

10 *g-7*

SEATTLE'S BEST COFFEE

Fans of SBC rave about the smooth and mellow taste of this brand, in part because the house blend uses lighter beans than Starbucks'. The company got its start in Seattle in 1970, one year before Starbucks opened. While it hasn't grown at the same rate, there are several dozen branches in the area and

more than 100 in the world. Beans, selected by founder Jim Stewart on his global travels, are roasted at the Vashon Island facility. Especially popular with environmentally conscious Seattle residents are the six organic, shade-grown varieties. Besides its stand-alone cafés, SBC's coffee bars are found in most QFC supermarkets. *Seaboard Building, 400 Pike St. (at 4th Ave.), Downtown, 206/624–1635.*

10 *e-6*

STARBUCKS

As a local you probably already know that the first Starbucks opened at the Pike Place Market in 1971. Now, with more than 100 locations in western Washington (and thousands more around the world), folks craving a caffeine fix needn't look far to find Starbucks' familiar green mermaid logo. From basic drip coffee to the frosty Frappucino drink, Starbucks has it all. You can buy it to brew at home, too, in whole bean or freshly ground. Check the phone book for other locations. *Pike Place Market, 1912 Pike Place (near Stewart St.), 206/448–8762.*

7 *f-3*

TEACUP

Stand in awe before the 150 varieties of tea—they even custom-blended tea for an expedition to Mt. Everest—and dozens of tea sets. Don't leave without sampling a refreshing cup. *2207 Queen Anne Ave. N (at W. Boston St.), Queen Anne, 206/283–5931.*

10 *g-7*

TULLY'S

The youngest of the major Seattle-based coffee chains, Tully's is vocal about its desire to compete with Starbucks. With dozens of shops in the Seattle area and more than 100 worldwide, it's already the third largest specialty coffee retailer in the country. When Tully's headquarters moved to the former Rainier Brewing Company near busy I-5, they gained a highly visible location. Then winning the exclusive rights to sell coffee at Safeco Field was another marketing coup. Tully's coffee quality and menu choices are similar to Starbucks. The company emphasizes a warm and comfortable café ambiance, with cozy chairs and couches, and even kids' play areas and fireplaces at some locations. *1401 4th Ave. (at Union St.), 206/625–0600.*

ethnic foods

9 f-6

BORRACCHINI'S BAKERY & MEDITERRANEAN MARKET

Folks come from all over for the great prices and endless variety of packaged Italian foods and wines, fresh and frozen pasta, and well-stocked deli. The bakery is full of goodies, too—from basic Italian breads and rolls to fancy napoleons and fruit tarts. Many a special occasion has been graced by a Borracchini's cake. Watch the decorators design it, then get some to-die-for spumoni to go with it. *2307 Rainier Ave. S (at S. College St.), Beacon Hill, 206/325–1550.*

10 e-6

DELAURENTI SPECIALTY FOOD MARKET

DeLaurenti has attracted Italian food fanatics for more than half a century. Crowded aisles are stocked with pasta, canned goods, olive oils, olives, dried fruits, chocolates, and Italian cookies and crackers. The deli carries Italian meats, salads, and more than 150 kinds of cheeses. Buy some of the artisan breads and a bottle from the selection of Italian wines for home. *1435 1st Ave. (in the Economy Market Bldg.), Pike Place Market, 206/622–0141.*

10 e-6

MEXICAN GROCERY

Though some Mexican groceries have come and gone, this small shop across from the Market Arcade has stood the test of time. The staff make fresh tortillas in varied styles and flavors, plus the store stocks authentic Mexican foods, including fresh salsas and lots of dried chiles. *1914 Pike Pl. (near Stewart St.), Pike Place Market, 206/441–1147.*

9 c-6

PACIFIC FOOD IMPORTERS (PFI)

Because it's a warehouse-style store, PFI can be hard to find, and the atmosphere is not one of glitz and orderliness. But the exotic food items are cheap. The best deals are found on the deli meats and cheeses (often the lowest price in town), spices, olives, pasta, dried beans, and olive oils. *1001 6th Ave. S (at S. Stacy St.), Beacon Hill, 206/682–2022.*

2 d-6

SALUMERIA

Salumeria is both a restaurant and a shop. Eat here (and you won't regret it), or buy what you need to take home and cook up your own feast. It stocks meats, cheeses, olives, baked goods, cooking equipment, and a good selection of wine. *4918 Rainier Ave. S (at Hudson St.), Columbia City, 206/760–7741.*

7 e-4

TRADER JOE'S

Healthful and affordably priced items have made Trader Joe's popular coast to coast. The store-brand items are top-notch and include ready-made packaged food to bulk and bagged snacks. Yet the store's emphasis is on interesting ethnic flavors and dishes, including Thai, Indian, Asian, Mexican, and Middle Eastern foods offered fresh and frozen. Discount prices are applied to beer and wine, dairy products, some toiletries, and the ever-changing items in the floral department. *112 W. Galer St. (at 1st Ave. W), Queen Anne, 206/378–5536 or 800/SHOP–TJS, www.traderjoes.com.*

5 g-7

4601 Roosevelt Way NE (near NE 45th St.), University District, 206/547–6299.

2 f-3

15400 NE 20th St. (at 156th Ave. NE), Bellevue, 425/643–6885.

fish & seafood

10 e-6

CITY FISH MARKET

One of several fishmongers in the Market, City Fish is known for high-quality products and attentive, expert service. Besides local fish and shellfish, the store carries some more exotic species, too. They'll ship overnight to anywhere in the United States. *1535 Pike Pl. (in the Main Arcade), Pike Place Market, 206/682–9329.*

9 f-6

MUTUAL FISH

This is where many top local restaurants buy fish, so you know it's got to be good. Shellfish can be selected from tanks; you can also buy Asian groceries here. *2335 Rainier Ave. S (near S. College St.), Beacon Hill, 206/322–4368.*

10 *e-6*

PIKE PLACE FISH MARKET

Home of the famous "flying fish," it's the obvious choice for fresh fish and shellfish, smoked fish, and gift items. And clearly, the workers here love what they do. *86 Pike St. (in the Main Arcade), Pike Place Market, 206/682–7181.*

7 *f-3*

QUEEN ANNE THRIFTWAY

Though the annual race among shops to procure the first-of-the-season Copper River salmon gets much media publicity, it's the day-in, day-out attention to quality at this grocery store's highly regarded fish counter that keeps customers coming back. *1908 Queen Anne Ave. N (at Howe St.), Queen Anne, 206/284–2530.*

1 *d-1*

SHORELINE CENTRAL MARKET

If you're up north, you don't have to go Downtown to get the freshest fish and seafood: Central Market has live fish, crabs, lobster, clams, mussels, and oysters in tanks, as well as an impressive selection of fresh and frozen fish. This is a full-service grocery store, too, with an immense produce section including Asian items, plus natural foods, bulk items, take-out Mexican, Chinese, and pizza, and an espresso stand. *15505 Westminster Way N (at NE 155th St.), Shoreline, 206/363–9226.*

4 *g-7*

WILD SALMON SEAFOOD MARKET

The fish you'll find here are just off the boat. You'll probably see at least one vessel docked here. Holding tanks are filled with shellfish; at the service counter, fillets and steaks are trimmed before your eyes. *1900 W. Nickerson St. (at Fishermen's Terminal), Magnolia, 206/283–3366.*

gourmet foods

7 *c-4*

CHEFSHOP.COM

Though they do a brisk business over the Internet, ChefShop.com opened a retail store in Seattle so that local foodies could taste-test and buy the goods first-hand: Imported olive oils, hard-to-find baking sugars, Asian and Indian

condiments, and tins of foie gras. *1435 Elliott Ave. (near W. Galer St.), Magnolia, 206/286–9988.*

3 *b-8*

HUSKY DELI

The popular deli is stocked with cheeses, meats, salads, and sandwiches and does a lot of catering. But come for the homemade ice cream (in more than 40 flavors) available by the scoop, in a thick milkshake, or hand-packed to take home. *4721 California Ave. SW (at SW Alaska St.), West Seattle, 206/937–2810.*

7 *f-6*

LARRY'S MARKETS

The locally owned Larry's chain pioneered the concept of the destination grocery store—prices aren't the point, so things can be expensive. Bargains can be found on packaged and canned foods, dairy, and frozen foods, but it's the unending selection of unusual and interesting products, which are not-so-discounted, that are the real temptation. The enormous cheese section has more than 200 varieties; other specialty sections include organic produce and foods, live seafood, meat from the service butcher, Asian macrobiotic products, fine chocolates, and baked goods. In short, the choices are awesome. *100 Mercer St. (at 1st Ave. N), Queen Anne, 206/213–0778.*

11 *c-2*

Broadway Market, 401 Broadway St. E (between Harrison and Republican Sts.), Capitol Hill, 206/322–6397.

2 *c-1*

Oak Tree Village, 10008 Aurora Ave. N (at N. 100th St.), Northgate, 206/527–5333.

14 *d-1*

699 120th Ave. NE (at NE 8th St.), Bellevue, 425/453–0600.

13 *d-1*

12321 120th Pl. NE (at NE 24th St.), Kirkland, 425/820–2300.

13 *g-4*

7320 170th Ave. NE (near Redmond Town Center), Redmond, 425/869–2362.

health & natural food

8 *c-8*

MADISON MARKET

Central Co-op expanded from their former Capitol Hill location into this bright and well-appointed natural foods market in 1998, adopting a new name in the process. It carries natural and organic foods, body-care products, vitamins, and health-care items, and there's a full service deli and large bulk-foods department. *1600 E. Madison St. (at 16th Ave. E), Capitol Hill, 206/329–1545.*

14 *b-1*

NATURE'S PANTRY
Nature's Pantry sells natural foods, organic produce, vitamins, supplements, cosmetics, and other nutritional products. The Northeast 10th Street store has a bakery and deli; the Crossroads shop has a juice bar. *10200 NE 10th St. (at 103rd Ave. NE), Bellevue, 425/454–0170.*

14 *g-1*

Crossroads Shopping Center, 15600 NE 8th St. (at 156th Ave. NE), Bellevue, 425/957–0090.

7 *g-1*

PCC NATURAL MARKETS
No longer just a destination for granola eaters, PCC is a full-line grocery store committed to providing you with a range of tasty and healthy food choices. Though it's still a consumer's co-op, and members' prices are discounted on some items, nonmembers are welcome, too. The bulk-food department is packed with whole foods; you can make your own peanut butter; and the deli has fresh pasta and take-out entrées, along with meats, cheeses, and salads. Besides food, PCC carries vitamins, nutritional products, and gift items. Sign up for classes on healthful cooking and nutrition. *716 N. 34th St. (near Fremont Ave. N), Fremont, 206/632–6811.*

5 *f-2*

7504 Aurora Ave. N (at Winona Ave. N), Green Lake, 206/547–6299.

3 *b-8*

2749 California Ave. SW (at SW Lander St.), West Seattle, 206/937–8481.

7 *e-4*

TRADER JOE'S
See Ethnic Food, *above.*

5 *g-4*

WHOLE FOODS MARKET
Whole Foods Market opened a shop here in 1999, and it quickly developed a loyal following. The produce department

is a vegetative artwork, the organic meats are incredible, and the wide range of natural foods and health remedies covers just about everything a health-conscious family could need. The cheese department must represent every cheese-making country of the world. Other impressive sections include the olive bar, the take-out foods, the walk-in wine cooler, the bakery, and the juice bar. *1026 NE 64th St. (at Roosevelt Way NE), University District, 206/985–1500.*

herbs & spices

10 *e-6*

WORLD MERCHANTS SPICE COMPANY
Owner Tony Hill scours the world to find the best and most unique spices, herbs, and teas. Everything is freshly harvested, so visit often to see what's in season. *1509 Western Ave. (near the Hillclimb), Pike Place Market, 206/682–7274.*

meat & poultry

7 *f-3*

A&J MEATS & SEAFOOD
Many swear the meat here is the best in town. Maybe it's the result of a half-century's experience smoking their own meats? A&J also sells ready-to-cook entrées like chicken cordon bleu, marinated leg of lamb, and stuffed pork chops. Ready-made accompaniments include potatoes, gravies, and rolls. Stop in at the adjacent McCarthy & Schiering wine shop to get a bottle to go with your meal. *2401 Queen Anne Ave. N (at W. McGraw St.), Queen Anne, 206/284–3885.*

10 *e-6*

DON & JOE'S MEATS
It carries all the basic fresh meats—beef, veal, pork, lamb, and chicken, and sells more diverse varieties, too, including game birds and organ meats. Tripe, anyone? *85 Pike St. (near 1st Ave.), Pike Place Market, 206/682–7670.*

1 *d-1*

SEATTLE'S FINEST EXOTIC MEATS
Getting bored of the usual? Wanna try something new? Come on Saturday from noon to 4 PM to sample something exotic, or just ask the helpful staff to fill you in on the interesting varieties here,

like ostrich and kangaroo. They're surprisingly low in fat. *17532 Aurora Ave. N (at N. 175th St.), Shoreline, 206/546–4922.*

pasta & noodles

6 *a-6*

PASTA & CO.

Find fresh pasta here, along with sauces, salads, and entrées to create a fab at-home meal. While you're at it get your imported olive oil here and some yummy baked goods, too. *2640 NE University Village (at 25th Ave. NE), University District, 206/523–8594.*

14 *b-1*

10218 NE 8th St. (at 102nd Ave. NE, near Bellevue Square), Bellevue, 425/453–8760.

7 *f-3*

2109 Queen Anne Ave. N (at Crockett St.), Queen Anne, 206/283–1182.

produce

Whether it's Seattleites' health-conscious approach to life or just the abundance of produce available from Northwest farmers, the Seattle area is blessed with many great produce providers. Pike Place Market has been connecting farmers with customers for decades and farmers markets sprout up every weekend from spring to fall in local communities. A drive along country roads in summer is sure to lead you to a produce stand or two, but for the best in Asian produce, head to the International District's small grocers or Uwajimaya, or north to the Shoreline Central Market.

wines & spirits

9 *b-7*

ESQUIN WINE MERCHANTS

Self-appointed sommeliers know they'll find excellent values and an impressive selection here, including bottles from France, Italy, and Australia, as well as from Northwest and American winemakers. Sales are frequent, with special by-the-case bargains, and the store will deliver orders over $100 to Seattle and Tacoma residents at no charge. The knowledgeable staff leads wine tastings twice a week. *2700 4th Ave. S (at S. Forest St.), SoDo, 206/682–7374.*

7 *f-3*

MCCARTHY & SCHIERING

The owners Daniel McCarthy & Jay Schiering live wine: They know it, they love it, they make suggestions with abandon, and rarely are customers dissatisfied. When you aren't, bring it back. They'll smell it, taste it, and try to figure out what went wrong. Take a moment to chat with these experts about the wine industry, and the adventurous and the traditional bottles they stock. Stop by on Saturday 11–5 for tastings. *2401B Queen Anne Ave. N (at W. McGraw St.), Queen Anne, 206/282–8500.*

5 *f-4*

6500 Ravenna Ave. NE (at NE 65th St.), University District, 206/524–9500.

8 *b-3*

PETE'S FINE WINES

Don't be confused by the sign that reads Pete's Supermarket; it's much more than a neighborhood grocery. Pete's Fine Wines, along with Pete's of Bellevue, carries more than 1,000 labels from around the world. Prices are good and monthly specials are even better. Come to the Bellevue shop on Saturday from 3 to 6 PM for tastings. If wine-shopping activates your appetite, try one of the hefty custom-made deli sandwiches. *58 E. Lynn (at Fairview), Eastlake, 206/322–2660.*

14 *b-1*

134 105th Ave. NE (near NE 2nd St., Bellevue, 425/454–1100.

10 *e-6*

PIKE & WESTERN WINE MERCHANTS

Once you've gathered up your produce and other items for a meal, let the purveyors glance into your shopping bag and help you select the right bottle to go with it. Wines are from the Northwest and around the world; plus there's also a selection of champagne. Stop by Friday afternoon 3 to 6 for tastings. *1934 Pike Pl. (between Stewart and Virginia Sts.), Pike Place Market, 206/441–1307.*

FRAMING

10 *e-6*

MARKET GRAPHICS

You can find the art you want—posters to reproduction prints—and get it framed, too. The design-savvy staff is tops. *1935 1st Ave. (near Pike Place Market),* Downtown, *206/441–7732.*

4 *f-5*

MCDOWELL'S U-FRAME-IT

In the early 1970s, Steve McDowell opened his first do-it-yourself framing shop; his business has since grown to include a dozen more from Mukilteo to Federal Way. The concept is still the same—the staff assists you in framing your art, simply and quickly. It usually takes just an hour. Nowadays some people are too busy even for that, so McDowell's offers custom framing, too. *5601 20th Ave. NW (at NW 56th St.), Ballard, 206/784–7565.*

14 *b-1*

11049 NE 8th St. (at 110th Ave. NE), Bellevue, 425/455–2622.

8 *b-7*

1822 Broadway (near E. Denny Way) Capitol Hill, 206/322–4455.

6 *b-7*

4530 Union Bay Place NE (near NE 45th St.), University District, 206/522–0968.

GIFTS

Interesting gifts and gift shops abound. Handcrafted items can be found at Pike Place Market, Fremont Sunday Market, and at seasonal festivals and fairs, including the annual Bellevue Arts Fair. Visit Country Village in Bothell and Gilman Village in Issaquah for a relaxing shopping experience at one-of-a-kind boutiques. The upscale University Village Shopping Center is home to a number of unique stores, including a fine candle shop, home-decor stores, and more. Finally, don't overlook the gift shops at museums, garden shops, zoos, and other local attractions.

5 *b-8*

BITTERS CO.

Sisters Amy and Katie Carson fill their rustic-chic shop with merchandise from around the world and they intermix it with locally crafted items. Jewelry, ceramics, furniture, textiles, clothing, and accessories are always stocked. Bits of found objects—driftwood, glass, metal, and natural fibers—have been used to create decor items; styles mix Scandinavian and Japanese simplicities. Look for fish-trap lamps, soft-bristle brooms, hand-loomed jute and cotton

rugs, and banana-fiber textiles in toffee- and chocolate-color plaids ($38/yard). Come hungry and you can have a sandwich or a snack at the café, or take a break at the wine bar before or after your shopping adventure. *513 36th St. N (between Dayton and Evanston Aves. N), Fremont, 206/632–0886.*

7 *f-1*

PORTAGE BAY GOODS

Funky Fremont is filled with similarly funky gift and antique shops; this one stands out for its environmental philosphy, with many items made of recycled materials, including glassware made from recycled glass and obsolete computer motherboards reincarnated as coasters and journals. *706 N. 34th St. (near Fremont Ave. N.), Fremont, 206/547–5221.*

9 *a-2*

YE OLDE CURIOSITY SHOP

The totally weird stuff never fails to shock or amaze. Yes, that's a shrunken head. And, behold, the mummified bodies. (These items aren't for sale.) For a century these bizarre items have been displayed; now they're accompanied by a fine collection of Native American art, including masks and totem poles; collectible figurines, music boxes, and antique weapons; imported arts and crafts; and loads of novelties and tacky souvenirs. *1001 Alaskan Way (Pier 54), Waterfront, 206/682–5844.*

HOME FURNISHINGS

Seattle's building boom has brought about dozens of new furniture stores, home-decor shops, and professional design studios. Before shopping or hiring someone, narrow down your work by having at least a rough idea of what you want and how much you're willing to pay. Bring a photo or sketch if you can, and be prepared to discuss such details as your current space limitations and desired color scheme.

For excellent design and remodeling advice, furniture shopping hints, and tips on the best deals in home and garden supplies, listen to "The Home Front," a home-improvement radio show hosted by local design expert Tammy Michaels, which airs on KOMO 1000-AM on Saturday at 9:30–11 AM.

architectural artifacts

`10` *f-8*

ANCIENT GROUNDS

Native American arts are the core of this gallery (with a coffee shop), but there's also a range of globally derived crafts. The collection of masks is top-notch, with pieces from Mexico, Japan, Africa, and Papua New Guinea. There's also pre-Columbian pottery. *1220 1st Ave. S (at University St.), Waterfront, 206/749–0747. Closed Sun.*

`12` *c-3*

CAROLINE STALEY FINE PRINTS

The spare gallery rooms highlight just a few quality items, mainly 19th- and 20th-century Japanese woodblock prints. A case in the back is filled with unframed reprints. *314 Occidental Ave. (between S. Main and Jackson Sts.), Pioneer Square, 206/621–1888.*

`12` *b-1*

KIBO GALERIE

Dress up your home with museum-quality African art, or handcarved furniture, chests, masks, statues, and collectibles. Bits and pieces from South Pacific islands are also displayed. *314 Occidental Ave. (between 1st and 2nd Aves. S), Pioneer Square, 206/621–1888. Closed Sun.–Mon. Sept.–May.*

bedding & bath

`10` *f-6*

BED, BATH & BEYOND

Browse here before buying elsewhere; prices are generally lower, and there are frequent sales on all the goods for showering, slumbering, plus everything in between. Look for everyday and high-end kitchen gadgets, stylish living-room accessories, and closet organizers. College students can get stuff for the dorm or first apartment; couples can sign up for the gift registry. Look to the terrific Web site for decorating tips and recipes. *1930 3rd Ave. (between Stewart and Virginia Sts.), Downtown, 206/448–7905, www.bedbathandbeyond.com.*

`2` *g-4*

Crossroads Shopping Center, 15600 NE 8th St. (at 156th Ave. NE), Bellevue, 425/564–0304.

`13` *g-4*

Redmond Town Center, 16495 NE 74th St. (between 164th and 165th Aves. NE), Redmond, 425/558–7978.

`10` *f-6*

LES PIAFS

Slim iron bed frames are decorated with frilly cushions, and vintage bath knick-knacks are hidden in shelf corners. If you're aiming to soften the look of your space, with romantic European- and American-style bed and bath items, this is the place to shop. *1921 2nd Ave. (between Stewart and Virginia Sts.), Belltown, 206/956–8366. Closed Sun.*

carpets & floor coverings

`7` *f-1*

CARAVAN CARPETS

The friendly owners of this corner shop not only have a wide range of new and used international carpets, but they'll also bend over backwards to make a deal. Trade in your old carpet for a discount on a new one. If you don't want to cover your whole floor, you can buy part of a rug—and you can exchange it for another if you don't like it when you get home. Cleaning, repairing, and appraisal services are available. *3500 Fremont Ave. N (at NW 36th St.), Fremont, 206/547–6666.*

`12` *b-3*

CHARLES ROBERTS ORIENTAL CARPET GALLERY

This large, museumlike gallery displays rugs under soft lighting that pops out their colors and sheen. There are hundreds of new carpets to choose from, and the expert staff will help you match the right one to your home's color scheme. You can also have your old rugs restored, cleaned, or appraised. *323 1st Ave. S (at S. Jackson St.), Pioneer Square, 206/621–9580.*

`12` *a-1*

DRISCOLL ROBBINS

The city's premier dealer in fine new and used Oriental carpets is also a favorite of interior designers. Choose from antique, tribal, Tibetan, and contemporary styles. Cleaning, padding, consulting, and delivery are available. *1002 Western Ave. (at Madison St.), Downtown, 206/292–1115.*

10 f-6

EHC

The Environmental Home Center offers fine-quality floor coverings that lessen the impact of home-decorating on the world. In addition to wool carpets and area rugs, you'll find plant-based coverings, recycled polyester carpet, and choices of all-natural fiber. Wood tiles, cork planks, and other smooth floor supplies are easy to install, and a full range of environmentally friendly home improvement accessories is offered. *1724 4th Ave. (between Stewart and Pine Sts.), Downtown, 206/682–7332, www.built-e.com.*

12 b-3

TURAN RUG GALLERY

You'll recognize this store by the weaving loom in the window—take a look at the books on international woven textiles around it, as well. The large carpets inside mostly hail from Asia; many have histories described in the books. If you're a serious buyer, plan to spend time here. Local delivery is free, and world shipping is offered. *410 1st Ave. (at S. Jackson St.), Pioneer Square, 206/749–9284.*

ceramic tiles & concrete

5 f-4

AMBIENTE EUROPEAN TILE DESIGN

Splashy, eye-catching iridescent tiles, bright, bold-patterned squares, and cookie-cutter shapes in all colors are available from this one-stop tile merchant. The upbeat showroom displays give you design ideas, but if you're not an artist, the staff will supply plenty of suggestions, free estimates, and installation. *227 NE 65th St. (between 1st Ave. NE and Latona Ave.), Green Lake, 206/ 524–2113, www.ambientetile.com.*

5 g-1

ART TILE CO.

From ceramic to stone, in do-it-yourself to professionally forged designs, this store inspires some of the city's top interior designers. The huge showroom covers thousands of shapes and hues, with tiles for every area in your home— complete with installation supplies and instructions. Note the handpainted and glass-block styles. *8511 Roosevelt Way NE (between NE 85th and 86th Sts.), University District, 206/523–3032. Closed Sun.*

2 h-3

CADMAN CONCRETE

Western Washington's largest concrete supplier also stocks and designs an extensive selection of decorative materials. Fifty-plus amazing styles can look like slate, brick, and wood and can be fashioned into any shape or color. Ask about the surprisingly durable Increte, material stamped with a symbol or pattern, which is often used to give a high-class touch to pool decks and living areas. The decorative concrete showroom highlights what they can do, but if you're further inspired, you'll want to check out the building materials warehouse. *18816 NE 80th St. (between 188th and 189th Aves. NE), Redmond, 425/868– 7334, www.cadman.com.*

12 c-2

NORBERRY TILE

Handmade Arts and Crafts tiles are the specialties here, and you can create your own or work with designers to get the look you want. Note the variety of inspiring samples, including glass, stone, and mosaics—the bronze imprints are outstanding. There's free parking around back, too. *207 2nd Ave. S (between S. Main and S. Washington Sts.), Pioneer Square, 206/343–9916, www.norberrytile. com. Closed Sun.*

china, glassware, porcelain, pottery, silver

1 g-3

ANDERSON'S CHINA, CRYSTAL & SILVER

Here you'll find more than 4,000 square ft of finery, including Gien, Haviland, Lenox, Mikasa, and Royal Doulton. You'll save 20%–40% on table settings and decorative items, and if you break something after you buy it they'll replace it at half the price. Plus, there's free gift wrapping. *Issaquah Meadows Shopping Center, 1480 NW Gilman Blvd. (between I–90 and Sammamish Rd.), Issaquah, 425/392– 4462 or 800/541–1241. Closed Sun.*

2 f-5

CHINA, SILVER & CRYSTAL SHOP

Get "ridiculous savings" on more than 700 patterns of china, plus sterling silver and stainless-steel flatware. Brides-to-be should note the extensive registry, complete with expert bridal consultants to help you wade through it all. A different manufacturer and pattern is featured each month. *10429 NE 2nd St. (between 104th and 105th Aves. NE), Bellevue, 425/462–4491 or 800/759–5817, www.chinasilvercrystal.com.*

`10` *f-6*

GALLERIES OF NIEMAN MARCUS

This is where Seattle's elite shop for crystal, china, and collectibles. If you can afford it, there's also jewelry and home decor. If that's not in your budget, you can still attend one of the store's artist receptions or holiday events. *Westlake Center, 400 Pine St. (at 4th Ave.), Downtown, 206/447–0901, www.niemanmarcus.com.*

`9` *e-6*

KUSAK CUT GLASS WORKS

The handblown, hand-cut crystal found at this century-old store is made on site in the owner's European tradition. The exquisite selection includes stemware, vases, and even crystal chandeliers. Look for big discounts during the spring and fall sales. *1911 22nd Ave. S (at Rainier Ave. S), Mt. Baker, 206/324–2931 or 800/ 426–9347, www.kusak.com.*

`12` *c-2*

LAGUNA

Collectors of ceramics need go no further for 20th-century American items. The range of designers includes Catalina, Fiesta, Franciscan, Rookwood, and Roseville, for starters. Some vintage items are also available. *116 S. Washington St. (between Occidental and 1st Aves. S), Pioneer Square, 206/682–6162, www.lagunapottery.com. Closed Sun.*

decorative glass

`12` *c-3*

GLASS HOUSE STUDIO

Seattle's oldest glassblowing studio and glass art gallery displays gorgeous iridescent art pieces backlit against black in cases along the high, exposed-brick walls. Watch the artists firing and shaping items in the glass-enclosed workshop in back, or just marvel at their creations. *311 Occidental Ave. S (between S. Main and Jackson Sts.), Pioneer Square, 206/682–9939.*

`10` *e-6*

GLASS EYE GALLERY

This small Market store sells all manner of glass ornaments, jewelry, and gift items. To protect the lovely selection of Venetian glassware, no kids are allowed. *1902 Post Alley (at Stewart St.), Pike Place Market, 206/441–3221.*

`10` *e-6*

PHOENIX RISING

One of the city's most famous glass shops, this gallery has everything from the medium: oversize plates, bowls, fountains, lamps, jewelry, and contemporary crafts. Look for modern crafts by over 200 local artists; receptions are scheduled throughout the year. *2030 Western Ave. (at Virginia St.), Pike Place Market, 206/728–2332, www.phoenixrisinggallery.com.*

`10` *e-5*

SEATTLE GLASSBLOWING STUDIO

Are unique handblown vases, bowls, lamps, and art pieces the objects of your affection? Have the pros create a line for you, even from your own design—or learn how to do it yourself. Demos and lessons are available daily. *2227 5th Ave. (between Bell and Blanchard Sts.), Downtown, 206/448–2181, www.seattleglassblowing.com.*

furniture

Seattle's booming housing market has resulted in an abundance of flourishing furniture stores. You'll find a bit of every style here, from classic handcarved woods to sleek modern designs, but be sure to shop around for bargains before you buy. Most stores are willing to discount sets, older items, and discontinued pieces, and many shops hold mid- and end-of-year sales.

`12` *b-1*

ARTE FORMA DESIGNS

There's a bit of everything beneath this store's exposed-beam ceiling, from country kitsch to classic European looks. It's a great place to shop for ideas or pick up a perfect side piece—a painted wooden bench, a sleek leather chair, a couple of velvet cushions, or a set created for you by the pro designers on staff. *997 Western Ave. (between Madison and Marion Sts.), Waterfront, 206/587–6663.*

12 *a-1*

BRASSWOODS FURNITURE

Rosewood furnishings, carved into exquisite shapes and inlaid with copper floral patterns, are the specialties of this shop, which opened in summer 2001. It's hard to believe that most of the polished armoires, bedframes, treasure chests, and tea trays are priced less than $1,000, but the owner is keen on jump-starting his business—buy soon, before prices rise. *1012 Western Ave. (between Seneca and Spring Sts.), Waterfront, 206/264–0957.*

12 *b-1*

DANIA

The office and home furniture at Dania's huge showrooms has futuristic, Jetsons-style lines and plain, bold colors. The slick wood and slim leather items are an improvement on IKEA's quality and the prices reflect this. But pieces are built to last, and the store is always less crowded. Work with the staff to decorate your space, and look for sample items on sale. *825 Western Ave. (between Marion and Columbia Sts.), Waterfront, 206/262–1001.*

2 *f-2*

12230 116th Ave. NE (at NE 122nd and 123rd Sts.), Kirkland, 425/823–9160.

5 *g-4*

6416 Roosevelt Way NE (between NE 64th and 65th Sts.), University District, 206/524–9611.

10 *f-8*

DIVA

This shop is full of ultramodern furnishings two steps ahead of the trend—this summer all in white leather. Look for B&B Italia, Fontana Arte, and Kartell designs. If you don't know what you're looking at, don't be intimidated—ask a one of the ultra-hip salespeople. *1300 Western Ave. (between Union and University Sts.), Waterfront, 206/287–9992.*

12 *c-3*

FINE NW WOODWORKING

This shop represents the work of more than 30 artist owner-members who value furniture craftsmanship and design. All pieces are original and created to show off the woods incorporated. You can find almost anything in the showroom or have it handmade for you at reasonable prices—a gorgeous walnut and bird's-eye maple–trimmed coffee table might sell for $2,275. *101 S. Jackson St. (at 1st Ave. S), Pioneer Square, 206/625–0542, www.nwfinewoodworking.com.*

1 *e-6*

IKEA

"Design-conscious home furnishings for the average homeowner" should be the motto for Seattle's most beloved, some-assembly-required shopping spot for the common folk. The enormous warehouse is laid out like a mansion: walkways lead you through room after room of cozy, intimately decorated demos. If you like the casual style, you'll find every type of furnishing and accessory here, right down to kitchen, bath, and backyard. Check out the bargain room in the corner between the warehouse displays and the exit, where returned merchandise often goes for 75% off the original price. There's a coffee shop, a Swedish café, and a child-care center (3 and up) with an enormous pit filled with balls to keep the wee ones busy while you shop. *600 SW 43rd St. (at Southcenter Pkwy.), Renton, 425/656–2980 or 800/570–4532, www.ikea.com.*

10 *f-8*

IN FORM

Furnishings are an art form in this showroom of extreme modern pieces. Some of it's fun, like the all-chalkboard table; other things look like they'd be more for conversation than comfort. The shop has top respect from the rich and cool Gen-Next set, who snap up pieces in minutes, so hesitation doesn't pay if you like something here. *1220 Western Ave. (between Union and University Sts.), Waterfront, 206/622–1608.*

12 *c-2*

LEATHERS

Only the richest leather furnishings and accessories—in 2,800 styles from 25 manufacturers—are sold in this dark, rustic showroom. Couches and chairs are done in deep, chocolate browns with a buttery sheen and set around old steamer trunks on the polished wood-plank floor. Suede items and wall hangings are also available. *220 S. Jackson St. (between 2nd and Occidental Aves.), Pioneer Square, 206/405–4444, www.leathersgallery.com.*

1 g-4

Gilman Village, 635 NW Gilman Blvd. (at Sammamish Pkwy. SE), Issaquah, 425/ 392–7632.

12 f-2

132 Central Way (at Market St.), Kirkland, 425/576–5700.

10 f-8

LIGNE ROSET

French contemporary furnishings are featured in this shop at the base of the Harbor steps. Look for simple, modern-style pieces in bright colors, with lots of glass items. 55 University St. (at Western Ave.), Waterfront, 206/341–9990.

12 a-1

MCKINNON FURNITURE

The handcrafted American furniture in warm-colored woods and country styles may include locally made Shaker-style pieces and other domestically wielded items. Prices are serious—a walnut dresser $2,850, a cherry media cabinet $3,175—but the quality of the merchandise is outstanding. You can also pick up chenille bedding and duvets ($519). 1015 Western Ave. (between Spring and Madison Sts.), Waterfront, 206/622–6474, www.mckinnonfurniture.com.

12 a-1

NORWALK FURNISHINGS

Whether you're a professional or a budding home designer, you'll be inspired, if not by the piles of big, thick decor books scattered around the displays, then by the displays themselves. Panels show off sections of wood-finish samples, and thousands of fabric squares line the back walls. Although most of the showroom furniture is in warm, deep colors like plum and amber, you're free to put together any look you like—with delivery in 35 days. 1010 Western Ave. (between Spring and Madison Sts.), Waterfront, 206/622–0280.

vintage, used, & discount furniture

Seattleites are not snobs—and they're not all Microsoft billionaires—but we do have good taste and we're keen on saving cash anywhere we can. Seattle has no shortage of sale furniture, but a lot of it's just cheap junk. Here's the scoop on where to find all the name-brand stuff on sale, and where to shop for the best-quality used items.

11 a-5

AREA 51

This is a fun place to look for unusual items—large, colorful chairs, offbeat couches, odd-angled tables. The turnover is quick, so stop back another day if you can't find what you want. 401 E. Pine St. (at E. Bellevue Way), Belltown, 206/568–4782.

1 e-6

BON MARCHÉ
FURNITURE GALLERY

Last season's home furnishings and sale items wind up here, often at deep discounts. But things are sold "as is," so look carefully for scratches, dirt marks, and tears before you buy—and if you still want it, you might get an even better deal if you bargain. Southcenter Mall, 17800 Southcenter Pkwy. (at I–5), Southcenter, 425/656–6671.

7 f-1

DELUXE JUNK

Bursting with cheap kitsch and collectibles, this landmark über-organized shop takes up the whole corner—and has for more than 20 years. Every space holds a set of treasures: Classic Hong Kong posters line the entryway, with harmonicas here, embroidered handkerchiefs there, chopstick sets to the left, and metallic slippers to the right. Furniture might include a happening glass-top table with four leopard-print chairs, a 6-ft credenza, or a wicker side table. As for clothes, this is the place to find that vintage dress in mint condition, or that paisley smoking jacket with matching handkerchief. 3518 Fremont Pl. N (at N. 36th St.), Fremont, 206/634–2733.

10 d-5

IT'S GOTTA GO

This discount warehouse for the Continental Furniture chain stores carries a variety of modern goods for every room. You'll find deep discounts on previous rentals and closeouts—albeit the original prices were inflated. Check the bargain loft, and feel free to haggle if you find something you like. Quick delivery is part of the service. 2200 Western Ave. (at Bell St.), Belltown, 206/441–0531.

12 a-1

MODELE'S

Although it's mostly consignment items—come Tuesday and Thursday mornings for the best selection—everything is in great condition. For $850 you can choose a new-looking 86″ sofa with five silk pillows, or a vintage cherry day table. If you'd like to sell your furniture, grab a consignment tip sheet first. Your items will be screened (and picked up free if they make the cut). There's also a design service if you'd like to order new furniture. *1001 Western Ave. (at Madison St.), Waterfront, 206/287–9942.*

2 *f-4*

NEWPORT FURNISHINGS

Deeply discounted name-brand furniture fills this national company's Seattle warehouse. You can pay half the retail prices on quality furniture—the catch is that you must order it: it takes four to six weeks, you pay at least half up front, and there's no home delivery. Appointments are mandatory, at which time you'll receive directions to the store. If you can live with this, you'll get big savings. Because the showroom is so crowded, though, bringing children is discouraged. *Bellevue, 425/643–8018, www.newportfurnishings.com.*

7 *f-7*

QUEEN ANNE PRE-OWNED FURNISHINGS

Gaze among the lounge chairs (how's flowered, 1960s-style in lemon-lime?), electric-blue wicker rockers, and polished curio cabinets. From baby-doll shoes to china tea cups, every piece in this roomy shop is displayed at its best angle—even the line of lamps hanging overhead near the back. There's free parking in back. *514 1st Ave. N (between Thomas and John Sts.), Queen Anne, 206/282–5489.*

2 *f-2*

URBAN COTTAGE

If you like quaint, classic pieces, come here for furnishings from the early to mid-1900s. Vintage lamps, mirrors, and chandeliers mingle with lace pillows and simple bed frames. You'll also find a number of unique original designs among the familiar-style used items. *218 Kirkland Ave. (at NE 116th St.), Kirkland, 425/828–3595.*

1 *e-6*

WHIMSICAL WHITES

Vintage collectibles, whitewashed furnishings, country-style housewares, and a menagerie of decorative items like frosted glass lamps and gilded mirrors are some of the items sold in huge white farmhouse with the weeping cherry tree out front. Look closely to see how doorknobs, candle holders, and linens have been recycled into unique items. *20224 108th Ave. SE (between SE 192nd and 208th Sts.), Kent, 253/520–0230. Closed Mon.–Tues.*

home accessories

The ever-expanding housing market, competitive interest rates, and the uneven stock market mean that home buyers here are always on the move, and the annual influx and exodus of students results in a massive redecorating movement. No matter what your style or budget, these housewares specialists know just what we need to make each new space our own—but you'll usually find the best selection of merchandise in late summer and early spring, and the deepest discounts after Christmas and Father's Day.

5 *b-8*

BITTERS CO.

See Gifts, *above.*

10 *g-6*

CHIASSO

Functional meets fun at this colorful modern housewares shop. The fruit-color lamps, furniture, and kitchen accessories have odd angles and lines, which give them a trendy edge. The goods are high-quality and offbeat; it's just the place to gift shop for someone who already has everything. Pick up a few attractive knickknacks—tea lights in frosted, pastel glasses, fish swizzle sticks—to add flavor to a party. There's also a bridal registry. *Westlake Center, 400 Pine St. (at 4th Ave.), Downtown, 206/624–2660, www.chiasso.com.*

11 *e-1*

CITY PEOPLE'S MERCANTILE

The humble wooden exterior belies the quality of the goods inside. Part hardware store (about half the store is devoted to such True Value hardware products as paint, hammers, and nails), part garden shop, and part gift shop, City People's is the 21st century's version of a general store. Once you have your apartment or house furnished, you can pick up all the accents here. Rustic Tuscan dinnerware, matchstick bamboo blinds, sparkly shower curtains, plus clothes, toys, hardware, and garden supplies fill the shelves. Come early to nab one of the free parking spaces. *500 15th Ave. E (at E. Republican St.), Capitol Hill, 206/324–9510.*

6 *d-6*

5440 Sand Point Way NE (at Princeton Ave. NE), University District, 206/524–1200.

10 *e-6*

COST PLUS WORLD MARKET

Seattleites love this international bazaar of housewares and furniture. The store stocks everything from bed frames to privacy screens to patio furniture, plus dishes, kitchen and bath accessories, pictures, baskets, and more. Many items are handmade in countries like Bolivia, Mali, India, and the Philippines. There's a terrific international wine section, as well as a gourmet foods emporium with lots of European imports. Don't miss the sample coffees, teas, and snacks. *2103 Western Ave. (at Lenora St.), Waterfront, 206/443–1055, www.costplus.com.*

2 *f-4*

10300 NE 8th St. (between NE 4th and 8th Sts.), Bellevue, 425/453–1310.

2 *f-4*

CRATE & BARREL

This trendsetting three-story home store opened in the summer 2001 and takes its name from when merchandise was simply displayed in its packing containers. The chain is known for its good quality at a reasonable price, and it's a favorite with first-time furniture buyers and those getting hitched. Also look for sheets and towels, colorful dinnerware, trendy party accessories, and a range of simple, functional furniture in traditional and modern styles. *Bellevue Square, Bellevue Way (between NE 4th and 8th Sts.), Bellevue, 425/646–8900, www.crate-barrel.com.*

12 *a-1*

DEEP INTERIORS

Professional design services and high-quality home accessories are what this store offers. Browse the crowded showroom to get a feel for your style, then sit down with a consultant and start sketching your plans. If you just need that special piece, there's lots to choose from here, as well. *1006 Western Ave. (between*

Spring and Madison Sts.), Waterfront, 206/621–1380.

12 *c-2*

FIREWORKS

See Folk Art & Handicrafts, *above.*

6 *a-6*

MILLER-POLLARD

UW students stock up on apartment furnishings here because they look so good—and can cost so little. Lamps, rugs, kitchenware, bath items, and more are available. You can even custom-order furniture if you don't find anything that's right for your space. Savvy shoppers wait for the mid-June sidewalk sale, when there's at least a 20% discount on everything. *University Village, 2673 NE University Village (at 25th Ave. NE), University District, 206/527–8748.*

7 *f-1*

PORTAGE BAY GOODS

Environment-conscious decorators buy from this store, which specializes in recycled, reworked housewares and gifts. Almost everything is handmade, including colorful quilts made from old T-shirts, and funky T-shirts made from old tea towels. There's a selection of handcarved furniture, recycled glassware, candles, and kitsch, each tagged with a story card to tell you its maker, history, and purpose. *706 N. 34th (at Fremont Ave. N), Fremont, 206/547–5221, www.portagebaygoods.com.*

10 *g-6*

POTTERY BARN

Once known for it's large array of tableware, Pottery Barn has recreated itself into a home-design store that pretty closely resembles Crate & Barrel. Wares now run the gamut from leather couches to armoires with a few lamps and picture frames thrown in for good measure. What you'll be hard pressed to find, however, are any diminutive items—furnishes are chunky and over-sized. The large, glass-enclosed shops have a department-store feel; take the escalator to the second-floor design studio, where experts can help you create a look for your home. Clothing for men and women is available, and there's a special Pottery Barn Kids section and Web site. *Pacific Place, 600 Pine St. (at 6th Ave.), Downtown, 206/621–0276, www.potterybarn.com, www.potterybarnkids.com.*

2 *f-4*
Bellevue Square, Bellevue Way (between NE 4th and 8th Sts.), Bellevue, 425/451–0097.

6 *a-6*
University Village, 4645 NE University Village (at 25th Ave. NE), University District, 206/522–6860.

10 *d-5*
RIFLESSI
An exquisite selection of fine Italian home accessories in vivid colors are brought to life against the pumpkin-orange cement floor, pea-soup-green painted walls, and a background of soft classical Italian music. Beautiful kitchen items include oversize plates, simple ceramic wine and water cups, and a cabinet of designerware with cards noting the artists and their inspirations. Don't miss the amazing selection of framed works, particularly the stained-glass scenes, or the majolica created in the traditional 13th-century method. The unusual, high-end items here are perfect for gifts—or sign up for the registry yourself. 2302 1st Ave. (between Bell and Battery Sts.), Belltown, 206/728–5840, www.riflessi-italia.com.

12 *d-4*
UWAJIMAYA
See Malls, above.

9 *e-2*
ZANADIA HOME FURNISHINGS
Eclectic, high-quality, and casual home furnishings fill the two stories of this shop. Velvet couches, cushions with gold brocade trim, pendulum clocks, and antiques contrast with the simple "puff chairs" made of soft pillows strung on black wire frames. Head downstairs to see the room full of couches and living room furniture. Lamps, pottery, and knickknacks decorate the empty spaces—and it's all for sale. Wallingford Center, 1815 N. 45th St. (between Wallingford and Burke Aves.), Wallingford, 206/547–0884, www.zanadia.com.

international accents

11 *c-2*
DAR SALAAM MOROCCAN IMPORTS
Shop here for gorgeous pottery from North Africa. Islamic mosaics and tiled mirrors share space with Arab overcoats, turquoise jewelry, and sequinned robes. Look for the handmade drum sets. 219 Broadway St. E (between Thomas and Harrison Sts.), Capitol Hill, 206/726–8265. Closed Mon.

12 *c-3*
HIMALAYAN TREASURES
Everything Nepalese, and some things Tibetan, can be found in this small store, including a variety of handwoven Nepalese carpets, all pure wool. Lanterns, candles, prayer flags, and other small home decorations fill the rest of the space. 200 1st Ave. S (at S. Washington St.), Pioneer Square, 206/233–9610. Closed Sun.

11 *c-2*
MALI INTERNATIONAL TRIBAL ARTS
African-style housewares, decorations, and gifts, all done in deep amber and eggplant hues, fill every inch of this cavernous shop. Stock up on inexpensive accents like baskets, jars, carvings, and knickknacks. Note the painted animal sets—the tallest giraffe is 10 ft high. Some clothes and a fantastic section of beaded jewelry are also available. 112 Broadway St. E (between Harrison and Thomas Sts.), Capitol Hill, 206/324–8060.

12 *c-2*
TAI DESIGNS
The Japanese owner makes the paper art objects sold here in the traditional manner, from the fiber of young mulberry trees. She takes orders—the framed art and half-finished crafts on display yield decoration ideas—or you can make decorations yourself; textiles woven from paper strips are just one of the innovative creations you can learn in her classes. 214 1st Ave. S (between S. Washington and S. Main Sts.), Pioneer Square, 206/343–5999.

kitchens

Seattle's diverse cultural mix has resulted in an array of international flavors that many of us long to bring into our own homes. Hence the number of speciality cooking stores stocking an appliance and implement for every cuisine—and you don't have to look much further than your local supermarket to find the right spices. For Asian ingredients, Uwajimaya is your best bet, though most kitchen stores and large grocers will order special items. The stores selected below have the best quality and most diverse merchandise, and many have excellent Web sites where you can log on for free recipes, decorating suggestions, magazines, and sale coupons.

10 g-6
CITY KITCHENS
Imagine all your dream implements and appliances for the kitchen; that's what's inside this big, friendly shop. The cookware selection is excellent, and you'll find an array of unusual but handy gadgets that once you buy you won't be able to live without. You can also rearrange your space with the attractive pot racks and butcher blocks. The gift registry is popular with young couples tying the knot. *1527 4th Ave. (between Pike and Pine Sts.), Downtown, 206/382–1138.*

8 h-4
COOKIN' AT MADISON PARK
This store looks like a kitchen used in *Metropolitan Home* spread: high ceilings, exposed-brick walls, lots of light, and casually arranged cooking goods. The front is filled with shining pots, square woks, ceramic dishes, and silver tools, but you'll also find oils, spices, and sauces to flavor them. Note the cute little accents—glass drink stirrers, decorative bottles, and scented candles—and the book section in back. *4224 E. Madison St. (between 42nd and 43rd Aves. E), Madison Park, 206/328– COOK or 206/328–2665.*

10 e-6
HABITS
Although it has general home merchandise, this shop concentrates on the kitchen and creating attractive places to enjoy a good meal. The setting and the staff inspire a fresh outlook on kitchen design, as well lend new dinner ideas. In addition to the typical cookware, you'll find crystal vases, unusual lamps, and a selection of comfortable, casual furniture. *2010 Western Ave. (at Virginia St.), Pike Place Market, 206/728–2828.*

4 e-5
KITCHEN 'N THINGS
There's a good mix of casual and fine kitchen and dining items at this store on the corner of the neighborhood's main shopping block. Crystal plates,

stemware, and cutlery mix with casual dishes and appliances. Brides-to-be commonly register here. *2324 NW Market St. (at 24th Ave. NW), Ballard, 206/784–8717.*

10 e-7
SUR LA TABLE
The original Market store is an Asian market-style jumble of more than 12,500 items whose purpose is to make cooking and dining a pleasure. It's a crowded mix of colors, with metal shelves stuffed full of dishes, glassware, and books; bunches of wooden spoons and silver whisks shoved into crocks; and a frightening display of knives on the wall. (You might want to get these from the mail-order catalog.) Celebrity chefs stop by regularly to shop Sur La Table's extensive inventory. *84 Pine St. (between 1st and Western Aves.), Pike Place Market, 206/448–2244, www.surlatable.com.*

2 f-2
90 Central Way (at Market St.), Kirkland, 425/827–1311.

10 g-6
WILLIAMS-SONOMA
Gourmet cooking and cookware (particularly French) is the foundation of this chichi chain kitchen store. The pots and pans, bakeware, tools, cutlery, and appliances are top-quality, with prices to match: If you're not into spending $400 for a toaster, you can watch to see if anyone does. But if you love being in the kitchen, you can't go wrong with anything here. Those who aren't so handy in the kitchen can pick up a few tips from the endless selection of books—or pick up a few bar goods and imported gourmet treats. If you like the kitchen styles, you'll also find housewares, linens, and basic furniture. As an added bonus, the store often samples the gourmet treats they sell through the catalog, too. *Pacific Place, 600 Pine St. (at 6th Ave.), Downtown, 206/621–7405, www.williams-sonoma.com.*

2 f-4
Bellevue Square, Bellevue Way (between NE 4th and 8th Sts.), Bellevue, 425/454–7007.

6 a-6
University Village, 2530 NE University Village (at 25th Ave. NE), University District, 206/523–3733.

lamps & lighting

5 *d-6*

HAROLD'S FINE HOME LIGHTING

What was once a small lamp shop has, in nearly a half-century, expanded into a full-scale lighting and design store. There are hundreds of styles to choose from, or for inspiration you can check the big idea books of shapes, shades, and finishes. If you don't see what you want, just bring in a sketch and the expert staff will help you design your own lamps or lighting systems. Hint: If you're looking for an unusual bulb, there's a whole wall of sizes and colors. *1912 N. 45th St. (between Burke and Meridian Aves.), Wallingford, 206/633–2557.*

12 *b-1*

HIGHLIGHTS

More than 40 collections of contemporary lighting, including such brands as Artemide, Foscarini, Leucos, Ron Rezek, and Resolute, are sold here. Styles range from classicly romantic to ultra-modern. Note the unusual designs—grape-bunch chandeliers, tall tube lights, and wiry metal creations. Get on the mailing list to shop the sample sales, where almost everything goes for under $200. *999 Western Ave. (between Madison and Marion Sts.), Pioneer Square, 206/382–9667.*

2 *f-4*

LAMPS PLUS

This chain store probably has the best selection of basic, conservative lamps for the home. There's something for every room, all in popular styles, shapes, and colors, but you can special-order more unique pieces. The prices are generally low, and you can schedule a free, in-home consultation. *11919 NE 8th St. (between 119th and 120th Aves. NE), Bellevue, 425/688–1033, www.lampsplus.com.*

12 *c-2*

SEATTLE LIGHTING FIXTURE CO. & DESIGN GALLERY

This is the Northwest's largest lighting-fixture supplier, and the beige Downtown warehouse is filled with light emanating from table lamps, sconces, chandeliers, and lanterns, among hundreds of other styles. Residential and commercial services are on site, as are hundreds of exclusive designs. You can even work with the professional staff to create your own lighting system, or attend free seminars on how to do it yourself. *222 2nd Ave. S (between S. Jackson and Main Sts.), Downtown, 206/622–2313, www.seattlelighting.com.*

2 *f-4*

12828 Bel-Red Rd. (between 128th and 129th Aves. NE), Bellevue, 425/455–2110.

HOUSEWARES & HARDWARE

11 *e-1*

CITY PEOPLE'S MERCANTILE

See Home Accessories, above.

6 *a-6*

MRS. COOK'S

Mrs. Cook's has an abundance of cooking gadgets, small appliances, cookware, and table linens and accessories. You'll find unique items here that you even the large department stores don't carry. *2810 NE University Village (at 25th Ave. NE), University District, 206/525–5008.*

6 *a-6*

RESTORATION HARDWARE

The theme at Restoration Hardware is "retro." From home furnishings to classic toys, the store is a browser's delight. Bargain hunters may pass on the classic but expensive furniture pieces, but few can resist buying at least one inexpensive blast from the past—like an original silver slinky or an atomic rocket. And yes, there's "real" hardware here, too, including unique and functional tools, cleaning supplies, and pricey cabinet fittings. *4635 NE University Village (at 25th Ave. NE), University District, 206/522–2775.*

10 *g-6*

Pacific Place, 600 Pine St. (at 6th Ave.), Downtown, 206/652–4545.

10 *e-7*

SUR LA TABLE

See Kitchens, above.

10 *g-6*

WILLIAMS-SONOMA

See Kitchens, above.

JEWELRY

antique & collectible items

2 *c-1*

ALANA ANTIQUE & ESTATE JEWELRY

If you're prone to impulse buying, be forewarned: the unique array of one-of-a-kind jewelry here is very tempting. The marriage-minded will want to see the collection of diamond rings set in platinum, white, and yellow gold. *Northgate Mall, Northgate Way (at 4th Ave. NE), Northgate, 206/362–6227.*

10 *g-7*

FACÈRÉ JEWELRY ART GALLERY

The jewelry here is "sculpture for wearing." Ramona Solberg's 200-square-ft store is packed with pieces made of traditional gold, silver, and gemstones; more unusual materials, too, like rubber, aluminum, and FIMO, a stiff polymer modeling clay; and antique jewelry from the late 1700s through the late 1890s. *City Centre, 1420 5th Ave. (at Pike St.), Downtown, 206/264–1400.*

6 *d-5*

MICHAEL WM. FARRELL JEWELERS

Antique collection pieces and estate jewelry are sold here, as are custom designs in platinum and gold. It's a good place for watch and jewelry repair, engraving services, bead stringing, appraisals, and consignment sales, too. *Sand Point Village, 5420 Sand Point Way NE (at Princeton Ave. NE), University District, 206/524–8848.*

11 *e-3*

324 15th Ave. E (at E. Thomas St.), Capitol Hill, 206/324–1582.

contemporary pieces

10 *g-6*

CARTIER

Well-heeled shoppers stand indecisively before Cartier and its neighbor, Tiffany & Co. Shop for ultralux, super-fine jewelry, watches, and accessories, including leather goods, pens, eyewear, and perfume. *Pacific Place, 600 Pine St. (at 6th Ave.), Downtown, 206/264–1400.*

7 *g-8*

E.E. ROBBINS THE ENGAGEMENT RING STORE

You may overhear the refrain, "forever is a long time", so the ring has to be right. Here the selection is vast and the sales help more than informed as to how to select the perfect ring. For the already-hitched, the store also sells anniversary rings. *2200 1st Ave. (at Blanchard St.), Belltown, 206/826–7464.*

6 *a-6*

SOMETHING SILVER

If you're looking for something that doesn't have to scream for attention, Something Silver is worth a visit. You'll discover everything imaginable for the new baby, all the way up to rings appropriate for marriage. They also specialize in charms of all varieties. Stop in and find something between $5 and $500. *2662 NE University Village (at 25th Ave. NE), University District, 206/523–7545.*

14 *b-1*

Bellevue Square, Bellevue Way (between NE 4th and 8th Sts.), Bellevue, 425/462–5261.

10 *f-6*

Westlake Center, 400 Pine St. (at 4th Ave.), Downtown, 206/621–7800.

8 *e-7*

2811 E. Madison St. (at 28th Ave. E), Capitol Hill, 206/860–6000.

10 *g-6*

TIFFANY & CO.

Diamonds may be everyone's best friend at Tiffany's, but you'll find all manner of sparkling jewels and keepsakes here. Fine china, crystal, sterling silver baby rattles and yo-yos, and much more will vie for your attention—and for the opportunity to be given to someone special in the signature Tiffany gift box. You can get practically anything engraved here, too. *Pacific Place, 600 Pine St. (at 6th Ave.), Downtown, 206/264–1400.*

10 *g-7*

TURGEON RAINE JEWELLERS

At the source of Seattle's modern architectural jewelry, see what old and new money is wearing. You'll find designs by owners Norman Turgeon and Jerry Raine, as well as pieces by European designers who use cutting-edge construction techniques. The tension-set diamond engagement rings are renown. If, among the jewelry cases, you don't find the exact piece you're looking for, they can arrange to have it made for you. *1407 5th Ave. (at Union St.), Downtown, 206/447–9488.*

LEATHER GOODS & LUGGAGE

10 *g-7*
BIAGIO
Biagio carries quality luggage, business cases, wallets, and other small leather goods, and travel accessories, as well as stationery and fine writing instruments. There are six Biagio stores in the greater Seattle area. *1405 4th Ave. (at Pike St.), Downtown, 206/623–3842 or 800/788–2808.*

2 *c-1*
Northgate Mall, Northgate Way (at 4th Ave. NE), Northgate, 206/362–6865.

14 *b-1*
Bellevue Square, Bellevue Way (between NE 4th and 8th Sts.), Bellevue, 425/454–5543.

10 *g-7*
LOUIS VUITTON
The Seattle Louis Vuitton store carries the full line of its signature luggage and handbags, as well as wallets and other accessories. *416 University St. (at 4th Ave.), Downtown, 206/749–0711.*

13 *g-4*
TODAY'S TRAVELER
Today's Traveler carries luggage, but they don't stop there. You'll find a world of helpful travel products here, including trip-friendly clothes by Ex-Officio, travel books, videos, maps, dual-voltage electronics, organizers, travel pillows, and other accessories. The store presents free and low-cost travel seminars and is also a full-service travel agency. *Redmond Town Center, 7311 164th Ave. NE, Redmond, 425/883–8400.*

MAPS

9 *a-2*
METSKER MAPS OF SEATTLE
Once you find this store, you'll have no excuse for getting lost again. Find maps galore, globes, travel books, compasses, puzzles and games to help you steer a course in the right direction. *702 1st Ave. (at Cherry St.), Downtown, 206/623–8747.*

10 *g-7*
RAND MCNALLY
If you're looking for maps, try this big, chain store, which stocks a full range of the company's famous local, regional, national and international maps. Rand McNally also carries other map brands from tiny-travel to wall-hanging sizes. It also has a good selection of travel guides. You can pick up some good travel accessories, too. *Four Seasons Olympic Hotel, 1218 4th Ave. (between Seneca and University Sts.), Downtown, 206/264–6277.*

5 *e-7*
WIDE WORLD BOOKS & MAPS
If most of your world wide adventures have been on the Web, expand your horizons with a visit to this shop. Stock up on maps, globes, language tapes, and travel books. Get trip tips from the well-traveled employees and then advance on your adventure by getting a passport photo. *4411 Wallingford Ave. N (at N. 45th St.), Wallingford, 206/634–3453.*

MUSIC

cds, tapes, & vinyl

12 *c-3*
BUD'S JAZZ RECORDS
Bud Young has been jazzing up the Northwest since 1982, with an inventory of jazz (and *only* jazz) recordings that number more than 10,000. It's one of the largest of such collections in the country, and jazz fans visiting Seattle make a point to include it on their itineraries. Most of the recordings are on CD, though Bud also carries some vinyl. *102 S. Jackson (at 1st Ave. S), Pioneer Square, 206/628–0445.*

5 *g-7*
CELLOPHANE SQUARE
Cellophane Square is well-known for its extensive vinyl section, carrying both new and used LPs. The University District store opened in 1972, so they've had decades to build up a formidable inventory. It's a great place to find used CDs, as well as all the newest releases Stop by on Saturday to catch the in-

store performances. *4538 University Way NE (at NE 45th St.), University District, 206/634–2280.*

14 *b-1*

322 Bellevue Way NE (at NE 4th St.), Bellevue, 206/329–2202.

11 *c-3*

130 Broadway Ave. E (at E. Denny Way), Capitol Hill, 206/329–2202.

3 *b-8*

EASY STREET

Explore the new and used music here on your own or the experienced staff is happy to make recommendations. If you've got some CDs you've grown bored with, bring them along and swap them for something new to listen to instead. If vinyl's your thing, check out the collection of new records upstairs. Blend your music shopping experience with a leisurely visit to the coffee bar and café. *4559 California Ave. SW (near SW Oregon St.), West Seattle, 206/938–3279.*

2 *c-2*

SILVER PLATTERS

Since the dawn of music compact discs, locally owned Silver Platters has been the place to find them. The selection is outstanding, with more than 60,000 titles, including extensive jazz and classical sections. Listening-before-you-buy is encouraged, and service is friendly and helpful. In addition to CDs, they also sell DVDs. Local artists frequently perform live at all stores. *9560 1st Ave. NE (at NE 95th St.), Northgate, 206/524–3472.*

13 *e-8*

14603 NE 20th St. (near 148th Ave. NE) Bellevue, 425/613–3472.

7 *g-6*

TOWER RECORDS, VIDEO, & BOOKS

Though part of a national chain, Tower manages to avoid the cookie-cutter corporate feel that some other music stores have. Of course their nation-wide connections are an advantage when you're looking for something special—if they don't have it (but there's a good chance that they will), they can get it for you. The store is well-organized, with numerous listening stations, and they stay open 'til midnight daily. *500 Mercer St. (at 5th Ave. N), Queen Anne, 206/283–4456.*

5 *g-7*

4321 University Way NE (at NE 43rd St.), University District, 425/632–1187.

musical instruments

7 *g-1*

DUSTY STRINGS ACOUSTIC MUSIC SHOP

Founders Ray and Sue Mooers opened this Fremont shop in 1979. Hammered dulcimers and folk harps are built here; they also carry many other acoustic instruments, including mandolins, banjos, fiddles, guitars, kazoos, and even tin whistles. The shop is packed with music in CD, video, and songbook format. *3406 Fremont Ave. N (at N. 34th St.), Fremont, 206/634–1662.*

7 *h-6*

GUITAR CENTER

This national chain brings the "superstore" concept to selling instruments, with big stores and a vast selection, including electric and acoustic guitars, basses, keyboards, drums, software, recording equipment, amps, DJ and lighting gear, and more. Each department is staffed by its own knowledgeable specialists who play the instruments they sell. Guitar Center also guarantees the lowest prices. *530 Westlake Ave. (at Mercer St.), Downtown, 206/287–9100.*

13 *d-1*

Upper Totem Lake Mall, 12608 120th Ave. NE (I–405 Exit 20B), Kirkland, 425/814–9640.

1 *d-1*

GUITARVILLE

Guitarville has been buying and selling vintage guitars and equipment since 1958. At any given time, it has hundreds of vintage instruments on display. The friendly staff lets you try out the guitars, and if you're looking for something rare, chances are they'll find it for you. *19258 15th Ave. NE (at NE 192nd St.), Shoreline, 206/363–8188.*

5 *f-7*

PETOSA MUSIC

The only manufacturer of accordions in America is right here in Seattle's Wallingford neighborhood. More than 100 antique models are on display in the store's museum. Besides accordions, Petosa Music carries state-of-the-art digital music products, including software, recording equipment, and computers. *313 NE 45th St. (at 4th Ave. NE), Wallingford, 206/632–2700.*

5 *b-1*

ROSEWOOD GUITAR

For the classical guitar aficionado, Rosewood is the place to visit. It carries flamenco and classical guitars, sheet music, and CDs, and arranges private lessons, too. *8402 Greenwood Ave. N (at N. 84th St.), Greenwood, 206/297–8788.*

5 *g-5*

TRADING MUSICIAN

Buy, sell, and, of course, trade instruments here. Find vintage guitars and amps, drums, keyboards, horns and winds, stringed instruments, harmonicas, and more. They also have a repair shop. *5908 Roosevelt Way NE (at 4th Ave. NE), Wallingford, 206/522–6707.*

sheet music

10 *g-5*

CAPITOL MUSIC CENTER

Capitol Music's forte is sheet music, and their selection is the best in the city. Particularly if you're looking for something obscure, don't bother going anywhere else. *718 Virginia St. (at 7th Ave.), Downtown, 206/622–0171.*

NEWSPAPERS & MAGAZINES

5 *g-7*

BULLDOG NEWS & FAST ESPRESSO

With nearly 3,000 newspapers and magazines, when you want to know what's going on in the world, this is the place to dash in, pick up a paper, a shot of espresso, and go. At the University District store, you can also find caffeine fulfillment, check E-mail, and surf the Internet. The first five minutes on-line is free with a coffee purchase, and you can surf at the low price of 25¢ per 10 minutes after that. *4208 University Way NE (at NE 42nd St.), University District, 206/632–6397.*

11 *c-2*

Broadway Market, 401 Broadway St. E (between Harrison and Republican Sts.), Capitol Hill, 206/322–6397.

14 *g-1*

EASTSIDE DAILY PLANET

Bellevue's Crossroads community is something of an ethnic melting pot, with Eastern European, Russian, Asian, Hispanic, African, and Middle Eastern immigrants contributing to the multicultural atmosphere. This newsstand serves the foreign language news needs for the diverse local community and greater Eastside, and also has a huge selection of magazines. *Crossroads Shopping Center, 15600 NE 8th Ave. (at 156th Ave. NE), Bellevue, 425/562–1519.*

10 *f-7*

READ ALL ABOUT IT INTERNATIONAL NEWSSTAND

Get here early for the popular papers, which usually vanish by mid-morning from the noisy corner shop at the Market entrance, or come for the international papers, in a section of their own amid the other often jumbled displays. You can also special-order papers from anywhere in the world. *93 Pike St. (at 1st Ave.), Pike Place Market, 206/624–0140.*

11 *c-3*

STEVE'S BROADWAY NEWS

Once you've spotted the blue awning, step inside quickly to pick up the most current papers or international periodicals. You have until midnight to grab what's left at the Capitol Hill store; the Fremont branch is open until 10 PM on weekdays and 11 PM on weekends. *204 Broadway St. E (at E. John St.), Capitol Hill, 206/324–7323.*

7 *f-1*

3416 Fremont Ave. N (at N. 34th St.), Fremont, 206/633–0731.

PET SUPPLIES

8 *f-6*

ALL THE BEST PET CARE

All the Best specializes in offering an alternative to mass-market pet food and supplies. They carry a wide selection of all-natural pet foods (some made of "human-quality" ingredients), nutritional supplements, and nontoxic flea products. You can buy homeopathic remedies here for such ailments as anxiety, cough, arthritis, sinusitis, and depression. *2713 E. Madison (at 27th Ave. E), Capitol Hill, 206/329–8565.*

5 *h-1*

8050 Lake City Way (at 15th Ave. NE),
Lake City, 206/524–0199.

7 *f-3*

2127 Queen Anne Ave. N (at W. Crockett
St.), Queen Anne, 206/283–3959.

13 *b-4*

1421 Market St. (at 14th Ave.), Kirkland,
425/889–2200.

for birds

14 *a-3*

DENISE'S PARROT PLACE

Find parrot-dise at Denise Mouroux's
shop, where you can visit or take home
hand-raised parrots and all their accoutrements, toys, perches, cages, etc.
Mouroux also sells her own blend of
bird-bean mix and bird muffin mix. *Tabit
Village Square, 7641 SE 27th St. (near 77th
Ave. SE), Mercer Island, 206/232–8115.*

for fish

5 *g-7*

FIN & FEATHER

Owner Sharon Wright carries a vast
selection of unique animals, and the
supplies to feed, house, and entertain
them in your own home. The knowledgeable staff provides personalized
attention, helping customers choose the
best habitats, food, and equipment for
birds, fish, small animals, reptiles, and
bugs. Don't miss the tarantula collection. *901 NE 45th St. (at 9th Ave. NE),
University District, 206/545–7958.*

for reptiles

13 *e-8*

PETS & THINGS

Not for the squeamish, this cozy-clut-
tered store tucked unexpectedly into a
strip mall is probably the area's most
complete reptile and reptile supply
store. Dealers of "Herpatat" (the complete professional snake cage), they can
outfit the classroom frog or rat as well
as your pet tarantula or 16 ft specimen.
Answers to "what the heck is this?" are
patiently addressed by the staff. Find
supplies for amphibians, reptiles,
insects, birds, and small animals. *14310
NE 20th St. (near 140th Ave. NE), Bellevue, 425/746–9782.*

for rabbits & rodents

1 *d-1*

BEST LITTLE RABBIT,
RODENT, & FERRET HOUSE

This nonprofit store has everything for
city-dwelling, indoor-only lagomorphs
(a.k.a. rabbits), ferrets, and rodents all:
from guinea pigs and rats to prairie
dogs and the occasional vole. Sandi
Ackerman directs BLRRFH (pronounced
blurf) and the House Rabbit Society's
Washington State adoption center with
near-manic energy and 20-plus years
experience in animal rescue. Her knowledgeable staff guide you to the right
books and videos and help you choose
from only the best food, toys, and
appropriate homes (not cages). Sandi's
hand-picked inventory includes made-
to-order pet condos; you can even have
one custom designed. *14325 Lake City
Way NE (near NE 145th St.), Lake City,
206/365–9105.*

PHOTO
EQUIPMENT

7 *h-6*

GLAZER'S CAMERA SUPPLY

The red-and-white building is hard to
miss in the heart of the Denny Regrade
neighborhood, although if you are looking to rent some pieces and purchase
others, you may have to walk a few
blocks between departments. (Glazer's
recently relocated its rental side two
blocks northwest of the main store.) The
bottom line is this: Glazer's is where the
camera pros shop. A large walk-in fridge
houses the most fragile film and camera
and film experts can be found about
every 5 ft. No pushy salespeople here;
they are real photographers who know
their stuff. Whatever your photo needs,
Glazer's will have it or help you find it.
*430 8th Ave. N (at Harrison St.), Down-
town, 206/624–1100.*

10 *h-2*

OPTECHS CAMERA SUPPLY

The focus at Optechs is on high-end
equipment and supplies for professionals. They are experts in digital imaging
and provide strong ongoing support
and service in that area. Optechs also
rents cameras, computers, and printers
on a daily basis; renters must be profi-
cient or take a two-hour training class
first. *433 Fairview Ave. N (at Republic
St.), Downtown, 206/343–9900.*

10 g-7

TALL'S CAMERA

Tall's has been serving the Seattle area since 1917, with experienced sales and repair services. They buy and sell used equipment and offer one-hour photo processing and five-minute passport photos. Besides still and video cameras, Tall's also sells binoculars, telescopes, and cellular phones. *1319 4th Ave. (at University St.), Downtown, 206/583–8111.*

14 b-1

Bellevue Square, Bellevue Way (between NE 4th and 8th Sts.), Bellevue, 425/455–2233.

6 a-6

2644 NE University Village (at 25th Ave. NE), University District, 206/522–6566.

SHOES & BOOTS

10 g-6

ADIDAS

Scan the glass display cases along the walls of this clean, spacious store, then take a seat on one of the round couches to sample a few styles. Shoes made the brand name famous, but you'll find all sorts of apparel and accessories for sports enthusiasts here. *1501 5th Ave. (between Pike and Pine Sts.), Downtown, 206/382–4317.*

10 g-6

BALLY OF SWITZERLAND

The world-famous footwear store has brought its line of top-quality shoes to Seattle. When you've made your choice, you can find a purse, accessories, and even luggage to match. *600 Pine St. (at 6th Ave.), Downtown, 206/326–5120. Closed Sun.*

2 b-2

CHUBBY & TUBBY

The name makes it sound like an ice cream shop, but this chain apparel store stocks hundreds of name-brand shoes and boots. If you want Adidas, Converse, New Balance, or Nike, this is your stop. Boots include Caterpillars, Lugz, and Western Chiefs. *7906 Aurora (at 80th St.), Greenwood, 206/524–1810.*

10 g-7

CHURCH'S ENGLISH SHOES, LTD.

Try this store for unique handmade English shoes and accessories suited for work, dress up, and casual wear. Odd sizes and special orders are also available. *402 University St. (at 4th Ave.), Downtown, 206/682–5043, www. churchshoes.com.*

12 c-2

CLOG FACTORY

Between the high, exposed-brick walls are shelves with clogs of all sizes lined up like brightly colored jelly beans. Shop for chic clunkers, chef shoes, garden scooters, or matching mother-daughter sets. *217 1st Ave. S (between S. Main and S. Washington Sts.), Pioneer Square, 206/682–2564.*

10 e-6

EDIE'S

Looking for funky footwear? Search this shop for retro styles, vintage heels, and '60s hoppers. Or just grab a plain pair of Northwest-style trailblazers. *319 E. Pine St. (between Bellevue St. and Crawford Pl.), Capitol Hill, 206/839–1111.*

10 e-6

J. GILBERT FOOTWEAR

Casual footwear for active lifestyles is what you'll find here. Check out the popular Campers, designed to get you where you want to go in style and comfort. *2025 1st Ave. (between Lenora and Virgina Sts.), Downtown, 206/441–1182, www.jgilbertfootwear.com.*

10 f-7

JOHN FLUEVOG SHOES

Inventor of the Angelic sole (protects against most earthly liquids "and Satan"), Fluevog carries big, thick shoes and boots. There's a Cuisinartlike blend of influences, platforms, geisha-style sandals, curvaceous heels, and extremely pointy toes. All are handmade. You never know who you'll find in the shop—fans, after all, include Madonna. *1611 1st Ave. (at Stewart St.), Downtown, 206/441–1065, www.fluevog. com.*

10 g-6

KENNETH COLE

The shoe shop that opened almost two decades ago in a movie trailer in a New York parking lot sold 40,000 pairs in two days, and business hasn't slowed since. Spiffed-up loafers, swingin' beige zip-up ankle boots, and tough-looking slip-on sandals come in a variety of shades and shapes, and rugged raised soles, flat-bottoms, clog fronts, and even low heels add punch to the styles. Dressed-down dress-up clothes, with thick colors and European lines, are the hallmarks of this store's newer apparel collections. For a complete look, add a sleek leather jacket, briefcase, or watch. There's also a line of women's clothes. *520 Pike St. (at 6th Ave.), Downtown, 206/632–5158 or 800/KEN–COLE, www.kennethcole.com.*

10 *e-6*

MAGGIE'S ITALIAN SHOES & CLOTHING

Voted the city's best shoe store by the *Seattle Weekly*, this Market store is a key place to snag European imports. More customers come for the shoes than the clothes, but it's nice to have options for matching your footwear finds. Bridal shoes and men's shoes are also available. *1927 1st Ave. (between Virginia and Stewart Sts.), Pike Place Market, 206/728–5837.*

10 *g-6*

MEPHISTO

The world's finest walking shoes, hand-crafted in Europe, are what you'll find in this open shop with accents of blue. Tall brown shelves display comfortable footwear and accessories, including loafers, sport shoes, and sandals. While you're there, pick up a pair of thick walking socks or a rugged, handcrafted briefcase. *1312 5th Ave. (between Union and University Sts.), Downtown, 206/622–3773, www.mephistoseattle.com.*

2 *f-4*

Bellevue Square, Bellevue Way (between NE 4th and 8th Sts.), Bellevue, 425/452–1414.

5 *d-7*

MIRAGE COMFORT SHOES

The shoes here are a blend of style and function, perfect for the active Northwest lifestyle. Lots of sandals and loafers are found on these shelves, with brands ranging from Blundstone and Dansko to Naot and Wolky. *417 Wallingford Ave. N (between N. 44th and 45th Aves.), Wallingford, 206/632–1449 or 800/326–6818, www.home.earthlink.net/~comfortshoes.*

10 *f-7*

MJ FEET

The first Birkenstock store in the United States started an international comfort footwear craze—and you can still see the brand treading dirt paths from Brazil to Bali. The open-toe, velcro-strap sandals for men (and women and kids) have non-skid soles and endless wearability. Be extra cool and wear them with the store's natural-fiber socks. Find discount merchandise at the Bellevue outlet store on 103rd Street, opened in summer 2001, or on the Web site. *1514 Pike Pl. (at 1st Ave.), Pike Place Market, 206/624–2929, www.mjfeet.com.*

5 *g-7*

4334 University Way NE (between NE 43rd and 44th Sts.), University District, 206/632–5353.

2 *g-4*

Bellevue Square, Bellevue Way (between NE 4th and 8th Sts.), Bellevue, 425/646–0416.

2 *f-4*

15 NE 103rd St. (at Main St.), Bellevue, 425/688–9139.

10 *g-6*

NIKETOWN

Way popular with teenagers, the two-story establishment is more than a store—it's an event, with sports shows running on wall monitors, rock music blasting, and occasional visits by sports stars. Niketown was one of Downtown's first mega-brand stores and the museum-style displays of celebrity shoes and high-cost lines bring in throngs of tourists. If you have a C-note (or more), drop it on a pair of these, or order footwear structured especially to your bones. Hint: For just $60, you can grab a pair of running-shoe clogs in a variety of jelly bean colors. *1500 6th Ave. (at Pike St.), Downtown, 206/447–6453, www.nike.com.*

10 *e-6*

PED

If you love shoes, you'll love this shop, which specializes in handmade European designer footwear. Dark leather men's work shoes and women's sandals bear names like Cydwok (they're very angular!) and Giraudon (these have perforations). Others styles are Gofreddo Fantini, Sigerson Morrison, and Jean Michael Cazabat. Be warned, though—

you'll want to stretch your budget on the delicious matching handbags and jewelry. *1115 1st St. (between Spring and Seneca Sts.), Downtown, 206/292–1767, www.pedshoes.com.*

10 *e-6*

SAN MARCO SHOES

Continental shoe styles and accessories are the specialties here. The focus is on good-looking, high-quality footwear that lasts—and makes you look like you just stepped off a Paris or Milan modeling runway. *1631 6th Ave. (at Pike St.), Downtown, 206/343–9138.*

5 *g-7*

WOOLLY MAMMOTH

Adventurers everywhere tout the comfort and quality of this store's casual brands. From rugged mud-brown sandals to funky, seafoam-green flip-flops. Look for Ecco, Naot, Stonefly, Wolky, and more. Psst—park free for up to two hours in any UDPA lot (but bring your ticket in for a stamp). *4303 University Way NE (at NE 43rd St.), University District, 206/632–3254.*

SPORTING GOODS & CLOTHING

6 *a-6*

FAST LADY SPORTS

Women will be stepping out in style and comfort for their fitness activities after a visit to this store. They carry shoes and apparel for running, swimming, cycling, aerobics, triathlon, cross-training, and hiking. Fast Lady Sports also hosts sports clinics and sponsors races, marathon training, and weekly group runs. *2710 NE University Village (at 25th Ave. NE), University District, 206/522–2113.*

13 *b-3*

5 Lake St. (at Park La.), Kirkland, 425/889–9433.

13 *g-4*

Redmond Town Center, 7501 166th Ave. NE (near NE 74th St.), Redmond, 425/558–7856.

10 *g-6*

NIKETOWN

See Shoes & Boots, *above.*

12 *b-1*

NORTH FACE

You can find The North Face's well-known brand of high-quality outdoor gear at most sporting goods stores. And you can find it right here, at their own retail shop. The backpacks are popular even with urban hill-climbers, and true mountaineers will find all they need to survive in the wilderness. You'll pay for the high-tech engineering and design of these products, but probably just once, since the merchandise comes with a life-time warranty. *1023 1st Ave. (at Madison St.), Downtown, 206/622–4111.*

10 *e-6*

PATAGONIA

For the fashion- and environmentally conscious, Patagonia offers high-quality clothes for outdoor wear. Comfortable natural fabrics and functional styles make this store a hit with the Seattle-area outdoorsy crowd. The fleece wear for kids is positively darling. Prices are rather spendy and Patagonia rarely has sales, but the clothes and gear here are durable and will stand the test of time. *2100 1st Ave. (at Lenora St.), Belltown, 206/622–9700.*

10 *h-3*

PLAY IT AGAIN SPORTS

Parents with growing kids swear by this chain, since they can trade in junior's old skis, boots, and other sports equipment when they're outgrown. Play It Again Sports buys, sells, trades, and consigns most kinds of sports gear, including bikes, skates, snowboards, skis, skateboards, and soccer, golf, baseball, softball, hockey, water sports, and tennis gear. Additional Puget Sound locations are in Woodinville, Lynnwood, and Renton. *1304 Stewart St. (at Denny Way), Downtown, 206/264–9255.*

13 *e-8*

14339 NE 20th St. (near 140th Ave. NE), Bellevue, 425/643–2599.

bicycles

6 *c-7*

AL YOUNG BIKE & SKI

This bike shop sells a good mix of bikes, including mountain, BMX, tandem, and low-riders. It sells and rents ski and snowboard equipment, and bikes can be rented by the hour to ride on the adjacent Burke Gilman Trail. *3615 NE 45th St.*

(at 36th Ave. NE), University District, 206/524–2642.

6 *c-7*
BICYCLE CENTER

This store calls itself the "family bike shop," and when you stop by you'll see plenty of kid-sized bikes lined up in front. They take trade-ins and also carry tandems, BMX, mountain, and recumbent bikes. You can rent bikes here to take for a spin on the nearby Burke Gilman Trail. *4529 Sand Point Way NE (near University Village), University District, 206/523–8300.*

5 *e-7*
BIKESMITH

Enter this small shop on the eastern edge of Wallingford to find an array of classic old bicycles—all at $100 or less. But the genius is in the workshop behind the counter, where bikes of all models and vintages are being hammered and welded back into shape. A small TV and a selection of biking videos in back keeps customers busy while they wait. *2309 N. 45th St. (between Bagley and Sunnyside Aves.), Wallingford, 206/632–3102.*

2 *g-4*
BICYCLES WEST

A new fleet of brand-name bikes, including specialized Trek and Schwinn styles, can be found at several branches around Puget Sound. Watch for sales, when you can pick up recent-model bicycles at deeply discounted prices. *Crossroads Shopping Center, 15600 NE 8th St. (at 156th Ave. NE), Bellevue, 425/747–2288.*

10 *f-8*
BLAZING SADDLES

Billed as the country's number-one bike touring company, these neat, well-organized shops are thoroughly stocked with bikes and biking materials. If you're already a rider, look here for first-class equipment. You can also pick up free maps and guides to the best places to ride in and around Seattle, or book a day tour of the area for $28–$48 (including helmet, front pack, rack, lock, and other essentials). *1230 Western Ave. (at University St.), Downtown, 206/341–9994, www.blazingsaddles.com.*

7 *f-6*
COUNTERBALANCE BICYCLES

The city's bike pros come here for parts and repairs, but you can also buy from the store's wide selection of brand-name cycles. If Fuji, Redline, and Voodoo ring bells, this is the place for you. The shop stocks mountain, BMX, cyclo-cross, and other bikes. *2 W. Roy St. (at Queen Anne Ave. N), Queen Anne, 206/352–3252, www.counterbalancebicycles.com.*

10 *d-6*
ELLIOTT BAY BICYCLES

Yes, it stocks the best brands, but it also can help you design and custom-build your own steel or titanium bike. Racing, touring, track, and off-road cycles are available. The store specializes in Davidson handbuilt custom bicycles. *2116 Western Ave. (between Blanchard and Lenora Sts.), Belltown, 206/441–8144, www.elliotbaybicycles.com.*

5 *f-3*
GREGG'S GREENLAKE CYCLE

All the brand names in mountain biking, racing, and touring bikes are here—it might have the region's largest selection of bikes—plus supplies for in-line skating, snowboarding, and other Northwest action sports. Custom styling is a big deal here, too. Rentals are also available, and the store is open late on weekdays. *7007 Woodlawn Ave. NE (between Ravenna Blvd. and E. Greenlake Dr.), Greenlake, 206/523–1822, www.greggscycles.com.*

5 *c-2*
7401 Aurora Ave. N (at N. 74th St.), Greenlake, 206/783–1000.

2 *f-4*
Bellevue Plaza, 121 106th Ave. NE (at NE 4th St.), Bellevue, 425/462–1900.

8 *e-3*
MONTLAKE BICYCLE SHOP

This shop has branched out into north Seattle as neighborhoods have expanded their waterfront trails and wooded parks. It has the brand-name equipment and basic services, plus quality used bikes and rentals. You can't beat the one-day repair service. *2223 24th Ave. E (at Lynne St.), Montlake, 206/329–7333.*

2 *f-5*

20 103rd Ave. NE (at Main St.), Bellevue, 425/462–8825.

1 *e-6*

211 Kirkland Ave. (between Main and 3rd Sts.), Kirkland, 425/828–3800.

boating

7 *c-2*

CAPTAIN'S NAUTICAL SUPPLIES

Captain's Nautical Supplies has been helping mariners navigate the seas for more than a century. They supply marine charts, books, nautical software, electronic navigation instruments, and also carry weather instrumentation and compasses, binoculars, and telescopes—basically anything that can help you find where you are and chart a course to where you're going. 2500 15th Ave. W (at W. Wheeler St.), Magnolia, 206/283–7242.

7 *h-3*

NORTHWEST OUTDOOR CENTER

NWOC specializes in kayaking. You can rent or buy kayaks, gear, and accessories here, and they offer comprehensive classes for beginners to pros. NWOC also leads guided trips on Lake Union and day trips to Northwest destinations. 2100 Westlake Ave. N (at Crockett St.) Lake Union, 206/281–9694.

camping & climbing

8 *a-6*

REI

This mecca for the outdoors enthusiast started here in 1938 by a group of mountain climbers, who set up shop as a consumers cooperative to buy climbing supplies, and the flagship store is somewhat of a tourist destination. Today there are more than 1.8 million active co-op members worldwide, shopping at more than 50 stores and via catalog and the Internet. Though you don't have to join the co-op to shop, it costs just $15 to become a lifetime member, and members receive patronage dividends and other perks. Besides selling all that you might need for your outdoor pursuits, including snow sports, hiking, biking, and kayaking, you can climb the 65-ft-high pinnacle (visible from I–5 Downtown); test out rain gear in the

rain simulator; and try out hiking boots and mountain bikes on the outdoor trails. Eastsiders will want to check out the Redmond store—it's about half the size but also has its own climbing pinnacle and the same great service and selection. 222 Yale Ave. N (at Thomas St.), Downtown, 206/470–4020.

13 *g-4*

Redmond Town Center, 16495 NE 74th St. (between 164th and 165th Aves. NE), Redmond, 425/882–1158.

fishing tackle & supplies

8 *b-3*

PATRICK'S FLY SHOP

As the name indicates, this shop is all about fly-fishing supplies. Learn to tie flies and build fly rods from owner Jimmy LeMert, or buy what you need for your next fishing excursion. 2237 Eastlake Ave. N (at E. Boston St.), Eastlake, 206/325–8988.

4 *g-5*

SALMON BAY TACKLE, GUIDES & OUTFITTERS

If you're fishing for salmon, trout, or steelhead, you'll find a great selection of fishing gear at Salmon Bay Tackle. They carry reels and rods, waders, pontoon boats, clothing, and accessories, and present classes on fly tying. 5701 15th Ave. NW (at 57th St. NW), Ballard, 206/789–9335.

golf

2 *c-1*

PUETZ GOLF SUPERSTORE

For more than half a century, Puetz has been outfitting Seattle golfers with all they need to hit the greens. It has all the major brands of clubs and equipment, as well as golf clothing and accessories. The Seattle store has a covered driving range and also offers lessons. 11762 Aurora Ave. N, North Seattle, 206/362–2272.

13 *e-8*

1645 140th Ave. NE (at Bel-Red Rd.), Bellevue, 425/747–0644.

2 *c-2*

PRO GOLF DISCOUNT

Pro Golf has a huge selection of golf equipment, with separate sections for left-handers and women. Try before you buy at the in-store driving range and putting green. There are seven Pro Golf locations in the greater Puget Sound area. *10409 Aurora Ave. N (at N. 105th St.), North Seattle, 206/527–7770.*

13 *e-8*

14121 NE 20th St. (near 140th Ave. NE), Bellevue, 425/641–6766.

kites

7 *h-1*

GASWORKS PARK KITE SHOP

Owner Kathy Goodwind not only sells kites, but she designs and manufactures them, too, a rarity for a woman in the kite industry. Her shop near Gas Works Park (and its popular kite-flying hill) is packed with colorful kites and wind toys. She carries the dual-line Prism kite, as well as the unique cylindrical Pop Kan Kite, designed and patented by her son Todd Hostetter. *3333 Wallingford Ave. N (near Gas Works Park), Wallingford, 206/633–4780.*

12 *c-3*

GREAT WINDS KITE CO.

Great Winds owner Ken Conrad encourages novice kite flyers to start out with easy-to-use kites like the delta kite and sled kite (he'll show you how to make one with a paper bag that costs 50¢). The store carries plenty of cool kites, kite parts, and equipment for experts, too, and sells kite building kits. *402 Occidental Ave. S (at S. Jackson St.), Pioneer Square, 206/624–6886.*

running

5 *f-3*

SUPER JOCK 'N JILL

This is the premiere shop in the area for runners. Whether you're just taking up jogging or training for the Seattle Marathon, they'll help you get set up with the best shoes and equipment. The store also promotes running by sponsoring races, camps, clinics, clubs, and fitness groups. *7210 Green Lake Dr. N (at N. 72nd St.), Green Lake, 206/522–7711.*

skating

7 *h-1*

URBAN SURF

Rent or buy in-line skates from the experts at Urban Surf, then roll your way onto the adjacent Burke-Gilman Trail for a cruise. It's less crowded than Green Lake—a great spot for beginners, too. Urban Surf also can help you get water and air-borne, with surf boards, windsurf gear, and classes, and kite-boarding supplies and instruction. In the winter they rent snowboards and sell snow sport equipment and clothing—whatever's left in summer goes for 40% off. *2100 N. Northlake Way (across from Gas Works Park), Wallingford, 206/545–9463.*

skiing

7 *c-3*

ALPINE HUT

Alpine Hut carries all the latest in ski and snow sports gear. They provide friendly and expert service and take the time to get to know their customers' needs. In the off-season, Alpine Hut stays busy selling bikes and in-line skates. *2215 15th Ave. W (at W. Newton St.), Queen Anne, 206/284–3575.*

13 *g-4*

7875 Leary Way NE (near Redmond Way), Redmond, 425/883–7544.

6 *a-6*

FIORINI SPORTS

Family-owned Fiorini Sports has been in business for more than three decades, providing personal, expert service to local skiers. They've got all you'll need for your downhill adventures and carry the newest in ski and snowboard styles. For more than 50 years, the Fiorinis have operated a ski school, too. Off-season, the store stays hopping with a busy tennis shop, in-line skate sales and rentals, and sales of sportswear, footwear, and eyewear. *4720 NE University Village (at 25th Ave. NE), University District, 206/523–9610.*

STATIONERY & OFFICE SUPPLIES

office supplies

10 *g-7*

OFFICE DEPOT

At this superstore, you'll find everything from pencils and paper clips to computers, fax machines, and furniture to outfit your office. More than just supplies, they offer office services, too—you can order business cards and stationery at the in-store print center and mail packages via UPS (no extra service charge). And, no need to cram that bookcase or file cabinet into your compact car—they provide free next-day delivery in the city for any purchase over $50. There are 13 locations in the greater Puget Sound area, call 888/GO–DEPOT to find out about the rest. *1423 4th Ave. (at Pike St.), Downtown, 206/748–9777.*

14 *c-1*

100 108th Ave. NE (at Main St.), Bellevue, 425/453–2900.

6 *a-6*

4900 25th Ave. NE (near University Village), University District, 206/527–3220.

13 *g-4*

Office Depot Center, 15301 NE 24th St. (at 152nd Ave. NE), Redmond, 425/747–9019.

5 *g-7*

UNIVERSITY BOOK STORE
See Bookstores, *above.*

pens & pencils

10 *g-7*

SEATTLE PEN
For the finest in writing instruments, Seattle Pen is the place to go. Visit the main showroom to see limited-edition pens and vintage pens, imported from around the world, and get personalized service. Exclusive brands include Montblanc, Parker, Waterman, and Sheaffer. The street-level boutique carries classic fine writing instruments, refills and supplies, and inexpensive gifts. *1411 4th Ave. (at Pike St.), Downtown, 206/652–4334.*

10 *g-7*

Seattle Pen Showroom, 1424 4th Ave. (in the 4th & Pike Bldg.), Downtown, 206/682–2640.

stationery

14 *b-1*

THE PAPER TREE
The Paper Tree carries a full line of custom invitations and announcements, business and personal stationery, cards, and gifts. Seasonal and holiday papers are available, along with many other styles, and the store has an in-house printing service. *Bellevue Square, Bellevue Way (between NE 4th and 8th Sts.), Bellevue, 425/451–8035.*

10 *g-7*

SILBERMAN/BROWN
For anyone who yearns for a return to the days before E-mail and other electronic communication, a visit to Silberman/Brown shows that the fine art of writing is not yet lost. You'll find all the supplies you need to add a personal touch to written communication—beautiful handmade papers, elegant fountain pens and vintage pens, creative invitations, and more. You can also find antique desk pieces and other desk accessories, leather-bound journals, agendas, photo albums, address books, and travel books. *1322 5th Ave. (at Union St.), Downtown, 206/292–9404.*

14 *b-1*

10220 NE 8th St. (across from Bellevue Square), Bellevue, 425/455–3665.

6 *a-6*

STYLUS PAPER & PEN STATIONERS
Open in University Village since 1979 (they started out as SabTec Stationers), Stylus is a pleasant place to shop for stationery, office, and art supplies. You'll find an excellent assortment of fine writing instruments, invitations and cards for all occasions, unique and fine imported paper, scrapbooks and photo albums, baby gifts, globes and other desk accessories, and general office supplies. The art department is well-stocked, too, and classes for kids and adults are offered through the Stylus Paper & Pen's School of Creative Arts. *4710 NE University Village (at 25th Ave. NE), University District, 206/523–2106.*

TOYS & GAMES

collectibles

4 *f-5*

ARCHIE MCPHEE'S
Quite simply, this is Seattle's most unique toy and novelty store—and perhaps the world's, too. As "outfitters of popular culture," it takes most seriously its mission to bring more wackiness to the world. Many of the products are also sold to other stores through their wholesale division, Accoutrements. So, it's not impossible to find items like the "Parking Space Goddess," the boxing nun puppet, and the Shiva lunchbox elsewhere. But you should immerse yourself in the quirky weirdness at least

When you pack your MCI Calling Card, it's like packing your loved ones along too.

Your MCI Calling Card is the easy way to stay in touch when you travel. Use it to call to and from over 125 countries. Plus, every time you call, you can earn frequent flier miles. So wherever your travels take you, call home with your MCI Calling Card. It's even easy to get one. Just visit **www.mci.com/worldphone.**

EASY TO CALL WORLDWIDE

1. Just enter the WorldPhone® access number of the country you're calling from.
2. Enter or give the operator your MCI Calling Card number.
3. Enter or give the number you're calling.

Aruba ⁝	800-888-8
Bahamas ⁝	1-800-888-8000

Barbados ⁝	1-800-888-8000
Bermuda ⁝	1-800-888-8000
British Virgin Islands ⁝	1-800-888-8000
Canada	1-800-888-8000
Mexico	01-800-021-8000
Puerto Rico	1-800-888-8000
United States	1-800-888-8000
U.S. Virgin Islands	1-800-888-8000

⁝ Limited availability.

EARN FREQUENT FLIER MILES

SEE THE WORLD
IN FULL COLOR

Fodor's Exploring Guides bring all the great sights vividly to life with hundreds of photographs, fascinating historical background, and colorful anecdotes. Detailed maps and practical information keep you headed in the right direction.

Pair a **Fodor's** Exploring Guide with your trusted Gold Guide for a complete planning package.

Fodor's EXPLORING GUIDES

At bookstores everywhere.

once. *2428 Market St. NW (at 24th Ave. NW), Ballard, 206/297–0240.*

2 *d-1*

CRANIUM'S COFFEE & COLLECTIBLES

Leon and Nancy Johnson opened their first store, Cranium's Cool Collectibles in a Lake City house in the mid-1990s. With three stories of rooms filled to the brim with vintage toys, games, and records, it quickly became a popular destination for baby boomers wanting to relive their childhood, or unload some of their own dust-gathering collectibles. When Cranium's moved to a new locale a few blocks away, on Lake City's main drag, they added coffee and food to the mix. All the pop culture collectibles are still on hand at the new location, including original Star Wars and Star Trek toys, Pez dispensers, posters, books, games, comics, and loads of LPs. *12301 Lake City Way NE (at NE 123rd St.), Lake City, 206/364–1924.*

2 *c-1*

KICKS HOBBY JAPAN

As a child in Hong Kong, Siu-Wai Ho was introduced early to Japanese toys. His love for the genre led him to focus exclusively on Japanese toys, games, and models later in life as a purvey of his favorite childhood objects. The concept seems to be working despite its nondescript location; the store stays busy selling the latest in Japanese video games and game systems, collectible action figures (especially Transformers), Gundam and Bandai models, *anime* (popular Japanese animation), soundtracks, and more. You can also shop via the Internet. *543 NE Northgate Way (near 5th Ave. NE), Northgate, 206/306–9060, www.kicks-hobby.com.*

13 *c-8*

ROSALIE WHYEL MUSEUM OF DOLL ART STORE

Doll collectors will go ga-ga over the antique dolls (and their prices, some in the thousands of dollars). Contemporary dolls and stuffed animals are not nearly as expensive, although you're likely a real collector if you'll willing pay $285 for Tigger. The store also carries some museum exclusives, miniatures, resource books, gift items, and wigs for antique dolls. Museum admission is not required to enter the store. *1116 108th Ave. NE (at NE 12th St.), Bellevue, 425/455–1116.*

new

3 *b-8*

CURIOUS KIDSTUFF

One of West Seattle's best-kept secrets, Curious Kidstuff wins raves from local parents. The store prides itself on stocking only nonviolent toys that are both fun and nurturing, and the selection is incredible. Toys are imported from all over the world and geared to all ages. Browsers are welcome and there are hands-on train and car tables for kids to try out. *4740 California Ave. SW (near SW Alaska St.), West Seattle, 206/937–8788.*

10 *g-6*

FAO SCHWARZ

The giant teddy bear that holds court outside FAO's entrance signals that this is no ordinary toy store. Within this fanciful world, trees talk, dinosaurs move, Humpty Dumpty comes alive, ruby slippers dance, and a plethora of toys are on display. The brightly attired store clerks play with the toys, and encourage customers to join in. Don't leave without seeing the floor-to-ceiling water tube filled with Barbie shoes or "playing" the giant keyboard with your feet—an FAO signature item made famous by Tom Hanks in the movie *Big. City Centre, 1420 5th Ave. (at Pike St.), Downtown, 206/ 442–9500.*

14 *b-1*

Bellevue Square, Bellevue Way (between NE 4th and 8th Sts.), Bellevue, 425/646– 9500.

5 *g-4*

SCIENCE, ART & MORE

Home-schooling parents and teachers will have a field day here as they discover all the makings for interesting science experiments and art projects. Who can resist an owl pellet dissection kit? If you sign up for the school support program, a percentage of your purchases are credited to your children's school for future purchases. Teachers (both the home and away variety) can also set up their own rebate account. *6417 Roosevelt Way NE (at NE 65th St.), University District, 206/524–3795.*

5 *b-1*

TOP TEN TOYS

Don't be fooled by the name, Top Ten Toys actually has thousands of toys. And it's the good stuff, too, not the mass market fare that you'll find at every discount store: Quality classic toys (no guns), musical instruments, costumes, arts and craft kits and supplies, puppets, dolls, play structures, trains, books and music, greeting cards, a big section of toddler and infant toys, and lots more. They'll even wrap your gifts. *104 N. 85th St. (near Greenwood Ave. N), Greenwood, 206/782–0098.*

2 *c-1*

TOYS R US

It seems that every kid wants to be a Toys R Us kid, and parents' overflowing shopping carts during the holidays assure that their wish comes true. It's the place to go to find all the mass market toys—from the perennial favorites, Barbie and Legos, to action figures from the latest movie or TV show. Wait a few months for the latter and you'll find them at bargain prices as the new fad-of-the-month clamors for precious shelf space. Toys R Us carries a great selection of baby supplies, furniture, and equipment; and lots of bikes, trikes, and other riding apparatus that kids can try before you buy. Branches are also in Tukwila, Lynnwood, Everett, and Federal Way. *Northgate Mall, Northgate Way (at 4th Ave. NE), Northgate, 206/361–1101.*

14 *c-1*

103 110th NE (near Main St.), Bellevue, 425/453–1901.

13 *g-4*

ZANY BRAINY

Practically every day there's some kind of free event—story-telling, crafts, face painting, themed weekends and more, for ages preschool through elementary. The emphasis is on interactive and educational toys that encourage children to use their imagination (not just the toys!) to have fun. *7215 170th Ave. NE (off NE Redmond Way), Redmond, 425/881–7334.*

VIDEOS

5 *b-8*

RAIN CITY VIDEO

National chains have challenged the survival of many independent video stores, but Rain City Video has survived by catering to film buffs with unmatched

variety and service. Owner Mark Vrieling focuses on the neighborhood needs at his three stores, carrying more family and new releases at the North Ballard store, eclectic and obscure films in Fremont, and the best of the best at the smaller Ballard store. All told, the chain boasts more than 40,000 films in its catalog, from recent blockbusters to foreign and independent films on VHS and DVD. *464 N. 36th St. (near Dayton Ave. N), Fremont, 206/545–3539.*

4 *h-5*

719 NW Market St. (at 8th Ave. NW), Ballard, 206/783–8367.

4 *d-3*

6412 32nd Ave. NW (at NW 65th St.), Ballard, 206/789–0132.

5 *g-6*

SCARECROW VIDEO

If it's available on video, you'll probably find it here. With more than 45,000 titles in Scarecrow's catalog, the store has the largest inventory in the Northwest. Besides renting and selling videos and DVDs, they carry laserdiscs and the high quality European PAL-format tapes that can only be played on European VCRs (you can rent the machine, too). *5030 Roosevelt Way NE (at NE 50th St.), University District, 206/524–8554.*

10 *f-6*

SUNCOAST MOTION PICTURE COMPANY

Movie fans won't be able to pass a Suncoast store at the mall without stopping in. The stores sell (but don't rent) videos, DVDs, and laserdiscs, from recent blockbusters to more obscure titles. There's a good selection of anime films, and loads of movie collectibles, action figures, and other paraphernalia. Other stores at Alderwood, Southcenter, SeaTac, and Everett Malls. *Westlake Center, 400 Pine St. (at 4th Ave.), Downtown, 206/343–7491.*

14 *b-1*

Bellevue Square, Bellevue Way (between NE 4th and 8th Sts.), Bellevue, 425/453–4795.

2 *c-1*

Northgate Mall, Northgate Way (at 4th Ave. NE), Northgate, 206/417–7567.

chapter 3

PARKS, GARDENS & SPORTS

parks

Years ago a local brewery promoted their product with the ditty "It's the water, and a lot more." The same could be said to describe Seattle's rich and varied parks. With a large body of water on the east and west, and numerous glacier-formed lakes and creeks inland, you're never far from a waterfront park.

Plus the water that falls from above and gives Seattle its rain-soaked, web-footed reputation creates lush greenery that's the envy of the drier side of the state. In fact, if you're an urban nature lover (that's no oxymoron around here), you're just minutes away from walking among 800-year-old trees, where you can also peek at wildlife in their wetland habitat, and explore miles of trails right in the city.

Outsiders may scoff at the lyrics of the '60s tune made famous by teen heart-throb Bobby Sherman "The bluest skies you've ever seen are in Seattle." Yet because we don't take them for granted, Seattleites really celebrate those blue-sky days by heading en masse to parks and beaches like Alki, Green Lake, Houghton, and Lake Sammamish to revel in the sunshine. With more than 400 parks and green spaces in Seattle alone (and more coming, thanks to the Parks Levy passed in 2000), the choices for recreation and relaxation seem endless. Add another 150 parks run by King County, and dozens more in neighboring suburbs, and you'll never run out of places to explore.

seattle parks

Parks without direct phone numbers can be reached through the **City of Seattle Parks and Recreation Department** (206/684–4075, www.cityofseattle.net/parks).

2 *b-6*

CAMP LONG

If you grew up in Seattle, you may have camped here as a Scout. Built by the Works Progress Administration in the late 1930s (who re-used materials from other projects around the city), it was created initially for organized groups. Since the mid-1980s, Camp Long has been open to the public and is the only city park that offers an urban camping experience. Ten rustic cabins rent for $35 per night and sleep up to 12 on double bunkbeds. Day-trippers will find nature trails to explore, and climbers can ascend 20-ft Schurman Rock or a simulated glacier. The park has its own naturalists who serve a significant role in the community as environmental educators. They lead a variety of free or low-cost nature field trips, classes, workshops, and walks for all ages. Evening program include night hikes, tide-pooling by flashlight, hayrides, campfire stories around a bonfire, stargazing, and more. Except for special evening events and overnight camping, the park is open Tuesday through Sunday, 8:30 to 5. *35th Ave. SW and SW Dawson St., West Seattle, 206/684–7434, www.cityofseattle.net/parks/environment/camplong.htm.*

PERMITS

You can't just grab a baseball diamond or a slew of tables for that outdoor family reunion. City park permits are required for lots of events, from sports to social picnics. The most common permits and their contacts are listed below. For other purposes and for parks in other cities, call the Parks Department.

Groups selling concessions (206/684–8002).

Special events (206/684–4080): This includes park weddings, charitable events, and commercial uses.

Reservations:

Athletic fields for individual groups (206/684–0477).

Athletic fields for leagues (206/684–4082).

Picnic areas for groups (206/684–4081).

Tennis courts for tournaments (206/684–4082).

Tennis courts for individual play (206/684–4077).

2 *b-1*

CARKEEK PARK

Carkeek has something other parks don't—salmon that return each fall to swim up Pipers Creek. Much credit goes to neighborhood residents and volunteers, whose conservation efforts have made the creek salmon-friendly again. Bridges cross the creek, making it easy to get a close-up look at the Northwest's signature fish. Nature trails lead through the forest and into meadows perfect for kite-flying. Walk over the pedestrian overpass to reach the 23-acre beach on Puget Sound. Railroad tracks run through the park, too—watch for trains from the overpass, but stay off the tracks in the park's woodsy areas. Park naturalists lead nature walks and classes, beach clean-up events, and other environmental education programs. Summer day camps are offered for children, too. The park's playground has a salmon slide (kids go in through the head and out through the tail) and fun public art. *950 Carkeek Park Rd. (entrance at NW 110th St. and 3rd Ave. NW), Broadview, 206/684–0877, www.cityofseattle.net/parks/parkspaces/carkeek.htm.*

4 *b-6*

DISCOVERY PARK

Magnolia has the city's largest park, with miles of trails traversing a 534-acre nature preserve. You could spend hours hiking, picnicking, observing wildlife, exploring the 2-mi beach, and gazing at magnificent views of Puget Sound and the Cascade and Olympic mountains. The park came into being when the army surplussed most of a former base, Ft. Lawton, to the city. Named after the HMS *Discovery*, the ship of Puget Sound explorer Captain George Vancouver, the park has been a place for nature discovery since the mid-1970s. While much of the property has been preserved as a natural area, there are two playgrounds, tennis courts, and a basketball court. On the beach, the historic West Point Lighthouse stands next to one of the least-appealing park sights, the waste-water treatment plant. With its strong commitment to education, the park doesn't ignore the plant; in fact it offers a free monthly program for ages 12 and up called "Where Does It Go When You Flush." Naturalists lead other free and low-cost programs, including nature walks every Saturday at 2 PM, bird tours on Saturday mornings (the park is home to more than 200 species of birds and wildlife), and occasional tours of the remaining historic military district. *Bordered by W. Lawton and W. Emerson Sts., 36th Ave. W, and Puget Sound (main entrance at 36th Ave. W and W. Government Way), Magnolia, 206/386–4236, www.cityofseattle.net/parks/parkspaces/discovparkindex.htm.*

8 *a-2*

GAS WORKS PARK

An industrial gas plant until the mid-1950s, in 1975 the site opened as a park that makes great use of the "re-use and recycle" concept. The former boiler room is now a picnic shelter; a children's play barn has taken over the old compressor room; and much of the old machinery has been painted and lives on as public art. Climb to the top of grassy Kite Hill to see the mosaic *Sundial*. Besides being one of the top kite-flying spots in the city, the park treats you to awesome views of

---

WHERE ROVER RUNS FREE

Dogs can play with other dogs, run about, and even swim at several off-leash dog areas in and around Seattle. Just don't try it at other parks, where the fines can be stiff—$50 for first-time offenders, with hikes for subsequent crimes. Beaches aren't dog-friendly either (except as noted); the fine can be a whopping $500 if Fido gets caught in a waterfront area, even on a leash. In addition to the off-leash dog areas listed in this chapter, additional sites are noted at the City of Seattle's "Yo Dogs" Web page: www.ci.seattle.wa.us/parks/parkspaces/yodogs.htm

Golden Gardens Park
The off-leash area is across the street and northeast of the beach (no waterfront access).

Luther Burbank Park
The park is in the northeast corner of park, with Lake Washington access.

Marymoor Park
It has 40 acres to roam, including access to the Sammamish River.

Sand Point Magnuson Park
The park is adjacent to northern boundary of park and Lake Washington.

the Downtown skyline and Lake Union boating activity. On the Fourth of July, a day-long festival here leads up to a spectacular fireworks show over the lake. *2101 N. Northlake Way, between Densmore Ave. N and Bagley Ave. N, Wallingford, www.cityofseattle.net/parks/parkspaces/gasworks.htm.*

5 *e-3*

GREEN LAKE PARK

For more than a century, Seattle residents have made Green Lake their recreation destination. More than a million people visit each year, and as you'd expect, the biggest crowds are on the weekends and warm summer evenings. For young singles, it's definitely one of the best "see and be seen" parks, where hard-bodied joggers, sun bathers in bikinis, and fun-loving Rollerbladers create a Venice Beach atmosphere. The park isn't just for singles though; children enjoy the huge playground, seasonal wading pool, swimming beach, and indoor swimming pool. The 2.8-mi trail that circles the lake has separate lanes, so dog-walkers and strolling couples can co-exist with cyclists and 'bladers. To get out on the lake, bring your own nonmotorized craft, or rent a paddle boat, rowboat, canoe, or sailboard. In July, human-powered boats made of milk cartons race for prizes in the annual Seafair Milk Carton Derby. On-land sport facilities include basketball and tennis courts, soccer fields, and a pitch-and-putt golf course. Although plenty of folks enjoy a picnic on the lawn, you can also visit one of the many cafés, restaurants, ice cream, and coffee shops on neighboring streets. *7201 E. Green Lake Dr. N, Bordered by E. Green Lake Dr. N, W. Green Lake Dr. N, E. Green Lake Way N, and W. Green Lake Way N, Green Lake, www.cityofseattle.net/parks/parkspaces/greenlak.htm.*

9 *c-3*

HING HAY PARK

As the main outdoor gathering spot in the International District, Hing Hay Park lives up to its English translation, "park for pleasurable gatherings." The small square is pleasurable to the eyes, too, paved in red bricks with a red and orange pagoda (donated by the city of Taipei) and a dragon mural on the north wall. There's no grass here, but Hing Hay has benches where you can sit and watch the sights and sounds of this diverse district. Crowds gather for live entertainment (music, dance, and martial arts), food, shopping, and crafts at the International District Summer Festival in mid-July. *650 S. King St., northwest corner of S. King St. and Maynard Ave. S, International District.*

7 *e-5*

KERRY PARK

Some say the views here are as good as you'd find at the top of the Space Needle. Certainly it's one of the best spots in the city to bring a camera for skyline shots. Come to meditate in solitude as the sun rises, or enjoy a romantic sunset with someone special. There's also a jungle gym for kid play. On the Fourth of July, the park is packed with people watching the fireworks over Elliott Bay. *211 W. Highland Dr., bordered by 2nd Ave. W, 3rd Ave. W, W. Highland Dr., and W. Prospect St., Queen Anne.*

2 *a-7*

LINCOLN PARK

This lovely seaside park, near the Fauntleroy ferry, has the city's only outdoor heated saltwater pool, Colman Pool, open in summer. Year-round, the park bestows stunning vistas of the Olympic Mountains and Puget Sound from its bluff-top location. Hike down through the forested bluff to get to the sandy beach and tidepools. Several trails run through the 130-acre park, popular with joggers and cyclists. There are also sports fields, tennis courts, horseshoe pits, and two playgrounds. Picnic tables and shelters are abundant, but for quiet and seclusion, insiders recommend the "secret" picnic area at the park's north end. *8011 Fauntleroy Way SW, bordered by Fauntleroy Way SW and Puget Sound, Othello St. SW, and Fauntleroy Ferry Terminal, West Seattle, www.cityofseattle.net/parks/parkspaces/lincoln.htm.*

7 *e-7*

MYRTLE EDWARDS PARK

Those who want nothing more than to admire beautiful scenery will enjoy lazing on this long strip of green and taking in the gorgeous views of Puget Sound, Mt. Rainier, and the Olympic Mountains. For the more athletically inclined, a 1.25-mi trail hugs the shoreline, connecting the park to Elliott Bay Park further north along the bay. The trail is shared by walkers, joggers, cyclists, strollers, scooters, and in-line skaters. The park is at the north end of the waterfront (adjacent to Pier 70) but there's no beach or water sports. Two major festivals fill the park each year: The free all-day Fourth of Jul-Ivars event on July 4 includes live music, an air show, hands-on fun for kids, and food booths, and culminates with a fireworks show over Elliott Bay at dusk. In August, HempFest attracts a liberal crowd, with live entertainment, speakers, food, and merchandise vendors. *3130 Alaskan Way W (entrance at Alaskan Way and Broad St.), Waterfront, www.cityofseattle. net/parks/parkspaces/medwards.htm.*

5 *h-5*

RAVENNA & COWEN PARKS

Take a walk through this forested glacier-carved ravine, flanked by Cowen Park on the west and Ravenna Park on the east, for sounds of chirping birds and the babbling Ravenna Creek to calm your urban-weary soul. Hidden from the 15th Avenue Northeast traffic above, the ravine is sometimes also unknown even to park-goers, who are busy playing at the tennis courts, playgrounds or picnicking and sunbathing on the green lawns. (There's also a softball field and wading pool.) In the late 1990s, Cowen Park developed a crime and transient problem. Neighborhood residents worked with city agencies to clean up the park, even finding resources for displaced homeless youth. Today the park, regularly patrolled by city police, is a safe and welcoming place. *Bordered by Brooklyn Ave. N, Ravenna Blvd. NE, NE 58th St., NE 62nd St., 20th Ave. NE (enter at Brooklyn Ave. NE on west, and 20th Ave. NE and NE 58th St. on east), University District, www.cityofseattle. net/parks/parkspaces/ravenna.htm.*

6 *h-4*

SAND POINT MAGNUSON PARK

Considering that it was once an airport, it's not surprising that the park terrain is relatively flat and open, in stark contrast to the city's more forested parks. (The U.S. Navy gave up some of the former Sand Point Naval Air Station property in the mid-1970s and in the late 1990s, the rest was decommissioned and the park almost doubled in size, gaining a slightly modified name, as well.) Yet the paved trails are wonderful for cycling, in-line skating, riding a scooter, and pushing a stroller. Many tots have learned to ride their two-wheelers here and a huge playground keeps the little ones entertained, too. Leashed dogs are welcome on the trails; a large off-leash area

includes one of the few public beaches where pooches can swim. Farther south on the mile-long shore, there's a swimming beach, a seasonal wading pool, and a boat launch. The park also has tennis courts, sports fields, and a terrific kite-flying hill. Be sure to look for the unique public art: *The Fin Project: From Swords to Plowshares* uses submarine fins to depict a pod of orca whales; *No Appointment Necessary* features two bright red chairs extended into the sky, and commemorates the international "Horsehead" outdoor art festival held here. At the adjacent National Oceanic and Atmospheric Administration (NOAA) campus (access at north gate near off-leash area), the wind interacts with steel pipes at *The Sound Garden*, producing tones for an art display that you can hear as well as see. *Bordered by NE 65th and 74th Sts., Sand Point Way NE and Lake Washington (entrances at 65th St. and 74th St.), Sand Point, 206/ 684–4946, www.cityofseattle.net/parks/ parkspaces/spmagnuson.htm.*

3 *a-8*

SCHMITZ PARK

Virtually unchanged since it opened in 1908, Schmitz Park has 50 acres of old-growth forest, including 800-year-old trees. It's an excellent park for nature study and quiet contemplation, but look to nearby Alki Beach if you want to picnic; there are no picnic tables (or even rest rooms) here. *Bordered by SW Admiral Way, Spokane St., 51st Ave. SW, and Schmitz Blvd. (entrance at Admiral Way and Schmitz Blvd.), West Seattle, www.cityofseattle.net/parks/parkspaces/ schmitz.htm.*

2 *d-6*

SEWARD PARK

Find quiet serenity in the forest with its towering trees, shimmering creek, and waterfall; experience summer madness of boom boxes, bikinis, and barbecues on the beach; or get creative at classes in the Art Studio, open to the public, which specializes in pottery. The park, on a Lake Washington peninsula, is surrounded by water. A 2.5-mi paved trail, popular with cyclists, walkers, and runners, circles the perimeter. Other trails lead into the woods, to the outdoor amphitheater, the native gardens, and the fish hatchery. Seward Park also has tennis courts, a playground, and scenic picnic spots. *5598 Lake Washington Blvd. S, (entrance at Lake Washington Blvd. S and S. Juneau St.),*

*Seward Park, www.cityofseattle.net/parks/
parkspaces/sewardpark.htm.*

8 *c-5*

VOLUNTEER PARK

One of several city parks and gardens
designed by the Olmsted Brothers firm
(led by John C. Olmsted, the step-son of
Fredrick Law Olmsted, who, with Calvert
Vaux, designed New York's Central Park)
in the early 20th century, Volunteer Park
has an air of elegance and tradition that
fits perfectly with the surrounding Capitol Hill mansions. Homage is paid to
the famed architects in the park's Water
Tower exhibit. An impressive art deco–
style building houses the Seattle Asian
Art Museum (the Seattle Art Museum
was here until it moved to its Downtown
digs); two sentinel lions stand guard
outside. On cold, rainy days, the Volunteer Park Conservatory (206/684–4743)
warms body and soul with the sights
and scents of colorful native and tropical plants. Admission is free and it's
open daily (including holidays), 10 to 4.
Near the conservatory, children play at a
nicely designed playground or splash in
the wading pool. The park has awesome
views of the city, sound, and mountains,
especially if you climb the 108 stairs to
the top of the 75-ft water tower. Concerts
and other performances are often held
in the park's bandstand, and picnickers,
joggers, and walkers find places to stop
for a scenic break along the park's circular drive. Bordered by 11th and 15th
Aves. E and E. Prospect and Galer Sts.
(enter at 12th Ave. E and E. Prospect
St.), Capitol Hill, www.cityofseattle.net/
parks/parkspaces/volpark.htm.

9 *b-2*

WATERFALL GARDEN PARK

This secluded Asian-inspired park may
be more of a secret than the district's
famed underground city. You'll likely hear
the 22-ft waterfall before you actually see
the gate to the tiny, fenced-in park, built
to commemorate the site where the
United Parcel Service began. Come early
at lunchtime to snag a bench or table for
a picnic. *219 2nd Ave. S (at S. Main St.),
Pioneer Square, 206/624–6096.*

10 *e-8*

WATERFRONT PARK

With the Seattle Aquarium to the north
and Pier 57's tourist shops to the south,
Waterfront Park is a break from the
area's indoor activities. Take a walk up
the sloped and stepped promenade to
the viewing towers equipped with telescopes. Gaze at fishing boats, ferries,
and other vessels on the sound, and
beyond to the Kitsap Peninsula. A
bronze fountain on the street side near
the aquarium blows gentle sprays when
there's a breeze. *1300 Alaskan Way
(between Piers 57 and 59), Waterfront.*

10 *g-6*

WESTLAKE PARK

Weary shoppers and Downtown workers
stretch their legs in Westlake Park. On
hot days, the park's Water Wall, a walk-
through arch, is popular not only with
children, but with business-clad adults,
as well. In summer, live musicians entertain around noon. During the holiday
season, the park takes on a festive air,
contributing the Holiday Carousel to
form a seasonal trivium with the Bon
Marché's Holiday Star and Westlake
Center's towering Christmas tree. *401
Pine St. (at 4th Ave.), Downtown, www.
cityofseattle.net/parks/parkspaces/
westlake.htm.*

east king county

13 *g-4*

ANDERSON PARK

Redmond's oldest park has two historic
cabins that can be rented, plus picnic
facilities, including a covered picnic
shelter and tables, a playground, and
eye-catching public art. The brick plaza
with its outdoor stage is the site for free
summer concerts on Sunday evenings.
*7802 168th Ave. NE (bordered by 168th
Ave. NE and Avondale Rd.), Redmond,
425/556–2300.*

14 *b-1*

**BELLEVUE
DOWNTOWN PARK**

A nice respite from shopping awaits you
just south of Bellevue Square Shopping
Center. Walk the half-mile promenade
that circles a waterfall and reflection
pools; or have a picnic on the vast green
lawn. Kids run straight for the castle-
themed playground. The park hosts the
city's annual Fourth of July Festival, and
an outdoor ice-skating rink, Wells Fargo
Ice Arena (425/453–1223), is open from
Thanksgiving to New Year's. *10201 NE
4th St. (bordered by NE 4th and 1st Sts.,
100th and 103rd Aves. NE), Bellevue, 425/
452–6881, www.ci.bellevue.wa.us/parks.*

14 g-8

COUGAR MOUNTAIN REGIONAL WILDLANDS PARK

In the "Issaquah Alps," King County's largest park has 3,000 acres with more than 36 mi of hiking trails. It's a hiker's heaven, with abundant natural resources—waterfalls, glacial boulders, creeks, wetlands, and wildlife. The park is also rich in history; you can explore the former coal-mining town of Newcastle and also view where the military placed Nike missiles and anti-aircraft guns during the Cold War. Naturalists often lead free walks and hikes, which are a great way to see this vast park. *SE Cougar Mountain Way and 178th Ave. SE (Exit 11A or 13 from I–90, follow signs), Issaquah, 206/296–4171, www.metrokc. gov/parks/rentals/pommar99.htm.*

1 f-1

DEYOUNG PARK

Shoppers and workers in downtown Woodinville take a break at this small, shady plaza across the street from Molbak's and adjacent to the Woodinville Town Center shopping area. A lunchtime free concert series in summer attracts families and nearby office workers. *13680 NE 175th St. (near 138th Pl. NE), Woodinville, 425/398–9327, www.ci.woodinville. wa.us/recreation/parks.asp.*

2 h-2

FARREL-MCWHIRTER PARK

Bring the kids to visit the barnyard animals here, or sign them up for one of the farm-related programs or pony rides. Besides the working farm, the park has picnic areas and several nature trails. *19545 Redmond Rd. (off Novelty Hill Rd.), Redmond, 425/556–2300.*

13 b-2

JUANITA BAY PARK

Be sure to bring your binoculars when you visit this wildlife sanctuary. More than 100 species of birds reside here; beavers, turtles, and other water-loving creatures also inhabit the marshy wetlands. Naturalists lead guided walks the first Sunday of each month at 1 PM. Interpretive signs along a mile of boardwalks and trails explain the park's plant and animal life. *2201 Market St. (at Forbes Creek Dr.), Kirkland, 425/828–1217.*

14 d-2

KELSEY CREEK COMMUNITY PARK & FARM

At Bellevue's farm-in-the-city you can wander through the barn to see animals and pet them through fences or cages or take tours and classes on arts, crafts, and nature topics. Elsewhere in the park, walk along the creek to see waterfowl and visit the children's playground, or hike on several trails through forest and wetland areas. A farm festival held in the fall, celebrates the harvest season with hayrides and crafts-making opportunities. *13204 SE 8th Pl. (SE 8th St. Exit and Lake Hills Rd. from I–405), Bellevue, 425/452–7688, www.ci.bellevue.wa.us/parks/major-parks/kelsey.htm.*

1 g-4

LAKE SAMMAMISH STATE PARK

In summer, the lake lures crowds to this day-use state park, with fishing, a big sandy beach, and a boat launch. The playground is popular as well, and the grassy fields and volleyball areas get plenty of use, too. Picnic tables and grills accommodate hungry folks. The beach area can get busy and noisy; for an escape from the frenzy, walk the nature trails along Issaquah Creek or take a bike ride and look for birds. *20606 SE 56th St. (Exit 15 from I–90 and follow signs), Issaquah, 425/455–7010, www.parks.wa.gov/parkpage.asp.*

14 a-3

LUTHER BURBANK PARK

Mercer Island's 77-acre waterfront park is especially loved by families—even the family dog can play in the designated off-leash area. At the lake there's a swimming beach, a fishing pier, and a dock for tying up boats and for sunbathing that's especially popular with teenagers. Away from the beach, the park has a playground, tennis courts, basketball hoop, picnicking facilities, a large grassy area, and meandering trails to explore and look for birds and wildlife. *2040 84th Ave. SE (at SE 24th St.), Mercer Island, 206/296–8687, www.metrokc.gov/parks/rentals/pomdec98.htm.*

13 b-4

MARINA PARK

Adjacent to Kirkland's downtown shops, restaurants, and galleries, Marina Park has a pleasant enough waterfront location, though there's no beach. You can get close to the water by walking out on the pier where boats dock. The outdoor pavilion gets put to use throughout the summer for the city's almost-free ($1 donation requested) concert series. 25

SUMMER SOUNDS

From July to mid-August, live music fills the air at community parks. Children's entertainers take to the stage at morning shows; evening concerts feature some of the best local groups and musicians— including brass bands, pop, rock, jazz, and zydeco. Unless otherwise noted, listings are found in Parks, above. Most concert series are free, but a few request a $1 donation.

City of Seattle

Carl S. English Botanical Gardens (see Botanical Gardens, above), Sunday 2 PM.

Gas Works Park, Golden Gardens Park (see Beaches, above) and Volunteer Park, Sunday noon–6. (Concerts alternate between parks. Call 206/729–5232 for schedule.)

Sand Point Magnuson Park, Sunday 2 PM.

East King County

Anderson Park, Sunday 5 PM.

Bothell Landing Park, Friday 6:30 PM.

DeYoung Park, Thursday noon.

Gene Coulon Beach Memorial Park, Wednesday 7 PM.

Marina Park, Tuesday and Thursday 7 PM, Wednesday 10 AM.

Mercerdale Park, Thursday and Sunday 7 PM.

Wilmot Gateway Park, Sunday 7 PM.

South King County

Angle Lake Park, Sunday 5 PM.

Lake Meridian Park, Thursday 7 PM.

Mill Creek Canyon Earthworks Park, Wednesday noon, Friday 7 PM.

Lake Shore Plaza (at Market St.), Kirkland, 425/828–1217, www.kirkland.net/parks/marina.htm.

13 g-5

MARYMOOR PARK

Over 600 acres and an array of amenities assure that there's something for everyone at Marymoor. Bird and wildlife watchers get close to nature on the park's interpretive paths; other trails connect to the Sammamish River Trail, popular with joggers and cyclists. History buffs should seek out the Willowmoor Farm and Clise Mansion, home of the Marymoor Museum. When it's not being used for bike races, cyclists can make a run around the banked oval Marymoor Velodrome. Built for the Goodwill Games, it's the only facility of its kind in the Northwest. Another unique park structure is the 45-ft-high climbing rock. Hobbyists fly model airplanes at a large field; other fields are used for baseball, soccer, and lacrosse. Additional recreation facilities include tennis courts, a fitness circuit, and a fishing pier. There are lots of picnic areas and two playgrounds. The park hosts several major community events, including the Heritage Festival the first weekend in July, a Fourth of July fireworks show, Evergreen Horse Classic, and WOMAD—World Music Arts and Dance Festival in late July. *6046 W. Lake Sammamish Pkwy. NE (take W. Lake Sammamish Pkwy. NE Exit to park off Hwy. 520), Redmond, 206/296–4232, www.metrokc.gov/parks/rentals/pomjun99.htm.*

14 c-3

MERCER SLOUGH NATURE PARK

See more than 170 species of birds and other wildlife in this 300-acre wetlands park. More than 5 mi of trails and boardwalks can be covered on foot, or take a canoe for an on-the-water look at this rich habitat. Guided nature walks are offered regularly, as are interpretive canoe tours. At the Environmental Education Center, programs are led by the Pacific Science Center, including summer camps, workshops, and birthday parties for kids. *2102 Bellevue Way SE (take SE 8th St. Exit from I–405, enter park at 112th Ave. SE or 118th Ave. SE), Bellevue, 425/462–2752, www.ci.bellevue.wa.us/parks.*

2 *e-5*

MERCERDALE PARK

This Mercer Island park has picnic tables, trails, and an outdoor concrete skateboarding area with a pyramid and quarter-pipe. An eye-catching, interactive water sculpture sprays mist on breezy days. The parks department hosts free summer concerts here in July and August. *78th Ave. SE and SE 34th St., Mercer Island, 206/236–5300.*

2 *e-1*

O.O. DENNY PARK

Follow winding Holmes Point Drive through the forested ravine to reach this waterfront park in the Juanita neighborhood. The small beach is great for swimming, sunbathing, and launching kayaks and canoes. A trailhead near the parking lot leads up into the forest of towering trees. *12032 Holmes Point Dr. NE (follow signs from Juanita Dr. NE), Kirkland, 206/296–4232.*

13 *c-4*

PETER KIRK PARK

In downtown Kirkland you'll find an outdoor swimming pool, playground, basketball court, and baseball field at this city park. Its skating area—open to skateboards and in-line skaters—is also a big draw. *202 3rd St. (at Central Way), Kirkland, 425/828–1217, www.kirkland. net/parks/pkirk.htm.*

2 *e-1*

ST. EDWARDS STATE PARK

Formerly a Catholic seminary, this large park is now open to the public for day use. Its trails are popular for hiking and mountain biking. A half-mile hike trail leads to the beach, where you can also fish. The park also has an Olympic-size indoor pool, tennis and handball courts, sports fields, and picnic areas. *14445 Juanita Dr. NE (near NE 142nd St.), Kenmore, 425/823–2992, www.parks.wa. gov/parkpage.asp.*

1 *h-3*

TOLT MACDONALD PARK & CAMPGROUND

Known for its location on the Snoqualmie River—for an in-the-air thrill, cross the 500-ft-long suspension bridge 28 ft above the river—Tolt MacDonald is also the only county park with overnight camping. Camping costs $15 per night

and is seasonal (mid-March through October). If you hike on the park's trails any time of year, you're likely to spot wildlife. The park has a children's playground, plus picnic shelters and sports fields. *31020 NE 40th St. (off Hwy. 203, southeast of Redmond), Carnation, 206/ 296–4232, metrokc.gov/parks/rentals/ pommay99.htm.*

14 *d-1*

WILBURTON HILL PARK

The Bellevue Botanical Gardens is Wilburton Hill's draw, but come weekends folks also head to the ballfields, picnic facilities, nature trails, and the first-rate playground, complete with a spider web to climb and a boat to play in. *12001 Main St. (at NE 2nd St.), Bellevue, 425/452–6881, www.ci.bellevue. wa.us/parks.*

1 *f-1*

WILMOT GATEWAY PARK

The sound of music fills the air at free summer concerts at Woodinville's first park, which opened in 1999. Besides the amphitheater and pavilion, it has a nice play area for children, covered picnic facilities, and a large grassy area. The park also has access to the Sammamish River Trail and a launch for non-motorized boats into the river. *17301 131st Ave. NE (near NE 175th St.), Woodinville, 425/ 398–9327, www.ci.woodinville.wa.us/ recreation/parks.asp.*

south king county

1 *a-1*

DASH POINT STATE PARK

The beach at Dash Point slopes so gradually that the water is almost warm in summer—at least it's warmer than any other Puget Sound beach near Seattle—so you won't be the only one in the water. There's also overnight camping here. *5700 SW Dash Point Rd. (take the 320th St. Exit from I-5 and follow signs about 6 mi), Federal Way, 253/661–4955, www.parks.wa.gov/parkpage.asp.*

1 *d-5*

ED MUNRO SEAHURST PARK

Burien's waterfront park is also a wildlife sanctuary, home to sea anemones, nudibranchs, and other creatures, plus an underwater "seapen" garden that divers can explore. Naturalists lead low-tide marine-life walks during the summer, or you can simply come visit the beach, forest trails, picnic areas, and playground. *13059 16th Ave. SW (at 140th Ave. SW and 16th Ave. SW), Burien, 206/ 988–3700.*

1 *d-7*

SALTWATER STATE PARK

Halfway between Seattle and Tacoma, city folk come to camp out in the woods and explore the beach. An underwater, artificial reef, which includes a series of tire reefs, an old pipeline, and a frame made of concrete beams, draws divers. Hiking, biking, fishing, bird-watching, volleyball, and sailboarding are popular activities here, too. The park is open for day use year-round, and for camping April to October. *25205 8th Pl. S (off Marine View Dr. S), Des Moines, 253/661– 4956, www.parks.wa.gov/parkpage.asp.*

park resources

CITY OF SEATTLE PARKS & RECREATION DEPARTMENT

The City of Seattle's Parks and Recreation Department is responsible for the vast majority of parks, beaches, playgrounds, courts, and public green spaces within city limits. The Department issues permits for events in parks, arranges reservations of sports fields and picnic areas, and staffs visitors centers and naturalist programs at several parks. You can always call to confirm whether a particular park diamond will be available. *206/684–4075, www. cityofseattle.net/parks.*

KING COUNTY PARKS & RECREATION

King County owns and manages many of the parks outside of city limits. *206/ 296–4232 for information and reservations, 206/296–4171 for interpretive programs, www.metrokc.gov/parks.*

WASHINGTON STATE PARKS

Several parks and overnight campgrounds in the greater Seattle area are state-managed properties. You can find a complete list on-line, plus camping information. *800/233–0321 for general information, 800/452–5687 for campsite reservations, www.parks.wa.gov/ parkpage.asp.*

other outdoor attractions

AMUSEMENT PARKS

Years ago, Seattle had a number of amusement parks, many at area beaches: Luna Park at Alki Beach was the "Coney Island of the West," Playland at Bitter Lake brought folks from around the state, and trolley lines transported fun-loving Seattle folks to Madison Beach's amusement park. Today Seattle Center's Fun Forest, built for the 1962 World's Fair, is the only such destination in the city.

10 *d-2*

FUN FOREST AMUSEMENT PARK

Traditional rides, dating to the park's inception when it was built for the '62 World's Fair, include a roller coaster and Ferris wheel; others reflect the city's aerodynamic legacy with names like Orbiter (an elevated, green, spinning machine) and Jetspin (an inverted spinning ride). Rides require tickets, with the most desirable ones garnering the most tickets. About 4 tickets per ride is common, at $1/ticket; purchase an all-day wristband to get the most bang for your buck. The park has a large kiddy-ride area and offers group birthday party packages. Outdoor rides are open seasonally; laser tag and video games can be played year-round at the indoor Entertainment Pavilion. *5th Ave. and Broad St., Seattle Center, Queen Anne, 206/728– 1585, www.funforest.com. Admission: free. Amusement park open June–Labor Day, daily noon–11; early Sept.–May, Fri. 7 PM– 11 PM, Sat. noon–11, Sun. noon–8. Entertainment Pavilion open year-round, Sun.– Thurs. 11–6, Fri.–Sat. 11–10.*

1 *d-8*

WILD WAVES/ ENCHANTED VILLAGE

It's not Disneyland, but it's western Washington's only theme park, and, as of 2001, owned by the Six Flags Theme Parks chain. Some love it so much they buy season passes. There are actually two parks—an amusement park and a water park; one ticket gets you into both. Enchanted Village has the carnival rides, about two dozen, including the triple corkscrew Wild Thing roller coaster. Tamer trips include a train ride or a spin on the antique carousel; a splash in the wading pool or taking in live music and dance on stage. The water park, Wild Waves, has water rides, slides, and a 24,000-square-ft wave pool. There are food concessions at Enchanted Village and you're welcome to bring your lunch in a cooler, but no food is allowed at Wild Waves. The parks are also open for special holiday events throughout the year. *36201 Enchanted Parkway S (Exit 142B off I–5), Federal Way, 253/661–8000, www.wild-waves.com. $24.99 adults, $20.99 children (under 48"), 2 and under free. Open mid-May–mid-June, Enchanted Village weekdays 9:30–4:30, weekends 10–6, Wild Waves daily 11–6; mid-June–July 4, Enchanted Village daily 10–6, Wild Waves daily 11–7; July 5–Labor Day, Enchanted Village daily 10–7, Wild Waves daily 11–8.*

BEACHES

With the Puget Sound to the west and 25-mi-long Lake Washington to the east, the Seattle area has miles and miles of waterfront speckled with beaches. Smaller lakes, products of ancient glacial movements, spring forth throughout the city and in neighboring suburbs, too. So, Seattleites are rarely far from a body of water. Many of the parks listed above have wonderful beaches; here are the best of the rest. Most Lake Washington beaches in Seattle, Kirkland, and Bellevue have lifeguards on duty in summer; in Seattle free swimming lessons are given at several beaches for ages 6 and up.

3 b-7
ALKI BEACH

In summer, cars inch along Alki Avenue, seeking a coveted parking space, all the passengers heading for this 2½-mi stretch of sandy beach. It's something of a California beach scene (except for the water temperature), with Rollerbladers, joggers, and cyclists sharing the walkway and sun-loving singles playing volleyball and flirting on the beach. Year-round, families come to build sandcastles, beachcomb, and fly kites; in winter, storm-watchers come to see the crashing waves. Check out the replica of the Statue of Liberty at 61st Avenue Southwest and visit the Coast Guard's Alki Point Light Station at 3201 Alki Avenue Southwest. Restaurants line the street across from the beach. *1702 Alki Ave. SW (from Duwamish Head to 63rd Ave. SW), West Seattle, www.cityof-seattle.net/parks/parkspaces/alki.htm. Drinking water, grills, picnic tables, phones, rest room.*

BRACKETT'S LANDING & EDMONDS UNDERWATER PARK

Edmonds beach has been designated a marine sanctuary. This means you can get an up-close look at native marine species in tidepools. Low-tide beach explorations are often led by beach rangers. Divers can get even closer to the marine life, as this is also the entry point to Edmonds Underwater Park, 27 acres of tide and bottomlands, with eight sunken structures, and numerous underwater trails to explore. Around Halloween, divers compete in an underwater pumpkin carving contest. *Main St. (north and south of Edmonds ferry dock), Edmonds, 425/771–0230. Drinking water, picnic tables, phones, rest rooms, showers.*

2 f-8
GENE COULON MEMORIAL BEACH PARK

At the south end of Lake Washington, not far from the Renton Boeing Plant, lies one of the lake's prettiest waterfront parks. On hot summer days a sandy swimming beach (lifeguarded from mid-June to Labor Day) gets plenty of action, as does the nearby playground. Boats also launch here, and windsurfers glide on the lake just outside of the swimming area. Pick up a meal at the Ivar's Fish Bar or Kidd Valley Burger concession stands or grill your own at one of the picnic shelters. The park also has tennis and volleyball courts, a fishing pier, horseshoe pits, and interpretive nature trails. Special events include a summer concert series and holiday light show. *1201 Lake Washington Blvd. N (NE Park Dr. Exit from I–405), Renton, 425/430–6700, www.ci.renton.wa.us/commserv/parks/coulon.htm. Drinking water, grills, picnic tables, phones, rest rooms, snack bar.*

4 d-1
GOLDEN GARDENS PARK

Puget Sound waters are bone-chilling cold, but that doesn't stop folks from jumping in to cool off. Besides brave swimmers, the park is packed with sunbathers in summer. In other seasons, beachcombers explore during low tide, and groups gather around bonfires to socialize and watch the sun go down. To the east of the beach, the park continues with hiking trails, grassy fields, and an off-leash dog area. *8498 Seaview Pl. NW (near NW 85th St.), Ballard, www.cityofseattle.net/parks/parkspaces/golden.htm. Drinking water, grills, picnic tables, phones, rest rooms.*

13 *b-5*

HOUGHTON BEACH PARK

On hot days, sun-worshipers and swimmers flock to this beach south of downtown Kirkland on the Lake Washington waterfront. The rest of the year, the playground attracts families and the fishing pier stays busy with anglers. *5811 Lake Washington Blvd. (between NE 58th and 60th Sts.), Kirkland, 425/828–1217. Drinking water, picnic tables, phones, rest rooms.*

13 *b-2*

JUANITA BEACH PARK

Directly across the bay from Juanita Bay Park's peaceful wetlands and wildlife, this beach hops with activity: children playing in the sand, sunbathers on the dock, swimmers in the closed-in swimming area, and picnickers in the park. *9703 Juanita Dr. NE (between 93rd and 97th Aves. NE), Kirkland, 206/296–4232. Drinking water, grills, picnic tables, phones, rest rooms, snack bar (seasonal).*

8 *h-4*

MADISON PARK

If you've been to Madison Park's shops and restaurants you may have already strolled down to this beach and park; beach users are glad to have the neighborhood's coffee shops and other amenities nearby. The sandy beach and sloping lawn fill quickly on warm days. Up the hill, children stay busy on the playground and tennis courts get lots of use. *2300 43rd Ave. E (at Madison St.), Madison Park. Drinking water, picnic tables, phones, rest rooms, showers.*

9 *h-1*

MADRONA PARK

Several beach parks and green spaces front the lake along Lake Washington Boulevard; Madrona Park is one of the largest. Young swimmers stay in the roped-in area while teens and adults swim out to a floating raft with diving board. A mile-long trail along the shore is popular with in-line skaters and joggers. Grassy areas encourage picnicking; a barbecue concession stand is open seasonally. Kids will like the sculpted sand garden and rocks and logs to climb on.

853 Lake Washington Blvd. (at Madrona Dr.), Madrona. Drinking water, grills, picnic tables, phones, rest rooms, showers.

2 *d-2*

MATTHEWS BEACH PARK

On warm summer days, the parking lot and nearby streets overflow with people visiting Seattle's largest freshwater swimming beach. The Burke-Gilman Trail runs through the park, making it a resting point for cyclists and joggers. Picnic areas, basketball hoops, and a big playground round out the park's amenities. *Sand Point Way NE and NE 93rd St., Sand Point, www.cityofseattle.net/parks/parkspaces/matthews.htm Drinking water, grills, picnic tables, phones, rest rooms, showers.*

14 *c-5*

NEWCASTLE BEACH PARK

Bellevue's largest waterfront park has a big swimming beach, fishing dock, nature trails, volleyball nets, and a large grassy area with picnic tables. The playground is a favorite, with a train that tots can sit in and older kids like to climb on and hop from car to car. *4400 Lake Washington Blvd. SE (off 112th SE Exit from I–405), Bellevue, 425/452–6881, www.ci.bellevue.wa.us/parks. Drinking water, picnic tables, phones, rest rooms.*

OLYMPIC BEACH

Fishing off Edmonds' Olympic Beach Fishing Pier and beachcombing along the shore you can sometimes see hardy souls cooling off by wading and swimming in the ice-cold Puget Sound water. Younger children like to climb on two bronze sculptures *Locals* and *School of Fish* at the south end of the park. To learn about Puget Sound sea life, visit the interpretive center at the pier. A nearby café serves up ice cream, espresso, and other treats; park yourself at one of the picnic tables with a snack and watch the ferries and seagulls on the Sound. *Dayton St. and Admiral Way, Edmonds, 425/771–0230, Drinking water, picnic tables, phones, rest rooms.*

1 *c-1*

RICHMOND BEACH SALTWATER PARK

At the city of Shoreline's waterfront park, explore tidepools on your own or join the low-tide walks led by naturalists. Free summer concerts are held in July and August. Families also make good use of the playground and picnic areas. *2021 NW 190th St. (at 20th Ave. NW),*

Shoreline, 206/546–5041, Drinking water, grills, picnic tables, phones, rest rooms.

BOTANICAL GARDENS

14 *d-1*
BELLEVUE BOTANICAL GARDEN

Visit the 36-acre Bellevue Botanical Garden in each season and you'll be rewarded with an ever-changing landscape of colorful blooms and greenery. The Perennial Border—a mixture of bulbs, shrubs, trees, and perennials—has won horticultural awards of excellence. At the Waterwise Garden, learn water conservation practices, including how to maintain a minimal-water garden. See plants native to other continents in the Alpine Rock Garden, behold brilliant blooms in the Fuschia Garden, and follow the Loop Trail to the Yao Japanese Garden. Filled with native plants and Japanese varieties, the Japanese Garden is especially vibrant in autumn. Don't miss the Botanical Garden's annual Garden d'Lights event; between Thanksgiving and New Year's, the park is decked out with more than 200,000 twinkling light displays depicting flowers blooming in the dark. Other special events include a Mother's Day Open House, plant sales, and gardening classes. Garden tours are the first Sunday of each month at 2 PM; groups can also arrange for tours at other times. The visitor center has a gift shop and park maps. *12001 Main St. (at 124th Ave. NE), Bellevue, 425/452–2750, www.bellevuebotanical.org. Open daily dawn–dusk, visitors center daily 9–4.*

4 *d-5*
CARL S. ENGLISH BOTANICAL GARDENS

Next to the Ballard (Hiram Chittenden) Locks resides a romantic English-style garden. Walk through 7 acres, planted with more than 500 species, including trees and shrubs from around the world and a bright display garden of fuschias. Free concerts are on Sunday afternoons. *3015 NW 54th St. (at 30th Ave. NW), Ballard, 206/783–7059, www.nws.usace.army. mil/opdiv/lwsc/garden.html. Open daily 7 AM–9 PM.*

1 *c-2*
E.B. DUNN HISTORIC GARDEN

Known as Seattle's "secret garden," because its location is only divulged to those with reservations, the Dunn Garden was designed by the Olmsted Brothers firm in the early 1900s. It's the only private Olmsted-designed garden open to the public. Since residents (including relatives of the original owner) live on the grounds, it's open only for reserved tours. *Broadview, 206/362–0933. Admission: $7 adults, $5 seniors and students, no children under 12. Open for tours by reservation only, Apr.–Sept., Thurs. 2, Fri. 10 and 2, Sat. 10.*

8 *f-3*
JAPANESE GARDEN

The Japanese Garden in the Washington Park Arboretum is a model garden of tranquility, designed by a Japanese landscape architect Juuki Iida. It uses hundreds of tons of stones hauled from the Cascades. In this compressed world of forests, mountains, rivers, and lakes, you'll spot a number of wild creatures—including turtles, ducks, and muskrats—and óne domestic one, the resident cat. Ceremonial tea demonstrations are held monthly at the garden's teahouse. Special events, including live music, festivals, and hands-on crafts are often presented. *1501 Lake Washington Blvd. E (Washington Park Arboretum), Capitol Hill, 206/684–4725, www.cityofseattle. net/parks/parkspaces/gardens.htm. Admission: $2.50 adults, $1.50 children. Open Mar.–Nov., daily 10–6.*

2 *d-7*
KUBOTA GARDEN

Somewhat hidden in south Seattle's Rainier Beach neighborhood, this garden is owned by the city of Seattle and maintained by a nonprofit foundation. Japanese gardening styles are integrated with Northwest native species, creating an inventive setting of hills and valleys. Paths and bridges crisscross the pools of recirculating water called the Necklace of Ponds, highlighting waterfalls and varied plantings. Drop by for a free guided tour on the last Saturday and Sunday of each month at 10 AM, or call to request a group tour for eight or more. *55th Ave. S (at Renton Ave. S), Rainier Beach, 206/725–5060. Open daily, dawn–dusk.*

8 *f-4*
WASHINGTON PARK ARBORETUM

Covering 200 acres of Seattle's Montlake and Capitol Hill neighborhoods, the Arboretum is home to more than 40,000 trees, shrubs, vines, and other plants, belonging to about 5,000 different species. Besides plant lovers, professional botanists are frequent visitors; the Arboretum is also a site for the University of Washington's botanical research. Walk along the ¾-mi Azalea Way to see flowering cherry trees and azaleas. At the north end, adjacent to the Museum of History and Industry, a ½-mi trail winds over bridges and wood walkways between Marsh and Foster Islands, just below the Evergreen Point Floating Bridge. In the Rhododendron Glen, see the official state flower in glorious bloom from March to June. Autumn brings glowing fall colors to trees; in winter, visit the Joseph A. Witt Winter Garden. The Arboretum's Japanese Garden (*above*) has traditional gardens, separate hours, and a small admission fee. Stop by the Graham Visitors Center to pick up a self-guided walking tour brochure or browse garden books and other items at the small gift shop. *2300 Arboretum Dr. E (at Lake Washington Blvd.), Capitol Hill, 206/543–8800, www.depts.washington. edu/wpa. Open daily 7 AM–dusk, visitor center daily 10–4.*

5 *c-6*

WOODLAND PARK ROSE GARDEN

Find floral bliss at this 2½-acre garden with more than 250 varieties of roses and over 5,000 rose bushes. It's one of just two dozen certified American Rose Test Gardens in the U.S., so you can take a peek at new hybrids before they've even been named. An interesting fact: Because it's adjacent to Woodland Park Zoo (*below*), the gardens get fertilizing help from the animals in the form of "ZooDoo." Visit between May and August to enjoy the roses at their peak. *5000 Fremont Ave. N (at 50th Ave. N), Fremont, 206/684–4863, www. cityofseattle.net/parks/parkspaces/ gardens.htm. Open daily 7 AM–dusk.*

ZOOS

1 *g-5*

COUGAR MOUNTAIN ZOOLOGICAL PARK

The Zoo's mission is to preserve endangered species and to educate the public. To do this, animals live in ten natural habitats, called "Worlds." Four of these—the Worlds of Mountain Lions,

Reindeer, Large Macaws, and Lemurs— are among the top three exhibits of their type in the U.S. Other Worlds mimic the habitats of antelopes, cheetahs, formosan elk, and cranes, and two rotating exhibits change each year. The zoo offers a number of education programs, tours, special events (including the Reindeer Festival in December), birthday-party packages, and school programs. *5410 194th Ave. SE (at SE 54th St.), Issaquah, 425/391–5508, www. cougarmountainzoo.org. Admission: $8 adults, $6.50 seniors (over 62), $5.50 children 4–15, $4 children 2–3, free under 2. Open Mar.–Oct., Fri.–Sun. 10–5.*

5 *c-6*

WOODLAND PARK ZOO

Consistently rated among the top ten zoos in the United States, Woodland Park showcases animals from around the world in elaborate natural habitats. Plan to spend several hours if you want to see it all, especially if there are baby animals to be seen—something about the little ones draws crowds and long waits. A recent such addition is Hansa (which means "supreme happiness"), daughter of Chai and the first Asian elephant born at the zoo. Around-the-world habitats include the Northern Trail, home to Northwest and Alaskan native species, including mountain goats, eagles, and grizzly bears. Look for giraffes and hippos in the African Savannah and swinging orangutans in the Trail of Vines. More than 50 exotic species of animals and thousands of plants live in the Tropical Rainforest. (It's a comfortable place to warm up on a winter day, too.) Kids enjoy the Family Farm, nearby play area, and pony rides in summer. A variety of special programs and events are offered, including day camps, zoo sleepovers, classes about animals and nature, and a summer concert series. *5500 Phinney Ave. N (at N. 55th St.); other entrances at N. 50th St. and Fremont Ave. N, and Phinney Ave. N and N. 59th St.), Fremont, 206/684–4800, www.zoo.org. Admission: $9 adults, $6.50 children 6–17, $4.25 children 3–5, free under 2. Open May–mid-Sept., daily 9:30– 6; mid-Sept.–Apr., daily 9:30–4.*

stadiums

The four major sports arenas in town are Safeco Field, where the Mariners

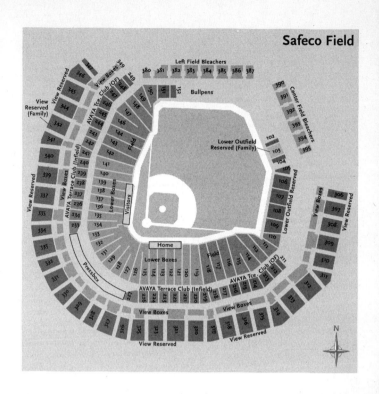

Safeco Field

Left Field Bleachers
380 381 382 383 384 385 386 387

Center Field Bleachers
389 390 391 392 393 394 395

View Boxes 347 348 349
View Tce. Club (OF)
View Reserved 346 345
AVAYA Tce. Club (Infield)
View Reserved (Family) 344 342 341
340 339 337 335 334 335 331
330 332 333
AVAYA Terrace Club (Infield)
Pressbox
Lower Boxes
Field
Visitors
Home
Lower Boxes
Field
Bullpens

Lower Outfield Reserved (Family)
102 103 104 105 106 107 108 109 110
Lower Outfield Reserved
View Boxes 306 307 308 309 310 311
View Reserved
AVAYA Tce. Club (OF)
211 312 313 314 315 318 319
View Boxes
View Reserved

View Boxes
View Reserved

N

Husky Stadium

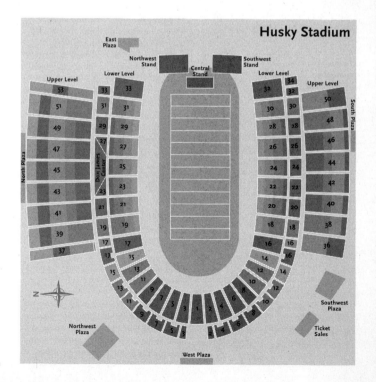

East Plaza
Northwest Stand
Central Stand
Southwest Stand

Upper Level
53 51 49 47 45 43 41 39 37

Lower Level
33 31 29 27 25 23 21 19 17 15 13 11

North Plaza

Don James Center

Lower Level
33 31 29

Central Stand

34 32 30 28 26 24 22 20 18 16 14 12

Lower Level
32 30 28 26 24 22 20 18 16 14

Upper Level
50 48 46 44 42 40 38 36

South Plaza

Northwest Plaza

West Plaza

Southwest Plaza

Ticket Sales

W

137

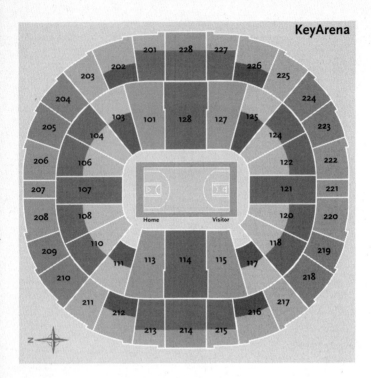

KeyArena

Seats: 201, 228, 227, 226, 225, 224, 223, 222, 221, 220, 219, 218, 217, 216, 215, 214, 213, 212, 211, 210, 209, 208, 207, 206, 205, 204, 203, 202

Court labels: 103, 101, 128, 127, 125, 124, 122, 121, 120, 118, 117, 115, 114, 113, 111, 110, 108, 107, 106, 104

Home / Visitor

play; Husky Stadium at the University of Washington; KeyArena, home of the Seattle SuperSonics; and the new yet-to-be-named Seahawks Stadium.

SAFECO FIELD

It may sound cliché but there really isn't a bad seat in the house. When it rains, the retractable roof deflects most of the rain. When it's sunny, you can watch the sun set over the Olympics (the mountains!) from behind the Mariners' second base. One local sports columnist refers to the venue, which opened in the summer of 1999—the most expensive stadium in recorded history and $100 million over budget—as "The Guilty Pleasure." *1st Ave. S and Atlantic St., 206/346–4000.*

HUSKY STADIUM

Look east from Husky Stadium and that's Lake Washington. Look at the field, and those are the Husky's, the UW's football team, the fans of which are responsible for the terrible traffic in the U-District during home games. *University of Washington, 3800 Montlake Blvd. NE (at N. 45th St.), University District, 206/543–2200.*

10 *b-2*

KEYARENA

Seattle Center has its hands full with the Seattle SuperSonics (NBA) and Seattle Storm (WNBA) but also the Seattle Thunderbirds (a minor-league hockey club) and all the major concerts. The surrounding area has plenty to offer post-game, with Tini Biggs to the south on 1st Avenue, Floyd's BBQ, or the venerable Sorry Charlies, a piano bar where a stately gentleman named Howard tickles the ivories. Traffic is a major problem on game nights at 7 and 10 PM. *Seattle Center, 1st Ave. N and Mercer St., Queen Anne, 206/283–3865.*

10 *c-1*

MEMORIAL STADIUM

Seattle Center, 5th Ave. N and Harrison St., Queen Anne, 800/796–5425.

12 *c-4*

"SEAHAWKS STADIUM"

Just in time for the 2002 season, a mere block away from Safeco Field the Seattle Seahawks will have their not-too-shabby $430 million football stadium on the site of the demolished Kingdome. It was unknown at press time which corpora-

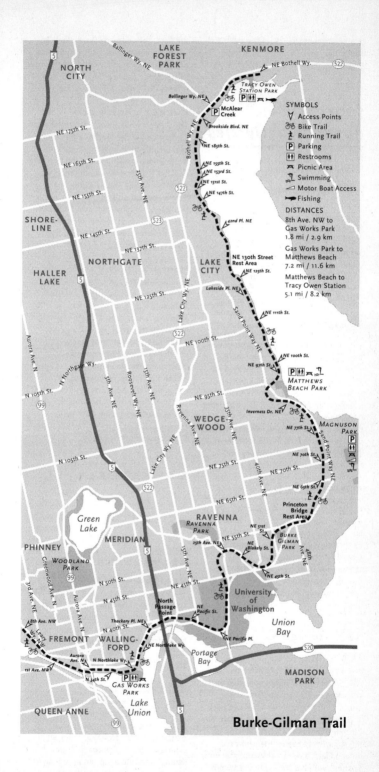

tion was slated to pick up the tab. *Occidental Ave. (between King St. and S. Royal Brougham), Sodo, 425/827–9777.*

sports & outdoor activities

It's just not all that unusual to meet people in Seattle who never stop exercising. They ski in the winter, run in the spring, hike/mountain bike/camp/sail in the summer, in-line skate in the fall. You can go to a 5K run in the morning and see the same people jogging around Green Lake later that afternoon or doing laps in the Queen Anne pool. The year is marked by sporting events, from the Jingle Bell 5K run through Downtown during Christmas through the summer STP (the 200-mi Seattle-to-Portland bike ride).

The laziest live vicariously through the city's spectator sports. Teams here attract an international following. People go to Sonics basketball games just to watch "Gary being Gary." (That's point guard Gary Payton.) The spanking-new Seahawks stadium will be ready for the 2002 season as well, which may just spark a renaissance in pro football in Seattle. Maybe.

BASEBALL

It's not just Seattleites who revel in a summer day spent at Safeco Field. The entire nation watched the 2001 season as the Mariners matched baseball's record for the most games won. The season normally runs from early April through September. The same goes for the minor leagues, which are nothing to sneeze at.

where to watch

12 *c-5*

SEATTLE MARINERS

Despite the crippling departure of all-stars Ken Griffey, Jr., Randy Johnson, and Alex Rodriguez, the Mariners keep coming back stronger every season. The Mariners play in the West Division of the American League; their home is Safeco Field, a retractable-roof stadium, opened (with big bucks) in the summer of 1999. Even if nothing's happening on the field, the walkways have plenty of stunning viewpoints that overlook the port's giraffelike cranes and the Olympic Mountains. *Safeco Field, 1st Ave. S and Atlantic St., Sodo, 206/346–4000.*

EVERETT AQUA SOX

The Everett Aqua Sox play short-season Class A ball in the Northwest League and are affiliated with the Mariners. Keep an eye out for Harold the Pig, who delivers balls to the pitching mound. Admission is $5–$10. Parking in the South Lot and on-street parking north of the stadium is free, but arrive about an hour early. *Everett Memorial Stadium, 3802 Broadway Ave. (Exit 192 off I–5), Everett, 425/258–3673.*

TACOMA RAINIERS

For some AAA Pacific Coast League action and a fabulous view of Mount Rainier, head south to see the Tacoma Rainiers, a Mariners' affiliate team. If you're totally broke, there's a grassy knoll outside of left field that you can watch the entire game from, but you didn't hear that from us. Take I–5 south to Exit 132, follow Highway 16 west for 2 mi, get off at the South 19th Street East Exit; take first right (Cheyenne St.), and follow road to stadium parking lots. *Cheney Stadium, 2502 S. Tyler (at 19th St.), Tacoma, 253/752–7707.*

BASKETBALL

The men's NBA season runs from November to April. The female counterpart, the WNBA, goes from mid-June to August.

where to watch

SEATTLE SUPERSONICS

Seattle SuperSonics of the National Basketball Association play at Key Arena. Single game tickets can be purchased at the KeyArena box office or by calling the NBA. *KeyArena, Seattle Center, 1st Ave. N and Mercer St., Queen Anne, 206/283–3865 or 800/4NBA–TIX.*

SEATTLE STORM

After the demise of the Seattle Reign, the first women's professional team in town, hopes were immediately pinned on the WNBA to pick Seattle for an expansion team. The coach dribbled through Downtown for an entire day once to win supporters to the cause.

Prayers were answered with the formation of the Storm. The Storm plays a 2½-month schedule June–August. *KeyArena, Seattle Center, 1st Ave. N and Mercer St., Queen Anne, 206/217–9622.*

UNIVERSITY OF WASHINGTON HUSKIES

The Huskies represent Seattle basketball in the Pac-10 Conference. In the 2000-01 season the Husky's tough women's team—which enjoys a very loyal (and loud) fan base—fell just short of a trip to the Final Four. The men's team, however, has had less than its share success. Games are played at what was formerly known as "Hec Ed." *Seafirst Arena at Hec Edmundson Pavilion, UW campus, 3870 Montlake Blvd. NE, University District, 206/543–2200 or 206/543–2210.*

where to play

The best pick-up games are at the outdoor court across the street from Seattle Center on Broad Street and at the indoor courts at Green Lake. The most serious action in town happens in the more dangerous streets of Central District.

BICYCLING

With more than 90 mi of signed bike routes—including 15 mi of bike lanes, Seattle is certainly a cycle-friendly city. It's estimated that 36% of Seattle's 520,000 citizens bike recreationally, with up to 8,000 people using pedal power to get to work.

biking resources

CASCADE BICYCLE CLUB

With more than 5,500 members, this club organizes rides for recreational and hard-core bikers virtually every day of the year and holds several major ride events during the year, the most famous being the Seattle-to-Portland Bicycle Classic. *206/522–2453, cascade.org.*

BICYCLE ALLIANCE OF WASHINGTON

These folks are a great resource for cycling-related information and are the state's largest advocacy group for city cyclists. *206/224–9252, www.bicycleallinace.org.*

BICYCLE SATURDAYS & SUNDAYS

The Seattle Parks Department sponsors this twice-a-month ride on different weekends May through September. On these days, a 4-mi stretch of Lake Washington Boulevard from Mt. Baker Beach to Seward Park is closed to motor vehicle traffic. Riders may continue around the 2-mi loop at Seward Park and back to Mt. Baker Beach to complete a 10-mi, car-free ride. *206/684–7045, www.pan.ci. seattle.wa.us/td/satsun.asp.*

KING COUNTY PARKS & RECREATION

In addition to trails within the city, King County has more than 100 mi of paved and nearly 70 mi of unpaved trails including the Sammamish River, Interurban, Green River, Cedar River, Snoqualmie Valley, and Soos Creek trails. *206/296–4258, www.metrokc.gov.*

SEATTLE BICYCLE PROGRAM

Affiliated with the City of Seattle, this program created the urban and multiuse trails (a.k.a. bike routes) around the city, along with wide shoulders and pedestrian paths—things, in other words, that benefit bicyclists. Check out their Web site for bike route maps. *206/ 684–7583, www.cityofseattle.net/td/ bikemaps.asp.*

where to ride

BURKE-GILMAN TRAIL

The Burke-Gilman Trail and the trail that encircles Green Lake are obvious choices for biking, but at Green Lake, joggers and walkers tend to impede fast travel. The city-maintained Burke-Gilman Trail, a much less congested path, extends 12.1 mi along Seattle's waterfront from Lake Washington almost to Salmon Bay along an abandoned railroad line. *Matthews Beach Park. See Burke-Gilman Trail map.*

13 *g-5*

MARYMOOR VELODROME

If you feel the need for speed, then the Velodrome is for you. The Friday Night racing series, which runs from mid-May through August, is a summer sports tradition; races are also held on Wednesday, 6 to 10 PM. The National Championship meets, regional Olympic trials and the Goodwill Games are held here, and this is where a number of

Olympians and National and World champions have trained. When not used for competitive racing, the banked oval is open to the public. *6046 W. Lake Sammamish Pkwy. NE (in Marymoor Park), Redmond, 206/227–5379, marymoor.velodrome.org.*

7 *e-7*

MYRTLE EDWARDS PARK
North of Pier 70, it has a path for jogging and bicycling. *See* City Parks, *above.*

BIRD-WATCHING

Bird-watching in Seattle is quickly becoming a favorite pastime, with many outdoorsy folks keeping extensive lists

---

WALKING IN NATURE

Nature abounds at most area parks; these are especially rich with opportunities to see and learn about the region's flora and fauna. Naturalist-led hikes and low-tide beach walks are offered at many; others have well-marked trails and trail-guide brochures so you can explore on your own.

City of Seattle
  Camp Long

  Carkeek Park

  Discovery Park

  Ravenna and Cowen Parks

  Schmitz Park

  Seward Park

East King County
  Bothell Landing Park

  Cougar Mountain Regional Wildlands Park

  Farrel-McWhirter Park

  Gene Coulon Memorial Beach Park

  Juanita Bay Park

  Kelsey Creek Park

  Luther Burbank Park

  Marymoor Park

  Mercer Slough Nature Park

  Newcastle Beach Park

  O.O. Denny Park

North of City (see Beaches, *above*)
  Richmond Beach Saltwater Park

  Brackett's Landing and Underwater Park

---

of species seen all over the Pacific Northwest. Because of Seattle's coastal proximity, all kinds of water and land birds following flight paths to summer nesting grounds or winter habitats make a way station of the area. Snow geese and trumpeter swans, for instance, arrive from Alaska every spring and take up residence in Skagit Valley fields. For general information or for group tours, educational lectures, and other bird-related events, contact **The Seattle Audubon Society** (206/523–8243, www.seattleaudubon.org).

4 *b-6*

DISCOVERY PARK
Within the city, Discovery Park—with over 500 acres of diverse landscape including dramatic sea cliffs, sand dunes, forest groves, and protected tidal beaches—attracts at least 200 different bird species year-round. In summer, park officials conduct free birding tours. *3801 W. Government Way, 206/386–4236.*

6 *d-6*

SEWARD PARK
The 277-acre park has good bird-watching and extensive bike and walking paths, hiking trails, and a native plant garden that serve binocular-toting folks. *5898 Lave Washington Blvd. S.*

SPENCER ISLAND
About a half-hour drive north of the city near Everett is Spencer Island; for better or worse, its proximity to a sewage treatment center attracts all kinds of waterfowl, while wetlands and wooded areas draw herons, eagles, hawks, owls, and a host of other birds year-round. There's a 3½-mi trail that loops along the top of the dike that surrounds the island. *From Seattle, take I–5 north to Exit 195 in Everett, go left on Marine View Dr., bear left on Hwy. 529 N, and cross the bridge over the Snohomish River. Go right at the first exit, following signs for Smith Island and Langus Riverfront Park (which has the area's only rest rooms). Go straight on Smith Island Rd. From the beginning of Smith Island Rd., it's 1.3 mi past the park to the Spencer Island parking lot. Follow the walking trail to Spencer Island.*

BOATING

Add up the protected waters of the Puget Sound, Lake Union, and Lake Washington and you've got a haven for boat owners.

sailboarding

URBAN SURF
Lake Washington and the Puget Sound are Seattle's most popular sailboarding spots, and Urban Surf is a popular sailboard renter year-round. *2100 N. North-lake Way (at Meridian Ave. N), Lake Union, 206/545–9463.*

hydroplaning

3 *g-8*

UNLIMITED HYDROPLANE RACES
A highlight of Seattle's Seafair festivities from mid-July to the first Sunday in August. Races are held on Lake Washington near Seward Park. The untold pleasure of this event is the people-watching. Well, that and the possibility of a big hydroplane crash. Tickets cost $15–$25. In summer, there are weekly sailing regattas on lakes Union and Washington. *206/728–0123 or Seattle Yacht Club, 206/325–1000 for schedules.*

where to boat

5 *e-3*

GREEN LAKE

1 *e-3*

LAKE WASHINGTON

2 *c-4*

LAKE UNION

marinas

2 *f-3*

YARROW BAY MARINA
Dock your own or rent a 17- and 20-ft runabouts for the day or week. *5207 Lake Washington Blvd. NE (near NE 52nd St.), Kirkland, 425/822–6066 or 800/336–3834.*

BOWLING

To get involved with a bowling team and for other bowling-related information, contact **The Greater Seattle Bowling Association** (6100 Southcenter Blvd., Suite 200, 206/923–3138, www.nwsports.com/gsba). The **Greater Seattle Women's Bowling Association** (206/878–4669) creates teams and organizes tournaments.

2 *c-2*

LEILANI LANES
The 36-lane alley hosts the Rock 'n' Roll Bowl Show every Saturday from 10 PM til midnight; cost is $12 per person (includes shoe rental) for the show featuring a live DJ and a laser light display. Regular bowling costs $2.70 per game per person before 6 PM and $3.50 per game per person evenings (shoe rental is $2.50). *10201 Greenwood Ave. N (N. 102nd St.), Greenwood, 206/783–8010.*

1 *e-5*

SKYWAY PARK BOWL & CASINO
Skyway's a veritable entertainment mecca with 24 bowling lanes, an 18-hole minigolf course, and a 14-table casino, where poker and blackjack are the games of choice. Bowling costs $3 per game per person Sunday through Thursday and $3.75 on Friday and Saturday—or a group can rent a lane for $12 per hour (shoe rentals, $3.25). During Cosmic Bowl (Wednesdays from 3:30 to 5:30 PM and Sunday 9 PM to midnight), the overhead lights are turned low and the gutters come alive with flashing lights: cost is $5 per person for two hours or $8 per hour per lane. *11819 Renton Ave. S (west of 72nd Ave. S), Skyway, 206/772–1220.*

4 *g-5*

SUNSET BOWL
Hard-core bowlers frequent the 26 lanes at Sunset, where the sun never sets: it's open 24 hours. A full restaurant, arcade, pro shop, and bar—with free karaoke on Wednesday, Thursday, and Saturday—makes it a favorite hangout for young and old alike. Weekdays, it costs $2.50 per person, per game before 6 PM; after 6 PM and on weekends and holidays, cost is $3.25 per person per game. Shoe rentals are $2. *1420 NW Market St. (at 14th Ave. NW), Ballard, 206/782–7310.*

BOXING

2 *d-6*

HILLMAN CITY BOXING GYM
Seattle is not a huge boxing center, for pro fights or for training, but Hillman serves most of the amateur and pro boxing community in this city. *5601 Rainier Ave. S (at S. Findlay St.), Rainier Valley, 206/722–3239.*

CRICKET

1 *e-6*

SEATTLE CRICKET CLUB

The Pacific Northwest's oldest and largest cricket club organizes four Seattle teams that compete around the region with other unofficial teams that play each other for fun. From late April to the end of September, you can usually find a game in progress most weekends (official games start at 1 PM and unofficial games start at 11 AM). Matches are at Fort Dent Park—the only public park with an exclusive cricket field in the Northwest. From Fort Dent Way, drive across the bridge into the park and the cricket field is on your right. *Fort Dent Park, 206/526–8793, www.seattlecricket.com.*

FISHING

Fishing's in this city's blood. Cruise over the Ballard Bridge in early summer, and you'll marvel at the number of fishing

---

GONE FISHING

Throw a pole off one of the park department piers. You may fish year-round for rainbow trout, cutthroat trout, and large- and smallmouth bass. Chinook, coho, and steelhead salmon are also available, but often subject to restrictions. Pier from north to south include:

Golden Gardens Park (Shilshoe Bay, north end of Seaview Ave.): Saltwater fishing.

Madison Park (43rd Ave. E and E. Madison St.).

Madrona Park (Lake Washington Blvd. S and E. Jefferson St.).

Magnuson Park (Sand Point Way NE and NE 65th St.).

Mount Baker Park (Lake Washington Blvd. S between Lake Park Dr. S and S. Horton St.).

Sayres Memorial Park (Lake Washington Blvd. S and 46th St. S).

Seward Park (Lake Washington Blvd. S and S. Juneau St.).

Waterfront Park (Elliot Bay piers 57–61 on the Downtown waterfront): Saltwater fishing.

---

boats that can cram into the canal after a winter of fishing off of Alaska. For the tamer fishing in the city's backyard, there are plenty of placid places to throw some bait. In fact, Seattle has many public fishing piers throughout the city.

Call the **Seattle Parks Department** (206/684–4075) for information on fishing locations, permits, and licenses. Regulations are printed in the "Sport Fishing Rules" pamphlet available at most sporting goods stores, where you can buy your license.

5 *e-3*

GREEN LAKE FISHING PIERS

Green Lake is stocked with more than 10,000 legal-size rainbow trout each year. Anglers also can vie for brown trout, largemouth bass, yellow perch, and brown bullhead catfish. The Parks Department maintains three fishing piers along the lake's shores: East Green Lake Drive at Latona Avenue Northeast; West Green Lake Drive North and Stone Avenue North; and West Green Lake Way North, just north of the shellhouse. You can't deny the bizarre combination of hooking one in while North Face clad moms jog by with their toddlers in sport utility strollers. *7201 E. Green Lake Dr. N, Bordered by E. Green Lake Dr. N, Green Lake, www.cityofseattle.net/parks/parkspaces/greenlak.htm.*

charter-fishing

Charter-fishing companies operating from Shilshole Bay run trips to catch salmon, rockfish, ling cod, flounder, and sea bass.

4 *c-4*

ADVENTURE CHARTERS

You pay $125 for a 6-hour trip with up to 6 anglers of all abilities. Trips depart from Shilshole Bay marina year-round. *Shilshole Bay marina, 7001 Seaview Ave. NW, Ballard, 206/789–8245.*

4 *c-4*

FISH FINDERS

You pay $135 for a 6- to 7-hour trip with about 6 anglers of all abilities. Trips leave year-round and include the cost of a two-day fishing license ($6). *Golden Tides*

Marina, 6019 Seaview Ave. N (next to
Ray's Restaurant), Ballard, 206/632–2611.

FLYING

Whether you're looking to learn to fly,
rent a plane for a weekend get-away, or
get a bird's-eye-view tour of the city, there
are plenty of companies willing to give
you wings, most of them centered
around Boeing Field near Sea-Tac airport.

1 d-5

AVIATION
TRAINING CENTER

This flight school has a variety of professional flight-training programs. 7201
Perimeter Rd. at Boeing Field, Tukwila,
206/768–1332 or 888/708–2180.

1 d-5

GALVIN FLYING

Aircraft rentals, scenic flights, and flight
training are available; it's open 24/7.
7001 Perimeter Rd. at Boeing Field, Tukwila, 206/763–0350 or 800/341–4102,
www.galvinflying.com.

8 c-4

SEATTLE SEAPLANES

With all the water surrounding Seattle,
seaplanes are very popular. With take-
offs and landings on scenic Lake Union,
it has both flight training classes and
aerial tours. 1325 Fairview Ave. E (south of
E. Galer St.), Capitol Hill, 206/329–9638,
www.seattleseaplanes.com.

FOOTBALL

The pro-football season runs from early
September through December. Starting
this year, all games will take place at the
new $400 million football and soccer
stadium, right next door to the
Mariners' Safeco Field. Nobody's quite
figured out why we have a roofed stadium for a sport that's played in the
summer and an open-air stadium being
built for a sport played in the winter.

12 c-4

SEATTLE SEAHAWKS

It's another civic project kick-started by
Microsoft co-founder and billionaire
Paul Allen, who also built the Experience
Music Project and saved the Cinerama
movie theater from destruction. He's
the Seahawks owner and is expected to

pick up a quarter of the cost. At press
time, the stadium was trying to attract a
major league soccer team to the city and
the new stadium, which is slated to
open with the 2002 football season.
Occidental Ave. (between King St. and S.
Royal Brougham), Sodo, 425/827–9777,
www.seahawks.com.

6 a-8

UNIVERSITY OF
WASHINGTON HUSKIES

Frankly, people get more excited about a
Husky game than a Seahawks home
game, considering how many UW grads
stay in town after graduating. Despite
the endless litany of player scandals that
included a former player robbing a drug
dealer, in 2001 these guys also made it
to the Rose Bowl. Although both football teams have been sharing the
Huskies' stadium, the Seahawks are
slated to move into their new home in
September 2002. Don't think that this
will solve the U-District's traffic congestion on game day. Husky Stadium, University of Washington 3800 Montlake Blvd.
NE (at N 45th St. NE), University District,
206/543–2200, www.gohuskies.com.

GOLF

As urban golf courses go, Seattle's got it
pretty good. City-run courses at Jackson
Park, Jefferson Park, and West Seattle
are considered among the best places to
play based on value, the quality of the
courses, and pace of play (it usually
takes less than 4.5 hours to finish a
round). The courses are open year-
round and you can reserve a tee time up
to 30 days in advance on-line at
www.seattlegolf.com.

There are, of course, dozens of other
facilities—both public and private—
throughout Greater Seattle. A fantastic
resource for any golf lover is www.seat-
tlegolfguide.com, which lists all 18- and
9-hole courses in the area, plus greens
fees and course maps.

13 e-6

BELLEVUE MUNICIPAL
GOLF COURSE

On the Eastside, Bellevue has a short
par-71 course with generous greens and
few hazards, plus a driving range. This
is one of the state's busiest courses, so
reservations are recommended, especially for weekend tee times. Call on

Monday for tee times. Greens fees are $27 Friday–Sunday and $23 Monday–Thursday; carts are $27; credit cards are accepted. *5500 140th Ave. NE (north of NE 40th St.), Bellevue, 425/452–7250.*

13 *f-8*

CROSSROADS GOLF COURSE

This course comprises nine par-3 holes with small flat greens throughout. Services are limited to a soda-vending machine and a putting green. Greens fees are $6, and tee times are first-come, first-served. *16000 NE 10th St. (at 160th Ave. NE), Bellevue, 425/452–7158*

5 *d-5*

GREEN LAKE PITCH & PUTT

This nine-hole pitch-and-putt course plays extremely short and easy. Cost is $4 for adults and $3 for juniors and senior citizens; it's open 9 AM–dusk, March–October. *5701 W. Green Lake Way N (at N. 57th St.), Green Lake, 206/632–2280.*

7 *c-2*

INTERBAY FAMILY GOLF CENTER

Interbay has a driving range ($5 per 50-ball bucket, $8 per 100, and $11 per 150), a 9-hole executive course ($13 on weekends and $11 weekdays), and a minigolf course ($6 for adults and $4.50 for kids). The range and minigolf course are open daily 7 AM–11 PM; the executive course is open dawn to dusk. *2501 15th Ave. W (at Gilman Dr. Ave.) Queen Anne, 206/285–2200.*

1 *d-1*

JACKSON PARK

There's an 18-hole course and a 9-hole executive course (weekdays, greens fees are $25 and $10, respectively, $28 and $12 on weekends, and $22 and $14 for a cart). *1000 NE 135th St. (10th Ave. NE), Hamlin Park, 206/363–4747, jacksonparkgolf.linkstime.com.*

9 *e-8*

JEFFERSON PARK

The par-27, 9-hole course has a lit driving range with heated stalls that's open from dusk until midnight. Greens fees are $12 on weekends, $10 weekdays. Carts are $14. The driving range charges $2 for a bucket of 30 balls. *4101 Beacon Ave. S (at S. Dakota St.), Beacon Hill, 206/762–4513, jeffersonparkgolf.linkstime.com.*

3 *c-8*

WEST SEATTLE GOLF COURSE

This 18-hole course has a reputation for being tough but fair. Greens fees are $25 weekdays, $28 weekends, and it's $22 for a cart. Junior and senior discounts are only honored on weekdays. *4470 35th Ave. SW (near SW Avalon Way), West Seattle, 206/935–5187, westseattlegolf.linkstime.com.*

13 *f-3*

WILLOWS RUN GOLF COURSE

Willows has it all: an 18-hole, links-style course; a 9-hole, par-27 course; and a lit, 18-hole putting course that's open until 11 PM. Thanks to an improved drainage system, Willows plays reasonably dry even in typically moist Seattle-area weather. Greens fees for 9 holes are $11 weekdays, $13 Friday through Sunday; and for 18 holes are $40 or $55. Carts are $27. Willows also has two pro shops and a driving range ($6 for 75 balls and $4 for 35). *10402 Willows Rd. NE (north of NE 95th St.), Redmond, 425/883–1200, www.willowsrun.com.*

HOCKEY

If you've got your heart set on playing ice hockey, you'll have to drive to satisfy your dreams: Seattle doesn't have a single rink within city limits.

leagues

GREATER SEATTLE HOCKEY LEAGUE

Though Seattle doesn't have in-city rinks of its own, there's no lack of hockey enthusiasts in this town. It's a recreational, organized league with both winter and summer seasons for both men and women; individual registration is $225 and gets you placed on a team with others of similar skill levels. *206/255–6739, www.gshockey.com.*

SEATTLE WOMEN'S HOCKEY CLUB

With roughly 50 members, it is open to all women in Greater Seattle who want to play ice hockey on teams that play season games and tournaments all over the Northwest (usually one game a week during the season that runs September through March). *Box 1224, Woodinville, 98072, 206/292–4970.*

TEAM SEATTLE HOCKEY

A member club of the International Gay and Lesbian Ice Hockey Association, Team Seattle Hockey is open to men and women of all skill levels. *206/910–5617.*

where to watch

10 *b-2*

SEATTLE THUNDERBIRDS

This major junior (class A) team plays in the Western League and, at the time of writing, was in the midst of a serious losing streak, placing at the bottom of their division. Top point earners were center Nate Thompson and left wing-man, Tyler Metcalfe. The best regular season finish was back in the 1989–90 season, when the Birds posted a 52-17-3 record, including a 33-2-1 mark at home. (Eight players were selected in the first round of the NHL draft in the 90s, with two of those, Peter Nedved in 1990 and Patrick Marleau in 1997, going number two overall.) Current Bench Boss is Dean Chynoweth who has replaced Don Nachbaur, the franchise's all-time coaching victory leader. You can catch a game from late September through the end of March. *KeyArena, Seattle Center, 1st Ave. N and Mercer St., Queen Anne, 425/869–7825 or 206/448–7825.*

where to play

1 *d-1*

HIGHLAND ICE ARENA

Pick-up games are held here twice a week in Shoreline on Wednesdays from 10:15 to 11:45 PM (cost is $10 per person) and on Saturdays, 6:15 PM to 7:45 PM (cost is $15). Adult and youth league teams are also organized through Highland Ice Arena. *18005 Aurora Ave. N (at N. 180th St.), Shoreline, 206/546–2431.*

1 *f-1*

KINGSGATE ICE ARENA

Adult hockey drop-in sessions change monthly. The arena also organizes a variety of youth and adult league teams. *14326 124th Ave. NE (near 144th Ave. NE), Kirkland, 425/823–1242.*

SNO-KING ICE ARENA

The area's only National Hockey League–size rink is just over the Sno-homish County line; hockey league teams, pick up games and hockey classes are all offered. *19803 68th Ave.*

W (between 196th and 200th Sts. NW), Lynnwood, 425/775–7511.

HORSERACING

1 *e-8*

EMERALD DOWNS

Take in Thoroughbred racing from April through September 15. The 166-acre track is about 15 mi south of Downtown, east of I–5. *2300 Emerald Downs Dr. (north of 15th St. NW), Auburn, 253/ 288–7000 or 888/931–8400, www. emeralddowns.com.*

HORSEBACK RIDING

You aren't going to find any horseback riding in the city, but a few outfitters take guided rides through the surrounding hills. For most of these horses, you're going to have to weigh less than 250 pounds.

where to ride

EZ TIMES OUTFITTERS

EZ Times has guided horseback-riding trips near Mount Rainier daily. *18703 Hwy. 706, Elbe, Pierce County, 360/569– 2449.*

SKYLAND RANCH

Skyland offers guided scenic tours along the Skykomish River. *43100 Reiter Rd., Gold Bar, 360/793–2611.*

TIGER MOUNTAIN OUTFITTERS

This Eastside outfitter leads three-hour, 10-mi scenic rides to a lookout point on Tiger Mountain. *24508 SE 133rd St. (at 246th Ave. SE), Issaquah, 425/392–5090.*

ICE-SKATING

There aren't a whole lot of ice-skating rinks in Seattle. To skate you'll most likely have to venture outside the city borders or head to the Seattle Center, which freezes an ice rink November and December each year for Winterfest, a month-long holiday festival of performing arts.

CASTLE ICE

It's birthday party central on not one but two rinks. It's open daily and costs about $9 for skates and admission.

12620 164th Ave. SE (at 128th Ave.), Renton, 425/254–8750.

HIGHLAND ICE ARENA
See Hockey, above.

SNO-KING ICE ARENA
Cheap Skate Night is on Wednesday, when admission is cut to $4.50, and Christian Skate Night is Friday at this multi-purpose rink. 19803 68th Ave. W (between 196th and 200th Sts. NW), Lynnwood, 425/775–7511.

IN-LINE SKATING

BURKE-GILMAN TRAIL
The nirvana of in-line skating in Seattle is a paved-over rail line that stretches 12.1 mi along Lake Washington for the pleasure of all, but especially joggers, cyclists, and skaters. There are people who live along this trail who use it as a commuter corridor. Matthews Beach Park. See Burke-Gilman Trail map.

10 b-2
GREEN LAKE PARK
And then there are those who prefer skating in circles. If you're in this camp, head for this little microcosm of mothers, babies in strollers, and 70-year-olds who will blow past you in sneakers and sweatbands. Bordered by E. Green Lake Drive N, W. Green Lake Dr. N, E. Green Lake Way N, and W. Green Lake Way N, Green Lake, www.cityofseattle.net/parks/parkspaces/greenlak.htm.

7 e-7
MYRTLE EDWARDS PARK
This park has waterfront views of the Puget Sound with a paved trail for in-line skaters. 3130 Alaskan Way W (entrance at Alaskan Way and Broad St.), Waterfront, www.cityofseattle.net/parks/parkspaces/medwards.htm.

LAWN BOWLING

9 e-8
JEFFERSON PARK LAWN BOWLING CLUB
Young and old alike can bowl daily at 1 PM—morning bowling is held Monday, Wednesday, and Friday starting at 10 AM with evening games on Mondays at 7 PM—or sign up for free lessons. 4103 Beacon Ave. S (west of the Jefferson Park

Golf Clubhouse), 206/762–2490 or 425/774–8152 for lessons.

5 b-5
WOODLAND PARK LAWN BOWLING CLUB
Bowl on a patch of grass just west of the Green Lake Amphitheater in the upper right corner of serene Woodland Park. Call for game times and lessons. Green Lake Park (enter at W. Green Lake Way N), 206/782–1515.

MARTIAL ARTS

Seattle's Martial Arts scene can sometimes be New Age-y, so you should explore the numerous martial arts studios for the combination of athletics, discipline, and philosophy that works for you.

7 f-7
ENSHIN KARATE
This Japanese dojo teaches traditional karate, as well as the pop art of Karobics. 2620 3rd Ave. (at Vine St.), Downtown, 206/443–6934.

11 g-8
SEVEN STAR WOMEN'S KUNG FU
Seven Star teaches a combination of karate, kung fu, and Chinese boxing to women and teenage girls. 525 21st Ave. (at Jefferson St.), Central District, 206/720–1046.

4 f-5
WORLD MARTIAL ARTS
This school teaches tae kwon do, the Korean art that focuses on flexibility and prizes kicking above all. 2002 NW Market St. (at 20th Ave. NW), Ballard, 206/782–7000.

MINIATURE GOLF

Rain prevents the proliferation of miniature-golf courses in Seattle, and the few ones that brave the weather are located outside the city confines.

1 d-5
FAMILY FUN CENTER
The center has the traditional 18-hole miniature-golf course with castles, windmills, and looping patches of Astroturf.

7300 Fun Center Way (at Southcenter Blvd.), Tukwila, 425/228–7300.

INTERBAY FAMILY GOLF CENTER
See Golf, above.

1 *e-5*
SKYWAY PARK BOWL & CASINO
The kitsch factor alone draws putters to this indoor course, inside a bowling alley and a casino. *11819 Renton Ave. S (west of 72nd Ave. S), Skyway, 206/772–1220.*

ROCK CLIMBING

Rock climbing is a sport Seattle likes to claim as its own. Many head for REI's flashy tourist ornament, but spots like Stone Garden and Vertical World are the favorites of local and serious enthusiasts.

CAMP LONG
See Parks, above.

8 *e-1*
CLIMBING ROCK
For a low-cost (i.e., "free") climb, you can crash this indoor facility. Although it's intended for use by UW students and staff, not to worry—enforcement of said policy is loose at best. You'll find mostly ropeless routes, and a few bolts for belaying here and there. Parking in campus lots is free Saturday afternoon and Sunday, but can be brutally difficult just about any other time. *Waterfront Activities Center, UW, south of Husky Stadium, 206/543–9433.*

8 *a-6*
REI
Every day around 200 people have a go at the Pinnacle, a 65-ft indoor climbing rock. You must schedule your climb in person. The sign-up is open Monday, Wednesday, Thursday, and Friday 10 to 7, Saturday 10 to 4, and Sunday 11 to 3. It's free for REI members; $5 for non-members, includes equipment. The wait can be anywhere from 30 minutes to four hours, but it's rare that you don't get to climb on the same day you sign up. *222 Yale Ave. N (at Thomas St.), Downtown, 206/223–1944.*

4 *c-8*
STONE GARDENS ROCK GYM
Stone Gardens has bouldering routes and top-rope faces. Although there's plenty to challenge the advanced climber, the mellow vibe is a big plus for families, part-timers, and aspiring novice-to-intermediate types. It costs $12, $10 for students. *2839 NW Market St. (at 28th Ave. NW), Ballard, 206/781–9828.*

3 *c-8*
VERTICAL WORLD
VW claims to be the first indoor climbing gym in the country. Opened in 1987, VW has 14,000 square ft of climbable surface, as well as a selection of weight-lifting equipment, and a separate bouldering section. The top-rope routes max out at 32 ft, which can seem pretty darn high when you scramble up under your own power. Tuesday and Thursday nights tend to be the busiest, though rainy weekend days also breed lines. The cost is $11 weekdays, $16 on weekends. Rental equipment is also available. *2123 W. Elmore St. (W. Commodore Way) West Seattle, 206/283–4497.*

RUGBY

SEATTLE RUGBY FOOTBALL CLUB
The club welcomes new members to its two men's sides and two women's sides. The club plays in Pacific Northwest and Canadian leagues. *10710 Lake City Way NE (NE 107th St.), Wedgewood, 206/728–4925.*

RUNNING & JOGGING

People in Seattle pretty much feel comfortable jogging anywhere in the city, although there are definitely destination running spots that on a sunny day will crowd up like a mall during a Labor Day sale.

BURKE-GILMAN TRAIL
See Matthews Beach Park in Beaches; see also Burke-Gilman Trail map, above.

5 *e-3*
GREEN LAKE PARK
Far and away Seattle's most popular jogging spot, this picturesque lake with a paved 3-mi circumference loop seems

custom-made for it. The lake has 2.7-mi and 3.1-mi trails and is populated with moms, strollers, 70-year-old marathoners, and in-line skaters. Then there are those odd groups of 10 who just decide to go out and stroll around the lake together, much to the exasperation of runners. *7201 E. Green Lake Dr. N, Green Lake, www.cityofseattle.net/parks/ parkspaces/greenlak.htm.*

8 *c-5*
VOLUNTEER PARK
See Parks, *above.*

SAILING

4 *c-1*
WIND WORKS RENTALS
First pick goes to its members, but Wind Works is ready and able to arrange rentals for nonmembers as well. Experienced sailors are allowed to skipper their own boats after a brief qualifying process. Skipper-yourself rates run from $96 on weekdays to $126 on weekend days for a 22-ft Catalina; corresponding rates are $324 to $452 for a 43-ft Hunter. Hiring a skipper and crew member from Wind Works gives you the option of half- or multiday rentals aboard the Catalina, as well as a 50% discount on the rate for either vessel. Skippering fees add $175 (half-day) or $250 (full-day), or $250 (multiday). Large groups (up to 30 people) might want to spring for the 1930s-era 61-ft racing yacht. While only Wind Works staff are allowed to skipper it, you have the option of booking weekday or weekend sunset sailings in summer. *Shilshole Bay, 7001 Seaview Ave. NW, Ballard, 206/784–9386.*

where to learn
CENTER FOR WOODEN BOATS
If you've got the desire but not the experience, then go to the where experienced hands will guide you. *1010 Valley (on the south end of Lake Union), 206/382–2628.*

SCUBA DIVING

It's not the Caribbean. But with so much water teeming with marine life, it should come as no surprise that Seattle has a lot to offer scuba divers. Both within the city and the larger area, there are all kinds of opportunities to get face-to-face with giant octopi or wander underwater through old wrecks.

lessons
If you want to learn to dive or become a certified instructor, there are plenty of Seattle scuba schools to get you into a wet suit and fins.

CRAIG GILLESPIE'S SCUBA SCHOOL GROUP
You can join a training program as a beginner or as a professional diver (with offices in California and Hawaii, too) and sign up for excursions throughout the Puget Sound area. After applicants pass a written test, they can be tested in the water at various city pools. *206/374–2937, www.seattlescuba.bizland.com.*

5 *h-1*
HARRY TRUITT'S SEATTLE LIGHTHOUSE DIVING CENTER
One of the country's oldest and most respected scuba centers has new and used scuba equipment for sale or rent, runs a variety of classes, and organizes local boat trips, excursions to the San Juan Islands, and tropical vacations. *8215 Lake City Way (at 17th Ave. N), Lake City, 425/771–2679 or 800/777–3483, www.lighthousediving.com.*

13 *e-8*
SILENT WORLD
Serving wanna-be divers and divers needing a challenge, classes are entry level through specialty courses and include diver first aid, wreck diving, and underwater photography. Open water sessions are held at Alki Point, Edmonds Underwater Park, and Keystone Jetty on Whidbey Island. *13600 NE 20th St. (between 132nd and 140th Aves. NE), Bellevue, 425/747–8842, www. silent-world.com.*

STARFISH ENTERPRISE
Serious recreational divers can take advanced courses in underwater rescue and CPR, Nitrox (which is enriched air used for additional safety), and other such specialties here. Before enrolling, you must already be certified in recreational open water diving. *600 W. Nickerson St. (at 6th Ave. W), Ballard, 206/ 286–6596, www.starfishenterprise.com.*

where to dive

EDMONDS UNDERWATER PARK

Edmonds is a labor of love for Bruce Higgins, an avid diver who, with the help of volunteers, built the extensive underwater park and marine preserve on an artificial reef. Guide ropes help divers move through the park where navigation and depth awareness are key, especially in the south end of the park, which is adjacent to active Washington State Ferries. The park was created so area divers could enjoy watching marine animals; no animals—which includes octopus, squid, flounder, and myriad other species—are allowed to be taken by hand, spear, or fishing pole. *Brackett's Landing N. (north of ferry terminal), Edmonds, 425/771–0230.*

HMCS CHAUDIERE

For a weekend trip head north on I–5 to Vancouver, BC, hop a ferry at Horseshoe Bay, and dive the wreck at Langdale. The decommissioned military ship was intentionally sunk to create a habitat for marine life. The 356-ft Destroyer Escort ship is billed as the largest man-made reef in North America. *Kunechin Bay, Sechelt Inlet, B.C., 70 mi north of Vancouver, dive.kingston.net/hmcschau.htm.*

1 *d-7*

SALTWATER STATE PARK

See South King County *in* Parks, *above.*

3 *c-7*

SEACREST PARK

With the Downtown skyline just across the bay, lights from office towers shimmer on the water's surface, making Seacrest especially known for its night diving. While below, divers can search out octopus and other marine species too numerous to list. Winter offers the best visibility; you can often see up to 25 ft. *1660 Harbor Ave. (near Fairmount Ave.), West Seattle.*

SKATEBOARDING

2 *e-5*

MERCERDALE PARK

See East King County *in* Parks, *above.*

12 *d-4*

RAIN CITY SKATE PARK

Beginners can take lessons at the on-site day camp that runs during the summer months. Both amateur and professional competitions are held here at the 12,000-square-ft park, which includes an 11½-ft vertical ramp, a mini ramp, concession stand, and a fully stocked pro shop. *1044 4th Ave. S (near Safeco Field), Downtown, 206/749–5511.*

7 *g-6*

SEATTLE CENTER SKATE PARK

This 8,900-square-ft concrete park has a 9-ft deep bowl, ledges, hand rails, and vertical walls that attract skateboarders and in-line skaters of all levels. *305 Harrison St. (at Seattle Center), Queen Anne, 206/684–7385.*

SKIING

Snow sports may be one of the few reasons to look forward to winter in Seattle. Here the rain becomes a boon for skiers and snowboarders, although a few years ago the rain was so heavy it shut down all the local resorts. Ski season usually lasts from November until April. A one-day adult lift ticket averages about $40, and most of the resorts rent and have restaurants. For Snoqualmie Pass ski reports and news about conditions in the more distant White Pass, Crystal Mountain, and Stevens Pass, call 206/634–0200 or 206/634–2754. For recorded messages about road conditions in the passes, call 800/695–7623.

ALPENTAL AT THE SUMMIT

Although it's part of The Summit at Snoqualmie complex, most advance skiers come directly here for the most concentrated vertical around—a lot of the runs are long and steep. (Giant Slalom gold medalist Debbie Armstrong trained here for the 1984 Olympics.) A one-day lift ticket will run you $38; equipment another $27. The resort is 50 mi from Seattle, but it's right off the highway so you avoid icy mountain roads. *Exit 52 off I–90, Snoqualmie Pass, 425/434–7669.*

CRYSTAL MOUNTAIN

Serious skiers will probably want to make the 2½-hour drive here, about 75 mi from Seattle. The slopes are challenging, the snow conditions good, and the mountain top has amazing views of nearby Mount Rainier. (There are only one or two hotels around here, so book ahead.) An adult one-day lift ticket costs about $45, and a full rental package costs $25. *33914 Crystal Mountain Blvd., Crystal Mountain, 360/663–2265, www.crystalmt.com.*

THE SUMMIT AT SNOQUALMIE
Chances are good that a local skier took his or her first run at Snoqualmie, the resort closest to the city. With three ski areas—Summit West, Summit Central, and Summit East—gentle slopes, rope tows, moseying chairlifts, a snowboard park, and dozens of educational programs, it's the obvious choice for an introduction to the slopes. *Exit 52 off I–90, Snoqualmie Pass, 425/434–7669 or 206/236–7277 Ext. 3372 for nordic center.*

WHISTLER
Whistler, 200 mi north of Seattle, is a best done as a three-day weekend trip. And you really can't call yourself a skier here and not go to Whistler at least once. Many consider it the best ski resort in North America. The massive resort is renowned for its nightlife, which is just at the foot of the slopes. You abandon your car outside the village upon arrival and negotiate the entire hotel/dining/ski area on foot. A one-day adult lift ticket costs about $60 (Canadian), and rental packages are about $40 (Canadian). Make sure you have chains or snow tires. *Hwy 99, Whistler, B.C., Canada, 800/766–0449.*

nordic/cross-country
Cross-country skiers will find a wide range of trails that vary in length and difficulty within a half-hour to two-hour drive from Seattle. Local nordic opportunities include undisturbed backcountry trails to groomed tracks at developed ski areas and resorts. Always call ahead for road conditions, which may prevent trail access.

To ski Washington state park trails you'll need to purchase a Sno-Park Pass, available at most sports stores (REI at Yale and John Streets.), ski shops, and Forest Service Ranger District Offices. For information on trails and trail conditions, contact the **State Parks information center** (800/233–0321, www.parks.wa.gov/winter).

HURRICANE RIDGE
The trails here have the best views of Mount Olympus and begin at the lodge.

The drive is 140 mi. *Olympic National Park, 17 mi south of Port Angeles, 360/452–0330 or 360/565–3131 for for road reports.*

MOUNT BAKER SKI AREA
Eight trails, passing through avalanche-prone areas, are accessible via Concrete or Glacier. You'll need a Forest Pass. *206/634–0200 or 360/856–5700.*

THE SUMMIT
See Alpine/Downhill, above.

SOCCER

leagues

2 *C-2*

GREATER SEATTLE SOCCER LEAGUE
The country's leading nonprofit adult soccer association, with spring, summer, fall, and winter seasons, gives you plenty of chances to get your kicks. The league has 20 skill divisions in four age groups in most neighborhoods around the city. *9750 Greenwood Ave. N (south of 100th St.), Greenwood, 206/782–6831.*

where to watch

10 *C-2*

SEATTLE SOUNDERS
The men's professional, A-League team, play a 13-game season from May through September, and are affiliated with the pro Colorado Rapids team. Tickets are $12, or $15 for reserved seating. *Memorial Stadium, Seattle Center, 5th Ave. N and Harrison St., Queen Anne, 800/796–5425, www.seattlesounders.net.*

1 *g-5*

SEATTLE SOUNDERS SELECT
The Select are in the United Soccer League's W-1 Women's league and play home games in Issaquah. Tickets are $8. *Issaquah High School, 700 2nd Ave. SE (south of SE Evans St.), Issaquah, 800/796–5425, www.seattlesounders.net.*

where to play
To reserve a soccer field, call the **Parks department** (206/684–4075).

SOFTBALL

where to watch

8 *e-1*

HUSKY SOFTBALL STADIUM

If you're a fan of women's softball, the University of Washington Husky team starts up in February and goes through the summer. *Softball field, UW (behind Husky Stadium, off Montlake Blvd. NE), University District, 206/543–2200, www.gohuskies.com.*

where to play

To reserve one of the many softball field in the city, call the **Parks department** (206/684–4075).

SQUASH

A number of fitness clubs have squash courts—we list some below— although they all have different policies regarding membership and guest privileges. Call for membership information or court rentals.

leagues, clubs & lessons

SEATTLE SQUASH RACQUETS ASSOCIATION

The nonprofit organization hosts tournaments, assembles city leagues, offers instructional clinics, and participates in local and national rankings of players; the organization doesn't have a phone, so the best way to contact organizers is through the Web. *www.ssra.c-labs.com.*

where to play

12 *d-1*

GATEWAY ATHLETIC CLUB

See Fitness Centers & Health Clubs, *below.*

10 *e-6*

SEATTLE ATHLETIC CLUB

See Fitness Centers & Health Clubs, *below.*

SOUND MIND & BODY

See Fitness Centers & Health Clubs, *below.*

10 *h-7*

WASHINGTON ATHLETIC CLUB

See Fitness Centers & Health Clubs, *below.*

9 *b-2*

YMCA

See Fitness Centers & Health Clubs, *below.*

SWIMMING

Seattle Parks and Recreation maintains eight indoor pools (Queen Anne, Ballard, Evans, Rainier Beach, Southwest, Medgar Evers, Helene Madison, and Meadowbrook) year-round and two outdoor pools (Colman and Mounger) Most cost $1.75–$4.

MOUNGER POOL

It's one of the summer-only outdoor facilities, which has a large children's area. *2535 32nd Ave. W (at W. Smith St.), Magnolia, 206/684–4708.*

QUEEN ANNE POOL

This indoor pool is only about a 10-minute drive from Downtown and has the added bonus of a sauna. *1920 1st Ave. W (at Howe St.), Queen Anne, 206/386–4282.*

PLAYGROUNDS

For swinging, sliding, and climbing, Seattle area kids and parents give the thumbs-up to these playgrounds. All are listed in Parks above, except where noted.

City of Seattle
  Carkeek Park

  Gas Works Park

  Green Lake Park

  Lincoln Park

  Matthews Beach Park (see Beaches, above)

  Sand Point Magnuson Park

East King County
  Bellevue Downtown Park

  Gene Coulon Memorial Beach Park

  Lake Sammamish State Park

  Luther Burbank Park

  Newcastle Beach Park (see Beaches, above)

  Peter Kirk Park

  Wilburton Hill Park

TENNIS

There are 151 public tennis courts in Seattle's parks; we just name a few. Note only three are lighted: Lower Woodlank, Miller Park (Capitol Hill), and Lincoln Park (West Seattle). Check your phone book for more. To schedule an outdoor court, call the Citywide Athletics Office, 206/684–4077.

resources

PUGET SOUND TENNIS TOUR

Tennis lovers throughout the region have gotten together to organize this tour that runs May through August. You can sign up for either singles or doubles matches and get linked with others at their skill level from Everett to Kent. The tour has advanced, intermediate, and beginner levels and tracks each player's games played on public and private courts. 425/424–2858, www.tennistour.org.

where to play

9 f-5

SEATTLE TENNIS CENTER

All ages are welcome to the facility, which has 10 indoor tennis courts, 4 outdoor courts, and a wide array of programs and lessons. You pay $15 (for 1¼hours) to reserve a court for singles play and $20 for doubles; it costs $6 (for 1½ hours) to reserve an outdoor court for both singles and doubles. November through May, the center is open weekdays from 6 AM to 10:30 PM and on weekends from 6:45 AM to 10:30 PM; June through September, hours are from 6 AM to 9:30 PM weekdays and from 7 AM to 7:30 PM on weekends.2000 Martin Luther King Jr. Way S (at Plum St.), Beacon Hill, 206/684–4764.

VOLLEYBALL

Call the **Parks Department** (206/684–4075) to find out about the parks with volleyball courts. The choicest spots are at Green Lake and Golden Gardens, which has beach volleyball on the shores of Shilshole Bay.

YOGA

Plenty of yoga studios city-wide let you choose from whether you're a Hatha, Ashtanga, or Kundalini devotee.

8 b-8

8 LIMBS YOGA CENTER

It welcomes drop-ins and manages to challenge the intermediate student without alienating the novice. Hatha, Ashtanga, Satsang, and Viniyoga are offered, plus prenatal and baby classes. 500 E. Pike St. (at Summit Ave.), Capitol Hill, 206/325–1511.

8 c-8

SAMADHI YOGA

It combines yoga with an aerobic workout surrounded by statues of Hindu deities. Classes have an Ashtanga focus. 1205 E. Pike St. (at 12th Ave.) Capitol Hill, 206/329–4070.

fitness centers & health clubs

PRIVATE HEALTH CLUBS

Although Seattleites would like you to believe that the gym is only an acceptable place of exercise when it rains, truth be told, there are plenty of gym rats in this city.

7 e-6

ALL STAR FITNESS

It's usually packed with 20- to 30-year-old urban professionals—maybe because it's one of the few gyms that has an indoor pool, plenty of Cybex weight machines, and a packed schedule of fitness classes, including yoga, kickboxing, and step. 330 2nd Ave. W (at Harrison Ave.), Queen Anne, 206/282–5901.

4 f-5

BALLARD HEALTH CLUB

An anomaly among clubs—Ballard is incredibly low-key and reasonably priced, with everything you need and nothing more: weights, cardio machines, a wide variety of classes including three kinds of yoga, a stretching room, and day care in the basement of an old Ballard building. 2208 NW Market St. (at 22nd Ave. NW), Ballard, 206/706–4882.

12 *d-1*

GATEWAY ATHLETIC CLUB

Designed to impress with its striking views, this tidy facility has attentive service. Besides the usual lineup of free weights, weight machines, and cardio equipment, you'll find an impressive offering of classes (including power cycling, ski conditioning, and water fitness), as well as a squash court and a swimming pool. *700 5th Ave., 14th fl. (at Cherry St.), Downtown, 206/343–4692.*

10 *e-6*

SEATTLE ATHLETIC CLUB

Beyond its deceptively modest entrance is more than 60,000 square ft of free weights, Cybex circuit machines, treadmills, Stairmasters, rowing machines, recumbent cycling machines, an indoor track, a full-size basketball court, racquetball and squash courts, and a swimming pool. The club also has a full slate of classes, from power cycling, step, and cardio to toning, tai chi, and yoga. *2020 Western Ave. (at Virginia Ave.), Downtown, 206/443–1111, www.sacdt.com.*

SOUND MIND & BODY

Free weights, Cybex machines, plus two floors of cardio equipment help you get buff. Yoga, Pilates, and kickboxing integrate the mind and the body. Locations in Madison Park and Eastlake. *437 N. 34th St. (at Phinney Ave. N), Fremont, 206/547–2086, www.smbgym.com.*

12 *c-1*

VAULT FITNESS CLUB

The aptly named gym is in a former bank and combines an extensive collection of equipment and classes (yoga, step, Pilates, and spinning) with some unusual recycled architectural features. The spa pool has an 8-ft waterfall emerging, it seems, from the corner of the ceiling. The main floor has free weights, treadmills, and Cybex, Hammer Strength, and rowing machines. A large aerobic studio, as well as rows and rows of various cardio machines facing a phalanx of television monitors, are on the loftlike second floor. Downstairs are saunas, steam rooms, and locker rooms. *808 2nd Ave. (at Columbia St.), Downtown, 206/224–9000, www.vaultfitness.com.*

10 *h-7*

WASHINGTON ATHLETIC CLUB

It may no longer be a men's club, but it's still where a lot of hobnobbing goes on. Five floors cover a varied fitness regime of everything from physical therapy to martial arts, plus weight training and fitness classes. *1325 6th Ave. (at Union St.), Downtown, 206/622–7900, www.wac.net.*

YMCAS

9 *b-2*

YMCA

The recently remodeled facility has sqaush courts, an indoor pool, free weights, and cardio machines, plus an indoor track. Classes range from tai chi and yoga to dance and cardio kick. *909 4th Ave. (at Madison St.), Downtown, 206/382–5010, www.seattleymca.org.*

chapter 4

PLACES
TO EXPLORE

galleries, gargoyles, museums, and more

The Emerald City, Jet City, Queen City—none of Seattle's nicknames truly captures its magic. This is a town of hidden treasures, with artwork embedded in its sidewalks, mythical creatures lurking under its bridges, and plenty of parks and gardens interrupting its concrete. Although some of Seattle's oldest landmarks have disappeared, many, still gritty with tradi-tion, have been fiercely protected by concerned community groups. Some have not only been preserved but also moved to new locations, resulting in bits of urban history in unlikely places. And many an old structure has been replaced by some wonderful new piece of eye candy that reflects contemporary Seattle and its citizens. Pick a neighborhood, slip into a comfortable pair of shoes, and

WHERE TO GO

Many of the organizations and parks listed here tell their stories on the Web. Here are some URLs to explore when you don't feel like leaving the house on a rainy day.

www.cityofseattle.net
Information straight from the city's leaders.

www.historylink.org
Find out about Seattle's past and present.

www.renttech.com
Find an apartment online.

www.seattlepi.com
The Seattle Post-Intelligencer is one of two daily newspapers in town. Its Web site is full of breaking local and national news.

www.seattletimes.com
The Seattle Times daily newspaper is one of the country's largest independently owned. Its Web site has frequently updated local news and entertainment information.

www.thestranger.com
Run by the irreverent weekly newspaper, The Stranger, this is a good place to find fun things to do—especially at night.

transit.metrokc.gov
Forget driving. Take the bus. Here's how.

www.wsdot.wa.gov/traveler.html
Here's the information you'll need to deal with Seattle's horrific traffic problems.

www.inballard.com
Information on all things Ballard.

www.seeseattle.org
Homepage for the Seattle–King County Convention and Visitors Bureau.

www.seattleweekly.com
The Weekly is the more staid of Seattle's two weekly newspapers, with strong focuses on local political coverage and entertainment.

www.speakeasy.net/~traceyb/thrift
Site for Seattle Slacker, a sensibly quirky repository for Seattle survival tips. Some of the information is outdated, but most has timeless appeal.

www.kexp.org
Web site for Paul Allen's experimental radio and Internet project KEXP-FM 90.3; also has the most comprehensive local concert listings.

students.washington.edu/ahvakana/pubart/home.html
An ever-growing chronicle of public art information.

www.ci.seattle.wa.us/arts/workshop/cultural.pdf
A good plan for an exploration of downtown art, sponsored by the City of Seattle Web site.

take a stroll any day of the week, rain or shine. And don't forget to grab a latte for the journey.

neighborhoods

3 *b-2*
BALLARD
What began in 1889 as its own town—built around the ship-building industry and populated by Scandinavian immigrants—became a part of Seattle proper in 1907. Since 1917 vessels have traveled from the fresh waters of Washington and Union lakes to Puget Sound's briny Shilshole Bay via the Ballard Locks. Ballard retains a small-town feel and strong ties to commercial fishing and boat building. Streets are lined with tidy working-class homes as well as stores that offer Scandinavian goods. At the same time, the neighborhood is popular with laid-back twentysomethings drawn to a small but thriving town center that offers an array of cafés, boutiques, and live-music as bars. *Bordered by Shilshole Bay, Lake Washington Ship Canal, 3rd Ave. NW, and NW 85th St.*

1 *d-6*
BELLEVUE
For decades Bellevue has been trying to become more than a bedroom community centered around a mall. So far, it has merely succeeded in becoming a bedroom community centered around a mall *and* a convention center. Nonetheless, this pleasant upscale community has interesting shops and rèstaurants, an art museum, and a charming old town with many early 20th-century buildings. *East of Seattle, bordered by Lake Washington, Lake Sammamish, SE 68th St., and NE 70th St.*

10 *d-5*
BELLTOWN
This area just north of Downtown isn't especially large, but it is especially popular with the food-lovin', club-hoppin' crowd. Its few blocks are crammed with swanky and/or funky eateries offering all types of dishes. Clubs such as the Crocodile Cafe and the Sit & Spin are stops for top-notch bands, and bars range from posh watering holes to low-end dives. Still, there's nothing divey about

Belltown: new condos are in big supply but only for those with big incomes. *Bordered by Elliott Bay, Denny Way, 6th Ave., and Virginia St.*

3 *f-5*
CAPITOL HILL
Capitol Hill demonstrates Seattle's diversity better than any other neighborhood. Here, the city's youth culture, old money traditions, and gay and lesbian scene converge amid theaters and churches, coffeehouses and nightclubs, and stately homes and student apartments. It also offers mind-blowing city and mountain views and some truly dynamic people-watching. Stroll down Broadway Avenue East between East Denny Way and East Roy Street or along Pike and Pine between Boren Avenue and Broadway and you'll find an eclectic collection of restaurants, bars, knick-knack shops, and vintage-clothing stores. You'll share the sidewalk with drag queens, punkers, club kids, college kids, and senior citizens. You'll see Capitol Hill's demure side in some residential areas, where tree-lined streets are home to mansions from an entirely different era. *Bordered by I–5, Pine St., 23rd Ave. E, and Lake Washington Ship Canal.*

9 *e-1*
CENTRAL DISTRICT
East of Downtown and adjacent to Capitol Hill and First Hill is the Central District, the cultural and residential hub for Seattle's African-American community. Here, mom and pop restaurants serve up soul food while Mount Zion Baptist Church and the First African Methodist Episcopalian Church serve up food for the soul. Over the years, the Central District has been through many ups and downs. In the 1940s, this was the part of town that nurtured a dynamic jazz scene, but the area also has suffered from neglect and economic blight. This neighborhood's high school (Garfield High) produced legends such as Jimi Hendrix and Quincy Jones, but gang activity also has plagued the streets. Today, the Central District is a neighborhood in transition. The economy is undergoing a renaissance as many business snap up property and wealthy white people buy up homes on the cheap. The changes have been both a boon and bane to long-time residents. *Bordered by I–90, Martin Luther King Jr. Way, E. Madison St. and 12th Ave.*

3 *d-6*

DOWNTOWN/WATERFRONT

Elliot Bay's brilliant waters push up against a striking skyline to form the heart of Downtown Seattle. Stretching along the Waterfront is historic Pike Place Market, where farmers and fishermen sell a cornucopia of goods. The Seattle Aquarium offers awe-inspiring displays of local marine life, and there's shopping galore in the three-story Westlake Center mall. Residential space is limited, although this neighborhood does have some apartments and upscale condominiums. For the most part, however, Seattleites live in the surrounding neighborhoods of Capitol Hill, Belltown and the International District. *Bordered by Elliott Bay, I–5, Columbia St., and Virginia St.*

3 *e-4*

EASTLAKE

This neighborhood on Lake Union's east shore is best known for its houseboat colony. These lovely buoyant abodes began bobbing up here in the 1940s and 1950s, built by a feisty group of writers, professors, and bohemian-spirited water lovers. The rest of the neighborhood is an assortment of single-family homes, apartments, condos, boatyards, restaurants, and small shops. *Bordered by Lake Union, I–5, Mercer St., and Ship Canal Bridge.*

3 *d-3*

FREMONT/WALLINGFORD

Fremont's residents—many of them artists—do little to change or challenge its funky, artsy, eclectic image. The Artists' Republic of Fremont, as many call it, brims with liberal attitude and free-thinking bravado. Its motto, *"De Libertas Quirkas"* ("The Freedom to Be Peculiar") is emblazoned on a 53-ft-high Russian rocket that towers over the business center. A few blocks away, under the Aurora Bridge, a giant concrete troll clutches a Volkswagen Beetle. Every June, Fremont hosts a wild Solstice Parade that's often crashed by nude bicyclists. But Fremont has had a personality crisis ever since software giant Adobe moved its offices here and pricey condos began to rise. Only time will tell whether hipness or yuppiness wins out. Both Fremont and the adjoining neighborhood of Wallingford (to the northeast) are known for their "community feel" and have an array of fun and unique shops, cafés,

bars, and restaurants. *Bordered by N. 50th St., Lake Washington Ship Canal, I–5, and 8th Ave. NW.*

5 *d-3*

GREEN LAKE

Seattle's recreational mecca is wrapped around a beautiful park that's wrapped around a lovely lake. The 342-acre Green Lake Park includes facilities for basketball, tennis, baseball, and soccer. A 3-mi jogging and bicycling trail rings the lake. The park is generally packed (about 1 million people visit each year), especially on weekday evenings, when many Seattleites here to be active *as well as* to see and be seen. Beyond the park are peaceful middle- and upper-class homes. The commercial district, on the lake's east side, is a good place to grab a fresh carrot juice before heading out to hunt for a new bicycle or gear for the great outdoors. Although many of the homes in Green Lake are heading towards the upscale end of things, the neighboring 'hoods of Greenwood and Phinney Ridge (to the west) remain a good place to buy a reasonably priced home or rent an affordable apartment. *Bordered by N. 60th St., N. 85th St., I–5, and Aurora Ave. N.*

12 *e-3*

INTERNATIONAL DISTRICT

The 40-block International District (I.D.) is a testament to Asia's influence on this port city. Chinese immigrants first came here during the mid-1800s to work in the lumber mills and on the railroads. The community has remained largely intact despite anti-Chinese riots and the forced eviction of Chinese residents during the 1880s. Today about one-third of the I.D.'s residents are Chinese, one-third are Filipino, and another third come from elsewhere in Asia or the Pacific islands. The district has many Chinese, Japanese, and Korean restaurants as well as herbalists; acupuncturists; antiques shops; and private clubs for gambling, karaoke, and socializing. *Bordered by Main St., S. Dearborn St., 4th Ave., and 8th Ave.*

13 *c-3*

KIRKLAND

Kirkland is a pleasant lakefront community on the eastern shore of 20-mi-long Lake Washington. Along with a very pedestrian-friendly downtown, Kirkland has shops, galleries, and waterside restaurants. *East of Seattle, bordered by Lake Washington, Redmond, Hwy. 520, and NE 124th St.*

3 *d-4*
LAKE UNION

Lake Union lies in the heart of Seattle, between Queen Anne to the west, and Capitol Hill to the east. It's also bordered by residential Wallingford to the north, and by the commercial and industrial flats of the Denny Regrade to the south. The natural freshwater lake was once a center of maritime industry but underwent an urban renaissance during the 1980s and 1990s, when condominiums, parks, and restaurants began to replace shipyards, gasworks, and mills. The lake's eastern and western shores are lined with houseboats, but a pretty paved footpath runs along the lake's southern waterfront past yacht docks and restaurants with waterfront decks.

3 *d-4*
MAGNOLIA

With its neat houses and manicured lawns this neighborhood has been a bastion of white middle- and upper-class living throughout Seattle's history. Although the area has become more diversified, it still retains this reputation. Magnolia Boulevard winds up a bluff that overlooks Puget Sound. Discovery Park (Seattle's biggest) and the Ft. Lawton Landmark District sit at the northwest end of this neighborhood. *Bordered by Puget Sound, Lake Washington Ship Canal, 15th Ave. W, and Magnolia Blvd.*

2 *e-6*
MERCER ISLAND

Microsoft cofounder and all-around rich guy Paul Allen keeps a house on this island to the east of Seattle—which paints a pretty accurate picture of just how upscale this neighborhood is. Elite country clubs and palatial estates as well as numerous parks and protected wetlands are the norm. The median price for a home is $575,000. Lots of old money lines these tidy streets, which are not, as one might expect, paved in gold. *In Lake Washington to the south, between Seattle and the Eastside.*

12 *c-2*
PIONEER SQUARE

Seattle's oldest neighborhood is a hub of activity, with a multitude of restaurants, shops, and Web development companies, as well as the city's largest concentration of art galleries. Streets lined with massive redbrick and sandstone buildings provide a glimpse of how Seattle appeared when it was rebuilt after the Great Fire of 1889. At the corner of Yesler Way and 2nd Avenue stands the 42-story Smith Tower, the tallest building west of the Mississippi when it was completed in 1914. Yesler Way was once called Skid Road, a term born when timber was slid down the street to a steam-powered mill on the Waterfront. At night this historic district drapes itself with party attire owing to its many rock clubs, sports bars, and taverns. *Bordered by Alaskan Way S, Columbia St., 4th Ave. S, and S. King St.*

7 *e-4*
QUEEN ANNE

This rolling neighborhood is split into two parts, each with its own personality. Upper Queen Anne, atop Queen Anne Hill, has upscale houses, a cluster of fashionable restaurants and shops, and spectacular views. Property prices have ballooned here almost as much as the size and luxuriousness of the many new homes. Although Lower Queen Anne, at the foot of the hill, has seen some gentrification, it remains more of a working-class neighborhood—one where it's still possible to find an affordable apartment. This part of town is also the setting for some of Seattle's most famous attractions, including the Space Needle, the Experience Music Project, and the Pacific Science Center. *Bordered by Lake Union, Denny Way, 15th Ave. W, and Aurora Ave. N.*

6 *b-4*
RAVENNA

This unpretentious neighborhood just north of the University District was named after a seaside district in northeast Italy. There's nothing flashy or quirky about these quiet, tree-lined streets, home to many middle-class single-family homes. And that's just fine by those who live here. They're proud of this residential neighborhood's "down-to-earth" feel with its family restaurants and homey shops. *Bordered by NE 75th St., I–5, 43rd Ave. NE, and Ravenna Blvd./NE 55th St.*

13 *g-4*
REDMOND
Home to software giant Microsoft, Redmond is one of the Puget Sound area's most affluent cities. In fact, so many wealthy people live in the neighborhoods and cities to the east of Seattle (Kirkland, Bellevue, Mercer Island, and Redmond), that region is now known as the Gold Coast. As if there weren't enough titles being bandied about, Redmond is also known as the "Bicycle Capital of the Northwest" because of its first-rate bicycle race track at Marymoor Park. *East of Seattle, bordered by NE 116th St., and the town of Kirkland, NE 24th St., and Avondale Rd.*

3 *f-3*
UNIVERSITY DISTRICT
The U-District surrounds the University of Washington (UW) and buzzes with a youthful vibe. Most of the neighborhood's residents are renters, moving in and moving out according to the school year's calendar. A stroll through the UW campus can include stops at its museums and Central Plaza, the nerve center for student activism. It's also known as Red Square not so much for the students' political leanings as for the red-brick paving. To get a whiff of the slightly anarchic energy that fuels this part of town, head off campus to what is affectionately known as The Ave., a shopping area along University Way Northeast (especially between 42nd and 50th streets). This is the hub of the U–District's social life, with great coffeehouses, cinemas, clothing stores, and cheap restaurants—as well as panhandlers and pockets of grime. *Bordered by Ravenna Blvd., Montlake Cut Waterway (connecting lakes Union and Washington), 25th Ave. NE, and I–5.*

2 *b-6*
WEST SEATTLE
South of the city and on a peninsula just across Elliott Bay lies West Seattle. It was here, in 1851, that a group of settlers known as the Denny Party first staked their claim to the land that would become Seattle. Today this neighborhood is a mix of rich and poor, upscale and downtrodden. As prices have skyrocketed in Seattle proper, many people have fled to West Seattle in search of affordable housing. On a drive through it you'll pass miles of beautiful beaches, cute shops and restaurants, cozy single-family homes, and crime-plagued low-income housing. Its center, called the Junction, is home to a shopping area as well as 10 of the neighborhood's 11 murals. Gorgeous Alki Beach sweeps around the area's perimeter, offering spectacular views of Puget Sound and the Seattle skyline as well as a good place to run, blade, and bike. *Bordered by Puget Sound, Alki Ave., SW Roxbury St., and W. Marginal Way.*

where to go

AQUARIUMS

It's no surprise Seattle and neighboring Tacoma are home to two of the Pacific Northwest's most amazing aquariums—water is everywhere. Aside from allowing visitors to get close to a stunning variety of marine life, these attractions also seek to foster awareness and respect for area residents' close, delicate relationship to their neighbors beneath the water's surface.

3 *f-8*
POINT DEFIANCE ZOO & AQUARIUM
Twenty-nine acres in Tacoma have been transformed into a wonderland of animals from around the Pacific Rim. Creatures native to Puget Sound swim in the North Pacific Aquarium complex's 140,000-gallon tank, the aquarium's centerpiece. Here, you can observe Puget Sound marine life, or watch fifty sharks swim in separate tanks as part of the "Sharks–The Survivors" exhibit, which also includes videos and graphics that burst myths and elaborate on conservation efforts. In the Discovery Reef Aquarium located in Point Defiance's South Aquarium building, you can watch and learn about a variety of colorful tropical fish. Although the Beluga whales are gregarious and charming, the Magellanic penguins that bray and waddle around Penguin Point steal the show. *5400 N. Pearl St. (at dead-end of Pearl St. off Hwy. 16), Tacoma, 253/591-5337, www.pdza.org. $7.25 adults, $6.75 senior citizens, $5.50 children 4–13, free children under 3. Memorial Day–Labor Day, daily 10–7; winter hours vary.*

10 *e-8*

SEATTLE AQUARIUM

Puget Sound is home to the world's largest octopuses, tipping the scales at 100 pounds with a 10-ft tentacle-to-tentacle spread. You can get up close and personal with the aquarium's resident cephalopod, but other exhibits in the ecologically aware aquarium equally exhilarate. Seals and sea otters gracefully swim in the pools and make doe eyes at you. A glassed-in tunnel affords views of glinting fish above and to each side. The Discovery Lab lets you see tiny marine life through high-power video microscopes, and the Tide Pool gives you a glimpse of creatures that dwell in the crevices of Washington's craggy coast. The educational and sobering "State of the Puget Sound" exhibit explores that body of water's ecology and the effect humans are having on it. *Pier 59 (on Alaskan Way), Waterfront, 206/386–4320, www.seattleaquarium.org. $7 adults, $6.25 senior citizens, $5.25 children 6–18, $3.25 children 3–5. Memorial Day–Labor Day, daily 10–7; Labor Day–Memorial Day, daily 10–5.*

ARCHITECTURE

Whether it's the Technicolor swoops of the Experience Music Project or the sky-piercing girders of the Space Needle, Seattle's architectural achievements make a statement. Although the city went through some serious architectural blahs in the 1960s and 1970s, the last decade has been a dazzling one, indeed. It's now home to buildings created by architects who have won Pritzker Prizes (the field's top honor) and who have lent real class to the skyline: Frank Gehry, Robert Venturi, and Rem Koolhaas.

9 *b-2*

BANK OF AMERICA TOWER (COLUMBIA TOWER)

(Martin Selig, 1985) The original design for the tallest building west of the Mississippi called for it to rise even higher than its 997.36 ft, but this plan was scrapped when it became clear that the structure would have obstructed the flight path to Seattle-Tacoma International Airport. Height isn't the only thing that makes it imposing: as it's sheathed in black glass, locals often refer to it as the Darth Vader Building. Its 76 stories contain 1.5-million square ft of office space. The Columbia Tower Club (on floors 75 and 76) is a popular space for private parties and functions and (of course) has a magnificent view of the city and its surroundings. There's also an observation deck on the 73rd floor. *701 5th Ave. (at Cherry St.), Downtown, 206/386–5151, www.columbia-tower.com. Observation deck: $5 adults, $3 senior citizens and children 12 and under. Observation deck: Weekdays 8:30–4:30.*

10 *g-7*

BENAROYA HALL

(Mark Reddington/LMN Architects, 1998) Taking up a full Downtown block, the home of the Seattle Symphony has an exterior—steel, limestone, sweeping panes of glass—that's as dramatic and elegant as the music that often fills its interior. The cylindrical four-story lobby is enclosed in majestic curving glass. Beyond are a 2,500-seat auditorium and a more intimate 541-seat recital hall. *200 University St. (entrance at 3rd Ave. and Union St.), Downtown, 206/215–4747, www.seattlesymphony.org. Free. Weekdays 10–6, Sat. 1–6; tours weekdays at noon and 1 PM.*

9 *b-1*

CENTRAL LIBRARY

(Rem Koolhaas, 2003) Many believe that, when it opens in 2003 on the site of the city's old library, the new 15-story Central Library will become Seattle's architectural star. World-famous Dutch architect Rem Koolhaas is behind its design, which calls for five platforms that zigzag upward and a facade that's encased in a meshlike metal skin. Intersecting beams, pipes, and trusses will ensure that the building can withstand earthquakes. Such daring doesn't come cheap: the budget is $159 million. *1000 4th Ave. (at Madison St.), Downtown.*

11 *c-7*

CHAPEL OF ST. IGNATIUS

(Steven Holl, 1997) "A Gathering of Different Lights" was the theme behind the design and construction of this stunning, 6,000-square-ft, Catholic chapel on the Seattle University campus. Outside, the building is fronted by a grassy "thinking field" and a large reflecting pool. The exterior has a modern angularity to it that seems a bit jarring. But inside, the deft use of color panels and natural and artificial light give the chapel a serene, spiritual grace. *900 Broadway (at E. Marion St.), First Hill*

206/296–6000, www.seattleu.edu/chapel.
Mon.–Thurs. 7 AM–10 PM, Fri. 7–7, Sat.
9–5, Sun. 9 AM–10 PM.

10 d-2

EXPERIENCE MUSIC PROJECT (EMP)

(Frank O. Gehry, 2000) Funded by Microsoft cofounder Paul Allen, Seattle's most controversial structure is a 140,000-square-ft interactive museum celebrating American popular music. Some love its bulbous exterior, and some simply hate it. But nearly everyone is sure not to miss it. Architect Frank Gehry drew inspiration from electric guitars to achieve its swooping design—and then he went wild. Made of glass, steel, and painted aluminum, the EMP is all over the color map. Red, silver, gold, baby blue, and purple adorn its surfaces. Interior spaces go from open and roomy to closed and cramped. They're also hard-wired for the latest and greatest technological wizardry. *5th Ave. (between Broad and Thomas Sts.), Queen Anne, 206/770–2700, www.emplive. com. $19.95 adults; $15.95 students, military, and senior citizens; $14.95 children 7– 12. Memorial Day–Labor Day, daily 9 AM– 11 PM; Sept.–May, Sun.–Thurs. 10–6, Fri.– Sat. 10 AM–11 PM.*

5 h-8

HENRY ART MUSEUM

(Carl Gould, 1927; addition by Charles Gwathmey, 1997) The original Gothic-style building containing UW's art museum was a small but respectable one made of redbrick and adorned with a wrought-iron entry. Seventy years later it underwent a renovation that quadrupled its size and was greeted with both cheers and jeers. According to one Seattle critic, "The old Henry was retained, but it wasn't respected." Still, the addition—done in glass, textured stainless steel, and cast stone—allowed for the creation of an auditorium, a multimedia gallery, a café, a bookstore, and a sculpture court among other things. The building has been praised for its open, airy gallery spaces. *Corner of 15th Ave. NE and NE 41st St., University District, 206/543–2280. www.henryart.org. $5 adults, $3.50 senior citizens, free high school and college students (with ID) and children 13 and under, free Thurs. 5 PM–8 PM. Tues.–Wed. 11–5, Thurs. 11–8, Fri.– Sun. 11–5.*

8 c-5

ST. MARK'S EPISCOPAL CATHEDRAL

(Dedicated in 1931; renovations by Olson Sundberg Architects, 1997) Thanks to its square exterior of stone, brick, and wood, this Episcopalian church is nicknamed the Holy Box. Inside, though, sunlight streams through the west wall's giant rose window (it's 21 ft in diameter) and floods vast open spaces. The building was supposed to be far more elaborate, but construction began in 1928, and the Great Depression made it impossible to raise funds for anything more than a modest structure. There was, however, money enough for significant renovations that began in 1997. *1245 10th Ave. E (at E. Galer St.), Capitol Hill, 206/323–0300, www.saintmarks.org.*

10 g-8

SEATTLE ART MUSEUM (SAM)

(Robert Venturi, 1991) SAM's entire collection was once housed in the beautiful, 1933, Carl Gould–designed building in Volunteer Park. When space became an issue, museum officials decided to build a new structure for most of the works and leave the Asian pieces in the original building, which has been renamed the Seattle Asian Art Museum. Venturi made the new, five-story, city-block-size museum a work of art in itself. He's renowned for his postmodern designs that incorporate historical references and images from contemporary pop culture. Here, large-scale vertical fluting adorns the limestone exterior, which is also accented by terra-cotta, cut granite, and marble. Inside a staircase with Chinese sculptures and bright-colored arches grandly ascends into the open space. The museum cost $64 million and was greeted upon opening by enthused patrons as well as fuming nay-sayers who didn't like the cost or the interior's somewhat quirky design. *100 University St. (at 1st Ave.), Downtown, 206/654–3255, www. seattleartmuseum.org. Suggested donation: $7 adults, $5 students and senior citizens, free children under 13, free 1st Thurs. of month. Tues.–Wed. 10–5, Thurs. 10–9, Fri.–Sun. 10–5.*

8 c-5

SEATTLE ASIAN ART MUSEUM

(Carl Gould, 1933) This graceful art moderne–style structure was built to house the extensive Asian art collection of Richard E. Fuller and his mother, Margaret MacTavish Fuller. At that time it was called the Seattle Art Museum, but over the years the collection grew and diversified until much of it was moved into a bigger building Downtown. Most of the Asian collection remained in the original location, and the building underwent a $1.7 million refurbishment. It was rededicated as the Seattle Asian Art Museum in 1994. The elegant edifice—perfectly symmetrical with delicate filigree scrollwork at the entry—harmonizes with the natural beauty of Volunteer Park. A plaza stretches from the front door to the edge of a bluff and foliage surrounds the rest of the building. *1400 E. Prospect St. (Volunteer Park), Capitol Hill, 206/654–3100, www.seattleartmuseum.org. Suggested donation: $3 adults, free children under 13, free 1st Thurs. and Sat. of month. Tues.–Wed. 10–5, Thurs. 10–9, Fri.–Sun. 10–5, and some Mon. holidays.*

10 *c-3*

SPACE NEEDLE

(Edward E. Carlson, John Graham Sr., Victor Steinbrueck, John Ridley; 1961) With its gargantuan steel legs and UFO-shape top, this futuristic structure is *the* symbol of Seattle. It was constructed for the 1962 World's Fair (the theme of which was "Life in the 21st Century") and designed to withstand a wind velocity of 200 mph. Twenty-five rods protect the tower from lightning. The observation deck, a 43-second elevator ride from street level, yields 360° vistas. The SkyCity restaurant, some 500 ft above the ground, also revolves 360° (in about 50 minutes). The Space Needle underwent a $20 million face-lift that not only revamped the SkyCity Restaurant but also created the Space Needle Pavilion—a 9,000-square-ft glass-and-metal structure that curves around the landmark's base. Designed by architect Gary Wakatsuki, it serves as an entryway and has a gift shop. *219 4th Ave. N (at Broad St.), Queen Anne, 206/443–2111, www.spaceneedle.com. $11 adults, $9 senior citizens, $5 children 5–12, free children under 5. Sun.–Thurs. 9 AM–11 PM, Fri.–Sat. 9 AM–midnight.*

5 *h-8*

SUZZALLO LIBRARY AT UW

(Charles H. Bebb and Carl Gould, 1926) When planning began in 1922, the architects intended this library to be "the

soul of the university," with all the hallowed glory of such traditional academic institutions as Oxford and Cambridge. And so they constructed a masterpiece of Gothic architecture with Tudor accents, common to the redbrick colleges in England. The exterior is adorned with 19 cast-stone figures depicting people who have contributed to Western culture; shields showing the coats of arms of various universities also decorate the outside. The interior is equally marvelous thanks to 11 35-ft-tall stained-glass windows, a curving double staircase, rows of chandeliers, and soaring arches. The library was named after Henry Suzzallo, the 15th UW president. *Center of UW Campus (near Central Plaza), University District, 206/543–0242, www.lib.washington.edu/Suzzallo. Mon.–Thurs. 7:30 AM–midnight, Fri. 7:30–6, Sat. 9–5, Sun. noon–midnight.*

ART GALLERIES

Seattle has a thriving gallery scene with many splendid and provocative exhibitions. Pioneer Square is especially hopping when it comes to art. As part of the First Thursday Art Walk many Downtown and Pioneer Square galleries stay open late on the first Thursday of each month to celebrate the openings of monthly shows. And when it comes to glass artists and glass lovers, this is definitely ground zero. As they say, "Seattle is the Manhattan of glass art."

12 *c-3*

CAROLYN STALEY FINE PRINTS

The speciality in this Pioneer Square gallery is fine Japanese prints. Among the offerings are traditional 18th- and 19th-century *ukiyo-e* prints depicting Kabuki actors, courtesans, landscapes, and legends. There are also 20th-century *shin hanga* prints that combine traditional styles with Western influences as well as the west coast's largest collection of Japanese woodblock prints. *314 Occidental Ave. (between 1st and 2nd Aves. S), Pioneer Square, 206/621–1888, www.carolynstaleyprints.com. Tues.–Sat. 10:30–5.*

10 *g-3*

ELLIOTT BROWN GALLERY

Although it has featured photography and mixed-media sculpture, this gallery specializes in glass works by a select group of acclaimed artists. Among them are Dale Chihuly, Richard Marquis, and Ann Robinson. The gallery organizes up to nine exhibitions a year. *215 Westlake Ave. N (between John and Thomas Sts.), Downtown, 206/340–8000, www. elliottbrowngallery.com. Tues.–Sat. 11–6.*

12 *b-2*

ESTHER CLAYPOOL GALLERY

As its space is split in half, this gallery often presents two solo shows simultaneously—sometimes allowing for interesting juxtapositions. The emphasis is on contemporary painting and works on paper, but the gallery also shows such top regional photographers as Arthur Aubry, Eduardo Calderón, Ford Gilbreath, and Glenn Rudolph. Luke Blackstone, Michael Dennis, and Pam Gazale have also showcased their sculptures here. *617 Western Ave. (between Columbia St. and Yesler Way), Pioneer Square, 206/264–1586, www.estherclaypool.com. Tues.–Fri. 11–6, Sat. 11–5.*

12 *b-2*

EYRE/MOORE GALLERY

Paintings, sculptures, photographs, and works that mix a variety of media have all been displayed at this gallery, which specializes in contemporary American artists who are just coming into their own or are midway into their careers. Exhibits range from minimal and conceptual to representational and figurative. *913 Western Ave. (at Marion St.), Downtown, 206/624–5596, www.eyremoore.com. Tues.–Sat. 11–6.*

12 *c-3*

FOSTER/WHITE GALLERY

One of the Northwest's largest galleries focuses on regional contemporary paintings, sculpture, ceramics, and glass. Emerging artists are represented as well as such established northwest greats as Mark Tobey, Morris Graves, and Kenneth Callahan. Foster/White also carries a good selection of work by acclaimed glass artists, including Dale Chihuly and William Morris. *123 S. Jackson St. (at Occidental Ave. S), Pioneer Square, 206/622–2833, www.fosterwhite.com. Mon.–Sat. 10–5, Sun. noon–5.*

13 *c-4*

126 Central Way (at Lake St.), Kirkland, 425/822–2305. Mon.–Wed. 10:30–6, Thurs.–Sat. 10:30–9, Sun. 11–5.

5 *b-3*

FRANCINE SEDERS GALLERY

Known for its outstanding northwest art, this gallery represents 35 artists with strong regional reputations, including the beloved figurative painter Jacob Lawrence. It also handles works from the estates of Wendell Brazeau, Boyer Gonzales, and Walter Isaacs as well as pieces by Guy Anderson, Mark Tobey, and Pehr. *6701 Greenwood Ave. N (at 67th St.), Green Lake, 206/782–0355, www.sedersgallery.com. Tues.–Sat. 11–5, Sun. 1–5.*

12 *c-3*

G. GIBSON GALLERY

Let G. Gibson take you on a visual excursion—one created by photographs from the 19th and 20th centuries. You might also be able to revel in exhibits of contemporary mixed-media works. *122 S. Jackson St., Suite 200 (at Occidental Ave. S.), Pioneer Square, 206/587–4033, www.ggibsongallery.com. Tues.–Fri. 11–5:30, Sat. 11–5.*

12 *c-2*

GREG KUCERA GALLERY

The wooden floors are so shiny that they practically reflect the art hanging on the walls above. Contemporary painting, sculpture, and works on paper by regional and nationally recognized artists are displayed in one of four indoor spaces or the outdoor sculpture deck. And there's no trepidation about presenting exhibitions that reflect sensitive social and political topics. Kara Walker's racially charged silhouettes have been shown here as have pieces by Robert Mapplethorpe. *212 3rd Ave. S (at Washington St.), Pioneer Square, 206/624–0770, www.gregkucera.com. Tues.–Sat. 10:30–5:30.*

12 *c-2*

GROVER/THURSTON GALLERY

This two-story space is a favorite among those who know their way around Pioneer Square's lively gallery district. Here northwest contemporary art reigns supreme. Paintings by Fay Jones are among the highlights, as are the cracked-glass and ceramic figurines by Judy Hill. *309 Occidental Ave. S (between Main St. and Jackson St.), Pioneer Square, 206/223–0816, www.groverthurston.com. Tues.–Sat. 11–5.*

7 h-8

HOWARD HOUSE

This bold, edgy gallery pushes the envelope with pieces by avant-garde painters and sculptors as well as digital-media and installation artists. Owner Billy Howard got his start by opening his home to the public for exhibitions. A year later he partnered up with an old college friend and the two opened a shared space with a furniture store in the front and a gallery in the back. It may sound odd, but the combo has worked. It's no surprise that this place is favored by hipsters. *2017 2nd Ave. (at Virginia St.), Belltown, 206/256–6399, www.howardhouse.net. Tues.–Sat. 11–6.*

8 a-7

911 MEDIA ARTS CENTER

Many a film and video artist has received support from this nonprofit media center. Fees to use its lights, cameras, production studio, and editing suites are lower than elsewhere. It also conducts workshops and screens (usually on Friday at 8 PM) independently made documentaries, experimental narratives, animated productions, and short films. The center's front window is an exhibition space: a recent installation had large bleary eyeballs staring out at passersby, their images broadcast from stacks of TVs. *117 Yale Ave. N (at Stewart St.), Downtown, 206/682–6552, www.911media.org. Weekdays 10–9.*

7 g-8

ROQ LA RUE

It ain't fancy, but this space has some of Seattle's coolest, quirkiest exhibits— from kitschy pop art to album cover art to the fine art of tattooing. It has also shown works by some of the country's best alternative comic book artists, including Charles Burns, Dan Clowes, and Chris Ware. Owner Kirsten Anderson says she tried "to create an atmosphere where big-buck art collectors as well as skate kids would feel welcome and comfortable." She's succeeded. *2224 2nd Ave. (at Blanchard St.), Belltown, 206/374–8977, www.roqlarue.com. Tues.–Fri. 2–6, Sat. noon–4.*

10 f-8

WILLIAM TRAVER GALLERY

On the second floor of a building that dates from 1910, this well-established gallery displays paintings and glass, clay, and mixed-media works under 17-ft-high ceilings. Exhibitions change monthly and have included elaborate champagne and martini glasses by Walter Lieberman; metal sculptures by Laura Griffith; paintings on glass by Dick Weiss; and sculptures made of bronze, tissue, and plaster by Eric Chesebro. *110 Union St., 2nd floor (at 1st Ave.), Downtown, 206/587–6501, www.travergallery.com. Weekdays 10–6, Sat. 10–5, Sun. noon–5.*

ART MUSEUMS

From ancient Asian artifacts to cutting edge digital media and from delicate glass sculptures to full-tilt rock music— the region's museums deliver a wonderful sampling of the many forms art has taken throughout history. Admission typically ranges from free to reasonably priced.

13 c-8

BELLEVUE ART MUSEUM

The Bellevue doesn't just display art, it also offers opportunities to learn about and create art. There's no permanent collection; instead, the museum features changing exhibits of contemporary visual works by artists from around the Pacific Northwest and the world. It also acts as a kind of studio and community center by hosting discussions, lectures, and courses. In January 2001, the museum moved to its new three-story, 36,000-square-ft building. Designed by architect Steven Holl, the structure is made of glass, aluminum, and textured concrete. Light reigns supreme here— windows, terraces, and skylights are prominent features. *510 Bellevue Way NE (at 6th St.), Bellevue, 425/637–1799, www.bellevueart.org. $6 adults, $4 senior citizens and students, free children under 6, free 3rd Thurs. of month. Tues.–Wed. 10–5, Thurs. 10–8, Fri.–Sat. 10–5, Sun. noon–5.*

10 d-3

EXPERIENCE MUSIC PROJECT (EMP)

The curvaceous, eye-popping structure designed by world-famous architect Frank Gehry contains an interactive museum dedicated to the art of rock and roll. The EMP celebrates America's love affair with music by displaying more than 80,000 instruments, stage costumes, fanzines, handwritten song lyrics, rare song sheets, photographs, films, and other items. There's also an extensive archive of recorded sound. At the museum's center is Trimpin's *Roots and Branches*—a giant tornado-shape sculpture made of more than 500 guitars and other instruments programmed and robotically controlled to play music. The Jimi Hendrix Gallery has the world's largest collection of Hendrix memorabilia. Another gallery displays guitars owned by the likes of Bob Dylan, Hank Williams, Kurt Cobain, and the bands Pearl Jam, Soundgarden, and the Kingsmen. There are often live music shows in EMP's Sky Church performance space. *5th Ave. (between Broad and Thomas Sts.), Queen Anne, 206/770–2700, www.emplive.com. $19.95 adults; $15.95 students, military, and senior citizens; $14.95 children 7–12. Memorial Day–Labor Day, daily 9 AM–11 PM; Sept.–May, Sun.–Thurs. 10–6, Fri.–Sat. 10 AM–11 PM.*

11 *a-8*

FRYE ART MUSEUM

In his will, Seattle businessman Charles Frye provided for the creation of a free public art museum to house and display the more than 230 works he and his wife, Emma, had collected starting in 1893. Charles died in 1940 at age 81, and this museum was opened in 1952. The collection includes many pivotal late-19th- and early 20th-century American and European realist works. Prized among them are German artist Franz von Stuck's *Sin*, a painting with impressionist leanings that predates the movement, and Alexander Koester's *Ducks*, an example of the Academy School of German painting. The Frye has a garden courtyard and a reflecting pool. *704 Terry Ave. (at Cherry St.), First Hill, 206/622–9250, www.fryeart.org. Free. Tues.–Wed. 10–5, Thurs. 10–9, Fri.–Sat. 10–5.*

5 *g-8*

HENRY ART GALLERY

On the western edge of the UW campus, the Henry was founded in 1927 and was Washington State's first public art museum. Part of its mission is to encourage experimentation so, the Henry tends to embrace modern and contemporary art, including many visually and conceptually challenging pieces. Among its more than 20,500 objects are 19th- and 20th-century paintings, an extensive photography collection, a textile and costume collection, and cutting-edge digital and other new-media works.

Highlights include Jacob Lawrence's *The Builders, No. 1*, as well as photos by Ansel Adams and Imogen Cunningham. *15th Ave. NE (at 41st St.), University District, 206/543–2280, www.henryart.org. $5 adults, $3.50 senior citizens 62 and older, free high school and college students (with ID) and children under 14, free Thurs. 5 PM–8 PM. Tues.–Wed. 11–5, Thurs. 11–8, Fri.–Sun. 11–5.*

MUSEUM OF NORTHWEST ART (MONA)

You have to drive about 1½ hours (78 mi) north of Seattle—to the town of La Conner, a haven for artists and writers—to reach MoNA, but it's well worth the drive. The museum celebrates the so-called Northwest School (or Northwest Tradition) of art, whose practitioners are influenced by the natural beauty of the environment as well as by Native American and Asian culture. On display are works by local artistic heroes from both the past and the present, including Morris Graves, Mark Tobey, Kenneth Callahan, and Guy Anderson. The museum also shows glass art, a Seattle specialty. *121 S. 1st St., La Conner, 360/466–4446, www.museumofnwart.org. $3 adults, free children 12 and under. Tues.–Sun. 10–5.*

10 *f-8*

SEATTLE ART MUSEUM (SAM)

Drive through Downtown and you can't miss Seattle's most prominent art museum—thanks in no small part to Jonathan Borofsky's 48-ft-high steel *Hammering Man* sculpture outside the front door. Step inside to find a large, airy, brightly lit hall enlivened by two ancient Chinese stone camels. More than 23,000 objects make up SAM's collection, which embraces African and Native American works as well as European decorative art. The museum also has a collection modern pieces by such artists as Agnes Martin, Andy Warhol, and Roy Lichtenstein. Jackson Pollock's 1947 *Sea Change* is a highlight. Although the Downtown branch has some examples of the extensive Asian art collection, most such works are at its sister facility—the Seattle Asian Art Museum—in Volunteer Park (a ticket purchased at SAM is valid at this branch if used within one week). The café, just off SAM's lobby, is one of Downtown's best lunch spots. *100 University St. (at 1st Ave.), Downtown, 206/654–3255, www.seattleartmuseum.org. Suggested*

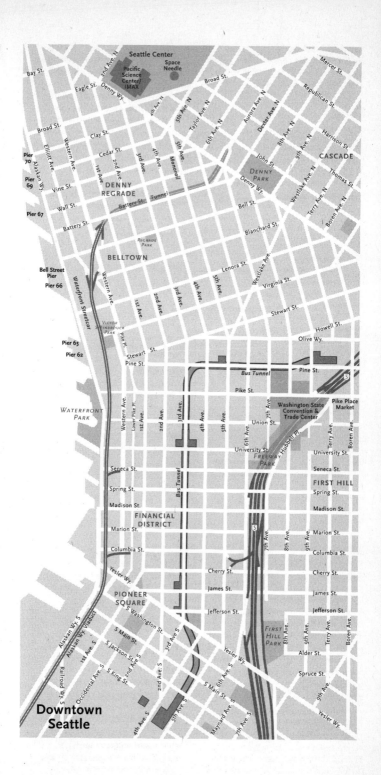

Downtown Seattle

169

donation: $7 adults, $5 students and senior citizens, free children under 13; free 1st Thurs. of month. Tues.–Wed. 10–5, Thurs. 10–9, Fri.–Sun. 10–5.

8 *c-5*

SEATTLE ASIAN ART MUSEUM

SAM's exquisite satellite houses Japanese, Chinese, Korean, Indian, Southeast Asian, and Himalayan art. Many of the thousands of paintings, sculptures, and textiles were acquired by the late Eugene Fuller, Seattle's most famous collector. Among the highlights are a 13th/14th–century Buddhist sculpture *Exalted Monk (Moment of Enlightenment)*, ancient Chinese funerary art, and early Thai ceramics. Although exhibits change constantly, the museum's holdings are so vast that it may be years before a favorite piece makes a reappearance. (A ticket to the Asian Art Museum is good for $3 off admission to SAM if used within one week.) *1400 E. Prospect St. (Volunteer Park), Capitol Hill, 206/654–3100, www.seattleartmuseum.org. Suggested donation: $3 adults, free children under 13; free 1st Thurs. and Sat. of month. Tues.–Wed. 10–5, Thurs. 10–9, Fri.–Sun. 10–5, some Mon. holidays.*

BRIDGES

With so many bodies of water—small and large—it's no wonder that Seattle has more than 150 bridges, including three drawbridges and one swing bridge. Here are some of the most impressive.

4 *g-7*

BALLARD BRIDGE

This 2,854-ft-span drawbridge was built in 1917 at the west end of the Lake Washington Ship Canal. It links the Magnolia and Queen Anne neighborhoods with Ballard and is the fourth and last of the canal bridges beneath which boats must pass to enter Puget Sound from Lake Washington. *15th Ave. NW from Magnolia to Ballard.*

2 *d-4*

EVERGREEN POINT FLOATING BRIDGE

Made of a string of pontoons connected end to end, this 1.4-mi-long bridge opened in 1963. It crosses Lake Washington from Union Bay just south of the UW campus to Evergreen Point in the city of Medina. The bridge isn't in great shape having suffered storm damage; it's also often jam-packed with traffic. As part of Highway 520 it's the main passageway for those who live in Seattle and work in the major tech companies of Redmond, Bellevue, and Kirkland. *Hwy. 520 from University District to Medina.*

7 *g-1*

FREMONT BRIDGE

Completed in 1917, this drawbridge opens vertically an average of 35 times a

---

WATER, WATER EVERYWHERE

Want to appreciate the aquatic marvels in and around Seattle? Here's where to go:

alki beach (viewpoints)
Walk, jog or rollerblade along this beach and adjoining park as it cuts a path along Elliott Bay and Puget Sound.

ballard locks (historic structures & streets)
Watch boats make their way from Lake Washington and Lake Union out to the Puget Sound.

center for wooden boats (history museums)
Watch boats as they're made, and dream about a life on the water.

discovery park (historic structures & streets)
Discover one of the most stunning views of Puget Sound at this park atop a bluff.

fremont bridge (bridges)
Stroll across this colorful overpass for a view of the tree-lined Lake Washington Ship Canal.

gasworks park (viewpoints)
Perched at the north end of Lake Union, this relaxing park offers a gorgeous view of the water and Seattle's skyline.

green lake park (neighborhoods)
This small-but-scenic inner-city lake (and the park that surrounds it) is one of Seattle's most popular outdoor destinations, and a hotspot for socializing, too.

seattle aquarium (aquariums)
Check out the octopus, starfish, and sea otter as you check out Pier 59 and Elliott Bay.

day—making it one of the world's busiest. It crosses the Lake Washington Ship Canal and links Fremont with Queen Anne. The bridge's current blue and orange color scheme was chosen by a 1985 poll of Fremont residents and by the Fremont Arts Council. When it's not open for marine traffic, the bridge sits 30 ft above the water. *Westlake Ave. N, Queen Anne to Fremont Ave. N, Fremont.*

7 *g-1*

GEORGE WASHINGTON MEMORIAL BRIDGE (AURORA BRIDGE)

You know that old story about the troll that lived under the bridge and gave the three billy goats a hard time? Well, Seattle has its very own bridge troll. This bridge is the part of the Aurora Highway/Highway 99, which crosses over the Lake Washington Ship Canal. Finished in 1932, it rises 167 ft above the water and is 2,945 ft long, linking the Fremont and Queen Anne neighborhoods. When you're in Fremont, stroll under the bridge at North 36th Street and you'll find the *Fremont Troll*—a giant, whimsical, concrete monster that jealously grips a Volkswagen Beetle. *Hwy. 99, Queen Anne to Fremont.*

2 *d-5*

LAKE WASHINGTON FLOATING BRIDGE

It took 18 months to build and was the largest bridge of its kind when it opened in 1940. It spans 3,387 ft (1¼ mi) and has 25 pontoons—each one 350 ft long and 59 ft wide—that are kept in place with 65-ton anchors. For 50 years its four lanes carried east- and west-bound traffic from the eastern side of Seattle to the north end of Mercer Island and on to the east side of Lake Washington just south of Bellevue. It became an important part of the I−90 corridor and allowed Mercer Island grow into a thriving suburb. In 1989, a second floating bridge opened next to it, adding three general-purpose lanes and two carpool lanes. In 1990, a week of high winds and rain sunk the original bridge; three years later it was reopened. *I−90 from East Seattle to Mercer Island.*

8 *e-2*

MONTLAKE BRIDGE

This gorgeous drawbridge, spanning 344 ft across the Lake Washington Ship Canal, is the first of four such bridges that boaters must pass beneath to cruise from Lake Washington to Puget Sound. Designed by renowned Seattle architect Carl Gould and opened in 1925, the bridge is watched over by two Gothic-style control towers. It connects the U−District to Capitol Hill and is the site of much celebration each May on boating season's opening day. *Montlake Blvd. from E. Shelby St., Capitol Hill to University of Washington, University District.*

8 *d-2*

SHIP CANAL BRIDGE

The segment of I−5 that crosses Portage Bay is a massive, high-level, double-decker bridge that carries 12 lanes of often heavy traffic. The bridge opened in 1962, and it's now a main north−south thoroughfare between the U−District and Eastlake. Although its lower deck has express lanes, this bridge can become extremely congested at rush hour. Residents' impatience with traffic reached particularly heinous heights on August 28, 2001, when a few passing motorists taunted a woman to jump while she held onto a railing for nearly four hours slowing morning traffic. (She was safely recovered but her suicide attempt and the cruel impatience of drivers gained national attention.) *I−5 from Eastlake to University District.*

5 *g-8*

UNIVERSITY BRIDGE

This drawbridge spans Portage Bay, the body of water between Lake Washington and Lake Union, and connects the U−District with Eastlake and Capitol Hill. It was built in 1919 and remodeled in 1933. Although it gets a lot of use, traffic has decreased in recent years since the nearby Ship Canal Bridge was built *Eastlake Ave. E from Furhman Ave. E, Eastlake to Northlake Way, University District.*

3 *d-8*

WEST SEATTLE BRIDGE

With a length of 11,800 ft and a height of 150 ft, this is Seattle's longest and tallest bridge. It links West Seattle with the south end of Downtown, crossing high above the Duwamish Waterway's busy shipping lanes. It also connects West Seattle with Highway 99 and I−5. The bridge was completed in 1984 and replaced a drawbridge that was destroyed when a freighter rammed into it. *Harbor Ave. SW, West Seattle to Highway 99.*

CHILDREN'S MUSEUM

10 C-2

SEATTLE CHILDREN'S MUSEUM

On the lower level of Center House in Seattle Center, kids can run and play safely in microcosms of the world. Cultural workshops and village re-creations teach children about daily life in faraway lands such as Ghana and the Philippines. A replica neighborhood—with a fire station, a grocery store, and a post office—aids in acclimating kids to things closer to home. Waterfalls and a large tree introduce a mountain wilderness area. And then there's Cog City—a sort of life-size version of Chutes and Ladders. Tots love to climb, slide, and bounce around a soft, padded area. There are also hands-on activities such as arts and crafts. *305 Harrison St. (at 5th Ave. N), Downtown, 206/441–1768, www.thechildrensmuseum.org. $5.50. Weekdays 10–5, weekends 10–6.*

KIDS IN TOW?

Save the frantic search for a babysitter for an evening out. On a nice day your wee one will enjoy scampering around these kid-friendly destinations.

center for wooden boats (history museums)
> *Make your kid the skipper in a family day out in an antique or Native American canoe.*

the children's museum (children's museums)
> *Plenty of colorful interactivity to romp around in.*

experience music project (art museums)
> *Unleash the musical prodigy within on the Sound Lab's state-of-the-art instruments.*

fremont troll (statues, murals, and monuments)
> *Climb up his shoulder to the top of his head—he won't bite your little billy goat gruff.*

lake view cemetery (graveyards and cemeteries)
> *Inspire a young martial arts student by paying homage at Bruce Lee's grave.*

museum of history and industry (history museums)
> *Find out what life was like for Seattle's earliest pioneers in "If I Were Back Then," presented Monday, Wednesday, and Friday mornings.*

pacific science center (science museums)
> *Creepy crawly fun can be had in the mole rat and insect exhibits, and everyone loves the butterfly room.*

wing luke museum (history museums)
> *Marvel at kites, dragon puppets, and beautiful artwork, backdrops to educational segments on Asian historical contributions.*

COLLEGES & UNIVERSITIES

Most Seattle residents are, at one point or another, engaged in some form of educational self-improvement. It's not unusual to bump into someone who's working toward a degree or taking recreational college courses for the simple joy of learning. That's understandable given the variety of nationally respected institutes both within the city limits and around Western Washington. Whether you're thinking about studying medicine or ponder flowering arrangement as a hobby, you'll have a number of first-rate schools from which to choose once you decide to get serious.

10 d-6

ART INSTITUTE OF SEATTLE

Teaching creative skills that are applicable in the business world is the emphasis at the Art Institute of Seattle, recently accredited by the Commission on Colleges of the Northwest Association of Schools and Colleges. Artistically inclined, corporate career–minded types come here to earn a two-year degree in interior and fashion design, animation, audio production, commercial photography, or other fields. Founded in 1946 as the Burnley School for Professional Art, it joined The Art Institutes, a national network of creative schools in 1982, and enrollment rose from 1,000 students to almost 3,000. *2323 Elliott Ave. (on Waterfront at Bell St.), Downtown, 800/275–2471 or 206/448–0900, www.ais.edu.*

8 b-6

CORNISH COLLEGE OF THE ARTS

With 650 students, Cornish may be the smallest of Seattle's colleges, but it definitely has an impact on the city's arts community. Students learn fundamental skills in their discipline while working with professionals in the field, many of whom teach at the school. Although it lacks campus attractions, developments are in the works to change this—and besides, the surrounding neighborhood has plenty to offer. The school is due to expand and centralize its facilities with a new three-story building that has a library, additional classrooms, and a common area with a gallery. *Cornish South, 710 E. Roy St. (off 10th Ave. E); Cornish North, 1501 10th Ave. E; Downtown; 206/726–5151; www.cornish.edu.*

PACIFIC LUTHERAN UNIVERSITY

Established in 1890 by Scandinavian immigrants, Pacific Lutheran is on 126 quiet Tacoma acres that are equidistant from Mt. Rainier and the Washington coast. The more than 3,600 students, 61% of them female, work toward liberal arts undergraduate and graduate degrees. Pacific Lutheran has a number of notable features, including the W.M. Keck Observatory; the Pacific Northwest's second largest children's literature collection; the Mary Fuch's organ, the largest all-mechanical pipe organ at a West Coast university; and KPLU 88.5, a National Public Radio affiliate that's Seattle's best jazz station on the FM dial. *121st St. S at Yakima Ave., Tacoma, 253/531–6900, www.plu.edu.*

8 b-7

SEATTLE COMMUNITY COLLEGES

More than 28,000 students attend classes at this nationally recognized community college's four campuses: Seattle Central in Capitol Hill, North Seattle in Northgate, South Seattle in West Seattle, and the Seattle Vocational Institute in the Central District. Students come from all walks of life to work toward two-year degrees, learn a new trade, or take professional enrichment classes. The main campus, Seattle Central, greatly influences the political and social scenes on the always-active Broadway strip. Its Broadway Performance Hall plays an important role in the city's cultural community, hosting plays, author readings, and dance performances. *Seattle Central, 1701 Broadway Ave. E, Capitol Hill, 206/587–3800, http://sccdweb.sccd.ctc.edu.*

2 c-1

North Seattle Community College, 9600 College Way N, Northgate, 206/527–3639.

3 b-8

South Seattle Community College, 6000 16th Ave. SW, West Seattle, 206/764–5300.

9 f-3

Seattle Vocational Institute, 2120 S. Jackson St., Central District, 206/587–4950.

7 e-1

SEATTLE PACIFIC UNIVERSITY

Forget about co-ed kegger hijinks—students caught smoking, drinking, or fraternizing on campus are subject to expulsion at this small Christian university, near the Ship Canal. A religious education is the focus of this small campus, a principle that this one-time seminary takes very seriously. Founded in 1891 by Free Methodist Church members as Seattle Seminary, the university didn't officially become known as Seattle Pacific University until 1977, after decades of expansion. Today Seattle Pacific's approximately 3500 students take advantage of the institution's strong liberal arts courses, particularly its education degree program, and adopt the school's evangelical mission. *3307 3rd Ave. W (at Nickerson St.), Queen Anne, 206/281–2000. www.spu.edu.*

11 d-7

SEATTLE UNIVERSITY

On the south end of Broadway, between Capitol Hill and First Hill, sits this four-year Jesuit School. Seattle University is more than a century old, but it adopted the SU name in 1948. Founded by Father Victor Garrand and Father Adrian Sweere as the Parish and School of the Immaculate Conception in 1891, it quickly expanded its property holdings and evolved into Seattle College in 1898. Eleven years later the school awarded its first bachelor of arts degrees, and in 1933 it became the first Jesuit college to admit women. Today SU has 43-acres that are strewn with tree-lined paths and gardens. Even the Quad, an open gathering spot in the center of the campus, is designed to resemble a Japanese rock garden. The school's curriculum stresses the notion of making learning a lifelong endeavor, integrating the pursuit of knowledge as a part of spirituality. *900 Broadway Ave., Capitol Hill, 206/296–6000, www.seattleu.edu.*

3 *f-8*
UNIVERSITY OF PUGET SOUND

Tudor Gothic buildings, views of the Cascade and Olympic mountains, and pungent fir groves make this 97-acre liberal arts school—35 mi south of Seattle in Tacoma—one of the region's most beautiful. Perhaps that's why many of its 2,725 undergrad and graduate students live on campus. It was founded in 1888 and is home to Kilworth Chapel, a New England–style church that pays homage to the school's Methodist heritage. In recent years the university has spent almost $50 million on improvements, including a new concert hall, athletic field, theater, and fitness center. The Kittredge Arts Complex houses a photo lab, sculpture and painting studios, and wood- and metalwork areas. The Kittredge Gallery regularly hosts changing art exhibits. Wheelock Center is the heart of campus social life, home to the student newspaper and radio station as well as a student-operated pizza joint and the Lawrence Street Station, an all-around eatery. *1500 N. Warner St., Tacoma, 253/879–3100, www.ups.edu.*

5 *h-8*
UNIVERSITY OF WASHINGTON

Top-notch research and graduate programs in social work, drama, nursing, oceanography, and physiology have earned UW national renown. Locals love it for its winning sports teams, and many Seattleites show their allegiance with purple and white Huskies bumper stickers. (Here's a tip: Only visitors or recent transplants refer to Seattle's best known university by its proper name. Around here, it's called U-Dub, saving you the trouble of saying "W.") The diverse, 35,000-strong student body flavors the entire neighborhood for miles. On weekends students amble down the Ave., a commercial strip near campus, or congregate in Red Square—named for its redbrick paving—to see performances, participate in political rallies, or simply to read a book or meet with friends. The school was originally located Downtown, but it moved to Denny Hall in 1895 and expanded from that first building. The Henry Art Gallery

and the Burke Museum of Natural History and Culture lend the campus considerable cultural cachet, and the National Public Radio affiliate KUOW FM is also associated with the university. *Visitor Information Center, 4014 University Way NE, University District, 206/543–9198, www.washington.edu. Daily 8–5.*

WESTERN WASHINGTON UNIVERSITY

The more than 12,000 students at this state university 90 mi north of Seattle can enjoy some of western Washington's best scenery. Lake Whatcom, Bellingham Bay, and the San Juan Islands are all nearby. Both Vancouver, BC and Mt. Baker are a mere hour's drive away. The 200-acre campus includes 38 acres of trees, flora in the Sehome Arboretum, and an impressive collection of 24 outdoor sculptures. Isamu Noguchi's famous *Skyviewing* sculpture sits at the campus's crossroads, called Red Square just like the one at its U-Dub cousin. Students relax indoors at the Viking Union or plant themselves around Fisher Fountain, Western's main meet-and-greet area. *South College Dr. (off I–5 and Hwy. 11), Bellingham, 360/650–3000, www.wwu.edu.*

GRAVEYARDS & CEMETERIES

Within the Seattle area's 30 or so cemeteries, you'll find epitaphs that tell stories about the adventurous spirits and iconoclasts who have been attracted to the city during its 150-year history.

6 *b-6*
CALVARY CEMETERY

A Catholic cemetery teeming with stone cherubim and majestic headstones, this the final resting place of Pike Place Market founder Giuseppe "Joe" Desimone, and "Tioga George" Burns, baseball's American League MVP in 1926. *5041 35th Ave. NE (at 50th St.), University District, 206/522–0996.*

2 *b-1*
EVERGREEN-WASHELLI CEMETERY

This North Seattle cemetery is popular with shutterbugs for its angels and elaborately carved monuments. Among a number of military graves are first settlers David T. Denny and his wife, Louisa Boren Denny, laid to rest here with their son, Jonathan, in the cemetery's first burial service. You'll also find the grave of George Washington Carmack, the man who discovered the Klondike Gold Fields and sparked the gold rush that changed the city. *11111 Aurora Ave. N (near 110th St.), Northgate. 206/362–5200.*

1 f-5
GREENWOOD MEMORIAL PARK

Greenwood receives a number of visitors because of its most famous resident, guitar god Jimi Hendrix. Fans congregate here to get rubbings of the plaque with the engraved guitar that marks his resting place or to leave flowers or guitar picks. Inquire at the office for directions to the site. *350 Monroe Ave. NE (at 3rd St.), Renton, 425/255–1511.*

8 c-4
LAKE VIEW CEMETERY

The city's oldest cemetery also happens to contain the graves of the legendary Bruce Lee and his son, Brandon, who are buried side by side atop a knoll. Martial arts practitioners and fans bring incense, flowers, and notes—you'll often find someone sitting in quiet contemplation on the bench before Bruce's red marker and Brandon's black one. Other Seattle big wigs who are buried here include Asa Mercer, one of the city's settlers; Princess Angeline, daughter of Chief Seattle, the Duwamish Tribe leader for whom the city was named; John Nordstrom, founder of the Nordstrom department store chain; and members of the Denny family, who first settled the region. On sunny days there are clear views of Lake Washington and Lake Union from here; such *vistas* and the hilly paths make the cemetery an interesting, if odd, route for the occasional jogger. *1554 15th Ave. E (just south of E. Garfield St.), Capitol Hill, 206/322–1582.*

HISTORIC STRUCTURES & STREETS

As far as cities go, Seattle is a pretty young one. Settlers didn't even show up here until 1851. Finding streets and structures that go way back is made even more difficult by two things—the Great Fire of 1889, which torched a large portion of the city, and the Denny Regrade, a construction project from 1906–11 that flattened Denny Hill and

took down all the old buildings and businesses that had been on it. Still, Seattle isn't entirely without landmarks.

12 c-1
ALASKA BUILDING

This stately stone building was Seattle's first steel-frame skyscraper and—with 14 stories—the city's tallest building for seven years. It lost that title to the Hoge Building (705 2nd Avenue), which was built in 1911 and had 18 stories. *618 2nd Ave. (at Cherry St.), Pioneer Square.*

3 a-8
ALKI POINT

In September 1851, David Denny, John Low, and Lee Terry arrived in what would become Seattle. They settled at Alki Point for six months before moving to what is now Pioneer Square. Today, a monument—a miniature version of the Statue of Liberty—marks the place where they first arrived. Alki Point and Alki Beach are now best known for their beautiful park and well-maintained biking and running path. *Corner of Alki and 63rd Aves. SW, West Seattle.*

4 d-5
BALLARD LOCKS/LAKE WASHINGTON SHIP CANAL

Thanks to manpower—and lots of it—a boat in freshwater Lake Washington can sail to freshwater Lake Union and on out to the salty waters of Puget Sound and the sea beyond. It took six years (1911–17) to carve the 8-mi Lake Washington Ship Canal into dry land. The Ballard Locks (officially the Hiram M. Chittenden Locks) on the canal's west end were completed in 1917 and serve 100,000 boats yearly by raising and lowering water levels anywhere from 6 ft to 26 ft. On the north side of the locks are a 7-acre ornamental garden and a visitors center with displays on lock and canal history and operation as well as several sculptures by local artists. Along the south side is a 1,200-ft promenade with a footbridge, a fishing pier, and an observation deck. You can watch the marine population make the same journey as the boats. The fish ladder's 21 levels form a gradual incline that allows an estimated half million salmon and trout to swim upstream each year. Several windows at the waterline afford views of the fish struggling against the current en route to their spawning grounds. *3015 NW 54th St. (at 32nd Ave.*

NW), Ballard, 206/783–7059, www.
nws.usace.army.mil/opdiv/lwsc. Free.
Locks daily 7 AM–9 PM; visitor center May
15–Sept. 15, daily 10–6; Sept. 16–May 14,
Thurs.–Mon. 11–4.

3 a-2

FT. LAWTON/ DISCOVERY PARK

In 1900 the U.S. Army established a military post on Magnolia Bluff. Known as Ft. Lawton, it was part of the defense system that protected Puget Sound from naval attack. Over the years thousands of soldiers called it home, and in 1903 President Theodore Roosevelt stopped by for a visit. The post was turned over to the city in 1970, and its lands became what is now the 534-acre Discovery Park. Here you'll find spectacular views of both the Cascade and the Olympic mountains; 2 miles of tidal beaches; and plenty of meadows, cliffs, forests, and streams. The city council made what was left of the military post a preservation district in 1988. Today, the Ft. Lawton Landmark District includes original army structures built between 1898, before the fort was dedicated, and 1908. 3801 W. Government Way (at 36th Ave. W), Magnolia, 206/386–4236. Free. Visitors center daily 8:30–5.

1·0 e-7

PIKE PLACE PUBLIC MARKET

This Seattle institution began in 1907 when the city issued permits allowing farmers to sell produce here from wagons, which were later replaced by stalls. At one time the market was a madhouse of vendors hawking their produce and haggling with customers over prices. (Even today some fishmongers still carry on this kind of frenzied banter.) Urban renewal almost killed the market, but city voters, led by the late architect Victor Steinbrueck, rallied and voted it a historical asset in 1973. Wander though the market today and you'll discover a colorful array of arts and crafts tables; booths that sell fresh seafood, produce, cheese, wine, bulk spices, tea, and coffee; and a great number of shops purveying curios, art, imports, and foodstuffs. Because the market is built along a bluff, its main arcade stretches down a cliff face for several stories. Many of the more interesting shops are "down under," that is, below the main arcade. Pike Pl. at Pike St. (west of 1st

Ave.), Downtown, 206/682–7453, www.
pikeplacemarket.org. Mon.–Sat. 9–6,
Sun. 11–5.

12 c-2

PIONEER SQUARE DISTRICT

This area started out as home to the Native American Duwamish tribe. In 1852 white pioneers settled here, and it evolved into the city's original Downtown. The Great Fire of 1889 razed 50 blocks of mostly wooden buildings in one day. But Seattle came back—this time with buildings made of brick, stone, and iron. The rebuilding helped spur the city's transformation from a logging town to a Pacific Rim shipping center and a haven for immigrants from Asia and the Pacific islands. In 1897 the S.S. Portland docked in Seattle with more than a ton of gold mined from the Yukon. Suddenly, the city became America's most important hub for those traveling to and from the Klondike. Gold rushers needed hotels, supplies, mining equipment, and entertainment, and so Pioneer Square boomed, becoming notorious for its brothels, bars, and opium dens. After the early 1900s, the city's business core began moving north and Pioneer Square headed into a nosedive. In 1970 the square was saved from the fate of becoming a parking lot when the area was designated Seattle's first historic district. A walk through this lively neighborhood reveals gorgeous turn-of-the-20th-century redbrick and stone buildings, examples of Renaissance Revival, Beaux Arts, and Richardson Romanesque architecture. Unfortunately, many of these old buildings suffered damage during an earthquake that rocked the city in February 2001. Many underwent serious repairs. Bordered by Alaskan Way S, Columbia St., 4th Ave. S, and S. King St.

12 c-2

SEATTLE UNDERGROUND/ UNDERGROUND TOUR

After the Great Fire of 1889, many of the new streets and buildings were constructed atop the old. Today, you can see storefronts dating from the 1890s on an official walking tour of the musty passageways beneath Pioneer Square. The Seattle Underground Tour starts in a public house that dates from 1890 and winds its way through five blocks of underground caverns. The guides are witty and knowledgable, and the tour offers a lively look at the city's wild west past. *608 1st Ave. (between Yesler Way and Cherry St.), Pioneer Square, 206/682–4646, www.undergroundtour.com. $9 adults, $7 senior citizens and students, $5 children 7–12, free children under 7. Ticket office daily 9:30–6; tour times vary but typically run 11–5.*

12 *C-2*

SMITH TOWER

At 42 stories, Smith Tower was the tallest building outside of New York when it opened on July 4, 1914. Lyman C. Smith—the structure's creator and namesake—was a businessman from New York who'd made his money from typewriters (he's the Smith in Smith-Corona). He began construction of the beautiful white terra-cotta–and–steel tower in 1911 but died before it was completed. Smith Tower remained Seattle's highest structure until the 605-ft Space Needle poked through the clouds in 1962. As with many of Pioneer Square's older buildings, the tower fell into disrepair in the 1960s and 1970s. In the 1990s, a $28 million renovation not only restored the building but also upgraded its wiring and added central air-conditioning. The 35th floor's Chinese Room is a beautiful space that you can rent for special occasions. It's surrounded by an observation deck with a 360° view of the Olympics, the Cascades, Mt. Rainier, Mt. Baker, and Elliott Bay. *506 2nd Ave. (at Yesler Way), Pioneer Square, 206/682–9393 to administration or 206/622–3131 to Chinese Room, www.chineseroom.com. Call Chinese Room for reservations.*

12 *C-2*

YESLER WAY

In 1852, businessman Henry Yesler built the Puget Sound's first steam-powered sawmill on a wharf at Elliott Bay. Timber logged off the hills was sent to the sawmill on Yesler Way, the original "Skid Road," a path made of small logs laid crossways and greased so the trees would slide down. Later, as Pioneer Square began to deteriorate, the street became known for the drunks and down-and-outers that hung out in the area. Today Yesler Way is the heart of the bustling Pioneer Square Historic District, popular with tourists and art enthusiasts as well as a few folks down on their luck. *Pioneer Square.*

HISTORY MUSEUMS

A tyke of a city from a historical point of view, Seattle nonetheless has an intriguing background that predates the arrival of the Denny settlers. Laden with tales of pioneer perseverance, gold rush dreams, and, interestingly enough, plucky generosity from some of the burgeoning city's ladies of the evening, you could never call Seattle's history boring.

5 *h-7*

BURKE MUSEUM OF NATURAL HISTORY & CULTURE

A regional natural history and culture museum, the Burke brings numerous visitors to the UW campus. The paleontological collection alone has almost 3 million specimens including mollusks and fossil flora. Standing exhibits surveying the northwest's indigenous cultures span 35 Native American tribes. The museum also hosts traveling exhibits such as the one on Sir Ernest Shackleton's doomed exploratory voyage to Antarctica in 1914. *17th Ave. NE (on northwest edge of UW at 45th St.), 206/543–5590, www.washington.edu/burkemuseum. Admission: $5.50 general, $4 senior citizens; additional fee for some special exhibits; add $1 for same-day admission to Henry Art Gallery. Mon.–Wed. 10–5, Thurs. 10–8, Fri.–Sun. 10–5.*

3 *e-5*

CENTER FOR WOODEN BOATS

Every spring young maritime explorers flock to this museum to watch boats being made or to browse the collection of antique vessels. Highlights include the 1897 schooner *Wawowa*, an 1869 Bristol Bay gilnetter, and Aleutian kayaks and canoes dating from the 19th century. You can also take a ride in one of many restored vessels (on Sunday such junkets are free between 2 and 3; rent rowboats and sailboats for between $12.50 and $23.50 weekdays, between $20 and $37.50 weekends) or watch carvers create a traditional cedar canoe. If you're lucky a craftsperson might stop his or her carving and pounding to tell you a story or sing you a song. Those enchanted sufficiently by the experience may be moved to join the center as a volunteer and embark on a restoration project of their own. *1010 Valley St. (near Terry Ave.), Eastlake, 206/382–2628, www.cwb.org. Free. Mon. and Wed.–Sun. 11–6.*

12 c-2

KLONDIKE GOLD RUSH MUSEUM

California may be synonymous with the Gold Rush of 1849, but Seattle experienced its own frenzy over the precious metal. Indeed, the 1896 discovery of gold in northwestern Canada drew fortune seekers from around the country to Seattle, irrevocably changing its history. This small museum illustrates the importance of the 1897–98 boom, when the city's small business district was forced to grow up to meet the needs of the Klondike Rush. Audio and video presentations explain the adversities northwest miners faced and introduce a few key historical figures. A gold-panning demonstration and a glimpse of the artifacts housed here, particularly photos of wizened miners and the cramped conditions they endured, make a visit more memorable. *117 S. Main St. (at 1st Ave. S), Pioneer Square, 206/553–7220. Donations encouraged. Daily 8–5.*

2 c-7

MUSEUM OF FLIGHT

Prepare for take off: The museum's collection of 131 airborne craft and nearly 20,000 flight-related artifacts is more than enough to boggle the mind of even the most technically savvy visitor. In the Red Barn, site of Boeing's original airplane factory, you can trace the history of human flight and peruse instruments, models, armament, tools, uniforms, photographs, and a galaxy of other flight-related items. Most people head straight for the vintage planes, though. In the Great Gallery, you'll find 25 World War II–era planes among other craft. Guided tours are free. *9404 E. Marginal Way S (at 94th Pl.), south of Seattle, 206/764–5720, www.museumofflight.org. $9.50 adults, $8.50 senior citizens, $5 children 5–17. Mon.–Wed. 10–5, Thurs. 10–9, Fri.–Sun. 10–5.*

4 d-3

NORDIC HERITAGE MUSEUM

As its name suggests, this museum is all about Nordic art, artifacts, and heritage—be it from Denmark, Finland, Iceland, Norway, or Sweden. Its nine permanent galleries provide an in-depth look at Scandinavian immigration to America and Nordic settlement in the Pacific Northwest. Among the finds are textiles, china, books, tools, and photographs brought from the old countries. The temporary galleries display paintings, sculpture, and photography by contemporary Nordic artists. *3014 NW 67th St. (at 32nd Ave.), Ballard, 206/789–5707, www.nordicmuseum.com. $4 general, $3 senior citizens, $2 students, free children under 5. Tues.–Sat. 10–4, Sun. noon–4.*

8 e-1

SEATTLE MUSEUM OF HISTORY & INDUSTRY

Few places are better equipped to help you get a handle on the northwest's history. Since 1952 this museum has collected objects—some dating as far back as 1780—that chronicle the region's economic, social, and cultural history. Factory and mining equipment, gramophones, clothing, and newspapers and other everyday items from yesteryear are all on display. Weekends see educational presentations and workshops for families. Students, teachers, and history buffs also make great use of the museum library, whose books, documents, and photographs number in the hundreds of thousands. *2700 24th Ave. E (by Husky Stadium, near Park Dr.), University District, 206/324–1126, www.seattlehistory.org. $5.50 adults, $3 senior citizens and children 6–12, $1 children 2–5. Daily 10–5.*

12 e-3

WING LUKE MUSEUM

Named for the first Asian-American elected official, this small but well-organized museum surveys 200 years of cultural and historic contributions by people from Asia and the Pacific islands who settled in the Pacific Northwest. The emphasis is on how immigrants and their descendants have transformed and been transformed by American culture. Displays contain photographs, costumes, fabrics, baskets, musical instruments, and other objects. The centerpiece exhibit, "One Song, Many Voices: The Asian Pacific American Experience" spans a multitude of cultures, including Chinese, Japanese, Cambodian, and Hawaiian. There are also exhibits that teach you about crafts and traditional medicines. And don't miss the handmade kites resembling birds, goldfish, turtles and other creatures. They dangle from the ceiling and complement a 35-ft-long Chinese dragon puppet and an even larger dragon boat. *407 7th Ave. S (at Jackson St.), International District, 206/623–5124, www.wingluke.org. $4* *adults, $3 senior citizens and students, $2 children 5–15. Tues.–Fri. 11–4:30, weekends noon–4.*

LIBRARIES

Seattleites love books—whether they're curling up with a good novel at the corner coffee shop or perusing endless stacks at the city's many libraries. For a complete list of Seattle's public libraries (there are more than 20), visit www.spl.org.

10 *h-6*

CENTRAL LIBRARY

Seattle's public library system includes this central Downtown location and 23 branches. Combined they have a massive collection of books as well as 3,000 different periodicals and newspapers. The system also a includes a business and technology department; an environmental information center; and the Seattle Collection, with books, maps, scrapbooks, videos, and documents related to the region. All locations provide card holders with 45 minutes of free Internet access per day on a first-come, first-served basis. At press time, Seattle Central Library's spectacular new building, designed by renowned architect Rem Koolhaas, was being constructed on the site of the old one at 1000 4th Avenue. Its temporary digs were on Pike Street, and about half of its collection was in storage; some items were retrievable and some weren't. *800 Pike St. (at 8th Ave.), Downtown, 206/ 386–4636, www.spl.org. Mon.–Thurs. 9– 9, Fri. 10:30–6, Sat. 9–6, Sun. 1–5.*

9 *f-2*

DOUGLAS TRUTH NEIGHBORHOOD LIBRARY

This branch of the Seattle Public Library is home to the African-American Collection that contains more than 9,000 books dealing with African-American experiences locally and around the world. *2300 E. Yesler Way (at 23rd Ave.), Central District, 206/684–4704. www.spl.org. Mon.–Thurs. 10–9, Fri. 11:30–6, Sat. 10–6, Sun. 1–5.*

5 *h-8*

SUZZALLO LIBRARY AT THE UNIVERSITY OF WASHINGTON

One of North America's premier research libraries—particularly in the areas of oceanography and Eastern European, East Asian, and Scandinavian studies—is also a spectacular example of Gothic architecture. Some 35 mi of book-filled shelves are housed in this building, which is the heart of the school's massive library system. It and the other 22 campus branches have more than 6 million catalogued volumes with an equal number of microform materials. You can use the library's resources, but you must have a UW library card to check materials out. If you're not a student but want a card, simply join the Friends of the University of Washington Libraries ($25 annually). *Center of UW campus (near Red Sq.), University District, 206/543–0242, www. lib.washington.edu/Suzzallo. Mon.–Thurs. 7:30 AM–midnight, Fri. 7:30–6, Sat. 9–5, Sun. noon–midnight.*

10 *g-4*

WASHINGTON TALKING BOOK & BRAILLE LIBRARY

A variety of books in formats suitable for visually impaired and physically challenged readers can be found at this branch of the Seattle Public Library system. In addition to Braille and large-type books, the library houses books and magazines on cassette. Special cassette and record players needed to play these materials are free to registered users. *2021 9th Ave. (at Lenora St.), Downtown, 206/615–0400, www.spl.org. Weekdays 8:30–5, Sat. 9–1.*

PLACES OF WORSHIP

Seattle's churches are steeped in the city's pioneer history. Most houses of worship are Christian—particularly Lutheran—and largely homogenous. Pews are often filled by folks whose ancestors were from Scandinavia or elsewhere in Europe. Still, the city also has a significant Jewish population as well as growing Hindu and Muslim communities. The city's newest mosque was built in 2001.

9 *d-7*

BEACON HILL FIRST BAPTIST CHURCH

At first glance this church looks more like a home than a place of worship, and perhaps that was architect Ellsworth Storey's intention. He designed it in 1910, opting for a Tudor style over traditional Gothic and Romanesque styles.

Although the structure has been modified over the years (its wooden shingles were replaced with asphalt shakes), Storey's adventuresome architecture won the church historical recognition by the Seattle City Council in 1981. Call for information on services. *1607 S. Forest St. (at 16th St.), Central District, 206/324–3350.*

11 *c-7*

CHAPEL OF ST. IGNATIUS

Stephen Holl's bold architecture marries spirituality with design at this recently built Roman Catholic church, which draws the majority of its parish from Seattle University and the surrounding Capitol Hill neighborhood. Thinking in terms of light and darkness, Holl designed the church as these elements correspond to Catholic ideas of consolation and desolation, positioning colored windows and lenses to affect sunlight as it reflects throughout the church during the day. It's open daily, with services Monday through Saturday at 12:05 PM and Sunday at 11 AM and 9 PM. *900 Broadway Ave. (between Madison and Marion Sts.), Capitol Hill. 206/296–6000, www.seattleu.edu/chapel.*

9 *d-2*

FIRST AFRICAN METHODIST EPISCOPAL CHURCH

AME has served as the African-American community's political and social nexus since 1886. Its spacious basement hall is the site of community discussions and lectures by a variety of intellectuals, authors, and artists throughout the year. The gospel choir is one of the city's best. Sunday services are held at 8 AM and 11 AM. *522 14th Ave. SW (between E. Mercer and E. Republican Sts.), Central District, 206/324–3664 or 206/324–3665.*

11 *a-5*

FIRST COVENANT CHURCH

The First Covenant congregation worships in a dome-covered, circular sanctuary with a central pulpit that symbolizes the centrality of God's word. Heavy oak and intricate stained-glass doors separate the entryway from the interior. Although the church was founded in 1889 by a group of Lutheran Swedish immigrants known as the Mission Friends, today its followers reflect the city's greater diversity. The structure itself has also changed: the church

moved to its current location in 1901, and the building's design was updated in the 1960s. Today it's a Pike Pine Corridor landmark whose gleaming golden cupola can be seen for blocks away. Office hours are weekdays 9 to 1; Sunday morning services are at 11. *400 E. Pike St. (at Bellevue Ave.), Capitol Hill. 206/322–7411, www.seafirstcov.org/sfcc/index.html.*

9 *b-2*

FIRST UNITED METHODIST CHURCH

The Methodist congregation's first service was held in 1853 in a log cabin and attended by the entire city—that is, 30 people. Two years later the Little White Church was officially established at Second Avenue and Columbia Street. From there the congregation that would become First United Methodist grew, and the humble building was ennobled by spires and arches that survived 1889's fire, which leveled most of the city. The church was moved to what is now the heart of Seattle's Downtown to accommodate the congregation's growing numbers—topping 1,000 at the turn of the century. The majestic baroque architecture is gone, replaced by a simpler, more utilitarian design. Even so, you can still experience services in the historic sanctuary, built in 1908. Its doors are open weekdays from 9 to noon and 1 to 4. Sunday morning services are held at 9 and 11. *811 5th Ave. (between Columbia and Marion Sts.), Downtown, 206/622–7278, www.firstchurchseattle.org.*

11 *g-5*

MOUNT ZION BAPTIST CHURCH

Home to the state's largest African-American congregation, this is where gospel-music fans come to catch the spirit through moving sermons and rousing song. The church's first gatherings began in 1890; back then its prayer meetings were held in people's houses and in a store. The church was incorporated in 1903, and after a number of moves, settled in its current simple but sturdy brick building. The interior design dates from 1975, when it was remodeled. Eighteen stained-glass windows, each with an original design that honors a key African-American figure, glow within the sanctuary. James Washington's sculpture *The Oracle of Truth*, a gray boulder carved with the image of a lamb, greets you at the entrance. Flanked by three flat stones, the work is dedicated to children struggling to find truth, and sits beneath a bell tower built in memory of influential African-American businessman Russell Gideon, who died in 1985. Services are held Sunday at 7:45 AM and 10:45 AM. *1634 19th Ave. (at E. Madison St.), Central District, 206/322–6500.*

12 *h-3*

SEATTLE BETSUIN BUDDHIST TEMPLE

Peaceful and majestic, this Jodo Shinshu temple was elevated to Betsuin status in 1954, acknowledged by the mother temple in Kyoto, Japan. The building was dedicated in 1941, but the temple's history dates from November 15, 1901, when Reverend Kakuryo Nishijima performed the Pacific Northwest's first Jodo Shinshu Buddhist service. The U.S. Maritime Commission took over the building during World War II; on August 4, 1946 it once again became a house of worship. It's one of a handful of U.S. temples that follows the dictates of a full temple compound, complete with the large ceremonial bell called a *bonsho,* a columbarium, and an auditorium. You're welcome to attend the 10 AM Sunday service, but call ahead or visit the Web site to find out about temple etiquette. *1427 S. Main St. (between 14th Ave. and 16th Ave.), International District, 206/329–0800, www. seattlebetsuin.com.*

11 *c-6*

SEATTLE FIRST BAPTIST CHURCH

On the cusp of Capitol Hill and First Hill, this Gothic church's green spire rises above the trees and rooftops. The congregation dates from 1869; the church itself was built in 1912. The 2001 earthquake damaged its stone facade (note the cracked parapets, which now serve as sculptures in flower beds out front). First Baptist prides itself in being one of the nation's most open and inviting congregations, and people of all races and sexual orientations joyfully worship here each Sunday. The office is open weekdays from 8:30 to 4 and on Sunday from 9 to 12:30; visitors are encouraged to call ahead. *1111 Harvard Ave. (at Spring St.), First Hill, 206/325–6051, www.seattlefirstbaptist.org.*

9 *c-1*

ST. JAMES CATHEDRAL

On Sunday you can hear the bells of St. James ringing throughout Capitol Hill.

The stirring claxon befits the Catholic cathedral's majesty, as do the voices of the Cathedral Choir or those of the Children's Schola Cantorum that often echo through its stone walls. Renovations in 1994 improved the acoustics and restored many of the aging interior details. Everything about the elaborate sanctuary—from its high carved ceilings to its golden holy-water basin—seem designed to excite the eyes and soothe the soul. The newest addition is a pair of bronze ceremonial doors that commemorate the Great Jubilee Year (2000) and which opened for the first time before midnight mass on Christmas Eve 1999. Masses are held on weekdays and Saturdays at 8:15 AM and 12:10 PM and on Sundays at 8:10 AM, noon, and 5:30 PM. Office hours are weekdays from 9 to 5; tours are available by appointment. *804 9th Ave. (between Marion and Columbia Sts.), Downtown, 206/622–3559, www. stjames-cathedral.org.*

8 *c-5*

ST. MARK'S EPISCOPAL CATHEDRAL

Regardless of their creed or denomination, many Seattleites are touched by St. Mark's at one time or another. Its services are broadcast each Sunday evening at 9:30 on KING FM 98.1, frequent classical music performances and dances are held within its sturdy walls, and the choir's annual performance of Handel's "Messiah" is a local holiday tradition. Music is as integral to the Episcopal church's identity as its tolerant philosophy, evident in its election of the Reverend Robert Vincent Taylor as dean, the first openly gay priest to lead an Episcopalian cathedral. Construction on the classical church began in the late 1920s but was delayed by the Great Depression. It was dedicated in 1931 and remained the same until 1997, when the west wall and rose window were renovated. Sunday services are at 8, 9, and 11 AM, and 7 and 9:30 PM. *1245 10th Ave. E (at Galer St.), Capitol Hill. 206/323–0300 or 206/323–1040 for concert information and tickets.*

8 *c-8*

TEMPLE DE HIRSCH SINAI

Age and seismic activity demanded that this landmark synagogue's original 1908 structure be either refurbished or destroyed; the congregation chose the latter in 1992. Today the stairway and classical columns at the entrance are all that's left of the original building. But the generous spirit of its namesake, Baron Moritz de Hirsch, is very much alive. The airy sanctuary of the replacement structure is reserved for the synagogue's reform services, but local groups book the Jaffe Room for fundraisers, concerts, and dances. The Chicken Soup Brigade, a local AIDS awareness organization, hosts its monthly bingo night here. These kitschy, pop culture–theme evenings are hosted by a drag performer, and are the temple's most popular social event. *1511 Pike St. (at 15th Ave.), Capitol Hill, 206/ 323–8486, www.tdhs-nw.org.*

SCIENCE MUSEUMS & OBSERVATORIES

Seattle isn't exactly over-run with science museums and observatories, but those that the city does have are well worth the visit—and lots of fun for both kids and adults.

10 c-3
PACIFIC SCIENCE CENTER
This romper-room masquerading as a science center contains 6 acres of hands-on exhibits—making it an excellent stop for children and adults. In the Body Works area, large, brightly colored machines amusingly analyze human physiology. In the Tech Zone, you can challenge a robot to a game of tic-tac-toe or play virtual-reality soccer. The Tropical Butterfly House (with hundreds of free-flying lepidopterans) is as mystical as the dinosaur exhibit is popular. IMAX screenings and laser light shows take place daily. The outdoor plaza, with fountains and concrete towers, dates from the 1962 World's Fair. *200 2nd Ave. N (at W. Denny Way), Queen Anne, 206/ 443–2001, www.pacsci.org. $8 adults, $5.50 senior citizens and children 3–13, free children under 3; IMAX and laser shows extra. Memorial Day–Labor Day, daily 10–6; early September–late May, weekdays 10–5, weekends 10–6.*

5 h-6
UNIVERSITY OF WASHINGTON CAMPUS OBSERVATORY
One of the first buildings on the UW campus contains one of the west's oldest working refractive telescopes. This antique isn't terribly large (a mere 6″ diameter), but it gives you a good look

at the moon, various planets, and other astral objects. No scientific research is performed here. The observatory is on the north end of the campus, surrounded by dense shrubbery. At press time, it was closed for renovations. When it's open, observation times vary depending on the season; admission is consistently free. Call for details. *Corner of NE 45th St. and 17th Ave. NE (UW campus), University District, 206/543– 0126, www.astro.washington.edu/dept/ campusobservatory.html. Free.*

STATUES, MURALS, MONUMENTS & PUBLIC ART

Look up, look down and you'll find art in the sidewalks, on buildings, hanging from lightposts—even the bus shelters are covered with colors worth admiring. There isn't nearly enough space to list everything worth cooing at along Seattle's streets. Instead, choose from this sample of entertaining public works.

3 b-7
ALKI MONUMENT
The marker showing where the Denny Party landed in 1851 was donated to the city in 1905 by Lenora Denny, Arthur Denny's daughter. Seattle's version of Plymouth Rock has a piece of the actual pilgrim landmark in its base. *Corner of Alki Ave. SW and 63rd Ave. SW, West Seattle.*

8 c-5
BLACK SUN
The sculpture in front of the Seattle Asian Art Museum frames the Space Needle from a right angle. It's speculated that this sculpture was the inspiration for the rock band Soundgarden's song "Black Hole Sun." *1400 E. Prospect St. (Volunteer Park), Capitol Hill.*

11 c-3
BROADWAY STEPS
Artist Jack Mackie inlaid seven sets of bronze dancing feet into the sidewalk along Broadway, each demonstrating the steps for the tango, the waltz, the foxtrot, the bus stop, and others. Look closely at the steps near Roy Street to see coffee beans in the concrete, a nod to the region's love affair with java. *Broadway Ave. E (between Pine and Roy Sts.), Capitol Hill.*

10 *d-3*

CHIEF SEATTLE

Stoically watching the business and revelry in Seattle Center, a statue of Chief Seattle, of the Duwamish tribe, stands with his right arm raised in welcome. Seattle was among the first Native Americans to have contact with the white explorers who came to the region. He was viewed as a great leader and peacemaker by his fellow tribesmen and as a friendly contact by the white settlers. The sculpture was created by local artist James Wehn in 1912 and dedicated by the chief's great-great granddaughter, Myrtle Loughery, on Founder's Day, November 13, 1912. After withstanding decades of rain and handling the statue was restored in 1975. *Intersection of 5th Ave., Denny Way, and Cedar St., near southeast corner of Seattle Center, Queen Anne.*

11 *g-1*

CITY IN THE SKY MURAL

If you visit the popular Kingfish Café, you can still see the 3-D mural designed by Don Barrie, which has succumbed to the elements since its creation in 1974. Based on a Hopi Indian legend about evolution, the 70- × 30-ft painting is a sweeping, dreamlike landscape of waves, green shores, and blue sky. You can sit and contemplate the mural on antique daybeds left outside by restaurant owners to handle the dining room's overflow. A foundation is seeking to restore the mural. *606 19th Ave. E (at Mercer St.), Central District.*

9 *g-1*

CRESPINEL MARTIN LUTHER KING, JR., MURAL

Heading west on Cherry Street in the Central District, you'll see a 17-ft-tall mural of Dr. Martin Luther King, Jr., gazing off in the distance thoughtfully. Pacific Northwest artist James Crespinel painted the mural in the summer of 1995 on the eastern face of the building that houses Catfish Corner, a soul food takeout place. *Corner of Martin Luther King Jr. Blvd. and Cherry St., Central District.*

7 *g-1*

FREMONT TROLL

Beneath the Aurora Bridge lurks a gigantic bearded troll with a gleaming eye and a pouty lip. Eighteen ft tall and not so handsome, the Fremont Troll clutches a Volkswagen Beetle in his massive left hand, and, in case you're wondering, the car is real. But the gray giant is far from a threat. Rather, he watches over the quirky Fremont neighborhood and allows people to crawl up on his shoulders for the obligatory photo, sometimes even getting a few "nose pickers" here and there. The troll appeared in 1991, commissioned by the Fremont Arts Council. The statue only looks frightening around Halloween, where he presides over a wild parade, is bedecked with a bicycle-wheel rim as a nose ring, and gets a giant spider pal to crawl on his shoulder. *N. 36th St. (under Aurora Bridge), Fremont.*

10 *f-8*

HAMMERING MAN

Jonathan Borofsky's 48-ft-tall, 26,400-pound, black metal sculpture has a counterpart almost twice its size in Frankfurt, Germany, as well as brethren in Los Angeles, Dallas, and Miami. The Seattle *Hammering Man* lords over the entrance to the Seattle Art Museum, his head bowed and motorized left arm wielding hammer up and down four times each minute. Borofsky's intent was to remind the office-bound people scurrying past the sculpture's feet of the city's vastly underappreciated blue-collar workers. At least once prankster Seattleites played a trick by attaching a ball and chain to one of his feet. *Corner of 1st Ave. and University St., Downtown.*

11 *c-5*

JIMI HENDRIX

Countercultural Capitol Hill wouldn't be complete without some dedication to the city's most worshiped rock-and-roll icon. His bronze effigy holds a guitar, of course, and from the looks of things he hasn't just kissed the sky, he's made out with it. Buckled at the knees with his hand up, head thrown back, and eyes squeezed shut, Seattle's legendary son is frozen in the midst of what seems a particularly ear-splitting riff at the south end of Broadway. Frequently someone will leave an offering—a flower, a cigarette, or even a joint—in his outstretched fingers. *Broadway Ave. (near Pine St.), Capitol Hill.*

5 *c-8*

LENIN

When Russian counterrevolutionaries knocked over a 7-ton statue of Lenin in 1989, they couldn't have known it would end up in Seattle's Fremont district. A

Seattle-area man named Lewis Carpenter toted the striding bronze Red from Slovakia to Seattle in 1989, and when he died in 1994, the statue made its way to the Fremont Sunday flea market. Soon he was ousted from this den of capitalism, and today he sits in front of a burrito joint on North 36th Street. Sometimes found holding cigarettes, burritos, or other goods, he can be your personal comrade for the low price of 150,000 (dollars, not rubles). *N. 36th St. (between Fremont and Evanston Aves.), Fremont.*

8 a-6
LINCOLN TOE TRUCK

The mascot of what was formerly Seattle's most beloved—or hated, if you're the one impounded—tow-truck company, Lincoln Towing, was created in 1979. It consists of a signature pink tow truck with five pink toes atop its cab. The big toe's massive nail greets commuters who take Exit 167 off I–5. The owners of Lincoln Towing have retired, and the land under the Toe Truck has since been sold, but the landmark remains for the time being. *Corner of Fairview Ave. N and Mercer St. (near entrance to I–5), Lake Union.*

10 g-7
METRO TRANSPORTATION TUNNEL

Bus shelters around the city are adorned with paintings to ease the boredom of waiting, but no work is more colorful than the mile-long bus tunnel that runs underground between the Convention Center (at Terry Avenue and Pine Street) and the International District. Among a variety of artworks near the route's six stations are three 35-ft-long city-sanctioned murals—designed and installed by local artists Fay Jones, Gene Gentry McMahon, and Roger Shimomura—that provide abstract, cartoonish interpretations of Downtown landmarks and street scenes in glorious palettes. And it's hard to miss the sculptures at the stops along the way. A favorite is the awe-inspiring *Temple of Music*, created by Erin Shie Palmer, which tantalizes concertgoers bound for Benaroya Hall from the University Street Station. Best of all, you don't have to pay to see these works, since the tunnel falls within the city's "ride free zone." Get off the bus to look at the art at all the stops, and zoom by the murals as much as you like. *Entrances at 9th Ave. and Pine St., Westlake Center Mall, Third Ave. between Union St. and Seneca St., Third Ave. between Jefferson St. and Yesler Way, and at 5th Ave. S and S. Jackson St., Downtown.*

12 b-2
PIONEER SQUARE PARK

Compared with Seattle's other parks, this swatch of land at the heart of Pioneer Square's entertainment strip is minuscule, but it's home to three well-known landmarks. The 50-ft-tall Tlingit Totem Pole is a replica of Puget Sound's first landmark, which was taken from an Alaskan village by a Seattle businessman in 1889. An iron pergola that served as a shelter for an underground rest room had been in the park since 1909, but a car accident recently felled it; at press time it was being restored. The park's stalwart is a bust of Chief Seattle, gazing at the hundred-fold residents who pass by each day. *100 Yesler Way (at Post Ave.), Pioneer Square.*

5 g-8
SADAKO PEACE PARK

In 1990, when Nobel Peace Prize–nominee Dr. Floyd Schmoe was 93 years old, he and a group of volunteers built this park from a pile of garbage, wrecked cars, and brush. The space, bought by Schmoe with money won from receiving the Hiroshima Peace Prize, commemorates the 45th anniversary of that city's bombing, and it has become a symbol of peace and understanding. Its centerpiece is a bronze statue of Sadako Sasaki, a young girl who survived the bombing, only to die of radiation sickness at age 12. Chains of origami paper cranes—brought as peace offerings—often hang around the statue's neck or from her hand. *Bordered by NE 40th St., Eastlake Ave., and 9th Ave. NE, University District.*

12 c-3
SEATTLE FALLEN FIREFIGHTERS MEMORIAL

Lest you forget that a massive fire destroyed most of Seattle more than a century ago, this memorial stands in the heart of Occidental Park, surrounded by art galleries, Persian carpet shops, and antiques stores. Four bronze figures in full emergency gear stand—as if fighting a four-alarm blaze—amid slabs of fallen stone. The statues are so lifelike that you'll occasionally see people who aren't watching where they're going mutter "pardon me" to one of the figures. *S.*

Jackson St. (between 1st and 3rd Sts.), Pioneer Square.

4 g-7
SEATTLE FISHERMEN'S MEMORIAL

Atop a white stone pedestal a fisherman is captured in bronze as he struggles with a catch, eternally battling the sea. Dedicated in 1988, the memorial honors the many local men and women who have lost their lives. More than 500 names are inscribed on a bronze plaque at the statue's base, and sadly new names are added every year at a memorial service on the first Sunday in May. In the busy Seattle Fishermen's Terminal, the statue overlooks Salmon Bay and provides a serene place to contemplate a sunset. *3919 18th Ave. W (at Emerson Pl.), Ballard.*

6 h-3
SOUND GARDEN

The most famous of Warren Magnuson Park's beachside artworks is a series of aluminum tubes of different lengths, mounted to catch the wind and create flutelike music. (And, yes, Seattle's famous band named itself after this sculpture.) On a windy day it fills the air with enchanting sounds that are audible from quite a distance. Early morning walkers and joggers often rest on one of the nearby whale-shape benches to watch sunrises over Lake Washington—a spectacle that's especially lovely when accompanied by this gentle soundtrack. *Sand Point Way NE (at 65th St.), Wallingford.*

3 a-8
STATUE OF LIBERTY ON ALKI BEACH

One of 195 Lady Liberty replicas around the country, this one was erected by Boy Scouts in 1952 as part of their national "Strengthening the Arm of Liberty" campaign. The so-called Miss Liberty (or Little Liberty) is a popular meeting point for beachfront picnics and dates. *Alki Point (near 2700 block of Alki Ave. SW), West Seattle.*

7 g-1
WAITING FOR THE INTERURBAN

Fremont's signature statue frequently fools visitors who drive by and wonder why this crowd looks so still and happy. In reality it's a cast aluminum sculpture of five figures, one of whom is holding a small child. Residents enjoy dressing and ornamenting the figures for holidays, birthdays, homecomings—just about any joyful occasion. Look closely at the dog circling the legs of one figure and you'll see it wears the face of a bearded, ornery-looking man. As the story goes, the one-time honorary mayor of Fremont, Armen Stepanian, was upset with Richard Beyer for choosing himself as the artist to create the statue when no one else applied to the Fremont Arts Council for the job. Beyer had the final word in the brouhaha by putting Stepanian's face on the canine. *N. 34th St. (just over Fremont Bridge at Fremont Ave.), Fremont.*

3 c-8
WEST SEATTLE JUNCTION

On a walk through West Seattle's business district, you'll come across works of art depicting scenes from local history. A few play tricks with perspective, reminiscent of the paintings Wile E. Coyote used in his attempts to trick the Roadrunner. *The Junction* is a perfect example: If not for the row of neatly trimmed laurel bushes just beneath the wall upon which it's painted, you might be tempted to walk right into the picture's 1918 street scene, painted from the perspective of a streetcar. Another mural is taken from a postcard of 1920s Alki. The most colorful, however, is the *The Hi-Yu Parade*, with its rendition of an award-winning *Wizard of Oz*–theme float reminding locals of a 1973 summer celebration. *Along California Ave. SW and Fauntleroy Way SW (between 44th and 47th Aves.), West Seattle, www.westseattle.com/site/murals.*

VIEWPOINTS

The skyline, mountains on all sides, a glittering Puget Sound . . . there's no shortage of feasts for the eyes in the city. During the cloudiest seasons, Emerald City residents console themselves with the knowledge that gorgeous views will return with the sunshine. Parks on hilltops, skyscraper lounges, and even well-situated workplace windows are lookouts that can make the most jaded person stop short and sigh, momentarily transfixed. Even the worst of days dissolve into memory at the merest sight on our cityscape, especially from the vantage points listed here.

At press time the observation deck at the Bank of America Building was closed for reasons associated with September 11, 2001, attacks on the World Trade Center. You might want to call ahead to confirm that such public facilities are open before heading out.

3 *a-7*

ALKI BEACH

A prime spot for picnics, sunbathing, or Frisbee games, Alki Beach is crowded on hot summer days with sunbathers and swimmers brave enough to test the chilly waters. You can see across the Puget Sound from this sandy strip, and views include the Olympic Mountains, the city skyline, and the interesting people around you. *1100 Alki Ave. SW, West Seattle, 206/684–4075.*

12 *d-1*

BANK OF AMERICA BUILDING (COLUMBIA TOWER) OBSERVATION DECK

The tallest building west of the Mississippi houses fast-paced white-collar workers, but you can kick back in one of the 73rd-floor observation deck's leather chairs. Sunny days afford views of the sound and Mt. Rainier—in fact, you can see all the way to Tacoma. *701 5th Ave. (at Cherry St.), Downtown, 206/386–5151, www.columbia-tower.com. $5 adults, $3 senior citizens and kids 12 and under. Weekdays 8:30–4:30.*

13 *g-6*

CASCADE VIEW PARK

Sometimes you can see this park's most beloved residents, a pair of red-tail hawks. Most visitors bring a picnic or a basketball or baseball for the courts or the diamond, playing and eating with an unobstructed eastern backdrop of the Cascade Mountains. *16202 NE 40th St. (at Dayton Ave.), Redmond.*

5 *f-8*

GASWORKS PARK

Stake out a space here early to see the Fourth of July fireworks. The site of working coal gasification plant until 1956, the spot was transformed into a park in 1975. Today kids dream of climbing all over the leftover pipes and workings. Put thoughts of tetanus out of your head and take a jaunt up the 60-ft hill, where you can read the park's sundial or take in glittering views of the skyline and Lake Union. It recently benefited from a full-scale clean up, but they left some of the pipes and industrial debris as artful remembrances. *3300 Meridian Ave. N (at Northlake Way), Wallingford.*

8 *c-4*

LOUISA BOREN LOOKOUT

Capitol Hill natives are loathe to tell people about this little park across from Lakeview Cemetery. Sit on the bench under the tree at the park's center, and gaze upon a carpet of treetops in Interlake Park below. Unobstructed views of Lake Washington and the U–District are available rain or shine, but on the clearest days the Cascade Mountains complete the picture. This is a great place to enjoy a summer sunrise or fall's foliage. To the right of the viewpoint is a path winding down to Interlaken Park, a popular route for runners looking for a hard workout. *1555 15th Ave. E (at Garfield St.), Capitol Hill.*

10 *c-3*

SPACE NEEDLE

Seattle's Jetsons-style landmark affords 360° city views. A 43-second elevator ride takes you to the observation deck, which fills with golden hues when the sun is setting. Queen Anne Hill looks beautiful from here, as does the Cascade Range when the skies are cloud free. *Seattle Center, 5th Ave. (at Broad St.), Queen Anne, 206/443–2111, www.spaceneedle. com. $11 adults, $9 senior citizens and children 11–17, $5 children 5–10, free for children under 5. Sun.–Thurs. 10 AM–11 PM, Fri.–Sat. 10 AM–midnight.*

8 *c-5*

VOLUNTEER PARK WATER TOWER

Seattle's finest free view resembles an Arthurian castle until you get up close. Then the modern metal steps bring you back to reality. Climb the curved staircase to the top of the 75-ft-tall structure, and your workout will be rewarded by 360° views of the city through openings in a large room. This place is a popular one for dates around prom season and for lovers at any time of the year, so be prepared for a little P.D.A. *15th Ave. E (near Prospect St.), Capitol Hill.*

chapter 5

ARTS, ENTERTAINMENT & NIGHTLIFE

Long before it was even a blip on the national arts scene, Seattle was carefully tending its arts community. Twenty-five years ago, a large and well-funded theater scene began developing, the Seattle International Film Festival was founded, and rock musicians were often seen carting their equipment between the city's many lively clubs. So when the high-tech boom of the 1990s drew the eyes of the nation to the Pacific Northwest, Seattle was ready for the spotlight. Its dynamic theater scene is now a highly regarded proving ground for Broadway, the film festival draws the finest in world cinema to the city each spring, and you can't get from Belltown to Capitol Hill without hearing rock or dance music echoing in the streets. From classical music in Downtown's state-of-the-art Benaroya Hall to outdoor cinema screenings in Fremont, there is no end to the city's entertainment options. Families enjoy the Seattle Children's Theatre and any of several summertime folk art and music festivals. Intrepid club crawlers are well rewarded within the city's many notable music and dance venues. Add a pint of traditional ale or a stem of Washington wine to your evening to complete the taste of the Northwest.

performing arts

tickets

You can buy advance tickets to most events by mail, in person at the box office, or on-line and by phone (with a credit card). At box offices you generally won't be charged a service fee, but watch out for small fees tacked on when ordering tickets over the phone or on-line. Be sure to ask about refund and cancellation, as they vary.

There are many ways to go out on the cheap—just be sure to do your research and read the fine print. Season subscriptions and group rates are frequently discounted. Also, look into preview, pay-what-you-can, senior citizen, and student discount tickets. Such tickets are usually only sold one to a customer on the day of the show, and you may need an ID to buy them. Most theaters also offer cheap seats 10 minutes before show time, for those who feel lucky.

Ticketmaster (206/628–0888, www.ticketmaster.com) sells tickets to most arts, entertainment, and sports events in the Seattle area by phone or on-line. The three locations of Ticket/Ticket (Broadway Market, 401 Broadway E, 2nd floor [at E. Republican St.], Capitol Hill, 206/324–2744; Pike Place Information Booth, Pike Place Market [1st Ave. and Pike St.], Downtown, 206/682–7453 Ext. 226; Meydenbauer Center, 11100 NE 6th St. [corner of NE 6th and 112th Sts.], Bellevue, 206/325–6500) sell half-price tickets to many events on the day of the performance (or the previous day for a matinee). Sales are cash and in-person only. The Broadway location's hours are Tuesday through Saturday from noon to 7 and Sunday from noon to 6; the Pike Place and Bellevue hours are Tuesday to Saturday from noon to 6 (for Monday performances, buy tickets on the previous Sunday). The independent company www.ticketweb.com sells local event tickets on the Web.

CONCERT HALLS & VENUES

Many places host myriad arts events in the Seattle area. The newer venues have incorporated state-of-the-art acoustical engineering and sound, so they have a leg up on the competition. The older, more classical halls, while beautifully grand in style, have suffered some from wear, tear, and attempts to fit new technology into old buildings not designed to accommodate it.

10 *g-8*

BENAROYA HALL

It's so state-of-the-art that every one of Benaroya's 2,500 main hall seats delivers acoustical purity. This makes seeing the Seattle Symphony, which is based here, a requisite for residents. The four-story lobby has a curved glass facade making intermission just as impressive as many of the big name performers. *200 University St. (at 2nd Ave.), Downtown, 206/215–4800.*

11 *c-5*

BROADWAY PERFORMANCE HALL

Saved from destruction by the Seattle Central Community College, this hall is now a beautiful monument to old Seattle. It's small, but it has outstanding acoustics as well as great sight lines, thanks to a steep descent toward the stage. The events calendar features many types of performances: the Seattle Asian Film Festival one week, poetry or dance the next, and then, perhaps, a touring company of circus jugglers. *1625 Broadway Ave. (at E. Pine St.), Capitol Hill, 206/325–3113.*

8 *b-6*

CORNISH COLLEGE OF THE ARTS

Cornish's Ned Skinner Theater serves as headquarters for distinguished jazz, dance, and other groups. Its superior student productions spotlight emerging talent. *710 E. Roy St. (at E. Boylston), Capitol Hill, 206/323–1400.*

10 *h-7*

FIFTH AVENUE THEATER

Long struggling to survive, this chinoiserie-style landmark (circa 1926) is currently the home of the Fifth Avenue Musical Theater Company. When the company is on hiatus, the theater hosts traveling musical and theatrical performances. *1308 5th Ave. (at University St.), Downtown, 206/625–1900.*

13 *b-4*

KIRKLAND PERFORMANCE CENTER

Bringing an interesting array of experiential performance art to the stage is this center's mission. Many of its productions are multicultural music, dance, or theater events, some of which involve mixed media. *350 Kirkland Ave. (in Peter Kirk Park), Kirkland, 425/893–9900.*

10 *f-5*

KING CAT THEATER

Here you've got a large concert venue that books national folk, blues, and alternative rock acts. A former cinema, it affords great views from every seat, and the all-ages policy makes it possible for families to enjoy a concert together. *2130 6th Ave. (at Blanchard St.), Downtown, 206/269–7444.*

13 *c-4*

MEYDENBAUER CENTER

State-of-the-art equipment and excellent acoustics are the hallmarks of this multifaceted, community-based facility. It hosts performances by children's theater troupes, the Ballet Bellevue, the Bellevue Civic Theater, and many other groups. *11100 NE 6th St. (at 112th Ave. NE), Bellevue, 425/637–1020.*

10 *e-6*

MOORE THEATER

Its beauty may have faded, but this grande dame still plays hostess to a variety of events. A quick peek at the prominent marquee clues you in to the audience of the moment—from jazz and instrumental enthusiasts to hard-rock and contemporary music fans. *1932 2nd Ave. (at Virginia St.), Downtown, 206/443–1744.*

10 *h-5*

PARAMOUNT THEATRE

A makeover has given the Paramount—once a grand music hall and movie palace—back its majesty. Its 2,800 comfortable seats are often filled by fans of big-name R&B, hip-hop, pop, and rock artists. Top comedians and dance troupes sometimes play here, too. *907 Pine St. (at 9th Ave.), Downtown, 206/682–1414.*

10 *d-7*

PIER 62 & 63 PARK

Tax dollars are put to good use here by bringing music to the community on parks department property. This glorious outdoor stage overlooking the bay is a great place to catch your favorite top-name acts, including many alternative music bands. If you're lucky enough to own a sailboat (or know someone who does), a show could very well be free. *200 Alaskan Way W (at Stewart St.), Waterfront, 206/281–8111.*

10 *c-2*

SEATTLE CENTER

This complex on the site of the 1962 World's Fair has several halls that present plays and operas as well as dance, music, and performance art productions. It's also home to Labor Day Weekend's Bumbershoot arts festival. *305 W. Harrison St. (at 3rd Ave. W), Queen Anne, 206/684–8582.*

DANCE

Seattle may not leap to mind as a hot spot for dance, but there are a few places where you can enjoy the art. And you don't have to limit yourself to an annual performance of *The Nutcracker,* either. A small number of venues ensures that each troupe finely tunes its seasons to accommodate a broad range of tastes, so there are many diverse and engaging new works. Renowned dance groups include the Emerald City on their tours as well; just be poised to pounce on tickets.

5 h-8

MEANY HALL FOR THE PERFORMING ARTS

This is the best known performance hall on the University of Washington (fondly known as U-Dub) campus, and rightly so. From September through May it hosts important national and international companies, with an emphasis on modern and jazz dance. This means that Meany showcases the brightest names in contemporary dance and choreography. *University of Washington, 15th Ave. NE (at 41st Ave. NE), University District, 206/685–2742.*

7 f-6

ON THE BOARDS

You'll often find nontraditional experimental performances here—think bold, controversial, and provocative. In addition to presenting contemporary dance productions, this company also stages plays, concerts, and multimedia events. The main subscription series runs from October through May, but there's something scheduled nearly every weekend year-round. *100 W. Roy St. (at 1st Ave. N), Queen Anne, 206/217–9888.*

10 c-1

PACIFIC NORTHWEST BALLET

Bringing both classical ballets and groundbreaking new works to the stage, this company and school is the heart of the city's dance scene. The Christmas-time production of *The Nutcracker,* with choreography by Kent Stowell and sets by Maurice Sendak, is a family tradition. *Opera House at Seattle Center, W. Mercer St. and 3rd Ave., Queen Anne, 206/441–2424.*

FILM

Although Seattle's multiplexes entice patrons with Surround Sound and food courts, a few smaller, kiosk-fronted theaters still evoke a bygone era. Most have attempted to match the comforts of the major chains with updated sound systems and revamped interiors. It's their traditional charm—combined with a tendency to support independent cinema—that keeps their seats full, though.

The strongest evidence of Seattle's passion for cinema is the wildly popular Seattle International Film Festival (206/324–9996) held each May and June. October's Gay & Lesbian Film Festival (206/323–4276) is an annual favorite. For show times and theater locations, call the *Seattle Times* InfoLine (206/464–2000 Ext. 3456).

10 e-5

CINERAMA

Billionaire Paul Allen scooped up and restored this theater, with its curved screen made for the 70-mm craze of the 1960s. With expert attention to detail, the design team went beyond mere renovation to create a showplace that is at once a retro pleasure and a state-of-the-art movie palace. *2100 4th Ave. (at Lenora St.), Downtown, 206/441–3080.*

11 c-5

EGYPTIAN THEATER

This art deco–style former Masonic Temple now screens first-run films and is the prime venue of Seattle's International Film Festival. Lines around the block often greet the ticketless, so come early, or plan to buy a ticket for a later show. Delicious treats and espressos are sold in the theater's café. *801 E. Pine St. (at Broadway Ave.), Capitol Hill, 206/323–4978.*

5 b-8

FREMONT OUTDOOR CINEMA

Believe it or not this "theater" consists of a cinderblock wall, a parking lot, and a projector set up on scaffolding. Throngs of young people and families drag their blankets, bean bags, or even couches out here to enjoy popular movies or cult classics under the stars. *U-Park Lot, 600 N. 34th St. (at N. Phinney Ave.), Fremont, 206/781–4230.*

5 *g-6*

GRAND ILLUSION CINEMA

In the 1930s this was simply a screening room. Today, its lovingly planned film schedule, knowledgeable staff, and coffee bar make it an outstanding home for fans of independent flicks, art films, and espresso. *1403 NE 50th St. (at University Way NE), University District, 206/523–3935.*

5 *e-7*

GUILD ON 45TH

One of the Guild's two theaters often features a major studio release while the other plays a fringe film. Throughout, the high-back seats are comfortably plush. In the smaller theater, raked rows allow screen views without the silhouette of the head in front of you. There's even a crying room for, well, criers. *2115 N. 45th St. (at Meridian Ave. N), Wallingford, 206/633–3353.*

11 *c-1*

HARVARD EXIT

A first-run and art-film house, the Harvard Exit is in the former home of the Women's Century Club, hence the quaint, antiques-filled lobby. It's small and somewhat hard to find, but once you get here, you'll feel right at home, particularly if you indulge in some spiced tea and one of a few modest snacks. *807 E. Roy St. (at Broadway Ave.), Capitol Hill, 206/323–8986.*

11 *f-8*

LITTLE THEATER

Film buffs truly love this intimate screening run by the same team that owns the Grand Illusion. It offers retrospectives and art-house programming. *608 19th Ave. E (at E. Cherry St.), Capitol Hill, 206/675–2055.*

4 *f-5*

MAJESTIC BAY

After being demolished and rebuilt, this theater emerged like a phoenix from ashes. It shows first-run films and has all the comforts of a modern cineplex as well as all the magic of an old-time movie house. *2044 NW Market St. (at 20th Ave. NW), Ballard, 206/781–2229.*

5 *g-7*

NEPTUNE

As its name suggests, this theater has a nautically themed interior and an epic

ambience. The seats aren't the most comfortable, and there's very little elbow room. Still, crowds of hip U-Dub scenesters stand in line to catch the latest buzz in filmdom. *1303 NE 45th St. (at University Way NE), University District, 206/633–5545.*

7 *f-6*

UPTOWN CINEMA

Its three screens and its comfortable seats allow the Uptown to cash in on artsy independents *and* Hollywood blockbusters. *511 Queen Anne Ave. N (at W. Republican St.), Queen Anne, 206/285–1022.*

5 *g-7*

VARSITY THEATER

The Varsity shows an eclectic roster of first-run, classic, and cult movies. As it's popular with students who need a break from studying, late night seating can be a problem. *4329 University Way NE (at NE 43rd St.), University District, 206/632–3131.*

OPERA & CLASSICAL MUSIC

The hype of the Northwest rock & roll scene has overshadowed top-notch opera and classical music offerings. However, a fiercely loyal local patronage supports the highly talented Seattle artists, who create and premier groundbreaking works here, in spite of, or because of, the lack of media attention.

13 *c-4*

BELLE ARTE CONCERTS

A season of five chamber music concerts is held in the Meydenbauer Center each year from September through April. Performances are always of the highest caliber, whether they feature local musicians or national acts. *11100 NE 6th Ave. (at 112th Ave. NE), Bellevue, 425/454–2410.*

4 *d-3*

MOSTLY NORDIC CHAMBER MUSIC SERIES

The Nordic Heritage Museum's calendar includes five separate concert series, each with music from one of the Scandinavian countries. *Nordic Heritage Museum, 3014 NW 67th St. (at 32nd Ave. NW), Ballard, 206/780–5707.*

10 g-8

NORTHWEST CHAMBER ORCHESTRA

For more than 20 years this chamber orchestra has presented classical works—from the baroque to the modern. Part of its seven-show season, which usually runs from September through May, is held on the grounds of the Seattle Asian Art Museum in Volunteer Park. *Benaroya Hall, 200 University St. (at 2nd Ave.), Downtown, 206/342–0445.*

10 g-8

SEATTLE MEN'S CHORUS

You don't have to love choral music to love this 180-member gay chorus—they're simply spectacular on so many levels. Outstanding traditional selections are a given, but the group always manages to knock the socks off the well-heeled set with one or two twists. *Benaroya Hall, 200 University St. (at 2nd Ave.), Downtown, 206/323–2992.*

10 c-1

SEATTLE OPERA

One of the nation's leading companies continues to sell out its innovative performances during an August through May season. Its lavish, adventurous productions have garnered international acclaim. *Seattle Center, Seattle Center Opera House, 3rd Ave. and Mercer St., Queen Anne, 206/215–4747.*

10 g-8

SEATTLE SYMPHONY

This exciting symphony has been nominated for 10 Grammy Awards. In addition to national and international acclaim, it has the superior acoustics and sight lines of Benaroya Hall, ensuring that your classical night out will be one to remember. *Benaroya Hall, 200 University St. (at 2nd Ave.), Downtown, 206/215–4747.*

THEATERS & THEATER COMPANIES

From classical to downright wacky, there's a stage for theater big and small—small, being the fringe theaters that pop-up, amaze and amuse, and quietly die off. Big, being the elaborate productions put on by well-funded and traditional companies. A good number of medium-size companies and theaters are distinguishable by their moderate budgets (and sometime big-name performers) that bridge the gap between experimental and conservative. Excellent theater coverage in local papers has helped to draw the long-standing patron and the newbie alike.

10 f-6

ANNEX THEATRE

Run by a collective of artists, the Annex's year-round productions run to the avant-garde, which often means funky, quirky, wacky—take your pick of these and similar adjectives. The musicals often spin new twists into classic themes, making them consistent favorites. *1916 4th Ave. (at Stewart St.), Downtown, 206/728–0933.*

10 h-7

A CONTEMPORARY THEATER

ACT launches new and exciting works by emerging dramatists, sometimes running three or four shows simultaneously to fill every nook and cranny of its space. *Late Night Catechism,* long running and well loved, has been dubbed the *Cats* of Seattle. *Eagles Auditorium, 700 Union St. (at 7th Ave.), Downtown, 206/292–7676.*

10 g-7

CRÊPE DE PARIS

Take a sophisticated French restaurant on the second floor of a mall, book side-splitting cabaret theater and musical revues into it, and, voilá—you have dinner theater à la Seattle. Both the food and the entertainment attract those of moderate means. *1333 5th Ave. (at University St.), Downtown, 206/623–4111.*

5 c-8

EMPTY SPACE THEATER

This theater keeps its promise to "bring audience and artist to common ground through uncommon works." Its 150 seats are packed tightly together—leaving very little empty space at all—and its maverick, out-there productions (November through June) keep audiences checking in to see what can possibly be next. *3509 Fremont Ave. N (at NW 34th St.), Fremont, 206/547–7500.*

10 g-7

FIFTH AVENUE MUSICAL THEATER COMPANY

The Fifth Avenue Theater's resident professional troupe mounts four lavish

musicals from October through May.
1308 5th Ave. (at University St.), Down-
town, 206/625–1900.

10 *c-1*

INTIMAN THEATER

The Intiman presents important classical and contemporary pieces from the world stage, adding just a dash of the experimental for spice. Extraordinary young talent freshens up tried-and-true classics. The season generally runs from May through November. *Playhouse at Seattle Center, 2nd Ave. N (at W. Mercer St.), Queen Anne, 206/269–1901.*

11 *d-5*

NEW CITY THEATER & ARTS CENTER

In keeping with the evolutionary vibe that prevails on Capitol Hill, this residence–turned–art house showcases experimental performances by local, national, and international artists. A small café—which also serves as a cabaret space and a gallery of all things provocative—rounds out the interior of what could pass for a farmhouse from the outside. *1634 11th Ave. E (at E. Pine St.), Capitol Hill, 206/323–6800.*

12 *e-2*

NIPPON KAN THEATER

This historic theater is an integral part of the Japanese-American arts experience. It has been renovated to allow for a mixture of cultural events, from meetings to concerts. *628 S. Washington Ave. St. (at 6th Ave. S), International District, 206/841–2521.*

11 *d-5*

NORTHWEST ACTORS STUDIO (STAGE 6)

Up some stairs in an office building you'll find the stage for one of the city's oldest independent acting schools. You'll uncover what's going on in the minds of local artists, as many of the performances here are in the works. *1100 E. Pike St. (at 11th Ave. E), Capitol Hill, 206/324–6328.*

2 *c-2*

NORTHWEST PUPPET CENTER

One of only a handful of the nation's full-time puppet centers is right here in Seattle. Shows based on folk tales are common, as are those about animals or holidays, and each performance clocks

in at under an hour. The theater is decidedly kid friendly with low bench seating, though most lounge on the floor. *9123 15th Ave. NE (at NE 92nd St.), University District, 206/523–2579.*

10 *g-2*

OPEN CIRCLE THEATER

A black-box performance space, the Open Circle features cutting-edge theater and one-person shows. Productions are usually, though not always, crazy, campy, and outrageous. *429 Boren Ave. N (at Terrace St.), Downtown, 206/382–4250.*

10 *c-2*

SEATTLE CHILDREN'S THEATRE

Top-notch productions of new works as well as adaptations from classic children's literature fill the six-play, September-to-June season. Kids sprawl out on the floor and climb over seats in theaters designed for tiny hands and roaming eyes. After the show, actors come out from behind the scenes to explain how things are done and answer questions, making this a wonderful place to introduce children to theater. *Charlotte Martin Theatre at Seattle Center, 2nd Ave. N (at W. Thomas St.), Queen Anne, 206/441–3322.*

10 *c-1*

SEATTLE REPERTORY THEATER

The Rep presents new and classic plays during its September through April season. Adoring fans flock to see new takes on choice classics as well as those fresh from the New York stage. *Bagley Wright Theater at Seattle Center, 155 W. Mercer St. (at 1st Ave. N), Queen Anne, 206/443–2222.*

5 *b-1*

TAPROOT THEATER

This quaint little theater puts on shows that convey Judeo-Christian values— plays rooted in themes of hope and faith. And it does so without biblical heavy handedness. *204 NW 85th St. (at Palatine Ave. N), Greenwood, 206/781–9705.*

12 *e-3*

THEATRE OFF JACKSON

Although the principal performances are from the Northwest Asian-American Theatre, other productions find their way to stage in this funky little taxi

garage–turned–theater. *409 7th Ave. S
(at S. Jackson St.), International District,
206/340–1049.*

14 *a-4*

YOUTH THEATER NW

Here's a theater of children, for children—no actor is over the age of 18. Its
six-play season is divided equally into
shows for children ages 3 to 8 and those
for the 9-and-up set. Performances of
new and classical works are scaled back
to no longer than 75 minutes. *8805 SE
40th St. (at 88th St. SE), Mercer Island,
206/232–4145.*

nightlife

Seattle's nightlife is as diverse and as it
is laid back. Whether you opt for a highbrow club, a hipster hangout, or a blue-
collar pub, there's no sense of
exclusivity. You won't be turned away
owing to your style of dress, whether it's
fancy, fanciful, or far from either. Some
of this is the result of state liquor laws,
which often force nightspot owners to
keep their minds and options open to
keep business booming.

BARS & TAVERNS

The Washington State Liquor Control
Board stipulates that places serving
hard alcohol must also serve food. As a
result, many taverns only serve beer and
wine, and a good number of bars offer a
food menu that just meets the basic
requirements they need to be granted a
full liquor license. Whether you want a
martini or a microbrew, be prepared to
order it before 2 AM, when bartenders
stop serving.

10 *f-7*

ALIBI ROOM

With a screenplay library of all things,
this is the film community's unofficial
watering hole. You've got music, eats,
drinks, and lots of the young and the hip
packed in elbow to elbow and wishing
they had come a little early for one of the
few tables with a window view. With any
luck, you might spy a local celebrity or
two. *85 Post Alley (at Pine St.), Downtown, 206/623–3180. Daily 11:30 AM–2 AM.*

4 *c-4*

ANTHONY'S HOMEPORT

Listen to the sound of the seals barking
and take in the spectacular views of
Shilshole Bay in the flagship of this
sophisticated northwest seafood chain.
The smartly dressed clientele is intent
on a festive night out. Although the
bartenders make delectable Bloody
Marys, all the drinks seem to taste
much better than elsewhere thanks to
the gentle sea breezes. *6135 Seaview
Ave. NW (at Shilshole Bay Marina), Ballard, 206/783–0780. Mon.–Sat. 11:30
AM–9:30, Sun. 10 AM–9:30 PM.*

10 *f-7*

ART BAR

High ceilings mean plenty of wall space
for the paintings and sculptures in this
long, narrow, bohemian space. The
crowd is as much a spectacle as the surrounding installations. Although the
ambience of offbeat Belltown is strong,
you'll find all manner of patrons here—
from art students to the after-work cocktail set. *1516 2nd Ave. (at Pike St.),
Downtown, 206/622–4344, Sun.–Thurs.
11 AM–midnight, Fri.–Sat. 3 PM–2 AM.*

11 *d-5*

BARCA

Spanish and Moroccan architectural
styles, a jewel-tone color scheme, velvet
upholstery, a mosaic-tile bar, and
wrought-iron details create a lavish setting. The beautiful people of Capitol Hill
mingle here, so the wise will put as
much effort into their "look" as the
place has into its. *1510 11th Ave. E (at
E. Pike St.), Capitol Hill, 206/325–8263.
Daily 4 PM–2 AM.*

9 *a-2*

BOOKSTORE BAR

Cigars and after-work martinis await the
finely dressed in this cozy, warmly lit bar
at the Alexis Hotel. *1009 1st Ave. (at
Madison St.), Downtown, 206/382–1506.
Sun.–Thurs. 11:30 AM–midnight, Fri.–Sat.
noon–midnight.*

5 *e-7*

THE BUNGALOW

A parlor atmosphere prevails at this
quiet little neighborhood hangout. Overstuffed chairs placed before a crackling
fire invite you to relax while your table is
prepared. It's easy to while away an
evening here, conversing and sipping

wine selected from some 60-plus varieties. *2412 N. 45th St. (Sunnyside Ave. N), Wallingford, 206/632–0254. Tues.–Thurs. 5–11, Fri.–Sat. 5–midnight.*

11 *b-5*
THE CAPITOL CLUB

The young, the beautiful, and the hip laze about amid colorful pillows on a velvet banquette that surrounds the room at this casual Moroccan-style spot—one that's really more Casbah than bar. The cocktails are often inventive, and there's a small but inviting balcony that overlooks the best Capitol Hill has to offer. *414 E. Pine St. (at Bellevue Ave. E), Capitol Hill, 206/325–2149. Daily 5 PM–2 AM.*

11 *b-5*
CHA CHA LOUNGE

Otherworldly red lights beckon you inside this lounge, which more than a few local rock-'n'-roll musicians consider a home away from home. The interior is over-the-top retro, and both staff and patrons are more likely to be pierced and tattooed than not. *504 E. Pine St. (at Bellevue Ave. E), Capitol Hill, 206/329–1101. Daily 4 PM–2 AM.*

8 *a-8*
CLOUD ROOM

A neighbor of the regal Paramount Theater, this Camlin Hotel hangout attracts a pre- and post-show drink crowd and has a bird's-eye view of Downtown. In warm weather, opt for a spot on the patio. *1619 9th Ave. (at Pine St.), Downtown, 206/682–0100. Tues.–Fri. 11:30 AM–1 AM, weekends 4 PM–1 AM.*

11 *c-5*
COMET TAVERN

Grunge devotees hunch around beer pitchers set on pock-marked wooden tables here, and a couple of old timers take their usual stools. The graffiti and posters make this seem a shrine to the local rock scene, where flyers and stickers touting new bands vie for precious wall space with those of the veterans. *922 E. Pike St. (at 10th Ave. E), Capitol Hill, 206/323–9853. Daily noon–2 AM.*

12 *c-2*
DOC MAYNARD'S

Favored by frat house rabble-rousers, Doc Maynard's is loud and raucous. The beer flows furiously on weekends when

hard rock bands take the stage. *610 1st Ave. (at Yesler Way), Downtown, 206/682–3705. Thurs.–Sat. 8 PM–2 AM.*

8 *b-3*
EASTLAKE ZOO

Harley Hogs are the only animals you'll find at the Eastlake Zoo, and they're an endangered species of late. Although it's a biker bar by reputation, nowadays the crowd is mostly locals who like cheap beer and pool. *2301 Eastlake Ave. E (at E. Lynn St.), Lake Union, 206/329–3277. Daily 11 AM–2 AM.*

11 *a-7*
FIRESIDE ROOM

At the Sorrento Hotel's classy lobby lounge, you can collapse into a comfy wingback chair and put your feet up. The warm glow from the fireplace is as comforting as the yummy cocktails and appetizers. This is a great place for get-togethers, whether your friends are casual types or sophisticated club-goers. *900 E. Madison St. (at 9th Ave. E), Capitol Hill, 206/622–6400. Daily 11:30 AM–1 AM.*

5 *g-7*
FLOWER'S

Smoke and mirrors are—literally—the predominate features of this flower shop–turned–booze house. Students, punks, and scenesters hover around flower-themed tables, puffing away on cigarettes and catching glimpses of themselves in the mirrored ceiling. *4247 University Way NE (at NE 43rd St.), University District, 206/633–1903. Daily 11 AM–2 AM.*

9 *b-3*
F. X. MCRORY'S

You can wait out sporting event traffic jams in the old-time setting of this large, boisterous sports bar, or catch a drink with pals after work. Its known for its single-malt whiskeys, its fresh oysters, and its proximity to *both* the pro baseball and pro football stadiums. *419 Occidental Ave. S (at S. Jackson St.), Pioneer Square, 206/623–4800. Mon.–Thurs. 11:30–10, Fri. 11:30–11, Sat. noon–11, Sun. 11:30–10.*

10 *h-7*
GALLERY BAR

Business executives and scenesters head to the Sheraton hotel's cozy bar for top-notch cocktails and excellent service. 1400 6th Ave. (at Union St.), Downtown, 206/387–5585. Daily noon–2 AM.

10 g-7
GARDEN COURT
The staff at the elegant lounge in the Four Seasons hotel serves cocktails with savoir faire. The atmosphere is perfect for a formal lunch, a romantic rendezvous, or a casual night out with your pals. 411 University St. (at 4th Ave.), Downtown, 206/621–1700. Tues.–Thurs. 5–midnight, Fri.–Sat. 5–2 AM.

4 f-5
HATTIE'S HAT
Hattie's didn't have to be remodeled to get a 1950s rockabilly look, it just had to be dusted off a little. This easygoing joint sincerely wants to be your favorite watering hole and restaurant. Many have heard this call. 5231 Ballard Ave. NW (at NW Vernon Place), Ballard, 206/784–0175. Weekdays 3 PM–2 AM, weekends 8 AM–2 AM.

10 f-7
IL BISTRO
This sexy little Italian number is perfect for a romantic evening. The low lights, low ceilings, and stiff drinks ensure a gauzy, idyllic night on the town. 93A Pike St. (at 1st Ave.), Downtown, 206/682–3049. Sun.–Thurs. 5:30–10, Fri.–Sat. 5:30–11.

11 c-5
LINDA'S
A moose head stares down at the friendly staff and the crazy mix of patrons in this bar whose motto is "A Nice Place for Nice People." The jukebox is one of Seattle's finest, with everything from lounge to punk. 707 E. Pine St. (at Harvard Ave. E), Capitol Hill, 206/325–1220. Weekdays 4 PM–2 AM, weekends 10 AM–2 AM.

10 d-2
LIQUID LOUNGE AT EMP
Drinks with the size and strength that rock stars have become accustomed to await you amid EMP's famous sights and sounds. Entry to the very cool lounge is free, so you can hook up here with friends before you take the pricey tour or make it your regular hangout. Seattle Center, 325 5th Ave. N (at N. Thomes St.), Queen Anne, 206/770–2777. Daily 5 PM–2 AM.

5 f-3
LITTLE RED HEN
Classic country-and-western tunes pour out of the jukebox to the delight of old school country fans. They aren't the typical health-conscious set usually found in the surrounding neighborhood; the smoke alone in this place is killer. 7115 Woodlawn Ave. NE (at NE 71st St.), Green Lake, 206/522–1168. Weekdays 6 AM–2 AM, weekends 8 AM–2 AM.

7 f-6
MECCA CAFE
Once an old timers' watering hole, the Mecca has been adopted by area hipsters for its dark, laid-back environment and its kickin' jukebox. 526 Queen Anne Ave. N (at W. Mercer St.), Queen Anne, 206/285–9728. Daily 6 PM–2 AM.

5 f-4
MONA'S
Sophisticated yet inviting Mona's offers plenty of cheery cocktails and candlelight. It's the perfect place to take a date or a small group of friends. 6421 Latona Ave. NE (at N. 65th St.), Green Lake, 206/526–1188. Daily 5 PM–2 AM.

10 c-6
THE MUDSHARK BAR
In the venerable Edgewater hotel, this bar takes its playful name from a bit of lore about some rock stars who decided to fish from the balcony. An easygoing atmosphere and great views of Elliott Bay and the Olympic Mountains are the draws here. 2411 Alaskan Way (at Wall St.), Waterfront, 206/728–7000. Daily 11 AM–2 AM.

7 g-1
NICKERSON STREET SALOON
It's easy to drop by this neighborhood favorite and sit for a spell with whatever brew suits you. The pub grub isn't bad, either. 318 W. Nickerson St. (at Fremont Ave. N), Fremont, 206/284–8819. Daily 11:30 AM–2 AM.

10 f-6
OLIVER'S
If you prefer to drink your cocktails in an atmosphere that seems better suited to taking high tea, head to the Mayflower Park Hotel's lounge. Wingback chairs, low tables, and lots of natural light make this a lovely respite. Masters of

mixology, the bartenders make truly delightful martinis. *405 Olive Way (at 4th Ave.), Downtown, 206/382–6995. Daily 11 AM–2 AM.*

10 *g-7*

PALOMINO

After a whirlwind Downtown shopping spree, reward yourself with a drink at this long-standing favorite. You may well be joined by hip young singles making their first toast to a night on the town as well as members of an older set enjoying pre-theater cocktails and appetizers. *1420 5th Ave. (at Union St.), Downtown, 206/623–1300. Mon. 11:30–10:30, Tues.–Thurs. 11:30–11:30, Fri.–Sat. 11:30–midnight, Sun. 4:30–10:30.*

10 *e-6*

PINK DOOR

Look for a lone light illuminating a pink door hidden away on Post Alley, just steps from Pike Place Market. Inside you'll find a cozy bar with tantalizing drink offerings. To while away a sunny afternoon sipping a signature violet martini on the covered deck is to know true bliss. *1919 Post Alley (at Virginia St.), Pike Place Market, 206/443–3241. Tues.–Sat. 11:30–11.*

10 *e-6*

QUEEN CITY GRILL

The young, the successful, and the fashionable come here to put on airs and enjoy dinner, drinks, and plenty of big city style. *2201 1st. Ave. (at Blanchard St.), Downtown, 206/443–0975. Mon.–Thurs. 11:30–11, Fri. 11:30 AM–midnight, Sat. 4:30–midnight, Sun. 4:30–11.*

10 *e-6*

RENDEZVOUS

Like many dives that have come before, this hole-in-the-wall gin joint attracts the artsy and the not-so-artsy alike. The house drinks will knock you hard on your heels. *2320 2nd Ave. (at Bell St.), Belltown, 206/441–5823. Daily 6 PM–2 AM.*

10 *c-3*

SPACE NEEDLE

If the night is clear, it really is worth paying the fare for the elevator ride up the Needle and splurging on the expensive drinks served at the top. The views seem especially grand if you're sharing them with someone special. *Seattle Cen-*

ter, 219 4th Ave. N (at Broad St.), Queen Anne, 206/443–2100. Sun.–Thurs. 4:30–9, Fri.–Sat. 4:30–10.

5 *g-4*

TEDDY'S TAVERN

An over-30, bike-loving, pool-playing, no-frills-beer-swilling crowd has made Teddy's all its own. *1012 NE 65th St. (at Roosevelt Way NE), University District, 206/526–9174. Daily 1 PM–2 AM.*

10 *b-3*

TINI BIGS

A successful-looking clientele gathers at this high-profile spot to enjoy 27 variations of the martini. Shiny tables, black walls, and dim pink lights ensure a sufficiently stylish stage on which to be seen. *100 Denny Way (at 1st Ave.), Downtown, 206/284–0931. Daily 4 PM–2 AM.*

5 *b-8*

TRIANGLE

This happening hangout really is a triangle. Fremont scenesters flock here as much for its cool ambience as for its cocktails. Get lucky and get one of the few outdoor tables in—you guessed it—a triangular patio. *3507 Fremont Pl. N (NW 34th St.), Fremont, 206/632–0880. Daily 11:30 AM–2 AM.*

10 *e-5*

TWO BELLS

A smoky haze hovers above the heads of this pub's artsy patrons. Well loved and well worn, the Two Bells still grills some of Seattle's best burgers; wash them down with a frosty pint. They're closed Wednesday. *2313 4th Ave. (at Bell St.), Downtown, 206/441–3050. Mon.–Tues. 11 AM–midnight, Thurs.–Sat. 11 AM–2 AM, Sun. 11–11.*

11 *a-7*

VITO'S

It's dark, and it looks and feels seedy—albeit in an oh-so-good way. The cigar-chomping types seem right at home in the dimly lit booths and amid the "I'll make you an offer you can't refuse" atmosphere. Recorded swing music and golden oldies as well as karaoke are on tap nightly. *927 9th Ave. E (at E. Madison St.), Capitol Hill, 206/682–2695. Daily 11 AM–2 AM.*

`10` *g-6*

VON'S

In the after-work hours, the stools and club chairs here are usually full. That may be because sophisticated martini drinkers haven't let the collegiate look and feel fool them. *619 Pine St. (at 6th Ave.), Downtown, 206/621–8667. Daily 11 AM–2:30 PM and 5 PM–10 PM.*

`10` *b-3*

WATERTOWN

Grab a comfy booth and check out the scene. The people-watching usually starts with happy-hour types and ends with trendy singles dancing to house music or old school favorites. *106 1st Ave. N (at Denny Way), Queen Anne, 206/284–5003. Sun.–Thurs. 5 PM–2 AM, Fri.–Sat. 8 PM–3 AM.*

`10` *g-8*

W SEATTLE HOTEL BAR

Classic concoctions and velvet-lined booths are among the hallmarks of this posh hotel lounge. Pull together the latest look in fashion to live the lush life here. *1112 4th Ave. (at Spring St.), Downtown, 206/264–6060. Sun.–Wed. 11:30 AM–midnight, Thurs.–Sat. 11:30 AM–2 AM.*

BLUES & JAZZ

In keeping with the feel of the music, the club scene here doesn't hit you over the head with a loud presence. But it's there: Pioneer Square's many stages come alive at night, but are imperceptible by day. The well-heeled go to Dimitriou's Jazz Alley but laid-back Larry's is often packed, too.

`4` *f-5*

BALLARD FIREHOUSE

A former firehouse is now Ballard's music mecca, with local and national blues acts and the occasional classic rock or oldies concert. Its high ceilings make quiet conversation impossible, but most folks come for music not chatter. *5429 Russell Ave. NW (at NW Market St.), Ballard, 206/784–3516. Daily 8 PM–2 AM.*

`10` *f-5*

DIMITRIOU'S JAZZ ALLEY

When they're in Seattle, all the big names seem to play at this club. Clean up a bit so you'll fit in with the shiny,

well-dressed set. *2033 6th Ave. (at Virginia St.), Downtown, 206/441–9729. Daily 6 PM–2 AM.*

`12` *c-2*

THE J&M CAFÉ

Expect to party at this gigantic Pioneer Square institution. Swinging singles gather at the large, long, picnic-style tables and rock to the loud, live blues that's featured most weekends. *201 1st Ave. S (at S. Washington St.), Pioneer Square, 206/292–0663. Daily 11:30 AM– 2 AM.*

`12` *c-2*

LARRY'S

This unpretentious tavern-restaurant serves up breakfast, burgers, and blues. It's usually packed and has live shows nightly. *209 1st Ave. S (at S. Washington St.), Pioneer Square, 206/624–7665. Daily 8 AM–2 AM.*

`05` *f-4*

LATONA PUB

Truth be told, this place was once a real dive, but now it's a funky, friendly neighborhood bar with local folk, blues, or jazz musicians playing nightly. The no-smoking policy is a plus for many, as is the array of locally brewed beers. *6423 Latona Ave. NE (at NE 64th), Green Lake, 206/525–2238. Weekdays 11:30 AM–2 AM, Sat. 1 PM–2 AM, Sun. 2–2.*

`12` *c-2*

NEW ORLEANS

Could be the Mardi Gras decor, could be the toe-tapping jazz, blues, or zydeco— whatever it is, it makes this restaurant and nightclub the closest thing to Bourbon Street bar that you'll find in these parts. Nightly shows feature top local performers, though national acts play here, too, on occasion. *114 1st Ave. S (at S. Washington St.), Pioneer Square, 206/ 622–2563. Mon. and Thurs. 11–10, Tues.– Wed. 11–11, Fri.–Sat. 11 AM–2 AM, Sun. noon–10.*

`12` *b-4*

OLD TIMER'S CAFE

Some pub crawlers are drawn straight from the sidewalk into this hot spot by the sultry sounds of the nightly blues and reggae shows. Others stop by routinely just to throw a few back. *620 1st Ave. (at Cherry St.), Pioneer Square, 206/ 623–9800. Daily 10–2 AM.*

5 g-4

SCARLET TREE

North of the U-District, this institution serves up great burgers and live rhythm and blues most nights. It caters to laid-back locals and grad students. *6521 Roosevelt Way NE (at NE 65th St.), University District, 206/523–7153. Weekdays 6:30 AM–2 AM, weekends 7:30 AM–2 AM.*

10 e-6

TULA'S

Passersby often pop into this comfortable Mediterranean café to get a better look at the local jazz or blues performers and the occasional belly dancer. *2214 2nd Ave. (at Blanchard St.), Belltown, 206/443–4221. Daily 3 PM–2 AM.*

BREWPUBS

There was a time when microbreweries were popping up faster than your corner latte stand, but like all fads, that time has passed. What have survived are the best of the best, "fermented" success if you will. Sure, the beer had better be on the mark, but to make a success out of one of these joints, you've got to create that casual comfort of a neighborhood pub and blend it with the freshest brews found anywhere. These pubs understand and deliver.

5 g-7

BIG TIME BREWERY

One look at the moose head on the wall and the memorabilia scattered about and you know that this pub caters to pint-loving U-Dub students. Pale ale, amber, and porter are always on tap; the imaginative specialty brews change monthly. *4133 University Way NE (at NE 42nd St.), University District, 206/545–4509. Sun.–Thurs. 11:30 AM–12:30 AM, Fri.–Sat. 11:30 AM–1:30 AM.*

11 d-5

ELYSIAN BREWING COMPANY

Golden Fleece Ale, Zephyrus Pilsner, and Immortal India Pale Ale flow from the taps of this large open pub. Even if the cute mythological brew names don't appeal, the dependable pub fare and eccentric Capitol Hill clientele will. *1221 E. Pike St. (at 12th St. E), Capitol Hill, 206/860–1920. Weekdays 11:30 AM–2 AM, weekends noon–2 AM.*

4 h-7

HALES ALES BREWERY & PUB

Hales serves up nine regular and seasonal offerings in a cheerful setting. Its signature brews are the pale and amber ales; order a "taster's flight" if you want to test the rest. *4301 Leary Way NW (at NW 43rd St.), Fremont, 206/782–0737. Mon.–Thurs. 11–10, Fri.–Sat. 11–midnight.*

4 g-6

MARITIME PACIFIC BREWING COMPANY

This smoke-free brewpub features yummy ales and seasonal brews amid the low-key atmosphere of a working-class neighborhood. The Salmon Bay Bitter is particularly delicious. *1514 Leary Way NW (at 15th Ave. NW, under Ballard Bridge), Ballard, 206/782–6181. Mon.–Thurs. 3–9, Fri.–Sat. noon–11.*

10 f-7

PIKE PUB & BREWERY

Proudly proclaiming itself to be "Beer Central," the Pike is operated by the brewers of the renown Pike Place Pale Ale. It also houses the Seattle Microbrewery Museum and an excellent shop with home-brewing supplies. *1415 1st Ave. (at Union St.), Downtown, 206/622–6044. Sun.–Wed. 11 AM–midnight, Thurs.–Sat. 11 AM–2 AM.*

12 b-5

PYRAMID ALEHOUSE

Just south of Pioneer Square, this alehouse brews a varied line of beers, including a top-notch hefeweizen, an apricot ale (it tastes much better than it sounds), and Thomas Kemper lagers. It's the perfect place to gather after a Mariners game. *91 S. Royal Brougham Way (at 1st Ave. S), Pioneer Square, 206/682–3377. Sun.–Thurs. 11–10, Fri.–Sat. 11–11.*

13 c-8

ROCK BOTTOM

Bellevue's khaki-clad sophisticates often stop at this fairly ubiquitous chain to lift a few house brews. The later the hour, the younger the patrons. Peek-a-boo brewing machines tempt the curious; when staffers have time, they conduct quick behind-the-scene tours. *550 106th Ave. NE (at NE 6th St.), Bellevue, 425/462–9300. Mon.–Thurs. 11 AM–1:15 AM,*

Fri.–Sat. 11 AM–1 AM, *Sun.* 11 AM–midnight.

11 *b-5*
SIX ARMS
This member of a chain of pubs operated by the McMenamin family of Portland, Oregon, has the same comfortably eccentric decor as its brethren. *300 E. Pike St. (at Melrose Ave. E), Capitol Hill, 206/223–1698, Mon.–Sat.* 11 AM–1 AM, *Sun. noon–midnight.*

5 *b-8*
THE TROLLEYMAN
The birthplace of local favorites Ballard Bitter and Redhook Ale has whitewashed walls, a no-smoking policy, a fireplace, and armchairs. The original Redhook Brewery is right next door—take the 45-minute tour before you pop into the Trolleyman for a pint. *3400 Phinney Ave. N (at 34th Ave. NW), Fremont, 206/634–4213.*

COFFEEHOUSES

You've no doubt heard all about Seattle's love affair with coffee—and everything you've heard is probably true. You can't throw a stick without hitting a Starbucks, a Seattle's Best Coffee, a Tully's, or one of the many thriving independents. The big boys count on getting you in and out in under a minute; the little guys entice you to linger—by yourself reading a book or chatting with a group of friends. Although just about any coffee shop or espresso cart will do in a pinch, most Seattleites have a favorite bean club.

11 *b-3*
B&O ESPRESSO
Midway up Capitol Hill is one of Seattle's earliest purveyors of the magical elixir known as the latte. It's a buzz of pit stoppers heading up or down the hill, and the on-site bakery turns out gorgeous desserts. *204 Belmont Ave. E (at E. John St.), Capitol Hill, 206/322–5028. Weekdays* 7 AM–midnight, *Sat.* 7 AM–1 AM, *Sun.* 9 AM–midnight.

11 *b-5*
BAUHAUS
The bookshelf-lined walls of this smart corner café are full of art and architecture books. Not surprisingly, intellectuals and hipster nerds fill its tables. *301 E.*

Pine St. (at Melrose Ave. E), Capitol Hill, 206/625–1600. Weekdays 6 AM–1 AM, *weekends* 8 AM–1 AM.

11 *c-5*
CAFFÉ VITA
Brooding chess players, punk activists, and scraggly poets vie for sidewalk seats at this haven for alternative lifestylers. Coincidentally, it also brews some of the most scrumptiously roasted beans in town. *1005 E. Pike St. (at 10th Ave. E.), Capitol Hill, 206/325–2647. Weekdays* 6 AM–midnight, *weekends* 7 AM–midnight.

11 *b-3*
COFFEE MESSIAH
"Caffeine Saves" is the motto of this over-the-top bean temple, which makes no apologies for its dense religious paraphernalia done tongue-in-cheek. The well-heeled worshipers tend to dress all in black. *1554 E. Olive Way (at Summit Ave. E), Capitol Hill, 206/860–7377, Sun.–Thurs.* 7 AM–midnight, *Fri.–Sat.* 7 AM–2 AM.

5 *b-2*
DIVA ESPRESSO
A warren of nooks and crannies makes this large, rambling coffee shop seem quite cozy. Although neighborhood types pick up a quick cup to go, many spread out their stuff on a table and settle in for a good long while. *7916 Greenwood Ave. N (at 80th St. NW), Greenwood, 206/781–1213. Mon.–Sat.* 6 AM–9 PM, *Sun.* 7–6.

11 *c-3*
HABITAT ESPRESSO
At this coffee collective, politics and coffee *do* mix. It donates much of its profits to charities. Smack in the middle of Capitol Hill's main drag, this is a good place to stop for a thoughtful interlude before or after a movie. *202 Broadway E (at E. Olive Way), Capitol Hill, 206/329–3087. Mon.–Thurs.* 7 AM–midnight, *Fri.* 7 AM–2 AM, *Sat.* 9 AM –2 AM, *Sun.* 9 AM–midnight.

4 *h-1*
THE LIBRARY
In the parlor of what was once a private home, this café invites you to relax and truly enjoy your coffee. No two of the comfy chairs are the same, and many of the funky antiques scattered hither and yon are for sale. *850 NW 85th St. (at 8th Ave. NW), Ballard, 206/789–5682. Daily* 8 AM–3 PM.

11 *c-3*

SEPTIÈME

Don't let the linen table cloths fool you: there's something a little seedy, but totally cool, about this café. Lattes are served in big white porcelain bowls that can't help but leave you with a foam mustache. On summer evenings, head out back to the patio, where you can sip coffee to rumba and salsa by the light of tiki torches. *214 Broadway E (at E. Olive Way), Capitol Hill, 206/860–8858. Daily 9 AM–12 AM.*

10 *e-5*

THE SIT & SPIN

Multi-taskers love this place. It has live music nightly plus a range of tasty health food *and* coin-op laundry facilities. *2219 4th Ave. (at Blanchard St.), Downtown, 206/441–9484. Sun.–Thurs. 9 AM–midnight, Fri.–Sat. 9 AM–2 AM.*

10 *e-5*

SPEAKEASY

Unlike many cyber cafés, this one has an inviting atmosphere and a computer-savvy staff. Download your E-mail, and enjoy some choice people-watching. *2304 2nd Ave. (at Bell St.), Downtown, 206/728–9770. Mon. 11 AM–7 PM, Tues.–Thurs. 11 AM–midnight, Fri. 11 AM–1 AM, Sat. noon–1 AM, Sun. noon–10.*

5 *b-8*

STILL LIFE IN FREMONT

This place is light, airy, and full of the bohemian flavor for which Fremont is famous. Locals enjoy the homemade soup as much as the coffee. *709 N. 35th St. (at Fremont Ave. N), Fremont, 206/ 547–9850. Daily 7:30 AM–10 PM.*

13 *b-4*

TRIPLE J CAFÉ

An upscale set lounges about on couches here, drinking all sorts of coffee concoctions. There's outdoor seating as well. *101 Central Way (at 1st St.), Kirkland, 425/822–7319. Mon.–Thurs. 5 AM–11 PM, Fri.–Sat. 6 AM–midnight, Sun. 6 AM–10 PM.*

7 *f-6*

UPTOWN ESPRESSO

A busy bus stop feeds the line in this fast-paced coffeehouse, but the well-trained staff keeps up. The baked goods are noteworthy as well. Weather permit-ting, the walls come down and the whole place spills out onto the sidewalk. *525½ Queen Anne Ave. N (at W. Mercer St.), Queen Anne, 206/285–3757. Weekdays 5 AM–10 PM, weekends 6 AM–11 PM.*

11 *c-3*

VIVACE ROASTERIA

Carefully trained baristas prepare each cup—made with the café's own blend—precisely. The high ceiling make things noisy, but the espresso is the best in town. *901 E. Denny Way (at Broadway E), Capitol Hill, 206/860–5869. Daily 6:30 AM–11 PM.*

5 *b-8*

WIT'S END

This combination bookstore, tearoom, and café hosts a variety of events. One day it's a comedy performance, the next it's a folk music show, and the following it's a meeting of an area Latin Club. *770 N. 34th St. (at Fremont Ave. N), Fremont, 206/547–2330. Daily 10–9.*

12 *c-3*

ZEITGEIST

Pioneer Square area's working Joes and Janes appreciate this coffeehouse's java as much as its light, airy atmosphere and its art exhibits. The baristas take their craft to heart, and there are plenty of sweets and savories to go with each delicious cup. *161 S. Jackson (at Occidental Ave. S), Pioneer Square, 206/583–0497. Weekdays 6 AM–7 PM, Sat. 8–7.*

COMEDY

The mainstream American comedy scene exploded in the late '80s, then went stale. Was it that people weren't laughing anymore? Were all the comics starring in their own TV shows? Who knows, but the clubs that made the grade kept it simple, with local and tour-ing standups, and letting the material keep 'em begging for more.

12 *c-2*

COMEDY UNDERGROUND

This club is literally underground, resid-ing beneath Swannie's restaurant. Stand-up comedy and open-mike ses-sions are held nightly. *222 S. Main St. (at 2nd Ave. S), Pioneer Square, 206/628–0303. Thurs.–Sun. 7:30–2 AM.*

5 *g-6*

GIGGLES

Locally and nationally known comedians
yuck it up Thursday through Sunday
with all-ages shows starting at 8:30 PM.
The underagers are shown the door for
the late show starting at 10 PM. There's
an open mic for all ages on Thursday
and Sunday. *5220 Roosevelt Way NE (at
NE 53rd St.), University District, 206/526–
5653. Daily 8:30–2 AM.*

5 *g-8*

JET CITY IMPROV

Here's a troupe that fuses improvisational comedy (often based on suggestions from the audiences) with music.
Shows start at 10:30 PM and go to when-
ever it's over. *Ethnic Cultural Center,
3940 Brooklyn Ave. NE (at NE 39th Ave),
University District, 206/781–3879, Fri.–
Sat. 10:30 PM.*

10 *f-7*

MARKET THEATER

The Market Theater's popular "theater
sports" shows make improvisational
comedy performances competitive.
Show duration varies. *1428 Post Alley (at
Pike St.), Downtown, 206/781–9273. Fri.–
Sat. 10:30 PM, Sun. 7 PM.*

DANCE CLUBS

Whether it's ballroom, swing, disco, or
drum 'n' bass that gets your toe a tap-
pin', there's a polished hardwood floor
for you. But don't limit yourself to just
one venue and genre, many a late-night
groove starts out as a Lindy hop. For the
latest in trip, hip, or techno, area DJs
rotate around clubs, making each and
every night a huge scene somewhere.
There are handbills galore in the coffee
shops.

11 *b-5*

THE BALTIC ROOM

What started life as a piano bar is now,
with its gorgeous mohair booths, a
sophisticated salon. Low-key acid jazz
meets daring house music meets contemporary rhythms—all meet some of
Seattle's sexiest people. *1207 E. Pine St.
(at E. Melrose Ave.), Capitol Hill, 206/
625–4444. Daily 5 PM–2 AM.*

11 *c-5*

CENTURY BALLROOM

What a place. Only leather-soled shoes
are allowed to dance across the polished
3,000-square-ft floor of this painstakingly
restored establishment. The music is
often live, and there are classes as well as
swing and other dances, so beginners
and long-time Lindy lovers feel right at
home. Hours vary depending on scheduled event. *915 E. Pine St. (at 10th Ave. E),
Capitol Hill. 206/324–7263. Daily.*

10 *f-5*

I-SPY

Its name is apt: this dance club knows
what's hip long before you do. Whether
you dress flashily or you call it good in
jeans and a T-shirt, you won't be out of
place. Visiting DJs frequent the turnta-
bles on the club's two levels. Note that
the entrance is in an alley, meaning you
have to be a bit of a spy to find it. *1921
5th Ave. (at Stewart St.), Downtown,
206/374–9292. Daily 9 PM–2 AM.*

12 *c-2*

THE LAST SUPPER CLUB

Pioneer Square's club people come here
for some serious dancing. Sometimes it
has the atmosphere of a frat house;
otherwise the vibe is more mixed. The
sound is mainly house and disco, and
the club's drag nights are a big favorite
with the gay and straight crowd that
jams the dance floor on weekends. *124
S. Washington St. (at 1st Ave. S), Pioneer
Square, 206/748–9975. Tue. 4 PM–10 PM,
Wed.–Sat. 4 PM–2 AM.*

10 *d-5*

PAMPAS ROOM

The mood is generally festive at this
1950s-style supper club. Its jazz, swing,
and Latin music seems to entice even
shy souls onto the dance floor. *90 Wall
St. (at 1st Ave.), Downtown, 206/728–
1377. Fri.–Sat. 6–2.*

7 *g-7*

POLLY ESTHERS & CULTURE CLUB

Part of a nationwide chain, this retro
dance club spins soul favorites from the
'70s and MTV standards from the '80s.
Nonstop drinking and dancing is the
aim of the attractive suburbanites, who
come here determined to raise a disco
fever. Weekends are a crush. *332 5th Ave.
N (at W. Harrison St.), Queen Anne, 206/*

279–1977. *Wed.–Thurs.* 9 PM–2 AM, *Fri.–Sat.* 8 PM–4 AM.

8 *a-7*
RE-BAR

Still groovin' after quite a few years, this art-crammed dance club is beloved by a mixed gay and straight clientele. Come for the festive feel and the friendly staff rather than great leaps of turntable imagination—the emphasis is on well-loved songs from the disco and house eras. *1114 Howell St. (at Boren Ave.), Queen Anne, 206/233–9873. Daily 10 PM–2 AM.*

10 *g-5*
700 CLUB

DJs spin soul, R&B, and hip hop, in this refreshingly racially mixed club. Sure it's a little small, but that just creates an intimate feeling when you're shaking your booty. *700 Virginia Ave. (at 7th Ave.), Downtown, 206/343–7518. Tues.–Sat. 8 PM–2 AM.*

11 *d-5*
THE VOGUE

The dark denizens of Seattle's Gothic scene keep their look alive by ritualistically converging here. At Sunday's Fetish Night, you can wear the leather bondage suit that hangs secretly in the back of your closet. Or maybe you'll just stop by to hear the deafening clang of industrial music. *1511 11th Ave. E (at E. Pike St.), Capitol Hill, 206/324–5778. Daily 9 PM–2 AM.*

10 *h-4*
THE WASHINGTON DANCE CLUB

If you long for a waltz, a tango, or a foxtrot, sashay into this studio for ballroom dancing on Friday and Sunday nights. Worry not if you're little rusty; there are workshops for a nominal fee held a couple hours before the glitter ball descends. You can even come alone and find a dance partner right there in your class. *1017 Stewart St. (at Lauren St.), Downtown, 206/628–8939, Fri. 9 PM–11:30 PM, Sun. 7 PM–9 PM.*

FOLK/ETHNIC

Though it may look like "folk" means Irish or Celtic, don't let the names of these places lull you into believing you'll hear only the song stylin's of a bonnie lass. There's plenty of acoustical performers taking the stage offering all manner of song. Look for that rockabilly revival or alternative country.

12 *c-2*
BOHEMIANS

Seattle's only reggae club has a marvelous calendar of shows by world-class recording artists and DJs who play not only reggae but also soul, hip hop, and Afro-pop music. Both the dreaded and the dread loving come for that special groove and peace-loving vibe. *111 Yesler Way (at James St.), Pioneer Square, 206/447–1514. Mon.–Sat. 4 PM–2 AM.*

4 *f-5*
CONOR BYRNE'S PUB

Your search for an immaculately drawn pint is over if you've landed here. Hipster singles and those with a yearning for a wee bit of Irish hospitality settle in along the upholstered benches. On weekends there's live Celtic music. *5140 Ballard Ave. NW (at NW Market St.), Ballard, 206/784–3640. Daily 1 PM–2 AM.*

5 *b-8*
DUBLINER

Funky Fremonters, area dot-commers, and a few real Irish blokes toss back the pints at this pub. If you're up on your traditional tunes, stop by for open mike night on Tuesday. Film lovers take note: you can see movies run by the Fremont Outdoor Cinema from the back patio. *3405 Fremont Ave. N (at NW 34th St.), Fremont, 206/548–1508. Daily 1 PM–2 AM.*

6 *c-1*
FIDDLER'S INN

Expect to hear some fiddle playing at this smoke-free pub's agreeable nightly folk, Celtic, and blues events. You'll also find excellent microbrews as well as a choice wine list. Bring your old band instrument and sign up for open mike Mondays. *9219 35th Ave. NE (at NE 92nd St.), University District, 206/525–0752. Mon.–Tues. 11:30 AM–2 AM, Wed.–Fri. 11:30 AM–1 AM, Sat. noon–1 AM, Sun. noon–11.*

10 *g-6*
GORDON BIERSCH

The ultra-upscale Pacific Place mall holds a joint—part of a national chain of brewpubs—that presents nightly performances by singer-songwriters. Despite the posh surroundings, there's never a cover charge. The array of ales, stouts, and porters will warm your heart. *600 Pine St. (at 6th Ave.), Downtown, 206/405–4205. Daily 11–9.*

11 *e-2*

HOPVINE PUB

By putting the spotlight on singer-songwriters and acoustic folk, this cozy, cheerful pub gives you the chance to preview original works by local musicians. *507 15th Ave. E (at E. Republican St.), Capitol Hill, 206/328–3120. Daily 11:30 AM–2 AM.*

5 *g-6*

IRISH EMIGRANT

Hoist your pint in this old-school Irish pub, and you'll be elbow to elbow with U-Dub students and transplants who still brandish a brogue. On weekends, the oh-so-boisterous residents of the university's Greek Row pack the place and party like it's St. Patty's Day. Midweek evenings tend to be mellow enough to actually enjoy the sights and sounds of the Emerald Isle. *5260 University Way NE (at NE 52nd St.), University District, 206/525–2955. Weekdays 4 PM–2 AM, weekends 11 AM–2 AM.*

10 *e-6*

KELLS

On a stroll along Post Alley, you're bound to encounter this small Irish pub near Pike Place Market. Although it's without airs or attitude, things get a little raucous on weekends, when Celtic music is featured. If it's a quiet pint you're after, arrive early. *1916 Post Alley (at Pine St.), Downtown, 206/728–1916. Daily 11:30 AM–2 AM.*

11 *b-5*

KINCORA PUB

If you'll be needing a well-drawn draft and cast-off furniture around a roaring fire, then take a load off here. No loudmouthed heavy drinkers spoil the calm of this Irish pub smack in the middle of Capitol Hill's hyped up scene. *518 E. Pine St. (at Boylston Ave. E), Capitol Hill, 206/325–0436. Daily 2–2.*

6 *a-7*

MURPHY'S PUB

This spacious pub with big comfy chairs has just the right vibe for the hippie/yuppie neighborhood that surrounds it.

On weekends, you'll find Irish and folk musicians on the small stage. Competitive darts games—with steel-tipped projectiles and old-fashioned cork boards—are also a possibility. *2110 N. 45th St. (at Meridian Ave. N), Wallingford, 206/634–2110. Sun.–Thurs. 11:30 AM–2 AM, Fri.–Sat. 11 AM–2 AM.*

12 *b-1*

OWL 'N' THISTLE IRISH PUB

Loaded with regulars, this cavernous but affable pub is the perfect place to drink a well-drawn pint of Guinness and listen to some folk music. Snooker is to be had in the back. *808 Post Ave. (at Columbia St.), Pioneer Square, 206/621–7777. Daily 10 AM–2 AM.*

12 *b-1*

TIR NA NOG

The name means "land of youth" in Gaelic, but young and old alike enjoy this tasteful spot. It's the hangout for many an Emerald Isle expat, though it's unclear whether they're drawn by the pints, the Irish bric-a-brac, or the traditional music that's performed several nights a week. *801 1st Ave. (at Columbia St.), Pioneer Square, 206/264–2700. Weekdays 11 AM–2 AM, Sat. noon–2 AM.*

4 *f-5*

TRACTOR TAVERN

This is the city's top spot to catch a roots or alternative country act. The large, dimly lit hall has all the right touches: an excellent sound system, wagon-wheel fixtures, exposed brick walls, and a cheery staff. *5213 Ballard Ave. NW (at NW 20th Ave.), Ballard, 206/789–3599. Daily 4 PM–2 AM.*

GAY & LESBIAN BARS & CLUBS

The good news is that Seattle has a thriving and eclectic gay scene, the bad news is that it's mostly for the boys and limited to Capitol Hill. Some venues have "Ladies Nights"—which is the closest thing to a second Lesbian club in town. (The Wildrose is currently the only girl bar.) If you live near Capitol Hill, hooray for you; you can sidle on up to a local bar for a casual drink, disco 'til dawn, shoot stick, and take your pick of niche bars.

5 e-7
CHANGES

Changes is one of the few gay bars *not* on Capitol Hill. Locals make a night of it on karaoke Mondays and Wednesdays. *2103 N. 45th St. (at Meridian St. N), Wallingford, 206/545–8363. Daily noon–2 AM.*

11 d-5
THE CUFF

Although it strives to be a manly leather bar, you'll find all shapes and sizes here. The dance floor—often loud and crowded—is tucked away downstairs, but the main floor bar and its open-air patio is the place to be on a warm night. *1533 13th Ave. E (at E. Pike St.), Capitol Hill, 206/323–1525. Daily 2–2.*

11 b-5
MANRAY

A wall of white metal plates that somehow defy graffiti marks Capitol Hill's newest high-tech hangout. Its retro-futuristic decor and sumptuous drink menu (there are 32 martinis alone) lend wit and style to the city's gay bar scene. The upscale clientele enjoys summer evenings on the lanai, complete with a gurgling fountain. *514 E. Pine St. (at Boylston Ave. E), Capitol Hill, 206/568–0750. Weekdays 11 AM–2 AM, weekends 4 PM–2 AM.*

11 c-5
NEIGHBORS

Seattle's oldest gay bar is hard to find (the entrance is in an alley that runs between Pike and Pine streets). But don't let this deter you. Trends come and go, but this bar and dance club keeps Capitol Hill's gay-male population happy with drag shows, theme nights, and an easygoing atmosphere. *1509 Broadway Ave. (at E. Pike St.), Capitol Hill, 206/324–5358. Sun.–Wed. 4 PM–2 AM, Thurs. 4 PM–3 AM, Fri.–Sat. 4–4.*

11 c-5
R PLACE

You can't miss this three-story club that caters to gay sports fans, pool players, and karaoke enthusiasts. It's able to pack people in by being laid-back and friendly as well as spacious. And it's the perfect haunt for those who want to be "out" without the burden of prep time demanded by the more fashionable. *619 E. Pine St. (at Boylston Ave. E), Capitol Hill, 206/323–8828. Daily 2–2.*

11 e-5
SEA WOLF SALOON

This neighborhood watering hole couldn't be pretentious if it tried. The drinks are mighty stiff, the patrons often wind up sharing the extra-long tables, and there's always a cheery group around the lone pool table. *1413 14th Ave. E (at E. Union St.), Capitol Hill, 206/323–2158. Daily 11 AM–2 AM.*

11 d-5
SPAGS TAVERN

Pool, darts, and beer are all on tap at this inconspicuous gay pub. It's refreshingly free of the glamorous types you encounter in some of the larger bars. *1118 E. Pike St. (at 11th Ave. E.), Capitol Hill, 206/322–3232. Daily 2–2.*

8 a-8
TIMBERLINE TAVERN

Seattle's only country-and-western dance club for gays and lesbians is beloved by fans of serious honky-tonk. Come early Tuesday through Thursday evenings for beginning and advanced dance lessons, and then let your feet do the talking. *2015 Boren Ave. (at Virginia St.), Downtown, 206/622–6220. Tues.–Sat. 6 PM–2 AM, Sun. 4 PM–2 AM.*

11 c-5
THE WILDROSE

Expect a mob nearly every night of the week at Capitol Hill's lone lesbian bar. The weeknight karaoke crowd is fun and good natured, cheering for singers whose voices range from sweet to sour. Weekends are raucous; grab a window table early and settle in for perpetual ladies' night. *1021 E. Pike St. (at 10th Ave. E), Capitol Hill, 206/324–9210. Sun.–Wed. 11 AM–midnight, Thurs. 11 AM–1 AM, Fri.–Sat. 11 AM–2 AM.*

POP & ROCK

Ask a kid toting a guitar case about "grunge" and you'll likely get a painful moan, perhaps with an accompanying gesture. Seattle has soooo moved on. Too few people truly know the mixed bag that is the rock scene. Here, there's a kid picking up a guitar every day, and in a few, he or she will be pasting up fliers and whipping up a frenzy on one of the local stages.

11 *d-6*

THE BREAKROOM

Styled as a working-man's hangout, this is a hip, comfortable spot to enjoy alternative bands. Although the action is on stage, where new bands begin their ascent to stardom, there are pool and air-hockey tables at the back. *1325 E. Madison St. (at 13th Ave. E.), Capitol Hill, 206/860–5155. Daily 4 PM–2 AM.*

10 *e-5*

CROCODILE CAFÉ

Seattle's most successful club books alternative music acts nightly except Monday. Depending on the bill, you'll find those from the grunge scene mixed with those barely able to make the 21 and over cut. The main room can get packed, but the back bar is always available for a mid-show getaway. *2200 2nd Ave. (at Blanchard St.), Downtown, 206/441–5611. Tues. 8 AM–11 PM, Wed. 11 AM–2 AM, Thurs.–Sat. 8 AM–2 AM, Sun. 9 AM–3 PM.*

10 *d-3*

DV8

If you're over 21, you might feel downright adult in this underage rock club. Big-name acts play to enthusiastic, scrubbed-clean crowds sporting grown-up duds. Bring your earplugs and steer clear of the mosh pit. *131 Taylor Ave. N (at Denny Way), Queen Anne, 206/448–0888. Mon.–Thurs. 9:30 PM–2 AM, Fri.–Sat. 9:30 PM–4 AM.*

10 *e-7*

GIBSON'S BAR & GRILL

This bar looks like it's been around the block a few times—it has. Stiff pours and hard-core drinkers set the scene. Up-and-coming punk bands refuse to give up the stage, much to the delight of fans. *116 Stewart St. (at 1st Ave.), Downtown, 206/448–6369. Weekdays 11 AM–2 AM, weekends noon–2 AM.*

8 *a-7*

GRACELAND

Graceland is a dimly lit club that specializes in alternative rock. The stage has the cramped feel of a ship's hold, but the raised seating at the rear offers excellent views of the rockin' and the stompin'. All-ages events are also held here regularly. *109 Eastlake Ave. E (at Denny Way), Downtown, 206/381–3094. Daily 4 PM–2 AM.*

13 *g-4*

THE OLD FIREHOUSE

An east side rarity is this all-ages hot spot. Underage music fans check out the best in local and touring alternative bands here. Show times vary, as do the days the club is open; doors typically open at 8 PM on show nights. *16510 NE 79th St. (at 164th Ave. NE), Redmond, 425/556–2370.*

5 *g-5*

PARADOX THEATER

Underage music fans pack this place thanks to its mix of punk, pop, hardcore, and the spoken word as well as its proximity to the U-Dub campus. *5510 University Way NE (at NE 55th St.), University District, 206/524–7677. Daily 7 PM.*

10 *f-7*

SHOWBOX

Like a cat with many lives, the Showbox continues to survive the fickle fates of fad, booking the latest in big-name acts. Rave nights and guest DJ appearances are also popular in this cavernous former ballroom. *1426 1st Ave. (at Pike St.), Downtown, 206/628–3151. Wed.–Sat. 3 PM–2 AM.*

SPORTS BARS & BILLIARDS

Armchair refereeing goes over a lot better when you're surrounded by dozens of fellow fans, huddled near a giant TV screen catching pay per view. Such is the appeal of the sports bar. For those who are more inclined to do more than recline, there are plenty of worthy pool halls to test your stick.

5 *g-7*

ALL AMERICAN SPORTS BAR & GRILL

Just a stone's throw from fraternities and dorms in the University District, you'll find the top gathering spot for Husky fans. The memorabilia-filled bar and restaurant has 24 TVs, so you can follow several games at once. *4333 University Way NE (at NE 43rd St.), University District, 206/545–7771. Weekdays 11:30 AM–2 AM, weekends 9 AM–2 AM.*

5 *b-8*

BALLROOM IN FREMONT

From its beer cans to its bars, Seattle loves to recycle. That said, take a former warehouse, give it a friendly no-nonsense name, throw in 15 well-kept pool tables, serve beer and wine, and you have this place. An inviting, neighborhood atmosphere prevails. *456 N. 36th St. (at Francis Ave. N), Fremont, 206/634–2575. Daily 4 PM–2 AM.*

10 d-6
BELLTOWN BILLIARDS

Don't expect to find sharks on the prowl; here you've got professionals who like to rack 'em up after work. It's an upscale, elegantly lit room, with 12 regulation tables and tasty southern Italian cuisine—not your average pool-hall fare. *90 Blanchard St. (at 1st Ave.), Downtown, 206/448–6779. Tues.–Fri. 11:30 AM–2 AM, Sat.–Mon. 4 PM–2 AM.*

13 b-4
DYNAMITE LOUNGE

You don't need to drive across the Lake Washington bridges to catch the big games or have a go at pool or darts thanks to this swanky, multifaceted lounge. You can hang out with your buddies here during the day or bring a date here in the evening for some dancing. *15 Lake St. (at Kirkland Ave.), Kirkland, 425/822–3474. Mon.–Thurs. 4 PM–1 AM, Fri.–Sat. 9 AM–2 AM.*

11 c-6
GARAGE

This one-time mechanic's garage is now a gigantic billiards hall, with well-spaced pool tables and spirited regulars. It's also a good place to spot a rock star or two. *1130 Broadway Ave. (at E. Madison St.), Capitol Hill, 206/322–2296. Daily 3 PM–2 AM.*

8 e-3
GRADY'S GRILLHOUSE

Here's a sports bar with a family-style atmosphere. You can bring the kids, catch the game, and be heard should you comment on a bad call or order up another pint. *2307 24th Ave. E (at E. Lynn St.), University District, 206/726–5968. Mon.–Thurs. 11:30 AM–midnight, Fri.–Sat. 11:30 AM–2 AM, Sat. noon–11.*

7 h-5
JILLIAN'S

Jillian's has everything a laid-back sports fan could ask for: plenty of space, pool tables galore, gigantic TV screens, video games, darts, air hockey, and much more. *731 Westlake Ave. N (at Valley St.), Downtown, 206/223–0300. Weekdays 11 AM–2 AM, weekends noon–3 AM.*

6 a-7
THE RAM RESTAURANT & BIG HORN BREWERY

The Ram is officially the unofficial watering hole for U-Dub sports fans. Preppy armchair quarterbacks fill the room with raucous commentary on the latest happenings at Husky Stadium. *4730 University Village NE (at 30th Ave. NE), University District, 206/525–3565. Daily 11 AM–2 AM.*

13 b-4
SHARK CLUB

Casual players fill this pool hall during the week; on weekends the sharks take over. You'll pay the club's hourly fee for your games; the sharks negotiate their own deals. *52 Lake Shore Plaza (at Central Way), Kirkland, 425/803–3003. Daily 4 PM–2 AM.*

12 c-3
TEMPLE BILLIARDS

This joint looks just like the ones you've seen in old movies—think chipped-plaster walls and low-wattage lighting. There's even a balcony with a lone table so you can re-create your favorite Minnesota Fats memory. *126 S. Jackson St. (at Occidental Ave. S), Pioneer Square, 206/682–3242. Weekdays 11 AM–2 AM, weekends 3 PM–2 AM.*

5 g-7
TOMMY'S NIGHTCLUB & GRILL

Tommy's sits on the Ave., the U-District's main drag, and plays host to mostly college students who enjoy the pub grub, microbrews, and billiard tables. It also has two areas for watching televised games and local rock bands after 10 PM. *4552 University Way NE (at NE 45th St), University District, 206/634–3144. Weekdays 11:30 AM –2 AM, Sat. 9:30 AM – 2 AM, Sun. 9:30 AM–midnight.*

chapter 6

HOTELS

To get the most out of Seattle's lodging scene spend some time identifying your preferences. Most properties specialize in one or two features. For some it's state-of-the-art business services, for others it may be romance and pampering. If it's a view you want—of the Cascades, the Olympics, Elliott Bay, or Lake Union—look to such high-rises as the Elliott Grand Hyatt, the Sheraton, and the Westin. The vistas from the floor-to-ceiling windows at the W Hotel are as dizzying as the beds are comfortable, and the panoramas at the Inn at the Market and the Edgewater Hotel almost make you feel part of the scenery. Suites at such moderately priced options as the Ace Hotel and Pensione Nichols are near their high-priced cousins, and take similar advantage of the striking views.

If unforgettably comfortable beds are important, try the Four Seasons Olympic. For pampering, choose the Alexis, with its on-site Aveda spa. For the best business services pick a hotel close to the convention center: the Elliott Grand Hyatt, the Madison, the Sheraton, the Westin, the W Hotel, or the Four Seasons Olympic. If an early morning flight has you worried about rush-hour snarls on I–5, opt for a hotel near the airport.

Most of Seattle's hotels are concentrated Downtown, but there are good deals to be had in the outlying neighborhoods, and some of those hotels offer complimentary transportation to and from Downtown sights. Both of the Marriotts at Lake Union, for example, offer a shuttle to the Pike Place Market, Westlake Center, the Space Needle, and Pier 70. Bed-and-Breakfasts on Capitol Hill are a manageable walk from Downtown, and are near boutiques, restaurants, bars, and movie theaters.

Less expensive but still tasteful lodging options (rates often include parking) are available in the University District, which is well served by the city's buses. The U-District typically caters to a more youthful crowd than other areas, with less expensive restaurants, trendy shops, and lots of pubs. Both Bellevue and Queen Anne attract a wealthier, more staid clientele. Bellevue is desirable to traveler's with business on the Eastside, shoppers, and those looking for proximity to the outdoor activities the nearby central Cascades provide. Queen Anne offers proximity to the many cultural events that take place on the Seattle Center grounds. While the Fremont neighborhood is busily attracting commercial and residential newcomers, there are no lodging facilities located within walking distance of this self-proclaimed "Center of the Universe." The closest bets are the Marriott Courtyard at Lake Union or the Chelsea Station near the Woodland Park Zoo.

Seattle's peak season is May through September, with August at the pinnacle. You aren't likely to have trouble booking a room during the rest of the year as long as you aren't competing with visitors in town for major conventions, arts, or sporting events. But to make sure you won't go sleepless, the best advice remains, book as far in advance as possible.

PRICE CATEGORIES

CATEGORY	COST*
Very Expensive	over $250
Expensive	$200–$250
Moderate	$150–$200
Budget	under $150

*All prices are for a standard double room, excluding 15.6% combined hotel and state sales tax.

VERY EXPENSIVE LODGINGS

12 *b-1*

ALEXIS HOTEL

The European-style Alexis occupies two 1901 neoclassical buildings near the waterfront. Upon your arrival, complimentary sherry awaits you in the lobby bar, a prelude to the attentive service you'll receive throughout your stay.

Rooms, painted in creamy yellows, have imported Italian and French fabrics as well as both antique and reproduction furniture. Some suites have whirlpool tubs or wood-burning fireplaces, and some baths have marble tiles. Unfortunately, views are limited, and rooms facing First Avenue can be noisy. But perhaps you're here for the Aveda spa, in which case you'll be in a world of your own. The spa is reason alone many stay here—even a few locals. More mundane hotel amenities include shoe shines, the morning paper, and access to a gym on-site. Pets are welcome. *1007 1st Ave. (at Madison St.), 98104, Downtown, 206/624–4844 or 800/426–7033, fax 206/621–9009, www.alex-ishotel.com. 65 rooms, 44 suites. 2 restaurants, bar, in-room data ports, minibars, room service, spa, steam room, gym, laundry service, concierge, meeting rooms, parking (fee). AE, D, DC, MC, V.*

14 *c-2*

BELLEVUE CLUB HOTEL

Warm earthtones incorporated into the decidedly modern setting, coupled with the clever use of lighting, create the illusion of sunlight inside this boutique hotel even when it's raining outside. Original oil paintings by Northwest artist Mark Rediske hang in each room. Pillows made from African Kuba textiles, Turkish area rugs, and Japanese *raku* pottery offset cherry furniture. All rooms have plush armchairs and large, spa-inspired, limestone-tile bathrooms with tubs and separate glass-enclosed showers. An on-site spa means you can fully relax with a facial or massage. *11200 SE 6th St. (112th Ave. SE), 98004, Bellevue, 425/454–4424 or 800/579–1110, fax 425/688–3101, www.bellevueclub.com/hotel.htm. 64 rooms, 3 suites. 2 restaurants, lounge, in-room data ports, in-room safes, minibars, refrigerators, room service, pool, spa, tennis court, basketball, health club, laundry service, concierge, business services, meeting rooms, parking (fee). AE, DC, MC, V.*

10 *c-6*

THE EDGEWATER

The only hotel on Elliott Bay, the Edgewater has spacious accommodations with balconies. Though some quarters face Alaskan Way, many offer views of the ferries and barges plying Puget Sound and the distant Olympic Mountains. All rooms have fireplaces and are decorated in rustic plaids and pale unfinished-wood furniture. From the lobby's comfortable sofas and chairs, you can sometimes see sea lions frolicking in the bay. A courtesy van shuttles you to and from Downtown. *Pier 67, 2411 Alaskan Way, 98121, Waterfront, 206/728–7000 or 800/624–0670, fax 206/441–4119, www.noblehousehotels.com. 232 rooms, 4 suites. Restaurant, bar, in-room data ports, minibars, no-smoking rooms, room service, gym, bicycles, laundry service, concierge, meeting rooms, parking (fee). AE, D, DC, MC, V.*

10 *h-6*

THE ELLIOTT GRAND HYATT

The Elliott was part of an expansion of the Washington State Convention Center. Both projects, it seems, were designed to fulfill the needs of Seattle's high-tech industry. The hotel offers state-of-the-art Internet access (100Mb/s), virtual private network technology (basically a closed circuit network carrying conference specific information accessible within a group of hotel guests), video conference rooms, two executive boardrooms, and a 151-seat theater with data ports at every seat. The warm rooms with natural color schemes are filled by cherry wood furnishings, Carrara marble floors, and Vesuvio granite counters; oversize tubs are standard in all baths. *721 Pine St. (at 7th Ave.), 98101, Downtown, 206/262–0700, fax 206/625–1221, www.seattle-grand.hyatt.com. 312 rooms, 113 suites. Restaurant, bar, café, in-room data ports, minibars, no-smoking rooms, room service, gym, laundry service, concierge, meeting rooms, parking (fee). AE, D, DC, MC, V.*

10 *h-7*

FOUR SEASONS OLYMPIC HOTEL

The 1920s Renaissance Revival–style Olympic is the grande dame of Seattle hotels. Marble, wood paneling, potted plants, thick rugs, and plush armchairs adorn public spaces. The skylit Garden Court is a relaxing spot for lunch, afternoon tea, or dancing to a swing band on weekends. The Georgian Room, the hotel's premier restaurant, exudes Italian Renaissance elegance. Shuckers oyster bar is more casual. Guest rooms, decorated in 1920's period reproductions, floral fabrics, and soft yellow or green wall coverings, are less luxurious than the public areas, but have a homey feel. All have sofas, comfortable reading chairs, and desks. Amenities include valet parking, chocolates on your pillow, complimentary shoe shines, the morning paper, and bathrobes. *411 University St. (at 5th Ave.), 98101, Downtown, 206/621–1700 or 800/223–8772, fax 206/682–9633, www.fourseasons.com. 225 rooms, 225 suites. 3 restaurants, lounge, in-room data ports, in-room safes, minibars, room service, indoor pool, health club, children's programs, laundry service, concierge, meeting rooms, parking (fee). AE, D, DC, MC, V.*

10 *h-8*
HOTEL MONACO
Goldfish in your room are among the fun touches at this luxury hotel, part of the Kimpton Group of hotels, inside a former office building in the heart of the financial district. The light, whimsical lobby has high ceilings and hand-painted nautical murals inspired by the fresco at the Palace of Knossos in Crete. A pleasing blend of bold colors and patterns graces the spacious guest rooms. In-room amenities include voice mail, fax machines, irons, hair dryers, coffeemakers, and stereos with CD players. The hotel welcomes pets—although the goldfish may not. *1101 4th Ave. (Spring St.), 98101, Downtown, 206/621–1770 or 800/945–2240, fax 206/621–7779, www.monaco-seattle.com. 144 rooms, 45 suites. Restaurant, bar, in-room data ports, no-smoking rooms, room service, exercise room, dry cleaning, laundry service, concierge, business services, meeting rooms, airport shuttle, parking (fee). AE, D, DC, MC, V.*

9 *b-1*
HOTEL VINTAGE PARK
As a tribute to the state's growing wine industry, each guest room in this stylish boutique property, part of a Northwest minichain, is named for a Washington winery or vineyard. The theme extends to complimentary servings of local wines each evening in the lobby, where you can relax on richly upholstered sofas and chairs arranged around a marble fireplace. Rooms—decorated in dark green, plum, deep red, taupe, and gold—have custom-made cherry furniture, and original works by San Francisco artist Chris Kidd. Hotel staffers will check out and deliver your choice of titles from the Seattle Public Library. You can also have exercise equipment brought to your room. Some of the best restaurants in the city are inside hotels; if where you eat is just as important to where you

stay, the Vintage Park hotel and Tulio restaurant are a terrific choice. *1100 5th Ave. (Spring St.), 98101, Downtown, 206/624–8000 or 800/624–4433, fax 206/623–0568, www.hotelvintagepark.com. 93 rooms, 33 suites. Restaurant, in-room data ports, minibars, no-smoking floors, refrigerators, room service, spa, laundry service, concierge, meeting rooms, parking (fee). AE, D, DC, MC, V.*

13 *b-8*
HYATT REGENCY BELLEVUE
Near Bellevue Square and other downtown area shopping centers, the Hyatt looks like any other sleek high-rise, but its interior is adorned with huge displays of fresh flowers and such Asian touches as antique Japanese chests. Rooms are understated, with dark woods and earthtones predominating. Deluxe suites include two bedrooms, bar facilities, and meeting rooms with desks and full-length tables. You have access to a separate health club and pool that shares a courtyard with the hotel (fee). The restaurant serves excellent and reasonably priced breakfasts, lunches, and dinners; an English-style pub and sports bar serves lunch and dinner. *900 Bellevue Way NE (NE 8th Street), 98004, Bellevue, 425/462–2626, fax 425/646–7567, www.hyatt.com. 353 rooms, 29 suites. Restaurant, sports bar, in-room data ports, no-smoking rooms, room service, concierge, meeting rooms, parking (fee). AE, D, DC, MC, V.*

9 *b-1*
MADISON
Rooms at this high-rise between Downtown and I–5 are decorated in deep green, burgundy, and brown, with dark-wood furniture. Good views of Downtown, Elliott Bay, and the Cascades can be had from rooms above the 20th floor. If you stay on a club-level floor (25, 26, or 27), you'll receive complimentary Continental breakfast and have your own concierge. Amenities on all floors include free coffee, the morning paper, and shoe shines. The health club has a rooftop pool and a hot tub. *515 Madison St. (at 6th Ave.), 98104, Downtown, 206/583–0300 or 800/278–4159, fax 206/622–8635, www.renaissance.com. 466 rooms, 88 suites. 2 restaurants, bar, in-room data ports, minibars, room service, laundry service, concierge, health club, meeting rooms, parking (fee). AE, D, DC, MC, V.*

`10` h-6

PARAMOUNT HOTEL

The châteauesque Paramount's location provides easy access to fine dining, shopping, and the convention center as well as to such high-tech entertainment sites as Gameworks, Niketown, and a 16-screen Cineplex Odeon. The comfortable lobby, with a fireplace, bookshelves, and period reproductions, looks like a country gentleman's smoking parlor. Rooms, quiet but small, are decorated in hunter green and beige with gray accents. All have work areas, lounge chairs, large bathrooms, and movie and game systems. *724 Pine St. (at 8th Ave.), 98101, Downtown, 206/292–9500 or 800/426–0670, fax 206/292–8610, www.west-coasthotels.com. 146 rooms, 2 suites. Restaurant, in-room data ports, no-smoking rooms, room service, gym, laundry service, concierge, meeting rooms, parking (fee). AE, D, DC, MC, V.*

`8` a-5

RESIDENCE INN BY MARRIOTT

An extended-stay hotel on scenic Lake Union, the Marriott is perfect for families. All accommodations are one- or two-bedroom suites, each with a living room and a fully equipped kitchen. Decorated in greens and blues, the comfortable suites get plenty of natural light. The lobby, in a seven-story atrium with a waterfall, has many areas in which to relax, watch TV, play games, or peruse the cookbooks displayed on bookshelves. Room rates include complimentary shuttle service within a 2½-mi radius of the hotel. *800 Fairview Ave. N (at Minor Ave. N), 98109, Lake Union, 206/624–6000 or 800/331–3131, fax 206/223–8160, www.marriott.com. 234 suites. Room service, no-smoking rooms, in-room data ports, indoor pool, sauna, gym, children's programs, parking (fee). AE, D, DC, MC, V. CP.*

`10` h-7

SEATTLE HILTON

Just west of I–5, the Hilton is a popular site for meetings and conventions. The tastefully nondescript rooms have soothing color schemes. The Top of the Hilton, providing excellent views of the city, serves well-prepared salmon dishes and other local specialties. An underground passage connects the hotel with the Rainier Square shopping concourse, the Fifth Avenue Theater, and the convention center. *1301 6th Ave. (at University St.), 98101, Downtown, 206/624–0500 or 800/426–0535, fax 206/682–9029, www.hilton.com. 237 rooms, 3 suites. 2 restaurants, piano bar, in-room data ports, minibars, no-smoking floors, room service, gym, laundry service, concierge, business services, meeting rooms, parking (fee). AE, D, DC, MC, V.*

`10` g-6

SEATTLE SHERATON HOTEL & TOWERS

Business travelers are the primary patrons of this 35-story hotel near the convention center. The lobby features an art-glass collection by well-known northwest artist Dale Chihuly. Rooms on the top five floors, larger and more elegant than those on lower floors, include concierge service and complimentary Continental breakfast. Dining options include Fullers, one of Seattle's best restaurants, and the casual Pike Street Cafe, which serves all-American cuisine. *1400 6th Ave. (at Pike St.), 98101, Downtown, 206/621–9000 or 800/325–3535, fax 206/621–8441, www.sheraton.com/seattle. 800 rooms, 40 suites. 4 restaurants, 2 bars, in-room data ports, in-room safes, minibars, room service, indoor pool, health club, laundry service, concierge, meeting rooms, parking (fee). AE, D, DC, MC, V.*

`11` a-7

SORRENTO

Built in 1909, the Sorrento was designed to look like an Italian villa, with a dramatic circular driveway around a palm-fringed fountain. Sitting high on First Hill, the hotel overlooks Downtown and Elliott Bay. Rooms are quiet and comfortable, though some are quite small. The largest are the corner suites, which have some antiques and spacious baths. The Hunt Club serves Pacific Northwest dishes. The dark-paneled Fireside Lounge, in the lobby, is an inviting spot for coffee, tea, or cocktails. Other amenities include free limousine service within the Downtown area and privileges at a nearby athletic club (fee). *900 Madison St. (at Terry Ave.), 98104, First Hill, 206/622–6400 or 800/426–1265, fax 206/343–6155, www.hotelsorrento.com. 76 rooms, 42 suites. Restaurant, bar, in-room data ports, minibars, room service, laundry service, concierge, meeting rooms, parking (fee). AE, D, DC, MC, V.*

10 · g-8

W HOTEL

Everything here is streamlined, stylized, and chic. Candlelight and custom-designed board games encourage you to linger around the lobby fireplace on comfortable purple couches with black-and-white faux-fur throw pillows. Nearby bookshelves hold a selection of old favorites, and rough-hewn wooden bowls cradle shiny green apples. Each room has two phone lines, a cordless phone, Ethernet laptop access, a TV with high-speed Internet access, and CD players and VCRs complete with libraries. Floor-to-ceiling windows maximize striking views of Puget Sound and the city. Decorated in black, brown, and French blue, rooms are almost austere, but beds are exceptionally comfortable with goose-down pillows and comforters. An iron, ironing board, coffeemaker, hair dryers, and luxurious cotton robes round out the room amenities. *1112 4th Ave. (at Seneca St.), 98101, Downtown, 206/264–6000 or 877/946–8357, fax 206/264–6100, www.whotels. com. 419 rooms, 16 suites. Restaurant, bars, in-room data ports, in-room safes, minibars, no-smoking floors, room service, gym, laundry service, concierge, business services, meeting rooms, parking (fee). AE, D, DC, MC, V.*

10 · f-5

WESTIN HOTEL

The flagship of the Westin chain often hosts U.S. presidents and other visiting dignitaries. Northeast of Pike Place Market, Seattle's largest hotel is easily recognizable by its twin, 47-story cylindrical towers. The innovative design gives all rooms terrific views of Puget Sound, Lake Union, the Space Needle, or the city. Airy guest quarters are furnished in a simple, high-quality style. Some are equipped with fax machines, speaker phones, and data ports. *1900 5th Ave. (at Stewart St.), 98101, Downtown, 206/ 728–1000 or 800/228–3000, fax 206/727–5896, www.westin.com. 822 rooms, 43 suites. 3 restaurants, 2 bars, in-room data ports, in-room safes, minibars, no-smoking floors, room service, indoor pool, beauty salon, massage, gym, children's programs, laundry service, concierge, business services, convention center, car rental, parking (fee). AE, D, DC, MC, V.*

1 · f-1

WILLOWS LODGE

Along the banks of the Sammamish River near the Red Hook Brewery, and the St. Michelle and Columbia Wineries, Woodinville is only slightly off the beaten path. The town is a splendid base camp for those doing business with the Eastside's giants of tech-commerce or if you're looking for a rejuvenating weekend getaway. A dramatically lit, Douglas fir greets you at the entrance to this spa hotel, as does the legendary Herbfarm Restaurant, with its French-country style and its nine-course meals. A floor-to-ceiling stone fireplace dominates the lobby, and contemporary Native American prints and sculptures by area artists adorn the walls and gardens. Timbers salvaged from a 19th-century warehouse lend rustic counterpoints to the sleek modernity throughout. All rooms have fireplaces, oversize tubs, and CD and DVD players. Bathrooms have stone sinks that resemble free-standing salad bowls and have austere, industrial-looking spigots. You can also take advantage of special dining and lodging packages that include a stay in one of the Herbfarm suites overlooking the kitchen gardens. The on-site spa specializes in facials, massage, and body wraps using Declor products. *14580 NE 145th St. (near Redhook Brewery), Woodinville 98072, 425/424–3900 or 877/424–3930, fax 425/424–2585, www. willowslodge.com. 83 rooms, 5 suites. 2 restaurants, bar, in-room data ports, in-room safes, minibars, refrigerators, room service, pool, spa, gym, laundry service, concierge, business services, meeting rooms, free parking. AE, D, DC, MC, V. CP.*

13 · b-6

WOODMARK HOTEL

Steps away from downtown Kirkland, 7 mi east of Seattle, the Woodmark is the only hotel on Lake Washington's shores. A circular staircase, descending from the lobby to the Library Lounge, passes a huge bay window with a panoramic lake view. The contemporary guest rooms face the water, a courtyard, or the street and are done in shades of café au lait, taupe, and ecru. Numerous amenities include terry-cloth robes, coffeemakers, irons, hair dryers, free shoe shines, and the morning paper. There's a fitness center nearby in Carillon Point, a residential-commercial complex. Waters

Bistro serves such Pacific Rim dishes as lemongrass steamed clams and grilled halibut with roasted onion-ginger relish. *1200 Carillon Pt., 98033, Kirkland, 425/822–3700 or 800/822–3700, fax 425/822–3699, www.thewoodmark.com. 79 rooms, 21 suites. Restaurant, bar, in-room data ports, in-room safes, minibars, refrigerators, room service, gym, laundry service, concierge, business services, meeting rooms, parking (fee). AE, DC, MC, V.*

EXPENSIVE LODGINGS

1 *e-6*

DOUBLETREE INN & DOUBLETREE SUITES

These two hotels across the street from each other are adjacent to the Southcenter shopping mall and convenient to business park offices. The inn is a classic Pacific Northwest–style lodge; its rooms are smaller and less lavish than those in the suites, but they're perfectly fine and cost at least $25 less. Suites have sofas, tables and chairs, and wet bars. *Doubletree Inn, 205 Strander Blvd. (at Southcenter Pkwy.), 98188, Southcenter, 206/575–8220 or 800/325–8733, fax 206/575–4743, www.doubletreehotels.com. 193 rooms, 5 suites. Bar, coffee shop, dining room, indoor and outdoor pools, meeting rooms, airport shuttle, free parking. Doubletree Suites, 16500 Southcenter Pkwy. (near Strander Blvd.), 98188, Southcenter, 206/575–8220 or 800/325–8733, fax 206/575–4743. 221 suites. Restaurant, bar, minibars, refrigerators, indoor pool, hot tub, sauna, health club, racquetball, meeting rooms, airport shuttle, free parking. AE, D, DC, MC, V.*

MOUNTAINS MAJESTY

Many hotels are positioned to take maximum advantage of breathtaking views of the Cascades and Olympics, Elliott Bay, Lake Washington, and the pièce de résistance, Mt. Rainier. The next time the clouds break, book a room at one of the following hotels, soak in the sights, and save your memories for the rainy days.

W Hotel (Very Expensive)
The floor-to-ceiling windows offer dizzying views from rooms from the fifteenth floor up.

The Inn at the Market (Expensive)
Elliott Bay and the Pike Place Market are right outside your window.

The Westin Hotel (Very Expensive)
These twin circular towers offer panoramic views of all the sights, natural and man-made.

Seattle Sheraton Hotel and Towers (Very Expensive)
An Olympic-sized pool and gym with a view are on the top floor of this 35-story hotel.

The Elliott Grand Hyatt (Very Expensive)
A view lounge on the 27th floor is available to guests on the concierge levels.

The Woodmark (Very Expensive)
Understated elegance on the shores of Lake Washington, the Woodmark is popular with visiting celebrities.

The Edgewater (Very Expensive)
Get a water-level view of ferries and other harbor traffic on Elliott Bay from this Pier 67 location.

Madison (Very Expensive)
The rooftop health club, complete with pool and hot tub, has a breathtaking view of the cityscape.

Pensione Nichols (Budget)
The suites have sweeping views of Elliott Bay and enclosed balconies.

University Tower (Budget)
This art deco U-District beacon has stunning views of Mt. Rainier, the UW campus, any of the city's lakes, or downtown skyline, depending on which way your room faces.

`10` f-8
INN AT HARBOR STEPS

On the lower floors of a high-rise residential building, this lodging is a departure for Four Sisters Inns, whose collection of small hotels focuses on quaint city and country properties. The entrance and corridors, in muted gray, tan, and sage, have something of a yuppie-dormitory feel, but the rooms are large and have high ceilings, gas fireplaces, and tidy kitchenettes. Bathrooms accommodate large tubs (some of them whirlpools) and oversize glass-enclosed showers. A tempting breakfast buffet is served in the dining room, and each afternoon sees complimentary hors d'oeuvres, wine, and tea in the library. The Wolfgang Puck Cafe is next door—and they'll deliver. *1221 1st Ave. (at University St.), 98101, Downtown, 206/748–0973 or 888/728–8910, fax 206/748–0533, www.foursisters.com. 30 rooms. In-room data ports, refrigerators, room service, indoor pool, sauna, basketball court, gym, coin laundry, laundry service, concierge, meeting room, parking (fee). AE, MC, V. BP.*

`10` e-7
INN AT THE MARKET

This sophisticated yet unpretentious property up the street from Pike Place Market is perfect for travelers who like boutique hotels with personality. The good-size rooms are decorated with comfortable modern furniture and small touches such as fresh flowers and ceramic sculptures. Coffee and the morning newspaper are complimentary. If your room lacks a view, head for the fifth-floor deck, where you can have a seat in an Adirondack chair and look out over the water and the market. The hotel can obtain day passes for you at the Seattle Western health club ($15 per day) or make appointments for you at the spa down the street. Restaurants here include Campagne, and the less formal yet equally romantic Café Campagne downstairs. *Pike Place Market, 86 Pine St. (at 1st Ave.), 98101, Downtown, 206/443–3600 or 800/446–4484, fax 206/448–0631, www.innatthemarket.com. 60 rooms, 10 suites. 3 restaurants, in-room data ports, no-smoking rooms, refrigerators, room service, laundry service, concierge, meeting room, parking (fee). AE, D, DC, MC, V.*

`10` b-1
MARQUEEN HOTEL

At the foot of Queen Anne Hill, just blocks from the Seattle Center—built for the 1962 World's Fair and now home of Space Needle, KeyArena, and Experience Music Project—the Marqueen is ideal for patrons of the opera, ballet, theater, or KeyArena sporting events. The hotel is in a brick structure that dates from 1918 and was once an apartment building. Its dark lobby has marble floors, overstuffed furniture, Asian-style lacquered screens, and a grand staircase looking out at a garden mural painted on a facing building. The spacious guest rooms, furnished with antique replicas, all have kitchens and sitting areas as well as beds adorned with down comforters in green, gold, pink, and burgundy that coordinate with the window treatments. A free newspaper is left outside your door each morning. *600 Queen Ave. N (at Roy St.), 98109, Queen Anne, 206/282–7407, fax 206/283–1499, www.marqueen.com. 47 rooms, 4 suites. Kitchenettes, in-room data ports, room service, laundry service, parking (fee). AE, D, DC, MC, V.*

`10` f-6
MAYFLOWER PARK HOTEL

Brass fixtures, antiques, and lacquered screens lend Asian undertones to the public and private spaces at this older property near the Westlake Center. Service here is smooth and unobtrusive. Rooms are on the small side, but the Mayflower Park is so sturdily constructed that it's much quieter than many modern downtown hotels. *405 Olive Way (at 4th Ave.), 98101, Downtown, 206/623–8700 or 800/426–5100, fax 206/382–6997, www.mayflower.com. 159 rooms, 13 suites. Restaurant, bar, no-smoking rooms, room service, gym, concierge, laundry service, business services, meeting rooms, parking (fee). AE, D, DC, MC, V.*

`8` a-8
SUMMERFIELD SUITES

Next to the convention center and overlooking I–5, Summerfield Suites is ideal for an extended business stay. Guest rooms are tastefully decorated in burgundies and greens. Suites have full kitchens, living rooms with gas fireplaces, and separate bedrooms. Street-facing rooms have balconies and views of Lake Union, but the fumes and noise from the traffic below will probably keep you inside. If you keep your doors and windows closed, your room will be remarkably quiet. A Continental breakfast is served each morning in the dining area off the lobby. *1011 Pike St. (at Boren Ave.), 98101, Downtown, 206/682–8282 or 800/833–4353, fax 206/682–5315, www.summerfieldseattle.com. 10 rooms, 183 suites. Breakfast room, air-conditioning, in-room data ports, no-smoking rooms, pool, sauna, gym, coin laundry, meeting rooms, parking (fee). AE, D, DC, MC, V. CP.*

10 e-5
WARWICK HOTEL
Service at this medium-size property is friendly and leisurely (but not slow), and the rooms are understated without being bland. Perhaps this is why the hotel has a more intimate feel than you might expect given the number of rooms. Most guest rooms have small balconies providing Downtown views. Brasserie Margeaux, the lounge, is a welcome respite after a day in this bustling neighborhood. The Warwick offers 24-hour courtesy transportation within Downtown. *401 Lenora St. (at 4th Ave.), 98121, Downtown, 206/443–4300 or 800/426–9280, fax 206/448–1662, www.warwickhotels.com. 225 rooms, 4 suites. Restaurant, bar, in-room data ports, no-smoking rooms, room service, indoor pool, hot tub, sauna, gym, concierge, parking (fee). AE, D, DC, MC, V.*

10 g-7
WEST COAST GRAND HOTEL
This former bank headquarters is now a comfortable business-oriented hotel convenient to the shopping and financial districts. Service here is warm and professional; the public spaces have high ceilings, tall windows, and dark-wood paneling. Lining the lobby are sitting areas with couches and overstuffed chairs upholstered in olive green and aubergine velvets and brocades. Guest rooms are mid-size and attractively appointed in a green and pink botanical theme. Rooms on the executive floors, 17–20, have exquisite views of Puget Sound or the skyline. All rooms are equipped with coffeemakers, hair dryers, irons, and ironing boards. *1415 5th Ave. (at Union St.), 98101, Downtown, 206/971–8000 or 800/325–4000, fax 206/971–8100, www.westcoasthotels.com. 287 rooms, 10 suites. Restaurant, in-room data ports, no-smoking rooms, room service, gym, laundry service, concierge, business services, meeting rooms, parking (fee). AE, D, DC, MC, V.*

MODERATELY PRICED LODGINGS

10 f-6
THE CLAREMONT HOTEL
This 1926 property languished for several decades as a low-income residential hotel. Its current owners have taken advantage of its enviable location and innate charm. All 10 of its floors have been refurbished; some have undergone major renovations. The small lobby has an understated beauty, with the original marble wainscoting and a fireplace accented by a rich terra-cotta finish. Guest rooms range from spacious suites, some with kitchens, to cramped and viewless cells. Bathrooms have all been restored in keeping with their original 1930's style, and many rooms have large walk-in closets. The hotel's two-story ballroom is popular for weddings and other festivities. *2000 4th Ave. (at Virginia St.), 98121, Downtown, 206/448–8600 or 800/448–8601, fax 206/441–7140, www.claremonthotel.com. 30 rooms, 80 suites. Restaurant, in-room data ports, no-smoking rooms, gym, laundry service, meeting rooms, parking (fee). AE, D, DC, MC, V.*

10 h-7
CROWNE PLAZA HOTEL
The Crowne Plaza is directly off I–5, midway between First Hill and the financial district. The lobby is small and plainly appointed in teal and cream with brass accents and houseplants. Rooms are quiet and spacious, with lounge chairs and work areas. All have views of Safeco Field and Harbor Island to the south and Elliott Bay and the Space Needle to the north. The relaxed, friendly staff is very attentive. *1113 6th Ave. (at Seneca St.), 98101, Downtown, 206/464–1980 or 800/521–2762, fax 206/340–1617, www.basshotels.com. 415 rooms, 28 suites. Restaurant, bar, in-room data ports, no-smoking rooms, room service, sauna, health club, laundry service, concierge, business services, meeting rooms, parking (fee). AE, D, DC, MC, V.*

11 e-4

GASLIGHT INN

Rooms here range from a crow's nest with peeled-log furniture and Navajo-print fabrics to suites with gas fireplaces and antique carved beds. There's also an apartment with a blown-glass chandelier and views of downtown and Elliott Bay. The large common areas have a clubby feel, with oak wainscoting, animal statuary, high ceilings, and hunter-green carpeting. One owner's past career as a professional painter is evident in the impeccable custom-mixed finishes throughout. Guests staying in the suites receive free off-street parking. *1727 15th Ave. (at Howell St.), 98122, Capitol Hill, 206/325–3654, fax 206/328–4803, www.gaslight-inn.com. 9 rooms, 7 suites. No-smoking rooms, pool. AE, MC, V. CP.*

7 g-6

HAMPTON INN & SUITES

During the week, this utilitarian property caters primarily to business travelers; on weekends it's an attractive choice for guests attending the various festivals and events held at the nearby Seattle Center. About half the rooms are suites, each with a gas fireplace, a kitchen, and a balcony. All rooms have irons, ironing boards, and coffeemakers. *700 5th Ave. N (at Roy St.), 98109, Queen Anne, 206/282–7700 or 800/426–7866, fax 206/282–3325, www.hamptoninn-suites.com. 124 rooms, 74 suites. In-room data ports, gym, meeting rooms, free parking. AE, D, DC, MC, V. CP.*

11 a-7

INN AT VIRGINIA MASON

As it's owned by the Virginia Mason Medical Center, this hotel draws quite a few "medical guests" from out of town whose treatment keeps them in the city for multiple days. Few folks know that it's open to the general public as well. The generously proportioned large rooms have a historic feel, a few of them even with original wood-burning fireplaces surrounded by beautiful 1920s tile work. In warmer months you're welcome to enjoy city views from the rooftop garden. The Rhododendron Restaurant, popular with guests and hospital staff, serves simple, healthful fare in the lobby or adjoining courtyard. *1006 Spring St. (at Terry Ave.), 98104, First Hill, 206/583–6453 or 800/283–6453, fax 206/223–7545. 78 rooms, 1 suite.*

Restaurant, in-room data ports, parking (fee). AE, D, DC, MC, V.

7 h-5

MARRIOTT COURTYARD

Comfort and convenience more than make up for what this hotel lacks in charm. The perks: Lake Union and Space Needle views, a courtesy shuttle (to and from the Space Needle, Convention Center, Westlake Center, Pike Place Market, and the Waterfront), inexpensive parking, a cozy lobby lounge, a pool, and a business center. Guest rooms are sunny and spacious, decorated in shades of green and burgundy. Each has a coffeemaker, an iron, and an ironing board. Rooms on the Lake Union side are popular with Fourth of July revelers who want a good view of the fireworks. Within walking distance you'll find critically acclaimed restaurants and popular national chains. The Wooden Boat Center is across the street, as is Kenmore Airs floatplane terminal. *925 Westlake Ave. N (Aloha St.), 98109, Lake Union, 206/213–0100 or 800/321–2211, fax 206/433–4443, www.courtyard.com. 250 rooms, 2 suites. Restaurant, bar, room service, in-room data ports, no-smoking rooms, indoor pool, hot tub, gym, coin laundry, business services, meeting rooms, parking (fee). AE, D, DC, MC, V.*

10 e-6

PENSIONE NICHOLS

It's hard to beat this B&B's location one block from Pike Place Market. Suites on the second floor have enclosed balconies, full-size kitchens, private baths, bedrooms, and large living rooms. Most third-floor rooms have skylights rather than windows and are decorated in light colors with antique and contemporary furnishings. *1923 1st Ave. (at Virginia St.), 98101, Downtown, 206/441–7125 or 800/440–7125. 10 rooms share 4 baths, 2 suites. AE, D, DC, MC, V. CP.*

12 b-2

PIONEER SQUARE HOTEL

A mid-1990s renovation trimmed this 1914 workmen's hotel down to 75 generously sized rooms and three suites. Furnishings are standard issue; the color scheme is predominantly pink. Rooms at the back of the hotel face an air shaft, creating dark but peaceful refuges. A stay here gets you access to a nearby health club. *77 Yesler Way (at Western*

Ave.), 98104, Pioneer Square, 206/340–1234, fax 206/467–0707, www.pioneer-square.com. 75 rooms, 3 suites. Coffee shop, pub, in-room data ports, no-smoking rooms, room service, laundry service, concierge, business services, meeting rooms, parking (fee). AE, D, DC, MC, V. CP.

5 *f-7*

UNIVERSITY PLAZA HOTEL

Families and business travelers like this full-service motor hotel across I–5 from the University of Washington. The mock-Tudor decor gives the place a dated feel, but the service is cheerful, and the rooms are spacious and appointed with teak furniture. Ask for a room away from the freeway. *400 NE 45th St. (4th Ave NE), 98105, University District, 206/634–0100 or 800/343–7040, fax 206/633–2743, www.travelbase.com/destinations/seattle/univ-plaza. 133 rooms, 2 suites. Restaurant, bar, no-smoking rooms, room service, pool, beauty salon, gym, meeting rooms, free parking. AE, D, DC, MC, V.*

10 *g-6*

WEST COAST ROOSEVELT HOTEL

The elegant lobby—with its grand piano, fireplace, Chinese lacquered screen, and walls of windows—is a great place to relax and watch the foot traffic outside. Small rooms are furnished with early 1900s reproductions upholstered in mellow pinks and greens. Thanks to the insulated windows you can enjoy city views without hearing street noise. Some bathrooms have their original tile work, but there isn't much counter space. The convention center and the shopping district are nearby. *1531 7th Ave. (at Pine St.), 98101, Downtown, 206/621–1200 or 800/426–0670, fax 206/233–0335, www.westcoasthotels.com. 138 rooms, 13 suites. Restaurant, bar, in-room data ports, no-smoking rooms, room service, gym, laundry service, meeting rooms, parking (fee). AE, D, DC, MC, V.*

BUDGET LODGINGS

7 *g-8*

THE ACE HOTEL

YOU ARE BEAUTIFUL is etched into every vanity mirror at this ultrahip, super-friendly hostelry. The darling of the nation's architectural and design elite offers the squeaky clean functionality of a Norwegian budget hotel. It serves the nightclubbing public in the most modern of styles; the decor is white on white. Half the rooms sleep "one or two humans" and share bathrooms. Suites are larger and have full private baths hidden behind rotating walls. Westerly facing quarters have views of Elliott Bay. Thoughtful amenities include condoms, energy bars, bottled water, and cool little address books and day planners. Hair dryers are available upon request. Pets are welcome. *2423 1st Ave. (at Wall St.), 98121, Belltown, 206/448–4721, fax 206/374–0745, www.theacehotel.com. 24 rooms, 9 suites. Restaurant, in-room data ports, no-smoking rooms, room service, parking (fee). AE, D, DC, MC, V.*

9 *e-3*

THE AMARANTH INN

A historic Seattle home just blocks from Chinatown has been restored and converted into a spacious, sunny B&B. The common areas include a sunroom, a parlor, and a formal breakfast room. Six guest rooms have private baths and gas fireplaces; all rooms are equipped with TVs and phones and are done in creams and pale greens with touches of lace and brocades in the bedspreads and window treatments. The full breakfasts served here range from straight forward egg dishes with sausage or bacon to French toast with seasonal fruit, and always include juice, pastries, coffee, and a selection of teas. Smoking is not allowed anywhere indoors. *1451 S. Main St. (at 14th Ave. S), 98144, International District, 206/720–7160 or 800/720–7161, fax 206/323–0772, www.amaranthinn.com. 8 rooms, 2 share bath. Breakfast room, free parking. AE, D, DC, MC, V. CP.*

8 *b-5*

BACON MANSION

On a tree-lined street a short walk from Volunteer Park and the bustle of Broadway, the grandly proportioned Bacon Mansion is surrounded by gardens. The first-floor common areas include a large living room filled with comfortable furniture, a grand piano, and lots of afternoon sunlight. All the guest rooms are pleasantly appointed with an array of collectibles old and new. Several rooms have hideaway beds in addition to the queen-size beds that are the norm here. The Capitol Suite has a fireplace and a view of the Space Needle. The Garden

Suite has its own kitchenette. *959 Broadway Ave. E (at E. Prospect St.), 98102, Capitol Hill, 206/329–1864 or 800/240–1864, fax 206/860–9025, www.baconmansion.com. 11 rooms, 2 share bath; 2 suites. In-room data ports. AE, D, DC, MC, V. CP.*

8 *b-6*

BED & BREAKFAST ON BROADWAY

Proprietors Don Fabian and Russel Lyons go out of their way to make you feel comfortable in their home on the north end of Broadway. (Broadway actually runs north–south despite being having an East in its name—this end of Broadway ironically veers west!) A Steinway grand piano dominates the music room, and antiques and art, including paintings by co-host Lyons, fill the living room. Queen-size beds with goosedown comforters are standard in the guest rooms, as are private baths and TVs. Two rooms have enclosed balconies. A Continental breakfast is served in the large kitchen or on the deck under a grape arbor. Although off-street parking is available, the inn is near restaurants, movie theaters, shops, and a bus stop, eliminating the need for a car. *722 Broadway Ave. E (at E. Roy St.), 98102, Capitol Hill, 206/329–8933 or 888/329–8933, www.chcs.com/bbonbroadway. 4 rooms. No-smoking rooms, free parking. AE, D, DC, MC, V. CP.*

5 *h-6*

CHAMBERED NAUTILUS

A resident teddy bear keeps you company at this Georgian Revival B&B built in 1915 by a professor of Oriental Studies at the University of Washington. Rooms all have baths, some with antique dressers converted into sinks and counters, as well as robes and well-stocked bookshelves. Most rooms also have private porches, and one has a fireplace. Breakfast might include stuffed French toast with orange syrup or a breakfast pie of salmon, dill, and Swiss cheese. *5005 22nd Ave. NE (at NE 50th St.), 98105, University District, 206/522–2536, fax 206/528–0898, www.chamberednautilus.com. 10 rooms. Dining room. AE, MC, V. BP.*

5 *c-6*

CHELSEA STATION

This B&B offers warm hospitality in a quiet locale across from the Woodland Park Zoo. The parlor and breakfast room are done in sage green and have Mission-style oak furniture, brocade upholstery, lace curtains, and works by local artists. Guest rooms in front have views of the Cascades, and all have a phone, a desk, and a mix of antique and contemporary furnishings. Several rooms have adjoining doors, useful for families or larger groups. One suite has a piano, another a kitchen. Breakfast can be tailored to suit special diets upon request, and the innkeepers will accommodate the needs of guests with allergies to environmental irritants within their control, such as down, dust, or cleaning products. *4915 Linden Ave. N (at N. 50th Ave.), 98103, Fremont, 206/547–6077 or 800/400–6077, fax 206/632–5107, www.bandbseattle.com. 2 rooms, 7 suites. Breakfast room, in-room data ports. AE, D, DC, MC, V. BP.*

14 *c-2*

DOUBLETREE HOTEL BELLEVUE

The 10-story Doubletree has an airy atrium filled with trees, shrubs, and flowering plants. The property also has a formal dining room, a lounge with two dance floors, and oversize guest rooms decorated in hunter green, burgundy, and beige. Rooms have either king- or queen-size beds. Two-room suites have wet bars and whirlpool tubs. *300 112th Ave. SE (SE 8th St.), 98004, Bellevue, 425/455–1300 or 800/733–5466, fax 425/455–0466, www.doubletreehotels.com. 348 rooms, 5 suites. 2 restaurants, bar, in-room data ports, room service, pool, gym, laundry service, concierge, business services, meeting rooms, free parking. AE, D, DC, MC, V.*

8 *c-7*

HILL HOUSE

An impeccably restored 1903 Victorian, the Hill House contains richly colored rooms with a mix of antique and contemporary furnishings. Two suites have phones and TVs. The rates include a filling breakfast and off-street parking, making this one of the city's best bargains. Book well in advance for summer weekends. *1113 E. John St. (at 11th Ave. E), Capitol Hill, 206/720–7161 or 800/720–7161, fax 206/323–0772, www.seattlebnb.com. 5 rooms, 3 with bath; 2 suites. Breakfast room, free parking. AE, D, DC, MC, V. BP.*

7 f-6
INN AT QUEEN ANNE

The setting for this reasonably priced inn is a brick 1920s structure that was once an apartment building. Its location is ideal: near the Seattle Center, a gourmet grocery, a movie theater, and Dick's Drive-In (a locally revered burger joint). Rooms are modestly decorated in shades of green and burgundy; each has a kitchenette, like a studio apartment, and a small bathroom. A Continental breakfast is served each morning in the lobby. *505 1st Ave. N (at Republican St.), 98109, Queen Anne, 206/282–7357 or 800/952–5043, fax 206/271–9719, www. innatqueenanne.com. 67 rooms, 1 suite. In-room data ports, kitchenettes. AE, D, DC, MC, V. CP.*

10 h-8
PACIFIC PLAZA

This 1929 property, which retains a period feel, is a good bargain for singles or couples. Families may find the non-descript rooms too small. The location is ideal if you want to be near the heart of the city. Restaurants, shopping, and the financial district surround this modest hotel. *400 Spring St. (at 4th Ave.), 98104, Downtown, 206/623–3900 or 800/426–1165, fax 206/623–2059, www.pacificplazahotel.com. 157 rooms, 1 suite. Restaurant, coffee shop, no-smoking rooms, concierge, parking (fee). AE, D, DC, MC, V. CP.*

8 d-6
SALISBURY HOUSE

Built in 1904, this craftsman-style house sits on a wide, tree-lined, Capitol Hill street. The spacious rooms are comfortably furnished with an eclectic collection of furniture, including some antiques. The basement suite has a private entrance and phone line, a fireplace, cable TV, and a jetted whirlpool bathtub. The Rose Room is decorated in rose chintz and has a canopy bed, the Lavender Room is furnished in white wicker, and the Blue Room has a private deck overlooking the garden. An expanded Continental breakfast is served in the sunny dining room. *750 16th Ave. E (at Aloha St.), 98112, Capitol Hill, 206/ 328–8682, fax 206/720–1019, www. salisburyhouse.com. 4 rooms, 1 suite. Dining room. MC, V. CP.*

8 a-5
TUGBOAT CHALLENGER

Guest quarters are snug on this 96-ft red tugboat moored at the south end of Lake Union. Built in 1944 for the U.S. Army, the *Challenger* was converted into a "bunk and breakfast" by Jerry Brown, its current owner. When weather permits, the vessel makes morning cruises around Lake Union and Lake Washington; in summer there are also overnight trips to the San Juan Islands. State rooms have single-, double-, or queen-size beds; five rooms have private baths. The Admiral's Cabin has an oversize tub with terrific views. If mist and drizzle make it too chilly for you to sit out on the upper deck, you can head to a seat by the fireplace in the cozy, carpeted living room. A full breakfast is served in the solarium. *1001 Fairview Ave. N (at Yale Ave. N), 98109, Lake Union, 206/340– 1201, fax 206/621–9208, www.gtesupersite. com/tugboatchallenger. 9 rooms (3 share bath), 1 suite. AE, MC, V. BP.*

5 g-7
UNIVERSITY INN

The no-nonsense rooms at this modern hotel are outfitted with light wood furniture and floral pattern fabrics. All have writing desks, and some have decks. Units in back are quieter. Enjoy the hot tub year-round and the outdoor pool in season. *4140 Roosevelt Way NE (at NE 42nd St.), 98105, University District, 206/ 632–5055 or 800/733–3855, fax 206/547– 4937, www.universityinn.com. 90 rooms, 12 suites. Restaurant, in-room data ports, in-room safes, no-smoking floors, pool, hot tub, gym, coin laundry, dry cleaning, meeting rooms, free parking. AE, D, DC, MC, V. CP.*

5 g-7
UNIVERSITY TOWER

This property was built in 1931 and has the art deco elegance to prove it. Bright red lounge chairs are bold touches in rooms that are bathed in soothing shades of white. Many rooms have calming views of Mt. Rainier, Green Lake, Lake Union, or the University of Washington. Amenities include coffeemakers, hair dryers, irons and ironing boards, free newspapers, and Continental breakfast. *4507 Brooklyn Ave. NE (at NE 45th St.), 98105, University District, 206/634–2000 or 800/899–0251, fax 206/547–6029, www.meany.com. 155 rooms. Restaurant, bar, in-room data* ports, no-smoking rooms, gym, laundry service, concierge, meeting rooms, free parking. AE, D, DC, MC, V. CP.

① c-4
VILLA HEIDELBERG
This 1909 craftsman-style home has a garden setting as well as views of Elliott Bay and the Olympic Mountains from its wraparound porch, its living room, and two of its guest rooms. The Garmish Room is sunny and bright with a private deck, and the spacious Heidelberg Room has its own fireplace, phone, and TV. A full breakfast is served in the formal dining room on a table bedecked with what seem to be different sets of china, linen, and glassware each day. 4845 45th Ave. SW (at SW Erskine St.), 98116, West Seattle, 206/938–3658 or 800/671–2942, fax 206/935–7077, www.villaheidelberg.com. 4 rooms with shared bath, 2 suites. AE, MC, V. BP.

⑩ d-5
THE WALL STREET INN
Built in the 1950s as a land base for merchant marines, this Belltown inn now serves as a warm and homey land base for tourists. Guest rooms are comfortably furnished in an appealing mix of styles, some with the original Murphy beds. Each room has a private bath, a hair dryer, robes, and slippers; some rooms have kitchenettes, and seven have peek-a-boo views of Elliott Bay and the Olympic Mountains. An extensive Continental breakfast is laid out each morning in the reception area for you to enjoy in front of the fire, out on the patio, or back in your room. 2507 1st Ave. (at Wall St.), 98121, Belltown, 206/448–0125, fax 206/448–2406, www.wall-streetinn.com. 20 rooms. In-room data ports, kitchenettes, refrigerators, business services, parking (fee). AE, MC, V. CP.

⑭ c-1
WEST COAST BELLEVUE
The town-house suites as this hotel, a 20-minute walk from Bellevue Square, are suitable for two to four people, with sleeping lofts and wood-burning fireplaces. Rooms facing the courtyard are larger and quieter than the others. A substantial, complimentary appetizer buffet, served in the lounge weekdays between 5 PM and 7 PM, includes seafood and roast beef. 625 116th Ave. NE (8th Ave. NE), 98004, Bellevue, 425/455–9444, fax 425/455–2154,

www.westcoasthotels.com. 160 rooms, 16 suites. Restaurant, bar, room service, pool, gym, laundry service, business services, meeting rooms, free parking. AE, D, DC, MC, V.

⑩ h-5
WEST COAST CAMLIN
On the edge of Downtown but near the convention center, this 1926 apartment-hotel has an elegant lobby with Asian carpets, large mirrors, and lots of marble. Rooms ending with the number 10 are the best: they have windows on three sides. Each room has a work space and a cushioned chair for relaxing. The noisy heating, air-conditioning, and ventilation system are drawbacks, but these (and the rest of the hotel) are slated to be upgraded. 1619 9th Ave. (at Pine St.), 98101, Downtown, 206/682–0100 or 800/426–0670, fax 206/682–7415. 132 rooms, 4 suites. Restaurant, bar, in-room data ports, room service, pool, dry cleaning, concierge, meeting rooms. AE, D, DC, MC, V.

⑩ g-5
WEST COAST VANCE
This historic hotel does a tidy little business as it puts budget travelers close to the major downtown attractions, including shops and the convention center. Guest rooms are clean, pretty, and get plenty of natural light. The street noise is less noticeable on the upper floors. 620 Stewart St. (at 7th Ave.), 98101, Downtown, 206/441–4200 or 800/426–0670, fax 206/443–5754, www.westcoasthotels.com. 169 rooms. Restaurant, concierge, parking (fee). AE, D, DC, MC, V.

HOSTELS

Independent hostels and those affiliated with Hostelling International (HI) are similar in price and style: they almost always have private rooms as well as dorms that sleep 4–12 people. Seattle has only two properties that fall into this category, and both are within blocks of each other near the Pike Place Market. In summer, a dorm-style bed in either establishment will cost around $20; a private room for two or three people runs $50–$60. Neither place has air-conditioning.

10 *f-7*

GREEN TORTOISE BACKPACKER'S HOTEL

Kitchen privileges are included with the accommodations at this hostel-like hotel one block from the Pike Place Market on a gritty stretch of Second Avenue. This facility is a bit grubby, and some of the front desk staffers are terminally crabby, but the price is tough to beat. For $20 you can let a bed in a dorm-style room and spend your days fraternizing with the young international clientele who make this place a vital travel hub for the adventurous. *1525 2nd Ave. (at Pike St.), 98101, Downtown, 206/340–1222, fax 206/623–3207, www.green-tortoise.net. 8 rooms with shared bath, 164 hostel-style beds. Coin laundry. MC, V.*

10 *f-8*

YOUTH HOSTEL: SEATTLE INTERNATIONAL

The neighborhood has grown decidedly upscale around this redbrick hostel near Pike Place Market. Common areas are clean and bright with views of Elliott Bay. For around $20 you can bed down dormitory-style, if you're lucky you can nab one of the private rooms with 3 beds for $60. Either way, you'll have access to the kitchen and the dining room. *84 Union St. (at Western Ave.), 98101, Downtown, 206/622–5443, fax 206/682–2179, www.hiayh.org. 3 rooms, with shared bath, 191 dormitory beds share bath. Library, coin laundry. AE, MC, V.*

HOTELS NEAR THE AIRPORT

1 *d-6*

DOUBLETREE HOTEL SEATTLE AIRPORT

The Doubletree is a full-service convention hotel whose large, bright rooms all have balconies, some of which are wrap-around and afford great views. Furnishings include comfortable chairs, a dining table, and a desk. *18740 Pacific Hwy. S (at S. 187th St.), 98188, Sea-Tac, 206/246–8600, fax 206/431–8687, www.doubletreehotels.com. 837 rooms, 13 suites. 3 restaurants, 2 bars, in-room data ports, room service, pool, beauty salon, gym, laundry service, meeting rooms, airport shuttle, parking (fee). AE, D, DC, MC, V. Moderately priced.*

1 *d-6*

HILTON SEATTLE AIRPORT & CONFERENCE CENTER

Only a half-hour drive from Downtown, and directly across the street from Sea-Tac, this newly minted hotel and conference center clearly seems to be designed with the business traveler in mind. Rooms are spacious cheery, decorated in pale yellows, greens and burgundy. All come equipped with work desks, iron, ironing board, hairdryer, and robes. In addition to a variety of smaller meeting rooms, a full service conference center which can accommodate up to 1,000 guests is connected to the hotel by a breezeway. *17620 Pacific Hwy. S (S. 176th St.), 98188, Sea-Tac, 206/244–4800, fax 206/248–4499, www.hilton.com. 390 rooms, 6 suites. Restaurant, bar, in-room data ports, pool, gym, coin laundry, laundry service, concierge, business services, meeting rooms, airport shuttle, free parking. AE, D, DC, MC, V. Expensive.*

1 *d-6*

MARRIOTT SEA-TAC

The luxurious Marriott has a five-story, 21,000-square-ft atrium complete with a waterfall, a dining area, an indoor pool, and a lounge. Rooms are decorated in greens and mauve with dark-wood and brass furnishings. *3201 S. 176th St. (Pacific Hwy. S–International Blvd.), 98188, Sea-Tac, 206/241–2000 or 800/643–5479, fax 206/248–0789, www.marriott.com. 454 rooms, 5 suites. Restaurant, lobby lounge, in-room data ports, no-smoking rooms, room service, indoor pool, hot tubs, sauna, health club, video games, laundry service, concierge, meeting rooms, airport shuttle, free parking. AE, D, DC, MC, V. Expensive.*

1 *d-6*

WESTCOAST GATEWAY HOTEL

Missed the last flight out? WestCoast Gateway provides inexpensive, straightforward accommodations close to the airport. The staff is helpful and unobtrusive. The quiet guest rooms are also done in shades of gray with burgundy accents. All have coffeemakers. *18415 Pacific Hwy. S (near S. 182nd St.), 98188, Sea-Tac, 206/248–8200 or 800/426–0670, fax 206/244–1198, www.westcoasthotels.com. 145 rooms. Breakfast room, in-room data ports, no-smoking floors, room service, gym, dry cleaning,*

meeting room, airport shuttle, free park-
ing. AE, D, DC, MC, V. CP. Budget.

1 *d-6*

WEST COAST
SEA-TAC HOTEL

The enthusiastic, helpful staff make this
hotel attractive to business or leisure
travelers. You're welcome to play the
baby grand piano in the small but comfortable lobby. All rooms are equipped
with Nintendo systems; rooms in the
rear have views of Bow Lake. *18220*
Pacific Hwy. S (near S. 182nd St.), 98188,
Sea-Tac, 206/246–5535 or 800/426–0670,
fax 206/246–9733, www.westcoasthotels.
com. 146 rooms. Restaurant, bar, room
service, pool, hot tub, sauna, gym, busi-
ness services, meeting rooms, airport shut-
tle, free parking. AE, D, DC, MC, V.
Budget.

1 *d-6*

WYNDHAM GARDEN HOTEL

The elegant lobby has a fireplace, a marble floor, and comfortable furniture.
Rooms have large desks, overstuffed
chairs, irons and boards, coffeemakers,
and hair dryers. *18118 Pacific Hwy. S (S.*
182nd St.), 98188, Sea-Tac, 206/244–
6666, fax 206/244–6679, www.wynd-
ham.com. 180 rooms, 24 suites. Restau-
rant, lobby lounge, in-room data ports,
no-smoking floors, room service, indoor
pool, gym, coin laundry, laundry service,
meeting rooms, airport shuttle, free park-
ing. AE, D, DC, MC, V. Very Expensive.

B&B
RESERVATION
SERVICES

If you're looking for a more personal
(and significantly cheaper) overnight
experience, choose a B&B. Seattle has
quite a few compared with other U.S.
cities its size. The city's zoning laws are
strict and difficult to navigate, so it's
rare when that part of the puzzle comes
together with other pieces such as a
convenient location, adequate parking,
and appropriate quarters. When everything does fall into place, a high-quality
lodging is the result. Seattle's B&B's are
primarily in historic homes with the
exception of the Wall Street Inn (in a former apartment building) and the Inn at
Harbor Steps (in a modern residential
high-rise).

Make reservations as far in advance as
possible; refunds are possible up to 10
days before arrival, but investigate
whether you can lose your deposit.
Sometimes a fine of $35 is levied for
cancellations.

Bed and Breakfast Association of Seattle
(Box 31772, Seattle, WA 98103, 206/
547–1020 or 800/348–5630, www.
seattlebandbs.com).

A Pacific Reservation Service (Box 46894,
Seattle, WA 98146, 206/439–7677 or
800/684–2932, fax 206/431–0932,
www.seattlebedandbreakfast.com).

chapter 7

CITY SOURCES

getting a handle on the city

BANKS

Commercial banks are generally open weekdays from 9 AM to 5 PM. Some are open later on Fridays evenings or half-day on Saturdays.

Cirrus Cash-Machine Locator (800/424–7787).

Plus ATM Locator (800/843–7587).

Bank of America (206/461–0800, www.bankofamerica.com): Seattle's largest American banking institution has more than 50 locations in the area, all with ATMs. Most are open weekdays 10–6 and some on Saturday 10–1.

Key Bank (206/447–5767 www.keybank.com): There are 36 branches, all with ATMs. Most are open Monday–Thursday 9–5 and Friday 9–6.

US Bank (800/872–2657, www.usbank.com): There are 29 Seattle locations, all with ATMs. Branch hours are weekdays 9–5. Some are open Saturday 9–1.

Washington Mutual (800/756–8000, www.wamu.com): There are 30-plus branches in greater Seattle. Most are open weekdays 9–6 and some Saturday 9–1.

Wells Fargo (800/869–3557, www.usbank.com): There are 30 Seattle locations, all with ATMs. Branch hours are weekly 9–6. Some are open Saturday 9–2.

DRIVING

There's no way to put it nicely—driving in Seattle sucks. Seattle has been twice rated the second-worst city for traffic congestion in the nation—both times beaten only by Los Angeles. Parking along the waterfront, in Downtown, or in Belltown can be a major hassle, too. After you've driven around for 20 minutes or so, you may think about trying to park in a paid lot (there are plenty of them but they'll cost you). Locals need patience and lots of it. A few guidelines: You may turn right at a red light (unless otherwise posted). General speed limits are 20 mph in a school zone, 25 mph on city streets, 50 mph on county roads, and 60 mph on state highways. Parts of interstate highways may be posted with higher maximum speeds.

licenses

After moving into Washington State, you've got 30 days to get a new driver's license. You can apply for one or get your current Washington driver's license renewed at any Licensing Service Office (LSO). You have to be at least 16 years old to get a driver's license, and you have to submit acceptable proof of identity and age (it must have your name, date of birth, signature, and photo—i.e., a license or ID card from another state or a military ID).

If you're an adult who has a valid driver's license in another state, bring that with you. You'll have to pass a vision and driving knowledge test. A driving skills test may be administered at the discretion of the LSO employee, as well. You will be charged $32 for your first five-year Washington driver's license ($7 for your examination and $25 for your license).

Your license expires on your fifth birthday after it's issued. Renew it at any LSO by bringing in your old ID and taking the vision test. It'll cost $25, plus another $10 if you renew more than 60 days after it expired. Also, you have 10 days to notify the Department of Licensing if you change address or change your legal name change. If your driver's license is lost, stolen, or so badly damaged nobody can read it, you can get a duplicate for $5. You'll need to have another proper picture ID for proof.

To register your car and get plates, go to a Vehicle Licensing office. You'll need the current title and registration; a Washington State Patrol inspection certificate (which verifies that the Vehicle Identification Number on the vehicle matches the title or registration documents) and certification that your car has passed a Washington emissions test (this depends on what year your car was made—call for details); a photo ID; and, if your vehicle is less than 10 years old, an odometer reading. (You and the previous owner have to sign an odometer disclosure statement if you're licensing a newly purchased car).

What you'll pay: $4 filing fee, a $15 local fee. A basic license fee of $30 for most cars. License fees for trucks are based on the weight—it's usually between $34 and $70. To renew your registration annually it's $30. Bring cash or a check from a local bank to pay the licensing fees. Plastic is not accepted.

DEPARTMENT OF LICENSING

Washington State Department of Transportation (www.wa.gov/dol): A helpful site with registration and renewal information, including local licensing office contact information.

The following are just a few of the places you can go to get your driver's license and your car registered in Seattle.

Washington State Department of Licensing—Main Office, Olympia (360/902–3900, weekdays 8–5): Get all your questions answered here.

Licensing Service Office—Downtown (380 Union St., 206/464–6845. Mon.–Wed., Fri. 8:30–4:30.; Thurs. 9:30–4:30): Get a driver's license here.

Licensing Service Office—North (907 N. 135th St., Bitter Lake, 206/368–7261, Mon., Wed., Fri. 8:30–4:30.; Tues. 8:30–5; Thurs. 9:30–4:30): Get a driver's license here.

Ballard Auto Licensing Agency (2232 NW Market St., Ballard, 206/781–0199, weekdays 9–6): License and register your vehicle here.

King County License & Regulatory Service Division (500 4th Ave., Room 401, Downtown, 206/296–4000. weekdays 8:30–4:30): License and register your vehicle here.

University License Agency (5615 Roosevelt Way NE, University District, 206/522–4090, weekdays 9–2:30): License and register your vehicle here.

traffic

The main east–west and north–south corridors will be packed at the peak rush hour times from 8 AM to 10 AM and between 4 PM and 7 PM. Heading east

---

ESSENTIAL NUMBERS & WEB SITES

PARKS

Seattle Parks and Recreation 206/684–7241 or 206/684–8020, www.ci.seattle.wa.us/parks.

King County Parks System 206/296–4258 for programs; 206/296–4232 for trail conditions; 800/325–6165 Ext. 4232, www.metrokc.gov.

Washington State Parks 800/233–0321 information or 800/452–5687 for campsite reservations, www.parks.wa.gov.

Washington State Department of Transportation Highway Information 206/368–4499 or 800/695–7623.

SPORTS

Seattle Post Intelligencer Score Line 206/448–8377, www.q13reports.com for NBA, MLB, NHL, and NFL results.

Seattle Mariners 206/622–4487 for tickets, http://mariners.mlb.com.

Seattle Seahawks 888/635–4195 for tickets, www.seahawks.com.

Seattle Sonics 800/462–2849 for tickets, www.nba.com/sonics.

Seattle Storm 206/217–9622, www.wnba.com/Storm.

Seattle Thunderbirds hockey 206/628–0888 for tickets, 206/448–7825, www.seattle-thunderbirds.com.

MISCELLANEOUS

City of Seattle offices www.cityofseattle.net/directory.

Citysearch http://seattle.citysearch.com/.

Pike Place Market www.pikeplacemarketnews.com or www.seattlespublicmarket.com.

Ticketmaster 206/628–0888.

Time and Temperature 206/361–8463.

and west, the trouble spots are on the two floating bridges—Evergreen Point Floating Bridge (across Highway 520) and the Lake Washington Floating Bridge (across I–90). Traveling north and south, watch out for I–5 through Downtown and, to a lesser degree, Highway 99. The West Seattle Bridge also tends to back up at rush hour.

How can you avoid these trouble spots? Go to work later and leave later. Or head to work earlier and leave earlier. It can also help to check the road conditions before you leave.

Washington State Department of Transportation (www.wsdot.wa.gov/traveler.htm): Those cursed cameras at many of the traffic trouble spots can help you plan your commute. So can the other information posted here.

GEOGRAPHY

Seattle is basically a strip of land boxed in and cut in half by water: On the west is Puget Sound. On the east is Lake Washington. In the middle—Seattle. The Lake Washington Ship Canal and Lake Union then divide the north end from the south end of the city. And I–5 divides the west from the east.

The major neighborhoods break down like this: In the center—Downtown and Belltown. A bit north are Queen Anne, East Lake, and Magnolia. North of the Lake Washington Ship Canal are Fremont, Ballard, and Wallingford. A bit south are Pioneer Square and the International District. Farther south is West Seattle. East of I–5 is Capitol Hill and First Hill. East of I–5 *and* north of the Lake Washington Ship Canal is the University District and Green Lake. Got that so far? Streets generally run north–south and avenues run east–west. However, because Seattle's geography is so hilly and wet, there is almost always an exception to any discernible pattern.

Odd-numbered addresses are on the west side of avenues and on the south side of streets. The directional designations such as "NW" or "S" will give you a general idea of which part of the city a particular address can be found relative to the central Downtown area. For example, "NW" streets or avenues would typically be found in the Ballard, Crown Hill, or Blue Ridge neighborhoods. No directional designations are used Downtown, or in the neighborhoods in the center of the city. The farther you go from Downtown, either north or south, the more streets and avenues adhere to a numeric grid pattern.

t's important to remember that for streets, the directional is commonly stated first. If someone says "NW 67th," it's safe to assume they are referring to Northwest 67th *Street,* not avenue. Conversely, if someone says a destination is on "33rd E," they are referring to 33rd *Avenue* East.

IAs far as major travel routes go, I–5 runs right through the middle of the city and acts as the main north–south arterial. Highway 99 (the Aurora Highway) is also a main north–south thoroughfare. Denny Way is an important east–west route within Seattle, especially for those trying to get from the waterfront or Lower Queen Anne to Capitol Hill.

When it comes to remembering the order of the Downtown streets, use the popular local mnemonic device. Beginning with Jefferson Street and working north, there are two streets for the first letter of each of the following words: "Jesus Christ Made Seattle Under Protest" (i.e., Jefferson and James, Columbia and Cherry, Marion and Madison, Spring and Seneca, University and Union, Pike and Pine).

With many of the tech companies headquartered in the smaller cities on the east side of Lake Washington (Redmond, Kirkland, Bellevue), there's a whole lot of traffic between Seattle and the Eastside. The two floating bridges—Evergreen Point Floating Bridge (across Highway 520) and the Lake Washington Floating Bridge (across I–90) are the only routes across that body of water.

HOLIDAYS

Seattle's banks, post offices, schools, offices, and many businesses close on these days.

New Year's Day (January 1).

Martin Luther King Day (3rd Monday in January).

Presidents' Day (3rd Monday in February).

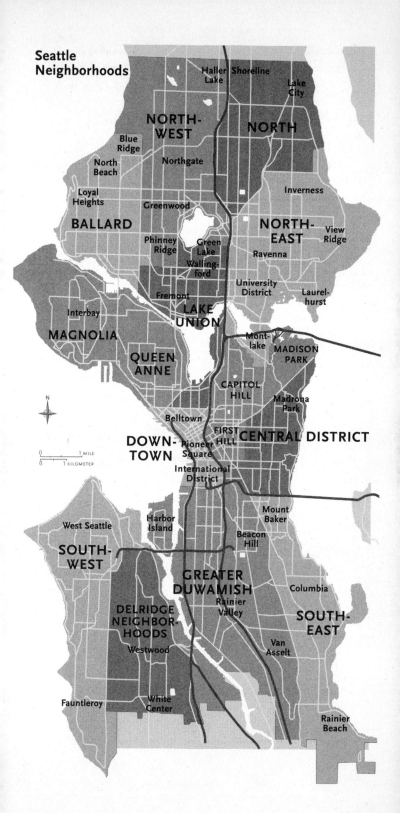

Seattle
Neighborhoods

Haller Lake
Shoreline
Lake City

NORTH-WEST
NORTH

Blue Ridge
North Beach
Northgate

Loyal Heights
Greenwood
Inverness

BALLARD
NORTH-EAST

Phinney Ridge
Green Lake
Walling-ford
View Ridge

Ravenna

Fremont
University District
Laurel-hurst

LAKE UNION

Interbay
Mont-lake

MAGNOLIA
MADISON PARK

QUEEN ANNE
CAPITOL HILL

Madrona Park

Belltown

FIRST HILL
CENTRAL DISTRICT

DOWN-TOWN
Pioneer Square

International District

Mount Baker

West Seattle
Harbor Island
Beacon Hill

SOUTH-WEST

GREATER DUWAMISH

DELRIDGE NEIGHBOR-HOODS
Rainier Valley
Columbia

SOUTH-EAST

Westwood
Van Asselt

Fauntleroy
White Center

Rainier Beach

N

0   1 MILE
0   1 KILOMETER

229

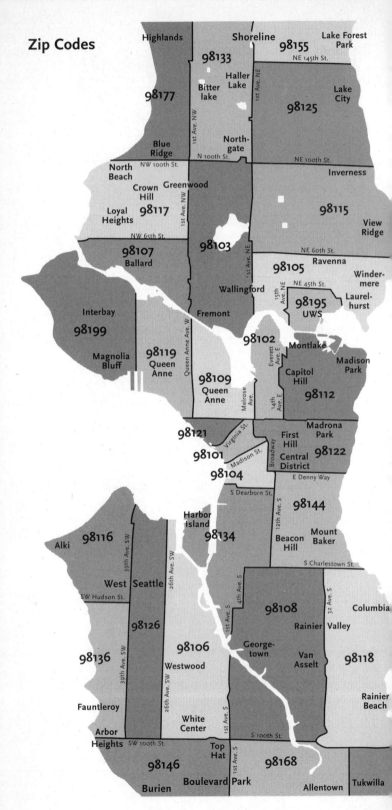

Zip Codes

Highlands

98133 Shoreline

98155 Lake Forest Park

NE 145th St.

Haller Lake

98177 Bitter lake

Lake City

98125

NE 145th St.

Blue Ridge

North-gate

N 100th St.

NE 100th St.

NW 100th St.

North Beach

Greenwood

Inverness

Crown Hill

98117

98103

98115

Loyal Heights

1st Ave. NW

1st Ave. NE

View Ridge

NW 6th St.

98107 Ballard

NE 6th St.

98105 Ravenna

Windermere

Wallingford

NE 45th St.

98195 UWS

Laurelhurst

Interbay

98199

Fremont

98102

Montlake

Madison Park

Magnolia Bluff

98119 Queen Anne

Queen Anne Ave. W

98109 Queen Anne

Melrose Ave.

14th Ave. E

Everett Ave. E

Capitol Hill

98112

Madrona Park

98121

Virginia St.

First Hill

98122

98101

Madison St.

Central District

Broadway

98104

E Denny Way

S Dearborn St.

Harbor Island

12th Ave. S

98144

98134

Beacon Hill

Mount Baker

S Charlestown St.

Alki

98116

39th Ave. SW

West Seattle

26th Ave. SW

4th Ave. S

1st Ave. S

98108

32 Ave. S

Columbia

SW Hudson St.

Rainier Valley

98126

98106

George-town

Van Asselt

98118

98136

Westwood

39th Ave. SW

26th Ave. SW

Rainier Beach

Fauntleroy

White Center

Arbor Heights

SW 100th St.

1st Ave. S

S 100th St.

98146

Top Hat

98168

Burien

Boulevard Park

Allentown

Tukwila

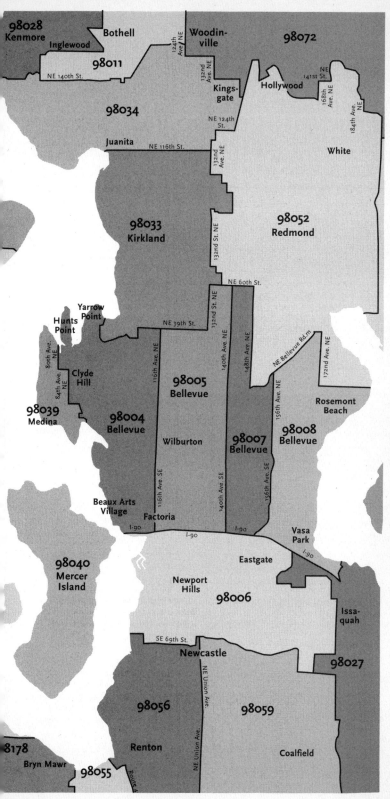

Seattle Street Designations

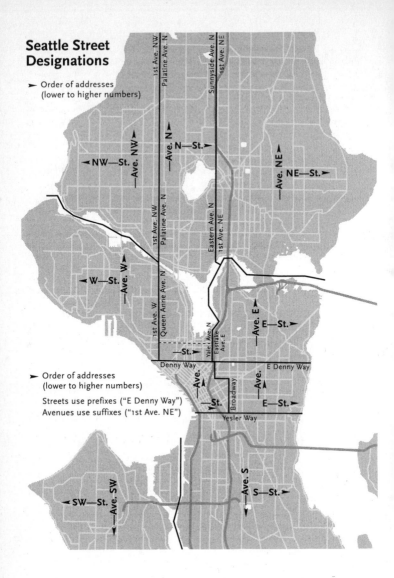

➤ Order of addresses (lower to higher numbers)

➤ Order of addresses (lower to higher numbers)

Streets use prefixes ("E Denny Way")
Avenues use suffixes ("1st Ave. NE")

Memorial Day (last Monday in May).

Independence Day (July 4th).

Labor Day (1st Monday in September).

Columbus Day (2nd Monday in October).

Election Day (1st Tuesday in November).

Veterans' Day (November 11th).

Thanksgiving (4th Thursday in November).

Christmas (December 25th).

LIQUOR LAWS

In Washington State beer and wine can be purchased at the local grocery store until 2 AM. However, the harder stuff (liquors such as vodka, whisky, and tequila) must be bought at a state-licensed liquor store. They usually open Monday through Saturday around 10 or 11 AM and close anywhere from 6 to 10 PM They are not allowed to open on Sundays. **Washington State Liquor Board** (www.liq.wa.gov): For liquor store locations.

As far as nightclubs go, establishments that are classified as "taverns" can only sell beer and wine, whereas "bars" can sell all alcohol types. The legal age for purchase and/or consumption is 21.

NO SMOKING

While smoking isn't officially outlawed in Seattle, you may get a few sideways glances from city dwellers who are proud their lungs are as clean as mountain snow. A number of establishments have instituted their own no-smoking policies, but by and large, most restaurants and bars have both smoking and non-smoking sections.

PARKING

rules & enforcement

You will get ticketed, you will get towed. Seattle police are serious about parking violations, so assume the worst, although you will occasionally get lucky. Scoring on-street parking—especially during the day and on weekend evenings—Downtown, on Capitol Hill, and Queen Anne Hill, is a practice in esoteric forms of patience known only to Bhuddists and Seattle drivers; circling blocks for up to 30 minutes isn't rare. Be sure to read the posted parking signs and be aware of curb markings.

Throughout the city are nearly 9,000 metered parking spaces with thousands more unpaid, unrestricted spaces. But with so many car-loving newcomers, parking has become something of a competitive sport. Parking in metered spaces is free after 6 PM and on Sunday and holidays. For residential parking, the **City of Seattle** (206/684–7623) has instituted a zone permit program: local residents with permits are exempt from the usual, two-hour maximums. Permits cost $27 and are good for two years.

If you're heading downtown after 5 PM, Pacific Place has some great deals: $2 parking for up to 3 hours.

DOWNTOWN PARKING GARAGES

Bon Marche (3rd Ave. and Pine St.).

Pacific Place Shopping Center (600 Pine St.).

Rainier Square (409 Union St.).

Washington State Convention Center (800 Convention Pl.).

Westlake Center (Olive Way, between 4th and 5th Aves.).

PARKING NEAR PIKE PLACE MARKET

To avoid typical Market traffic, take Western Avenue, turning on to Lenora or Madison Street. Here you'll find both metered parking or the Public Market Garage.

Public Market Garage (1531 Western Park): The garage is free if you're back in under an hour and cheap if you're not: $2.25/hour.

Self-pay lots (1615 Western Ave., at Pine St.; 50 Lenora St., between Western and 1st Ave. E).

PARKING NEAR SAFECO FIELD

The Seattle Mariners' home diamond, **Safeco Field,** is located at 1st Avenue and South Atlantic Street. There are 4,500 on-street parking spaces within a three block radius along with a 2,100-stall parking garage across South Atlantic Street from the stadium; season ticket holders and people with disabilities can reserve spots by calling 206/346–4233.

PARKING NEAR SEATTLE CENTER

Paid-parking lots are a hot business, where all-day spots can cost $10 to $15 with slightly lower rates for early birds and nighthawks. During festivals and other events, parking at Seattle Center can be difficult since the cheapest spaces—city-run lots—fill up fast. There are two garages and six lots.

Call the Seattle Center and KeyArena Traffic Hot Line for parking prices, carpool discounts, and event dates (206/233–3989).

Lots are located on 1st Avenue, between John and Thomas streets; on Third Avenue North, between Mercer and Roy streets; and on Fifth Avenue North, at Republican. In commercial lots around Seattle Center, lot attendants stand in the street, waving wands to direct your car into their property. Expect to pay $25 to park your car close to KeyArena for a few hours on an event night.

PARKING NEAR UNIVERSITY OF WASHINGTON'S HUSKY STADIUM

Husky Stadium, home to University of Washington teams and the Seattle Seahawks while their stadium is under construction, is on Mountlake Boulevard, just north of Northeast Pacific Street. There are numerous lots; one is on the east side of the University of Washington campus on Pend Oreille Road, just off of 25th Avenue Northeast; the main campus lot is accessible when you turn off Northeast 45th Street onto 17th Avenue Northeast and turn right into the main entrance to campus; another football parking lot is on Brooklyn Avenue Northeast, off Northeast 45th Street. There are plenty of signs to direct you to public football parking.

PERSONAL SECURITY

As almost-large cities go, Seattle is pretty safe. Still, women—and an increasing number of men—have recently been harassed or attacked in Belltown and Pioneer Square; other incidents have occurred as individuals have exited buses in neighborhoods throughout the city. Risk-reduction strategies include using bus schedules to minimize wait times at bus stops or, if walking, using a planned route to avoid lonely areas, parks, parking lots, garages, and alleyways in favor of well-lit areas. If you have to be out at night alone, carry minimal possessions, consider wearing low-profile shoes and clothing, and walk with purpose to project an assertive image. If you drive, get in the habit of locking your car (whether you're driving or parked) and hiding possessions in the trunk since the number of car break-ins—whether you're parked curb-side or in a garage—has exploded in the last few years.

Crime Stoppers (206/343–2020): If you have information on a crime, you can call here anonymously.

Community Crime Prevention Office (206/684–7555): For safety tips, contact this office of the Seattle Police Department, which is also a part of the Block Watch program.

Seattle Police Department (206/625–5011 general non-emergency or 911 for emergency www.ci.seattle.wa.us/seattle/spd/spdpan.htm): The non-emergency phone number can be used for reporting things like loud neighbors. Check out the latest police news, including 911 calls from citizens and crimes being investigated on-line. The Web site

also lists other important city-wide contact numbers.

PUBLICATIONS

Seattle is among only a handful of cities its size to have two daily, competitive papers duking it out for readers. The fallout from a 49-day strike in 2000 by employees at both *The Seattle Times* and the *Seattle Post Intelligencer* is still uncertain, with many speculating one or the other may fold in the coming years. The two papers operate under a Joint Operating Agreement; while news and editorial operations are separate and competitive, *The Seattle Times* manages most business functions for both papers. The Sunday newspaper has a joint masthead with *Post-Intelligencer* staff providing three pages of editorials and feature stories, with the rest of the content produced by *The Seattle Times*.

Seattle Post-Intelligencer (101 Elliott Ave. W, 206/448–8000 for the main operator or 206/448–8350 to report breaking news, fax 206/448–8166, http://seattlep-i.nwsource.com): Seattle's oldest newspaper, with its massive neon-and-metal globe perched atop its office on the Elliott Bay waterfront, is also an important city landmark. The P-I is known as a feisty paper with strong coverage of breaking news. Columnists include Art Thiel, known locally as "The Wild Wit of the West" (sports); Pulitzer Prize winning cartoonist David Horsey (newsroom); and Robert Jamieson, whose frank pieces on race have gotten Seattle talking.

The Seattle Times (1120 John St., 206/464–2200 newsroom or to report breaking news or 206/464–2204, fax 206/464–2261 newsroom or 206/382–6760 for letters to the editor, www.seattletimes.com): More than 1.25 million copies are distributed weekly, making it the region's most widely read newspaper. Known for its investigative reports, in-depth news coverage and strong feature and arts and entertainment sections, it has been awarded seven Pulitzer Prizes in its history. Columnists Jean Godden (city), Ron Judd (sports), and Kay McFadden (television) enjoy local popularity and national repute.

The weekly *Gay Standard* (29th Ave. E, 206/322–9027, www.gaystandard.com) is an industry leader in providing news, features, and other information for Seattle's lesbian, gay, bisexual, and transgender community. Classifieds and LGBT business listings are valuable resources both in print and on-line.

Puget Sound Business Journal (720 3rd Ave., Suite 800, 206/583–0701 or 206/583–0701 for subscriptions, fax 206/447–8510, http://seattle.bcentral.com/seattle): This regional weekly focuses on international business and the area's innovative practices within a global marketplace.

Real Change (2129 2nd Ave., 206/441–3247, www.realchangenews.org): Created monthly by Seattle's homeless population and homeless activists, *Real Change* broaches poverty and social justice issues. Homeless people get a portion of the sales plus all donations above the $1 charge.

Seattle Daily Journal of Commerce (83 Columbia St., 206/622–8272, fax 206/622–8416, www.djc.com): Construction, real estate, technology, and the arts and entertainment industries are all covered with the local corporate folk in mind.

Seattle Gay News (206/324–4297, fax 206/322–7188, www.sgn.org): Distributed weekly (mostly in newspaper boxes on Broadway in Capitol Hill), Seattle's major pink paper lists gay-positive businesses and community events, and local features range from same-sex marriage debates to the police's role in hate crimes.

Seattle Weekly (1008 Western Ave., Suite 300, 206/623–0500, fax 206/467–4338, www.seattleweekly.com): Like other Village Voice Media Group papers, the *Weekly*'s real strength is in covering environmental, labor, and social justice issues—hot-button topics in Seattle's politically liberal urban milieu.

The Stranger (1535 11th Ave., 3rd floor, 206/323–7101, fax 206/323–7203, www.thestranger.com): Covering the music and entertainment scene, this free weekly has syndicated columnists Rob Breszny ("Free Will Astrology") and Dan Savage ("Savage Love"). Popular local columns include the incredibly funny "I, Anonymous", written by locals-with-a-beef, and "I Saw You", in which Seattleites write in, hoping to connect with a stranger who caught their eye.

PUBLIC TRANSPORTATION

Seattle's public transportation system, as in many West Coast cities, isn't nearly as comprehensive as New York's or Chicago's. By and large, this is a car-loving town, and, despite a voter initiative and years of discussion, plans for a subway or light-rail transit system haven't materialized, mostly because of the cost to build it. Still, hundreds commute to work by bus and via the brand-new commuter trains that link cities south of Seattle with Downtown.

buses

Seattle's Ride Free Area is a nice perk. Between 6 AM and 7 PM, you can ride the bus for free in the area that extends to Battery Street in the north, South Jackson Street to the south, east to 6th Avenue and west to the waterfront. Buses that go through a tunnel beneath the city are included in the Ride Free Area.

The Metro Bus Tunnel, the nation's first designed for dual-power buses that operate with electrical power inside the tunnel and diesel power on city streets, operates from 5 AM to 7 PM on weekdays and 10 AM to 6 PM on Saturday. The 1.3-mi tunnel runs through the heart of Downtown, serves thousands of commuters daily, and has colorful murals, clocks, and electronic art.

There are five tunnel stations: The Convention Place Station is at Ninth Avenue and Pine Street; Westlake Center Station, Westlake Avenue and Pine Street; University Street Station, University Street and Third Avenue; Pioneer Square Station, James Street and Third Avenue; and the International District Station, South Jackson Street and Third Avenue.

The cost for adults is $1.25 during peak hours (6 to 9 AM and 3 to 6 PM) and $1 during nonpeak hours. Youth, ages 5 to 17, pay 75¢ and senior citizens and persons with disabilities pay 50¢ at all times. Exact change is required. On buses traveling out of Downtown, you pay your fare as you exit; if you're traveling into Downtown, pay when you board. If you need to change buses, be sure to get a transfer at the time you pay (transfers are good for 1½ to 2 hours, depending on the route).

The bus system is divided into zones: the City of Seattle is one zone and all other areas outside the city within King

County comprise a second zone. Any time you cross Seattle city limits, you must pay the two-zone fare, which varies depending on the length of your travel.

King County's Transit (206/287–8463 automated schedule information or 206/553–3000 route planning assistance, http://transit.metrokc.gov): Find out how and where to catch the local buses on-line.

BUS PASSES

Month-long, 3-month, and 12-month bus passes are available; the cost depends upon your regular commuting distance. Also available is the Puget Pass, a regional transit pass accepted on King County Metro Transit vehicles, as well as those operated by Community Transit of Snohomish County, Pierce Transit, Everett Transit, and Seattle's Sound Transit Service.

Through the Puget Pass system, you can also purchase Ship-to-Shore Passes which combine ferry fare from Bainbridge Island with transit fare. Monthly passes for adults range from $76.50 to $131.75.

Sound Transit Rider Information Line (888/889–6368 or 206/624–PASS): Ticket booth locations and transit pass information.

LONG-DISTANCE BUS

Greyhound (811 Stewart St., 800/229–9424 or 206/628–5526).

ferries

The Washington State Ferry System is United States' largest, operating 25 ferries over nine routes and serving 20 terminals. The ferry run from Seattle to Bainbridge Island has spectacular views of Seattle, Elliott Bay, and Puget Sound and takes about 35 minutes. The ferries leave from Colman Dock on Pier 52 along the waterfront every 40 to 60 minutes. If you're looking to take a ferry on a Friday night or a summer weekend, get in line at least an hour ahead of your departure time because ferries fill up fast.

Washington State Ferry System (206/464–6400, www.wsdot.wa.gov/ferries/index.cfm): For schedule and route information.

waterfront streetcar

The 1927 Australian streetcars were brought to Seattle from Melbourne in the early '80s and are popular with tourists and Seattle newcomers because they provide easy access to the International District, Pioneer Square, Myrtle Edwards Park, and various stops along the Elliott Bay waterfront. Even though it operates within the downtown Ride Free Area, fare is collected on the Streetcar at all times. Adult cash fare is $1 or $1.25 depending on time of day. You can hop on and off—transfers are good for 90 minutes and streetcars run about every 20 minutes, daily. For more information, call 206/553–3000.

seattle center monorail

Built for the 1962 World Fair, the monorail is a quick and convenient link from Downtown to Seattle Center and the Space Needle. The monorail operates from 7:30 AM to 11 PM on weekdays and 9 AM to 11 PM weekends with at least one round-trip every 15 minutes from stations at Seattle Center, across from the Space Needle, to Westlake Center at the corner of Fifth Avenue and Pine Street. Round-trip fare for adults is $2.50, $1 for youth (ages 5 to 12) and senior citizens (ages 65 and over). Passengers with disabilities and children under age 4 ride free.

taxis

Taxis do not randomly cruise about Seattle looking for fares. Unless you're near a downtown hotel or outside a busy nightclub, telephone requests are the best way to score one and cabs arrive within five minutes of most calls. You can also walk up to taxi stands outside the Westin Hotel on Fifth Avenue and the Washington State Convention & Trade Center on Pike Street, near Seventh Avenue.

Far West Cab (206/622–1717).

Graytop Cab (206/282–8222).

Orange Cab (206/522–8800).

Yellow Cab (206/622–6500).

commuter rail

Sounder Trains are still a new phenomenon in Seattle—and as such, you can only travel north to the city in the mornings and south from Downtown during weekday evenings. Plans are in the works to create more round-trips and to extend service to communities north to Everett and from Lakewood to Tacoma. For now though, there are two trains that leave Tacoma—one at 6:15 AM and another at 6:45 AM—with stops in Puyallup, Sumner, Auburn, Kent, and Tukwila before arriving in Seattle. Southbound trains leave Seattle at 5:10 and 5:35 PM.

Depending on your travel distance, a one-way adult fare costs between $2 and $4 and can be purchased at automated ticket boxes inside the stations. One-week, two-week, and monthly passes are also available. Transfers from Sounder Trains are accepted on buses throughout the region.

Sounder Trains (888/889–6368, www.sounder.org).

King County train-to-bus information (206/553–3000): Information about bus routes that connect with Sounder service.

Pierce Transit information (253/581–8000): Bus–Sounder connection information.

LONG-DISTANCE TRAINS
Amtrak (King Street Station, 303 S. Jackson St., 800/USA–RAIL [800/872–7245] or 206/382–4125).

RADIO STATIONS

am
570 KVI Talk

710 KIRO Sports

770 KNWX Business

820 KGNW Christian

880 KIXI Oldies

950 KJR Sports

1000 KOMO Talk/news

1090 KYCW Country

1150 KSRB Classic R&B

1210 KBSG Oldies

1250 KKDZ Disney

1300 KKOL Talk

1380 KRKO Snohomish County news

1400 KITZ Silverdale community news/talk

1420 KRIZ R&B/Soul/Gospel

1490 KBRO Classic rock

1540 KXPA World

1560 KZIZ Gospel/Spanish

fm
88.5 KPLU NPR/Jazz/Pacific Lutheran University

89.5 KNHC Dance/house

89.9 KGRG Green River Community College

90.3 KEXP University of Washington/Experience Music Project

90.9 KVTI Top 40

91.3 KBCS Bellevue Community College/jazz/folk/blues

91.7 KBTC Classic rock

92.5 KLSY Classic rock

93.3 KUBE Rap/R&B

94.1 KMPS Country

94.9 KUOW NPR/University of Washington

95.7 KBTB '80s/R&B

96.1 KXXO Easy listening

96.5 KYPT '80s/rock

96.9 KGY Country

97.3 KBSG Oldies

98.1 KING Classical

98.9 KWJZ Light jazz

99.9 KISW Rock

100.7 KQBZ Talk

101.5 KPLZ '80s/'90s

102.5 KZOK Classic rock

103.7 KMTT Alternative

104.3 KAFE Adult contemporary

104.9 FNK Alternative/rock

105.3 KCMS Christian

106.1 KBKS Top 40

106.9 KRWM Soft rock

107.7 KNDD Alternative/rock

RECYCLING

Seattle Public Utilities (206/684–3000, www.cityofseattle.net/util/services/recycling): The city conscientiously collects paper, plastic, paper, and metals from the curb every other week, on the same day as garbage pick-up. Glass should be sorted from plastic, paper and metals and placed in the specific glass recycling bin. For other rules visit the Web site.

TAX & TIP

sales tax & beyond

Washington's sales tax varies from 7% to 8.8% and is applied to all purchases except groceries and prescription drugs. At restaurants you'll pay a 9.1% meal tax. Hotel room tax is 15.6%, car rental tax is 28.5%, and parking lot tax is 8.8%.

tipping

Tips and service charges are usually not automatically added to your bill. If service is satisfactory, give foodservers, taxi drivers, barbers, hairdressers, and so forth 15% to 20% of the total bill. Bellhops, doormen, and porters at airports and train stations are generally tipped $1 for each bag. There's no local system for tipping concierges, but a gratuity of $2–$5 is suggested if a small service is performed, such as restaurant reservations, theater tickets, or a town car, and $10–$20 if the service is more extensive or unusual, such as having a large bouquet of roses delivered on a Sunday.

TELEVISION

major broadcasters

Channel 4–KOMO (ABC)

Channel 5–KING (NBC)

Channel 6–KONG

Channel 7–KIRO (CBS)

Channel 9–KCTS (PBS)

Channel 11–KSTW (UPN)

Channel 13–KCPQ (FOX)

Channel 22–KTWB (WB)

cable

Channel 8–DSC

Channel 12–KBCBI

Channel 16–QVC

Channel 17–HSN

Channel 19–ODSY

Channel 21–GOVACC

Channel 23–TVW

Channel 24–CSPAN

Channel 25–CSPAN2

Channel 27–UWTV

Channel 28–SCCTV

Channel 29–KWOG

Channel 30–FSN

Channel 31–ESPN

Channel 32–ESPN2

Channel 34–SPVN

Channel 35–FOOD

Channel 36–TRAVEL

Channel 37–THC

Channel 38–TLC

Channel 39–FOXFAM

Channel 40–NICK

Channel 41–DISNEY

Channel 42–TOON

Channel 43–APL

Channel 44–CNN

Channel 45–HN

Channel 46–CNBC

Channel 47–MSNBC

Channel 48–FNC

Channel 49–COURT

Channel 50–OXYGN

Channel 51–LIFE

Channel 52–A&E

Channel 53–FX

Channel 54–TNT

Channel 55–TBS

Channel 56–BET

Channel 57–TNN

Channel 58–USA

Channel 59–SCIFI

Channel 60–COMEDY

Channel 61–CMT

Channel 62–VH1

Channel 63–MTV

Channel 64–MTV2

Channel 65–E!

Channel 66–BRAVO

Channel 67–AMC

Channel 68–HBO

Channel 69–SHOW

Channel 71–MAX

Channel 72–TMC

Channel 73–ENCORE

Channel 74–STARZ!

Channel 76–UWTV2

Channel 77–PUBACC

Channel 78–TWC (Weather Channel)

VOTER REGISTRATION

Anyone who wants to vote has to register 30 days prior to an election. You must be a U.S. citizen by birth or naturalization, 18 years old before election day, and a legal resident of the state, meaning your residence in Washington is your permanent or principal residence. If you miss the 30-day cut-off, you can register in person at the Elections Office up to 15 days before election. Mail-in registration forms can be downloaded from the Elections Office Web site or picked up from King County community centers, city and town clerks, Seattle Community Service Centers, public libraries, any public school, most fire stations or the League of Women Voters.

Elections Office (500 4th Ave., Room 553, at James St., Downtown, 206/329–4848, www.metrokc.gov/elections/register.htm for a registration form; open weekdays 8:30 AM–4:30 PM).

WEATHER

For about 10 months of the year, the weather waffles between two modes: rain and about-to-rain. The average annual rainfall of 38″ is actually less than many Northeast cities, but the permanent mist and cloud-hang makes it seem much wetter.

The rainy season lasts roughly between October and May. June and September are intermittently sunny, and July and August will bring the edenic summer that Seattleites say makes all the rainy days worth it—sunny and 75°. Sun and rain will split the week in the spring and fall—and don't rely too heavily on the weather forecast.

At its coldest, winter will get down to the low 40s during the day. The city will get a snow dusting once or twice a year, although the snow doesn't usually stick. As observed with natives, the Northwest uniform of a fleece and a waterproof shell will serve you well in almost any weather.

National Weather Service (www.nrh.noaa.gov/Seattle).

Weather Channel (Channel 78): All-day weather information.

resources for challenges & crises

BABY-SITTING SERVICES

Best Sitters (206/682–2556): Recommended by most hotels in town, it uses licensed, bonded baby-sitters, all of whom are older than 25 and have had previous experience as nannies and care givers.

CATERING

Gourmet delicatessens in Seattle's many high-end grocery stores can put together small or large orders for you, including Larry's Markets and Thriftway.

grown-up parties
Famous Northwest Catering Company (313 E. Madison St., between Lake Washington Blvd. and 32nd Ave. E, Madison Park, 206/324–3663): A small café in

front does a good take-out business thanks to the tempting baked goods. The real deal goes down in back, where wedding cakes and other delectables are assembled.

Lisa Dupar Catering (17825 NE 65th St., Suite A140, between NE Marymoor Way and E. Sammamish Rd. N, Redmond, 425/881–3250, www.lisaduparcatering. com): Celebrity chef Lisa Dupar whips up renowned Southern-inspired creations that incorporate European influences from her Swiss training. She runs the gamut from money-is-no-object weddings to business lunches.

Lowell-Hunt Catering (1111 Fairview Ave. N, at Yale Ave., Lake Union, 206/264–0400): Its most famous clients include the Clintons during their visit to Seattle, as well as Bill Gates Sr. and Jr. (Junior is the Microsoft magnate. Senior is a prominent attorney in town.) Indoor, outdoor, five guests or five thousand, Lowell-Hunt can handle it all, including providing banquet facilities on Lake Union.

Villa Victoria Catering (1123 34th Ave., at E. Spring St., Madison Park, 206/329–1717): For a south of the border event, try chef-owner Naomi Andrede Smith, who makes some fantastic carne asada and tamales. If you can't wait for a party, make a trip to her kitchen's take-out window in Madrona.

kids' parties
Spring Rain Toys & Parties (425/432–9962): If you're planning a children's party, check out these folks who specialize in food and entertainment for the junior set.

CHARITIES

Computer Bank Charity (206/365–4657): If you have a used computer you'd like to donate, the organization takes donations on Saturday, and refurbishes the computers with new software and gives them to families in need and community centers.

Seattle Goodwill (206/329–1000, 1400 S. Lane St., at the corner of Dearborn Pl. S, Rainier Valley www.seattlegoodwill. org): The 22 donation centers in the Puget Sound area accept used clothes, housewares, books, and small appliances. Call to find a donation center near you.

Salvation Army (800/958–7825, 1010 4th Ave. S, between S. Royal Brougham Way and Jackson St., Downtown): For the lazy yet well intentioned, Sally Ann will pick up used clothes, household items, and some furniture—no couches or mattresses. Call for a pickup.

Secretary of State's charity line (800/332–4483, www.secstate.wa.gov/charities): Worried about whether the charity soliciting your donations is pulling a fast one? Call these folks.

CHILD CRISIS

Child Abuse and Neglect 24-Hour Reporting Line (206/721–6500).

Childhaven (206/624–6477 or 206/328–5437 for crisis nursery): Resources and parenting courses.

Child Protective Services (206/721–4115): Available 24 hours.

Children's Home Society (206/524–6020).

Children's Mental Health Intake (206/328–5774).

Crisis Line (206/461–3222).

Parents Anonymous (206/233–0139): Resources and parenting courses.

CITY GOVERNMENT

The City of Seattle (206/684–8811, www.ci.seattle.wa.us): Call this general line for complaints and information regarding all city departments. The Web site has information on government contacts and city events, plus construction updates for parks and stadiums and downloadable forms for permits.

COAST GUARD

Emergency Search and Rescue (206/220–7001).

General Information (800/652–8813).

CONSUMER PROTECTION

Attorney General's Consumer Help Line (800/551–4636).

Better Business Bureau (206/431–2222).

City Department of Consumer Affairs (206/386–1298).

State Consumer Protection Complaints and Inquiries (206/464–6684).

U.S. Consumer Product Safety Commission (800/638–2772).

COUNSELING & REFERRALS

aids advice & services
AIDS/HIV Health Care Referral (206/284–9277): Offers confidential referrals to testing clinics and medical providers.

AIDS Info Line (206/205–7837): City of Seattle information line covers related issues, including HIV and STDs, and offers counseling and referrals.

Harborview STD Clinic (206/731–3590).

King County Crisis Line (206/461–3222).

Seattle AIDS Support Group (206/322–2437): Support services for people living with HIV.

Seattle Gay Clinic (206/299–1623): Counseling, STD and HIV testing, and hepatitis vaccinations, treatment referrals.

Washington State HIV/AIDS Hotline (800/272–2437): Information about HIV, counseling, and referrals.

alcoholism treatment
Alcoholics Anonymous Hotline (206/587–2838): This 24-hour hotline also has a schedule of all Seattle AA meetings.

crime victims
Crime Victims Hotline (206/461–3222 or 800/244–5767): 24-hour counseling and referrals.

Office of Crime Victims Advocacy (800/762–3716): Provides legal information and financial assistance to crime victims.

Seattle Police Department Victim Assistance Section (206/684–7777).

domestic violence
Domestic Abuse/Women's Network (206/656–4305).

Domestic Violence Hotline (800/562–6025): 24-hour counseling and shelter referrals.

King County Crisis Line (206/461–3222).

New Beginnings Shelter (206/522–9472): 24 hours.

drug abuse treatment
Drug Abuse 24-hour Hotline (800/562–1240).

Narcotics Anonymous (206/329–1618): Referrals to meetings, counseling, and services for people addicted to drugs.

Teen Drug Abuse 24-hour Hotline (206/722–4222).

Washington State Division of Alcohol and Substance Abuse (360/438–8200): Referrals to community services and financial assistance for treatment.

gay & lesbian
Advocates for Abused & Battered Lesbians (AABL, 206/547–8191).

Gay, Lesbian, Bisexual, and Trans-gendered Youth Info Line (206/322–7900).

Lambert House (Youth) (206/322–2735).

Lesbian Resource Center (206/322–2735).

Parents, Families, and Friends of Lesbians and Gays (PFLAG) (206/325–7724).

Seattle Counseling Services for Sexual Minorities (206/323–0220 or 800/527–7683).

Stonewall Recovery Services (206/461–4546).

mental health information & referral
Mental Health 24-hour Hotline (206/461–3222): 24-hour counseling and referrals.

Washington Advocate for Mentally Ill (206/789–7722).

rape crisis
Abused Deaf Women's Advocacy Services (TDD only, 206/726–0093).

Communities Against Rape and Abuse (CARA, 206/322–4856): Grassroots approach to anti-rape activism, with monthly meetings and volunteer opportunities.

Harborview Center for Sexual Assault and Traumatic Stress (206/521–1800).

King County Sexual Assault Resource Center (KCSARC, 206/632–7273 or 800/825–7273): 24-hour hotline.

Sexual Assault Center (206/521–1800).

DOCTOR & DENTIST REFERRALS

Dental Referral Service (800/511–8663): A national referral service.

Pediatric Care Referral (206/284–0331).

Swedish Medical Center Physician Referral (800/793–3474).

University of Washington Physician Referrals (800/826–1121 or 800/826–1121).

FAMILY PLANNING

Downtown Public Health Center (2124 4th Ave., between Blanchard and Lenora Sts., Belltown, 206/296–4960 clinic or 206/296–4772 teen clinic): Counselling, pregnancy tests, birth control, emergency contraception, and STD and HIV screening. The clinic is open 7:30 to 5 weekdays with a teen walk-in clinic on Thursdays between 2:30 and 5 PM.

Family Planning Informational and Referral Line (800/770–4334).

King County public clinics (206/296–4600, www.metrokc.gov/health/fam-sched.htm): Consult them for a full list of locations.

Planned Parenthood Seattle Clinic (2001 E. Madison St., at 20th Ave. E, Downtown, 206/328–7700 clinic; 206/328–7724 HIV and AIDS services; 206/328–7711 information line): Provides abortion services, birth control, emergency contraception, pregnancy testing, and STD and HIV screening.

Planned Parenthood University Clinic (4500 9th Ave. NE, Suite 324, just north of NE 45th St., University District, 206/632–2498, fax 206/633–0838): Birth control, emergency contraception, abortion services, and STD and HIV screening. Hours vary so always call ahead.

FIRE

Dial **911** in case of fire.

The **Seattle Fire Department** (206/386–1338 or 206/684–7274 for CPR classes,

www.firesafe.com) has educational resources on its Web site, plus a community outreach program and CPR classes.

GAY & LESBIAN CONCERNS

Seattle has a vibrant and politically active gay and lesbian community centered on Broadway in the city's Capitol Hill neighborhood. A good source for community information is GayCity, an on-line magazine, www.gaycity.org or *Seattle Gay News*. *See also* Gay and Lesbian Nightlife *in* Arts, Entertainment, & Nightlife.

crisis & counseling

Domestic Violence 24-hour Hotline (800/562–6025): Counseling and support services.

Seattle Counseling Services for Sexual Minorities (206/323–1768 or 800/527–7683).

Ingersoll Gender Center (206/329–6651): Transgendered services.

political groups

Equality Washington (206/323–5191).

Harvey Muggy Lesbian and Gay Democrats (206/233–8065).

Legal Marriage Alliance of Washington (206/464–3009).

self-defense & anti-violence services

Q Patrol (206/325–9128): Volunteers patrol city streets and parks to keep them safe for gays and lesbians.

Seattle Police Department Gay bashing/Hate crimes Line (206/233–3898).

religious & spiritual organizations

Dignity Seattle (206/325–7314).

Metropolitan Community Church (206/325–2421).

MultiFaith Works (206/324–1520).

HOMEWORK HELP

The time of the dial-up hotline has run its course. Now kids can log-on for help.

The King County Library System
(www.kcls.org/webkids/hmwtop.html):
For both elementary and high-school
students with topics ranging from architecture to rain forests, from the Holo-
caust to Egyptian mathematics.

The Seattle Public Library
(www.spl.lib.wa.us/youngad/hmwork.ht
ml): A fun, informative site to help kids
plow through research papers and
nightly assignments.

HOUSECLEANING AGENCIES

Maid in the Northwest (206/622–7783,
www.maidinthenw.com): Licensed,
bonded, and insured maids provide
one-time and regular cleaning services.

Merry Maids (206/527–2984 University
District, 206/937–7083 West Seattle,
www.merrymaids.com): A range of
cleaning services in Greater Seattle.

**Western Washington Better Business
Bureau** (www.orwwabbb.org): Lists rep-
utable housecleaning services.

LANDLORD/ TENANT ASSISTANCE

Attorney General's Office
(www.wa.gov/ago/consumer/lt/ffi.html)
: Information on Washington's land-
lord/tenant laws.

**Attorney General's Consumer Informa-
tion Service** (800/692–5082): General
information via recorded messages on a
variety of landlord/tenant topics.

City of Seattle Renters' Rights Service
(206/684–7899): A complaint hotline for
tenants having problems with landlords.

The Tenants Union (3902 S. Ferdinand
St., 206/723–0500 or 800/752–9993,
www.tenantsunion.org): The Union provides legal referrals and can advise you
of your rights.

LEGAL SERVICES

**American Civil Liberties Union of Wash-
ington** (705 2nd Ave., Room 300, at
Cherry St., Pioneer Square, 206/624–
2180): File complaints or get referrals.

Columbia Legal Services (101 Yesler Way,
Suite 300, at 1st Ave., Pioneer Square,

206/464–5911 or 206/464–5933): Free
legal advice and possible representation
for those with limited English-speaking
skills and their advocates.

Lawyer Referral Service (206/623–2551):
Free legal services and referrals by the
Seattle/King County Bar Association
over the phone.

Legal Action Center (100 23rd Ave., at E.
Yesler Way, Downtown, 206/324–6890):
Free legal assistance and referrals for
low-income tenants with eviction
notices; help for low-income King
County residents with tenant/landlord
problems, consumer protection, and
debtor/creditor problems.

**Northwest Women's Law Center's Infor-
mation and Referral Service** (206/621–
7691): Information and referrals by
phone only on family law, child support,
domestic violence, and sexual harass-
ment; free legal representation is available for selected women's cases.

NW Immigrant Rights Project (909 8th
Ave., at Marion St., First Hill, 206/587–
4009 or 800/445–5771): Immigration
legal services are free or by donation.

LOST & FOUND

at airlines & airports
Seattle-Tacoma International Airport
(Mezzanine Level, Room 6016, in the
central part of the main terminal, 206/
433–5312 or 206/431–4444; 206/433–
5312 for after-hours pick up, fax 206/
439–6620): Open weekdays 7 AM–5 PM;
Saturday 10 AM–5 PM; picture ID is
required for pick up.

Air Canada (206/433–4172).

Alaska (206/431–5674).

America West (206/433–5710).

American (206/433–3968).

Asiana (206/246–0755).

British Airways (206/433–5712).

Continental (206/901–5662).

Delta (206/439–4300).

Frontier (206/431–0445).

Harbor (206/433–5330).

Hawaiian (206/431–7715).

Horizon (206/834–3068).

JetBlue (800/JET–BLUE [800/538–2583]).

Northwest (206/433–3605).

Reno Air (206/433–5707).

Southwest (206/439–2800).

TWA (206/433–5729).

United (206/433–4172).

US Airways (206/433–7853).

on other public transportation

King Street Amtrak Station (206/382–4125).

Metro Buses Lost & Found (206/553–3090).

lost animals

PetShelter Network (206/297–9055, www.petshelter.net): You can post a notice of your lost pet on PetShelter's Web site. PetShelter reunites owners with their pets and looks for volunteers to open their homes to strays and uncollected homeless pets. It does not have a drop-off service.

Seattle Animal Control/Seattle Animal Shelter (2061 15th Ave W, 1 mi south of the Ballard Bridge, Ballard, 206/386–PETS, www.cityofseattle.net/rca/animal): To locate or report lost-and-found pets, contact the Lost Pet Hotline between 7 AM and 7:30 PM weekdays. After 9 PM or on weekends, call the same number and hit option 1 to hear a full description of animals picked up within the last 48 hours. Or consult the Found Animal Roster on-line. Stray animals are held for three business days; after that, they are either placed for adoption, put in foster care, or euthanized. Owners searching for pets are encouraged to visit the shelter. Shelter hours are Tuesday through Saturday noon to 6, Sundays noon to 4.

lost credit cards

American Express (800/992–3404).

Discover Card (800/347–2683).

Master Card (800/307–7309).

Visa (800/336–8472).

lost traveler's checks

American Express (800/221–7282).

Master Card (800/223–9920).

Visa (800/227–6811).

MEDICAL EMERGENCIES

Emergency 911.

Ambulance Services and Advanced Life Support, which is required for life-threatening situations, is provided by paramedics who work for fire departments throughout King County.

ambulance

American Medical Response (206/444–4444): Non-emergency ambulance service in Seattle and King County, provides Basic Life Support or critical-care transport, usually scheduled in advance to move patients among nursing homes, hospitals, and urgent-care facilities.

hospital emergency rooms

Children's Hospital (4800 Sand Point Way NE, south of NE 50th St., Sand Point, 206/526–2222).

Evergreen Hospital Medical Center (12040 NE 128th St., at 120th Ave. NE, Kirkland, 425/899–1700).

Harborview Medical Center (325 9th Ave., at Alder St., First Hill, 206/731–3074): This is the region's only Trauma One care center, so it's here that the sickest and most badly injured patients are taken.

Northwest Hospital (1550 N. 115th St., west of Meridian Ave. N, Northgate, 206/368–1765).

Overlake Medical Center (1035 116th Ave. NE, between Lake Bellevue Dr. and NE 8th St., Bellevue, 425/688–5200).

Providence Seattle Medical Center (500 17th Ave., at E. Jefferson St., Downtown, 206/320–2111).

Swedish Medical Center (747 Broadway Ave., between Cherry and Marion Sts., Capitol Hill, 206/386–6000).

Valley Medical Center (400 S. 43rd Ave., at SE Carr Rd., Renton, 425/251–5185).

Virginia Mason Hospital (1100 9th Ave., at Spring St., First Hill, 206/583–6433).

poison control center

Poison Control Center (800/732–6985 or 206/526–2121): Call in case of accidental poisoning.

suicide prevention

Crisis Clinic Of King County (206/461–3222 for adults, 206/461–4922 for teens).

King County's Children's Crisis Response Team/Children's Hospital Kids' Line (206/915–7803).

King County suicide prevention agencies (http://suicidehotlines.com/washington.html): A complete directory of suicide prevention agencies.

The National Hope Line (800/784–2433 or [800/SUICIDE]): 24 hours.

Seattle Community Psychiatric Clinic (206/461–3614).

Seattle Counseling Services For Sexual Minorities (206/323–0220 or 800/527–7683).

Seattle Mental Health Crisis Line (206/224–2840).

ON-LINE SERVICES

These three ISP (Internet service provider) giants will sign you up by phone or on their Web sites. Expect to pay about $20 a month for unlimited service and $40 for high-speed cable or DSL connections.

America Online (800/827–0035, www.aol.com).

AT&T Internet Services (800/967–5363 or 800/487–5200, www.att.com).

Earthlink (800/327–8454 or [800/EARTHLINK], www.earthlink.com/join).

The following Web sites get a lot of hits from Seattle residents:

Amazon.com This is one of the biggest Internet companies based in Seattle. At www.amazon.com you can order CDs, books, small electronics, and much more.

City of Seattle Visit www.cityofseattle.net for lots of information straight from the city's leaders.

Groovetech Watch and listen to some of the best DJs perform at www.groovetech.com.

History Link Lots of great historical information about Seattle can be found at www.historylink.org.

Microsoft Here's the homepage to the world-famous software giant—www.microsoft.com (see also www.msn.com).

RealArcade Kill some of your free time at Real Network's on-line gaming Web site www.realarcade.com.

Rent Tech This site (www.renttech.com) is a great way to find an apartment from the comfort of your computer.

Seattle Public Libraries The city's public library system has not only some great physical outposts, but a great Web site as well at www.spl.org.

Washington State Department of Transportation Tired of getting stuck in traffic? Check out www.wsdot.wa.gov/traveler.htm for the information you'll need to deal with Seattle's horrific traffic problems.

PETS

adoptions

Humane Society for Seattle/King County (13212 SE Eastgate Way, at 129th Pl. SE, Bellevue, 425/641–0080, www.seattlehumane.org): This nonprofit organization has been dedicated to finding good homes for animals since it was founded in Seattle in 1897. (It is not animal control and isn't part of any national humane organization.) It also has a public boarding kennel and a spay and neuter center.

Progressive Animal Welfare Society (PAWS, 15305 44th Ave. W, off 148th St. and west of Hwy. 99, Lynnwood, 425/787–2500, www.paws.org): The Pacific Northwest's largest animal advocacy and care organization has a Wildlife Center where they care for and rehabilitate injured wild animals; a Companion Animal Shelter from which you can adopt various domesticated cats, dogs, and rabbits (in Lynnwood); and an adoption center, "Cat City," created especially for felines (in Greenwood).

Cat City (8503 Greenwood Ave., at N. 85th St., Greenwood, 206/782–1700).

Seattle Purebred Dog Rescue (206/654–1117. www.spdrdogs.org): This nonprofit referral organization places unwanted purebred dogs into suitable homes. The volunteer-run organization works cooperatively with breeders, animal shelters, breed clubs, and individuals and handles more than 3,500 dogs a year. This service is open to those who would like to put dogs up for adoption as well as for people who are looking to adopt.

dog-walking services

Dog Trots Walking & Sitting (206/280–3647): Dog walking in West Seattle.

Fantastic Dog & Cat Sitting Service (206/547–5947, http://home.att.net/~fantasticdog/): This in-home animal-sitting and dog-walking service is a good alternative to kennels. The long-time pet lovers who run this business come straight to your home. They can arrange group and individual walks.

Urban Pet (206/378–0464, www.urban-pet.com): Whether you want your pet taken for a 15-minute stroll or on an hour-long romp, this team of pet lovers will accommodate dog's exercise needs, with a variety of dog walking packages.

grooming

Kristi's Grooming Company (8501 35th Ave. NE, at NE 85th St., Wedgewood, 206/522–0500; 2407 10th Ave. E, at E. Miller St., Capitol Hill, 206/320–0100): A highly recommended grooming business in two locations.

Loving Care Mobile Cat Salon (206/523–3013): They come to you and your kitty.

Petco (8728 Holman Rd. NW, at NW 87th St., Ballard, 206/784–0524; 4732 California Ave SW, at SW Alaska St., West Seattle, 206/932–9003; 809 NE 45th St., at 8th Ave. N, University District, 206/548–1400): This pet supply chain has the usual food and goodies as well as grooming. There are nine stores in the Seattle area open daily.

sitting & boarding

Happy Camper Pet Services (206/784–5291, www.happycamperpets.com): This is a small operation run by long-time animal care-giver Heidi Freeman. She will come to your home and also provides some away boarding, described as "luxury suites" with heat, air-conditioning, TV, and radio.

Pet Sitters of Puget Sound (206/622–7387): Pet sitter referral line.

Purrfect Cat Boarding (1511 NE 166th St., at 15th Ave. NE, Shoreline, 206/367–3325): This boarding service specializes in cat care and has large cages, plus a playroom.

training

Academy of Canine Behavior (4705 240th St. SE, at 47th Ave. SE, Bothell, 425/486–9567, www.aocb.com): Classes, counseling, and seminars on dog training, plus grooming and boarding.

Canine Behavior Center (206/367–8071 or 425/898–1341, www.caninebcenter.com): Obedience classes at seven locations, as well as seminars and in-home consultations.

veterinary hospitals

Animal Surgical Clinic of Seattle (4102 Stone Way N, N. 41st St., Wallingford, 206/932–3308): Specializes in surgery.

Broadway Veterinary Hospital (1824 12th Ave., at Denny Way, Capitol Hill, 206/322–5444): Handles medical, surgical, and dental care. Also offers prescription diets and behavior counseling.

Crown Hill Veterinary Hospital (9069 Holman Rd. NW, at NW 90th St., Crown Hill, 206/782–6363): A member of the American Animal Hospital Association.

Emerald City Emergency Care (4102 Stone Way N, at N. 41st St., Wallingford, 206/634–9000): Specializes in after-hours emergencies.

West Seattle Animal Hospital (4714 42nd Ave. SW, in Jefferson Square, West Seattle, 206/932–3308): Open daily. Takes everything from ferrets to dogs.

veterinarian referrals

Animal Emergency & Referral Center (19511 24th Ave. W, 196th St. SW, Lynwood, 425/745–6745): 24-hour emergency and critical care.

Seattle Veterinary Medical Association and Washington State Veterinary Medical Association (425/454–8381).

PHARMACIES OPEN 24 HOURS

Rite Aid (3905 Factoria Sq. Mall SE, off 128th Ave. SE, Bellevue, 425/644–2925 or 800/748–3243 or [800/RITEAID] for other locations).

Walgreens (14510 Aurora Ave. N, at N. 145th St., Shoreline, 206/361–8826 or 800/925–4733 for other locations, www. walgreens.com).

POLICE

Emergency Dial 911.

Seattle Police Department (206/625–5011): Non-emergency police services including reporting a burglary or auto theft, general information, and the location and phone number of the precinct nearest you, available 24 hours daily.

POSTAL SERVICES

Post offices hours range everywhere from weekdays 10–5 to 8–6, depending on the branch. Many are open for a few hours on Saturday as well.

Main Station (301 Union St., at 3rd Ave., Downtown): Open weekdays 7:30–5:30.

Ballard Station (5706 17th Ave. NW, at NW 57th St., Ballard).

Columbia Center Station (701 5th Ave., at Cherry St., Downtown).

East Union Station (1110 23rd Ave., at E. Spring St., Capitol Hill).

Greenwood Station (8306 Greenwood Ave. N, at N. 83rd St., Greenwood).

Lake City Station (3019 NE 127th St., at 30th Ave. NE, Lake City).

Magnolia Station (3211 W. McGraw St., at 32nd Ave. W, Magnolia, 800/275–8777), www.usps.com).

federal express

Federal Express (800/463–3339, www. fedex.com) for locations and pickups.

Wanderers' Mail Service FedEx Authorized ShipCenter (1916 Pike Pl., Suite 12, at Stewart St., Downtown).

FedEx World Service Center (1200 6th Ave., at Seneca St., Downtown).

East Union Station (1110 23rd Ave., at E. Spring St., Capitol Hill).

FedEx World Service Center, Bank of America Tower (701 5th Ave., at Cherry St., Downtown).

FedEx World Service Center Industrial Area (1926 6th Ave S, at S. Holgate St., Downtown).

Natco FedEx Authorized ShipCenter (4509 Interlake Ave. N, at N 45th St., Wallingford).

ups

UPS (800/742–5877, www.ups.com): For pickup and locations.

The Home Office (2606 2nd Ave., at Vine St., Downtown).

Mailbox (300 Lenora St., at 3rd Ave., Downtown).

Office Depot (1423 4th Ave., at Union St., Downtown).

Pike Place Parcel (1916 Pike Pl., at Stewart St., Downtown).

UPS Store (1514 4th Ave., at Pike St., Downtown).

SENIOR CITIZEN SERVICES

Mayor's Office for Senior Citizens (206/386–1001): Programs and services for seniors and people with disabilities in the Seattle-King County area.

Senior Information and Assistance (888/435–377).

Senior Rights Assistance (206/448–5720): Sixty-plus trained volunteers (under the supervision of an attorney) advise seniors on a one-on-one basis about everything from insurance to Social Security to legal referrals.

Senior Services of Seattle/King County (206/448–5766, www.seniorservices. org): The area's largest nonprofit agency serving 70,000 seniors through its nine Senior Centers.

TELEVISION— CABLE COMPANIES

There are only two cable companies in the area. Call one of the below for service, repairs, and general information.

AT&T (877/824–2288).

Millennium Digital Cable (800/829–CABL).

UTILITIES

gas
Puget Sound Energy (425/452–1234).

electric
Seattle City Light (206/684–3000).

telephone
Qwest (800/244–1111 customer service; 800/573–1311 24-hr repair reporting).

water
Seattle Public Utilities (206/684–3000).

VOLUNTEERING

how to
Seattleites tend to have a philanthropic and activistic inclination. If you're one of them, there are plenty of groups and organizations that would be thrilled to have your help—from the City Volunteer Program to the United Way.

organizations
Food Not Bombs, Seattle (206/985–2247, www.scn.org/activism/foodnotbombs): Serves vegetarian meals to people in need.

Seattle City Volunteer Program (206/684–4075): Operated through the Parks and Recreation Department.

Seattle Community Network (206/365–4528, www.scn.org): A network of volunteer and activism organizations. Also offers free E-mail and computer training to those without access.

Seattle Food Banks (206/626–6462).

United Way of King County (206/461–3700, www.uwkc.org): An established charitable organization that raises money for many worthy social programs—from women's shelters to organizations that provide food and health care to the needy. United Way also pairs would-be volunteers with programs.

ZONING & PLANNING

Department of Design, Construction, and Land Use (700 5th Ave., Suite 2000, in Key Tower, Downtown, 206/684–8600): Handles zoning questions and complaints.

Department of Neighborhoods–Historic Preservation (700 3rd Ave., 4th floor, in the Arctic Building, Downtown, 206/684–0464): Preserves Seattle's historic buildings, neighborhoods, and landmarks.

Seattle Planning Commission (600 4th Ave., Suite 300, Downtown, 206/684–0433): Gathers public input and advises the mayor, City Council, and city departments on broad city goals, policies, and plans for the physical development of the City.

learning

ACTING SCHOOLS

Freehold Studio/Theatre Lab (1525 10th Ave., at Pike St., Capitol Hill, 206/323–7499, www.freeholdtheatre.org): The school was formed in 1991 through the merger of the Pasquilini-Smith Studio and the Mark Jenkins Actors' Workshop; thousands of students and artists participate in performances, which are a large part of the local drama scene.

Northwest Actors Studio (1100 E. Pike St., at 11th Ave., Capitol Hill, 206/324–6328,www.nwactorsstudio.org): Provides theater arts conservatory space for emerging companies and individual artists.

Seattle Children's Theatre (201 Thomas St., at Seattle Center 206/443–0807, www.sct.org): Has classes and workshops for children, including a deaf-youth drama program, which serves 3,300 students annually.

ADULT EDUCATION IN PUBLIC SCHOOLS

University of Washington Extension Program (5001 25th Ave. NE, between NE 48th St. and NE Blakeley St., University District, 206/543–2320, www.extension.washington.edu): Evening classes and on-line distance learning courses are available in almost every subject the university offers its matriculated students. The fees tend to be pretty steep, though—almost twice that of community college courses.

ART SCHOOLS

Cornish College for the Arts (710 E. Roy St., at Boylston Ave., Capitol Hill, 206/726–5151, www.cornish.edu): Non-matriculated students may take classes in art, dance, design, music, performance production, and theater.

Seattle Academy of Fine Art (University Heights Center, 5031 University Way NE, University District, 206/526–2787, www.realistart.com): The adult program has studio classes in traditional techniques of realist art and summer workshops in New Mexico and on the Olympic Peninsula.

film & video

911 Media Arts Center (117 Yale Ave. N, at Stewart St., Lake Union, 206/682–6553, www.911media.org): The nonprofit media center offers workshops, editing suites, and use of its equipment.

photography

Photographic Center Northwest (900 12th Ave., at Marion St. and Broadway Ave., Capitol Hill, 206/720–7222, www.pcnw.org): Classes in black-and-white and color photography.

BALLROOM DANCING

Century Ballroom (915 E. Pine St., at 10th Ave., Capitol Hill, 206/324–7263 www.centuryballroom.com): Five-week salsa and swing lessons are held in a restored grand, old ballroom when it's not open for dancing. This is where the young Gap-clad crowd congregates.

Washington Dance Club (1017 Stewart St., at Terry Ave., Downtown, 206/628–8939, www.seattle2000.com/wdc): A traditional ballroom dancing scene where you can pick up and polish the tango, waltz, and foxtrot.

COMMUNITY COLLEGES

Seattle Central Community College (1701 Broadway, Capitol Hill, 206/587–5450 admissions, 206/587–4133 information, www.seattlecentral.org): Known for its diverse student life and innovative, interdisciplinary coordinated studies program, it's a regional leader in arts education.

Seattle Vocational Institute (2120 S. Jackson St., 206/587–4950, http://sviweb.sccd.ctc.edu): Open-entry vocational programs and adult learning courses include GED preparation, English as a second language, and basic adult education. Most programs take six months to a year to complete.

North Seattle Community College (NSCC, 9600 College Way N, North Seattle, 206/527–3664 admissions, 206/527–3639 information, www.gonorth.org): About 5 mi north of Downtown, NSCC occupies a 62-acre campus that includes 11 acres of environmentally protected wetlands. NSCC is known for its Physical Education Wellness Center and a state-of-the-art High Technology Learning Center. Adults, senior citizens, and distance-learners are welcome.

South Seattle Community College (6000 16th Ave. SW, West Seattle, 206/764–5300 registration, www.sccd.ctc.edu/south for information and application forms): The college regularly hosts student and community art shows and has a lovely campus with walking paths, gardens, a reflecting pool and gazebo, and a gorgeous arboretum. Many facilities—including the college beauty center, art gallery, arboretum, flower shop, and library—are open to the public. Evening, weekend, and distance learning classes are offered.

COMPUTER CLASSES

In high-tech Seattle, it should come as no surprise that just about anyone who wants to learn computer skills can find an abundance of computer classes, many of them for free.

Asha Computer Education Program (Microsoft Campus, 156th Ave. NE, between Bellevue-Redmond Rd. and NE 40th St., Redmond, 425/869–8074, www.ashanet.org/seattle/acomp.html): Beginners and those with experience are taught by Microsoft professionals at the Microsoft campus. Classes, which generally cost $75–$100 are small (about five people), with all money going to help educate under-privileged children in India.

Chinese Information and Service Center (409 Maynard Ave. S, at S. Jackson St., International District, 206/624–5633): Free or mostly free computer classes.

Delridge Community Center (4501 Delridge Way SW, at 22nd Ave. SW, West Seattle, 206/933–8629): Open to the public with sliding-scale classes and free public computer access.

Garfield Community Center (2323 E. Cherry St., between 23rd and 24th Aves., Downtown, 206/684–4788): Hosts various multimedia classes with open access to its network of 10 workstations for its mostly low-income clientele.

Seattle Central Community College's Community Education Program (206/587–5449): Any group of seven or more—friends, students, employers, or staff members—can request customized beginner to intermediate computer classes.

Seattle Community Centers provide free classes for low-income youth, ages 8 to 18, with computer access for youth and adults.

Miller Community Center (330 19th Ave. E, north of E. Thomas St., Capitol Hill, 206/684–4753).

Yesler Community Center (835 Yesler Way, at Broadway Ave., Capitol Hill, 206/386–1245).

The Seattle Public Library System (206/386–4636, www.spl.org/calendar/netclass.html): Has free computer classes and free public access to computer workstations. Class dates, times, and locations vary from month to month and registration is usually required. Contact them for current schedules and library locations.

COOKING SCHOOLS

Bertrand Chez Vous (4756 University Village Pl. NE, south of NE 50th St., University District, 206/729–1554, www.bertrandchezvous.com): A native Frenchman, Bertrand studied at Paris's Cordon Bleu School of Cooking and runs a unique cooking school, whereby people volunteer their homes and invite friends over for a cooking party or series of classes; a number of businesses have also used classes as team building exercises.

Blue Ribbon Cooking School (1611 McGilvra Blvd. E, 206/328–2442, www.blueribboncooking.com): Virginia Duppenthaler opened her first school in Vancouver, BC, in the '70s, and is one of

a handful of North Americans to reach the highest level of culinary achievement recognized by the International Association of Culinary Professionals. She and her husband Mike run the show here.

DANCE SCHOOLS

Seattle's salsa recent explosion hasn't lost any of its heat, and in fact, it has spawned interest in a variety of other dance styles. You don't have to be part of a duo to learn to dance—and in fact, it may be to your benefit since plenty of clubs around town will offer you opportunity (and no doubt a host of willing partners) to strut your new skills during special dance events.

Dance Sport International (12535 Lake City Way NE, just north of NE 125th St., Lake City 206/361–8239, www.dancesportseattle.com): Private and group lessons in everything from ballroom and swing to the cha-cha and competitive dancing. Beginner to advanced-level classes are available for $10 per person per class (minimum of 6 pre-paid classes); you can go weekly or drop-in for classes when your schedule allows. Two 45-minute private lessons are available for couples for $75.

The Fifth Avenue Dance Studios (2211 3rd Ave., at Blanchard St., Downtown, 206/621–9824): Private and group lessons for singles and couples in ballroom dancing, swing, and Latin, and salsa—*not* on Fifth Avenue.

Living Dance Traditions (2442 NW Market St., at 24th Ave. NW, Ballard, 206/781–1238, www.ltdance.com): Lindy hop, waltz, salsa, tango, nightclub two-step, and other dances are taught at beginner and intermediate levels; several levels of swing are taught. Courses are six-weeks long and cost $55 per person. All classes except tango are held at the Swedish Club (1920 Dexter Ave. N). Tango classes are held at All That Dance (5507 35th Ave. NE, in Seattle's Ravenna neighborhood.

LANGUAGE SCHOOLS

Berlitz Language Center (415 112th Ave. NE, at NE 4th St., Bellevue, 425/451–0162): Immersion courses for individuals and groups—in nearly all spoken languages.

Language Institutes (200 W. Mercer St., Suite 504, at 2nd Ave. W, Queen Anne, 206/217–9644, www.cultural.org.): Learn a multitude of languages at three locations.

Seattle Language Academy (340 15th Ave. E, at E Thomas St., Capitol Hill, 206/325–4109): Spanish, Italian, Sanskrit—this school covers the globe. It has both day and evening classes and teaches English as a second language.

Washington Academy of Languages (98 Yesler Way, at 1st Ave., Pioneer Square, 206/682–4463, www.wal.org): Eleven languages—from French to Thai—taught at a many different levels.

MUSIC SCHOOLS

Music Works Northwest (14360 SE Eastgate Way, Suite 102, at 142nd Pl. SE, Bellevue, 425/644–0988, www.musicworksnw.or): Among the music education programs at this nonprofit organization are music therapy, jazz theory, composition and arranging, music history, recording and music technology classes, and young child music programs. It also has jazz ensembles, chamber music ensembles, choirs, orchestras, world music ensembles.

vacation & travel information

AIRLINES

Aeroflot Airlines (206/464–1005).

AirBC/Air Canada (800/247–2262).

Air Mobility Command (877/863–1463).

Alaska Airlines (800/426–0333).

America West (800/235–9292).

American Airlines (800/433–7300).

American Trans Air (800/435–9282).

Asiana Airlines (800/227–4262).

British Airways (800/247–9297).

Continental Airlines (800/525–0280).

Delta Airlines (800/221–1212).

EVA Air (800/695–1188).

Frontier Airlines (800/432–1359).

Harbor Airlines (800/359–3220).

Hawaiian Airlines (800/367–5320).

Horizon Air (800/547–9308).

Iberia Airlines (800/772–4642).

Japan Airlines (800/525–3663).

JetBlue (800/538–2583).

KLM Royal Dutch Airlines (800/374–7747).

Lufthansa (800/645–3880).

Northwest Airlines (800/225–2525).

Scandinavian Airlines (800/221–2350).

Shuttle by United (800/748–8853).

Southwest Airlines (800/435–9792).

Sun Country Airlines (800/359–6786).

Trans World Airlines (800/221–2000).

United Airlines (800/241–6522).

United Express (800/241–6522).

US Airways (800/428–4322).

AIRPORTS

Seattle-Tacoma International Airport (Sea-Tac, Pacific Hwy. S [Hwy. 99], off I–5 at Exit 154B, 15 mi south of Downtown Seattle, 206/431–4444, www.portofseattle.org/seatac): Airline information, paging, ground transportation information, parking information. Sea-Tac is currently undergoing a massive facelift, so expect to encounter lots of detours, opening-soon Starbucks signs, and an extra 10 minutes to get to your gate.

OAG (www.oag.com/web/default.asp): Real-time flight status—check before you head out.

getting there by public transportation

Your least expensive transportation option ($2; cash only) is a Metro Transit city bus. You can catch one from the bus tunnel Downtown for the 45-minute ride to Sea-Tac. Take Express Tunnel Bus 194 or regular Buses 174 or 184.

BY LIMOUSINE

Limousine fare is $45 to Downtown and is charged by the car, not by the passen-

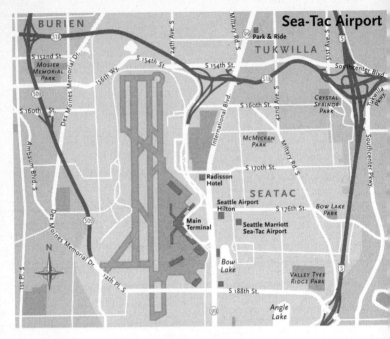

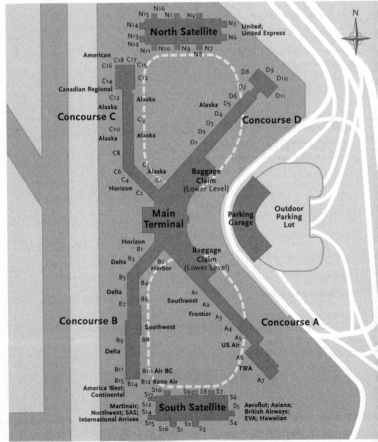

AIRLINES	GATE LOCATIONS
Aeroflot Airlines *(206) 464-1005*	SS
AirBC / Air Canada *800 247-2262*	NS
Air Mobility Command *877 863-1463*	SS
Alaska Airlines *800 426-0333*	C/D
America West *800 235-9292*	B
American Airlines *800 433-7300*	C *(dom)* SS *(intl)*
American Trans Air(ATA) *800 435-9282*	SS
Asiana Airlines *800 227-4262*	SS
British Airways *800 247-9297*	SS
Continental Airlines *800 525-0280*	B
Delta Airlines *800 221-1212*	B
EVA Air *800 695-1188*	SS
Frontier Airlines *800 432-1359*	SS
Hawaiian Airlines *800 367-5320*	SS
Horizon Air *800 547-9308*	B/C/NS *(dom)* SS *(intl)*
Iberia Airlines*	C *(dom)* SS *(intl)*
Japan Airlines*	C *(dom)*
JetBlue Airways *1-800-JETBLUE*	B
KLM Royal Dutch Airlines**	SS
Lufthansa***	NS
Northwest Airlines *800 225-2525*	SS
Scandinavian Airlines *800 221-2350*	SS
Shuttle by United*** *800 748-8853*	NS
Southwest Airlines *800 435-9792*	B
Sun Country Airlines *800 359-6786*	*Service temporarily suspended effective 10/10/01*
Trans World Airlines *800 221-2000*	SS
United Airlines *800 241-6522*	NS
United Express *800 241-6522*	NS
US Airways *800 428-4322*	SS
World Airways†	SS

*See American Airlines with questions.
**See Northwest Airlines with questions.
***See United Airlines with questions.
†Serving Air Mobility Command; see AMC with questions.

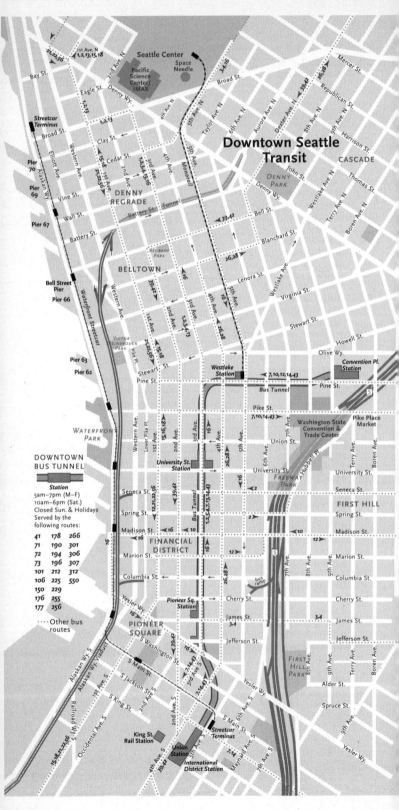

Downtown Seattle Transit

CASCADE

DENNY REGRADE

BELLTOWN

WATERFRONT PARK

DOWNTOWN BUS TUNNEL

Station
5am–7pm (M–F)
10am–6pm (Sat.)
Closed Sun. & Holidays
Served by the following routes:

41	178	266
71	190	301
72	194	306
73	196	307
101	212	312
106	225	550
150	229	
176	255	
177	256	

···· Other bus routes

FINANCIAL DISTRICT

FIRST HILL

FIRST HILL PARK

PIONEER SQUARE

Seattle Center

Space Needle

Pacific Science Center/IMAX

Streetcar Terminus

Pier 70
Pier 69
Pier 67

Bell Street Pier
Pier 66

VICTOR STEINBRUECK PARK

Pier 63
Pier 62

DENNY PARK

REGRADE PARK

Westlake Station

Convention Pl. Station

Pike Place Market

Washington State Convention & Trade Center

FREEWAY PARK

University St. Station

Pioneer Sq. Station

Bus Tunnel

bus ramp

King St. Rail Station

Union Station

Streetcar Terminus

International District Station

ger (cars hold up to four people). Drivers meet you on the third floor of the Parking Garage.

Atlas Towncar (206/860–7777 or 888/646–0606, www.atlastowncar.com).

BY SHUTTLE & SHUTTLE BUS

Metro Transit (206/553–3000, transit.metrokc.gov/bus/flymetro.html): Service to Downtown hotels costs $8.50.

Gray Line Airport Express (206/626–6088, www.graylineseattle.com): The bus costs $8.50, $14 round-trip; departs twice an hour, with service to and from major Downtown hotels. Airport pick-up is at doors 6 and 26 on the lower level at baggage claim.

Shuttle Express/Express Car (206/622–1424 or 800/487–7433 in WA, www.shuttleexpress.com): 24-hour door-to-door Town Car service serving Greater Seattle; from the airport to Downtown the flat-rate fare is $20. You can make reservations at the Shuttle Express counter upon arrival. For trips to the airport, make reservations at least 24 hours in advance.

BY TAXI

A metered cab service will cost you $25–$30, though several taxi companies offer a flat rate of $25 for trips between Downtown and the airport. Allow at least 40 minutes for the trip. Taxis are available on the third floor of the Parking Garage.

Far West Cab (206/622–1717).

Graytop Cab (206/282–8222).

Orange Cab (206/522–8800).

Yellow Cab (206/622–6500).

getting there by car

By car the trip will probably take you about 20 minutes on a good day, 45 minutes during the worst traffic of the day. From Downtown, take I–5 south to Exit 154B to Sea-Tac Airport and merge onto Route 518. Take the Hwy. 99 exit toward Sea-Tac airport. This is the fastest route, but in cases of total gridlock, take Hwy. 99 south from downtown to Tukwila, turn right on South 160th Street, left onto Air Cargo Road and follow the signs to the airport.

General parking is available on the top floors of the garage for $2 per half-hour or $20 per day; automated pay stations mean you take your parking ticket when pulling in, and carry it with you into the airport. You pay for parking at one of 29 pay station machines before returning to your car.

Short-term parking (for up to two hours), in the garage across the street from the terminal, costs $2 per hour (or $3 an hour after 2 hours, up to $30 maximum per day). Remember to take your parking ticket with you.

An assortment of off-site long-term lots surround the airport, which charge about $10 a day and offer shuttle service to the airport.

Valet parking (206/433–5308): Available in the short-term garage and costs $20 per hour for up to four hours, $30 per hour after that.

CAR RENTAL

Rates in Seattle begin at $25 a day and $115 a week for an economy car with air-conditioning, automatic transmission, and unlimited mileage. This does not include the car-rental tax of 18.5%. Renting a car at the airport, where rental fees are higher, means you can pay an additional 10% in airport tax. However, you can quickly find yourself eating up the savings in rates and airport tax after the cost of shuttles or taxis to an off-airport rental agency. As you think it over, consider whether you'll want to go with a local or national rental agency. The price difference isn't typically that significant.

major agencies
Alamo (800/327–9633).

Avis (800/331–1212).

Budget (800/527–0700).

Dollar (800/800–4000).

Hertz (800/654–3131).

National Car Rental (800/227–7368).

Thrifty (800/847–4389).

local agencies
Ace Extra Car Rentals (206/246–7510).

Advantage (800/777–5500 or 206/824–0161).

Century/Rent Rite (206/246–5039).

Express Rent-A-Car (206/241–3760).

EZ Rent-A-Car (206/241–4688).

U Save (206/242–9778).

CURRENCY EXCHANGE

Allworld Currency Exchange (1411 3rd Ave., Suite 1401, at Union St., Downtown, 206/464–0204): Foreign currency wire transfers, foreign currency drafts, and foreign currency banknotes.

American Express Travel Agency (600 Stewart St., at 6th Ave., 206/441–8622): Traveler's checks, travel services, and foreign currency exchange.

Bank of America (701 5th Ave., at Cherry St., Downtown, 206/461–0800): A retail banking chain with multiple Seattle locations.

566 Denny Way, at 6th Ave., Belltown.

100 Mercer St., at 1st Ave. W, Queen Anne.

230 Broadway Ave. E, at John St., Capitol Hill.

4701 University Way NE, at 48th Ave. NE, University District.

525 S. Jackson St., at 5th Ave. S, International District.

Custom House Currency Exchange (1900 5th Ave., at Olive Way, 206/269–6353): Buys and sells international currencies and handles corporate accounts.

Thomas Cook Currency Services (Sea-Tac, main terminal behind the America West ticketing counter, 206/248–0401: Exchanges foreign currencies.

Washington Mutual (1201 3rd Ave., at Seneca St., Downtown, 800/756–8000): A retail banking chain with multiple city locations.

301 Broadway Ave. E, at John St., Capitol Hill.

1417 Queen Anne Ave. N, at Galer Ave., Queen Anne.

4020 E. Madison St., at 40th Ave., Madison Park.

4300 Brooklyn NE, at 43rd Ave. NE, University District.

CONSULATES

British Consulate (900 4th Ave., Suite 3001, 206/622–9255).

Canadian Consulate General (Plaza 600, Suite 412, at 6th Ave. and Stewart St., 206/443–1372).

Consulate General of Japan (601 Union St., Suite 500, 206/682–9107).

Consulate General of Russia (Westin Building, 1900 5th Ave., Suite 2323, between Western Ave. and Virginia St., 206/728–1910).

Consulate General of the Republic Of Korea (2033 6th Ave., 206/441–1011).

Consulate of Belgium (2200 Alaskan Way, Suite 470, 206/728–5145).

Consulate of Denmark (6204 E. Mercer Way, Mercer Island, 206/230–0888).

Consulate of France (2200 Alaskan Way, Suite 490, 206/256–6184).

Consulate of Mexico (2132 3rd Ave., 206/448–3526).

Consulate of Sweden, (1215 4th Ave., Suite 1019, 206/622–5640).

Hungarian Consulate (Kirkland, 425/739–0631).

Norway Consulate (1402 3rd Ave., Suite 806, 206/623–3957).

INOCULATIONS, VACCINATIONS & TRAVEL HEALTH

Before taking off on a far-flung vacation, make an appointment with your doctor to make sure you're caught up on all your vaccinations, especially tetanus, tuberculosis, and typhoid—a Hepatitis A vaccine is also a good idea. It's always a good idea to pack sun protection—sunblock, sunglasses, and a broad-brimmed hat. Long-sleeved shirts and long pants also help protect the skin from harmful sun exposure. And, if you're prone to motion sickness, don't leave home without Dramamine or some other preventative medicine. Keep all personal medication in your handbag or a small pack; not in your checked luggage.

The Centers for Disease Control Hotline (404/639–2572 or 800/311–3435, www.cdc.gov): For specific information about health concerns in the area you'll be traveling.

The Hall Health Travel Clinic (1959 NE Pacific St., University of Washington Medical Center, 206/616–2495): Consultations by appointment (for adults, cost is $57) and includes the writing of needed prescriptions.

The Travel Medicine Service (1959 NE Pacific St., University of Washington Medical Center, 206/598–4888): Complete medical services by appointment, including vaccinations and inoculations; Open Monday through Saturday with evening hours.

PASSPORTS

To get a passport, you must show up in person at the Federal Passport Office with proof of U.S. citizenship (a previous U.S. passport or certified birth certificate), present proof of identity (can include a naturalization certificate, certificate of citizenship, a current valid driver's license, or government or military identification), two passport photos (measuring 2″ × 2″ and taken within the last six months; photos can be either in color or black-and-white) and payment for the applicable fee (generally, major credit cards, debit cards, exact cash, checks, money orders, and bank drafts are accepted). A new U.S. passport costs $65 ($40 for those under 18); a renewal costs $55. Normal processing time for a passport is four to six weeks.

If you need an emergency passport for travel within 10 days, you'll pay an additional $30 fee for "expedited processing"; bring your plane ticket with you to the office.

Passport *renewal* is handled most easily through the mail. Renewal forms are available at many post offices, passport centers, or on the postal service Web site and can be submitted by mail or at any passport acceptance agency.

To renew by mail, sign the application and attach to it: your most recent passport, two identical passport photos and the appropriate fee (fees change often so call ahead to find out how much you'll need to send; passports renewed by mail in the United States can only be forwarded to your U.S. address).

If you're short on time and/or don't have Internet access, you can obtain passport information and forms by phone, for a fee. Call the National Passport Information Center at 900/225–5674 (35¢ per minute) or, with a major credit card, 888/362–8668 ($4.95 flat rate). In a grave emergency after hours (such as the death of a relative abroad), call the passport duty officer at the U.S. State Department in Washington (202/647–4000).

Federal Passport Office (915 2nd Ave., between Union and Madison Sts., Room 992, Downtown, 206/808–5700): Open 8 AM to 3 PM weekdays.

United States Postal Service (http://travel.state.gov/passport_renewal.html): Passport renewal applications.

passport processing

Regular, non-expedited passports are also issued through Community Neighborhood Service Centers around the city (the service centers also have applications for mail renewals). Days and hours for passport processing vary from location to location.

Community Neighborhood Service Centers (206/615–0725).

Ballard (2305 NW Market St.).

Central (2301 S. Jackson St., Suite 208).

Lake City (12707 30th Ave NE).

Southeast Center (4859 Rainier Ave. S).

Southwest (5405 Delridge Way SW).

University Center (4534 University Way NE).

passport photos

Photo and copier stores around the city will snap your mug. Remember: you will need to submit two identical photos, 2″ × 2″ in either color or black-and-white, with your passport application form.

Film Stop (708 3rd Ave., Downtown 206/624–5180): Quick turn-arounds on passport photos.

(1001 4th Ave., Downtown, 206/682–5666).

(1826 6th Ave., Downtown, 206/682–5060).

(617 Broadway E, Capitol Hill, 206/322–4086).

(508 3rd Ave. W, Queen Anne, 206/285–2111).

Ken's Camera (1327 2nd Ave., Downtown, 206/223–5553): If you have to visit the Federal Passport Office, Ken's is just about four blocks away, and can produce passport photos instantly.

Kinko's (1335 2nd Ave., Downtown, 206/292–9255): Instant passport photos available 24 hours at this and other area locations. Note: It's always good to call ahead to make sure the camera is working.

TOURIST INFORMATION

Seattle/King County Convention and Visitors Bureau (520 Pike St., Suite 1300, at 5th Ave., Downtown, 206/461–5800, www.seeseattle.org).

Seattle Visitor Center (Washington State Convention Center, 800 Convention Pl., at Union St., Downtown, 206/461–5840).

Washington State Convention & Trade Center (800 Convention Pl., at Union St., Downtown, 206/447–5000, www.wsctc.com).

Washington State Tourism Development Division (Box 42500, Olympia, WA, 98504-2500, 360/725–5050, www.tourism.wa.gov).

TRAVELER'S AID

Traveler's Aid Service (Family Services Travelers Aid, 1100 Virginia St., Suite 210, at Boren Ave., Downtown, 206/461–3888, www.travelersaid.org): This nationwide service helps crime victims, stranded travelers, and wayward children and works closely with the police.

U.S. CUSTOMS

U.S. Customs Service Refers you to the appropriate authority on importation of goods (206/553–0770 or 800/697–3662, www.customs.ustreas.gov).

VISA INFORMATION & TRAVEL ADVISORIES

Call the embassy or consulate of the country you plan to visit for up-to-date information on visa requirements, travel advisories, and service strikes.

U.S. State Department Overseas Citizens Services (202/647–5225, http://travel.state.gov/travel_warnings.html): For travel advisories on specific countries.

Ask Immigration (800/375–5283): Answers questions on immigration, citizenship, visas, relatives abroad, and more.

DIRECTORIES

restaurants by neighborhood

index

NORTH AURORA

Doong Kong Lau Hakka Cuisine (Chinese), 10

PHINNEY RIDGE

Le Gourmand (French), 21

Mae's Phinney Ridge Cafe (American), 3

Red Mill (American casual), 4–5

PIKE PLACE MARKET

Alibi Room (American casual), 4

Cafe Campagne (French), 20

Campagne (French), 20

The Crumpet Shop (English), 19

Delcambre's Ragin' Cajun (Cajun/Creole), 9

El Puerco Lloron (Mexican), 31

Emmett Watson's Oyster Bar (seafood), 35

Etta's (seafood), 35

Jack's Fish Spot (seafood), 36

Kells Irish Pub & Restaurant (Irish), 24

Lowell's (American), 3

The Market Grill (American casual), 4

Matt's in the Market (eclectic), 18

Maximilien (French), 21

Oriental Food Mart (Philippine), 33

Pink Door (Italian), 26

Place Pigalle (French), 22

Sisters European Snacks (American casual), 5

Three Girls Bakery (American), 4

PIONEER SQUARE

Cafe Hue (Vietnamese), 45

Cafe Paloma (café), 7

New Orleans (Cajun/Creole), 9

Salumi (Italian), 26

Taco del Mar (Tex-Mex), 42

Trattoria Mitchelli (Italian), 27

QUEEN ANNE

Bahn Thai (Thai), 42

Bamboo Garden (Chinese), 10

Bamboo Garden Vegetarian Cuisine (Kosher), 29

Banjara (Indian), 23

Canlis (steak), 39

Chinoise Cafe (Pan-Asian), 32

Chutney's (Indian), 23–24

El Diablo Coffee Company (Cuban), 17

Figaro Bistro (French), 21

Kaspar's (contemporary), 14

Mediterranean Kitchens (Middle Eastern), 32

Pandasia (Pan-Asian), 32

Panos Greek Taverna Kleftiko (Greek), 23

Perche No (Italian), 26

Ponti Seafood Grill (seafood), 37

Racha (Thai), 43

Roy St. Bistro (English), 19

Sam's Sushi (Japanese), 28

Sapphire Kitchen & Bar (Moroccan), 32

10 Mercer (contemporary), 12

Tup Tim (Thai), 43

Zeek's (pizza), 36

RAINER VALLEY

Jones Barbeque (barbecue), 6

Jumbo (Chinese), 11

RAVENNA

Queen Mary Tearoom (tea), 41

REDMOND

Desert Fire (Southwestern), 38

Epiros Greek Restaurant (Greek), 22–23

Typhoon (Thai), 43–44

ROOSEVELT

Scarlett Tree (American casual), 5

SEA-TAC

Bai Tong (Thai), 42

SKYWAY (SOUTH SEATTLE)

Ezell's Famous Chicken (Southern), 38

SHORELINE

Black Pearl (Chinese), 10

UNIVERSITY DISTRICT

Aqua Verde (Mexican), 30–31

Boat Street Cafe (French), 20

Caffe Brazil (Brazilian), 6

Irish Emigrant (Irish), 24

Lotus (Thai), 43

My's (Vietnamese), 45

Pagliacci Pizza (pizza), 33

Rain Dancer (contemporary), 15

Sunlight (vegetarian & macrobiotic), 45

Tandoor (Indian), 24

Tempero Do Brasil (Brazilian), 6–7

Ugly Mug (café), 8

WALLINGFORD

Asteroid Cafe (Italian), 25

Bizzard Italian Cafe (Italian), 25

Bungalow Wine Bar & Cafe (café), 7

Eva's Restaurant & Wine Bar (eclectic), 18

Jitterbug Cafe (American casual), 4

Kabul (Afghan), 2

Luau Polynesian Lounge (Hawaiian), 23

Teahouse Kuan Yin (tea), 41

WATERFRONT

Anthony's Pier 66 (seafood), 34

Elliott's Oyster House (seafood), 35

Ivar's Acres of Clams (seafood), 36

Ivar's Seafood Bar (seafood), 36

The Shanty (American), 3–4

Waterfront (seafood), 38

WEDGEWOOD

Black Pearl (Chinese), 10

WEST SEATTLE

Alki Bakery (café), 7

Backdoor BBQ (barbecue), 5–6

Ephesus Restaurant (Greek/Turkish), 22, 44

Luna Park Cafe (American), 3

Pegasus Pizza & Pasta (pizza), 33–34

Saffron Cow (Mediterranean), 30

Salty's on Alki (seafood), 37

Sunfish Cafe (seafood), 37

index

CITY NOTES